THE ROUTLEI
OF QUEER ......

MW01201297

The Routledge History of Queer America presents the first comprehensive synthesis of the rapidly developing field of lesbian, gay, bisexual, transgender and queer US history. Featuring nearly thirty chapters on essential subjects and themes from colonial times through the present, this collection covers topics including:

- Rural vs. urban queer histories
- Gender and sexual diversity in early American history
- Intersectionality, exploring queerness in association with issues of race and class
- Queerness and American capitalism
- The rise of queer histories, archives, and collective memory
- Transnationalism and queer history

Gathering authorities in the field to define the ways in which sexual and gender diversity have contributed to the dynamics of American society, culture and nation, *The Routledge History of Queer America* is the finest available overview of the rich history of queer experience in US history.

Don Romesburg is Professor of Women's and Gender Studies at Sonoma State University, USA.

The Routledge Histories

The Routledge Histories is a series of landmark books surveying some of the most important topics and themes in history today. Edited and written by an international team of world-renowned experts, they are the works against which all future books on their subjects will be judged.

THE ROUTLEDGE
HISTORY OF
QUEER AMERICA

Edited by Don Romesburg

Routledge
Taylor & Francis Group

LONDON AND NEW YORK

First published 2018
by Routledge

2 Park Square, Milton Park, Abingdon, Oxfordshire OX14 4RN
52 Vanderbilt Avenue, New York, NY 10017

Routledge is an imprint of the Taylor & Francis Group, an informa business

First issued in paperback 2019

Library of Congress Cataloging-in-Publication Data
Names: Romesburg, Don, editor.
Title: The Routledge history of queer America / edited by Don Romesburg.
Description: New York, NY : Routledge, 2018. |
Series: The Routledge histories | Includes bibliographical references and index. |
Identifiers: LCCN 2017042154 (print) | LCCN 2017050744 (ebook) |
ISBN 9781315747347 () | ISBN 9781138814592 (alk. paper)
Subjects: LCSH: Gays—United States—History. | Sexual minorities—United States—History.
Classification: LCC HQ76.3.U5 (ebook) | LCC HQ76.3.U5 R697 2018 (print) |
DDC 306.76/60973—dc23
LC record available at https://lccn.loc.gov/2017042154

ISBN: 978-1-138-81459-2 (hbk)
ISBN: 978-0-367-22279-6 (pbk)

Typeset in Bembo and Minion Pro
by Florence Production Ltd, Stoodleigh, Devon, UK

To David, Asha, and Shailoe,
for making queer history with me every day.

CONTENTS

Contents

Contents

CONTRIBUTORS

Katie Batza, Assistant Professor of Women, Gender, and Sexuality Studies at the University of Kansas, researches the intersection of health, politics, and sexuality in the United States. Her publications to date examine the creation of gay medical clinics and national health networks before AIDS, chart lesbians' struggle for access to fertility treatments, and contribute to the National Park Service's LGBTQ Theme Study and subsequent efforts to preserve and interpret more LGBTQ historical sites.

Jennifer Brier is Associate Professor of Gender and Women's Studies and History at the University of Illinois at Chicago. She wrote *Infectious Ideas: U.S. Political Response to the AIDS Crisis* (University of North Carolina Press, 2009) and curated, with Jill Austin, "Out in Chicago," the Chicago History Museum's award-winning exhibition on LGBT history. She currently directs "History Moves," a community engagement and public history project that provides space for community organizers and activists to share their histories with a wide audience.

Elizabeth Catte is a public historian and educator whose work appears in museums and heritage sites worldwide. She holds a PhD in public history from Middle Tennessee State University and specializes in memory and commemoration.

Elizabeth Clement is Associate Professor of History at the University of Utah. Her first book, *Love for Sale*, came out in 2006 (University of North Carolina Press). She has two new projects. The first focuses on queer relationships to family. The second, *AIDS and the Silent Majority*, addresses family, religion and caregiving in Utah. The AIDS project has involved the creation of an archival and oral history collection on Utah's response to the AIDS epidemic.

Rachel Hope Cleves is Professor of History at the University of Victoria in British Columbia. She is author of *Charity and Sylvia: A Same-Sex Marriage in Early America* (Oxford University Press, 2014), winner of the Stonewall Honor from the American Library Association and the James C. Bradford Prize from the Society for Historians of the Early American Republic. Cleves is presently at work on a project titled "Good Food, Bad Sex," and on a biography of Norman Douglas.

Kate Eichhorn is Associate Professor of Culture and Media Studies at The New School University and the author of *The Archival Turn in Feminism* (Temple University Press, 2013) and *Adjusted Margin: Xerography, Art and Activism in the Late Twentieth Century* (MIT Press, 2016).

Finn Enke is Professor of History and Gender and Women's Studies at the University of Wisconsin, Madison. He is the author of *Finding the Movement: Sexuality, Contested Space, and Feminist Activism* (Duke University Press, 2007), and editor of *Transfeminist Perspectives: In and Beyond Transgender and Gender Studies* (Temple University Press, 2012), which won the Lambda Literary Award for Best 2013 Book in Transgender Nonfiction.

Julie R. Enszer is a scholar and poet. Her book manuscript, *A Fine Bind: Lesbian-Feminist Publishing from 1969 through 2009*, tells stories of a dozen lesbian-feminist publishers, to consider the meaning of the theoretical and political formations of lesbian-feminism, separatism, and cultural feminism. Her research has appeared or is forthcoming in *Southern Cultures, Journal of Lesbian Studies, American Periodicals, WSQ, Frontiers, Feminist Studies*, and other journals.

Marcia M. Gallo is Associate Professor of History at University of Nevada, Las Vegas, an activist scholar and the author of two award-winning books, *"No One Helped": Kitty Genovese, New York City, and the Myth of Urban Apathy* (Cornell University Press, 2015) and *Different Daughters: A History of the Daughters of Bilitis and the Rise of the Lesbian Rights Movement* (Seal Press, 2006). She has contributed essays and book chapters exploring post-World War II feminisms, progressive queer politics and culture, and oral history to journals and edited collections.

Richard Godbeer is Director of the Humanities Research Center, and Professor of History at Virginia Commonwealth University. He received his B.A. from Oxford University and his Ph.D. from Brandeis University. Godbeer is the author of *Sexual Revolution in Early America* (Johns Hopkins University Press, 2002) and *The Overflowing of Friendship: Love Between Men and the Creation of the American Republic* (Johns Hopkins University Press, 2009), as well as several books on witchcraft in colonial New England.

Emily K. Hobson is the author of *Lavender and Red: Liberation and Solidarity in the Gay and Lesbian Left* (University of California Press, 2016). A historian of LGBTQ activism and radical social movements in the postwar United States, she serves as Assistant Professor of History and Gender, Race, and Identity at the University of Nevada, Reno, and earned her Ph.D. in American Studies and Ethnicity at the University of Southern California.

Pippa Holloway is Professor of History at Middle Tennessee State University. She is the author of *Living in Infamy: Felon Disfranchisement and the History of American Citizenship* (Oxford University Press, 2013) and *Sexuality, Politics, and Social Control in Virginia, 1920–1945* (University of North Carolina Press, 2006). She teaches courses in US history, focusing on southern history, LGBT history, the history of mass incarceration, and historical research methods. Her current work examines the right to testify in court and the history of rules of evidence.

Kwame Holmes is Assistant Professor of Ethnic Studies at the University of Colorado Boulder. He is the author of "What's The T: Gossip and the Production of Black Gay Social History" in *Radical History Review* (Spring 2015) and a manuscript, *Chocolate to Rainbow City: Liberalism and Displacement in the Nation's Capital, 1957–1999*, which narrates how middle-class racial, gender and sexual diversification in the wake of civil rights, women's and gay liberation struggles in the Washington Metropolitan Area foreclosed the possibility that "Chocolate City" could belong to the city's working-class black majority.

Loraine Hutchins co-edited two anthologies on bisexuality: *Bi Any Other Name: Bisexual People Speak Out* (1991, re-released with new 25th anniversary introduction in 2016, Riverdale Avenue Books) with Lani Ka'ahumanu, and *Sexuality, Religion and the Sacred: Bisexual, Pansexual and Polysexual Perspectives* (Routledge, 2011) with H. Sharif Williams. She co-founded BiNet USA: The National Bisexual Network and AMBi—the Alliance of Multicultural Bisexuals in Washington, D.C. She teaches multi-disciplinary sexuality courses at Montgomery College in Maryland.

Lara Kelland is Assistant Professor of History and Public History at the University of Louisville, where she teaches and practices oral, public, and digital history. Her forthcoming book, *Clio's Foot Soldiers: Twentieth-Century US Social Movements and the Uses of Collective Memory*, comparatively examines the uses of history by activists within the Civil Rights, Black Power, Women's, Gay Liberation, and American Indian Movements. As a public history practitioner, she has worked on a variety of museum, archival, and community-based projects.

Amanda H. Littauer is Associate Professor of History and Gender Studies at Northern Illinois University. She earned her Ph.D. from UC Berkeley in 2006. Her research and teaching focuses on twentieth-century sexual culture, the history of women and girls, and LGBT studies. Her first book, *Bad Girls: Young Women, Sex, and Rebellion before the Sixties*, was published by University of North Carolina Press in 2015. Her current project is a social and activist history of queer youth in the twentieth-century United States.

Eithne Luibhéid is Professor of Gender and Women's Studies at the University of Arizona. Her research focuses on the connections among queer lives, state immigration controls, and justice struggles. Luibhéid is the author of *Pregnant on Arrival: Making the 'Illegal' Immigrant* (University of Minnesota Press, 2013) and *Entry Denied: Controlling Sexuality at the Border* (University of Minnesota Press, 2002). She is the editor of "Queer Migrations," a special issue of *GLQ* (2008), and the co-editor of *A Global History of Sexuality* (Wiley-Blackwell, 2014) and *Queer Migrations: Sexuality, Citizenship, and Border Crossings* (University of Minnesota Press, 2005).

Jen Manion is Associate Professor of History at Amherst College, author of *Liberty's Prisoners: Carceral Culture in Early America* (University of Pennsylvania Press, 2015), and co-editor of *Taking Back the Academy: History of Activism, History as Activism* (Routledge, 2004). Jen has essays in *Radical History Review, TSQ: Transgender Studies Quarterly, QED: A Journal of GLBTQ World-making, Signs: Journal of Women in Culture and Society*, and tweets at @activisthistory.

Andrea J. Ritchie is Researcher-in-Residence on Race, Gender, Sexuality and Criminalization at the Barnard Center for Research on Women, and was a 2014 Senior Soros Justice Fellow. She is author of *Invisible No More: Police Violence Against Black Women and Women of Color* (Beacon Press, 2017) and co-author of *Say Her Name: Resisting Police Brutality Against Black Women* (African American Policy Forum, 2016) and *Queer (In)Justice: The Criminalization of LGBT People in the United States* (Beacon Press, 2011).

Daniel Rivers is Associate Professor in the Department of History at The Ohio State University and a citizen of the Choctaw Nation of Oklahoma. His first book is *Radical Relations:*

Lesbian Mothers, Gay Fathers, and Their Children in the United States since WWII (University of North Carolina Press, 2013). He is currently working on a second book project on the history of LGBT/Two-Spirit Native Americans from 1940 to the present.

Don Romesburg is Professor in the Sonoma State University Women's and Gender Studies Department. He has published in numerous journals and anthologies with queer takes on public history as well as the histories of adolescence, sex work, transracial adoption, and queer/trans performers. He was the lead scholar working to bring LGBT content into the State of California's 2016 K-12 History-Social Science Framework, and trains educators and administrators to ensure ongoing implementation. Dr. Romesburg is also one of the founders of the GLBT History Museum in San Francisco.

Clare Sears is Associate Professor of Sociology and Sexuality Studies at San Francisco State University. She is author of *Arresting Dress: Cross-Dressing, Law and Fascination in Nineteenth-Century San Francisco* (Duke University Press, 2014), which was shortlisted for a Lambda Literary Award in 2016. She has also published articles in *Women's Studies Quarterly* and *GLQ*. Her current research investigates the historical emergence of emotional disturbance as an administrative and diagnostic category in special education law.

David Serlin teaches in the Department of Communication at UC San Diego, where he is also affiliated with the programs in Critical Gender Studies, Science Studies, and the Interdisciplinary Group in Cognitive Science. His books include *Replaceable You: Engineering the Body in Postwar America* (author; University of Chicago Press, 2004), which was the recipient of the Alan Bray Memorial Book Award from the Modern Language Association; *Imagining Illness: Public Health and Visual Culture* (editor; University of Minnesota Press, 2010), *Keywords for Disability Studies* (coeditor; NYU Press, 2015), and *Window Shopping with Helen Keller: Architecture and Disability in Modern Culture* (University of Chicago Press, forthcoming). He is a member of the editorial collective for the *Radical History Review*, an editor-at-large for *Cabinet*, and a founding editor of *Catalyst: Feminism, Theory, Technoscience*.

Nayan Shah is Professor and Chair of American Studies and Ethnicity at the University of Southern California. His research examines historical struggles over bodies, space and the exercise of state power, and contributes to studies of race and queer studies. He is the author *Stranger Intimacy: Contesting Race, Sexuality and the Law in the North American West* (University of California, 2011) and *Contagious Divides: Epidemics and Race in San Francisco's Chinatown* (University of California, 2001). He served as co-editor of *GLQ*, 2011–2014.

Sara R. Smith-Silverman is Assistant Professor of History at American River College and earned a Ph.D. in US History from University of California, Santa Cruz. Her work focuses on the racial, gender, and sexual politics of labor organizing in US history, as well as the relationship between the history of social movements and the labor movement.

Marc Stein is the Jamie and Phyllis Pasker Professor of History at San Francisco State University. He is the author of *City of Sisterly and Brotherly Loves: Lesbian and Gay Philadelphia, 1945–1972* (University of Chicago Press, 2000), *Sexual Injustice: Supreme Court Decisions from Griswold to Roe* (University of North Carolina Press, 2010), and *Rethinking the Gay and Lesbian Movement* (Routledge, 2012). He also served as the editor-in-chief of the *Encyclopedia of LGBT History in America* (Charles Scribners & Sons, 2003).

Whitney Strub is the author of *Perversion for Profit: The Politics of Pornography and the Rise of the New Right* (Columbia University Press, 2011) and *Obscenity Rules: Roth v. United States and the Long Struggle over Sexual Expression* (University Press of Kansas, 2013). His work has appeared in several scholarly journals, Salon, Vice, and OutHistory. Most recently, he co-edited *Porno Chic and the Sex Wars* (University of Massachusetts Press, 2016).

Sharon Ullman is Professor of History at Bryn Mawr College. She received her Ph.D. from the University of California at Berkeley. She is the author of *Sex Seen: The Emergence of Modern Sexuality in America* (University of California Press, 1997) and with Kathleen Kennedy, *Sexual Borderlands: Constructing an American Sexual Past* (Ohio State University Press, 2003). She is currently working on a project about the 1970s and cultural amnesia.

Beans Velocci is a Ph.D. student in History and Women's, Gender, and Sexuality Studies at Yale University. They earned their M.A. from the University of Utah in 2015 and their B.A. from Smith College in 2011. Beans currently works on race and the construction of normative gender in the nineteenth-century United States, with a focus on transgender history.

Stephen Vider is Visiting Assistant Professor in Museum Studies at Bryn Mawr and an Andrew W. Mellon postdoctoral fellow at the Museum of the City of New York. His book, *Queer Belongings: Gay Men, Lesbians, and the Politics of Home After World War II* (forthcoming from University of Chicago Press), examines how American conceptions of domesticity have shaped LGBT relationships and politics from 1945 to the present. His writing has also appeared in *American Quarterly* and *Gender & History*.

Margot Weiss is Associate Professor of Anthropology and American Studies at Wesleyan University. She is the author of the award-winning *Techniques of Pleasure: BDSM and the Circuits of Sexuality* (Duke University Press, 2011); her current book project, *Visions of Sexual Justice*, explores the intellectual work of queer activism in the midst of political impasse. She is Co-Chair of the Association for Queer Anthropology.

Kay Whitlock is coauthor of *Considering Hate: Violence, Goodness, and Justice in American Culture and Politics* (Beacon Press, 2015) and *Queer (In)Justice: The Criminalization of LGBT People in the United States* (Beacon Press, 2011). She lives in Missoula, Montana.

ACKNOWLEDGMENTS

First and foremost, I'd like to say to the people who warned me not to take on an editorial project of this scope that you were right: It took much more time and effort than I could have imagined. That said, it has been a profoundly enriching experience to collaborate with the thirty-one authors who produced this exceptional book, which is a major contribution to the field of queer US history. I don't think I'm overstating when I say that thanks to their care, nuance, clarity, and sophistication, they have made *The Routledge History of Queer America* a go-to text that will be referenced and taught for many years to come. It moves the field forward and captures what we've collectively built in getting here. I hope they all feel as proud of their efforts and our collaboration as I do.

There are many others to also thank. At Routledge, the editorial staff changed several times throughout the journey from start to finish, so many played a key role at different moments. Before she moved on to another press, Kimberly Guinta talked me into taking this gig and saw the book proposal through approval, and Genevieve Aoki steered the project through its infancy. Ted Meyer was vital through the last stages of chasing down truant authors and remote illustrations as well as being a supportive all-around cheerleader for the project. History editor Eve Mayer saw the book through to publication with grace and efficiency. Stephanie Gilmore was my intrepid indexer. At Sonoma State, the School of Social Sciences provided summer grants for several years, which allowed me to focus on this project. Finally, to my family: Heartfelt appreciation to David, for putting up with several years of both my excited monologuing about inspiring chapters and my grumblings when things hit a snag. Apologies to my oldest daughter, Asha, who, as I scrambled to get the manuscript to the publisher, had to give up the week of Daddy Day Camp we normally have between the end of her semester and the start of her summer camps. I promise I'll make it up to you next year. And thanks to my little one, Shailoe, for keeping me laughing.

INTRODUCTION

Having a Moment Four Decades in the Making

Don Romesburg

As this book goes to press, queer history is having a moment. In 2016, the National Park Service released its sprawling *LGBTQ America: A Theme Study of Lesbian, Gay, Bisexual, Transgender, and Queer History*. That year in July, in California, the state's Department of Education approved its latest K-12 History-Social Science Framework, in which, for the first time in any state, substantial lesbian, gay, bisexual, and transgender (LGBT) content appears in elementary, middle, and high school US history education. In 2017, despite the darkening national political landscape for LGBT people, momentum continued. In February, ABC aired the miniseries *When We Rise*, which chronicles the history of the modern LGBT rights movement across the last five decades. A few months later, Netflix secured worldwide distribution rights to *The Death and Life of Marsha P. Johnson*, a documentary about the legendary Stonewall Riots veteran and activist. Film festivals across North America screened *The Lavender Scare*, a documentary about post-World War II antigay government persecution, based on historian David Johnson's book of the same name. In New York, historian Stephen Vider curated "AIDS at Home: Art and Everyday Activism" at the Museum of the City of New York, while in San Francisco, the Board of Supervisors passed two history-related resolutions. The first unanimously endorsed the Gay, Lesbian, Bisexual and Transgender (GLBT) Historical Society's plan to secure a permanent location for its museum by 2020. Supervisors also legislated plans for the nation's first transgender historic district in the city's Tenderloin neighborhood. That summer, the city's South of Market neighborhood opened what is thought to be the first LGBT leather-focused historic park in the world, the Ringold Alley Leather Memorial. And these are just a few things happening in queer history beyond academia. After over 40 years of scholarly research into the queer past, this new level of public recognition signals the civic and cultural importance of LGBT history.

The scholarly fields of LGBT and/or queer history—more on terminology later—have come a long way since initial efforts in the 1970s and early 1980s. As Gerard Koskovich describes, previous historical work had been done in the 1950s and 1960s by those in the homophile movement. Beginning in the 1970s, though, a handful of scholars began taking deep dives into archives and generating rigorous analytical historical theses about same-sex sexuality and gender diversity. In this sense, publications by Carroll Smith-Rosenberg and Jonathan Ned Katz represent origins for our contemporary field. Smith-Rosenberg's 1975 article, "The Female World of Love and Ritual: Relations between Women in Nineteenth-Century America," and Katz's 1976 book, *Gay American History: Lesbians and Gay Men in the USA*, were grounded in the era's turn toward social history. Both explored how larger systems and structures of power interacted with the lives of everyday people. Additionally, both located within the American past inspirations for liberatory possibility in the present and, as Marc Stein has recently noted, "a specific vision for the future."[1]

Smith-Rosenberg's article is based on extensive analysis of late eighteenth- and nineteenth-century diaries and letters of white elite and middle-class women. It made three major assertions that have shaped the field ever since. The first was that same-sex sexuality and affective relations should be understood to be structured through historically specific social and cultural contexts rather than ascribed merely to individuals' psychological and developmental processes. The second was that intense and lasting ties between girls and women in that time and place were not issues of deviance but rather "defining configurations of legitimate behavioral norms and options." Third, within gender segregated structures not centrally of their own making, these girls and women produced networks of "emotional proximity" that generated lasting affective, physical and sometimes sensual ties that were central to who they were and to a life well lived.[2] Together, the arguments evidenced that sexuality is socially constructed and historically contingent, that social norms regarding sexuality and intimacy differ by time and place, and that within each era women find ways to make meaning of their connections to one another. These findings had profound implications for how to think about gender, love, intimacy, and community, both historically and in the worldmaking 1970s movements of second-wave feminism, lesbian feminism, and gay liberation.[3] The insights continue to speak to us today.

Unlike Smith-Rosenberg, who was a professor at the University of Pennsylvania with a Columbia University Ph.D. in History, and who at the time of her academic article's publication was going through divorce and coming out as a lesbian, Jonathan Ned Katz was an openly gay community scholar-activist when a popular press published *Gay American History*. As Jim Downs describes in *Stand by Me: The Forgotten History of Gay Liberation*, Katz, working with the Gay Socialists Action Project, drew on black and women's history methodologies and Marxist analysis to account for how religious, medical, and legal systems developed over time to identify and oppress same-sex sexuality and gender diversity. He also underscored innovative ways in which sexually and gender diverse people asserted agency through personal, cultural, and political resistance. Scouring archives, he compiled a stunning array of primary sources spanning from the 1500s to the 1970s in North America, arranging them into chapters on "Trouble," "Treatment," "Passing Women," "Native Americans/Gay Americans," "Resistance," and "Love."[4]

Today we would take issue with the limits of Katz's analysis and framing of, most obviously, indigenous people and those we could interpret through trans-historical lenses.[5] Such critiques should not, however, prevent us from being awestruck by *Gay American History*'s two profound contributions. First, the sheer volume and diversity of primary sources and their careful organization announced an unassailable presence for such as field as "gay history." These made it possible for professors to bring these sources into their teaching and research, which opened the field to professional development. At the same time, across the rest of the 1970s and 1980s, much of the field's foundational work was still being done by community scholars, often working in collaboration. Katz's book encouraged them to dig deeper into their local archives to unearth similar material and develop interpretations that had been, as a 1989 lesbian and gay history anthology phrased it, "hidden from history." Second, Katz's analysis blended social history's focus on structure and agency with an historical accounting for the social construction of homosexuality (and heterosexuality) as medical, legal, political, and personal categories of meaning, oppression, and resistance.

The Routledge History of Queer America seeks to capture the expansive and diverse fields of LGBT and queer US history, forty-odd years on from the early works of Smith-Rosenberg and Katz. Both became touchstones for the hundreds of books, articles, theses, and dissertations on LGBT and queer history that have followed. In 2015, Smith-Rosenberg's article received a 40-year retrospective conference panel at the Organization of American Historians. A year later, the New School hosted "Gay American History @ 40: Lesbian, Gay, Bisexual, Transgender, Queer History: Past, Present, Future," at which Smith-Rosenberg and Katz both gave talks, as did many leading and emerging scholars from this now-mature field.[6] The methods, analytical concerns, and lines of inquiry from those early works persist, even as the field has expanded far beyond them.

Today, queer history scholarship frequently appears in specialized journals such as the *Journal of the History of Sexuality* and *Radical History Review*, but also in preeminent journals of US history, such as the *American Historical Review* and the *Journal of American History*. It also finds its way into interdisciplinary journals from the queer- and trans-directed *GLQ* and *TSQ* to journals in American studies, women's and gender studies, and ethnic studies. Scholarly driven queer history also appears online in blogs such as NOTCHES: (re)marks on the history of sexuality, the ever-evolving OutHistory.org, and more mainstream sites from the *Atlantic* to Slate and the Huffington Post. Numerous academic presses have long had either history of sexuality series or an ongoing commitment to queer history as an important element of their catalogues. Queer US history has been the subject of many dozens of monographs, anthologies, and articles over the past four decades. In the last decade, it has been the subject of survey textbooks, including Leila Rupp's *A Desired Past*, Susan Stryker's *Transgender History*, Vicki Eaklor's *Queer America*, Michael Bronski's *A Queer History of the United States*, and Marc Stein's *Rethinking the Gay and Lesbian Movement*. Recent edited methodology anthologies include Nan Boyd and Horatio Roque Ramirez's *Bodies of Evidence: The Practice of Queer Oral History*, Leila Rupp and Susan Friedman's *Understanding and Teaching US LGBT History*, Amy L. Stone and Jaime Cantrell's *Out of the Closet, Into the Archives: Researching Sexual Histories*, and Susan Ferentinos' *Interpreting LGBT History at Museums and Historic Sites*.

Beyond scholarly and popular publications, the field has also seen explosive growth in the last decade through its institutionalization inside and outside of the academy. The Committee on LGBT History has a prominent presence at the annual American Historical Association conference, filling every session time with programming, while the Organization of American Historians has its own Committee on the Status of LGBTQ Historians and Histories and popular sessions. Conferences involving queer history occur across North America with frequency. Since the 2011 launch of the GLBT History Museum in San Francisco and the Pop-Up Museum of Queer History in New York, and more major exhibitions at mainstream institutions on related topics happening periodically, queer public history has been enjoying new prominence. Lesbian and gay historical scholarship has also played a significant role in US Supreme Court rulings (especially *Lawrence v. Texas* and *Obergefell v. Hodges*, where historians' *amicus* briefs are specifically cited by the court).

Additionally, queer history is a central aspect of interdisciplinary queer studies, especially in the last fifteen years as it has taken turns toward the archival and the historical.[7] Stand-alone LGBT and queer history courses are also being offered across North America, either as part of the growing number of queer and/or sexuality studies undergraduate and graduate degree programs or within history departments. Furthermore, many faculty are seeking to integrate the history of sexuality, and queer history specifically, into courses ranging from US surveys to more specialized courses in cultural, social, and political history. As K–12 history incorporates the LGBT past, especially in the wake of California's 2011 FAIR Education Act and the 2016 History-Social Science Framework, more secondary school teachers and education graduate programs need synthetic and accessible scholarship that encapsulates and interprets this now large and complex area of US historiography.

Still, the field of queer history, for all of its accomplishments, continues to struggle under conditions of, as queer studies scholar Heather Love noted during the Q&A of the closing session of Gay American History @ 40, "incomplete institutionalization."[8] Those studying and teaching the queer past, especially as LGBTQ scholars, graduate students, and educators, continue to face discomfort, disregard, and at times outright discrimination from some administrators, colleagues, publishers, funders, politicians, and community members. Many of us do all sorts of labor, hidden and visible, on our campuses and off, to support LGBTQ students and faculty, students and faculty of color, women, immigrants, and others marginalized by the systems, structures, and interpersonal dynamics we unevenly face. We also push our institutions and communities toward more expansive potentialities under conditions that render the prospects of structural change daunting—and often make precarious our own employment, advancement, and security.[9] It is worth noting that while some of the contributors to this book have tenure-track jobs, many others work term-to-term as contingent faculty or do their scholarly work without academic institutional affiliation.[10] More starkly, during the developmental process of the book's creation, one planned contributor, esteemed queer Latino historian Horacio N. Roque Ramírez, passed away. His absence in this collection is deeply registered. Horacio is not the only beloved queer scholar of color who we have lost far too young.

Additionally, our history is still rarely taught meaningfully outside of specialized courses. For many Americans, the assertion that kids in primary and secondary school should be learning about the LGBT past as integrated into the broader sweep of US history is still provocative—simply the notion that LGBT people have a meaningful history at all seems strange. Even at the college level, queer history plays a minor role, if any, in most US historians' scholarship and survey classrooms, despite decades of published work that should compel shifting analyses, narrative frames, and research approaches.

For both the reasons that queer history is a dynamic field gaining, at this moment, explosive momentum, and because its institutionalization and incorporation is still far from complete, *The Routledge History of Queer America* is a timely grounding text for many audiences, providing 28 innovative synthetic essays on the state of this now sprawling field. What follows is a brief guided tour through its major parts and their constitutive chapters.

Before I get there, though, two brief points of interest for readers on how to use this book. First, why is this a book about "queer America" rather than "LGBT" and/or the more precise "United States?" The former is a matter of substance, the latter one of form. Much ink has been spilled since the late 1980s over "why *queer*?" Rather than rehearse the whole discussion here, I humbly suggest that "queer" captures three central elements of the field's key concerns better than "LGBT." First, it most obviously operates as a loose umbrella term for all those sexually and gender-diverse people, activities, relations, categorizations, and identities that fall outside the norms of either their time and place or ours. Second, queer highlights the social construction and historical contingencies of sexuality and gender as fields of social power and meaning-making. Third, at its best, queer compels, as Cathy Cohen has famously argued, and Nayan Shah extends in his chapter here, an intersectional approach to institutional, social, cultural, and political operations of power. Grappling with mutually constitutive processes of racialization, gendering, sexualization, nationalizing, ascribing of socioeconomic class, and ability/disability gets us closer to describing the lived realities of the past even as it opens up the utility of queer history to understanding our present and producing more expansive and livable futures.

Although "LGBT," its subsets (such as "gay" or "bisexual"), or extended remixes ("LGBTQQIATSP" and so on) do not fundamentally prohibit the above approaches, they tend toward categories of identity. While the questions of how lesbian, gay, bisexual, and transgender people (as well as "queer," "questioning," "intersex," "asexual," "two-spirit," and "pansexual," to name a few) came to be identities and communities are key lines of historical inquiry, queer history seeks this and much more. How, for example, have people been queered by nation, as Eithne Luibhéid and Emily Hobson explore in their chapters, or by urbanization, as Kwame Holmes posits, or by slavery, as Clare Sears asks? Certainly, there are limits to the utility of "queer." It can tend toward a collapse back into dominant modes, such as gay over transgender, lesbian, and/or bisexual, as Finn Enke, Julie Enszer, and Loraine Hutchins, respectively, unpack in their chapters. Still, for the purposes of this book, queer does the best job of capturing all this unruly field has to offer.

I plead for tolerance on the question: Why "America" instead of "United States?" The titling format of the Routledge History of . . . series constrains wordplay, and I assert that *The Routledge History of Queer America* just sounds better than the clunkier *Routledge History of the Queer United States*. Moreover, in using "America," the title follows the form of the two major associations of the US history field, namely the Organization of American Historians and the American Historical Association. Let the record show that numerous contributing authors push the volume in more transnational directions and challenge the framing of US history as "American." While the book's focus is on the US, the nation's relationship to settler colonialism, immigration, and transnational flows in LGBT movements, politics, and culture means that the book also has global threads throughout.

Second, some suggestions on reading the book. The *Routledge History of Queer America* coalesces subject matter into topical and chronological chapters centered on historiographical synthesis, with detailed assessments of the state of the field and possible future directions. I trust this structure and form will be valuable to those with an interest in US history and/or those who wish to find connections with queer history in their own areas of research, teaching, and learning. Contributors come mostly from history departments, but given the field's interdisciplinarity, some have institutional homes in gender studies, ethnic studies, anthropology, sociology, cultural studies, communications, law, American studies, and literature. Hopefully there's a little something for everyone.

More specifically, for those seeking a general overview of the queer US past, I suggest you read Part One, the "Times" section, first, from start to finish. The contributors collectively do an excellent job of telling that big story and raising some of the main questions and concerns for those studying these particular eras. For those seeking specific questions of subject or concerns about analytic frame, the second two parts of the book ("Spaces and Places" and "Themes") will give you plenty of inspiration and direction for further inquiry and readings. For all readers, be sure to explore the extensive cross-referencing between the chapters and parts. My hope is that even if you begin with the intention of reading just one chapter for some project or syllabus you're working on, the cross-references will have you adventuring down multiple other paths and discovering the rich and diverse territory covered by this remarkable assemblage of scholars and the decades of work they weave together. Take notice, also, that many of the citations historians are used to finding in endnotes have been consolidated into the "Further Reading" sections at the end of each chapter. Of course, I invite everyone to read the book cover to cover. You will be dazzled, I promise.

On with the tour. Part One: Times is organized chronologically, and chapters are intended to orient students and scholars of various eras to LGBT and queer contexts. Read in its entirety, this section demonstrates transformative change over the long sweep of American history as well as the substantial and diverse queer historiography for every major period. In his chapter on colonial North America, Richard Godbeer invites close attention to how early Americans made uneven meaning of gender diversity and same-sex desire and intimacy among colonial, indigenous, and enslaved people, often depending on people's status in communities. Exploring the late eighteenth and early nineteenth centuries, Rachel Hope Cleves asserts that while American independence may have expanded boundaries for same-sex erotic expression among some white youth, the formation of the settler-colonial US state limited indigenous expressions and expanded sexual exploitation in the US slave system. Clare Sears takes up the limited position that slavery currently occupies in nineteenth-century queer historical scholarship to urge its incorporation into the more familiar aspects of the era's sexual and gender diversity, namely industrialization and western expansionism.

The late nineteenth and early twentieth centuries are deservedly seen as especially crucial to understanding the queer US past. As Elizabeth Clement and Beans Velocci argue in their chapter, the modern institutionalization of sexual categories in medicine and law forged with industrialization and urbanization to produce both vibrant queer subcultures and regimes of normalcy versus perversion. By the mid-twentieth century, policing and governing systems on the one hand and blossoming queer life on the other led to unprecedented persecution and resistance. In her chapter, Amanda Littauer explains how this era forged early civil rights groups, urban queer spaces, alternative domesticities, trans possibilities, strategic navigations of self-disclosure, and playful encounters with an often cruel and tragic popular culture. By the mid-1960s, as Whitney Strub details in his chapter, rising radicalism blossomed into what would, by the early 1970s, become gay liberation. A remarkably diverse movement rather than a monolith, liberation brought new meanings and agendas for trans people of color, middle-class gay white men, white lesbian separatists, black lesbian socialists, and bisexual activists, all of whom often strove for multiracial, cross-class coalition, yet struggled with inclusion and efforts to align the movement with liberal electoral politics and urban reform. By the 1980s, AIDS would come to dominate queer life in the US, but as Jennifer Brier argues in her chapter, HIV/AIDS history and queer history are not synonymous. Rather, HIV/AIDS history in the 1980s and 1990s tells a queer history of how LGBT people were transformed by the epidemic in ways that redefined how we challenged systems, structures, and ideologies of normativity. Finally, Margot Weiss, an anthropologist, provides a brief queer history of our long present era of neoliberalism, arguing that since the 1970s, and with increasing force since the 1990s, the privatization of social services, emphasis on citizens as consumers, and promotion of corporate welfare and urban redevelopment pits some "deserving" gay people against "undeserving" queer others in politics, culture, and economics. She urges us to grapple with this past in order to comprehend and take action on the queer politics of our time.

Part Two: Spaces and Places is organized into major literal and figurative spatial arrangements through which US queer historical scholarship has been arranged, from the most local scope (the body) through the most expansive (the transnational). First, though, it begins with the main site from which our historical scholarship has emerged—the archive. As media studies professor Kate Eichhorn traces in her chapter, early community LGBT archives from the 1970s and 1980s emerged out of private collections going as far back as the 1940s. By the 1990s and 2000s, these archives found a diversity of institutional homes with varying politics, access, resources, and archival practices. The "archival turn" in queer studies more generally has also expanded the meaning of the archive itself, as an assemblage of "seemingly disparate objects of study" and a way to stand in for those absences in the formal archive that nonetheless leave a queer trace, both of which encourage innovative practices for queer historians.[11]

From there, David Serlin traces the ways in which science, politics, and culture have been used across time in different ways to distinguish some idealized or normalized American bodies from queer others. He marks the interlocking ways that race, gender, able-bodiedness, and sexuality figure in ongoing efforts to produce the normative. In the twentieth century, queer bodies began assembling into LGBT social and political organizations, the diversity of which, Marcia Gallo asserts, reflect the eras in which they labored, the aspirations they shared to produce collective change from the experiences of marginalized individuals, and the limits their organizers placed on the scope of their collective vision.

A central spatial tension in queer US history relates to the domination of the urban over the rural. Given the near-hegemony of urban history within most queer scholarship, it might seem too great a provocation when contributor Kwame Holmes wonders if we are at the "end of queer urban history." His core assertion though, that those people who have been queered by urbanization have always exceeded easy categorization as "LGBT," leads him to center black queer and feminist analyses. He argues that to continue to speak to our present and future, queer urban history moving forward must incorporate all those straining against the city's normative forces of sexuality and gender in their time and place. Pippa Holloway and Elizabeth Catte argue that the question is less how to better do urban in queer history than how to reframe it through the rural, from the colonial era through the present. They focus on the ways in which rural spaces and places have over time accommodated and constrained sexual and gender diversity in distinct ways, and they challenge the urban/rural dichotomy as a false binary in the construction of the queer past.

Scholarship on US nationalism and transnationalism have been substantially deepened and complicated through histories of sexuality and gender. They suggest that, on the one hand, queer sexualities and diverse genders have been central to the project of US state nation-making and, on the other, they have flowed through imperial, globalizing, and transnational circuits of desire, capital, culture, and state power. The last two chapters in Part Two take on these large spatial scales. Eithne Luibhéid explains how the concepts of "queer" and "nation" have always been mutually constitutive, and traces this braided tension across processes of colonization, slavery, capitalism, empire, and the elaboration of the modern state. Similarly, Emily Hobson utilizes transnational and queer approaches to US history to denaturalize the nation-state, explore racialized knowledge productions about sexuality and gender, challenge the limits of sexual citizenship, and map out transnational LGBT activism since the mid-twentieth century.

Finally, Part Three constitutes the largest number of chapters, in an attempt to synthesize the rich content of major thematic concerns of both US queer history and queer studies more generally. These essays should enjoy a wide interdisciplinary audience, given the importance of historical analysis to their topics and frames. There is a loose method to their arrangement. The first five tackle vexing and productive tensions between trans, lesbian, bi, and queer of color identity categories and differential critical lenses for studying the past. The next seven address major issues that flow throughout much US history, and point in new directions where queer scholarship might head. The book then ends where this introduction begins, exploring how public history beats at the heart of the project of generating narratives of the queer past.

Jen Manion begins Part Three with an essay tackling the "acts vs. identities" question at the core of queer history—who did what, when, why, and what does that make them, then and now, to us? Manion acknowledges that as communities in search of our pasts, LGBTQ people need to be able to claim histories as ours. But which "ours?" We must strive to make historically useful claims while minimizing the exclusionary tendencies of extending our identifications into the past. Manion calls upon historians to embrace uncertainty and highlights trans and queer of color methodologies as central tools for our craft moving forward.

Finn Enke takes up trans historiographic methods and theoretical frameworks in his chapter. Like Manion, Enke looks to the nineteenth century and earlier, before modern categories of gender, sexuality, and race became relatively established, to urge historians to suspend their assumptions and to critique narratives and frames that marginalize trans analyses. Often, queer and trans histories and methods are placed into false opposition with lesbian histories, identities, and methods, as if one cancels out the other. In her chapter, Julie Enszer urges a "spiraling" approach to lesbian history that recognizes the multiple community-based, scholarly, and communal historiographic practices that have built lesbian history to date. In addition, she urges us to reject viewing queer and trans tensions with lesbian history as threatening, and to instead embrace them as generative "twists and turns along the spiral of its creation."[12] While lesbian history can at times be seen as under threat from other methodologies, bisexual history has yet to see its day in the sun. In her chapter, Loraine Hutchins calls upon historians of the queer past to reject bisexual erasure and embrace analytics, methods, and archives that open history to bisexual realities. Nayan Shah's chapter takes up the concept of estrangement that grounds his 2011 book, *Stranger Intimacies: Contesting Race, Sexuality and the Law in the North American West,* and extends it through queer of color histories of the technologies of estrangement from the colonial period to the present. The approach allows historians to reconceive of the innovative ways that indigenous, African American, Latinx, and Asian American people have produced queer and trans worldmaking and resistance.

Despite the presence of LGBT marriage and families in the political and media landscape of the last two decades, the scholarly history of queer families is still quite young. In his chapter, Daniel Rivers describes how self-defined lesbian, gay, and bisexual parents have been raising children since at least World War II, and he argues that while the gay liberation and lesbian-feminist movements would prove crucial to families with kids, it would take until the 1990s for queer family politics to take a central place in the modern LGBT rights movement. A crucial issue for lesbian, gay, and bisexual parents, and many others, was the depathologization of homosexuality as a mental illness, which finally occurred in 1973 when the American Psychiatric Association removed it from its *Diagnostics and Statistics Manual.* In Katie Batza's chapter, she explores the long queer history of sickness and wellness, and argues that since the 1880s through medicalization, access to healthcare, and freedom from it, sexually diverse and gender diverse people have unevenly negotiated related social norms regarding race, class, nationality, and ability. Indeed, as Andrea Ritchie and Kay Whitlock argue in their chapter, those same norms drove queer criminalization from the colonial period to the present. In myriad ways sexually and gender diverse people have resisted criminalization and, since the twentieth century, demanded legalization, with uneven success. In his chapter, Marc Stein takes up the question of how we should evaluate success—or progress—in terms of narrating queer law and politics over time. Rather than resolving the conflict between a progress narrative and queer critiques of that narrative, Stein suggests that the achievement of rights and freedoms for some LGBT people has come at the same time as intersecting forces have exacerbated structural divisions among queer people.

While the forces of law, politics, and medicine have long saturated the existences of sexually diverse and gender diverse people in the United States, economic and material realities and ideologies have also been central to how we have lived, loved, expressed ourselves, and been represented. John D'Emilio's still-relevant 1983 essay, "Capitalism and Gay Identity," linked the rise of industrial capitalism and urbanization to the transformation of same-sex desires into extrafamilial networks, subcultures, and identities. Since that essay was published, many scholars have taken up its analysis to explore queer work, class, and consumption, although, as Sara Smith-Silverman notes in her chapter, queer labor history is still a relatively underdeveloped subfield. Smith asserts that this is a shame, because changes in economic systems that structure labor have profoundly shaped queer history and the queer labor movement that has grown since the 1970s. Stephen Vider's chapter takes on the other side of the capitalist coin, namely consumerism. He asserts that since the early twentieth century, if not earlier, queer consumption has helped produce LGBTQ identities and communities in everything from bars and bathhouses to comportment, aesthetic sensibility, and target marketing. At the same time, the seductive incorporation of LGBT peoples into mainstreaming systems of consumer citizenship has been uneven, often creating winners and losers along intersecting lines of race, gender, and class. Many activists continue to see political economy and historical materialism as a central site for queer resistance. Many have also long understood how, in a consumer capitalist society, representation in popular culture is crucial to how queer people make sense of themselves and how others understand us. In her chapter, Sharon Ullman takes the long view of queer presence in popular culture, tracking major representations from early America through the new millennium. As she observes, popular culture's play with dressing up, make-believe, and multiple meanings have always made it a little queer, and the collective experience of popular culture's spectatorship has always produced a politics of empathy (as well as antipathy) for queer people. Understanding how and why queer representations took shape in particular ways in particular times and places allows us to appreciate the changing material, affective, and relational conditions of diverse LGBTQ people.

In the book's final chapter, Lara Kelland showcases the remarkable efforts through which LGBT people have, since the 1970s, had made queer history public. What began as grassroots efforts to build history cooperatives and cultural expressions based in gay liberation and lesbian feminism, evolved by the 1980s and 1990s into institutions committed to the preservation, interpretation, and accessibility of LGBTQ history for ourselves and for a wider world. Kelland explains how queer models of public history, both from within our own actions and organizations and from our growing presence within mainstream museums, galleries, libraries, and civic landscapes, grant the LGBT movement civic recognition of our remarkable presence (as the gay lib saying goes, "We Are Everywhere"). Such queer public histories also testify to our long evolution and celebrate our tenacious persistence.

The Routledge History of Queer America testifies to the depth and range of a momentous conversation from the last four decades about seven centuries of the American past. Queer history matters now more than ever, and not just because it is currently having a moment. Its contributions to the ways we comprehend and narrate the US past enrich and transform academic, public, and civic projects of history. Present and future stakes are high in synthesizing and sharing this rich past, as we collectively determine how sexual and gender diversity belong to and constitute American society, culture, polity, and nation.

Notes

1 Marc Stein, "Jonathan Ned Katz Murdered Me: History and Suicide," Process: A Blog for American History, Organization of American History, March 8, 2016, www.processhistory.org/stein-katz/. Accessed October 18, 2017.

2 Carroll Smith-Rosenberg, "The Female World of Love and Ritual: Relations between Women in Nineteenth-Century America," *Signs* 1, no. 1 (1975): esp. 2–3, 10, 24–29. For another early scholarly extension of how the period's patriarchal and separate sphere structures and ideologies produced opportunities for female same-sex sexual agency, intimacy, and relationality, see also Nancy F. Cott, "Passionlessness: An Interpretation of Victorian Sexual Ideology, 1790–1850," *Signs* 4, no. 2 (1978): 219–236. For brief analyses that extend and critique Smith-Rosenberg's analysis and claims, particularly as related to its limitations regarding race and its downplaying of sexual activity, see, in this volume,

Rachel Hope Cleves, "Revolutionary Sexualities and Early National Genders (1770s–1840s)" and Clare Sears, "Centering Slavery in Nineteenth-Century Queer History (1800s–1890s)."

3 For a discussion of Smith-Rosenberg's article as the first work of "authorized" lesbian history, see, in this volume, Julie Enszer, "Lesbian History: Spirals of Imagination, Marginalization, Creation and Erasure."

4 For another discussion of Katz's chapters and the historical politics of identity, see, in this volume, Jen Manion, "Language, Acts and Identity in LGBT History."

5 See, for example, Susan Stryker's generous yet focused critique in her keynote at the Gay American History @ 40 conference, "1973: Remembering Queer History Otherwise," May 5, 2016, New College, New York, www.youtube.com/watch?v=y3nI2uKH39Y. Accessed October 20, 2017.

6 For the Smith-Rosenberg roundtable, see "Organization of American Historians Annual Conference", St. Louis, April 17, 2015, www.oah.org/meetings-events/2015/highlights/women/. Accessed October 21, 2017. The *Gay American History @ 40* conference program can be found at www.yumpu.com/en/document/view/55468475/gah40-program. Accessed October 22, 2017. Debbie Richards assembled a fascinating roundup on Storify of conference-related tweets at "Gay American History @ 40" #GAH40, https://storify.com/amdial/gah40-roundup-572eb6f40f03d50002afbfe8. Accessed October 22, 2017.

7 For the uses for history of the archival turn in queer studies, see, in this volume, Kate Eichhorn, "Queer Archives: From Collections to Conceptual Framework."

8 The conference's closing session, featuring Katz along with John D'Emilio, Esther Newton, and Carole Vance, can be found at www.youtube.com/watch?v=o-A2i9OtYR0. Accessed October 19, 2017.

9 See, for example, the Committee on LGBTQ Status within the Profession, *LGBTQ Task Force Final Report* (American Historical Association: 2015): www.historians.org/Documents/FINALLGBTQREPORT31615.pdf. Accessed October 22, 2017. For a more general discussion of the strain and challenge of doing institutional "diversity work" as queer, trans, or feminist scholars, particularly those of color, see Sara Ahmed, *On Being Included: Racism and Diversity in Institutional Life* (Durham: Duke University Press, 2012) and *Living a Feminist Life* (Durham: Duke University Press, 2017); Roderick A. Ferguson, *The Reorder of Things: The University and Its Pedagogies of Minority Difference* (Minneapolis: University of Minnesota Press, 2012).

10 This tracks with professional discussions surrounding the *LGBTQ Task Force Final Report*, cited above. See Allison Miller, "Scholars on the Edge: The LGBTQ Historians Task Force Report and the AHA," *Perspectives on History*, February 2016, www.historians.org/publications-and-directories/perspectives-on-history/february-2016/scholars-on-the-edge-the-lgbtq-historians-task-force-report-and-the-aha. Accessed October 19, 2017.

11 This volume, p. 132.

12 This volume, p. 245.

Further Reading

Boyd, Nan Alamilla and Horacio N. Roque Ramírez, eds. *Bodies of Evidence: The Practice of Queer Oral History*. New York: Oxford University Press, 2012.

Bronski, Michael. *A Queer History of the United States*. Boston: Beacon, 2012.

Cohen, Cathy. "Punks, Bulldaggers, and Welfare Queens: The Radical Potential of Queer Politics?" *GLQ* 3, no. 4 (1997): 437–465.

D'Emilio, John. "Capitalism and Gay Identity." In *Powers of Desire: The Politics of Sexuality*, eds. Ann Snitow, Christine Stansell and Sharon Thompson, 100–113. New York: Monthly Review Press, 1983.

Downs, Jim. *Stand by Me: The Forgotten History of Gay Liberation*. New York: Basic Books, 2016.

Duberman, Martin, Martha Vicinus, and George Chauncey, Jr., eds. *Hidden from History: Reclaiming the Gay and Lesbian Past*. New York: Dutton, 1989.

Eaklor, Vicki. *Queer America: A People's GLBT History of the United States*. New York: New Press, 2011.

Ferentinos, Susan. *Interpreting LGBT History at Museums and Historic Sites*. Lanham, MD: Rowman and Littlefield, 2014.

Johnson, David K. *The Lavender Scare: The Cold War Persecution of Gays and Lesbians in the Federal Government*. Chicago: University of Chicago Press, 2004.

Katz, Johnathan Ned. *Gay American History: Lesbians and Gay Men in the USA*. New York: Thomas Y. Crowell Company, 1976.

Koskovich, Gerard. "The History of Queer History: One Hundred Years of the Search for the Share Heritage." In *LGBTQ America: A Theme Study of Lesbian, Gay, Bisexual, Transgender, and Queer History*, ed. Megan E. Springate, 04-1-04–38. Washington, DC: National Park Foundation, 2016.

Rupp, Leila. *A Desired Past: A Short History of Same-Sex Love in America*. Chicago: University of Chicago Press, 2002.

Rupp, Leila and Susan Friedman, eds. *Understanding and Teaching US LGBT History*. Madison: University of Wisconsin Press, 2014.

Shah, Nayan. *Stranger Intimacies: Contesting Race, Sexuality and the Law in the North American West*. Berkeley: University of California Press, 2011.

Stein, Marc, ed. *Encyclopedia of Lesbian, Gay, Bisexual, and Transgender History in America*. New York: Charles Scribner's Sons, 2003.

Stein, Marc. *Rethinking the Gay and Lesbian Movement*. New York: Routledge, 2012.

Stone, Amy and Jaime Cantrell, eds. *Out of the Closet, Into the Archives: Researching Sexual Histories*. Albany: State University of New York, 2015.

Stryker, Susan. *Transgender History*. Berkeley: Seal Press, 2008.

PART ONE

Times

1

COLONIAL
NORTH AMERICA
(1600s–1700s)

Richard Godbeer

How do we write about what today is called lesbian, gay, bisexual, and transgender history when dealing with periods before the fundamental categories of sexual identity that modern westerners now take for granted (such as 'gay,' lesbian,' and 'homosexual') came into existence? Some scholars, such as Rictor Norton, argue that men attracted to men and women attracted to women in whatever period can legitimately be described as gay and lesbian because their desires, however labeled at the time, were similar if not identical to those experienced and expressed by people today. Others, most notably David Halperin, have countered that these modern and western categories are freighted with assumptions that simply do not apply in other historical and cultural contexts. Indeed, some have suggested that the actual experience of desire might be shaped at least in part by the categories available to us, so that subjectivity is to some degree contingent upon discourse. This chapter's approach is closer to the latter position: men and women in the North American colonies who desired intimacy with members of the same sex experienced and expressed those desires in ways that were shaped by the cultural vocabulary available to them. We cannot possibly understand their feelings and experiences without taking seriously the discursive environment in which they moved. That is not to suggest that colonial Americans were entirely passive prisoners of a larger cultural discourse. Even though we are all handed a cultural script with which to articulate our desires, we each pick and choose which parts of the script to adopt and sometimes add our own lines. Early Americans sometimes tried to find words that would describe feelings and behavior that official language failed to encapsulate. But until very recently men-loving men and women-loving women did not think in terms of sexual orientation or identity; to impose subjectivities such as these onto their lives is simply to re-invent them as a mirror of ourselves instead of trying to understand them on their own terms.[1]

Historians investigating same-sex desire and gender diversity in the colonial period face a number of obstacles. Individuals were understandably reluctant to admit sexual behavior that carried the death penalty, while their neighbors were often eager to avoid acknowledging the occurrence of same-sex intimacy in their communities. The vocabulary that colonial Americans used to describe sexual attraction or activity was sometimes ambiguous; a reference to "unclean" behavior, for example, might indicate something sexual, but quite possibly not, given the Christian position that any sinful action polluted the body and soul of the persons involved.

Archivists and historians have, furthermore, sometimes ignored, suppressed, or even destroyed evidence of sexual and gender nonconformity that they found perplexing or distasteful.

★　★　★

Willful silence and suppression played a significant role in the manufacturing of Virginia's early history. Jamestown was initially an all-male colony; though women did migrate to the Chesapeake in subsequent years, they remained relatively few in number for several decades. The Chesapeake's skewed sex ratio made it extremely difficult for men to establish conventional family households or to find female sexual partners; there seems, furthermore, to have been little sexual contact with Indians during those years. Early settlers often paired off to form all-male households, living and working together. As historian Mary Beth Norton has remarked, "it would be truly remarkable if all the male-only partnerships lacked a sexual ingredient."[2] Some men may have engaged in sexual relations with each other out of desperation; others may have taken advantage of an unusual situation to form relationships that would have been stigmatized under normal circumstances.

Just as householders elsewhere on both sides of the Atlantic sometimes assumed that they had a right to the bodies as well as labor of their servants, so early seventeenth-century Virginians who had male indentured servants working for them may well have pressured or forced their dependants into having sex with them. One male servant was found dead with his thighs badly bruised; another who had been working for an all-male household hanged himself for no apparent reason. We can only wonder if these deaths were prompted, at least in part, by sexual coercion. One servant did formally accuse his master of raping him. As a result of that servant's testimony, Captain Richard Cornish was convicted of sodomy and hanged in 1625. In this case, the only trial for sodomy known to have taken place in the early Chesapeake, Cornish's execution aroused heated controversy. The death sentence was certainly open to question, given the lack of corroborative testimony: no one had witnessed the captain's alleged assault of his servant. Edward Nevell, for example, declared that the captain had been hanged "for a rascally boy wrongfully." The government was clearly determined to silence those who criticized its handling of the case. Nevell was arrested for his criticism of the court and sentenced "to stand on the pillory with a paper on his head showing the cause of his offense in the market place, and to lose both his ears, and to serve the colony for a year."[3] As women were now arriving in greater numbers, enabling the formation of more conventional households and marriages, the authorities may have wanted to make an example of Cornish. Critics of the court may have been anxious about the vulnerability of other men, perhaps including themselves, especially if they were to be convicted as a result of uncorroborated accusations. It is striking that none of the reported conversations about this case suggested any revulsion toward sodomy itself. Some Virginians may have feared that a veil of silence regarding sexual activity between men in the colony was being ripped away. That veil of silence was soon back in place and would remain there, lifted only recently by a few scholars who have begun to ask questions about fragmentary evidence that survives about male liaisons in the early Chesapeake.

In sharp contrast, sodomy would figure as a regular topic of public discourse further north in seventeenth-century New England, where Puritan leaders were eager to protect their New Israel from pollution, sexual or otherwise, through vehement denunciation of sin in all its manifestations. Though officials there were exceptionally energetic and vigilant in their campaigns against illicit sex, the assumptions that underlay those efforts were not unusual. In common with settlers in other British American colonies, New Englanders made a number of assumptions about what we would call sexuality that differed radically from our own.

Perhaps most fundamentally, Puritans did not think about sexual impulses in terms of a distinct sexuality or sexual orientation that impels men and women toward members of the same or opposite sex. They thought in terms of specific sexual acts that were divided into two fundamental categories: sex between a husband and wife, and all other sex (including premarital sex, casual sex between a man and a woman, masturbation, sex between two men or between two women, and bestiality). They explained all non-marital sex just as they did any other sin, such as drunkenness or falling asleep during a sermon: they were all caused by innate moral corruption which every human being inherited from Adam and Eve. Ministers held that sodomy and bestiality were "unnatural" and so more sinful than illicit sex between a man and a woman. But official teaching did not conceive of sodomy as fundamentally distinct from any other manifestation of human sin. Nor did it see particular men or women as constitutionally inclined or limited to any one form of sexual offense. In other words, the fundamental issue was not sexual orientation, but moral orientation.

Anglo-American laws against sodomy reflected this official preoccupation with particular acts rather than sexual identity or orientation, so that courts were interested primarily in finding out whether a specific act of sexual intercourse had occurred. Neither intent nor an attempt could justify conviction, which carried the death penalty. Because most people committing illicit sexual acts had the common sense not to do so in a public place, conviction rates were remarkably low: it was rare that witnesses came forward with unequivocal statements that they had seen sexual intercourse taking place; and liaisons involving members of the same sex could not be exposed through a resulting pregnancy. This was, of course, good news for individuals who might otherwise have been convicted and hanged.[4]

Not only were executions for sodomy rare, but prosecutions were also remarkably sparse, even in the bracing moral climate of New England. Local communities preferred to handle problematic behavior through informal channels. They resorted to ecclesiastical discipline or the legal system only when private exhortation or informal arbitration failed to resolve the situation. The narrow framing of the laws against sodomy and the rigorous demands of the legal system, which required two independent witnesses for a conviction, may well have deterred some New Englanders from initiating formal action against offenders. Addressing the situation through non-juridical channels was, moreover, less dire than invoking capital law and so would have appealed to those who disapproved of sodomy but did not want the accused to hang. In several cases of sodomy that came before courts or church congregations, it emerged during the proceedings that the accused had long been locally notorious for their sexual interest in men, but that it had taken an extraordinary turn of events to bring about a formal charge. Any number of local incidents and controversies involving sodomy may have escaped record because of this preference for non-institutional forms of social control. When Nicholas Sension, a farmer in Windsor, Connecticut, was brought to trial for his "sodomitical actings" in 1677, it became clear that he had been making sexual advances to local men for over three decades. There had been several informal investigations into his behavior, but his aggressive interest in other men did not become a legal issue until Sension prosecuted one of his own servants for slander. The young man had told neighbors that his employer was making unwanted advances toward him, and when several people came forward to refute Sension's charge of slander by confirming that he was a serial aggressor, the court initiated a sodomy trial. Had Sension not made this disastrous tactical error, we would most likely know nothing about his reputation or behavior.[5]

The transcripts that survive from that case are rich and revealing in a number of respects. Not least, they show just how restrictive and rigorous the courts were in handling cases such as these. Although many men came forward to testify that Sension had made sexual advances toward them or other male neighbors, only one witness claimed to have seen Sension penetrate a male partner and so Sension could not be hanged. The Sension transcripts also suggest that incidents of sodomy or attempted sodomy sometimes failed to reach the courts because locals were either less outraged by such behavior than clerical tirades and legal prohibitions might lead us to expect, or weighed their disapproval of sodomy with other considerations. Nicholas Sension was in most respects a popular man. One fellow who was summoned to describe an occasion on which Sension had tried to rape him expressed his reluctance to do Sension any harm because the accused had been so kind to him and his wife when they needed help. In determining an individual's social worth, most colonists appear to have found nonsexual aspects of that person's behavior more significant even than an allegedly heinous sin and crime such as sodomy. Risking the loss of a good neighbor struck many practical-minded settlers as too high a price to pay for moral cleansing.

Sension was also a prominent landowner and employer in the community where he lived. When in his twenties, he had made advances to men of roughly the same age as himself. But in later years, most of the men whom he approached were teenagers or young adults and at least two of them were his own servants. In other words, Sension appears to have been interested in men whose age and status placed them in a position subordinate to himself. For most sodomy prosecutions in the colonial period there survives only a brief record of the charge and outcome; in some cases, we do not even know the names of those involved, let alone their age or relative status. Contemporaries often referred to servants as "boys" or "girls" regardless of their age, making it difficult to ascertain how old they really were unless other information survives. (William Couse, the servant who accused Richard Cornish of raping him, was twenty-nine years old, but Edward Nevell described him as "a rascally boy.") Yet at least in Sension's case, sexual aggression, hierarchy, and power were closely intertwined. That power dynamic might also help to explain why most of Sension's neighbors took so long to protest his behavior. Scholars have shown that social status was crucial in determining whether individuals would be held accountable for crimes such as rape. At least some of those who were aware of sexual aggression toward servants understood that behavior in terms of the power dynamic involved: as historian Barbara Lindemann has written, "many instances of coerced sexual relations were probably not perceived as rape, even by the victim, and certainly not by the assailant or the neighbors," because it was seen instead as "an expression of male control."[6] Sension may have believed that his aggressive behavior was justified by his status as a male householder and employer; others may have felt the same way, even if they did not approve of his behavior.

The Sension case also gives us a tantalizing glimpse of neighbors trying to understand and describe a man's persistent desire for physical intimacy with other men in a period that had no vocabulary to capture that ongoing attraction. They clearly perceived in Sension's actions a persistent inclination toward sodomy that was specific and transcended individual incidents or acts. For them the issue was not sinfulness in general, but a specific sin, repeated over and over again. Sension himself apparently characterized his repeated sexual overtures toward other males as a distinct realm of activity. When neighbor William Phelps berated Sension for attempting to seduce various men in the vicinity, Sension reportedly admitted that he had "long" practiced "this trade." It is not clear from Phelps's deposition whether he or Sension introduced the word "trade" into their conversation; indeed, Phelps may have used it retroactively. But "trade" implied a specific calling or way of life: use of that word to describe Sension's behavior, by whomever, indicated a sense of its significance, distinctiveness, and permanence in his life. The designation "trade" went well beyond the act-oriented view of sodomy propounded in official statements and fitted Sension's own experience much better than did authorized categories. Phelps's deposition, then, provides a rare glimpse of ordinary people creating their own sexual taxonomy. To argue that New England townspeople and villagers identified a distinct sexuality would stretch the evidence too far. But observation of men such as Nicholas Sension does seem to have led neighbors and acquaintances to treat sodomy as a specific and consistent impulse: it became in their minds a habitual course of action that characterized some men throughout their lives. When Sension's neighbors told court officials about his long history of attraction toward young men, their remarks were of little use in proving a legal charge of sodomy, yet relating Sension's male-oriented sexual appetite made sense to them.

If official discourse provided no conceptual tools for understanding a man's lifelong desire for other men, it was even more impoverished in its discussion of women who desired women. Ministers included in their definitions of "unnatural" sex not only the coupling of men with men but also of women with women. Yet they had remarkably little to say about the latter and the laws against sodomy focused much more specifically on male sex. That was due in large part to the legal system's conception of sex as an act of phallic intercourse. Because lawmakers and magistrates understood sex in terms of penetration, they found it difficult to conceive of a sexual scenario that did not involve a penis along with a male to which it was attached. As a result, there was little room for the recognition or prosecution of sex between women. On only two known occasions did women appear before New England courts on charges of "unclean" behavior with a person of the same sex. In one case the magistrates described the behavior under consideration as "unseemly" and in the other as "lewd." The use of these vague adjectives probably reflected the judges' uncertainty as to how sexual intimacy between women should be classified, and also, perhaps, a reluctance to describe the acts in particular. Without a penis to hold on to, they were lost.[7]

Surviving evidence about individuals whom we might characterize today as transgender is also sparse for the colonial period.[8] Early reports from the New World had described a category of Native American men who lived as women, dressed in female clothing, and engaged in sexual relations with other men. There were also Indian women who assumed male clothing and roles, though this phenomenon seems to have been less widespread. European observers expressed amazement that Indians apparently revered men who lived as women, especially given that they made themselves sexually available to other men in their communities. Indian acceptance of and respect for behavior that was criminalized in Europe as whoredom and sodomy exemplified for these writers the immorality and savagery of Indian culture. Europeans used the word 'berdache' (an Arabic word meaning male prostitute) to describe such men. Yet Indians often referred to them as "half-man/half-woman."

The specific characteristics and functions of the "half-man/half-woman" varied from nation to nation, but in general s/he combined male and female attributes, remaining anatomically male and in some nations wearing both male and female articles of clothing. Such individuals could not attain the honor associated with male-identified roles that they had forsaken, but they were esteemed for unique contributions made possible by their gender-mixing. Whereas Europeans saw the "berdache" as an emblem of sin and disorder, from an Indian perspective the "half-man/half-woman" embodied and promoted the harmony that resulted from reconciling opposites within the physical and spiritual realms. Their composite identity as "half-man/half-woman" enabled them to mediate between the polarities of male and female as well as between those of spirit and flesh. Particular boys were prompted by dreams or visions to become "half-man/half-woman," made the transition through established rituals, and then assumed a prominent role within the ritual life of their communities. Some scholars have suggested that the presence of the "half-man/half-woman" may have worked to the advantage of other men in terms of gender politics within native communities: the incorporation of female qualities into male ceremonies without actually involving women may have appealed to Indian men who wished to symbolize the coming together of male and female without sacrificing their monopoly over certain aspects of ceremonial life. The "half-man/half-woman" sometimes married a man, but unless or until he did so he was sexually available to other men within his community, which would have given both married and unmarried men a sexual outlet that avoided potential conflict over access to women.[9]

Europeans who to sought to convert and "civilize" Indians insisted that setting aside native customs relating to sex and gender should play an important part in that process. Colonial leaders meanwhile sought to prevent European settlers from adopting Indian customs, sexual and otherwise, or from exhibiting any pattern of behavior that challenged official sexual and gender codes, which they saw as crucial to the establishment of an orderly society in the New World.[10] One tantalizing court case from Virginia in 1629 focused on a servant known sometimes as Thomas and sometimes as Thomasine Hall, who seems to have shifted back and forth between male and female attire. According to Hall's own testimony, s/he made these shifts so as to obtain access to gendered occupations that ranged from soldiering to sewing, though Hall may also have taken pleasure in adopting both male and female personae. Local curiosity and anxiety about Hall focused on the servant's genitalia, which neighbors forcibly examined on more than one occasion. Opinion was divided as to whether Hall's genital organs were male or female; but when asked if s/he was a man or woman, Hall replied that s/he was both. On both sides of the Atlantic, anatomical ambiguity was seen as having worrying implications for sexual relations and gender performance, though in practice few people were identified as such. Hall was rumored to have engaged in unmarried sexual relations with a female servant and so identifying his/her anatomical sex became crucial in determining what kind of offense had been committed. Establishing whether Hall was male or female would also dictate what kinds of labor s/he could be expected to do as a servant.

The court declined to address the issue of fornication or to identify Thomas/ine as male or female, instead announcing that the defendant was both and must henceforth wear a combination of male and female clothing. This would prevent Hall from switching back and forth as convenient. The sentence was clearly not designed to legitimize a hybrid gender or sexual identity but branded Hall as a freakish anomaly, reaffirming gendered and sexual order in a fledgling colony that was struggling to establish order of any kind. It is tempting to wonder if an awareness of the "half-man/half-woman" tradition had any impact on this decision. The magistrates made no such reference in their judgment, but if any of them did draw a parallel between the "berdache" figure and the sentence they imposed on Hall, they would doubtless have seen this as a measure of the defendant's personal degradation.[11]

Elsewhere in British America, men and women were occasionally presented in court for cross-dressing and in 1696 Massachusetts passed a law criminalizing transvestism, though why the legislative assembly saw fit to do so at this particular time is unclear. In early modern England boys and young men had to dress as women when they played female roles on the stage and some commentators worried that doing so might encourage sodomy in two ways. First, other men might become attracted to them in their feminized guise; and second, cross-dressing actors might become transformed temperamentally in ways that would lead them to think, feel, and desire like women, which might include welcoming or even initiating sexual relations with other men. Yet colonial Americans do not appear to have made any connection between cross-dressing and sodomy. Court cases and occasional scandals involving cross-dressing (as when enemies of Lord Cornbury, governor of New York in the first decade of the eighteenth century, accused him of wearing women's clothes) did not include any allegations or even insinuations of same-sex intimacy; and none of the defendants in sodomy cases during the colonial period were accused of cross-dressing.

★ ★ ★

During the years between Nicholas Sension's trial in 1677 and the outbreak of the American Revolution, attitudes toward same-sex intimacy across the Atlantic underwent a dramatic transformation. The emergence of "sodomite" as a social category—referring to a specific cadre of men with a consistent sexual interest in other men—represented a significant shift away from earlier typologies. Sodomy was increasingly associated with a particular personality type and also a specific subculture, especially in the metropolis. Male Londoners drawn to members of the same sex could now find partners and social camaraderie in recognized gathering places such as the so-called "molly houses" scattered across the city, where cross-dressing men who also sought sexual intimacy with other men embodied a new sexual and gendered order in which sodomy and effeminacy were now firmly conjoined. Surviving evidence from colonial cities in North America gives no signs of a subculture such as London offered. But new metropolitan conceptions and concerns did establish a foothold in print culture on both sides of the Atlantic alongside older paradigms. Readers of eighteenth-century newspapers encountered items describing police raids on "molly houses" in London and the prosecution of those who were found there. References to such men as "sodomites" amounted, as historian Thomas Foster has pointed out, to the depiction of sodomy as "a character trait" or "marker of personhood," even though such representations were by no means equivalent to "the modern medicalized and psychologized homosexual subject." Meanwhile, older religious frameworks that understood sodomy in terms of moral corruption inviting divine retribution still exerted a powerful influence, especially in eighteenth-century New England.[12]

The mid-eighteenth-century case of Stephen Gorton highlights this blend of perceptions. Gorton, minister at the Baptist church in New London, Connecticut, was suspended from his pastorate in 1756 for "unchaste behavior with his fellow men." Gorton had apparently exhibited an attraction to men for many years. In 1757 the General Meeting of Baptist Churches judged that his behavior indicated "an inward disposition" to this "sin of so black and dark a dye." The meeting did not explain what it meant by "inward disposition," but went on to recommend that Gorton absent himself from the Lord's Supper for several months and then give "effectual evidence" of his repentance and reformation. The assumption that Gorton could overcome his proclivities suggests that the meeting viewed his "sin" in terms consistent with earlier religious formulations, as an expression of moral corruption that sinners could defeat with Christ's support. Yet the phrase "inward disposition" depicted Gorton's depravity as expressing itself in a particular and consistent form. The official judgment did not assert a permanent sexual orientation, but it pushed religious categories to their limits in accommodating local impressions of Gorton's behavior and increasingly widespread representations of sodomy as a persistent, specific impulse.[13]

Despite this transformation in perceptions, there were even fewer prosecutions for sodomy in the eighteenth century than in the seventeenth century. In addition to the factors that had worked against formal censure of even those notorious for "sodomitical actings" in earlier decades, three additional developments now militated against prosecution. First, the courts paid less attention to moral regulation in general as financial and commercial issues dominated their caseloads. That redirection of legal energies did not mean that local communities had lost interest in addressing problematic behavior informally, but it did represent a significant change in the tone of public life. At the same time a growing preoccupation with privacy and increased aversion to the public exposure of malefactors made New Englanders eager to avoid formal proceedings. A third development involved the linkage of sodomy to commercial corruption, urban development, and foreign vice. Descriptions of English sodomy cases in eighteenth-century newspapers often linked sodomites to the seamier aspects of commercial enterprise. Concern about the potentially corrupting impact of economic development and specifically urban life was not new, but it took on additional significance in the late colonial and revolutionary periods as Americans sought to distance themselves from what they depicted as a decadent metropolitan culture across the Atlantic.

Eighteenth-century Philadelphians, for example, were well aware of the new models for understanding same-sex intimacy that had emerged across the Atlantic. Through a painstaking examination of printed matter that circulated in eighteenth-century Philadelphia, historian Clare Lyons has demonstrated that a wide social spectrum of city-dwellers were exposed to imported images of the sodomite through accounts of police raids and prosecutions in London as well as through fictional works. Yet there is no sign of these models being incorporated into Philadelphians' understanding of their own sexual culture or of any efforts to police same-sex relations in the city. Indeed, the local historical record is almost completely silent on the subject of sex between men. Lyons suggests that Philadelphians may have been making a deliberate choice not to acknowledge or police such behavior in their midst as "a way of not integrating the social type of the sodomite *into* colonial and early national society." Because sodomy served as a handy measure of British corruption, Americans were reluctant to acknowledge its presence in their own communities. The silence of the eighteenth-century historical record thus points not to the absence of sodomy but to its implication in American assertions of cultural as well as political independence.[14]

★ ★ ★

Because sodomy trials focused on specific physical acts and not desire or emotion, we rarely glimpse in the surviving court records any feelings that defendants may have had for one another. But other sources from the colonial era such as letters and diaries reveal that men often expressed affection and love for each other in ways that would become suspect and even dangerous in later periods. Following the late-nineteenth-century fusion of romantic and erotic attraction into new concepts of sexual orientation, love and sexual desire became closely entwined in the minds of Americans, making expressions of intense affection for members of the same sex problematic and perilous because they were now linked to same-sex eroticism; but earlier Americans felt much more comfortable declaring same-sex love because it was not yet tainted by such associations. In September 1763, to give just one example, Joseph Hooper, a recent graduate from Harvard College, sat down in Marblehead, Massachusetts, to compose a letter, addressed to his former classmate, Benjamin Dolbeare. He wrote as follows:

> The sun never rose and set upon me since I parted from you, but he brought to my longing imagination the idea of my bosom friend; my faithful memory daily represents him in all the endearing forms that in his presence ever rose in my mind. My fancy paints him in the most beautiful colours, and my soul is absorbed in contemplating the past, wishing for a reiteration and longing to pour forth the expressions of friendship, and receiving those that would calm the gloom, soften the horrors, and wholly extirpate the distractions that your absence creates—but I must have done and have scarce time to tell you how much I am your friend.[15]

Declarations such as this would not automatically have suggested to relatives or neighbors that Hooper desired Dolbeare sexually, let alone that sexual relations might be taking place. Indeed, most Anglo-Americans living in the colonial period treated emotional ties between male or female friends as quite distinct from sexual desire. Whereas sodomy was illegal and denounced by religious leaders as an abominable sin, non-erotic love between men or women was seen as decent, honorable, and praiseworthy. Acceptable expressions of love included not only words, either written or spoken, but also physical affection. Friends often referred to the pleasure that they took in touching and holding one another. There may well have been cases in which this validation of same-sex affection and love provided a cover for erotic intimacies, but we cannot simply assume that people who said they loved one another must have wanted to have sex, or that they actually did so. From a modern perspective, it might seem that these men and women were in denial about the true nature of their feelings for one another, but such a response is anachronistic: instead of imposing our own assumptions and sexual categories onto such relationships, we need to recognize that sexualized love was just one possibility in a rich repertoire of possibilities open to pre-modern men and women as they explored their feelings for friends of the same sex. That much broader range of licit possibilities for relating to one another included intensely loving and even physical yet non-sexual relationships.[16]

Early Americans used biblical and classical models to provide a worthy lineage for loving same-sex friendships. Ministers invoked the relationship between David and Jonathan as well as that between Ruth and Naomi as inspiring examples of men's and women's capacity for loving and virtuous same-sex friendship; they accorded such friendships a central place in their vision for the creation and sustenance of godly communities. Loving friendships also acquired legitimacy through their characterization as a form of kinship. Family incorporated not only biological kin and conjugal relatives but also friends with whom one felt a sense of kinship. Friendship and family membership overlapped as categories of association: people often referred to blood relatives as friends and addressed friends to whom they had no biological relationship as if they were kinfolk. The characterization of friends as family members was neither perfunctory nor merely honorary: it indicated a very real and meaningful connection between individuals. The love and loyalty associated with friendship seem for the most part to have complemented rather than clashed with those of blood and marriage. Early Americans took it for granted that loving relationships between men and between women could coexist with heartfelt love for a person of the opposite sex.

As men and women developed loving friendships with members of the same sex, they did so with the active approval and encouragement of their biological families and of society as a whole. Early Americans believed that friendship not only made people happy but also nurtured qualities that would radiate outward and transform society as a whole, encouraging those involved to look beyond their own selfish interests so as to empathize with the interests and feelings of others. Early Americans routinely asserted that ties between friends had a broad public significance. They believed that personal friendships informed and enriched social and public interactions, creating affective bonds between individuals that would then serve as the emotional sinews of a larger identity. They envisaged society not as an abstract entity but as the sum of individual and intensely personalized relationships, including loving friendships between men and between women.

That legitimization and celebration of loving friendship would acquire a particular and explicitly political significance for North Americans during the revolutionary period, when the encouragement of intense and loving friendships came to be seen as crucial to the nation-building project and its creation of worthy republican citizens. As Americans grappled with the challenge of translating republican principles into practice, male friendship became doubly significant: first, as a way of encouraging empathy between citizens in a society that no longer cohered through shared loyalty to a monarch; and second, as part of a larger project to re-imagine the family in ways appropriate to a new and somewhat democratized era. Republican thinkers crafted a blueprint for nationhood that shifted attention away from patriarchal authority toward fraternal collaboration and called for the active encouragement of brotherly love between friends. Such friendships would nurture social and moral instincts crucial to the well-being of a post-revolutionary society.[17]

Much of that post-revolutionary conversation about state-building focused on male friendship as a foundation for enlightened male citizenship. Yet printed discussions of same-sex friendship often depicted the nurturing of affection and love as a duty and pleasure that men and women shared in common. Literate women wrote of their feelings for one another in letters that bore a remarkable resemblance to those passing back and forth between male friends. Indeed, some men were eager to learn about the experience and expression of sympathetic friendship from female relatives and neighbors. Male friends developed relationships that quite self-consciously paralleled female friendships and used a similar language to express their devotion to each other. Because women living in the seventeenth-century and early eighteenth-century colonies left behind them far fewer letters and diaries than did men, and because male diarists and letter-writers were for the most part from the upper ranks of colonial society, we know much more about elite male friendships in the colonial period than about those of women and less privileged men. Yet we can be confident that a broad range of Americans were exposed to a public conversation about friendship that celebrated same-sex love: many colonists would have heard sermons lauding friendship and encountered the hundreds of articles on male friendship and love that were printed in eighteenth-century newspapers, either because they read these publications themselves or because they heard them being read aloud in taverns or at home. From the perspective of early Americans, same-sex intimacy was multi-potential: depending on the mode of its expression, it could nurture and reinforce or corrupt and undermine authorized cultural endeavors. Early Americans denounced sex between men or between women as sinful and dangerous, but actively encouraged same-sex love as a personal, social, and political good.

Notes

1 Rictor Norton, *The Myth of the Modern Homosexual: Queer History and the Search for Cultural Unity* (London: Cassell, 1997); David M. Halperin, "One Hundred Years of Homosexuality," in *One Hundred Years of Homosexuality and Other Essays on Greek Love* (New York: Routledge, 1990), 15–40.

2 Mary Beth Norton, *Founding Mothers and Fathers: Gendered Power and the Forming of American Society* (New York: Knopf, 1996), 354.

3 H.R. McIlwaine, ed., *Minutes of the Council and General Court of Colonial Virginia, 1622–1632, 1670–1676* (Richmond: Virginia State Library, 1924), 34, 78, 81, 83, 85, 93; John M. Murrin, "Things Fearful to Name," *Pennsylvania History* 65 (1998): 12.

4 For a detailed discussion of criminalization of gender and sexual diversity from the colonial period to the present, see in this volume, Andrea J. Ritchie and Kay Whitlock, "Criminalization and Legalization."

5 For the surviving transcripts from Sension's trial, see Richard Godbeer and Douglas Winiarski, eds., "The Sodomy Trial of Nicholas Sension", *Early American Studies* 12 (2014): 402–457.

6 Barbara S. Lindemann, "'To Ravish and Carnally Know': Rape in Eighteenth-Century Massachusetts," *Signs* 10 (1984–1985), 79, 81. Alan Bray contends that sex between men in early modern England often expressed the "prevailing distribution" of economic and social power and that this contributed to "a sluggishness in accepting that what was being seen was indeed the fearful sin of sodomy," which in turn would have protected perpetrators from social or official retribution as well as from condemnation by their own consciences. Alan Bray, *Homosexuality in Renaissance England* (London: Gay Men's Press, 1982), 49–51, 56, 76.

7 See Richard Godbeer, *Sexual Revolution in Early America* (Baltimore: Johns Hopkins University Press), 363n42.

8   For a discussion of trans history from the colonial era to the present, and the challenges of marking the past as transgender, see in this volume, Finn Enke, "Transgender History (and Otherwise Approaches to Queer Embodiment)."

9   See Sue-Ellen Jacobs, Wesley Thomas, and Sabine Lang, eds., *Two-Spirit People: Native American Gender Identity, Sexuality, and Spirituality* (Urbana: University of Illinois Press, 1997), Will Roscoe, *Changing Ones: Third and Fourth Genders in Native North America* (New York: St. Martin's Press, 1998), and Walter L. Williams, *The Spirit and the Flesh: Sexual Diversity in American Indian Culture* (Boston: Beacon Press, 1986).

10 For discussion of Anglo-American attitudes toward gender, which were in some respects extremely rigid and in others remarkably fluid, see Richard Godbeer, "Performing Patriarchy: Gendered Roles and Hierarchies in Early Modern England and Seventeenth-Century New England," in Francis J. Bremer and Lynn Botelho, eds. *The Worlds of John Winthrop: England and New England, 1588–1649* (Boston: Massachusetts Historical Society, 2005), 290–333.

11 This case is discussed in Kathleen M. Brown, *Good Wives, Nasty Wenches, and Anxious Patriarchs: Gender, Race, and Power in Colonial Virginia* (Chapel Hill: University of North Carolina Press, 1996), 75–80; Mary Beth Norton, *Founding Mothers and Fathers: Gendered Power and the Forming of American Society* (New York: Knopf, 1996), 183–197; and Elizabeth Reis, *Bodies in Doubt: An American History of Intersex* (Baltimore: Johns Hopkins University Press, 2009), 10–14, 16.

12 Thomas A. Foster, *Sex and the Eighteenth-Century Man* (Boston: Beacon Press, 2006), 163, 165, 174.

13 The surviving documentation for this case can be found in the Backus Papers (Andover-Newton Theological School, Newton Center, Mass.), box 7.

14 Clare A. Lyons, "Mapping an Atlantic Sexual Culture," *William and Mary Quarterly* 60 (2003): 121, 137–138, 152.

15 Joseph Hooper to Benjamin Dolbeare, 4 September 1763, Dolbeare Family Papers, Massachusetts Historical Society.

16 For an alternative perspective, see William Benemann, *Male–Male Intimacy in Early America: Beyond Romantic Friendships* (New York: Haworth Press, 2006).

17 In the following chapter, "Revolutionary Sexualities and Early National Genders (1770s–1840s), Rachel Hope Cleves describes in more detail the dynamics of sexual and gender diversity in the new nation.

Further Reading

Foster, Thomas A. *Sex and the Eighteenth-Century Man: Massachusetts and the History of Sexuality in America.* Boston: Beacon Press, 2006.

Foster, Thomas A., ed. *Long Before Stonewall: Histories of Same-Sex Sexuality in Early America.* New York: New York University Press, 2007.

Godbeer, Richard. " 'The Cry of Sodom': Discourse, Intercourse, and Desire in Colonial New England," *William and Mary Quarterly* 52 (1995): 259–286.

Godbeer, Richard. *Sexual Revolution in Early America.* Baltimore: Johns Hopkins University Press, 2002.

Godbeer, Richard. *The Overflowing of Friendship: Love Between Men and the Creation of the American Republic.* Baltimore: Johns Hopkins University Press, 2009.

Godbeer, Richard, and Douglas L. Winiarski, eds. "The Sodomy Trial of Nicholas Sension, 1677: Documents and Teaching Guide." *Early American Studies* 12 (2014): 402–457.

Halperin, David M. "One Hundred Years of Homosexuality," in *One Hundred Years of Homosexuality and Other Essays on Greek Love*, 15–40. New York: Routledge, 1990.

Jacobs, Sue-Ellen, Wesley Thomas, and Sabine Lang, eds. *Two-Spirit People: Native American Gender Identity, Sexuality, and Spirituality.* Urbana: University of Illinois Press, 1997.

Lyons, Clare A. "Mapping an Atlantic Sexual Culture: Homoeroticism in Eighteenth-Century Philadelphia." *William and Mary Quarterly* 60 (2003): 119–154.

Myles, Anne G. "Queering the Study of Early American Sexuality." *William and Mary Quarterly* 60 (2003): 199–202.

Norton, Rictor. *The Myth of the Modern Homosexual: Queer History and the Search for Cultural Unity.* London: Cassell, 1997.

Reis, Elizabeth. *Bodies in Doubt: An American History of Intersex.* Baltimore: Johns Hopkins University Press, 2009.

Roscoe, Will. *Changing Ones: Third and Fourth Genders in Native North America.* New York: St. Martin's Press, 1998.

Smithers, Gregory D. "Cherokee 'Two Spirits': Gender, Ritual, and Spirituality in the Native South." *Early American Studies* 12 (2014): 626–651.

Talley, Colin L. "Gender and Male Same-Sex Erotic Behavior in British North America in the Seventeenth Century." *Journal of the History of Sexuality* 6 (1996): 385–408.

Thompson, Roger. "Attitudes towards Homosexuality in the Seventeenth-Century New England Colonies." *Journal of American Studies* 23 (1989): 27–40.

Warner, Michael. "New English Sodom," in Jonathan Goldberg, ed., *Queering the Renaissance*. Durham, NC: Duke University Press, 1994.

Williams, Walter L. *The Spirit and the Flesh: Sexual Diversity in American Indian Culture*. Boston: Beacon Press, 1986.

2

REVOLUTIONARY SEXUALITIES AND EARLY NATIONAL GENDERS (1770s–1840s)

Rachel Hope Cleves

Shortly before members of the Constitutional Convention gathered in Philadelphia in May 1787 to write a new frame of government for the United States, a young author named Noah Webster moved to the city of brotherly love and set his own pen to addressing the nascent nation's challenges. Only a revolution in manners, he argued, more significant than "all the laws of power, or the little arts of national policy," could secure true independence. The problem, Webster worried, was that the changes to American society he witnessed under way in Philadelphia were pointing in the wrong direction. American women were dressing like French coquettes and American men were behaving like English "bucks and bloods." Far from improving in morals, the nation appeared to be on the point of losing its virtue.[1]

Did the United States undergo a sexual revolution during its first decades of independence? Did the rallying cry of liberty extend beyond the statehouse to the bedrooms, barrooms, and barns where the nation's citizens engaged in their own sessions of congress? An emerging historiographical consensus suggests that the Revolution licensed an expanding range of non-marital and non-normative erotic expression for white youth. On the other hand, the strengthening of the independent American state may have limited the range of sexual expression for people of color, most especially native Americans. If there was a sexual revolution in the early republic (1770s–1840s), historians must consider carefully the geographic and demographic limits of that transformation.

Print Culture

The loosening of sexual codes for white men and women can first be observed in the late-eighteenth-century's growing North American print culture, centered in Philadelphia. As revolutionary sentiments shook up the established hierarchies of colonial society, the impact appeared in the diversified offerings of the port city's book-importers and presses. Their inventories stretched far beyond political prints that debated the cause of independence or the proper composition of the new state, to more risqué sexual prints, many featuring humorous or sensational representations of same-sex sexuality.[2]

Clare A. Lyons uses the book advertisements printed in the city's newspapers, almanacs, and catalogues to track the circulation of homoerotic texts in Philadelphia after the 1750s. British novel *Roderick Random*, which featured the queer characters Captain Whiffle and Lord Strutwell, proved especially popular in the century's final decades, and the novel underwent its first local reprint in 1794. Another popular British import, the pornographic *Memoirs of a Woman of Pleasure*, featured sex between women as well as between men. Local authors also contributed to the city's bawdy print culture with texts such as *The Philadelphiad*, a 1784 pamphlet that illustrated the "modern characters of both sexes" who walked the city's streets, including sodomitical fops and whores.[3]

Early national Philadelphia's best-known local author, Charles Brockden Brown, explored a range of homoerotic possibilities in his novel *Ormond, or the Secret Witness* (1799). In *Long Before Stonewall*, literary critic Stephen Shapiro calls *Ormond* the most radical novel written by an American before 1850. The gothic novel's main love story takes place not between its endangered heroine, Constantia Dudley, and her sinister male suitor, Ormond, but between Constantia and her girlhood friend Sophia Courtland, who indulges a "romantic passion" for the damsel in distress. After Constantia engages in a long flirtation with Ormond's cross-dressing sister Martinette, who explains that she feels herself a "stranger to sexual distinction," the heroine kills Ormond and runs off to live happily ever after with Sophia.[4]

The sexually ambiguous and gender-bending character of Martinette is hardly unique, however, to revolutionary and early national print culture. Greta LaFleur discovers numerous examples of variant gender and sexual expression in eighteenth-century North American sources, and most especially in texts from the 1790s. Like Lyons, LaFleur examines both texts authored in North America and those accessible through importation and reprinting. John Bennett's *Letters to a Young Lady*, which circulated in North America after 1791, included lengthy attacks on "effeminate" men and "virago" women, both of whom threatened to upset the proper conduct of heterosexual relations. Texts about the gender-switching spy Chevalier d'Eon, who lived as a man for the first half of his life, then as a woman until she died, likewise enjoyed popularity in North America—and Philadelphia in particular—during the 1790s. LaFleur speculates that d'Eon served as the inspiration for battle-hymn-of-the-republic composer Julia Ward Howe's incomplete 1840 novel *The Hermaphrodite*, featuring a character like Virginia Woolf's Orlando who changes sex throughout the novel.

The figure of the female husband appeared far more frequently in revolutionary and early national prints than the hermaphrodite, popping up in newspapers, periodicals, and books, both local and imported. The prototypical female husband character was a working-class woman who had chosen to assume male garb at some time in her youth, then lived her life as a man to the point of marrying another woman, before her sex was accidentally exposed (most often by death or arrest). Female husband stories often alluded to the illicit sexual desires that might have motivated the subject's sex change, although newspapers and periodicals were constrained by the era's obscenity laws from stating the lesbian content in these stories. Notably, the female husband was rarely portrayed as an object of hatred or revulsion. Rather she appeared as an anti-hero in most narratives: a disreputable, yet admirable, plucky go-getter unwilling to be subordinated by her society's strict limits on the boundaries of female behavior.

Women who passed as men to serve in the era's wars figured as especially popular characters in period prints. Al Young's work on narratives about the real-life Deborah Sampson, who served as Robert Shurtliff in the American Revolution, and Daniel A. Cohen's work on narratives about the fictional characters Lucy Brewer and Almira Paul, who supposedly served as sailors during the War of 1812, indicate that allusions to women's same-sex desire constituted an important element of these tales. Female soldier narratives demonstrated what Cohen calls a "playful gender radicalism," intended to amuse a readership of youth, sailors, and prostitutes (although, no doubt, the old, land-bound, and monogamous also sneaked peeks).[5]

In general, revolutionary and early national print culture featured more accounts of women than men who crossed gender and sexual boundaries, but exceptions can be found. In a digital exhibit for OutHistory.org, Jen Manion discusses a pair of matching tales aimed at youth, "Lucy Nelson; Or, The Boy Girl" (1831) and "Billy Bedlow; or, The Girl-Boy" (1832), which treated male and female gender variance even-handedly. In both stories, the author instructed children about the necessity to correct gender-crossing behavior. As Manion points out, however, young gender-variant readers may have found recognition in these tales and re-imagined the stories' endings to better suit their own emotional needs.

Anti-masturbation tracts were another genre of early national didactic literature that raised queer possibilities. Historians have long puzzled over why masturbation suddenly came to be perceived as a social problem afflicting youth in the mid-eighteenth century. Perhaps it had something to do with the expanding expression of same-sex desire at the time. As pioneer historians of sexuality Vern Bullough and Martha Voght argued in a 1973 article, masturbation and homosexuality often overlapped in religious and medical literature. British author Samuel Solomon's *Guide to Health* (1800), an extended advertisement for the author's anti-masturbatory patent medicine the "Cordial Balm of Gilead," warned that children often learned masturbation from school friends or same-sex instructors. American experts during the 1830s, such as Boston doctor Samuel Bayard Woodward, related similar concerns. Woodward argued that children should be discouraged from sharing beds in boarding schools and factory dormitories to cut down on mutual masturbation. The surprisingly explicit treatment of same-sex intimacy, even between girls, in these respectable tracts confirms historian April Haynes' observation that "antimasturbation discourse legitimized almost any type of public sexual speech."[6] It is hardly surprising that pornographers took advantage of this leeway, leaving a legacy of textual confusion between sources intended to instruct and those designed to titillate.

Revolutionary Youth

Did early national society share the queer possibilities found in its dynamic print culture? The first wave of Revolutionary social history, published during the 1970s and 1980s, focused attention on the era's gender reformations, as seen in the rise of companionate marriage, republican motherhood, and the affective family.[7] As historians debated whether these developments yielded a revolution for women, however, they skirted over concurrent social developments that pointed away from the heterosexual family. Since 2000, a growing body of work has suggested that many women in the revolutionary and post-revolutionary periods sought to avoid marriage and motherhood, pursuing personal liberty as single women, despite their limited earning power and legal rights.

Lee Virginia Chambers-Schiller's 1984 social history *Liberty, a Better Husband* offers a foundation for this new scholarship by demonstrating the huge uptick of unmarried American women after the Revolution. Whereas only 2–3 percent of New England women during the colonial era remained unmarried for life, that figure rose to over 22 percent by 1870. The critical turning point came in the 1780s.[8] More recently, Martha Tomhave-Blauvelt has asserted that many young women in the post-revolutionary period feared marriage as an end to their freedom, a change in status that would entail endless labor as well as repeated exposure to the grave physical dangers of pregnancy and childbirth. Some chose to remain single for the attractions that the unmarried life provided, in particular the opportunity to focus on intimacies with other women. Lisa L. Moore's recent work on Sarah Pierce, founder of Connecticut's Litchfield Academy, discusses this early woman educator's dream of creating a household with fellow Litchfield-native Abigail Smith. Pierce exchanged letters with Smith's brother, doctor and writer Elihu Hubbard Smith, discussing their mutual aversion to heterosexual marriage. According to Moore, "Connecticut of the 1790s provided a context of sexual liberation, [and] antimarital gender egalitarianism."[9]

Such sentiments may have flourished among Pierce's set of literary men and women friends, but it cannot be said to have extended generally throughout post-revolutionary America, which remained aggressively pro-conjugal. The rejection of marriage and maternity should be understood, in and of itself, as a queer choice for women of the time, whether or not an erotic interest in other women went alongside. Following this logic, Kathryn Kent writes about the mid-nineteenth-century spinster as an "emergent, queer, protoidentity," a conclusion echoed in work by Heather Love.[10]

Many women who married nonetheless participated in the cultural revolution in attitudes towards sexuality by pushing back against what historian Susan Klepp calls the "enslavement" of a lifetime of childbearing. Newly politicized women demonstrated their capacity for citizenship by exercising the masterful art of self-restraint, particularly in physical relations with men. New brides in the mid-Atlantic states resisted old customs that dictated they endure being kissed by all the male attendants at their weddings. More importantly, new wives resisted dictates to bear as many children as fate delivered. Instead, women self-administered abortifacient herbs and restricted their sexual relations, often over their husbands' objections. By the 1830s, the demand for family planning had led to the expansion of contraceptive choices in the United States, with female syringes and male condoms both becoming more widely available.[11]

Not all men resisted these attacks on reproductive sexuality. A sizable number also chose singlehood. Sarah Pierce's friend Elihu Smith stayed a bachelor until he died at age twenty-seven in the arms of friends Samuel Latham Mitchill and Edward Miller. The Revolution inspired new and vigorous defenses of the single life. During the Colonial era, Thomas Foster argues, bachelors were stigmatized as deviant sexual types who disrupted the marital order. After the Revolution, according to John McCurdy, the new state government abolished laws that had targeted bachelors as subjects of regulation and special taxation. Changes in attitudes toward bachelorhood fit with the increasingly commonplace role of sexual experimentation in American youth culture. Diaries kept by a handful of Virginia bachelors in the 1780s and 1790s describe a "world charged with sexual opportunity and activity." Often that activity was heterosexual, but sometimes it was not, which caused concern for moral authorities. The argument made by a bachelor essayist in the *American Universal Magazine* that if instead of marrying women, "we could make it convenient . . . to marry one another, perhaps the married state might be less tormenting," gave credence to long-held suspicions that bachelors had queer tendencies.[12]

Those tendencies found expression in the fad for romantic friendships that spread during the late eighteenth and early nineteenth centuries. In this form of relationship, promoted by transatlantic sentimental literature, unmarried youths shared intense same-sex attachments characterized by expressions of deep love and devotion. A historiographical debate has long raged over the question of whether such intimacies should be understood as sexual. Caroll Smith-Rosenberg's field-defining article "The Female World of Love and Ritual" (1975) and Lillian Faderman's chapter on romantic friendships in *Surpassing the Love of Men* (1981) shared in an early consensus that the relationships were not erotic except in rare exceptions. These early works inspired vociferous reactions in the 1990s from scholars such as Lisa L. Moore and Marylynne Diggs, who offer strong evidence that not only were some romantic friendships sexual, but the potential for erotic expression within these relationships was well understood at the time.

Scholars of men's romantic friendships have also challenged Smith-Rosenberg's and Faderman's claims that romantic friendships were specific to women and emerged from nineteenth-century constructions of femininity. Yet here too are debates over the presumed asexuality of such relationships. For example, literary critic Caleb Crain describes the revolutionary-era intimacy between Philadelphia bachelors John Fishbourne Mifflin, James Gibson, and Isaac Norris as "*a fortiori* sexual," whereas the historian Richard Godbeer describes the triad as bound by platonic affection. Godbeer directs readers to set aside "modern assumptions about love between members of the same sex" and accept that men could forge deep emotional ties without concurrent sexual desire. Godbeer's caution extends even to his reading of a seemingly indiscrete letter from Brown College student Virgil Maxcy to his friend William Blanding. Maxcy, who had previously shared a bed with his friend, wrote to Blanding bemoaning their separation, "for I get to hugging the pillow instead of you. Sometimes I think I have got hold of your doodle when in reality I have hold of the bed posts." Blanding signed his letter "your cunt humble." This letter might read like a smoking gun, but Godbeer disagrees, concluding simply, "one cannot help but wonder."[13]

There seems little room to debate about the sexual content in the letters between South Carolinian college students Thomas Jefferson Withers and James Henry Hammond, penned in the 1820s. These are so explicit that when Martin Duberman originally sought to publish the documents the archive denied him permission. He went forward anyway, analyzing the letters in a landmark 1981 article in the *Journal of Homosexuality*. In the first letter Withers writes "I feel some inclination to learn whether you yet sleep in your Shirt-tail, and whether you yet have the extravagant delight of poking and punching a writhing Bedfellow with your long fleshen pole—the exquisite touches of which I have often had the honor of feeling?" In the second, Withers speculates that during their separation Hammond has been wielding his "elongated protuberance . . . at every she-male you can discover." This second letter indicates that close friendships served as a theatre of possibility not only for same-sex sexual behavior, but also for the development and expression of queer identities. Withers's "she-male" fits into a queer lineage extending backwards in time to the eighteenth-century sodomitical fops from *Roderick Random*, and forwards in time to the sexual inverts found in the writings of late nineteenth-century sexologists, like Richard von Krafft-Ebing.[14]

Evidence of same-sex behavior and identity can likewise be found in the letters between Massachusetts-born Charity Bryant and her romantic friends during the late eighteenth century. Bryant's correspondence might have escaped close inspection if not for the remarkable marriage she later established with Sylvia Drake in Weybridge, Vermont, which lasted from 1807 to 1851. Viewed from the perspective of her subsequent union, Bryant's earlier friendships can be seen as instrumental in the development of her lesbian persona. Letters written by Bryant's friends (she instructed recipients to burn the ones she authored), describe the joys of sleeping in each other's arms and of pressing heads to breasts, in an act that historian Karen Hansen, writing about a post-Civil War female couple, has called "bosom sex."[15] At rare moments, the surviving letters hint at genital intimacies and suggest Bryant's formation of a sexual identity focused on giving pleasure rather than receiving. This assumption of an active male role, as it was understood at the time, resonated with Bryant's later identity as the female husband within her marriage to Drake. It is also in keeping with the sexual practices of Anne Lister, the contemporaneous British gentlewoman whose coded diaries offer historians the most explicit window onto lesbian sexuality at the time.[16]

Figure 2.1 Silhouettes of Sylvia Drake and Charity Bryant framed with locks of their hair.
Collection of Henry Sheldon Museum of Vermont History, Middlebury, Vermont.

Law and Society[17]

Tight restraints on sexual speech for respectable citizens, especially women, limit the extent of direct textual evidence we have of individuals' erotic experiences during the late eighteenth and early nineteenth centuries. This holds true particularly for same-sex experiences, which remained under powerful social proscriptions. However, if same-sex lovers risked their reputations by inscribing too explicit declarations of mutual desire in their letters, for the most part they did not risk the graver punishments that had haunted colonial-era offenders. As colonies became states and British institutions were reinvented for American independence, the Revolution unleashed a wave of legal reforms, which disarmed capital statutes regulating sodomy.

Recent work by B. R. Burg, one of the founders of gay history, indicates that this wave of legal change began, as most waves do, at sea, and only later swept the land. In 1775, John

Adams drafted a set of regulations for the new navy of the United Colonies, which broke from British precedent by omitting the provision to punish buggery and sodomy with death. Adams's omission was sustained by several subsequent updatings of the US naval code, and no trials for sodomy took place within the American navy until 1805. Those charges resulted in no punishment for the accused; neither did charges in an 1835 case. The testimonies in the latter case, however, did reveal a well-developed same-sex subculture within the antebellum US navy, involving relations between young "chickens" and older sailors, who went "chaw for chaw" (mutual masturbation) or engaged in anal sex.[18]

Changes to legal codes within the new states followed soon after independence. Pennsylvania downgraded sodomy from a capital crime to one punishable by imprisonment in 1786. New York and New Jersey did the same in 1796, followed by Rhode Island (1798), Massachusetts (1805), and Connecticut (1821). In the South, Thomas Jefferson proposed revising Virginia's legal code in 1777 to punish male sodomy through castration and female sodomy by nose-boring, but the punishment was not reduced until 1800 (when it was replaced with imprisonment). Maryland began punishing sodomy with hard labor in 1793. Georgia strangely had no sodomy statute at all until it instituted a punishment of life imprisonment in 1816. In 1826, Delaware instituted the least severe punishment for sodomy of any state—a maximum jail time of three years, plus the already-archaic practice of flogging. Later Delaware brought back the pillory for convicted sodomites, harkening back to the seventeenth century. Only a few states retained capital punishment for sodomy until after the Civil War, including North and South Carolina. Many southern states applied differential harsher punishments for slaves than for free people. Despite its early liberalism, Virginia continued to define sodomy as a capital crime for slaves until the Civil War. Finally, with a few exceptions, the new states that entered the union after the Revolution punished sodomy through imprisonment.[19]

The lightening of statutory punishments for sodomy was matched by an easing of the laws' application. During the early national era, prosecutions for sodomy were very rare, continuing a trend from the colonial era. Already by the 1760s, prosecutions for all sexual crimes were on the decline. The loosening of sexual regulations provoked anxiety on the part of many old-fashioned moralists, which may explain the two surprising capital sentences for bestiality handed down in New England during the 1790s, the first in the region for over a century. Neither sentence, however, was carried through. As Doron S. Ben-Atar and Richard D. Brown argue, these prosecutions proved to be the last gasp of the old order, not a sign of things to come. The Revolution's expansion of personal liberties for free citizens had extended its reach to the sexual realm.

Both Mark E. Kann and Kelly A. Ryan have argued, however, that social regulation of sexuality picked up where legal regulations slackened. Ryan points to how elites in Massachusetts used strategies of wealth and race-based segregation to regulate sexuality within the family after the state's laws relaxed. Popular seduction narratives contributed to the social regulation of sexuality by emphasizing the values of female purity and passionlessness. Kann argues that the same social regulation of sexuality for the preservation of patriarchy took place nationally.

Slaves and Natives[20]

The Revolution's impact on the sexual lives of slaves and Native Americans does not fit well under the rubric of expanding personal liberty. Most contemporary historians of slavery agree that the Revolution ultimately strengthened American commitment to the institution by expanding access to lands that reinvigorated its profitability. Throughout the early national era, increasing numbers of women and men became subject to slavery and to the patterns of sexual exploitation that feminist historians have described as part of slavery's burden. Most research has focused on free white men's sexual domination of enslaved women through practices including rape, concubinage, and forced "breeding." Yet there is also evidence that free white women's abuse of female slaves could include erotic dimensions. Runaway slave Harriet Jacobs memoir of her sexual victimization by her master Dr. James Norcom, which offers one of the most lucid windows into this painful history, contains evidence of white women's role in sexual abuse. When Norcom's wife grew suspicious of her husband's relationship to Jacobs, she began sneaking up to Jacobs' bed at night and imitating her husband's voice to whisper sexual propositions in Jacobs' ear and judge the girl's reaction. Jacobs experienced this treatment as a sexual violation on a par with Norcom's own insistence on harassing her with sexual language.[21]

Scholars have been slower to explore the sexual abuse of male slaves. A recent article by Thomas Foster re-examines the research to call attention to the victimization of enslaved men by both white women and men. Testimony to the American Freedman's Inquiry Commission, convened in 1863, suggests that light-skinned enslaved men were fetishized, like their female counterparts, as sexually desirable. And a small handful of sources, including Harriet Jacobs' memoir, document white men's use of rape as a means to dominate enslaved men. As John Saillant suggests, white abolitionists, though not guilty of sexual abuse, also sometimes utilized homoerotic undertones in their writings on the enslaved male body.

The source base offers no evidence for reconstructing volitional same-sex intimacies among enslaved people. Although such relations must have taken place, they were of little interest to the literate whites whose writings provide the majority of evidence about the history of the peculiar institution. White authors did express interest, on the other hand, in the role that same-sex sexuality played in indigenous societies across North America. This evidence of sexual savagery, as white observers understood it, became another rationalization for conquering native peoples and imposing white authority. The strengthening of the American state in the wake of the Revolution, and the consequent extension of control over ever greater stretches of native land between the 1770s and 1840s, entailed a loss not only of indigenous sovereignty but also of sexual expression.

Many of the native societies that American settlement overspread during these decades of vigorous western expansion permitted the expression of sexualities and gender identities that would be judged queer today, although they may have been normative within their own cultures. Historians have focused particular attention on the role of two-spirits (a modern term), or individuals whose social sex differed from their embodied sex. Two-spirits often took spouses of the same biological sex, a practice that generated repeated expressions of shock within settler accounts. While indigenous languages used many different words to describe two-spirits, Anglophone scholarship has often referred to native men who lived as women as *berdaches*, an archaic term derived from an Arabic word for a boy prostitute. No single English word was applied as consistently to native women who lived as men, suggesting that the disproportionate concern within settler society over sexual conduct between males, versus between women, extended outwards.

Source limitations have resulted in vigorous debates among historians about both the extent and meaning of two-spirit identities. For example, only one anonymous source from the 1820s explicitly records the presence of two-spirits within the Cherokee nation, producing an evidentiary puzzle that Gregory D. Smithers unravels in a 2014 article. Far more extensive sources record the presence of two-spirits among southwestern indigenous groups such as the Zuñi and Apache, but scholars debate whether they were figures of respect or ridicule.[22]

There can be no debate that settler cultures regarded two-spirits with disdain. After the Revolution, when the United States initiated a "civilization program" to force the acculturation of indigenous peoples living east of the Mississippi River, federal agents demanded that groups such as the Cherokee restructure their gender roles to conform to settler culture. Women, who farmed the land in Cherokee tradition, were directed to take up domestic production, like weaving. Men, who had hunted, were instructed to take charge of the fields. Unbeknownst to the putative civilizers, this shift had homoerotic overtones for the Cherokee. Historian Theda Perdue argues that prior to European settlement, "some evidence suggests that a kind of sexual reclassification occurred for men who preferred to farm and that these men functioned sexually as well as socially as women."[23] Despite this irony, the overall effect of the civilization program was to exert pressure on indigenous groups to eliminate queer gender and sexual expressions.

Indigenous groups experienced less direct pressure to transform gender and sexual roles from the settler-traders they encountered in areas not under the direct control of the federal government during the antebellum era. Edwin Thompson Denig, who manned the American Fur Company's post at Fort Union on the upper Missouri River (in contemporary North Dakota), bought skins from Woman Chief, a Crow woman who had taken on a warrior role and acquired wives to dress her furs.[24] Likewise, Alexander Ross and David Thompson, two early nineteenth-century traders at Fort Astoria on the mouth of the Columbia River (in contemporary Oregon), recorded their profitable dealings with a Ktunaxa man who was female-bodied and had previously been known to them as a woman.[25] Denig, Ross, and Thompson expressed the customary surprise at these queer encounters, but they continued with business as usual. Unfortunately, as the federal government exerted increasing control over the continent, western peoples would also experience pressure to abandon such gender-bending practices. Later in the century, federal agents on the Crow and Hidatsa reservations forced two-spirit women to cut their hair and assume male dress.[26]

Revolution's End

The mid-nineteenth century may have introduced tighter constraints on queer gender and sexual expression by settlers as well as natives.[27] Prior to the Gold Rush, the frontier had served as a space of enlarged possibility for people like Charity Bryant, who found the newly settled town of Weybridge, Vermont, more hospitable to her masculinized femininity and woman-centered eroticism than was her hometown of North Bridgewater, Massachusetts, just outside Boston. As scholar Scott Larson has recently described, the Publick Universal Friend, a turn-of-the-century prophet who was born female but claimed reincarnation as a genderless spirit following a 1776 illness, dressing afterwards in a mixture of men's and women's clothing, settled a religious community on Iroquois land in western New York after encountering violent reactions in the east. Mother Ann Lee, who founded the celibate Shaker sect and was regarded as a female incarnation of Christ, also endured violence in long-settled areas of New England and built her first community in remote Niskayuna, New York, to avoid persecution.[28]

Following the onslaught of settlers to the far west in 1849, Clare Sears argues that states across the continent began passing new laws to control sexual and gender nonconformity. By 1900, thirty-four cities in twenty-one states had passed laws against cross-dressing.[29] Just as women's demands for expanded rights in the post-revolutionary era inspired a patriarchal backlash, as Rosemarie Zagarri argues, the queer possibilities of the frontier era may have prompted an attempt to reconsolidate the prewar sexual hierarchy. During the second half of the nineteenth century, medical and scientific discourse about same-sex sexuality increased in volume, newly categorizing same-sex attracted individuals and gender-benders as disciplinary subjects. This growth in discourse, of course, had unintended consequences as well—contributing to the formation of new sexual identities that would become a foundation for subsequent rights movements. The early national era may have been a revolutionary moment in the sexual lives of free American citizens, but it would not be the only such moment. Perhaps in the future, those revolutionary moments might even extend more broadly.

Notes

1 Noah Webster, *A Collection of Essays and Fugitiv Writings* (Boston, 1790), 93–97.
2 For the longer history of queer popular culture, see, in this volume, Sharon Ullman, "Performance and Popular Culture."
3 *The Philadelphiad; Or, New Pictures of the City* (Philadelphia, 1784), title page, 37.
4 Charles Brockden Brown, *Ormond, or The Secret Witness*, ed. Philip Barnard and Stephen Shapiro (Indianapolis: Hackett Publishing Group, 2009), 154, 197.
5 Daniel A. Cohen, *The Female Marine and Related Works: Narratives of Cross-Dressing and Urban Vice in America's Early Republic* (Amherst: University of Massachusetts Press, 1997), 20.
6 April Haynes, "Riotous Flesh: Gender, Physiology, and the Solitary Vice, 1830–1860," PhD diss., University of California, Santa Barbara, 2009, viii.
7 Ellen Rothman *Hands and Hearts: A History of Courtship in America* (New York: Basic Books, 1984); Linda Kerber, *Women of the Republic: Intellect and Ideology in Revolutionary America* (Chapel Hill: University of North Carolina Press, 1980); Philip Greven, *The Protestant Temperament: Patterns of Child-Rearing, Religious Experience, and the Self in Early America* (Chicago: University of Chicago Press, 1977).
8 Lee Virginia Chambers-Schiller, *Liberty, a Better Husband: Single Women in America: The Generations of 1780–1840.* (New Haven: Yale University Press, 1984): 3–5.
9 Lisa L. Moore, *Sister Arts: The Erotics of Lesbian Landscapes* (Minneapolis: University of Minnesota Press, 2011), 127–129.
10 Kathryn K. Kent, *Making Girls into Women: America Women's Writing and the Rise of Lesbian Identity* (Durham: Duke University Press, 2003), 21; Heather Love, "Gyn/Apology: Sarah Orne Jewett's Spinster Aesthetics," *ESQ: A Journal of the American Renaissance* 55, no. 3–4 (2009): 305–334.
11 Susan E. Klepp, *Revolutionary Conceptions: Women, Fertility, & Family Limitation in America, 1760–1820* (Chapel Hill: University of North Carolina Press, 2009), 6, 93, 190, 206.
12 John Gilbert McCurdy, *Citizen Bachelor: Manhood and the Creation of the United States* (Rochester: Cornell University Press, 2009), 193, 187. See also, in this volume, Richard Godbeer, "Colonial North America (1600s–1700s)."
13 Caleb Crain, "Leander, Lorenzo, and Castalio: An Early American Romance," in *Long Before Stonewall*, 243; Richard Godbeer, *The Overflowing of Friendship: Love Between Men and the Creation of the American Republic* (Baltimore: Johns Hopkins University Press, 2009), 2, 58.
14 Martin Bauml Duberman, "'Writhing Bedfellows': 1826 Two Young Men from Antebellum South Carolina's Ruling Elite Share "Extravagant Delight"," *Journal of Homosexuality* 6, no. 1–2 (1981): 87–88.
15 Karen V. Hansen, ""No *Kisses* Is Like Youres": An Erotic Friendship between Two African-American Women During the Mid-Nineteenth Century," in *Lesbian Subjects: A Feminist Studies Reader*, ed. Martha Vicinus (Bloomington: Indiana University Press, 1996), 199–200.
16 Rachel Hope Cleves, *Charity and Sylvia: A Same-Sex Marriage in Early America* (New York: Oxford University Press, 2014), 71–72.
17 For a discussion of criminalization of sexual and gender diversity from the colonial period to the present, see, in this volume, Andrea J. Ritchie and Kay Whitlock, "Criminalization and Legalization."
18 B. R. Burg, "Sodomy, Masturbation, and Courts Martial in the Antebellum American Navy," *Journal of the History of Sexuality* 23, no. 1 (2014), 60.
19 George Painter, *The Sensibilities of our Forefathers: The History of Sodomy Laws in the United States*, www.glapn.org/sodomylaws/sensibilities/introduction.htm (accessed January 27, 2015).
20 For discussions of queer history as it relates to enslavement and indigeneity, see, in this volume, Nayan Shah, "Queer of Color Estrangement and Belonging," and Clare Sears, "Centering Slavery in Nineteenth-Century Queer History (1800s–1890s)."
21 Linda Brent [Harriet Jacobs], *Incidents in the Life of a Slave Girl* (Boston: 1861), 54.
22 Richard C. Trexler, "Making the American Berdache: Choice or Constraint?" *Journal of Social History* 35, no.3 (2002): 613–636.
23 Theda Perdue, *Cherokee Women: Gender and Culture Change, 1700–1835* (Lincoln: University of Nebraska Press, 1998), 37.

24 Edwin Thompson Denig, "Of the Crow Nation," *Anthropological Papers* 151, no. 33 (1953), 63.

25 O.B. Sperlin, "Two Kootenay Women Masquerading as Men? Or Were They One?" *The Washington Historical Quarterly* 21, no. 2 (1930), 120–130.

26 Leila J. Rupp, *A Desired Past: A Short History of Same-Sex Love in America* (Chicago: University of Chicago Press, 1999), 66.

27 For more on shifts in gender and sexual diversity across the nineteenth century, see the following chapter in this volume, Clare Sears, "Centering Slavery in Nineteenth Century Queer History."

28 Stephen Stein, *The Shaker Experience in America: A History of the United Society of Believers* (New Haven: Yale University Press, 1992), 8, 72–75.

29 Clare Sears, *Arresting Dress: Cross-Dressing, Law, and Fascination in Nineteenth-Century San Francisco* (Durham: Duke University Press, 2014), 3.

Further Reading

Ben-Atar, Doron S. and Richard D. Brown. *Taming Lust: Crimes against Nature in the Early Republic.* Philadelphia: University of Pennsylvania Press, 2014.

Blauvelt, Martha Tomhave. *The Work of the Heart: Young Women and Emotion, 1780–1830.* Charlottesville: University of Virginia Press, 2007.

Bullough, Vern L. and Martha Voght. "Homosexuality and Its Confusion with the 'Secret Sin' in Pre-Freudian America." *Journal of the History of Medicine and Allied Sciences* 28, no. 2 (1973): 143–155.

Cleves, Rachel Hope. "'What, Another Female Husband?': The Prehistory of Same-Sex Marriage in America." *Journal of American History* 101, no. 3 (2015): 1–27.

Diggs, Marylynne. "Romantic Friends or a 'Different Race of Creatures'? The Representation of Lesbian Pathology in Nineteenth-Century America." *Feminist Studies* 21, no. 2 (1995): 317–340.

Faderman, Lillian. *Surpassing the Love of Men: Romantic Friendship and Love between Women from the Renaissance to the Present.* New York City: William Morrow, 1981.

Foster, Thomas A. "The Sexual Abuse of Black Men under American Slavery." *Journal of the History of Sexuality* 20, no. 3 (2011): 445–464.

Haynes, April. *Riotous Flesh: Women, Physiology, and the Solitary Vice in Nineteenth-Century America.* Chicago: University of Chicago Press, 2015.

Kann, Mark E. *Taming Passion for the Public Good: Policing Sex in the Early Republic.* New York: New York University Press, 2013.

LaFleur, Greta. "Sex and 'Unsex': Histories of Gender Trouble in Eighteenth-Century North America." *Early American Studies: An Interdisciplinary Journal* 12, no. 3 (2014): 469–499.

Larson, Scott. "'Indescribable Being': Theological Performances of Genderlessness in the Society of the Publick Universal Friend, 1776–1819." *Early American Studies* 12, no. 3 (2014): 576–600.

Lyons, Clare. "Mapping an Atlantic Sexual Culture: Homoeroticism in Eighteenth-Century Philadelphia." *William and Mary Quarterly* 60, no. 1 (2003): 119–54.

Manion, Jen. "Transgender Children in Antebellum America." http://outhistory.org/exhibits/show/trans genderchildrenantebellum (accessed 10 March 2015).

Moore, Lisa L. "'Something More Tender Still Than Friendship': Romantic Friendship in Early Nineteenth-Century England." *Feminist Studies* 18, no. 3 (1992): 499–520.

Ryan, Kelly A. *Regulating Passion: Sexuality and Patriarchal Rule in Massachusetts, 1700–1830.* New York: Oxford University Press, 2014.

Saillant, John. "The Black Body Erotic and the Republican Body Politic, 1790–1820." *Journal of the History of Sexuality* 5, no. 3 (1995): 403–428.

Shapiro, Stephen. "In a French Position: Radical Pornography and Homoerotic Society in Charles Brockden Brown's *Ormond or the Secret Witness.*" In *Long Before Stonewall: Histories of Same-Sex Sexuality in Early America,* ed. Thomas A. Foster, 357–383. New York: New York University Press, 2007.

Smith-Rosenberg, Carroll. "The Female World of Love and Ritual: Relations between Women in Nineteenth-Century America." *Signs* 1, no. 1 (1975): 1–29.

Smithers, Gregory D. "Cherokee 'Two Spirits': Gender, Ritual, and Spirituality in the Native South," *Early American Studies: An Interdisciplinary Journal* 12, no. 3 (2014): 626–651.

Solomon, Samuel. *A Guide to Health; or, Advice to Both Sexes: With an Essay on a Certain Disease, Seminal Weakness, and a Destructive Habit of Private Nature.* New York: Robert Bach, 1800.

Woodward, Samuel Bayard. *Hints for the Young in Relation to the Health of Body and Mind.* Boston: George W. Light, 1840.

Young, Alfred F. *Masquerade: The Life and Times of Deborah Sampson, Continental Soldier.* New York: Vintage, 2004.

Zagarri, Rosemarie. *Revolutionary Backlash: Women and Politics in the Early American Republic.* Philadelphia: University of Pennsylvania Press, 2007.

3

CENTERING SLAVERY IN NINETEENTH-CENTURY QUEER HISTORY (1800s–1890s)

Clare Sears

Introduction

Over the past few decades, scholars have produced a wealth of research on nineteenth-century queer history. This scholarship has shone a spotlight on industrial northern cities and the western frontier, detailing conditions that facilitated both the proliferation and restriction of non-normative genders and sexualities. By emphasizing the transformative effects of industrialization and westward expansion, however, the field of queer history has generally overlooked the sexual dynamics of slavery, an institution whose persistence, abolition, and aftermath was central to nineteenth-century life. Recent scholarship by Omise'eke Tinsley, Aliyyah Abdur-Rahman, and Vincent Woodard demonstrates that this omission is unjustified. Queer historical studies of slavery are not only academically viable but also politically necessary to foreground the specificities of black queer histories and center slavery's constitutive role in modern sexualities. In this chapter, I review the field of nineteenth-century queer history by discussing its central exclusion (slavery) in relation to its dominant themes (industrialization and western expansion). In doing so, I consider how the field would productively shift if queer histories of slavery were centered.

Slavery, Ships, and Plantations[1]

Queer history's neglect of slavery is startling, given the institution's centrality to economic and political life in the nineteenth century. Slavery's roots in the Americas, of course, stretch back to a much earlier period, when Spanish explorers first brought kidnapped Africans to Santo Domingo in 1501 and English colonists transported enslaved Africans to Jamestown, Virginia in 1619. Fortified rather than undermined by the Declaration of Independence, slavery expanded rapidly in the early nineteenth century, after the invention of the cotton gin in 1793 enabled large-scale production of a highly profitable export crop. In 1808, US Congress banned the international slave trade, but allowed the domestic trade to grow, which tripled the slave population by 1860, when four million African Americans lived in captivity. Ultimately, political disagreements over the economics of slavery, states' rights, and the federal government's authority to prohibit slavery in western territories prompted the Civil War in 1861. Following the war's end in 1865, Congress ratified the 13th Amendment to the US Constitution, which signaled slavery's legal end.

To date, scholars have presented scant primary evidence of volitional same-sex intimacies between African Americans held captive during slavery. Nonetheless, as Omise'eke Tinsley argues, histories of enslaved peoples must be open to different evidentiary possibilities. Tinsley, for example, traces the etymology of the Suriname word *mati*, which Creole women use to describe their female lovers. The word translates as "my girl," but has its roots in shipmate, as in "she who survived the Middle Passage with me."[2] Colonial records point to similar shipmate intimacies in multiple Caribbean sites, between African women—and men—who were kidnapped and transported to the "New World" together. Tinsley argues that enslaved women and men, aboard ships and on plantations, formed erotic same-sex bonds, some likely sexual, some not. Regardless of their sexual content, Tinsley frames these relationships as queer, as they radically disrupted a violent social order that denied the sentience of African peoples.

In *A Desired Past*, Leila Rupp presents additional fragmentary evidence of same-sex intimacies between enslaved women during the nineteenth century. Specifically, Rupp recounts the legal case of a white woman who sought monetary compensation after a person she enslaved, named Minty, escaped to British troops during the War of 1812. A witness in the case testified that Minty had used two surnames: she adopted the first (Gurry) when she married her husband and the second (Caden) when she left her husband and entered "an intimacy with a negro woman." As Rupp explains, this evidence points to the existence of same-sex relationships among enslaved women as well as their acknowledgement by whites.[3]

Although evidence of consensual same-sex relationships on US plantations remains fragmentary, a remarkable first-hand account of Cuban slavery paints a richer picture. Esteban Montejo was born into slavery in 1860 and a full century later narrated his memories for publication as *Biography of a Runaway Slave*. Montejo described life on a plantation where men far outnumbered women. In this context, some men opted for celibacy while "others had sex with each other and didn't want anything to do with women. Sodomy, that was their life." According to Montejo, these sexual practices were not temporary aberrations, but embedded in long-term relationships, with clear gender roles, where one man would cook and clean for his "husband."[4] In "Toward a Black Gay Aesthetic," Charles Nero analyzes Montejo's writings to establish the existence of same-sex intimacies between enslaved men in the Americas. Certainly, different conditions may have facilitated or inhibited same-sex intimacies on US plantations and these await their own excavations. Nonetheless, as Tinsley argues, black queer scholarship can usefully transgress national boundaries to foreground the oceanic crossings and traumatic dislocations that shaped slavery's trajectories.

The forced transportation and confinements of slavery were matched by coerced sexual encounters on ships and plantations. As historians have documented, sexual assault was endemic in these sites, as white men and women subjected enslaved peoples to multiple violations, including rape, concubinage, and forced reproduction. In this context, it is unsurprising that same-sex sexual abuse occurred. For example, Harriet Jacobs' *Incidents in the Life of Slave Girl*, published in 1861, presented a harrowing account of the multiple sexual assaults she witnessed before escaping from slavery. Some of these involved white masters and enslaved black men. In one passage, Jacobs describes a white master's sexual assault of a man named Luke. According to Jacobs, the unnamed master had become "prey to the vices growing out of the 'patriarchal institution'" and suffered from "extreme dissipation," a nineteenth-century sickness believed to result from sodomy. The man required constant care and kept Luke naked and chained to his bed, where he subjected him to "freaks . . . of a nature too filthy to be repeated." Contemporary scholars interpret this passage in different ways. In *Against the Closet*, Aliyyah Abdur-Rahman argues that Jacobs strategically deployed Luke's violation to subvert dominant ideologies of black perversity and highlight white men's degeneracy. More critically, in *The Delectable Negro*, Vincent Woodard claims that Jacobs' narrative promoted a politics of racial uplift that marginalized sexually ambiguous men such as Luke. Regardless of the interpretation, Jacobs' account provides clear evidence that at least some white men raped the black men they enslaved during the nineteenth century.[5]

Jacobs also describes her own experience of same-sex sexual torment at the hands of a white woman, Mrs. Flint, the plantation master's wife. The ordeal began when Mrs. Flint brought Jacobs to sleep near her bedroom, ostensibly to protect her from rape by the master. However, Flint soon began her own sexual invasions, visiting Jacobs during the night, leaning over her sleeping body, and whispering sexual propositions in her ear, "as though it were her husband who was speaking to me."[6] Jacobs explains Flint's actions in terms of jealousy, but according to Woodard, this obscures the white woman's own erotic interests in Jacobs, including her desire for sexual access and domination. After all, white women entered complex power-laden relationships with enslaved women, and multiple opportunities for coercive sex existed. It should come as no surprise then (although it often does) that other enslaved women described sexual assault by white mistresses, including the African American abolitionist and women's rights activist Sojourner Truth.

Alongside consensual and coerced same-sex intimacies, slavery instituted gender arrangements among captive peoples that diverged significantly from dominant white norms. This could take several forms. In her influential essay, "Mama's Baby, Papa's Maybe," Hortense Spillers makes the compelling case that slavery had "ungendering effects." Specifically, for those held captive, slavery substituted hard physical labor for the domestic sphere, erasing a terrain that was foundational to white bourgeois fictions of men and women's "separate spheres." Moreover, by transferring ownership of enslaved children from parents to masters, slavery obliterated the kinship ties and reproductive meanings that nineteenth-century gender norms typically required. Ultimately, slavery transformed humans into commodities to be traded, bought, and sold. Under such logic, although consistently resisted, African peoples ceased to be subjects of gender and became objects of property. For Spillers, slavery's ungendering effects unleashed "amazing. . . pansexual potential," not as a source of fluid identifications and multiple pleasures, but as "an open vulnerability to a gigantic sexualized repertoire," through which white men, white women, or both could commit sexual assault.[7]

Dominant white ideologies also expelled enslaved peoples from normative gender through depictions of masculine black women and feminine black men. As Woodard documents, white audiences frequently accused Sojourner Truth of being a man in women's clothes. At one event in Indiana, Truth bared her breasts to white women backstage to authenticate her gender, although not before lambasting the crowd for their possessive sexual demands of black women's bodies. Similarly, white men often imagined black men to be servile maternal figures who nursed them when sick and placed older black men, in particular, into grandmotherly roles. According to Woodard, these cross-gender representations extended to "the race" as a whole, as whites positioned "Negros" as a feminine race unable to resist European-American domination, while claiming masculine superiority for themselves.[8]

Gender variance was not just an unwanted imposition, however; some black men identified with and took pleasure in their femininity during slavery, just as some black women lived and embraced their masculinity. Woodard, for example, reframes the gender ambiguity of Jacobs' character Luke, from *Incidents in the Life of a Slave Girl*, arguing that he is not the epitome of degradation due to his coerced sexual and domestic service, but "a different type of representative black man who . . . offers a nonconforming and complicated understanding of black male sensibility." Woodard also foregrounds moments of pleasurable gender crossings in Frederick Douglass's writings, including his performance of femininity in relation to "gallant" and "chivalrous" white men who supported abolition.[9]

Nineteenth-century sources further document the female masculinity of Harriet Tubman, who escaped from slavery and became active in the underground railroad, shepherding more than three hundred people to freedom in the north. Some black women wore men's clothing as disguise when fleeing captivity, but Barbara McCaskill argues that Tubman's masculinity was more pervasive and enduring. Remembered as the "Moses of her people," Tubman demonstrated physical strength and valor that often outstripped male peers. Fellow abolitionist John Brown exclusively used male pronouns when praising the colleague he named "General Tubman": "He [Harriet] was the most of a man naturally that I ever met with."[10] Certainly, Brown's language may have reflected his failure to imagine strength and courage as female characteristics and it risked replicating racist narratives that denied black women's femininity. Still, such descriptions may have reflected Tubman's identification with masculinity and appreciation for such prose.

Acknowledging sexual and gender variance during slavery not only enriches understandings of the antebellum period, but also sheds new light onto the sexual politics of emancipation. After the Civil War, African American citizenship developed in complex relationship to sexual propriety and gender normativity, as Roderick Ferguson documents. The federal government played a central role in this, creating the Bureau for the Relief of Refugees, Freedmen and Abandoned Lands in 1865. Tasked with managing the newly enfranchised black population, the Freedmen's Bureau (as it was popularly known) promoted institutions that linked economic and moral development, including marriage. Queer histories of slavery provide important context for these developments.

According to Katherine Franke, the Freedmen's Bureau used state marriage laws to regulate African Americans' sexual practices and foster normative citizenship. Incorporation into the state institution of marriage narrowed the field of acceptable intimacies and delegitimized a wide-range of relationships that had flourished in enslaved communities. According to Brenda Stevenson, these included opposite-sex "sweethearting" (short-term non-monogamy), "taking up" (long-term non-monogamy), and "abroad marriages" (marrying but living apart from a spouse from another plantation). Stevenson does not discuss the queer possibilities of these relationships, but Mattie Udora Richardson suggests that abroad marriages may have facilitated same-sex relationships, allowing people to have infrequent contact with a distant spouse, while maintaining regular intimate contact with a same-sex partner. Post-emancipation marriage laws disrupted these queer arrangements and funneled black sexualities into opposite-sex monogamy. African Americans who did not comply with state marriage laws risked prosecution for sexual offenses; if convicted, they faced jail time and forced labor under the convict lease system. As a result, state marriage laws did more than disavow queerness and discipline black sexualities. They also supported the new system of racial subjugation that arose in slavery's wake.

Evidence for queer histories of slavery in the nineteenth century is readily accessible, both through well-known primary sources, such as slave narratives, and through less conventional means, such as etymology. Utilizing this evidence, recent scholarship documents a wide range of same-sex intimacies and gender diversity during slavery, including long-term relationships on Cuban plantations; erotic intimacies aboard slave ships; same-sex interracial rape on US plantations; whites' imposition of masculinity onto black women and femininity onto black men; and some enslaved peoples' embrace of cross-gender identifications.

Remarkably, the field of queer history tends to neglect this evidence and overlook slavery as a site of sexual and gender variance. Instead, the field—as often taught in college classrooms and synthesized in written reviews—centers the industrial northeast and western frontier as preeminent queer sites.[11]

Industrialization and Northeastern Cities[12]

Queer histories of the nineteenth century frequently focus on the northeastern United States, positioning the region's industrial capitalist cities as the cradle of recognizable queer life. These studies build upon John D'Emilio's pathbreaking 1983 essay "Capitalism and Gay Identity," which asserted the centrality of an industrial capitalist economy to the formation of modern gay identity. D'Emilio acknowledged that his analysis led with white experience and was thus limited. He also recognized that the northern industrial labor market excluded the vast majority of African Americans who remained tied to southern agriculture well into the twentieth century.[13] By replicating this framework, however, scholars tend to presume slavery's marginality to queer history and push African Americans to the periphery, unless or until they migrated from the south to the north.

Certainly, industrialization brought massive changes to economic, social and sexual life in the northeast. At the beginning of the nineteenth century, the US economy was based in agriculture, with production and consumption taking place on southern slave plantations and on northeastern and frontier family farmsteads. As the century unfolded, new developments in technology and transportation brought an industrial revolution, encouraged by federal legislation that supported big business and capitalist accumulation. Historians debate slavery's role in these developments, but generally agree that slave labor produced profitable export crops, particularly cotton, that financed industrialization.

The shift from an agricultural economy to an industrial one produced new working conditions and inequalities, drawing ever more people into a capitalist system that generated great prosperity for the nascent corporate elite and immense deprivation for the rapidly expanding working-class. Eventually, these changes consumed the nation, but they first took root in northeastern cities, only later extending to the war-torn south and western frontier. As a result, industrialization engendered geographic transformations, alongside economic ones, as rural Americans and European immigrants moved to northeastern cities in search of work. Very few African Americans made this journey before slavery ended; in 1860, for example, only 10 percent of African Americans were free and only a minority of those lived in the north. In the decades following Reconstruction's end (1870s to 1890s), African Americans did leave the south in greater numbers, fleeing a new system of racial subjugation marked by endemic poverty, Jim Crow segregation, criminalization, and lynching. Nonetheless, even by the turn of the twentieth century, most African Americans lived in the south and were largely untouched by the economic and social changes occurring in the north and west.

For people who did live in the urban northeast, the rise of an industrial economy transformed social and sexual life in several ways. First, as D'Emilio emphasized, industrialization facilitated key changes in the family by increasing opportunities for mobility and decreasing the economic necessity of reproduction. In the northeastern agricultural economy, production and consumption had previously taken place within the family, making it extremely difficult to live outside of this unit. By extension, sexuality was generally tied to reproduction, as families produced multiple offspring to ensure their farmstead's current and future productivity. The shift to an industrial economy disrupted the necessity of reproduction, as children became an economic liability rather than a benefit. Additionally, the rise of industrial cities gave people the freedom to live outside of traditional family units and move to large urban areas where sexual possibilities decoupled from reproduction or family sanction became more viable.

Rapid industrialization and urbanization, for example, facilitated the development of street subcultures conducive to sex between men. In *City of Eros*, Timothy Gilfoyle documents the world of commercial sex that flourished in mid-nineteenth century New York. Although Gilfoyle focuses on female prostitution, he includes evidence that male prostitutes worked in city brothels too. Urban life also facilitated cross-class sexual encounters, as upper and middle-class men cruised city streets for "rough trade." Walt Whitman, for example, is best known for his homoerotic poetry, but his writings also describe multiple late-night encounters with working-class boys in the streets, bars, and bathhouses of New York City and Washington D.C., just south of the Mason–Dixon line. Gender variance characterized these street scenes, as effeminate fairies plied their trade alongside masculine hustlers, and some city prostitutes identified as female, even as the law labeled them male. In 1836, for example, New York City police arrested an African-American woman named Mary Jones for pickpocketing a john, only to identify her as a man who lived in a local brothel. Similar to Jones, many sexual and gender dissidents fell afoul of the law and spent time in prison. They encountered a prison culture that facilitated sex among inmates, typically structured by gender variance or age difference, as Regina Kunzel and Mack Friedman document.

By the late nineteenth century in most northeastern cities, commercial entertainment districts augmented street-based subcultures, housing bars and clubs that offered sexual and gender transgressive pleasures. Urban vice investigations provide ample evidence of these venues, but first-hand reports also exist. Most notably, Ralph Werther (aka Jennie June and Earl Lind) documented New York City's commercial sexual underground, describing his identification as an androgyne (a feminine man who desires sex with men), visits to a "sex resort" named Paresis Hall, and involvement with the Cercle Hermaphroditos, an organization that fought against persecution. Most sources focus on the practices of whites, but one report on Washington D.C. in the 1890s spotlights African American men who donned women's clothing, attended drag parties, ogled naked men, and took part in "an orgie of lascivious debauchery beyond pen power of description." As Beth Clement and Beans Velocci explain in the subsequent chapter, such reports informed sexologists' theories of "inversion" that explained same-sex desire in terms of cross-gender identification.[14]

Finally, the northeastern industrial economy facilitated another form of same-sex intimacy with general social acceptance: romantic friendships. These relationships had roots in the late eighteenth century, as Rachel Cleves documents in the previous chapter. They gained new ground in the nineteenth century as industrialization produced novel gender arrangements among the predominantly white middle-class. Emerging from capitalist relations of production, the middle-class was marked by a specific gendered division of labor that placed men and women into radically different economic roles. Certainly, white men and women performed different productive tasks in the colonial agricultural economy, but these were typically interrelated and took place within the shared space of the home. In an industrial economy, the separation of men and women's labor was spatialized and expanded, as middle-class men left the home to enter the public sphere of paid employment and political life, while middle-class women were confined to the private sphere. The ideology of separate spheres legitimized this division, contrasting white men's strong, competitive and rational character with white women's weak and submissive nature. Unsurprisingly, there was a sexual dimension to this ideology, which granted men exclusive claim to lust and passion and denied women access to sexual desire.

Ironically, the ideology of separate spheres supported "romantic friendships" among middle-class women. Carroll Smith-Rosenberg first documented these relationships in her influential article "The Female World of Love and Ritual." As Rosenberg and subsequent scholars describe, romantic friendships were characterized by intense emotional attachment and physical affection between two women, which included kissing, caressing, bed-sharing, and declarations of enduring love. Women often imagined their romantic friend to be their lifelong soul mate, even as they entered conventional marriages with men. Most studies of romantic friendships have focused on women, but Jonathan Katz and Leila Rupp also describe romantic friendships among men, the most famous being Abraham Lincoln, who formed a long-term relationship with Joshua Speed. Similar to women's relationships, men's romantic friendships were socially accepted, but they were expected to end when men got older and married.

As Cleves explains, historians disagree on the sexual nature of romantic friendships, with early accounts insisting on emotionally intense but non-sexual dynamics and more recent work claiming that participants knew of their relationship's sexual potential, as did society at large. Feminist scholars also discuss the relationship of women's romantic friendships to first-wave feminism. Adrienne Rich, for example, situates romantic friendships on a "lesbian continuum" that she defines through intimate bonding rather than sex. As part of this continuum, romantic friendships always resisted heteropatriarchal power and carried feminist potential. In *Surpassing the Love of Men*, Lillian Faderman focuses on change over continuity, arguing that society tolerated romantic friendships for most of the nineteenth century because they posed little threat to patriarchal power. This changed at the century's end, however, as first-wave feminism brought new educational and professional opportunities to middle-class women, raising the specter of economic independence and sexual autonomy. Most analyses of romantic friendships center on the experiences of middle-class whites who were the primary subjects of separate spheres ideology. However, Farah Jasmine Griffin and Karen Hansen document the romantic friendship of two freeborn African American women who lived in the north in the 1860s: Rebecca Primus, a schoolteacher from a prominent Connecticut family, and Addie Brown, a domestic worker from Connecticut and New York City.[15]

From prostitution to romantic friendship, studies of the urban northeast provide compelling documentation of same-sex intimacy and gender nonconformity during the nineteenth century. Foregrounding the effects of industrialization, these studies connect large-scale economic developments with transformations in sexual life. Problems arise for the field of queer history, however, when individual studies are folded into an origin story that centers industrialization as the sole facilitator of modern sexual identities and overlooks the predominantly agrarian slave economy in the south. In part, the problem consists of a narrow regional focus that easily morphs into racial neglect: African Americans sometimes appear in these studies, but only when engaging in relationships and subcultures already marked as white. Conceptual problems also arise, as queer histories of northeastern cities foreground social processes and dynamics that are stunningly inapplicable to studies of slavery, including free labor, geographic mobility, a declining reproductive imperative, and the rise of separate spheres ideology. Slavery, of course, was defined by the absence of freedom, both in terms of labor and movement. It also erased the gender divisions of labor that underlay separate spheres ideology, hijacked enslaved women's reproductive capacities for plantation profits, and denied sexual autonomy. To better appreciate the regional and racial specificity of scholarship on northeastern cities, we need to consider its relationship to queer histories of slavery, as well as to work on the west.

Western Frontiers

Over the past two decades, nineteenth-century queer history has increasingly supplemented its emphasis on northeastern cities with a focus on western expansion. Expansion was of paramount importance during this period, stretching the nation's borders to the Pacific Ocean and triggering monumental changes in sexual and gender possibilities. To varying degrees, queer historical scholarship documents these changes, addressing their disparate effects on whites, Chinese Americans, Latino/as, and Native peoples. This scholarship, however, continues to bypass the sexual and gender dynamics of slavery even as "the peculiar institution" spread into vast new western territories.

Western expansion was propelled by the ideology of Manifest Destiny and the economics of land ownership. Proponents of Manifest Destiny believed that the United States had a divine right to possess and rule the northern continent from the Atlantic to Pacific coast, imposing their dominion on peoples who already occupied the land. For some adherents, manifest destiny was a religious edict that would bring Christianity to "heathen" Natives. For others, economic motives dominated, as new land promised new wealth and opportunity, particularly after the discovery of gold in California in 1848. Manifest destiny ideology fueled genocidal federal policies toward sovereign Indian nations, driving thousands of people from their ancestral homelands and effecting massive loss of life and land. Manifest destiny also legitimized the Mexican-American War, which transferred a full half of Mexico's territory to the United States in 1848. Finally, manifest destiny facilitated a massive westward migration of European immigrants and white Americans who settled in the hotly contested and newly conquered territories of the frontier.

As the nation's borders moved westward, possibilities for same-sex intimacies and gender diversity fundamentally altered. For European immigrants and white Americans, westward migration could lead to new possibilities and pleasures in frontier towns. In large part, these opportunities were structured by a profound gender imbalance among white migrants, as men were far more likely to head west than women. This opened up multiple spaces for cross-gender practices and same-sex intimacies, such as those that occurred at men-only dances in gold rush camps. In *Roaring Camp*, for example, Susan Johnson describes dances in the Calaveras County mines, where men attached large canvas patches to their pants to indicate their availability as a "lady" dance partner for the evening. At other dances, men would wear women's clothing, shoes and wigs to effect a more convincing transformation, as I document in my book *Arresting Dress*. By the end of the century, these dance practices were distant memory, but new entertainment venues emerged that encouraged same-sex erotics and gender-crossings. For example, at least two bars (Bottle Meyer's and The Dash) in San Francisco's vice district employed female impersonators who plied patrons with alcohol and had sex with men for money on the premises.

Westward expansion also facilitated multiple forms of gender crossing among migrants who wore men's clothing on bodies the law deemed female. Some of these people identified as women but dressed as men to facilitate a safer journey, while others fully identified as men. In one of the first studies of queer California history, the San Francisco Lesbian and Gay History Project recounted the story of Charley Parkhurst, who identified and lived as a man for thirty years in the mid-nineteenth century, until a coroner classified his body as female after his death. My book also documents cross-dressing practices among female sex workers who wore men's clothes to advertise their availability for commercial sex. Other women brought cross-dressing and prostitution together in different ways, by wearing men's clothing, hanging out in brothels, and forming intimate relationships with those who worked there. These clothing practices did not exist in a legal vacuum and during the second half of the nineteenth century, many towns and cities, particularly in the West, passed laws against cross-dressing.

While thousands of white Americans headed west for gold rush camps and frontier towns, Chinese migrants traveled east to these territories, typically migrating from Guangdong Province on China's southern coast to the port of San Francisco. Many traveled inland, but others settled in San Francisco where a distinct Chinese neighborhood took root, shaped by legal discrimination, residential segregation, community development, and merchant initiatives. Here, a series of homosocial living arrangements emerged that Nayan Shah describes as "queer domesticities" in *Contagious Divides*. These arrangements were not necessarily characterized by erotic activity between men, although this surely sometimes occurred. Instead, they were characterized by same-sex intimacies and gender expressions that diverged from dominant norms. In lodging houses and opium dens, for example, Chinese men enjoyed physical proximity to one another and forged emotional ties that counteracted the loneliness of living overseas in a hostile land. Additionally, in white households, Chinese men worked as houseboys and nursemaids, providing domestic services that inverted masculine norms. The concentration of Chinese men in domestic work stemmed from a racially stratified labor market, but many white observers interpreted it as evidence of Chinese inferiority and white American dominance.

When white and Chinese migrants came to the US southwest, they settled in highly contested borderland territory. Seized from Mexico in 1848, these borderlands were home to thousands of Mexicans who lost significant power, wealth, and status over the following decades. Historians have examined race, class and gender dynamics across these socio-geographic spaces, but as Emma Perez and Maria Elena Martinez argue, in-depth queer histories of the post-conquest borderlands have yet to be written, hampered by inadequate sources. Victor Manuel Macias-Gonzalez's work on northern Mexico's borderland cities provides one exception, documenting a proliferation of homosocial spaces that facilitated sex between men in the late nineteenth century, including bars, gymnasiums, bathhouses and jails. Several studies of borderland towns in the United States also present evidence of gender variance among the region's Latino/a populations.

Susan Johnson, for example, uses gold rush diaries to document multiple cross-gender practices among Mexican and Chilean miners who lived in California's southern mines during the 1850s. These include a matador named Señorita Ramona Perez, who revealed herself to be a man in women's clothing during a bullfight in Tuolumne County and an unnamed "Chilean hermaphrodite" who caught the attention of a white man named Alfred Doten. Peter Boag also presents evidence of cross-gender practices in *Redressing America's Frontier Past*, including those of a Mexican woman named Mrs. Nash. Nash worked as a laundress for General Custer's Seventh Cavalry at Fort Lincoln in Dakota and she married several times. Upon her death in 1878, a medical examiner announced that Nash had a male body and following significant teasing from fellow soldiers, her husband of five years committed suicide shortly after.

Representations of Mexican cross-dressing also appeared frequently in mid-nineteenth century literature. In *American Sensations*, Shelley Streeby analyzes popular sensationalist fiction of the 1840s and 1850s that regularly featured cross-dressing Mexican women soldiers. Authors typically represented these characters as elite, light-skinned women who donned men's clothing to defend their country, fell in love with a US soldier, and subsequently returned to a traditional female role. As Streeby explains, these popular stories usually featured weak and effeminate Mexican men, narrating a gendered crisis in Mexican nationality that legitimized US military incursions. Boag also analyzes representations of Mexican cross-dressing, focusing on male bandits who wore women's clothing in the post-war years. According to Boag, these representations delegitimized resistance to US domination by framing Mexican bandits as unmanly and deceitful men.

Mexicans, of course, were not the largest group of people who inhabited the southwest before white and Chinese migrants arrived, and for Native peoples who already occupied these lands, western expansion radically constricted the possibilities for same-sex intimacies and cross-gender pleasures. Most notably, many Native tribes recognized a third or fourth gender category beyond the man/woman binary familiar to white Americans. Different tribes used different terms to describe these genders—boté among the Crow, for example, winkte among the Lakota, nadleeh among the Navajo. Unwilling to accept non-binary genders, white settlers condemned Native peoples for instituting social and sexual practices that seemed at odds with their sex, including "cross-dressing" appearance and "same-sex" sodomy. From the early days of conquest, European explorers used Native gender and sexual difference to legitimize genocide. Throughout the nineteenth century, the US government pursued the extermination of Native peoples via war and forced migration across deadly terrain.

At the same time, the government launched interventions aimed at cultural extermination via assimilation and education. These explicitly targeted Native gender differences and related sexual possibilities. Some of these interventions took place on reservations. From the 1830s onward, the federal government systematically forced many Native peoples to leave their ancestral lands and move within the strict spatial boundaries of a reservation. Although Native tribes maintained sovereign status on reservations, confinement greatly constrained their capacity for self-determination and survival, particularly when boundaries were redrawn and territory reduced in violation of treaty agreements. The federal government established agencies on reservations, under the Bureau of Indian Affairs, which became mechanisms for eradicating gender and sexual difference. Evidence of these efforts dates back to the 1870s, when one agent forced a third-gender miati of the Hidatsas nation to endure a haircut and change of clothing in simulation of white masculinity. Later in the century, government agents on Crow land pressured botés to wear men's clothes and adopt a social and sexual role that mirrored that of white men, punishing those who refused to conform. One turn-of-the-century anthropologist reported that government agents particularly focused on a highly respected boté named Osh-Tisch, and "repeatedly tried to make him put on masculine clothing, but the other Crow protested, saying it was against his nature."[16]

Recognizing that Native reservation communities could undermine US efforts at cultural genocide, beginning in the 1870s government officials created Indian boarding schools to "civilize" Native youth away from home. Attendance was mandatory and over 100,000 Native children were sent to live in these schools and learn the ways of white Christian culture. For children who did not identify as "boy" or "girl," boarding school life could be especially devastating. Many children were forced to abandon their gender, while others ran away and sought sanctuary on reservations. Some youth remained in school and tried to avoid detection, risking harsh punishments if discovered. Historian Walter Williams, for example, describes a Navajo nadleeh child at the famous Carlisle Indian School in Pennsylvania who successfully lived in the girls' dormitory until a lice infestation forced all students to disrobe in front of school officials. Interpreting the child's body as male, officials removed the student from the premises. Receiving no information from government or school officials, the student's family endured horrific uncertainty and never discovered whether their child had been transferred to another institution, incarcerated, or killed.

Similar to studies of northeastern cities, many queer histories of western expansion emphasize freedom and mobility as constitutive of sexual and gender possibility. Some of these histories, however, complicate the field's reliance on mobility as a foundational concept. Williams' work on Native peoples, for example, emphasizes the traumatic loss of mobility that western expansion engendered, with confinement on reservations restricting sexual and gender diversity and furthering physical and cultural genocide. Additionally, Shah's research on San Francisco's Chinese community shows how confinement in a racially segregated labor and housing market facilitated sexual and gender practices that can be conceptualized as queer. These studies enrich the conceptual apparatus of nineteenth century queer history and broaden the field's regional and racial focus. Despite these important developments, however, the field continues to over-look the south and to neglect slavery as a queer historical site. To disrupt this troubling trajectory, queer histories of slavery must be centered, facilitating critical and constructive dialogue with established research on the west and north.

Throughout this chapter, I have reviewed the omissions and inclusions of nineteenth century queer history, documenting the viability and vitality of queer histories of slavery. One task for the field as a whole, however, is not simply to add slavery but to ask how knowledge, methods, and narratives of the queer nineteenth century would shift if slavery were centered. For example, how might understandings of women's same-sex eroticism differ if the paradigmatic example was not romantic friendships born of separate spheres, but *mati* relationships born of slavery or eroticized violence between mistress and enslaved? Similarly, how might understandings of sexuality in male-only environments shift if we began with the sex-segregated holds of slave ships, in the early nineteenth century, rather than the sex-segregated dances of gold rush towns, fifty years later? Finally, how might understandings of non-normative gender differ if we traced sexology's theories of inversion back to slavery's ungendering dynamics, as Abdur-Rahman suggests, rather than to gender variant subcultures in northeastern cities? Certainly, these shifts would center captivity and violence as constitutive of sexual possibility, displacing the field's almost exclusive focus on mobility and volition in this century. Additionally, they would push queer history to grapple more extensively with the interplay of racism and eroticism, as Sharon Holland urges. Undoubtedly, the resulting historical narratives would offer less celebratory and romantic accounts of the queer past. These accounts, however, would also be less partial and distorted, and ultimately more reflective of queer life—and death—in the nineteenth century.

Notes

1 For another discussion of enslavement as it relates to queer US history of the nation, see also Eithne Luibhéid, "Queer and Nation," in this volume.
2 Omise'eke Natasha Tinsley, "Black Atlantic, Queer Atlantic: Queer Imaginings of the Middle Passage," *GLQ* 14, no. 2–3 (2008): 192.
3 Leila Rupp, *A Desired Past* (Chicago: University of Chicago Press, 1999), 42.
4 Esteban Montejo, *The Biography of a Runaway Slave*, ed. Miguel Barnet, translated by W. Nick Hill (Connecticut: Curbstone Press, 1994), 40.
5 Harriet Jacobs, *Incidents in the Life of Slave Girl: Written by Herself*, ed. Jean Fagan Yellin (Cambridge: Harvard University Press, 2000 [1861]), 192. According to Woodard (*The Delectable Negro: Human Consumption and Homoeroticism within the U.S Slave Culture*, New York: New York University Press, 2014), Frederick Douglass also made multiple allusions to male rape when writing of his experiences under slavery.
6 Jacobs, *Incidents*, 34.
7 Hortense Spillers, "Mama's Baby, Papa's Maybe: An American Grammar Book," *Diacritics* 17, no. 2 (1987): 77.
8 For more on racialized representations of sexual and gender deviance, see, in this volume, Sharon Ullman, "Performance and Popular Culture."
9 Woodard, *The Delectable Negro*, 130–131.
10 Letter from John Brown. Quoted in Jean Humez, *Harriet Tubman, the Life and the Life Stories* (Madison: University of Wisconsin Press, 2003), 295.
11 See the Queering Slavery Working Group tumblr, organized by Vanessa Holden and Jessica Marie Johnson, for further discussion. http://qswg.tumblr.com. Accessed November 14, 2016.
12 For the longer history of urbanization in queer history, see, in this volume, Kwame Holmes, "The End of Queer Urban History?"
13 For an extended discussion of queer labor history, see, in this volume, Sara Smith-Silverman, "Labor."
14 Ralph Werther—Jennie June, *The Female Impersonators* (New York: The Medico-Legal Journal, 1922), 146–152; Charles H. Hughes, "Postscript to Paper on Erotopathia: An Organization of Colored Erotopaths," *Alienist and Neurologist* 14, no. 4 (1893): 731–32.

15 For further discussion of respectability strategies by people of color in queer US history, see Nayan Shah's chapter in this volume, "Queer of Color Estrangement and Belonging."
16 Robert Lowie, *The Crow Indians* (New York: Farrar and Rinehart, 1935), 48, quoted in Walter Williams, *Spirit and the Flesh: Sexual Diversity in American Indian Culture* (Boston: Beacon Press, 1986), 179.

Further Reading

Abdur-Rahman, Aliyyah. *Against the Closet: Black Political Longing and the Erotics of Race*. Durham: Duke University Press, 2012.

Boag, Peter. *Redressing America's Frontier Past*. Berkeley: University of California Press, 2011.

Chauncey, George. *Gay New York: Gender, Urban Culture, and the Making of the Gay Male World, 1890–1940*. New York: Basic Books, 1994.

D'Emilio, John. "Capitalism and Gay Identity." In *Powers of Desire: The Politics of Sexuality*, eds. Ann Snitow, Christine Stansell, and Sharon Thompson, 100–113. New York: Monthly Review Press, 1983.

Faderman, Lillian. *Surpassing the Love of Men: Romantic Friendship and Love Between Women from the Renaissance to the Present*. New York: William Morrow, 1981.

Ferguson, Roderick. "Of Our Normative Strivings: African American Studies and the History of Sexuality." *Social Text* 23, no. 3–4 (2005): 85–100.

Franke, Katherine. "Becoming a Citizen: Reconstruction Era Regulation of African American Marriages." *Yale Journal of Law and the Humanities* 11, no. 2 (1999): 251–309.

Friedman, Mack. *Strapped for Cash: A History of American Hustler Culture*. Los Angeles: Alyson Publications, 2003.

Gilfoyle, Timothy. *City of Eros: New York City, Prostitution, and the Commercialization of Sex, 1790–1920*. New York: Norton, 1992.

Griffin, Farah Jasmine, ed. *Beloved Sisters and Loving Friends: Letters from Rebecca Primus of Royal Oak, Maryland, and Addie Brown of Hartford, Connecticut, 1854–1868*. New York: Knopf, 1999.

Hansen, Karen. " 'No Kisses is Like Youres': An Erotic Friendship between Two African-American Women during the Mid-Nineteenth Century." *Gender and History* 7, no. 2 (1995): 153–182.

Holland, Sharon. *The Erotic Life of Racism*. Durham: Duke University Press, 2012.

Johnson, Susan Lee. *Roaring Camp: Social Relations in the California Gold Rush*. New York: W.W. Norton and Company, 2000.

Katz, Jonathan Ned. *Love Stories: Sex Between Men Before Homosexuality*. Chicago: University of Chicago Press: 2001.

Kunzel, Regina. *Criminal Intimacy: Prison and the Uneven History of Modern American Sexuality*. Chicago: University of Chicago Press, 2008.

Macias-Gonzalez, Victor Manuel. "A Note on Homosexuality in Porfirian and Post-Revolutionary Northern Mexico." *Journal of the Southwest* 43, no. 4 (2001): 543–548.

Martinez, Maria Elena. "Archives, Bodies and Imagination: The Case of Juana Aguilar and Queer Approaches to History, Sexuality, and Politics." *Radical History Review*, no. 120 (2014): 159–182.

McCaskill, Barbara. " 'Yours Very Truly': Ellen Craft—The Fugitive as Text and Artifact." *African American Review* 28, no. 4 (1994): 509–529.

Nero, Charles. "Toward a Black Gay Aesthetic: Signifying in Contemporary Black Gay Literature." In *Brother to Brother: New Writings by Black Gay Men*, ed. Essex Hemphill, 229–251. Boston: Alyson Publications, 1991.

Perez, Emma. "Queering the Borderlands: The Challenges of Excavating the Invisible and Unheard." *Frontiers* 24, nos. 2/3 (2003): 122–131.

Rich, Adrienne. "Compulsory Heterosexuality and Lesbian Existence." *Signs* 5, no. 4 (1980): 631–660.

Richardson, Mattie Udora. "No More Secrets, No More Lies: African American History and Compulsory Heterosexuality." *Journal of Women's History* 15, no. 3 (2003): 63–76.

San Francisco Lesbian and Gay History Project, " 'She Even Chewed Tobacco': A Pictorial Narrative of Passing Women in America." In *Hidden from History: Reclaiming the Gay and Lesbian Past*, eds. Martin Duberman, Martha Vicinus, and George Chauncey, 183–94. New York: New American Library, 1989.

Sears, Clare. Arresting Dress: *Cross-Dressing, Law and Fascination in Nineteenth Century San Francisco*. Durham: Duke University Press, 2015.

Shah, Nayan. *Contagious Divides: Epidemics and Race in San Francisco's Chinatown.* Berkeley: University of California Press, 2001.

Smith-Rosenberg, Carroll. "The Female World of Love and Ritual: Relations between Women in Nineteenth-Century America." *Signs* 1, no. 1 (1975): 1–29.

Stevenson, Brenda. *Life in Black and White: Family and Community in the Slave South.* New York: Oxford University Press, 1996.

Streeby, Shelley. *American Sensations: Class, Empire and the Production of Popular Culture.* Berkeley: University of California Press, 2002.

Tinsley, Omise'eke Natasha. "Black Atlantic, Queer Atlantic: Queer Imaginings of the Middle Passage." *GLQ* 14, no. 2–3 (2008): 191–215.

Woodard, Vincent. *The Delectable Negro: Human Consumption and Homoeroticism within U.S. Slave Culture.* New York: New York University Press, 2014.

4

MODERN SEXUALITY IN MODERN TIMES (1880s–1930s)

Elizabeth Clement and Beans Velocci

The late nineteenth century brought a profound shift in the way people thought about sexuality in the United States. Religious and legal authorities had condemned acts of sodomy for centuries, but committing them had not made you a particular kind of person. It just made you a sinner, and in some states, only if you got caught and prosecuted, a criminal. Though small queer subcultures had existed in the United States earlier in nineteenth century, these communities grew larger, became more visible, and began to produce new ways of understanding both queer sexualities and queer gender performances. After the 1870s, medical discourses from sexology and eugenics began to assert that certain kinds of sexual acts and gender transgressions made an individual a specific type of person: the "invert" or "homosexual."[1] What had been seen in the colonial period as just an isolated sexual act became the basis for a whole identity. Together, the growth of queer communities and the rise of a medical discourse about sexuality made the late nineteenth and early twentieth centuries a profoundly important—and distinctly modern— era in queer US history. Historians have spent the last four decades tracking the complex story of how and why those new communities and identities developed, and why sexual identity became a central part of how we think about who we are.

The language used to describe various sexualities and genders shifted significantly during the time under study (1880–1940). At the beginning of this period, for example, the word "homosexuality" referred to gender inversion—which was *centrally* about exhibiting traits of a gender other than the one you had been designated at birth. Desire for people of the same sex represented one symptoms of gender inversion, but it was not the only or the most import- ant one. By the end of the 1930s, though, the meaning of "homosexuality" had largely shifted toward our contemporary understanding of being attracted to people of the same sex, *whether or not* this had a relationship to gender identity. Some terms, like "queer" and "bisexual," had very different meanings than they do today, while others, like "gay," "lesbian," and "trans- gender," had not yet come into widespread use. Due to the instability of these terms, we have tried to use the language people used at the time when possible, rather than impose modern definitions backwards through time.

The transition from a world in which people committed acts of sodomy to one in which people belonged to categories such as "homosexual"—which historians generally call the shift from acts to identities—came about at the end of the nineteenth century as a result of dramatic changes in the economic system of the United States.[2] As John D'Emilio details in "Capitalism and Gay Identity," for most of its history, people in what would become the United States lived in rural areas and worked on small family farms. Regardless of their sexual desires, most people married because everyone needed family for economic survival. Beginning in the 1820s, however, factories brought industrialization, cheap manufactured goods, and most crucially, wage labor to America's cities. Many people who had the freedom to move (that is, people who were not either held in slavery or confined to the newly created reservations for Native Americans) responded by leaving rural areas in search of economic opportunity. The emergence of industrial capitalism also disrupted economies in Europe and Asia, driving huge numbers of *economic influence* immigrants to booming US cities. By 1920, a majority of Americans lived in urban areas and worked in non-farm jobs.[3]

As the individual began to replace the family as the main economic unit of society, wage labor freed some white men from economic dependence on marriage and children. Men could earn wages to support themselves rather than work as part of a family unit. This allowed men attracted to other men to organize their lives around their affective and sexual desires, which some of them then began to do. It is hard to say, though, which came first. Did men with same-sex desires move to the city for the freedom, or did they move to the city for opportunities, and discover it also freed them to have sex with other men? The answer is probably both. Either way, changes in the economy shaped how Americans organized sexuality between 1880 and 1940. As D'Emilio convincingly argues, wage labor, urbanization, and freedom from family supervision brought about our modern categories of homosexuality and heterosexuality, as well as the idea that all people fit into these categories.[4]

Gendered relationships to paid labor and family authority kept a majority of women from experiencing the freedom that wage labor offered. Employers assumed that men, as fathers or husbands, supported women, and they used this reasoning to keep women's wages to half those of men's, which in turn raised profits by keeping wage costs low. As Alice Kessler-Harris asserts, this enormous wage gap ultimately produced women's *actual* dependence on men. Because most women could not support themselves, much less parents or children, on the wages they earned, most women had to marry men just to survive. The sexual double standard embraced by most white Americans also limited women's ability to organize their lives around same-sex desire. For respectable middle-class white women in the 1870s and 1880s, marriage and family precluded any opportunity to work outside the home. While the middle class subscribed to the most rigid sexual double standard, the working-class also judged women and men differently for the same sexual transgressions. Families of all classes thus remained far more invested in the sexual purity of their daughters, and exerted significantly more control over them. When combined with appallingly low wages, family investment in women's sexual purity created a significant lag in the development of a visible lesbian community. Many women may have experienced sexual and emotional attraction to other women, but they lacked both the freedom and the financial resources to organize their lives around it. Thus, even in cities such as New York and Chicago, where communities of same-sex loving and gender transgressive men flourished, public spaces catering to women remained rare in the early twentieth century. This lack of a visible community compounds historians' problems analyzing women's experiences, as it means that we have far less evidence about them.[5]

Despite these limitations, we know some upper middle-class women possessed both the desire and the financial resources to avoid marriage. Most of these women were white, though there is anecdotal evidence of African American middle-class women doing so as well. However, as Linda Gordon has shown, middle-class black women involved in reform work married at much higher rates that white middle-class women engaged in the same kinds of work. Along with pursuing college education, pairing with another woman allowed some women to become much more involved in public life without risking the accusation that they neglected their families to do so. Between the 1880s and the 1920s, the historical record is filled with women who intervened in a wide variety of public policy issues and who also remained unmarried but sustained intense, sometimes life-long partnerships with other women. Jane Addams, founder of Hull House and the profession of social work, for example, took Mary Rozet Smith as her "devoted companion." When Addams and Smith traveled, Addams always wired ahead to hotels for a bed to share.[6] Even though it might be tempting to claim women like Jane Addams as lesbian foremothers, the privacy afforded to middle-class white women and the sexual passivity attributed to women more generally makes it very difficult to know exactly what these relationships meant. Were they romantic, sensual, sexual, or something outside our modern relationship categories?

Asking a different question—"how did contemporaries see this ambiguous canoodling?"—offers a more satisfying answer. As these women sought increasing political power, white men opposed to changes in women's status leveraged accusations of female masculinity and homosexuality against them to discredit their demands for meaningful employment and the vote. Before the development of homosexuality as a category, intense relationships between women had gone largely unremarked upon. "Smashes," in which two young women courted each other, complete with passionate letter-writing, gifts, kissing, and fondling, were accepted as part of life at women's colleges. Scholars Carroll Smith-Rosenberg, Sherri Inness and Nancy Sahli argue that as women demanded more power in the public sphere and as detractors gained the language of homosexuality, intense female friendships came under increased scrutiny. Arguments that college education shriveled women's ovaries, that a desire for the vote equaled a desire for sex with other women, or that "female sexual perverts" dominated all women's political movements demonstrates the emerging use of women's same-sex relationships to vilify all women's aspirations for a larger role in society. While these women did not call themselves lesbians, and while what they did in their long-term committed relationships remains shrouded in private domesticity, by the 1920s a particularly virulent form of homophobia had emerged to contain the threat they represented to men's political and economic dominance.

Much more sexually explicit evidence from the African American musical tradition indicates that black working-class women engaged in queer sexual practices and gender identities at the turn-of-the century. Certainly the blues, a working-class musical genre that migrated north with African Americans in the early twentieth century, contains extensive references to same-sex sexual desire and practices. "B.D. [Bull Dagger/Bull Dyke] Woman's Blues," originally recorded in 1935 by Bessie Jackson (Lucille Bogan), cast butch women as financially independent and sexually desirable: "B.D. women, you know they work and make their dough. And when they get ready to spend it, they know just where to go."[7]

Most of the songs in this tradition position same-sex desire as a part of cross-gender identification (the exception would be Monette Moore's "Two Old Maids in a Folding Bed," 1936). Jackson's "B.D. woman" walks "just like a natch'l man," while Ma Rainey's narrator wears "a collar and a tie." These gender-bending women desired the freedom, independence, and sexual access to women that men enjoyed. However, the songs do not identify their feminine partners as gender or sexual non-conformists, opening up the possibility that all women might find B.D. women an attractive alternative to heterosexuality. As with white middle-class women like Jane Addams, evidence from women blues musician's lives supports not so much our modern understanding of "lesbianism," as both sexual and gender queerness. First-person accounts of their wild parties indicate that some women blues musicians had sexual

Figure 4.1 Harlem blues legend Gladys Bentley, promotional postcard, c. 1946. Collection of the Smithsonian National Museum of African American History and Culture.

relationships with both women and men, found women sexually desirable, and on occasion, cross-dressed either privately or in performance.[8]

If some women's relationships remain difficult to interpret today, historians agree that by 1890 big cities hosted small but visible subcultures of same-sex attracted men in working-class neighborhoods. These communities and their practices differed significantly from what we understand today as "gay." Organized around "fairies" and their interactions with other men, "gayness" or "homosexuality" in these communities involved gender inversion more than it did desire for sex with other men. As George Chauncey explains, classified as male at birth, fairies viewed their sexual attraction to men as an outgrowth of their gender identity rather than a marker of a particular sexual "orientation." Some fairies dressed and lived exclusively as women. Others dressed as men, but relied on flamboyant symbols like a red tie, a green suit, or plucked eyebrows to signal their femininity and sexual interest in other men. Fairies' presence on the streets and in bars and dancehalls made them the most visible symbol of same-sex male desire. People of all classes thus came to imagine gender inversion as the primary marker of same-sex desire.

In 1916, a self-described fairy named Loop-the-loop posed for a portrait later published in the *American Journal of Urology and Sexology*. After giving an interview in male attire, Loop-the-loop donned a dress, stockings, and wig and told the doctor, "Ha! I feel more like myself now."[9] As Loop-the-loop's obvious preference for women's clothing shows, fairy identity had more to do with gender than it did with what modern readers might think of as sexual orientation, which poses interesting questions of interpretation. While fairies can be seen as "gay," they can just as easily be read as transgender: people who did not conform to the gender identity they had been assigned. Of course, fairies lived at a time before today's categories existed. It would be more accurate to say that fairies were neither gay nor trans but rather, simply, fairies. Working-class neighbors clearly recognized fairies as a third gender category and tolerated them in their midst, but that is not to say that they accepted them. Being a fairy involved giving up masculine privilege, something unthinkable to the majority of working-class people. The identity of fairy could allow one to express queer gender or desire, but also positioned the person as effeminate and thus subordinate in working-class society. This left fairies subject to harassment, rape and other violence ordinarily directed at women.

The identity of fairy crossed ethnic and racial boundaries. Native-born whites, immigrants, and African Americans all took up the identity of fairy, and the identity interacted in contradictory ways with white supremacy. In the 1920s, drag balls in African American neighborhoods such as Harlem drew thousands of people, including black and white fairies and black and white spectators. As Chad Heap has argued, white slumming in black neighborhoods upheld white supremacy because the location of these interracial balls in black neighborhoods upheld racist images of African Americans as "primitive" and prone to perversity. However, George Chauncey points out that balls also gave black spectators the unusual opportunity to watch, and by extension, judge, the behavior of white fairies. Balls thus both upheld and undermined white supremacy.

The Harlem Renaissance, an outpouring of black artistic production in the 1920s, highlights the ambivalent relationship of the African American community to queerness. As the discussions of blues musicians and drag balls have shown, working-class black communities tolerated open expressions of sexual and gender difference, at times even celebrating it in lyrics and performances. However, nationally, the small black middle-class chose a strategy of empowerment that historian Evelyn Brooks-Higginbotham has labeled "the politics of respectability."[10] The politics of respectability emphasized embracing middle-class sexual and gender values to deny racist sexual stereotypes about African Americans and thus prove their worthiness of the citizenship rights (most obviously the right to vote) that had been lost by most blacks in the 1890s. Or, to put it another way, the politics of respectability strategically deployed the performance of middle-class sexual and gendered values for explicitly political purposes. When W.E.B. Du Bois and other race leaders supported a blossoming of the black arts in the 1920s, they explicitly encouraged artistic expression as a form of propaganda about black worthiness for political rights. This led the NAACP's magazine the *Crisis* (which Du Bois edited) and other black publications to call for art that presented African Americans as embracing middle-class sexual values.[11] Queerness, by definition, violated the positioning of blacks as respectable citizens unjustly deprived of their civil rights. Despite the fact that a significant number of the artists involved in the Harlem Renaissance embraced queer sexual and gender styles, older and more conservative leaders like Du Bois and Alain Locke attempted to repress representations of queerness in the art they sponsored. As scholars such as A. B. Christa Schwarz and Eric Watts argue, discussions of queerness still happened, but need for patronage from black political elites and their white allies made it hard for black artists, regardless of their sexual identities, to represent queerness.[12] Divisions of class, and classed strategies of empowerment, then, marked "queerness" as dangerous to black aspirations for full citizenship, and limited positive depictions of the queerness so obviously present in Harlem and other centers of black life.[13]

Regardless of race, age and class position mattered a great deal in whether, and for how long, men might take up the role of fairy. Though most fairies came from the working class, some were middle class. Middle-class fairies, however, took great care to reveal their feminine mannerisms only in working-class settings, which is to say, like whites visiting Harlem in the 1920s, they went slumming. Unlike the working class, the middle class had no sense that people could exist in the space between male and female, and no tolerance for femininity in men. Middle-class men would also have paid a high professional (and thus financial) price for openly presenting as fairies. Young, working-class fairies, on the other hand, often made their living through sex work, which allowed them to express their gender identity while earning wages higher than those they would have earned as working-class men.[14] Some fairies took on the identity permanently, but most lived as fairies only temporarily because outward femininity represented the only visible template for structuring male-male sexual desire. Once they had found a community of like-minded men, many abandoned fairy style, especially in public, though they might "camp it up" in gay settings. The older fairies got, and/or the more middle-class their position, aspirations or job prospects, the more likely they were to shed their fairy identity and project a public gender presentation closer to normative masculinity.

Fairies most frequently sought sex with masculine men, called variously "normal," "jam," or "trade." Most Americans today identify sexuality as being about object choice (that is, who you want to have sex with) rather than gender performance. At the turn-of-the century, though, gender performance mattered far more than object choice: men who had sex with fairies remained "normal" as long as they presented as masculine and took the penetrative role in sex. In fact, these men tended to view women, fairies, and sometimes younger men, as inter-changeable. Their masculinity lay in their role, enacted through domination and/or penetration of women, fairies, or boys rather than in the assigned sex of the bodies they penetrated. Interestingly, these rules applied even to men who persistently preferred sex with fairies. For example, the fairy Loop-the-loop's partner, who consistently took the normatively masculine "active part" in their relationship, received the author's approval in the *American Journal of Urology and Sexology* article as an "intelligent young man" who "presented himself tidily in uniform."[15]

Rapid industrialization the 1880s and 1890s fueled the emergence of a related set of practices, particularly among transient male laborers known as hobos. In this stage of capitalist development, the economy depended on large pools of male labor that it could dismiss at will. In eastern cities men worked casually in construction and shipping. In the west they worked in mining, fishing, and lumber. All of these jobs provided poor wages to the young, unmarried men who moved from work site to work site and lived in all-male environments in flop houses and man camps. In hobo culture as well as in other same-sex environments such as prisons, men organized sex by age. Older men called "wolves" or "jockers" provided protection, resources and guidance for young men and boys, called "lambs" or "punks," in exchange for sex and other domestic services. In these situations, the young men did not need to be—and most often were not—effeminate, but the provision that the older man be masculine and take the penetrative role remained. Peter Boag argues that western cities such as Seattle and Portland that relied heavily on extractive industries had a much smaller fairy culture than in the east. In addition, both Boag and Nayan Shah have found that in the west reformers and police associated same-sex sexuality with the assumed "perversity" of racial minorities—particularly Asian men, despite the fact that police raids in cities in the Pacific Northwest entrapped men of all races as they solicited sex with other men.

Although gender inversion served as the dominant symbol of male-male sexuality in the early twentieth century, and transient culture required an age-based power difference for acceptable male-male relationships, some men rejected the idea that their desire for other men necessarily marked them as feminine. Describing themselves as "queers," by the 1920s and 1930s these largely middle-class men pioneered our modern understanding that object choice rather than gender identity defines "homosexuality" or "gay identity." As noted earlier, middle-class men who desired other men risked their class status, income, and family connections if they marked their desire for other men publicly. Some queer men looked down on fairies, and blamed fairies' visibility and flamboyant behavior for the hostility that society exhibited towards all men who desired each other. Many queers also viewed their love of other men as part of a masculine and noble tradition, or as an expression of egalitarian modernity, rather than a sign of innate femininity. As Chauncey explains, this denial of gender inversion as the basis of their desire, however, did not preclude many queers from developing an effete style involving an embrace of the arts and upper-class culture, which many in the working class viewed as effeminate (see Figure 4.2). It is understandable how outsiders might conflate fairies and queers, but people who identified this way saw themselves as very distinct from each other. It would take sexology and the emergence of modern heterosexuality to bring all forms of same-sex sexual activity into the singular category of modern homosexuality.

Across the late nineteenth and early twentieth centuries, US culture and sexual science increasingly identified heterosexuality with physiological, psychological and social "normalcy" and proper gender adjustment. Gender historians like to joke that masculinity is always in crisis, but the early twentieth century marked a time when white middle-class men did have a lot to be anxious about, and the emerging category of "heterosexual" offered a solution for these problems of masculine identity. The woman's suffrage movement and women's demands to participate more fully in paid labor threatened the male exclusivity of political participation and employment, which, some feared, blurred the line between men and women. At the same time, trade unions and urban political machines made up of working-class immigrant men challenged middle- and upper-class white men's power. As birth rates among the white middle class declined, large-scale immigration produced an increasingly diverse and populous society, which led some to fear Anglo "race suicide." While the end of Reconstruction and the emergence of Jim Crow reasserted white supremacy in the South, mass migration of African Americans to the north fueled white fears of slipping dominance. Finally, the closing of the western frontier served as a perceived death knell for the rugged (white) masculinity that many viewed as a core quality of US vitality. In reaction to these intertwined phenomena, as Kevin Murphy and Gail Bederman explain, middle-class white men began to define proper, normal "manhood" not broadly in terms of the power and privileges they exercised but instead much more narrowly through sexual object choice, a cool but tough emotional style, athleticism, and hard bodies. As the old race and gender order seemed to crumble around them, they looked to the burgeoning authority of science to uphold the hierarchies of gender, race, and class from which they had always derived their power. Sex and sexuality became powerful tools in this defense.

Figure 4.2 A flamboyant pansy tries to check into a women's rooming house.
Broadway Brevities comic, December 14, 1931 (scan courtesy of Will Straw).

Ironically, sexology, the scientific study of sex, initially began in Europe in the 1860s, not as a way to maintain hierarchies but instead as a way to explain and protect men who desired men. Karl Heinrich Ulrichs developed the first medical categories for men attracted to other men to describe himself. Ulrichs had no formal medical training, but turned to science after being barred from practicing law following an 1854 "unnatural fornication" conviction.

Ulrichs published a series of essays throughout the 1860s proposing a theory that "urnings"—people with male bodies and female souls—constituted a third sex with both masculine and feminine characteristics. Ulrichs argued that urnings should not be punished, because though they had male bodies, their female souls made their desire for other men natural, rather than sinful or criminal. Enormously influential among later sexologists, Ulrichs' work helped enshrine gender inversion as the primary marker of homosexuality. Although the 1870s and 1880s witnessed vigorous debates over the causes, significance, and possible treatments for homosexuality and inversion, Jennifer Terry explains that these debates took on an increasingly negative analysis and tone. Even as they drew on Ulrich's framework, by 1900 most European scientists largely agreed that homosexuality represented either a disease or evolutionary degeneration.

From the 1880s through the 1930s, the sexological category of inversion covered a range of gender non-normative bodies, behaviors, and identities, of which same-sex sexual object choice was only one.[16] Inversion might manifest in transvestitism, and Peter Boag explains that cross-dressing served as a primary marker of inversion in US sexological writings. Europeans began experimenting with surgery and hormones by the 1910s, in an attempt to treat gender inversion. Unsurprisingly, the ambiguity and slippage in the term "inversion" rendered the category less than useful, since so many falling into its diagnosis did not express all of its constitutive elements. As sexologists from the 1910s through the 1940s increasingly came to split gender inversion into homosexuality (object choice) and what they would later call transsexuality (gender identity), as Joanne Meyerowitz shows, surgery and hormones became the solution to gender difference. Even within the scientific literature, the distinction between homosexuality and gender inversion was never complete, however, which led, by the 1930s, to hormonal therapies to attempt to treat homosexuality as well.

In US sexology during the 1910s and 1920s, white middle-class male doctors adapted European theories about gender inversion to their own specific social and political environment. As Jennifer Terry and Peter Boag explain, these men saw America as an exceptional experiment, where people of European descent had, at least until 1900, avoided the mistakes Europe had made in modernization, urbanization, and industrialization. To prevent the corruption and sexual deviance that they believed had overtaken Europe (after all, those German sexologists must have gotten their research subjects from somewhere) as Julian Carter elaborates, Americans used the study of sex as a way to uphold a white, middle-class system of gender and race as their country also industrialized and urbanized. Arguing that the subordination of women to men and non-whites to white was natural, timeless, and rooted in biology, middle-class white male doctors used sexuality, and specifically the sorting of people into "normal" and "abnormal" categories of sexual identity and behavior, as one way to uphold patriarchy and white supremacy.

With significant numbers of women of all races agitating for the vote by 1900, sexologists and social commentators used the concept of gender inversion to explain away women's demands for expanded access to political power and meaningful work outside the home. As we have discussed, scientists coded women's demands for social power as sexual inversion. James G. Kiernan, a prominent American sexologist, noted in a 1914 article that his colleagues did not "think every suffragist an invert," but regarded "the very fact that women in general of today are more and more deeply invading man's sphere" as "indicative of a certain impelling force [sexual inversion] within them."[17] Normal, healthy women, American sexologists argued, happily submitted to men's authority, thus defining "normal" femininity as a cheerful acceptance of men's legal and physical dominance in both family and society.

Sexologists further pathologized inversion by framing it within the simultaneously developing theory of evolution. As Lisa Duggan explains, biologists, anatomists, and anthropologists working in the 1880s and 1890s agreed that significant differences between men and women (for example, characterizing men as "aggressive" and women as "passive" and thus "opposites" of each other) and women's subordination to men signaled higher stages of evolutionary progress. Because doctors regarded some degree of gender inversion as the primary cause of same-sex desire, they viewed homosexuality among whites as representative of either arrested development (getting stuck at a particular stage) or degeneration (actually moving backwards, and becoming less racially fit), and as such, a threat to the "white race." At the same time, Siobhan Somerville notes, race scientists determined the "primitivism" of their African American subjects, based particularly on the bodies of women, which they frequently compared to the bodies of white female inverts (that is, lesbians). American sexologists combined ideas about race and sexual inversion while working to uphold white supremacy in the aftermath of Reconstruction and the rise of Jim Crow. Homosexuality, then, became a way that scientists identified racial inferiority, and vice versa.

Duggan draws on evidence from both sexological and newspaper sources to show how white men imagined both black men and lesbians of all races (envisioned as masculine inverts) as threats to the white family who would steal "normal" white women, corrupt them, and sully the purity of the white race. American sexology thus not only drew on the existing European racialization of sexual inversion through ideas about race and evolution, but also modified it to fit a distinctly American agenda of segregation and defense of white racial purity. Armed with this framework of racialized homosexuality, sexologists set to work naming any breach in gender norms pathological, and simultaneously created a group of "normal" heterosexual people who performed gender, race, and class correctly.

The so-called closing of the American frontier in 1890 also spurred racialized concerns about sexuality, as Peter Boag explains. In the American imagination, if not in lived reality, the frontier preserved proper roles for men and women and reinforced masculinity in particular. The end of the frontier plunged America into modernity, and as a result, threatened to emasculate the nation. Framing the frontier as a place of normative masculinity masked the ways in which it teemed with gender and sexual diversity (as is underscored in Clare Sears' chapter in this volume). Sexologists sought to cordon this diversity off by juxtaposing the supposedly proper gender roles of settler colonialism with the inferiority of Native American sexual and gender deviance. Certainly, many (though not all) tribes allowed for what are today called "two-spirit" people in between or outside the categories of male and female, and often afforded them respect and spiritual power. Perhaps more importantly, many Native American families organized themselves according to different gender principles than Anglo families. Matrilineage, female authority over land and agriculture, and significant related political and economic power for women all violated Anglo gender norms. Mark Rifkin shows how advocates of white US settler colonialism had long justified war, missionary work, schooling, and the outright seizure of land, through references to the "wrongness" in the ways Native Americans organized gender and sexuality. Sexology became yet another tool in this arsenal.[18]

Assertions about the inherent morality of white, middle-class people fueled even more splitting in the classifications of homosexuals. Researchers tended to lump white, middle-class homosexuals into what they called the "true" invert group. Not surprisingly, sexologists saw pathological attraction to people of the same sex among the white middle class as a private, individual problem, best dealt with through treatment rather than punishment. Jennifer Terry explains that through a differential diagnosis for what was largely the same behavior, sexologists tended to view homosexuality among people of color and the working class as willfully immoral and criminal. White middle-class homosexuality, then, could be explained away as an aberration from the norm, while anyone else's same-sex desire defined the abnormality and inferiority of their entire group.

Like homosexuality, heterosexuality had to be invented, and it emerged specifically through the production of a "normal" category against which to compare supposedly deviant sexualities. In order for writers like Krafft-Ebing to determine which desires and behaviors counted as diseased they had to delineate the existence of a properly expressed sexual instinct. Initially they defined "normal" sexuality as reproductive, but later, with the rise of companionate marriage, they shifted to defining it as involving different (or as they would put it, "opposite") sexed people. Though most sexologists argued for immutable differences between heterosexual and homosexual people, and thus, rejected the idea that people could move between these categories, heterosexuality quickly began to appear fragile, difficult to achieve or maintain. Sigmund Freud, for example, proposed that each individual had to actively achieve normality through the repression of perverse instincts, and that development could easily go awry during childhood and adolescence. Constantly under siege from the threat of perversion, heterosexuality had to be protected and enforced. New fields such as child psychology and the burgeoning juvenile justice system developed to target problem behaviors and guide American youth on the path towards proper expressions of masculinity or femininity, culminating in heterosexual marriage and childrearing. Only through this process of maturation could white, middle-class American civilization survive and progress. Indeed, the American eugenics movement rapidly took up these ideas in the hope of guiding the healthy growth of the nation by controlling who could and could not reproduce.

As American sexologists sought to create neat hierarchies that emphasized the normal, they found more homosexual behavior among those understood to be white heterosexuals than they had anticipated. Homosexuals were supposed to be specific *types* of people, a small minority, aberrations with odd affect and style. Just as inversion could not hold all those supposedly categorized within it, the splitting of individuals into homosexual and heterosexual categories created a fundamentally unstable system, because scientists had to account for the huge numbers of apparently heterosexual people who engaged in same-sex sex under certain circumstances, such as in prisons (as Kunzel shows), communities of migrant laborers (as Boag and Shah show), the military (as Chauncey shows), and in adolescence (as Sahli, Inness, and Romesburg show). Sexologists responded by placing homosexuals into two groups: those who were truly mentally ill or degenerate and those who were just immoral. Or, to paraphrase Jennifer Terry, those who were born that way and those who had caught the gay. Thus, even as sexologists created a strict binary between homosexual and heterosexual, invert and normally gendered, they had to invent "tendencies," "phases," and "situational homosexuality" through which otherwise "normal" people still engaged in same-sex sex activities and gender transgressive behaviors. These moves allowed researchers to insist that there really was a stark line between heterosexual and homosexual, even when their own data indicated there was not.

Policing sexuality served as another way of clearly marking acceptable and unacceptable sexuality, though it of course reveals again that preserving the supposedly "natural" category of heterosexuality required significant state resources. Between 1880 and 1930, the federal government in the United States remained weak, and most regulation of queer sexuality and queer gender performance occurred at the local level. Rather than use sodomy laws to persecute homosexuality specifically, local law enforcement often arrested queer people on the basis of anti-prostitution, alcohol, or public disturbance statutes. In San Francisco in 1917, for example, vice crackdowns focusing on prostitution decimated the Barbary Coast district, where female impersonators and other gender-transgressive sex workers and entertainers had previously drawn massive crowds.

When the federal government did step in to regulate sexuality in this period, it also avoided using sodomy laws, and instead relied on other means to persecute queer people. During the early years of the twentieth century, the Bureau of Immigration, for example, refused entrance to people exhibiting indeterminate sex characteristics, including male prostitutes and people with ambiguous genitalia (those today called intersex), on the basis of their likelihood to become a "public charge" and need financial support from the state, rather than on the basis of perverse sexual acts. This policing came within a larger push to create safer public spaces for middle-class families and resulted in the broad regulation of the working-class. Unlike what would come in later decades, vice reform did not constitute a concerted attempt to target queerness. It was only during World War I that social reformers and police began to focus on homo-sexuality itself, imagined as a wartime problem imported from decadent Europe. Convictions for homosexual solicitation in New York increased eightfold from 1916 to 1920 as anti-vice societies deliberately investigated queer communities. Because reformers saw homosexuality as distinctly related to the war, though, their anxiety about policing it dropped off again as Americans regained a peacetime sense of normalcy, and as enforcing Prohibition became reformers' primary concern.

By the 1930s, the economic crisis of the Great Depression prompted the New Deal, and a new federal commitment to intervening in the sexuality of its citizens. Catastrophic rates of unemployment across the country spurred anxieties that men would abandon breadwinning as an ideal form of masculinity they were unlikely to be able to realize. The government feared that men would turn to the hobo lifestyle and the accompanying sexual perversity of transience. This fear was not unwarranted—rates of marriage and childbearing dropped precipitously during the Great Depression as men and women faced extreme difficulty supporting themselves, much less spouses and children.[19]

In *The Straight State*, Margot Canaday details how the government responded to the massive migration of unemployed men and boys by enacting economic relief programs that supported a model of heterosexual family characterized by male breadwinners with dependent wives and children. For example, the young men who joined the Civilian Conservation Corps (CCC) had to name a dependant who received a portion of their monthly earnings. Government officials characterized this requirement as teaching otherwise rootless young men responsible hetero-sexual masculinity. The Social Security Act also provided extra benefits to support the wives of married men. Thus, while the federal government acted to shore up men's power within families, it did so, at least initially, by rewarding favored heterosexual expression, rather than by explicitly punishing homosexuality. In incentivizing heterosexual marriage, the state constructed an appealing closet, which encouraged all people, regardless of their sexual desires, to embrace at least the appearance of heterosexuality. As a result, plenty of people with same-sex attraction married in this period. In the coming decades, the federal state would use its increasing powers to enforce the new heterosexual/homosexual binary that had emerged at the turn of the century and to punish those on the homosexual side.

By the 1930s, the homosexual and heterosexual had each become a type of person. The rise of wage labor spurred the growth of communities and identities centered around same-sex desire and gender diversity. As these communities became larger and more visible to out-siders, sexologists began to conduct research into them, as well as in prisons and mental hospitals. Sexologists took what they found and fashioned the homosexual/heterosexual binary to shore up the faltering gender, race, and class hierarchies. Science's framing of inversion, homosexuality, and heterosexuality reinforced existing power relations, and eventually provided the state with new ways to police people's sexual and gendered behavior. In turn, this allowed the state to enshrine the new concept of "heterosexuality" as an ideal for all citizens. However, queer communities continued to grow, and by the late 1940s, these communities began to resist state repression.[20] From the 1880s through 1940, gay identities emerged and helped produce gay communities. By the end of World War II, these communities began to create a political movement as they faced the increasingly dangerous federal state bent on actively shaping the intimate lives of its citizens.

Notes

1 Michel Foucault famously argued that in the European context after 1870, "the sodomite had been a temporary aberration; the homosexual was now a species." Michel Foucault, *The History of Sexuality, Volume I: An Introduction*, trans. Robert Hurley (New York: Vintage Books, 1990 [1978]), 43.

2 For an extended discussion historicizing queer identities, see, in this volume, Jen Manion, "Language, Acts, and Identities."

3 For the long history of urbanization and queerness, see, in this volume, Kwame Holmes, "An End to Queer Urban History?"

4 Also see, in this volume, Sara Smith-Silverman, "Labor."

5 For romantic friendships in the earlier nineteenth century, see, in this volume, Rachel Hope Cleves, "Revolutionary Sexualities and Early National Genders (1770s-1840s)" and Clare Sears, "Centering Slavery in Nineteenth-Century Queer History (1800s-1890s)."

6 Lillian Faderman, *Odd Girls and Twilight Lovers: A History of Lesbian Life in Twentieth-Century America* (New York: Columbia University Press, 1991), 25.

7 For discussions of same-sex desire expressed in blues music, see Maria Johnson, "Jelly Jelly Jellyroll: Lesbian Sexuality and Identity in Women's Blues" *Women and Music* 7 (December 2003): 31–52; Jana Evans Braziel, "Bye, Bye Baby: Race, Bisexuality, and the Blues in the Music of Bessie Smith and Janis Joplin," *Popular Music and Society* 27, no. 1 (2004): 3–26; Angela Davis, *Blues Legacies and Black Feminism: Gertrude "Ma" Rainey, Bessie Smith, and Billie Holiday* (New York: Vintage, 1999).

8 Braziel, 9–11.

9 R. W. Shufeldt, "Biography of a Passive Pederast," *American Journal of Urology and Sexology* 13 (1917), 460.

10 Evelyn Brooks-Higginbotham, *Righteous Discontent: The Women's Movement in the Black Baptist Church, 1880–1920* (Boston: Harvard University Press, 1993) 185–230. See also, Victoria Wolcott, *Remaking Respectability: African American Women in Interwar Detroit*, (Chapel Hill: University of North Carolina Press, 2001). Queer scholars have also taken up this analytic tool when discussing pre-Stonewall queer activism. See Marc Stein, *City of Sisterly and Brotherly Loves: Lesbian And Gay Philadelphia, 1945–1972* (Philadelphia: Temple University Press, 2004).

11 For discussions of Du Bois and other African American leaders interest in using art as a form of propaganda to combat racism, see A. B. Christa Schwarz, *Gay Voices of the Harlem Renaissance*, (Bloomington: University of Indiana Press, 2003), 29–32 and Thomas H. Wirth, ed., *Gay Rebel of the Harlem Renaissance: Selections from the Work of Richard Bruce Nugent* (Durham: Duke University Press, 2002), 47–8.

12 Eric King Watts, "Queer Harlem: Exploring the Rhetorical Limits of a Black Gay 'Utopia,' in *Queering Public Address: Sexualities in American Historical Discourse*, ed. Charles E Morris III (Columbia: University of South Carolina Press, 2007), 174–194.

13 For a fun and sexually explicit discussion of queer Harlem, see James F. Wilson, *Bulldaggers, Pansies, and Chocolate Babies: Performance, Race, and Sexuality in the Harlem Renaissance* (Ann Arbor: University of Michigan Press, 2011), 11–42.

14 See George Chauncey, *Gay New York* (New York: Basic Books, 1994), Chad Heap, *Slumming* (Chicago: University of Chicago Press, 2008), and Don Romesburg, " 'Wouldn't a Boy Do?': Sex Work and Male Youth in Early 20th-Century Chicago," *Journal of the History of Sexuality* 18, no. 3 (Fall 2009): 367–392. Despite being morally despised, prostitution also paid better than all women's work,

and most work available to working-class men. See Elizabeth Clement, *Love for Sale: Courting, Treating, and Prostitution in New York City, 1900–1945* (Chapel Hill: University of North Carolina Press, 2006).

15 Shufeldt, 456. This system in which men can maintain their "normal" masculinity as long as they take a penetrative role in sex has persisted in a number of communities. Even today, sex between men in prison, for example, configured through these roles, can remain acceptable within the bounds of masculinity. Sociologist Tomás Almaguer argued that in the 1980s and 1990s, for Mexican and Latin American sexual systems, and by extension among Chicano men in the United States, an active/passive distinction continued to be more important than a gay/straight binary. See Regina Kunzel, *Criminal Intimacy: Prison and the Uneven History of Modern American* Sexuality (Chicago: University of Chicago Press, 2008); Tomás Almaguer, "Chicano Men: A Cartography of Homosexual Identity and Behavior," *The Lesbian and Gay Studies Reader*, ed. Henry Abelove, Michèle Aina Barale, and David M. Halperin (New York: Routledge, 1993): 255–273.

16 For an extended discussion of sexual categories and medicalization, see, in this volume, Katie Batza, "Sickness and Wellness."

17 James Kiernan, "Bisexuality," *Urologic and Cutaneous Review* 18 (1914): 375. For more on bisexuality in sexual categorization and as a historical analytic, see, in this volume, Loraine Hutchins, "Bisexual History: Let's Not Bijack Another Century."

18 See also, in this volume, Eithne Luibhéid, "Queer and Nation"; Nayan Shah, "Queer of Color Estrangement and Belonging."

19 Walter LaFeber, Richard Polenberg, and Nancy Woloch, *The American Century: Volume 1: A History of the United States from 1890 to 1941* (New York: M.E. Sharpe, 2013), 155.

20 For the development of LGBT organizations, see Marcia Gallo, "Organizations," and for the unfolding of community and political development from the 1940s to the 1960s, see Amanda Littauer, "The Apex of Heteronormativity," both in this volume.

Further Reading

Bederman, Gail. *Manliness & Civilization: A Cultural History of Gender and Race in the United States, 1880–1917*. Chicago: University of Chicago Press, 1995.

Boag, Peter. *Same Sex Affairs: Constructing and Controlling Homosexuality in the Pacific Northwest*. Berkeley: University of California Press, 2003.

——. *Re-Dressing America's Frontier Past*. Berkeley: University of California, 2011.

Boyd, Nan Alamilla. *Wide Open Town: A History of Queer San Francisco to 1965*. Berkeley: University of California Press, 2003.

Canaday, Margot. *The Straight State: Sexuality and Citizenship in Twentieth-Century America*. Princeton: Princeton University Press, 2009.

Carter, Julian. *The Heart of Whiteness: Normal Sexuality and Race in America, 1880–1940*. Durham: Duke University Press, 2007.

Chauncey, George. "Christian Brotherhood or Sexual Perversion? Homosexual Identities and the Construction of Sexual Boundaries in the World War I Era." In *Hidden from History: Reclaiming the Gay and Lesbian Past*, eds. Martin Dauml Duberman, Martha Vicinus, and George Chauncey Jr., 294–317. New York: New American Library, 1989.

——. *Gay New York: The Making of the Gay Male World, 1890–1940*. New York: Basic Books, 1994.

Davidson, Arnold I. "How to Do the History of Psychoanalysis: A Reading of Freud's Three Essays on the Theory of Sexuality." Critical Inquiry 13, no. 2 (Winter 1987): 252–277.

D'Emilio, John. "Capitalism and Gay Identity." In *The Lesbian and Gay Studies Reader*, eds. Henry Abelove, Michèle Aina Barale, and David M. Halperin, 467–476. New York: Routledge, 1993.

Duggan, Lisa. *Sapphic Slashers: Sex, Violence, and American Modernity*. Durham: Duke University Press, 2000.

Gordon, Linda. "Black and White Visions of Welfare: Women's Welfare Activism, 1890–1945." In *Unequal Sisters: A Multi-Cultural Reader in U.S. Women's History*, eds. Vicki Ruiz and Ellen Dubois, 157–185. New York: Routledge, 1994.

Heap, Chad. *Slumming: Sexual and Racial Encounters in American Nightlife, 1885–1940*. Chicago: University of Chicago Press: 2008.

Inness, Sherrie A. "Mashes, Smashes, Crushes, and Raves: Woman-to-Woman Relationships in Popular Women's College Fiction, 1895–1915." *NWSA Journal* 6, no. 1 (Spring 1994): 48–68.

Kessler-Harris, Alice. *A Woman's Wage*. Lexington: University Press of Kentucky, 1990.

Meyerowitz, Joanne. *How Sex Changed: A History of Transsexuality in the United States*. Cambridge: Harvard University Press, 2002.

Murphy, Kevin. *Political Manhood: Red Bloods, Mollycoddles, and the Politics of Progressive Era Reform*. New York: Columbia University Press, 2008.

Rifkin, Mark. *When Did Indians Become Straight? Kinship, the History of Sexuality, and Native Sovereignty*. New York: Oxford University Press, 2011.

Romesburg, Don. "The Tightrope of Normalcy: Homosexuality, Developmental Citizenship, and American Adolescence, 1890–1940." *Journal of Historical Sociology* 21, no. 4 (December 2008): 417–442.

Sahli, Nancy. "Smashing: Women's Relationships Before the Fall." *Chrysalis* 8 (1979): 17–27.

Smith-Rosenberg, Carroll. "The Female World of Love and Ritual: Relations between Women in Nineteenth-Century America." *Signs* 1, no. 1 (1975): 1–29.

Terry, Jennifer. *An American Obsession: Science, Medicine, and Homosexuality in Modern Society*. Chicago: University of Chicago Press, 1999.

5

SEXUAL MINORITIES AT THE APEX OF HETERONORMATIVITY (1940s–1965)

Amanda H. Littauer

In the two decades following World War II, American culture idealized the white, patriarchal, heterosexual, middle-class family. Institutions of every kind rendered this exclusionary ideal into a punishing social, political, and economic imperative. In barracks and classrooms, movie theaters, offices and hospitals, those whose sexual desires and gendered subjectivities fell outside increasingly rigid norms confronted accusations that they were sick, deviant, and dangerous. Influenced by psychoanalysis and social science, "experts" de-emphasized homosexuality's association with gender inversion and stressed the potential that anyone could harbor queer inclinations.[1] Nevertheless, suspicion of effeminate men and masculine women actually intensified at the same time that Cold War political ideology converged with homophobia in what became a hegemonic formation: the homosexual as an invisible and insidious threat to national security.

Cast as outsiders who would never belong to the American democratic community, diverse queer people responded by actively pursuing both community and national belonging, expressing what Craig Loftin calls the civil rights impulse. Many people encountered that impulse in early gay civil rights organizations and publications, urban bars and neighborhoods, domestic spaces, and rural networks, though social hierarchies of gender, race, and class restricted access to safety and security. Mining sexual science, newly created lesbian and gay newsletters, and popular fiction, they situated themselves in broader queer worlds and used camp sensibility to read past stridently negative literary and visual representations in search of queer forms of being and desire. LGBT people staked claims to recognition and pleasure in all manner of places, from church choirs to suburban coffee klatches, and from reform schools to queer bars. Men and women pursued public recognition in distinct yet collaborative ways, insisting that authorities acknowledge their shared humanity and their rights as a minority population. Starting in the mid-1950s, transgender people, many of whom were poor, young, and of color, led defenses of queer public spaces against persistent police harassment. Trans people also navigated the medical system in pursuit of self-determination, while middle-class gay men and lesbians criticized psychiatric denigration of homosexual adjustment and maturity. Institutional oppression and queer resistance existed in dynamic relation to each other in the contentious postwar years, when policymakers and average people alike struggled over the question of which Americans truly belonged.

World War II

World War II was one of the most disruptive events in American history, uprooting millions, transforming the economy, and creating the military-industrial complex. The population shifted from rural areas and small towns to homosocial military communities and urban centers, where people encountered difference and many embraced the chance for reinvention. War-time mobility catalyzed widespread non-marital sexual self-expression, straight and queer alike. As Allan Bérubé's work has shown, military service created unprecedented opportunities to experience homosocial intimacy and homosexuality. At the same time, military leaders began assembling the mechanisms through which the armed forces might become a stridently hetero-sexual institution. Gay, lesbian and bisexual service members used camp, slang, and other self-protective strategies to create a place for themselves within a rapidly changing and increasingly hostile institution.

Building on World War I-era court-martialing cases for sodomy and sexual assault, and empowered by the state's massive infusion of resources during World War II, the military began policing not just sexual acts but homosexual status. In collaboration with psychiatrists, military officials devised a discharge system to get rid of gay, lesbian, and bisexual soldiers on the basis that they suffered from mental illness. As Allan Bérubé and Margot Canaday have detailed, military psychiatrists began screening out people with homosexual "tendencies" as early as 1941, and in 1943 authorities created the category of the "confirmed pervert." Even those determined to possess "latent" homosexual desires but who did not engage in same-sex sexual behavior were defined as undesirable and served under the constant threat of the so-called blue discharge (named for the color of the paper on which undesirable discharges were printed).

During World War II the US military first created a permanent presence for women. As authorities worked to create the new category of "female soldier," they sought to retain the military's fundamental patriarchy and racial segregation. As Leisa Meyer explains, the Women's Army Corps anticipated controversy about women service members' gender and sexual non-conformity by defensively policing both heterosexual sexual activity and assertive lesbian behavior. WAC leadership downplayed the extent of lesbianism, inadvertently creating conditions for a lesbian subculture in which women crafted strategies for mutual recognition, socialization, sexual encounters, and community. But butch lesbian soldiers—who embodied gendered and sexual power—directly threatened the military's construction of the feminine female soldier and suffered from traumatizing investigations that previewed the more wide-spread lesbian purges of the immediate postwar years.

The full effect of dishonorable discharges for homosexuality became clear at the war's end, when Veterans Administration officials excluded any solider with a blue discharge "because of homosexual acts or tendencies." Home and business loans, employment assistance, college and vocational training, and unemployment compensation were now out of reach for over 9,000 service members. Since most employers and many universities checked military discharge papers, vets marked by such designations struggled to secure jobs and higher education. Thousands more gay men, bisexuals, and lesbians who managed to secure honorable discharges were able to enjoy GI Bill entitlements only so long as they continued to conceal their sexuality from authorities. Some vets challenged the exclusion, reaching out to a range of civil rights organizations and social service agencies for assistance. But as the federal government began to

Figure 5.1 World War II Women's Army Corps radio technician Phyllis Abry (L) with her lover, Mildred, c. 1943.

Courtesy of GLBT Historical Society.

purge homosexuals in what became known as the "Lavender Scare," anti-homosexual policies only gained support.[2]

The GI Bill was the first time that the federal government explicitly excluded homosexual people from a major benefit, creating what Margot Canaday calls a "clear line between homosexuality and heterosexuality in federal citizenship policy."[3] As one of the most important pieces of social welfare legislation in US history, the GI Bill created a hierarchy of citizenship that reduced the life chances of those who "failed" to achieve the white heterosexual male ideal. It funneled resources directly to men, adding incentives for women to leave the lucrative industrial workforce and to depend on husbands for support. African American veterans (straight and queer alike) found that racially exclusionary Federal Housing Administration policies left them unable to take advantage of the GI Bill's mortgage assistance program. Thousands of black families were shut out of the mushrooming postwar middle class and subsequent generational housing equity, directly contributing to today's massive racialized wealth disparities. With unprecedented resources to distribute, state authorities carefully offered full citizenship only to white heterosexual men.

The Cold War State and the Lavender Scare

In the past, historians attempted to explain the intensity of state-sponsored homophobia in the early 1950s by pointing to the Cold War. Cold War culture trafficked the idea that subversive influences corroded American democracy surreptitiously, circulating not only in government institutions but also in the realms of popular representation, consumer culture, family life, and the individual psyche. As homosexuality became less clearly associated with gender non-conformity in favor of sexual object choice, queerness seemed to become less visible and therefore more pernicious. Anxiety about the threat that homosexuality apparently posed to mature hetero-sexual adulthood and to the nuclear family manifested in political institutions, where McCarthy and other leaders took advantage of the "homosexual menace" as a way to consolidate political power.

Newer research shows that this largely accurate narrative is incomplete. A more robust under-standing must account for additional political considerations, such as the rapid growth of the bureaucratic state and the highly partisan and opportunistic nature of postwar politics. According to Canaday, the simultaneous development in the early-mid twentieth century of the federal bureaucracy and the category of homosexuality helps to explain how and why citizenship was defined as exclusively heterosexual. Immigration, military, and welfare officials came to care about gender and sexual nonconformity before World War II, but the massive infusion of resources into wartime and Cold War military-industrial complex empowered government and professional authorities to police a "homosexual" population whose parameters they themselves helped to create. The 1952 McCarran–Walter Act prohibited those with "psychopathic" personalities (later "sexual deviates") from immigrating to the United States, while the military stepped up its harassment and exclusion of lesbians by defining female homosexuality as char-acterized not only by same-sex activity or gender nonconformity, but also through relationships, culture, and community.

State Department leaders initiated anti-gay witch hunts well before McCarthy galvanized national attention to the so-called communist menace. David Johnson argues that many pol-iticians, journalists, and citizens regarded homosexuals as a more serious national security threat than Communists. Congressional Republicans initiated this claim, but it quickly became a source of moral panic that saturated political culture. Campaigns to remove both Communists and homosexuals began in 1947; both groups were portrayed as "alien subcultures that recruited the psychologically maladjusted to join in immoral behavior that threatened the nation's survival."[4] Unlike Communists, however, federal authorities deliberately concealed the iden-tities of their queer targets, allowing gay people to become invisible phantoms who evoked Americans' worse fears about the declining moral fiber of society. And unlike the short-lived Red Scare, the "Lavender Scare" persisted through the 1970s. The purges ultimately destroyed the livelihoods (and sometimes the lives) of thousands of civil servants.

Even those without jobs in the federal government experienced the purges' ripple effect. In public schools, for instance, the unmarried women who had previously dominated the profession now faced intense scrutiny and pressure to marry, and both men and women were compelled to display perfect gender conformity in their mannerisms, appearance, and insti-tutional position. Teachers became targets when panic about sexual "psychopaths" erupted in the mid-1950s. As Jackie Blount describes, *Time* magazine published a sensational story in 1955 claiming that a "ring" of gay male teachers in Boise, Idaho had "corrupted" teenage boys who then went on to "infect" others. When the story broke, gay and lesbian teachers and other Boise residents fled out of fear that they would be arrested or committed to psychi-atric institutions without grounds, as were queer people in Boise and other cities around the nation.[5] As the bureaucratic state ballooned in size and power, public leaders increasingly defined citizenship itself as heterosexual and reduced queer Americans' access to rights and resources.

The Civil Rights Impulse

Across the country, queer people digesting news stories about anti-homosexual purges and persecution felt not only scared but also motivated by outrage. Responding to military discrimination, several hundred gay men organized the Veterans Benevolent Association in New York in 1945, and a diverse coalition of vets and their advocates fought the exclusion of those with blue discharges from GI Bill benefits. Some early victims of government firings used the courts to resist the police harassment that formed the basis for the purges. In 1948, for instance, Edward Kelly, an analyst with the Public Health Service lost his job after he was arrested for inviting an undercover officer in Washington, D.C. back to his apartment for drinks and sex. As Genny Beemyn explains, Kelley contested his arrest and won a legal victory when the US Court of Appeals ruled that courts had to exercise "great caution" when there was no corroborating evidence of an invitation to sodomy, and created guidelines for local courts known as "Kelly counsels" for similar future cases. As a result, more men challenged their arrests, and conviction rates in Washington D.C. dropped immediately.[6]

Similarly, early gains for transgender politics came when individuals such as Virginia Prince challenged government definitions of obscenity. While still living as a cross-dressing man and exchanging erotic letters with a friend, Prince was charged with distributing obscenity through the mail. As Susan Styker explains, the move was part of an attempt to restrict circulation of Prince's *Transvestia* magazine, the first long-running transgender periodical in the US. Postal law was one venue through which government agencies policed the speech and self-expression of LGBT people, and Prince's 1962 success in deflecting censorship of the magazine and evading penalties for the obscenity charge represented a victory for the right to free speech for queer and trans people.

Many individuals who did not take direct action nonetheless expressed their belief that they had the right to live as they were. Loftin argues that a broad swath of the gay and lesbian population was thinking about sexuality in political terms, not only those who became involved with early gay civil rights organizations. One individual who insisted upon her right to self-determination was Christine Jorgensen, a former (male) GI who entered the public spotlight in 1952 when newspapers around the world announced that she had completed successful genital transformation surgery in Copenhagen, Denmark. She became an instant media sensation; reporters juxtaposed photos of her as a man in military uniform and as a beautiful and elegant white woman. Though Jorgensen never saw herself as an activist, her story inspired letters of gratitude and recognition from hundreds of transgender people. Her fame also helped to define the modern understanding of transsexuality (as distinct from homosexuality or intersexuality).

Between 1950 and the late 1960s, homophile organizations challenged political and cultural stigma and advocated for the full inclusion of gay men and lesbians into American society. Although only occasionally touching on issues of transsexuality and bisexuality, generally accepting mainstream ideas about male/female difference, and prioritizing the experiences of white, middle-class people over others, homophile leaders crafted an effective reformist approach that responded dynamically and creatively to the harsh realities of Cold War culture.[7]

Emerging from leftist political networks and influenced by the Marxist concept of oppressed national minorities, Harry Hay decided that homosexuals would have to resist their persecution politically and began advocating for sexual privacy in the late 1940s. He had heard stories of the first wave of State Department purges of gay civil servants and feared that employment discrimination would soon spread to the private sector. In late 1950, he and six other white gay men founded the Mattachine Society in Los Angeles, adopting the secrecy, hierarchical structure, and centralized leadership of the Communist Party. In his analysis of Mattachine, Daniel Huerwitz emphasizes the "affirmative positive model" of simultaneous personal and political passion that Hay imported from his experiences with the Communist community and the sense of belonging that Mattachine members enjoyed. John D'Emilio and others stress the significance of their political analysis, which stemmed from the men's examination of their own experience. Their 1951 statement, "Sense of Value," posited the theory that homosexuals were a distinct and oppressed cultural group, "a social minority imprisoned within a dominant culture."[8] Although subsequent leaders of Mattachine demanded a more reformist agenda focused on public education, social service, and integration of homosexuals into the larger heterosexual society, this early articulation of a gay minority contributed to the subsequent rise of lesbian and gay identity politics.[9]

As Marc Stein explains, identity politics wasn't the only model for early homophile activism. The early movement was characterized by a remarkable diversity of perspectives on sex, gender, race, sexuality, and political ideology. Influenced by socialism, anarchism, and libertarianism, activists advocated for sexual privacy and civil liberties and incorporated organizing tactics from movements for racial justice. Popular social science, particularly Alfred Kinsey's *Sexual Behavior in the Human Male* (1948), helped advocates make the case that a significant percentage of Americans engaged in at least intermittent same-sex behavior and that gay men and lesbians should not be singled out. Some activists saw homosexuality and bisexulality not as identities but as universal human potentials. Transnationally, struggles for human rights and sex law reform and against colonialism also fueled the intellectual ferment of homophile leaders. Loftin's analysis of *ONE* suggests that editors were aware of and emboldened by successful efforts to decriminalize homosexuality in Europe.[10]

The homophile movement adapted to escalating state-sponsored homophobia and anti-communism by steering the nascent movement in the direction of recognition, reform, and integration. Working within the confines of Cold War nationalism, organizational leaders worked to promote social change by downplaying differences between straight and gay citizens.[11] The homophile movement made a tangible difference in the lives of thousands of queer Americans, particularly (though not exclusively) those from the white, middle class. As Stein points out, homophile leaders skillfully adapted strategies and goals from the black civil rights movement and regularly analogized between racial and sexual oppression, but they did not attract sustained participation from queer people of color. Working-class men and women may have been turned off by the public and overtly political orientation of homophile organizations, but they nonetheless contributed and benefited.

Women played significant roles at certain times in male-dominated groups such as Mattachine and *ONE*, but as Marc Stein observes, their experiences and priorities were different from those of gay men. While gay men were perhaps overly visible to a public that stereotyped them as deviant, psychopathic, and dangerous, lesbians were largely invisible and had distinct concerns about employment, reproduction, parenthood, and domestic and sexual violence. In 1955, four San Francisco lesbian couples started the Daughters of Bilitis (named for an obscure mythical seductress of Sappho). Marcia Gallo argues that the Daughters "slowly lifted the veil of secrecy that surrounded lesbians' daily lives in mid-twentieth-century America."

The organization took a strong stand against racial segregation, achieved significant membership of African American, Latina, and Asian American women, and elected two black lesbian presidents, but the DOB was nonetheless primarily an organization of white, middle-class lesbians. DOB's leadership viewed social acceptability as the means to achieve integration and strived to correct negative and pathologizing stereotypes about lesbians. The organization emphasized "providing safety, proving normality, and winning acceptance" but also offered increasingly critical social commentary. By 1963, certain chapters were pressing the national officers to allow picketing, which helped to transform activists "from female homophiles into lesbian rights activists."[12]

Written by and for women, the DOB publication *The Ladder* arrived in mailboxes across the country in an unmarked envelope. It was not the nation's first lesbian-centered publication—in 1947, Edythe Eyde (aka Lisa Ben) had published *Vice Versa* out of Los Angeles—but *The Ladder* connected many married and unmarried women to a lesbian community for the first time. With book reviews, opinion pieces, letters, and creative work, the magazine allowed lesbians to share their thoughts and feelings. The magazine presented a more positive image of lesbians than did paperback novels or psychological commentary, and its fiction reviews also guided women to the passionate lesbian sex scenes and attractive characters that only the pulps could offer.[13]

Although only a small percentage of queer people in postwar America joined homophile organizations, homophile publications introduced isolated individuals into an "imaginary community" and mapped out "a geography of the gay and lesbian world."[14] In *Contacts Desired*, Martin Meeker details how these communication networks helped to give gay men and lesbians a public voice that resisted mainstream cultural and political authorities' harmful claims. Between formal organizations and the much wider reach of their publications and visibility, the homophile movement constitutes an important chapter in the history of LGBT civil rights in the United States.

Queer Culture

In print, on stage, and on screen, representations of queerness proliferated in the postwar era. The vast majority spread the destructive notion that homosexuals were sick and infectious, deviant and dangerous. A 1964 photo essay in *LIFE* magazine, entitled "Homosexuality in America," for instance, referred to gay men as "sad and sordid" and featured an image of a Santa Monica, California, bar owner in front of a sign he put up that read, "Fagots [sic] Stay Out." Other cultural texts left more room for interpretation, and a small group of cultural commentators—most of them secretly gay themselves—crafted stories and arguments in which lesbian and gay people found the potential for enjoyable, meaningful, and even playful queer lives.[15]

In Hollywood, the Production Code explicitly forbade the naming of homosexuality, and gay or bisexual actors—such as Rock Hudson and James Dean—protected their careers by keeping their sexuality private. Nonetheless, films represented a range of outcasts and liminal types that conveyed strong messages about gay and lesbian people. Hollywood's primary contribution to Cold War sexual culture was to entrench the homophobic construction of gay men and lesbians as dangerous and psychologically crippled figures who threatened national security. In *North by Northwest*, for instance, the main character's involvement in the Communist underworld—which is marked by sexual deviance—stemmed in part from his over-devotion to his mother.

Popular psychoanalytic thought in the postwar years attributed all manner of "maladjustment" to failures of Oedipal development; mothers could inadvertently foster homosexuality and communist sympathies in their male or female children by being either excessively distant or adoring. The resulting psychopathology, the logic went, was difficult to detect. Postwar social science seemed to support the threat of invisible sexual corruption; Alfred Kinsey's finding that a substantial proportion of Americans had engaged in homosexual behavior suggested that same-sex desire was more pervasive and homosexual identity less fixed or stable than commonly believed. Cold War film exploited the apparent difficulty of distinguishing gay from straight men, suggesting that the ability of queer people to hide in plain sight made them insidious not only politically, but socially and culturally, as well.

In Alfred Hitchcock's *The Rope* (1948) and *Strangers on a Train* (1951), implicitly queer characters were predatory and even murderous. *Suddenly, Last Summer* (1959), based on the play by Tennessee Williams, represented a poet, Sebastian, who is scarred by his relationship with his mother and preys on boys until he meets his own gruesome and apparently inevitable end. A review of the film in the lesbian magazine, *The Ladder*, criticized the popular film's "ugliness and horror" and "predatory" theme, as Sherry points out.

More subtle treatments of homosexuality characterized films such as *Caged* (1950), which implies a destructive (yet entertaining) lesbian homoeroticism among women prison inmates, and *Rebel without a Cause* (1955), in which Plato is an artistic outsider who, in typical queer fashion, is doomed to die. In *Tea and Sympathy* (1956), an effeminate boy emerges into creative heterosexual adulthood thanks to healthy maternal influence and despite the proximity of a coach with a "contemptible" fondness for boys.[16] In *A Streetcar Named Desire* (1951), Marlon Brando expressed an intensity of emotion previously limited to female characters. Rumored to have sexual relationships with women, Barbara Stanwyck played several brassy and masculine characters, including lesbian Jo Courtney in 1962's *Walk on the Wild Side*.

Unlike mainstream cinema, film noir made gay men more visible but only in homophobic contrast to the straight "hard-boiled hero." Corber argues that film noir resisted dominant constructions of white masculinity—represented by the "organization man" who embraced workplace cooperation and suburban domestic life—by romanticizing homosocial spaces and bonds between men. In order to reassure the viewer of the hero's heterosexuality, noir film-makers iconographically linked gay men to the femme fatale through effeminate mannerisms, high taste, and luxurious surroundings. Despite the homophobic and sexist elements of this strategy, noir films rendered gay men legible on the silver screen.

"Camp" extended the connection between gay men and film beyond the bounds of legibility and representation and into the realm of aesthetics and affect. Scholars have associated camp with artistic sensibility, satire and mockery, theatricality, artifice, ironic respectability, skepticism, insistent uncertainty, fantasy, and the suspension of belief and disbelief. Camp offers insight into dominant culture from the position of an outsider. Michael Trask underscores its stringent antiessentialism, pointing out that the drag queen performs ironic femininity in ways that "insistently slacken" the binary opposition between maleness and femaleness.[17]

In the postwar era, gay male film spectators enlisted camp in their desire for leading men by identifying with leading women, particularly actresses such as Joan Crawford, Elizabeth Taylor, and Judy Garland, who expressed not only passion, allure, and vulnerability but also persistence. As Michael Bronski explains, "the woman stars of the 50s reflected the condition of many gay men: they suffered, beautifully."[18] Mourning over the death of Judy Garland reportedly contributed to the state of agitation that fueled the Stonewall Riots in 1969.

Those looking for more descriptive and explicit renderings of queer life than they could find in the movie theater turned instead to a burgeoning print culture. By the 1960s, hundreds of publications portrayed "homosexuals" in American society. From pornography and pulp to respectable magazines and journals, an unprecedented volume of text meant that no single claim about gay men or lesbians could go uncontested. Nearly every newspaper in the nation covered

Kinsey's findings about American sexual behavior, including homosexuality, and works of "pulp sexology" brought popularized and sensationalized versions of social scientific studies to the shelves of thousands of newsstands and bookstores.

Lesbian pulp novels illustrate the extent to which queer life infused popular culture. By 1965, a survey identified 348 lesbian pulp novels, most of which were written by men for men and perpetuated negative stereotypes of lesbians. But a small group of lesbian authors— such as Valerie Taylor, Ann Bannon, and Paula Christian—depicted strong characters who experienced pleasure and even autonomy despite the unhappy endings mandated by publishers. Lesbian mystery writer Katherine Forrest recalled her first encounter with Bannon's *Odd Girl Out* when she was 18 years old in 1957:

> I did not need to look at the title for clues; the cover leaped out at me from the drugstore rack. . . . Overwhelming need led me to walk a gauntlet of fear up to the cash register. . . . I stumbled out of the store in possession of what I knew I must have, a book as necessary to me as air. . . . It opened the door to my soul and told me who I was.[19]

Women such as Forrest used lesbian-authored pulps as maps as they struggled to understand themselves and to locate lesbian subcultures, whose bars and clubs figured in the plots of the novels. As I discuss in *Bad Girls*, fiction was one place where readers and authors alike could imagine desiring and desirable lesbian lives. Patricia Highsmith's lesbian novel, *The Price of Salt* (1952), was especially significant for its relatively happy ending.[20]

Gay men had a wider range of representational options, including the visual pleasures of homoerotic physique magazines and the erotic poetry of Beat poets such as Allen Ginsberg. The queerness of Beat culture is illuminated by Ginsberg's 1947 poem, "In Society," in which a peek inside a meat sandwich at a gay party reveals a dirty asshole. Gay male identity and community are visible in the poem, but the emphasis is on explicit male sexuality, outsider status, and disdain for social norms. Beat poets such as Ginsberg, Kerouac, and Burroughs lived complicated and contradictory sexual lives, but as D'Emilio has pointed out, their work enabled mid-century gay and bisexual male readers to celebrate their sexuality and to see themselves not as deviants but, rather, as nonconformists and rebels.[21]

Prominent literary figures such as Tennessee Williams, James Baldwin, and Gore Vidal shared the Beats' construction of queerness as a form of oppositional consciousness and embraced sex as an emancipatory force. According to Corber, however, these writers were more attuned to oppression than their Beat contemporaries. Williams, for instance, focused on and politi- cized female experience in ways that intersected with homoerotic themes, while Vidal crafted a gay macho style that rejected experts' (waning) view of homosexuality as defined by gender inversion. Baldwin promoted political solidarity by importing race, ethnicity, and sexuality into the class-centered tradition of social protest literature. All three authors insisted on placing private life in a broader public context, in ways that anticipated liberationist movements of the late 1960s.[22]

Writing under the pseudonym Donald Webster Cory, gay (or perhaps bisexual) Edward Sagarin was the lone nonfiction author in the postwar years to offer a sympathetic, in-depth account of gay male life (with a nod toward lesbians). In 1951, at the same time that Harry Hay was formulating his own analysis of a homosexuality as a legitimate minority, Cory published *The Homosexual in America*, which brought the same idea into wide circulation in the United States for the first time. Martin Duberman notes the book's additional groundbreaking claims, such as the notion that many homosexuals were less "queer" than many heterosexuals and that sexual categories themselves were contingent, shifting, and fluid. Despite his own decision to "hide behind the mask" during that extraordinarily hostile era—and his descent into homophobic conservatism in the 1970s—Cory/Sagarin ended the book by naming a "reservoir of protest" that would, in fact, invigorate the following generation. Given the rise of nonfiction paperbacks in the early 1960s that exuded contempt and alarm, *The Homosexual in America* remained for decades a valuable resource for LGBT people.

As D'Emilio writes, a common thread throughout most fiction and nonfiction literature about gay and lesbian people, even the 1964 *LIFE* Magazine photo essay, is the "implicit recognition that gay men and women existed in groups with a network of institutions and resources to sustain their social identity." Though distorted by misunderstanding, discourse thus reflected a robust and undeniable queer social world.[23]

Queer Space and Queer Life

In wartime and postwar years, bars were critically important sites of queer connection, community, and resistance. In the 1940s, bars and nightclubs that attracted a mixed queer and straight clientele and catered to tourists and businessmen could nonetheless, writes Nan Alamilla Boyd, help "establish a public culture for homosexuals." San Francisco's Finocchio's, for instance, featured female impersonators and "lured audiences with the titillating appeal of sexual deviancy and display." By the mid-1950s, gay men and lesbians had carved out devoted spaces for themselves. In the Black Cat, a gay male bar in 1950s San Francisco, Latino drag performer José Sarria cultivated a defensive and sarcastic style that artfully displaced gay audience members' sense of shame or anonymity with a "surge of cultural pride." He incorporated political themes in his performances and promoted the political and cultural visibility of queer people of color.[24]

Lesbians also created thriving bar-based communities in the 1950s. In San Francisco, there were between four and seven lesbian bars in the North Beach neighborhood in the 1950s. No other city enjoyed such a distinct lesbian district at mid-century, but studies of lesbian bar culture in Buffalo, Denver, and Detroit reveal lesbian commercial subcultures that served the needs of white, working-class women, in particular. A defining characteristic of these subcultures was their embrace of gender difference.

Butch/stud/masculine and fem/broad/feminine identities structured the terms of bar-based (and often intimate) interactions. In their groundbreaking study of mid twentieth-century Buffalo, oral historians Elizabeth Kennedy and Madeline Davis argue that a vibrant lesbian bar culture emerged in the 1940s and became "defiant" in the 1950s, when butch-fem couples "outraged society by creating a romantic and sexual unit within which women were not under male control."[25] Oral history narrators recall finding in bars a strong sense of belonging and pleasure but also risk, since occupying public space in this period exposed queer people to scrutiny, harassment, and alcoholism. Violence was common, not only because of police abuse, but also because butches were expected to defend themselves and their fem girlfriends. White and black tough bar lesbians fought "to expand their public presence and to control their environment," while fems welcomed newcomers, hosted social gatherings, mediated conflicts, enhanced lesbian visibility by appearing publicly at butches' sides, and participated actively in erotic relationships that fueled their communities.[26] This persistent self-assertion in the face of homophobic persecution was part of the long struggle for LGBT civil rights.

Racism limited the access of lesbians of color to bar culture. Bouncers demanded multiple forms of identification from black and Latina women, for instance, and bar owners regarded groups as a potential problem. A white oral history narrator openly admitted that she would never sleep with a black woman and preferred to stay "with my own color." White lesbians who regarded themselves as less racist than straight whites nonetheless minimized the existence of racism in lesbian bars, leaving women of color feeling invisible and unwelcome.[27]

As I have written about elsewhere, teenagers also tried to connect with adult lesbians through bars, with mixed results; most bars turned them away out of fear of attracting law enforcement, but certain bar owners protected teens by ushering them out the back door first when the police showed up. Some girls got creative, exploring lesbian bars on dates with their boyfriends or sneaking past bouncers by hiding in the middle of groups of older lesbians.[28]

In cities around the country, gay men of diverse race and class backgrounds congregated and cruised in public parks, such as Washington D.C.'s Lafayette Park, only one block from the White House. As Beemyn and Loftin explain, the Lafayette neighborhood included rooming houses, restaurants, and cultural institutions such as the YMCA that were centers of gay social life in the 1940s, though anti-gay policing and purges suppressed gay socializing in the 1950s.[29]

LGBT people also gathered in commercial sites such as Cooper's Donuts in Los Angeles and Dewey's cafeteria in Philadelphia, where sex workers, drag queens, and homeless gay and trans youth asserted their right to patronize and socialize as they pleased. According to Susan Stryker, Cooper's was an all-night coffeehouse in a rough neighborhood where Latino, African American, and other male hustlers and drag queens socialized with one another and with the men who picked them up or paid them for sex. On one night in May 1959, police came in and did what they usually did—demanding identification and arresting drag queens for vagrancy, loitering, or prostitution—but this time, customers fought the police with doughnuts and fists, and some of the queens under arrest managed to get away. Stryker points out that this kind of spontaneous act of defiance probably occurred frequently in the years before journalists or middle-class activists were paying attention.

Similarly, Marc Stein details how Dewey's coffeehouse and lunch counter had been popular with the late-night gay, lesbian, drag queen, and prostitute crowd since the 1940s but started refusing service to cross-dressing queer youth in 1965. When two teen boys and one teen girl refused to leave on April 25th, they and a gay lawyer defending them were arrested, and the local gay community picketed the restaurant and staged a successful sit-in. Dewey's management agreed to stop denying service based on gender nonconformity. As Stryker points out, the Dewey's incident illustrates that gay and transgender activism overlapped in poor and working-class urban areas and that the strategies of minority rights movements cross-fertilized to a significant extent. Many of Dewey's patrons were queer people of color whose lives represented the intersection between black and queer struggles for civil rights.

In the years before LGBT people boldly asserted their right to occupy public spaces such as bars and cafes, they nonetheless crafted opportunities to explore their queer desires and identities within dominant institutions. Homosocial settings in public and private schools allowed same-sex relationships to thrive. According to memoirists and oral history narrators, even coercive environments such as the military, reformatories, psychiatric institutions and prisons were sites of humanizing emotional and physical connections between men and among women.

Some of the most compelling recent research has focused on religious institutions. Despite efforts of most mainstream churches to exclude homosexual parishioners, Loftin finds that many gay Christians found ways to reconcile their religious beliefs with their sexuality. Similarly, before the politics of respectability became paramount to the civil rights movement, black churches brought queer people together. E. Patrick Johnson's black gay male narrators recall expressing effeminate theatricality in church choirs and enjoying sexual encounters beneath church pews. When religious leaders expressed homophobia, gay parishioners remained engaged spiritually and socially by selectively rejecting pastors' interpretations. Since the black church was (and remains) central to African American culture and community, particularly in the South, queer black people went to great lengths to preserve their membership. Johnson argues that the black church has been a "contradictory space" where doctrine and practice conflict and where negative attitudes toward homosexuality coexist with gay men's feelings of acceptance and belonging.[30]

Despite associations of postwar LGBT communities with large urban areas, recent studies have shown that rural spaces—particularly in the South—presented distinctive possibilities for the enactment of queer desire and identity among men. Southerners' preference for euphemistic and indirect approaches to sexuality created discursive space for young men to experiment with homosexuality. John Howard explains that "homosexuality and gender insubordination were acknowledged and accommodated with a pervasive, deflective pretense of ignorance" and concludes that "around deviant sexuality . . . a quiet accommodation was the norm."[31] At the same time, open rural landscapes and a lack of close supervision gave men literal room to move and breathe. Roadsides, barns, and fields were among the many places that boys and men could have sex undisturbed.

From a rural vantage point, the chronology of queer history actually looks quite different; historians stress that anti-gay harassment and enforcement picked up in the 1960s in reaction to the rise of more explicit and confrontational identity politics. Colin Johnson ends his book on rural sexualities, for instance, with a 1962 police sting on public highway restrooms in Ohio, which he interprets not as an example of rural traditionalism but, rather, as evidence that rural officials were importing regulatory mechanisms designed by urban police in response to growing queer subcultures. Future research should bring women into this picture of rural queer life.

For LGBT people in postwar America, domestic spaces served a diverse range of queer purposes that varied widely by region, race, and class. Rochella Thorpe's research shows that African American lesbians in Detroit satisfied their social needs and circumvented racism by hosting and attending parties in private homes. Kennedy and Davis found that the black lesbian community in Buffalo recognized and respected fem leaders, who not only organized and hosted house parties but opened their homes to those who needed their help, including queer youth. E. Patrick Johnson's southern black gay narrators recall legendary house parties featuring music, dancing, food, and drinks. Middle- and upper-class people often avoided socializing publicly in order to protect their jobs and reputations, preferring private and discrete social gatherings in their homes.

Suggesting that perhaps Cold War fears about the pervasiveness of queer desire were not entirely unfounded, Lauren Gutterman has argued that postwar suburbs housed untold numbers of married white women who formed romantic and sexual relationships with one another. Only a small number of these women encountered a public lesbian culture. Rather, the women transformed their own homes into queer spaces, meeting each other in the neighborhood, at work, or in church and enjoying sex while their husbands were at work. Although most wives tried to hide their same-sex relationships from their husbands, some managed to work out alternative marital arrangements.[32]

Married queer people had to be extremely careful in what Daniel Rivers has called "difficult and dangerous years for lesbian and gay parents and their children." Participating in gay life meant risking arrest, which could result in parents' legal separation from their kids. The Daughters of Bilitis recognized parenting rights as a top priority in the 1950s, and the first major court case to uphold the rights of lesbian and gay parents came down in 1967, but countless mothers and fathers lost custody of their children.[33]

Few of the same-sex desiring housewives in Gutterman's research described themselves as homosexual, gay, lesbian, or bisexual. Women's own words—such as references to "being able to live both ways" in a "two-way house"—evoke bisexual subjectivity, but bisexuality was an unfamiliar idea for most mid-century Americans. Psychological experts described married women's attraction to other women as evidence of "latent lesbianism" caused by flawed parent-child relationships, and as Marc Stein has pointed out, homophile groups at the time tended include anyone experiencing same-sex attractions under the category of gay or lesbian, even those who also had cross-sex attractions, relationships, or marriages. Avoiding labels allowed married women to frame affairs with women as consistent with their normative, feminine lives.[34]

In her analysis of diaries and correspondence, Heather Murray argues that young people faced a conflict between a growing consciousness of their own sexual difference and the post-war imperative of family togetherness and heteronormativity. Instead of frankly disclosing their sexual identities, Murray finds that most embraced an "ambiguous strategy of discretion as a way of maintaining both their gay and their family relationships." An adult daughter might inform her parents that she and her "close friend" would be living together permanently without acknowledging the romantic or sexual nature of their relationship. Murray notes that many people in the 1950s found this kind of code quite workable, though some found that living a "double" life took a toll on them emotionally. Analyzing letters to *ONE*, Loftin notes that when individuals told parents that they were gay, they did not experience uniformly hostile reactions but, rather, varied and complex responses that included not only rejection but also compromise, accommodation, and even acceptance.[35]

Strategic discretion was critical to postwar queer life generally. LGBT people in the 1940s and 50s did not use the term "coming out" to mean a public disclosure of sexuality. A more common metaphor was "wearing masks." As Loftin explains, "gay people controlled when to put on or remove their masks depending on the context and situation." By choosing when and where to pass as heterosexual, they exercised "adaptation and resilience" and created the security necessary to embrace queer worlds at the same time. Martin Meeker provides deeper insight into this perspective by arguing that homophile activists often, rather than being simply assimilationist and gender conforming, wore the "mask of respectability" as a skillful and learned strategy.[36]

Despite moments of radicalism, strident self-defense, and joyous defiance, queer life in the 1940s through the early 1960s was most often a struggle for recognition, inclusion, and ultimately belonging. In parks, bars, living rooms, churches, and the pages of *ONE* and *The Ladder*, queer people found each other, creating relationships and networks of support while state and private institutions systematically targeted those people who were associated with homosexuality and excluded them from civic life. But queer people shared many of the desires of mainstream society; they acted to preserve their membership in their families, workplaces, and communities at the same time that they constructed and represented new forms of queer kinship. On screen, stage, and the page, they tethered homosexuality to nonconformity, contesting repressive norms and delighting in cultural subversion. They also shared a civil rights impulse that nurtured a sense of dignity and encouraged nascent demands for rights and respect.

Notes

1 For the longer queer history of medicalization, see, in this volume, Katie Batza, "Sickness and Wellness."
2 Margot Canaday, *The Straight State: Sexuality and Citizenship in Twentieth-Century America* (Princeton, NJ: Princeton University Press, 2011), 138–142.
3 Canaday, *The Straight State*, 138.

4 David Johnson, *The Lavender Scare: The Cold War Persecution of Gays and Lesbians in the Federal Government* (Chicago, IL: University of Chicago Press, 2006), 21, 38.

5 Jackie M. Blount, *Fit to Teach: Same-Sex Desire, Gender, and School Work in the Twentieth Century* (Albany, NY: SUNY Press, 2005), 80–96.

6 Genny Beemyn, *A Queer Capital: A History of Gay Life in Washington* (New York: Routledge, 2014), 142.

7 For a longer queer organizational history, see, in this volume, Marcia Gallo, "Organizations."

8 Quoted in John D'Emilio, *Sexual Politics, Sexual Communities: The Making of a Homosexual Minority in the United States, 1940–1970* (Chicago, IL: University of Chicago Press, 1998), 65.

9 Johnson, *The Lavender Scare*, 170; Stein, *Rethinking the Gay and Lesbian Movement* (New York: Routledge, 2012), chapter two.

10 See also, in this volume, Emily Hobson, "Thinking Transnationally, Thinking Queer."

11 In this volume, Eithne Luibhéid's "Queer and Nation" explores the queer history of US nationalism.

12 Marica Gallo, *Different Daughters: A History of the Daughters of Bilitis and the Rise of the Lesbian Rights Movement* (Emeryville, CA: Seal Press, 2007), 73, 90, 117.

13 For lesbian history making as a movement and analytic, see, in this volume, Julie R. Enszer, "Lesbian History: Spirals of Imagination, Marginalization, Creation and Erasure."

14 Craig Loftin, *Masked Voices: Gay Men and Lesbians in Cold War America* (Albany: Suny Press, 2012).

15 For the longer history of queerness and popular culture, see, in this volume, Sharon Ullman, "Performance and Popular Culture."

16 Michael S. Sherry, *Gay Artists in Modern American Culture: An Imagined Conspiracy* (Chapel Hill: University of North Carolina, 2007), 59–60. See also, Cael Keegan, "Queer Sensations: Postwar American Melodrama and the Crisis of Queer Juvenility," *Thymos: The Journal of Boyhood Studies*, 7, no. 2 (Fall 2013).

17 Michael Trask, *Camp Sites: Sex, Politics, and Academic Style in Postwar America* (Palo Alto, CA: Stanford University Press, 2013), 6–9.

18 Michael Bronski, *Culture Clash: The Making of a Gay Sensibility* (Boston, MA: South End Press, 1984), 104.

19 Katherine V. Forrest, ed. *Lesbian Pulp Fiction: The Sexually Intrepid World of Lesbian Paperback Novels 1950–1965* (San Francisco: Cleis Press, 2005), ix.

20 See also, in this volume, Sharon Ullman's "Performance and Popular Culture" and Stephen Vider's "Consumerism," which explores camp, pulps, and physique magazines in the broader contexts of queer histories of consumer culture.

21 Regina Marler, ed. *Queer Beats* (San Francisco: Cleis Press, 2004), xx, xxxiii.

22 Robert Corber, *Homosexuality in Cold War America* (Durham: Duke University Press, 1997), 4–6.

23 D'Emilio, *Sexual Politics, Sexual Communities*, 139.

24 Nan Allamilla Boyd, *Wide Open Town: A History of Queer San Francisco to 1965* (Berkeley: University of California Press, 2005), 55–60.

25 Elizabeth Papovsky Kennedy and Madeline Davis, *Boots of Leather, Slippers of Gold: The History of a Lesbian Community* (New York: Routledge, 1993), 26.

26 Kennedy and Davis, *Boots of Leather, Slippers of Gold*, 25.

27 Rochella Thorpe, "'A House Where Queers Go': African American Nightlife in Detroit, 1940–1975," in Ellen Lewin, ed., *Inventing Lesbian Cultures in America* (Boston: Beacon Press, 2006). 48.

28 Amanda Littauer, *Bad Girls: Young Women, Sex, and Rebellion before the Sixties* (Chapel Hill, NC: UNC Press, 2015), chapter five.

29 For the longer history of queer urban life, see, in this volume, Kwame Holmes, "The End of Queer Urban History?"

30 E. Patrick Johnson, *Sweet Tea: Black Gay Men of the South* (Chapel Hill: University of North Carolina Press, 2008), 183. See also, in this volume, Nayan Shah, "Queer of Color Estrangement and Belonging."

31 John Howard, *Men Like That: A Southern Queer History* (Chicago: University of Chicago Press, 2001), xi, 142. See also, in this volume, Pippa Holloway and Elizabeth Lambert, "Rural."

32 Lauren Jae Gutterman, "'The House on the Borderland': Lesbian Desire, Marriage, and the Household, 1950–1979," *Journal of Social History* v. 46 n. 1 (fall 2012), 1.

33 Daniel Rivers, *Lesbian Mothers, Gay Fathers, and Their Children in the United States since World War II* (Chapel Hill, NC: UNC Press, 2015), 12. See also, in this volume, Daniel Rivers, "Families."

34 Gutterman, "'The House on the Borderland,'" 2–5, 8, 9. On latent lesbianism, see Amanda Littauer, *Bad Girls: Young Women, Sex, and Rebellion before the Sixties* (Chapel Hill, NC: UNC Press), 149–151. On bisexuality, see Stein, *Rethinking the Gay and Lesbian Movement*, 7 and, in this volume, Loraine Hutchins, "Bisexual History: Let's Not Bijack Another Century."

35 Heather Murray, *Not in This Family*, 2, 18, 40; Loftin, *Masked Voices*, 24.

36 Loftin, *Masked Voices*, 11; Meeker, "Behind the Mask of Respectability: Reconsidering the Mattachine Society and Male Homophile Practice, 1950s and 1960s," *Journal of the History of Sexuality* 10, no. 1 (2001): 78–116.

Further Reading

Duberman, Martin. "Donald Webster Cory: Father of the Homophile Movement," in *The Martin Duberman Reader: The Essential Historical, Biographical, and Autobiographical Writings.* New York: The New Press, 2013: 173–205.

Huerewitz, Daniel. *Bohemian Los Angeles: and the Making of Modern Politics.* Berkeley: University of California Press, 2008.

Johnson, Colin R. *Just Queer Folks: Gender and Sexuality in Rural America.* Philadelphia: Temple University Press, 2013.

Johnson, E. Patrick. *Sweet Tea: Black Gay Men of the South.* Chapel Hill: University of North Carolina Press, 2008.

Meeker, Martin. *Contacts Desired: Gay and Lesbian Communications and Community, 1940s–1970s.* Chicago: University of Chicago Press, 2006.

Meyer, Leisa. *Creating GI Jane: Sexuality and Power in the Women's Army Corps During World War II.* New York: Columbia University Press, 1998.

Meyerowitz, Joanne. *How Sex Changed: A History of Transsexuality in the United States.* Cambridge: Harvard University Press, 2004.

Stein, Marc. *City of Sisterly and Brotherly Loves: Lesbian and Gay Philadelphia, 1945–1972.* Philadelphia: Temple University Press, 2004.

Stein, Marc. *Rethinking the Gay and Lesbian Movement.* New York: Routledge Press, 2012.

Stryker, Susan. *Transgender History.* Berkeley: Seal Press, 2008.

Thorpe, Rochella. "'A House Where Queers Go': African American Nightlife in Detroit, 1940–1975," in Ellen Lewin, ed, *Inventing Lesbian Cultures in America.* Boston: Beacon Press, 2006.

6

GAY LIBERATION (1963–1980)

Whitney Strub

In 1972, Marsha P. Johnson expressed what she saw as the "main goal" of gay liberation: "to see gay people liberated and free and to have equal rights that other people have in America," with her "gay brothers and sisters out of jail and on the streets again." Lest that sound like an echo of liberal civil rights discourse, she added in the heightened rhetoric of the times, "We believe in picking up the gun, starting a revolution if necessary." Johnson, the vice president of STAR, the Street Transvestite Action Revolutionaries, embodied the radical potential of gay liberation. As a black self-identified transvestite and drag queen, she also lived in its margins, and marked her exclusion from white gay activist circles. Johnson noted that members of the Gay Activists Alliance (GAA) "weren't friendly at all" and mostly just gawked at her when she attended a meeting.[1] While the largely white GAA membership skewed toward graduate students, journalists, and others with middle-class concerns, STAR drew from street hustlers, homeless youth, and gender outlaws.

While they differed in membership, politics, and image, both STAR and GAA developed under the gay liberation umbrella. Less a coherent ideology or unified political formation than a structure of feeling marked by pride, visibility, affirmation, defiance, and boldness, "gay liberation" serves as an historical marker for the years between the Stonewall rebellion of 1969 and the twin catastrophes of 1981, as Ronald Reagan took office and AIDS was first identified. Neither date withstands closer scrutiny as a precise boundary; Stonewall was simply the most iconic moment in an escalating queer resistance across the mid-to-late 1960s, and its radical impulses continued well past the early 1980s. This essay examines gay liberation's emergence, successes, and failures, and enduring legacies.

The Rising Tide of Resistance

In the years leading up to the June 1969 Stonewall Rebellion, a series of episodes reflected the rising tide of an often youth-driven queer resistance. Activists pushed against the antigay violence of the US state that manifested in policing, incarceration, institutionalization, and exclusion from jobs, schools, and other sites of citizenship and upward mobility. They also tore through the strictures of the liberal politics of respectability in the homophile movement.

For the homophile movement, the need to combat pernicious myths and win acceptance from mainstream heterosexual Americans often guided their assimilationist approach. In this, the homophiles followed a course charted by the black civil rights movement, the labor movement, and other progressive causes forced to adapt to Cold War containment. For the second generation of gay activists, though, anxieties over red-baiting and other Cold War tactics to suppress dissent were greatly reduced. The student-led New Left had set the agenda for a new politics, as did black nationalism and Third World national liberation movements, particularly that of the Vietnamese people who resisted US imperialism. The rhetoric of the Black Panther Party and the antiwar movement, filled with anger, sarcasm, and incisive critique, provided the template for gay liberation. Moreover, where respectability had set the homophile movement's tone, sexual revolution and youth counterculture shaped gay liberation.

Growing tensions could be seen in such places as Philadelphia, where, as Marc Stein details, longtime leader Franklin Kameny, as late as 1969 in the annual Reminder picket, refused to allow same-sex demonstrators to hold hands. Rambunctious resistance to oppressive police and business owners erupted into numerous spontaneous demonstrations, from the strike at Dewey's in Philadelphia mentioned by Amanda Littauer in the last chapter, to the riot at Compton's Cafeteria in San Francisco in August 1966, where a group of "gay hustlers, 'hair fairies,' queens, and street kids of every gender who were too poor, too young, or too gender transgressive to be allowed in the bars" launched a spontaneous uprising against a Tenderloin establishment for its "service fees," perceived as discriminatory.[2]

The Compton's Cafeteria riots built on the infusion of energy provided by new groups that began to push the homophile movement into more radical directions. In San Francisco, the Society for Individual Rights (SIR) had been founded in 1963, and by early 1965 counted 300 members, more than the combined total of the other homophile groups in the city. Using a "bold language of social activism" closer to that of the Student Nonviolent Coordinating Committee (SNCC) than the Mattachine Society or Daughters of Bilitis, SIR combined assertive politics with social functions, holding well-attended dances that linked activism to more intimate means of community formation and enjoyment.[3] Meanwhile, Vanguard, began in July 1966, defined itself as "an organization of, by, and for 'the kids on the street'"—exactly the organizational infrastructure that empowered the marginalized patrons at Compton's Cafeteria to revolt.[4]

Even as the homophile national network expanded with the North American Conference of Homophile Organizations (NACHO), which held its first conference in 1966 in Kansas City, these generational tensions grew steadily more apparent. The same year in Los Angeles, gay liberationists established PRIDE (Personal Rights in Defense and Education) specifically in response to the perceived "stodginess of the homophile movement." When the notoriously violent and homophobic Los Angeles Police Department stepped up ongoing bar raids with a brutal invasion of the Black Cat, a Silver Lake bar that allowed for a New Year's kiss among couples as 1967 began, PRIDE led protests and leafleted drivers in the aftermath.[5] Schisms related to the Vietnam War further highlighted generational cleavages. While NACHO demanded gay inclusion in the military, new groups such as the Committee for Homosexual Freedom, established in early 1969 in San Francisco, were fundamentally linked to antiwar organizing. Indeed, as Justin Suran details, later that year Gay Liberation Theater in Berkeley debuted its performance of *No Vietnamese Ever Called Me a Queer*. Early gay liberation's collective resistance was inseparable from commitments to participatory democracy and community self-determination in the decade's broader left movements.[6]

Gay cultural production furthered the promise of liberation through a mixture of overt expression and eroticism. While Hollywood studio films, gay and lesbian pulp novels, and other representations of queer life offered pleasures that often required against-the-grain reading tactics, and writers such as James Baldwin, Gore Vidal, and Tennessee Williams authored important works, cultural production in the late Sixties again reflected larger social shifts. As obscenity laws—which had historically targeted queer texts with great frequency—grew harder for authorities to enforce, more proudly erotic representations began to circulate. In place of deliberately desexualized homophile magazines, Clark Polak's *Drum* pioneered male full-frontal nudity alongside political articles, beginning in 1965.

Similar transformations occurred in erotic gay film. Bob Mizer, editor of the squeaky-clean physique magazine *Physique Pictorial*, had since the 1950s shot dozens of short films, offering loin-clothed wrestling and other physical action. Beginning in the summer of 1968, however, enterprising young filmmaker Pat Rocco began showing his gay erotic short films at the Park Theatre in downtown Los Angeles. Rocco's *Hey Look Me Over* (1968) and *A Very Special Friend* (1968) presented openly gay, happy, romantic scenarios of attractive young men enjoying one another's bodies. As I argue in "Mondo Rocco," Rocco's pioneering full nudity and tender kissing announced a new era.

Such works circulated within a growing gay consumer infrastructure that forged communities and political consciousness, as historian David Johnson argues. Although the homophile movement had held this world at arm's length, by May 1967 even longtime Mattachine leader Hal Call opened the Adonis Bookstore in San Francisco. A few months later, Craig Rodwell followed suit with the Oscar Wilde Memorial Bookshop in New York City. In a reminder that generational position did not wholly determine cultural politics, the younger Rodwell disavowed material he considered smutty, while Hall screened stag films in his "Sex Education Film Series," which gradually grew into what he called the Cinemattachine, as Martin Meeker notes.

The Stonewall rebellion, built on this decades-long collective struggle, was both a culmination of and a schism in gay politics and culture. Early in the morning of June 28, 1969, police invading the Stonewall Inn on Christopher Street in Greenwich Village expected a formulaic raid of the sort urban police had undertaken for decades, a shakedown combined with harassment and humiliation of patrons. Without advance planning, the community fought back. As a report from the homophile press described, the police behaved with typical "bad grace," until the community began to throw pennies, "then beer cans, rocks and even parking meters. The cops retreated inside the bar, which was set afire by the crowd."[7] Once the skirmish was subdued, action resumed the next night, as the Stonewall reopened as a "free store" (having been charged with unlicensed liquor sales) and crowds gathered. Gay and straight people taunted police, and as tensions mounted, efforts to disperse the crowd by force failed, leading to several days of repeated congregation and resistance.

No clear record exists of who threw the first bottle or brick at Stonewall. The bar, in keeping with the racist norms of the day, catered to a mostly white clientele. But even homophile leader Dick Leitsch credited "nelly" gays with rushing the police. Later they led such chants as "We are the Stonewall girls/We wear our hair in curls/We wear no underwear/We show our pubic hair"—a mode of resistance that, as Martin Duberman notes, traded "traditionally macho" forms for "at least the glimpse of a different and revelatory kind of consciousness."[8] Stonewall was infused with the theatricality, flamboyance, and confrontation that came from the most marginalized, particularly street queens of color such as Marsha P. Johnson and Sylvia Rivera. As historian Tim Rezloff details, Rivera, born in 1951, had already survived repeated trauma, beginning with the suicide of her mother when she was an infant. Coming out as Sylvia, she was living on the street and turning tricks by early adolescence. For the Puerto Rican-Venezuelan Rivera and the African American Johnson, Stonewall represented a revolutionary uprising, where the "freaks" could triumph.

The impact of Stonewall registered immediately. Gay poet Allen Ginsberg, notorious for the graphic imagery of his 1956 "Howl" that had so shocked Cold War America, famously declared "that wounded look that fags all had ten years ago" had now gone.[9] Young activists quickly declared it a tipping point away from postwar liberalism's appeals to tolerance and equality and toward gay *liberation*.

Liberation in Theory and Praxis

"What is a lesbian?" asked the Radicalesbians at the start of their widely republished and read 1970 manifesto, "The Woman-Identified Woman." Their answer: "A lesbian is the rage of all women condensed to the point of explosion." No piece of writing better captures gay liberation's visceral rhetoric and radical theoretical underpinnings. Lesbianism, "like homosexuality," explained the Radicalesbians, "is a category of behavior possible only in a sexist society characterized by rigid sex roles and dominated by male supremacy."[10]

For the Radicalesbians and other early liberationist groups, patriarchal heterosupremacy operated through two layers of social regulation. First, rigid sex roles were secured by demanding women submit to "femininity," defined through meekness, passivity, dependence, and sexual availability. As their cutting phrasing had it, "when you strip off all the packing, you must finally realize that the essence of being a 'woman' is to get fucked by men." This hierarchy in place, the system then sorted men and women into straight and gay, with the latter term used as an insult to keep women further in place. "Lesbian," they explained, "is a label invented by the men to throw at any woman who dares to be his equal." In response to this oppressive system, the Radicalesbians and other gay liberation groups declared both gender and sexual identities "inauthentic" in their fixed forms. Instead, they advocated the polymorphous perversity encouraged by Herbert Marcuse, the influential theorist whose work in the 1950s and 60s had fused Marx and Freud in a critique of capitalist sexuality.

Not every gay liberationist engaged with theory in the same way. Dennis Altman, in his pioneering book *Homosexual: Oppression and Liberation* (1971), proclaimed himself "particularly indebted" to Marcuse and expanded upon his theory of "repressive tolerance" through which society controls sexuality by commodifying it. On the other hand, that same year in his *Dancing the Gay Lib Blues*, journalist and activist Arthur Bell joked that "I didn't exactly know what Machiavellian was," much less arcane terms of Marxism or psychoanalysis.[11] The short-lived but iconic Gay Liberation Front that mobilized in the wake of Stonewall, was "not, in general, very sophisticated" in its theoretical analysis, according to historian Terence Kissack.[12] Where it and other liberationist groups did flourish, however, was in its freewheeling, joyous, angry, and assertive approach to activism, premised on a politics of visibility and demands for the right to public space.

If the finer points of theory never settled into consensus, one central political belief was nearly unanimous: the urgent necessity to "come out." Indeed, the first words of the first issue of *Come Out*, a magazine begun in 1969 "by and for the gay community" (in this case, the GLF), were "Come out for freedom! Come out now! Power to the people! Gay power to gay people!"[13] When the GLF sought to represent coming out visually in a summer 1970 poster that quickly became iconic, photographer Peter Hujar shot a group of a dozen-plus members carousing down a street arm-in-arm, long hair flowing and smiles wide, a true "army of lovers."[14] The difference between this countercultural comportment and homophile respectability could not have been more stark. The pride marches that began in 1970 with Christopher Street Liberation Day became, as Timothy Stewart-Winter writes, "the crowning achievement of the new gay liberation politics."[15] When thousands of gay men, lesbians, and transsexuals and transvestites embodied the call "out of the closets, into the streets," theory here mattered less than audacious visibility.

The GLF declared "unity with and support for all oppressed minorities who fight for their freedom." While the group's solidarity with the Black Panthers, perceived as a homophobic group, caused internal friction, it led to a remarkable turnaround from leader Huey Newton, who declared homosexuality revolutionary in 1970, asking his fellow Panthers to stop using "fag" as a slur. Some GLF members who found its "paralyzing inefficiency intolerable," bogged down in chaotic meetings and consensus governance, split to form the Gay Activists Alliance in late 1969.[16] The GAA declared itself "completely and solely dedicated" to gay rights in its constitution, preemptively preventing intersectional coalitions. While conservative in contrast to the GLF, the GAA nonetheless affirmed a gay liberationist ethos of the "right to make love with anyone, anyway, anytime, provided only that such action be freely chosen by the individuals concerned."[17]

The Radicalesbians, GLF, and GAA provided some of the key theoretical texts of gay liberation in a movement animated by a spirited new praxis. The GLF and GAA, and radical lesbian feminist groups, for instance, shared a commitment to "zaps," or planned disruptions that interrupted the normal flow of oppressive heterosexism. Activist Arthur Evans explained that these were intended to both unnerve the "straight oppressor" and "rouse closet gays from their apathy," forging a new solidarity.[18] Targets ranged from the ostensibly hip, but actually homophobic, *Village Voice*, to New York University, which denied gay student groups dance permits. Liberationists hounded political candidates relentlessly, which paid off when they began to both recognize gay political power and seek refuge from interruptions. By late 1970, New York gubernatorial candidate (and former Supreme Court justice) Arthur Goldberg, after dodging earlier efforts to commit him to a position on gay rights, became the first candidate in the state's history to declare his support.[19]

If anger and defiance characterized gay activism of the early 1970s, so too did a joyous and celebratory mood that affirmed gay identity. "Gay" itself, after all, had long circulated as a term among those in the know, but now reflected a deliberate rejection of "homosexual," which carried the baggage of medicalization, criminalization, and pathologization. The homosexual had been defined by straight self-declared experts; gayness would be articulated by the community itself. To activist and writer Allen Young, gay meant "not homosexual, but sexually free."[20] Student activist Charles Thorpe went one step further in 1970, calling *gay* and *homosexual* "opposites," the latter coming from "our sick-psychiatrist friends' definition of us."[21]

Awareness of the ways social hierarchies such as race, class, and gender worked in tandem permeated gay liberationist writing. Still, race often remained a dividing line. For Ron Vernon, a black gay man abused from childhood on for being a "sissy," and a survivor of incarceration and daily experience with racism, gay identity alone was not enough to forge a solidarity that would skirt over other fault lines. He noted that, just as he had felt excluded from the Black Panther Party despite identifying with black nationalism because of the group's frequent homophobia, he thought that "black gay men and white gay men have an awful lot of consciousness-raising before they can understand women's oppression."[22] In the meantime, Vernon organized around his *whole* identity with Third World Gay Revolution, a group that fused anti-colonial and anti-racist politics with gay liberationist ones, pioneering a queer of color analysis. In its 1971 manifesto, "What We Want, What We Believe," Third World Gay Revolution laid out a sixteen-point program. Many of the points (and the title) came from the Panthers' Ten Point Program but expanded upon them to include gay people, so that the demand to "abolish the existing judicial system" elaborated that "all Third World and gay people" be tried by a jury of their peers. Other points returned to central concerns of gay liberation: "the right to be gay, anytime, anyplace; the right to free physiological change and modification of sex on demand," and "the abolition of the institution of the bourgeois nuclear family."[23]

Just as race consciousness became a challenge to the limits of gay liberationist thought and action, recognition of male privilege within gay lib did not eliminate it. Former New Left community organizer and activist Carl Wittman acknowledged in his widely read "A Gay Manifesto" (1969) that his views were "determined not only by my homosexuality, but by my being white, male, middle-class." Yet even as he wrote that "all men are infected with male chauvinism," he somewhat blithely declared that for gay men, chauvinism "is not central. . . . We can junk it much more easily than straight men can."[24] For many lesbians, annoyed and often silenced by the aggressive masculinity that led men to frequently dominate gay groups, this came as news. Within gay liberation, lesbians found themselves talked over by men, relegated to gendered roles in organizations, and otherwise treated with condescension. In a piercing critique of gay men, Daughters of Bilitis co-founder Del Martin denounced gay male chauvinism in a 1970 essay, "Good Bye to All That" (modeled on Robin Morgan's recent critique of New Left male sexism). That same year, most of the female members of GLF-Los Angeles left the group to form the Los Angeles Women's Center.[25]

Lesbians had already grappled with the sexism of straight New Left men and homophile organizations. But animus from straight feminists also persisted. Within the leading mainstream liberal feminist group, the National Organization for Women, leader Betty Friedan had famously labeled lesbianism "the lavender menace." Within NOW, purges reduced the visibility and centrality of prominent lesbians, and while the group passed a resolution in support of lesbian rights in 1971, it did little to quell bad feelings. As Stephanie Gilmore and Elizabeth Kaminski explain, tensions within local branches lingered into the 1980s. Things were not always better among radical feminists, either; Karla Jay and Rita Mae Brown (a victim of the NOW purges) found the New York group Redstockings "downright heterosexist."[26]

These tensions culminated in lesbian separatism. The Furies in Washington, D.C., were particularly influential, partly because they published a widely read newspaper bearing their name from 1971–72. Member Ginny Berson articulated their politics: "lesbianism is not a matter of sexual preference, but rather one of political choice which every woman must make if she is to become woman-identified and thereby end male supremacy."[27] This effectively posited lesbianism as the *only* true feminism. While debates over the politics and meaning of lesbianism continued across the decade, separatism manifested in numerous community-building efforts, from rural communes to such groups as Cincinnati's Labyris, formed in 1973 and reaching 30–40 members in its brief but regionally influential existence, which historian Susan Freeman argues laid the infrastructure for subsequent groups.

While lesbian separatism responded to some needs, it disregarded others. All twelve founding members of the Furies, for example, although based in the nation's premier Chocolate City (as the funk band Parliament would title its 1975 album in tribute to D.C.), were white women. On the other hand, critically engaged with the links between and among black power, feminism, and gay liberation, the Combahee River Collective (CRC) in the Boston area defined itself as a black lesbian socialist group. It pioneered what would later be called an intersectional analysis, premised on recognizing "the fact that the major systems of oppression are interlocking." Linking heterosexism to capitalism, the CRC in its 1977 Statement rejected any revolution short of a *complete* revolution: "the liberation of all oppressed peoples necessitates the destruction of the political-economic systems of capitalism and imperialism as well as patriarchy."[28]

While this challenged both feminist analyses that insisted on the primacy of gender as well as black nationalist analyses that overlooked gender and sexuality, the CRC nonetheless asserted its solidarity with both movements. Against the separatism that had become common-place among many radical movements, the CRC advocated an "identity politics" based on mobilizing around their own experiences and maintaining coalition with others. "Our politics initially sprang from the shared belief that Black women are inherently valuable, that our liberation is a necessity not as an adjunct to somebody else's may because of our need as human persons for autonomy," the Statement asserted, adding, "no other ostensibly progressive movement has ever considered our specific oppression as a priority." By putting black lesbians at the center of gay, black, and women's liberation, and demanding that gay politics, black and Third World activism, feminism, and Marxist thought all account for one another, the Combahee River Collective set the stage for much of the most important radical thought of the next several decades—even if white gay activists of the 1970s did not necessarily register this. Other groups, such as gay Latino/as, continued to struggle. As historian Horacio N. Roque Ramirez documents, the Gay Latino Alliance, established in San Francisco in 1975, reflected the "browning" process of racial consciousness that many were forced to undergo upon encountering the casual racism of such things as multiple-ID demands at Bay Area gay bars. Eric Wat describes how it would take until 1980 for the first Asian American gay group to form in Los Angeles, the Asian/Pacific Lesbians and Gays.[29]

Sexuality and Culture

Gay liberation was perhaps the Sexual Revolution's most revolutionary expression. For gay men in particular, already historically accustomed to more spatial liberty in public places than women, the years after Stonewall allowed for unprecedented expressions of sexuality and desire. Rejecting marriage as a "rotten, oppressive institution," Carl Wittman called for intimacy beyond possessive monogamy and forced distinctions between friends and lovers.[30] As the antigay policing that had inspired the Stonewall rebellion began, incrementally, to decline under the weight of gay political power, expanding bar cultures, bathhouses, and other venues afforded men growing sexual freedoms. Meanwhile, legal surveillance of "obscenity" faced pressure from the lucrative adult industries that proliferated in storefront movie theaters and adult bookstores, affording gay sexuality more legal space.

The two most iconic gay pornographic films of the early 1970s both positioned themselves within a spirit of liberation. Hardcore porn showing graphic sexual depictions had just begun to supplant the softcore of the 1960s when Wakefield Poole's *Boys in the Sand* (1971) and Fred Halsted's *L.A. Plays Itself* (1972) arrived onscreen. Predating the infamous hetero-hardcore film *Deep Throat* (1972), each found a large and unashamed audience. Vastly divergent in tone and temperament—*Boys* an enticing Fire Island reverie, *L.A.* a darker, S/M-tinged trip—they nonetheless shared the gay lib zeitgeist. Poole featured *Boys* star Casey Donovan (a blond Adonis who enters the film running naked out of the ocean) reading the liberationist newspaper *Gay*. Poole told reporters, "The whole time I made the film I thought of the gay lib slogan, Gay Is Beautiful. I wanted a film that gay people could look at and say, 'I don't mind being gay—it's beautiful to see those people do what they're doing!' "[31] Halsted, who preferred to identify as a *pervert* over *gay*, nonetheless allowed publicist Stuart Byron, himself a gay activist and journalist, to send promotional materials for his film addressed "Dear Gay Liberationist." Adopting movement language, Halsted explained, "making the film was my liberation, my coming out of the closet." When the homophobic *New York Times* insisted on using "all-male" in *L.A. Plays Itself* ads rather than "homosexual," Halsted successfully challenged it, allegedly the first time the paper had accepted the word in an ad.[32]

Proudly sexual representations saturated gay media, from bar ads to the liberationist press, with newspapers in every major metropolitan area. In New York, *Gay Power* and others combined naked images of men with political and cultural reporting, extending the project begun in Philadelphia by Clark Polak's *Drum*. San Francisco's *Gay Sunshine* carried everything from poetry to interviews to explicitly pornographic images. This sheer, unbridled sexual celebration was inherently political, and central to a conception of gayness that emphatically rejected the straight world's efforts to shame, silence, or control it.

Such public displays of sexuality often splintered along gender lines. Oppressed for their sexuality, gay men still benefitted from a society that afforded men more sexual freedom. For lesbians, pride coexisted with an awareness that their sexuality was constantly co-opted for voyeuristic straight male pleasure. As San Francisco Bay Area Gay Women's Liberation member Judy Grahn wrote in an influential 1970 essay, lesbianism was too often defined through the "pornographic fantasy" of straight men.[33] Foregrounding the sexual side of lesbian life had to be carefully navigated as lesbians built a culture celebrating their sexualities and identities. When filmmaker Barbara Hammer shot her erotic, experimental films that often included graphic lesbian sex, she carefully distinguished it from pornography. Indeed, her *Dyketactics* (1974), *Menses* (1974), or *Superdyke* (1975) would not have likely played well for the men in Times Square porn theaters.

Part of Hammer's project was to "reclaim public space for lesbian use," as film scholar Greg Youmans writes, and her vivid location shooting from rural communes to areas all over San Francisco did so powerfully.[34] As Finn Enke details, other lesbians claimed space through other means and venues; in Minneapolis, for instance, the Amazon Bookstore (est. 1970), the Wilder Ones softball team, and A Woman's Coffee House all offered relative safety and visibility to lesbians in the 1970s.

Cultural production centrally defined lesbianism in the 1970s. Joanne Passet describes the remarkable influence of Barbara Grier, the longtime book reviewer for the homophile *Ladder* who established Naiad Press as a lesbian publishing firm in 1973. That same year, Rita Mae Brown's *Rubyfruit Jungle* arrived. As a novelist, Brown reached a wider audience with the celebration of lesbianism she had begun in Radicalesbians and the Furies. Initially published by a small Vermont publisher, *Rubyfruit Jungle* quickly became a classic and joined the roster of the mass-market Bantam. Meanwhile, as Bonnie Morris explains, another influential company founded in part by former Furies, Olivia Records, debuted with singer-songwriter Meg Christian's *I Know You Know* in 1974, and immediately found a large and appreciative audience.

Even as lesbians and gay men built expansive cultures, they frequently shut transpeople and bisexuals out—the creation of an umbrella "LGBT" collective sentiment would have to wait. Early trans groups had overcome enormous odds. As Stephen Cohen details, STAR in New York had focused on prison issues and homelessness, opening STAR House, the first shelter for street transvestites, in the East Village in late 1970. By 1971, they were evicted. Leader Sylvia Rivera found little solace at GAA meetings, where founder Arthur Bell admitted the group was "frightened of Sylvia," and "by street people" in general.[35] Some gay liberation groups celebrated transsexuality, as when a Berkeley GLF member in 1970 called rejecting the gender binary "the most profoundly revolutionary act a homosexual can engage in," but after the burst of immediate post-Stonewall radicalism had passed, such support waned.[36]

By 1973, some of the greatest hostility toward transsexuals emanated out of lesbian and feminist circles. That year, the San Francisco Daughters of Bilitis expelled singer-songwriter Beth Elliott, who had been their vice president. At the West Coast Lesbian Conference that year, keynote speaker Robin Morgan called her "an infiltrator, and a destroyer—with the mentality of a rapist."[37] That same year, Sylvia Rivera was blocked from addressing the fourth pride march in New York. "How many of you white, middle-class motherfuckers have been in jail?," she asked upon taking the stage; "Been raped? Had your noses broken? . . . what are you doing about it? *Nothing!*" The grief it caused led Rivera to abandon the movement for many years.[38]

Groups such as the Miami-based Transsexual Activist Organization (TAO) endured, as historian Susana Peña recounts, but transsexuals remained under attack throughout the 1970s. Olivia Records came under recurring condemnation for employing transsexual sound engineer Sandy Stone. Joanne Meyerowitz explains how Olivia attempted to defend her, but Stone ultimately left in 1979, the same year Janice Raymond's book *The Transsexual Empire* launched the most sustained and vitriolic feminist assault yet, accusing transwomen of raping women's bodies, among other atrocities.[39]

Meanwhile, bisexuals had been seemingly hailed by the rhetoric of gay liberation, with its celebration of polymorphous perversity and sexual fluidity. Yet while Carl Wittman, for instance, had applauded bisexuality in his gay manifesto, in practice bisexuals found themselves frequently disparaged from all angles. Despite the pioneering visibility of then-bisexually identified glam rock icon David Bowie, the straight press joined gays and lesbians in trivializing bisexuality as a faddish "chic," or a form of indecisiveness. As with street queens and lesbians, bisexuals needed community space, and the establishment of the Bisexual Center in San Francisco in 1976, founded by Maggi Rubenstein and others, helped pave the way and combat bisexual invisibility, as Jay Paul has noted.[40]

Mainstreaming a Movement

As the move to marginalize trans people suggests, by the mid-Seventies, much of the radical and revolutionary movements were moving toward working within the very systems they had previously sought to dismantle. At times this resulted from government repression; FBI plants, illegal COINTELPRO tactics, and targeted violence such as the police murder of Chicago's Fred Hampton in 1969 devastated the Black Panther Party and other groups. Activist burnout and internal disarray also took a toll, witnessed most spectacularly in the implosion of SDS into factionalism in 1969. Another factor was pragmatism. If capitalism, or the nuclear family, for instance, proved impervious to overhaul, the damage they inflicted could still be mitigated. Black Panthers such as Bobby Seale and Elaine Brown ran for city office in Oakland, while radical feminists began building infrastructures related to women's health, domestic violence, and other areas where women remained underserved.

Gay liberation's own success also facilitated mainstream accommodation. If the wider American public remained at best indifferent and more often hostile to gay visibility, urban politics and culture had reached an accommodation with the flourishing "gay ghettos" such as Chelsea in New York City, West Hollywood in Los Angeles, and San Francisco's Castro. A growing sense of community comfort and safety accompanied a decrease in outwardly oppositional politics.

From the mid-1970s onward, gay activists who had previously denounced policing as oppressive began to flex political influence in order to forge tentative links to the very police forces that had historically subjugated them, as Christina Hanhardt details in *Safe Space*. In Los Angeles, for instance, LAPD chief Ed Davis continued an aggressively homophobic approach, refusing press accreditation to the *Advocate* into the 1970s and obstructing attempts to create police/community liaisons. As late as 1975, two years after the American Psychiatric Association removed homosexuality from its list of mental illnesses, he continued to call it "an emotional disorder." The new gay political power could be seen, however, when several members of city council denounced the LAPD's harassment of gay spaces as expensive and pointless. When police arrested sixteen men at a Hollywood bathhouse in 1980, city attorney Burt Pines declined to press charges, a public rebuke to antigay policing.[41] In Chicago, as Timothy Stewart-Winter details, the militant Alliance to End Repression had forged black-gay coalitions against police violence, but the group faded as its gay white members declared success with the decreased policing of gay bars. By the end of the 1970s, gay groups often worked *with* police rather than *against* them, setting the template for the neoliberal politics Margot Weiss describes in her chapter.

This shift toward working within mainstream systems was read by many gay critics as an abdication of liberationist politics. Roger Streitmatter describes how, when Wall Street investment banker David Goodstein purchased the *Advocate* for $1 million in 1974, he immediately signaled a new editorial direction, supplanting the paper's political reporting with an emphasis on consumerism. The first issue published under his control carried the subtitle, "Touching Your Lifestyle," and hailed the ideal reader: "You are employed and a useful, responsible citizen. You have an attractive body, nice clothes, and an inviting home." Sylvia Rivera and Marsha Johnson, still toiling on the streets, were clearly not invited. Later in the decade, Larry Kramer's acerbic novel *Faggots* (1978) skewered what he saw as the empty and idle pursuit of sex, drugs, and fashion that had come to dominate gay life. Even gay pornography, Jeffrey Escoffier explains, shifted toward polish and glamour. Upstart studios like Falcon highlighted the chiseled clone body and attire of new superstar Al Parker.[42]

New groups, particularly the National Gay Task Force (NGTF, est. 1973), emphasized the quest for equality through law and policy, rather than militant grassroots action. This model found remarkable success, with thirty-six local governments adding sexual preference to their antidiscrimination laws by 1975. In Miami, the Dade County Coalition for the Humanistic Rights of Gays embodied this stance, adopting "a moderate approach to gay rights, with emphasis on working within government structures," in their own words. The group's politics of respectability were not ultimately successful during a vicious local campaign through which local voters repealed a gay-inclusive rights ordinance in 1977.[43] That same year Harvey Milk's election as San Francisco county supervisor reflected gay success in municipal politics, offering a beacon of hope across the nation. Other victories were won through the legal sphere, as Marc Stein and others have noted: sodomy law reform, increased rights for gay and lesbian parents, and the 1973 decision by the Civil Service Commission to stop denying employment on the basis of sexual orientation.[44]

By the time the socially moderate Jimmy Carter entered the Oval Office in 1977, the NGTF had become consummate insiders, trading confrontational language for access and speaking, as Claire Bond Potter writes, "the language of capitalism and the Constitution." Unprecedented gay access to the halls of power, particularly in the form of presidential aide Margaret "Midge" Costanza, came at the cost of the intersectional analysis being pioneered by the Combahee River Collective.[45] In this framework, gay rights would be defined by a formal legal equality that elided structural and systemic sources of inequality that affected primarily queer youth, queers of color, the homeless, sex workers, and other marginalized groups.

The limits of this activism were keenly felt by those marginalized. When white gay activists attempted to link their plight to that of African Americans, but failed to base it on multiracial community work, such efforts fell flat. Kevin Mumford describes how, at 1975 city hearings in Philadelphia, white gay activists employed racial analogies that alienated black city legislators, who saw it as co-optation rather than true solidarity. Only several years later, after more serious multiracial organizing that placed black gay voices in the forefront to prevent gay issues from being reduced to a "white" issue, did Philadelphia enact an antidiscrimination ordinance.

By that point, a vicious national antigay backlash was well under way, as discussed by Jennifer Brier in the next chapter. Yet the animating spirit of gay liberation survived even the intense antigay antipathy and fear-mongering of Anita Bryant and the New Right, the 1978 assassination of Harvey Milk, and the advent of the AIDS epidemic. When Queer Nation took up its radical prose in the late 1980s, it sounded like nothing so much as a return to Martha Shelley writing, "Look out, straights . . . we are the extrusions of your unconscious minds—your worst fears made flesh" in 1970.[46] The gaps and omissions of white-dominated activism became opportunities for Third World women of color to create their own infrastructures, such as Kitchen Table: Women of Color Press, founded in 1980 by Combahee River Collective member Barbara Smith and poet Audre Lorde. Bisexual organizing continued in the face of AIDS-related backlash, with such groups as West Coast BiPol and the Boston Bisexual Women's Network (both est. 1983). And when queer theory emerged as a scholarly discipline in the 1990s, many of its central analytical precepts returned to the radically deconstructive ethos of the early 1970s.

In our post-marriage-equality landscape, LGBT people seem inheritors less of liberation than assimilation into liberalism. Yet throughout the US and beyond, artists continue to push collectively toward liberatory aims. Activists with organizations such as the Sylvia Rivera Law Project still advocate an intersectional politics that draws upon the revolutionary spirit of its namesake and the insights of the Combahee River Collective. In the lower frequencies and utopian longings of queer life today, gay liberation still registers.

Notes

1 "Rapping with a Street Transvestite: An Interview with Marcia [sic] Johnson," *Out of the Closets: Voices of Gay Liberation*, eds Karla Jay and Allen Young (New York: Quick Fox, 1972), 113, 118.

2 Members of the Gay and Lesbian Historical Society, "MTF Transgender Activism in the Tenderloin and Beyond: Commentary and Interview with Elliot Blackstone," *GLQ: A Journal of Lesbian and Gay Studies*, 4, no. 2 (1998): 355.

3 Nan Alamilla Boyd, *Wide Open Town: A History of Queer San Francisco to 1965* (Berkeley: University of California Press, 2003), 227.

4 Ad for Vanguard (c.1966), in *Screaming Queens: The Riot at Compton's Cafeteria* (dir. Susan Stryker and Victor Silverman, 2005).

5 Lillian Faderman and Stuart Timmons, *Gay L.A.: A History of Sexual outlaws, Power Politics, and Lipstick Lesbians* (New York: Basic, 2006), 187–190.

6 For the longer history of LGBT organizations, see, in this volume, Marcia Gallo, "Organizations."

7 Dick Leitsch, "Police Raid on N.Y. Club Sets Off First Gay Riot," (orig. Sept 1969), Chris Bull, *Witness to Revolution: The Advocate Reports on Gay and Lesbian Politics, 1967–1999* (Los Angeles: Alyson, 1999), 12.

8 Leitsch, 14; Martin Duberman, *Stonewall* (New York: Dutton, 1993), 201.

9 Duberman, *Stonewall*, 208.

10 Radicalesbians, "Woman-Identified Woman" (1970), available at http://library.duke.edu/digital collections/wlmpc_wlmms01011/. Accessed October 19, 2017. For a more extended analysis of lesbian history production and movement building, see, in this volume, Julie R. Enszer, "Lesbian History: Spirals of Imagination, Marginalization, Creation, and Erasure."

11 Dennis Altman, *Homosexual Oppression and Liberation* (New York: New York University Press, 1993; orig. 1971), 82, 106; Arthur Bell, *Dancing the Gay Lib Blues* (New York: Simon & Schuster, 1971), 126.

12 Terence Kissack, "Freaking Fag Revolutionaries: New York's Gay Liberation Front, 1969–1971," *Radical History Review* 1995, no. 62 (1995): 105–134, 113.

13 *Come Out* 1.1, Nov. 1969, p1., at http://outhistory.org/files/original/42b46f17f4fd7c6d62f105c1489d 7b47.pdf. Accessed October 19, 2017.

14 Richard Meyer, "Gay Power circa 1970: Visual Strategies for Sexual Revolution." *GLQ: A Journal of Lesbian and Gay Studies* 12, no. 3 (2006): 448.

15 Timothy Stewart-Winter, "Gay Pride Day," *Encyclopedia of American Holidays and National Days*, ed. Len Travers (Westport, CT: Greenwood, 2006), 291.

16 "What is Gay Liberation," n.d. (c.1970), International Gay Information Center, Ephemera, box 7, file: Gay Liberation Front-Los Angeles, New York Public Library; Toby Marotta, *The Politics of Homosexuality* (Boston: Houghton Mifflin, 1981), 142.

17 Gay Activists Alliance, Constitution and Bylaws (n.d., 1969), reel 17, GAA Records, New York Public Library.

18 Arthur Evans, "How to Zap Straights," *The Gay Liberation Book*, eds. Len Richmond and Gary Noguera (San Francisco: Ramparts, 1973), 112.

19 Donn Teal, *The Gay Militants* (New York: St. Martin's, 1994 [orig.1971]), 238.

20 Allen Young, "Out of the Closets, Into the Streets," in *Out of the Closets*, 28.

21 Elizabeth Armstrong, *Forging Gay Identities: Organizing Sexuality in San Francisco, 1950–1994* (Chicago: University of Chicago Press, 2002), 71.

22 "Sissy in Prison: An Interview with Ron Vernon," *Out of the Closets*, 110.

23 Third World Gay Revolution, "What We Want, What We Need," *Out of the Closets*, 363–367.

24 Carl Wittman, "A Gay Manifesto," *Out of the Closets*, 330, 332.

25 Faderman and Timmons, *Gay L.A.*, 220.

26 Duberman, *Stonewall*, 174.

27 Anne Valk, *Radical Sisters: Second-Wave Feminism and Black Liberation in Washington, D.C.* (Urbana: University of Illinois Press, 2008), 143.

28 Combahee River Collective Statement (1977), available at http://circuitous.org/scraps/combahee.html. Accessed October 19, 2017.

29 See also, in this volume, Nayan Shah, "Queer of Color Estrangement and Belonging."

30 Wittman, "Gay Manifesto," 333.

31 Donn Teal, "Wakefield Poole adds new dimension to porn," *Advocate*, March 1, 1972, 17.

32 Stuart Byron, "Dear Gay Liberationist" mailing, March 17, 1972, Arthur Bell Papers, box 92, file: Movies, NYPL; Donn Teal, "Halsted's porn," *Advocate*, May 10, 1972, 23; "S&M flicks cause furor," ibid.

33 Chelsea Del Rio, "Voicing Gay Women's Liberation: Judy Grahn and the Shaping of Lesbian Feminism," *Journal of Lesbian Studies* 19 (2015): 360.

34 Greg Youmans, "Performing Essentialism: Reassessing Barbara Hammer's Films of the 1970s," *Camera Obscura* 27, no. 3 (2012): 117.

35 Jessi Gan, " 'Still at the back of the bus': Sylvia Rivera's Struggle," *Centro Journal* 19, no. 1 (2007), 133.

36 Betty Luther Hillman, " 'The Most Profoundly Revolutionary Act a Homosexual Can Engage In': Drag and the Politics of Gender Presentation in the San Francisco Gay Liberation Movement, 1964–1972," *Journal of the History of Sexuality* 20, no.1 (2011): 172.

37 On this and other feminist transphobia, see Susan Stryker, *Transgender History* (Berkeley: Seal, 2008), 101–111; Robin Morgan, "Lesbianism and Feminism: Synonyms or Contradictions?" (1973), available at www.onearchives.org/wp-content/uploads/2015/02/Lesbianism-and-Feminism-Synonyms-or-Contradictions-by-Robin-Morgan-April-14–1973.pdf. Accessed October 19, 2017.

38 Martin Duberman, *Cures: A Gay Man's Odyssey* (New York: Dutton, 1991); Sylvia Rivera's speech was filmed, and can be seen at www.youtube.com/watch?v=9QiigzZCEtQ. Accessed October 19, 2017.

39 For a trans analytic lens on US history, see, in this volume, Finn Enke, "Transgender History (and Otherwise Approaches to Queer Embodiment."

40 See also, in this volume, Loraine Hutchins, "Bisexual History: Let's Not Bijack Another Century."

41 "Gay Paper Seized in Porn War," *Advocate*, May 24, 1972; Ed Davis to Robert Stevenson, January 16, 1975, City Council File 74–2967, Los Angeles City Archives; "No Charges Filed in Raid on Gay Spa," *Los Angeles Times*, November 20, 1980.

42 On mainstreaming and consumerism in queer US history, see, in this volume, Stephen Vider, "Consumerism."

43 Gillian Frank, "The Civil Rights of Parents: Race and Conservative Politics in Anita Bryant's Campaign against Gay Rights in 1970s Florida," *Journal of the History of Sexuality* 22, no. 1 (2013): 140–141.

44 See also, in this volume, Sara Smith-Silverman, "Labor."

45 Claire Bond Potter, "Paths to Political Citizenship: Gay Rights, Feminism, and the Carter Presidency," *Journal of Policy History* 24, no. 1 (2012): 106.

46 Martha Shelley, "Gay is Good," *Out of the Closets*, 31.

Further Reading

Cohen, Stephan. *The Gay Liberation Youth Movement in New York: "An Army of Lovers Cannot Fail."* New York: Routledge, 2008.

Enke, Finn. *Finding the Movement: Sexuality, Contested Space, and Feminist Activism.* Durham: Duke University Press, 2007.

Escoffier, Jeffrey. *Bigger Than Life: The History of Gay Porn Cinema from Beefcake to Hardcore.* Philadelphia: Running Dog Press, 2009.

Freeman, Susan K. "From the Lesbian Nation to the Cincinnati Lesbian Community: Moving Toward a Politics of Location." *Journal of the History of Sexuality* 9, nos. 1/2 (2000): 137–174.

Gilmore, Stephanie, and Elizabeth Kaminski. "A Part and Apart: Lesbian and Straight Feminist Activists Negotiate Identity in a Second-Wave Organization." *Journal of the History of Sexuality* 16, no. 1 (2007): 95–113.

Hanhardt, Christina. *Safe Space: Gay Neighborhood History and the Politics of Violence.* Durham: Duke University Press, 2013.

Johnson, David. "Physique Pioneers: The Politics of 1960s Gay Consumer Culture." *Journal of Social History* 43, no. 4 (2010): 867–892.

Kramer, Larry. *Faggots.* New York: Random House, 1978.

Littauer, Amanda. "Sexual Minorities at the Apex of Heteronormativity (1940s-1965)." *Routledge History of Queer America.* New York: Routledge, 2018.

Meeker, Martin. "Behind the Mask of Respectability: Reconsidering the Mattachine Society and Male Homophile Practice, 1950s and 1960s." *Journal of the History of Sexuality* 10, no. 1 (2001): 78–116.

Meyerowitz, Joanne. *How Sex Changed: A History of Transsexuality in the United States.* Cambridge: Harvard University Press, 2002.

Morris, Bonnie. "Olivia Records: The Production of a Movement." *Journal of Lesbian History* 19 (2015): 290–304.

Mumford, Kevin J. "The Trouble with Gay Rights: Race and the Politics of Sexual Orientation in Philadelphia, 1969–1982." *Journal of American History* 98, no. 1 (2011): 49–72.

Murray, Heather. "Free for All Lesbians: Lesbian Cultural Production and Consumption in the United States during the 1970s." *Journal of the History of Sexuality* 16, no. 2 (2007): 251–275.

Newton, Huey. "The Women's Liberation and Gay Liberation Movements" (1970), available at www.historyisaweapon.com/defcon1/newtonq.html. Accessed October 19, 2017.

Passet, Joanne. "Barbara Grier and the World She Built." *Journal of Lesban Studies* 18 (2014): 315–332.

Paul, Jay. "San Francisco's Bisexual Center and the Emergence of a Bisexual Movement." *Bisexualities— The Ideology and Practice of Sexual Contact with both Men and Women.* Erwin Haeberl and Rolf Gindorf, eds. New York: Continuum, 1998, 130–139. Available at www.sexarchive.info/BIB/bicent.htm. Accessed October 19, 2017.

Peña, Susana. "Gender and Sexuality in Latino/a Miami: Documenting Latina Transsexual Activists." *Gender & History* 22, no. 3 (2010): 755–772.

Raymond, Janice. *The Transsexual Empire: The Making of the She-Male.* Boston: Beacon, 1979.

Retzloff, Tim. "Eliding Trans Latino/Queer Experience in U.S. LGBT History: Jose Sarris and Sylvia Rivera Reexamined." *Centro Journal* 19, no. 1 (2007): 141–161.

Roque Ramírez, Horacio N. ""That's My Place!": Negotiating racial, sexual, and gender politics in San Francisco's Gay Latino Alliance, 1975–1983." *Journal of the History of Sexuality* 12, no. 2 (2003): 224–258.

Stein, Marc. *City of Sisterly and Brotherly Loves: Lesbian and Gay Philadelphia, 1945–1972.* Philadelphia: Temple University Press, 2004.

Stein, Marc. *Rethinking the Gay and Lesbian Movement.* New York: Routledge, 2012.

Stewart-Winter, Timothy. "Queer Law and Order: Sex, Criminality, and Policing in the Late Twentieth-Century United States." *Journal of American History* 102, no. 1 (2015): 61–72.

Streitmatter, Roger. *Unspeakable: The Rise of the Gay and Lesbian Press in America.* Boston: Faber & Faber, 1995.

Strub, Whitney. "Mondo Rocco: Mapping Gay Los Angeles Sexual Geography in the Late-1960s Films of Pat Rocco." *Radical History Review* 113 (2012): 13–34.

Suran, Justin David. "Coming out against the War: Antimilitarism and the Politicization of Homosexuality in the Era of Vietnam." *American Quarterly* 53, no. 3 (2001): 452–488.

Wat, Eric. *The Making of a Gay Asian Community: An Oral History of Pre-AIDS Los Angeles.* Lanham: Rowman & Littlefield, 2002.

Weiss, Margot. "Queer Neoliberal Times." *Routledge History of Queer America.* New York: Routledge, 2018.

7

AIDS AND ACTION
(1980–1990s)

Jennifer Brier

Unlike any disease before it, Acquired Immune Deficiency Syndrome (AIDS) changed the relationship between illness, people who are sick, and political structures. It also fundamentally transformed the lives of LGBTQ people and in the process marked a critically important moment in the history of sexuality. Because AIDS, as both a disease and a reaction to it, came into form in the United States over the course of the 1980s, it was profoundly influenced by broader concurrent political and social transformations. Some of the most vociferous and progressive arguments against the rise of conservatism (and neoliberalism, as is described in the next essay) came out of AIDS activism. Almost as soon as health care professionals and public health researchers began to report groups of gay men falling ill in 1981, people affected by the disease began to think of themselves as "people with AIDS," a group with specific needs requiring action *and* empathy. Developing a system to care for people who were dying was first and foremost the work of LGBTQ people.

The struggle of people with AIDS in the 1980s (today called people living with HIV/AIDS) also exposed the limits of the US welfare state, the prevalence of racism and its effects on health, and the homophobia that undergirded a wholesale abandonment of people with AIDS. In that respect, the first people to agitate as, and on behalf of, people with AIDS not only pushed back against a biomedical model that suggested all solutions would be medical in nature, but also developed a stunningly diverse and engaged response, which made stark the reality that AIDS travelled along lines of structural inequality and that fighting it required expansive and intersectional intervention. Action organized in response to AIDS needs to be understood in relation to queer history, but cannot be collapsed with it. The history of AIDS, therefore, pushes queer history beyond LGBT subjects, and toward an interrogation of the systems, structures, and ideologies of normativity that produce marginalization and precarity—and the ways in which those queered by such forces demand viability and justice.[1]

People with AIDS: The First Queer AIDS Activists Before HIV

AIDS wreaked havoc on the people made sick and the communities in which those people lived, received care, and very often died. It is impossible to overestimate the extent of suffering and fear AIDS wrought in its first years of existence in the United States. The combination of unknown etiology, fear of infections and the physical and visible manifestations on the bodies of gay white men, meant that thousands of people, most of whom were, at least at the outset, gay men living in cities, died very painful deaths. Initially called Gay Related Immuno-Deficiency (GRID), and manifesting in Kaposi's Sarcoma (KS) lesions on the skin or pneumocystis pneumonia (PCP) in the lungs, AIDS, as it was called by 1983–84, and the gay men who "had it," were feared and isolated. Calls by some ultra-conservative politicians to forcibly quarantine people with AIDS and the abandonment of people with AIDS at doors of emergency rooms underscored both the longstanding association between gayness and sickness and the virulent homophobia that propelled much of the reaction to AIDS.

While gay white men were at first the most visible cases, they were never the only communities affected. From the start, communities of color, particularly African American gay and bisexual men, were particularly hard struck, even as their suffering largely remained invisible because gayness was always assumed to be white. Throughout the first half of the 1980s, we learned of several other disparate groups who were among the earliest cases, including people who used intravenous drugs, female (at the time this was reported as "women" but we now know that it included both cisgender and transgender women) sex workers, hemophiliacs, and Haitians living in the United States and on the island of Haiti. This combination of people was often referred to as the "4-Hs": homosexuals, heroin users, hemophiliacs, Haitians, and sometimes a fifth H, hookers. With its focus on singular identity (people did not fall into two categories) and populations at risk, public discussions of AIDS effectively made a set of four social pariahs, and one group of "innocent victims," hemophiliacs. The language of risk groups, including the invisibility of gay and bisexual men of color in the category of "homosexuals", also allowed people to think that if they did not identify as one of these groups they were safe. It would take sustained action by and on behalf of people with AIDS for the focus to shift from identity to behavior. In the meantime, AIDS became a national epidemic and then a global pandemic within less than a decade. In the process AIDS became a political, social and health crisis, or what social theorist Paula Triechler calls an "epidemic of signification."[2]

State silence and inaction magnified the fear and isolation experienced by people living with, and dying from, AIDS. Across all levels of government people with AIDS witnessed a failure to respond to the epidemic and the needs it produced. Early activists called out mayors of large cities, including New York, San Francisco, and Los Angeles for a general slowness to action, while they also devised stinging critiques of the federal bureaucracy represented by agencies such as the Centers for Disease Control and the National Institutes of Health. But, as I detail in my published work, the most forceful and across-the-board criticism was lodged against Ronald Reagan's presidential administration. While President Reagan said almost nothing to the public about AIDS during his eight years in office, people who worked for the administration did a great deal to develop a response to AIDS based in ideological opposition to homosexuality. Examples of this run the gamut, from the White House press secretary and press corps laughing when reporters posed questions about AIDS in the briefing room, to the development of educational policy contraindicated by health care providers including Surgeon General C. Everett Koop. The Reagan administration spoke much more than the president and in the process advanced a set of governmental actions that contradicted much of the publicly facing material designed by LGBTQ people and other allies in the budding AIDS sector.[3]

In response to the sustained failure of municipal, state, and federal governments to act sufficiently, gay men and lesbians were among the first to will into being ways to care for people with AIDS and prevent the disease's spread. They did this in myriad venues and voices, sustaining arguments about health, sex, and the state that became central components in progressive political agendas emerging to critique the ascendant Religious Right. Writing in gay newspapers that had been built over the course of the 1970s, gay men, lesbians, and bisexuals answered profound fear and uncertainty by questioning the scientific establishment's focus on identity over behavior, and suggesting that gay, bisexual, and feminist notions of liberation could make desire and sex healthy in the age of AIDS.

Two gay men, in particular, led some of the earliest efforts at preventing the spread of AIDS. Michael Callen and Richard Berkowitz had both done sex work, worked as writers, and were among a community of gay men who suffered from numerous sexually transmitted infections. They took it upon themselves to talk publicly about their lives as sex-positive men struggling to rethink their sexual practices in the age of AIDS. In 1983, they self-published *How to Have Sex in an Epidemic,* which served as one of the first articulations of what would soon be called safe sex and later "safer sex." Joining liberationist material geared toward gay sexual health made by groups such as the Sisters of Perpetual Indulgence, Callen and Berkowitz called on men to use condoms, care for one another even during the most fleeting sexual encounters, and refuse accusations that they were sick because they were gay. While a vociferous debate ensued about the causal connection between AIDS and gay liberation, Callen and Berkowitz insisted that sex and love needed to be part of a response to AIDS instead of focusing on eliminating sex.

In addition to their arguments about prevention, Callen and Berkowitz were active in the People with AIDS Coalition, an organization that pushed the medical establishment to develop more ethical and positive treatment and care. In 1983, they were among a dozen or so white men who crafted the Denver Principles, one of the most important documents by and about people with AIDS, at the Fifth National Lesbian and Gay Health Conference. It read in part: "We condemn attempts to label us as victims, a term which implies defeat, and we are only occasionally patients, a term which implies passivity, helplessness, and dependence upon the care of others. We are people with AIDS." Combining prevention and treatment meant that people with AIDS foreshadowed argument that later AIDS activists would make that prevention and treatment needed to go hand in hand if either were to succeed.

The racial homogeneity of these fledgling organizers was indicative of an emerging racial politics of the AIDS epidemic, one structured by various forms of invisibility and refusal to see the conditions under which HIV/AIDS would become an epidemic that disproportion-ately affects communities of color, particularly African American men who have sex with men. While a small percentage of the first cases between 1981 and 1984, African American men were certainly among the first documented as affected. At the outset, the numbers reflected long standing racial segregation in gay communities, that kept white and black gay communities largely separate, especially when it came to sexual interactions. As scholars including Cathy Cohen and Darius Bost have noted, this initial white racialization of AIDS allowed most black gay men to construct AIDS as a disease that only affected white gay men and therefore not something that rose to the level of attention or action. Fighting racism in white gay communities took priority over AIDS in the early years of the epidemic. Bost suggests that this began to shift around 1983, when the extent of the epidemic's reach in African American communities became apparent.

Despite the initial limited numbers, some black gay men, especially writers, poets, and cultural producers began to imagine how to respond to AIDS in black queer spaces. Joined by black lesbians, Michelle Parkerson, Audre Lorde, and Barbara Smith, Joseph Beam, Essex Hemphill, Melvin Dixon, and Marlon Riggs, crafted a Black Gay renaissance, which had as one of its main concerns the health of black gay people. Down the East Coast, from New York, to Philadelphia, to Washington D.C., these writers formed intentional groups, such as the Other Countries writers collective and held fora about AIDS in black gay bars, such as the ClubHouse in D.C.[4]

An interracial coalition of gay men, lesbians, and bisexuals became the central drivers of community networks that filled the painful and often deadly gaps in care for people with AIDS, at the same time that many of them also made a case for seeing the intersection of homophobia, biphobia and racism. With names such as "Us Helping Us," created by black gay men in Washington D.C., the Los Angeles AIDS Hotline, where volunteers fielded calls day and night, and the San Diego Blood Sisters, an organization of mostly white lesbians who made blood donations in the name of gay men who were banned from doing so (a law in place from 1983 to 2015), and the Third World AIDS Advisory Taskforce in San Francisco, these nascent volunteer organizations set the stage for the development of a new form of care and treatment provision: AIDS Service Organizations (ASO).

Lesbians and bisexual women not only provided physical and emotional support in the early years of AIDS, they also actively developed tools for talking about what safer sex for all (heterosexual, lesbian and bisexual) women needed to look like. Refusing a common trope at the time—that women were vectors for the spread of disease—women activists, many of whom had been central figures in both the women's health movement and gay liberation movement, paid careful attention to the reality that women who have sex with women (WSW) needed to talk how HIV/AIDS affected them by talking about a list of behaviors that included having sex with men and women, using IV drugs and engaging in exchange sex with men. In 1987, Cindy Patton and Janice Kelly, two lesbian journalists, worked with cartoonist Alison Bechdel, to produce *Making It: A Woman's Guide to Sex in the Age of AIDS*. Printed in English and Spanish in the same volume, the book promised "to address one of the critical questions: How can women—heterosexual, lesbian and bisexual—enjoy full sex lives *and* protect themselves from this deadly disease?" The authors answered this question with a frank discussion of the myriad ways women had sex with one another and with men, as well as the reality of IV drug use as a risk factor for lesbian and bisexual women. But the cartoon did so in a way that rejected a budding notion that bisexual men and women served as a bridge that exposed heterosexuals to HIV/AIDS. It became one of the first outreach documents to address the overlap between people with same sex desire and people who use IV drugs, and it did so by centering the sexual experiences of women.

As the 1980s wore on, general consciousness about the epidemic expanded in part because notable people came out as having HIV/AIDS. In 1985, the 1950s movie star Rock Hudson died a few months after publicly announcing he was sick. Hudson's transformation from what cultural theorist Richard Meyer called a "starbody" into an "anti-body" surprised many of his heterosexual fans who knew him as a heart throb. Many saw Hudson's death as an opportunity to talk about how AIDS affected everyone. Gay men had an entirely different interpretation: they knew Hudson was gay and witnessed Hudson's fellow actor Ronald Reagan, and First Lady Nancy Reagan, refuse to provide Hudson with any care. In that respect, Hudson, and a handful of other famous heterosexuals who announced their serostatus later, including Magic Johnson in 1992 and Charlie Sheen in 2016, raised visibility about HIV/AIDS but did not necessarily address how inequality produced the conditions under which the overwhelming majority of people became infected with HIV, nor how their care and treatment was stunted by structural conditions of racism and homophobia.

A growing body of theatrical, literary, and popular work on the subject also expanded popular understandings of AIDS in the second half of the 1980s, at the same time that it focused attention on the experiences of white gay men as a stand-in for the experience of all gay men living and dying from AIDS. These early pieces did not substantively take up questions of racial inequality or the health effects of poverty. Although limited in substantive content on safer sex, some of the cultural material worked to humanize AIDS by focusing on how white gay communities responded to the epidemic. For example, in 1985, *An Early Frost* won NBC a Golden Globe for a depiction of a young white gay man's death with his economically comfortable family of origin; and Larry Kramer's caustic and realist play, *The Normal Heart*, premiered at the Public Theatre in New York City, with an all-white cast. Visual artist Keith Haring's then partner, Juan Rivera or Juanito Xtravaganza, a young Puerto Rican gay man who moved in and out of homelessness, served as a muse and an artist's assistant, and helped Haring produce arresting public art and graffiti around New York that made a case that art could induce political change. But while Haring regularly attended to issues of drug use and urban inequality, it rarely intersected visually with his work on AIDS.[5]

In a more stinging critique of both gay communities and the federal government, in 1987, journalist Randy Shilts released his hugely successful non-fiction account of the AIDS epidemic, *And the Band Played On*. The bestseller introduced two arguments about AIDS that have long outlasted the book: the profound lack of federal response to AIDS, and the concept that we could isolate and identify the first person with AIDS to enter the United States. Shilts identified Gaetan Dugas, a gay French Canadian flight attendant, as this person and called him Patient Zero, defined as the person who brought AIDS to the United States from his travels on the African continent and in Haiti. Disproven before the book even came out, the myth of Patient Zero exemplified for many Shilts's internalized homophobia and the racist tropes of AIDS's origin in central Africa. Historians Phil Tiemeyer and Richard A. McKay are rewriting Dugas's story, with his sense of self and agency at the center, as a way to again disprove Patient Zero, but do not fully decenter the blame that is placed on black people around the world as the original source of HIV/AIDS.

AIDS Service Organizations and the Beginning of the AIDS Service Industry

As the epidemic continued to kill people, and it was increasingly clear that state action was never going to be sufficient to care for and prevent the spread of AIDS, voluntary and non-profit organizations emerged to formalize AIDS service provision. Cities across the country witnessed the opening of institutions including the San Francisco AIDS Foundation (SFAF), the Gay Men's Health Crisis (GMHC) in New York, and the evolution of existing ones such as the Whitman–Walker Clinic in D.C., which began as the Gay Men's VD Clinic in 1973, and Howard Brown Health Center in Chicago that started the same year, all with the goal of providing an infrastructure to promote health in lesbian, gay, and bisexual communities. The institutional evolution was far from even, however. Few institutions effectively addressed the structural inequality laid bare by the AIDS epidemic. Often, the legacy of racial divisions in political and community organizing intersected with marginalizations of bisexual and transgender people to directly affect AIDS service work.[6]

De facto racial segregation of gay communities also produced the conditions under which African American gay men went from being almost imperceptible in the first cases of AIDS to representing more than a quarter of cases in 1986. Without attention to how racial disparities functioned in queer communities, comprehensive AIDS education, care and prevention was deaf to the realities of why race mattered for the epidemic. Queer people of African descent and queer Latinos pushed back against this model, and developed alternatives to racist arguments that connected people of color, particularly, to disease. Dan Royles describes AIDS work in Philadelphia, where Blacks Educating Blacks About Sexual Health Issues (BEBASHI) formed in 1985 at the same time as the Third World AIDS Advisory Taskforce began its work in San Francisco, about which I have written. Both of these organizations advanced a much more expansive notion of what it meant to do effective prevention work. They focused on issues of mass incarceration, drugs, and the evisceration of the welfare state at the same time as they developed sexual and reproductive health information for LGBTQ and heterosexual people of color. Scholarship on intersectionality and issues of structural inequality has been produced by the likes of Darius Bost, Dagmawi Woubshet, Juana Maria Rodriguez, Jesus Ramirez-Valles, and the late Horacio Roque Ramirez.

Bisexual communities also faced harsh criticism from the public health establishment and from gay and lesbian communities. The attacks were varied, ranging from accusations that bisexual men served as the "bridge" that brought HIV from gay men to heterosexuals, to claims that bisexual men were indistinguishable from gay men or simply unwilling to come out as gay. This biphobia functioned to reify notions that certain individuals were more dangerous than others and that male bisexuals were often deceitful with their female partners. Named "being on the down-low," when talking about African American men, meant that black bisexual men were further demonized as causing the spread of HIV/AIDS. Writing against this model, the Reverend Dr. Ibrahim Farajajé [AKA Elias Ferajajé-Jones] argues that "bisexuals were included in name, but not in reality," suggesting that bisexual communities had long practiced sexuality that centered affirmative consent and condom use, even though very little prevention material was ever directed toward them. We know even less about bisexual women, who were often engaged in sexual relationships with men and women who had sex with men and women, but only appear under the category of sex worker.[7]

By the mid-1990s, AIDS service providers and activists began using the phrase "men who have sex with men" or MSM as a way to call attention to sexual practices and move away from an identity-based model. This was a double-edged sword for self-identified bisexual men, who no longer could be named as distinct from gay men in name or reality.

The powerful effects of structural inequality on the course of the HIV/AIDS epidemic have manifested disproportionately on trans and gender non-conforming people, particularly transgender women of color. With higher rates of infection than almost any other group, trans women face a set of social and political conditions that put them at risk of contracting HIV, including higher rates of incarceration, sexual and gender-based violence, drug use, and practices of survival sex. Historians have not done nearly enough work to detail where the HIV/AIDS epidemic fits in trans history, especially in terms of what it means for trans people to live with HIV/AIDS. One of the few examples comes from Susan Stryker, who recounts the life of Lou Sullivan, a white gay transman who served as a "hub of the organized FTM community," and the gay community. Sullivan recognized the imperative for trans people to collect and hold their history to fight the invisibility they faced in many different sectors. Near the time of his death in 1991, Sullivan spoke a clarion call for gender and sexual autonomy in the face of HIV/AIDS: "You told me I couldn't live like a gay man, but now I am going to die like one."[8]

Fight Back/Fight AIDS: ACT UP and the Power of Direct Action

Fear and anger continued to percolate within gay communities and communities of people affected by AIDS. By the end of the 1980s, many activists and people living with AIDS decided they had enough of willful ignorance, governmental indifference, and corporate greed (often singling out pharmaceutical manufacturers). In response they started AIDS Coalition to Unleash Power (ACT UP), activating systemic direct action to fight back and fight AIDS. As detailed in a growing body of historical work by scholars such as Deborah Gould, Erin Rand,

and myself, activists insisted that AIDS was more than a health crisis, it was a political crisis. A comprehensive response required fundamental change to the health care system, artistic direct action and community organizing. Chanting and carrying graphically arresting picket signs, ACT UP used cultural production and a new politics of emotion to affect political change. They harnessed their anger into action and also shamed people whose inaction or obstructionism allowed the AIDS crisis to continue. ACT UP's activism on AIDS became one of the most forceful and vociferous reactions to the era's political conservatism.

ACT UP, with chapters across the country each with their own history, was a coalition of activists who shared a commitment to direct action as a means to get "drugs into bodies." Local chapters, particularly the first and largest one in New York City, orchestrated huge protests on Wall Street and at the headquarters of particular pharmaceutical companies, while national coalitions of chapters turned their attention to federal institutions, including the National Institutes of Health and the Centers for Disease Control. Led by the Treatment Action Group (TAG), protests produced significant changes to the way pharmaceutical companies and the federal government develop, test and distribute drugs. Their efforts produced the conditions under which combinations of drugs were given to people with AIDS, making it possible to ultimately bring combination therapy using protease inhibitors to market in 1996.

In addition to its action on treatment, ACT UP had a wide range of other caucuses, which produced a broad political agenda focused on the social health and political well-being of people living with AIDS, including the Majority Action Committee and the Women's Caucus. They attended to issues of housing instability, sexism and misogyny in the medical profession and

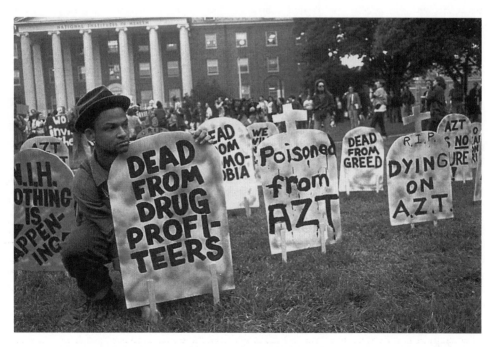

Figure 7.1 On May 21, 1990, as part of a "Storm the NIH" day of die-ins and building occupation, ACT UP (AIDS Coalition to Unleash Power) protestors take the lawn in front of the James Shannon building of the National Institutes of Health to push for more rapid HIV/AIDS drug development and more equitable access to treatment.

Courtesy of Donna Binder.

popular culture, and structural racism's magnifying effect on incarceration and policing of IV drug users. Scholars debate the extent to which racism affected ACT UP's work, but they agree that at the heart of the disagreement was who was imagined as the archetypal person with AIDS. Sociologist Deborah Gould writes, "Because issues of racism, sexism, and poverty in the AIDS epidemic did not establish that link for most of the HIV-positive, white, middle-class men in the group, those concerns seemed to some to be 'not about AIDS'."[9]

This fight over what was to be defined as "about AIDS" and "not about AIDS" became one factor in the diminution of members and actions out of New York City's chapter by the mid-1990s. Still, as the ACT UP/NY Women & AIDS Book Group, and more recently, historian Tamar Carroll document, activists initiated a national campaign to expand the medical definition of AIDS so that women could be diagnosed with AIDS and receive Social Security benefits as a critical piece of comprehensive care. Led by women with HIV, many of whom had recently been released from prison, and a handful of lawyers who worked to secure their federal benefits, the protestors made the case that "Women don't get AIDS, they just die from it." This was because HIV/AIDS did not manifest in women's bodies the same way it did in men's. Women dying from AIDS often had cervical cancer or pelvic inflammatory disease, while men often had KS or PCP. This meant that federal definitions of disability were only understood as appearing in men's bodies. ACT UP refused this, and in some of the most gender integrated and racially mixed series of protests, forced the Social Security Administration to expand the definition of AIDS to include a focus on t-cells and a longer list of accompanying infections. This not only gave women access to SSI, but also IV drug users of all genders, who were visible as deserving federal support.

It was with this forcefully expanded definition of AIDS that activists, health care providers, and scientists arrived at the Eleventh Annual AIDS Conference in Vancouver 1996 with talk of a cure for AIDS in the form of combination therapy using protease inhibitors. While activists insisted on and ultimately produced the conditions under which efficacious treatment emerged, many were also among the first to insist that treatment alone could not be defined as a cure. In his opening ceremony speech to thousands of attendees, ACT UP member Eric Sawyer said, "The headlines that PWAS want you to write from this conference would read: 'Human Rights Violations and Genocide continue to kill millions of impoverished people with AIDS.' That is the truth about AIDS in 1996." He ended leading a chant, "Greed Kills, Access for All."[10]

AIDS Service, Culture and Activism after ACT UP

Focusing exclusively on ACT UP, especially in its heyday from 1987 to1992, risks missing the longer-term effects of AIDS service, culture and activism in the lead up to the discovery of protease inhibitors in 1996 and the period after that when it was clear that treatment alone, would not be able to address the structural inequality that made the AIDS epidemic look as it did. For example, in 1992, GMHC, which had long been one of the leading AIDS service organizations in the country, started the Lesbian AIDS Project (LAP) under the leadership of long-time feminist and lesbian activist Amber Hollibaugh. LAP insisted that lesbians and women who have sex with women (WSW) needed to understand AIDS not necessarily because their risk came from their sexual practices with other women, but rather because of their sexual experiences with men and drug use. That is, their identity would not protect them, especially since the public health establishment often defined lesbians as women who exclusively had sex with other women, a definition that failed to reflect the lived experiences of many women who have sex with other women.

The expansion of cultural expression throughout the 1990s exposed queer and general audiences to ideas about HIV/AIDS and its relationship to other political and cultural struggles. Writers, visual artists, and filmmakers produced a significant body of AIDS-related materials, including Tony Kushner's 1991 *Angels in America: A Gay Fantasia on National Themes*, a day-long play in two parts that ran in theatres around the country with a fantastic narrative about death, Mormonism, racial politics, conservative politics and McCarthyism; Jonathan Demme's 1993 feature film, *Philadelphia*, which exposed a general audience to the life and death of a white gay lawyer played by Tom Hanks at the same time that it told a racialized narrative that marked black communities as more homophobic than white ones; Marlon Riggs's posthumous 1994 documentary *Black Is. . . Black Ain't*, which made a case for how anti-black racism fueled AIDS; choreographer and dancer's Bill T. Jones 1994 *Still/Here* about survival through movement and dance; and the photographic and installation art of Felix Gonzalez-Torres, the Cuban-American artist, who in 1991 produced a series of twenty-four billboards that appeared around New York City, of an unoccupied bed made empty by the death of his lover. As film scholars Roger Hallas and Alexandra Juhasz observe, alternative video projects filmed in response to HIV/AIDS also exploded in the 1990s as hand-held equipment became affordable and public access television provided a venue for experimental content.

Culture producers fighting the HIV/AIDS epidemic consistently made the case that their work was central to the efficacy of treatment and prevention efforts, especially in the period after protease inhibitors become available. By the turn of the twenty-first century this claim found powerful voice in the black queer ballroom communities of cities across the United States. Ethnographer Marlon Bailey suggests that the community networks brought into being and expanded through the balls enacted a form of "intravention," where young men of color who have sex with men become both the consumers of AIDS prevention and the producers of it, such that the "focus [is] on culture, as an arsenal of resiliency strategies upon which marginalized communities rely to survive the social crisis."[11] In Chicago, HIV/AIDS prevention and treatment targeting Latino communities takes form in Vida/SIDA (Live/AIDS), a grassroots organization that is housed in the Puerto Rican Cultural Center and centers cultural preservation alongside health.

While many chapters of ACT UP had slowed or ceased actions by 1996, ACT UP Philadelphia was at a point of major transformation. Forming Project TEACH (Treatment Education Activists Combating HIV), the chapter built activist leadership among communities of color, many of whom were also gender non-conforming and same gender loving. Sociologist and oral historian Pascal Emmer details how subsequent strategies and protests centered AIDS in macroeconomic debates about globalization, immigration, and economic security for the poor. ACT UP Philly connected US AIDS activists with activists around the world, making a case that effective treatment required guaranteed access to combination therapy, proper food and clean water, and affordable health care.

How AIDS is Remembered: Or What End Are We At?

As we approach a second major medical transformation in treatment and prevention of the HIV/AIDS—Pre-Exposure Prophylaxis (PrEP), the ability to take a small dose of protease inhibitors to prevent HIV infection—we need to, as Kane Race urges, refocus our attention on how we will narrate the history of the epidemic in the twenty-first century.

Centering the diverse experiences of people living with HIV/AIDS is one of the lessons we should take with us into the history books. With a plethora of oral history projects devoted to collecting the histories of people who provided care to people with HIV/AIDS as well as ones that capture the individual histories of long-term survivors, other people living with HIV/AIDS, and people who have died from AIDS, we have an opportunity to stitch together a larger public history of AIDS in the United States that also expands and deepens our understandings of the LGBTQ past.[12] The growing digital archive has already been used to produce both important web-based projects that will sustain historical work, including documentary films made by queer filmmakers, many of whom were activists in ACT UP.[13] Hopefully this growing work will not shy away from addressing how racism functioned and continues to affect the course of HIV/AIDS. We need to see historical work on long-term survivors who are not white men, and paint a richer picture of activism by and service provision for people of color living with HIV/AIDS.

We also need to continue to question how resources related to the treatment and prevention of HIV/AIDS are shared. This is put in the sharpest relief when we focus on the evolution of laws criminalizing how people living with HIV have sex. In 2015, Michael Johnson, a black gay college student, was sentenced to 30 years in Missouri prison for infecting one of his partners with HIV without disclosing his status. The state's disproportionate response to Johnson reflected the deep and long-standing connections between homophobia and racism as well as the links between HIV/AIDS and mass incarceration. It also suggests that we cannot think about treatment and prevention/treatment as prevention outside a larger context of structural inequality.

Activists had long presaged the racism and homophobia that structured Johnson's unequal treatment. In 1988, ACT UP New York member and filmmaker Vito Russo delivered a speech in Albany, NY called "Why We Fight," where he talked about how people with AIDS died: "So, if I'm dying from anything, I'm dying from homophobia. If I'm dying from anything, I'm dying from racism. If I'm dying from anything, it's from indifference and red tape, because these are the things that are preventing an end to this crisis."[14]

Notes

1 For the longer queer history of medicalization and activism, see, in this volume, Katie Batza, "Sickness and Wellness."
2 Paula A. Treichler, *How to Have Theory in an Epidemic: Cultural Chronicles of AIDS* (Durham: Duke University Press, 1999), 11.
3 For a short film on the press room see Calonico, Scott, *When AIDS Was Funny*, 2015, www.youtube.com/watch?v=yAzDn7tE1lU. Accessed October 19, 2017.
4 See also, in this volume, Nayan Shah, "Queer of Color Estrangement and Belonging."
5 For the longer queer history of popular culture, see, in this volume, Sharon Ullman, Performance and Popular Culture."
6 These fit into a longer history of LGBT organizations. See, in this volume, Marcia Gallo, "Organizations."
7 See also, in this volume, Loraine Hutchins, "Bisexual History: Let's Not Bijack Another Century."
8 Susan Stryker, *Transgender History* (Berkeley: Seal Press, 2009), 117–120.
9 Deborah B. Gould, "ACT UP, Racism, and the Question of How to Use History," *Quarterly Journal of Speech* 98, no. 1 (February 2012): 58.
10 Eric Sawyer, "Remarks at the Opening Ceremony," July 7, 1996, www.actupny.org/Vancouver/sawyerspeech.html. Accessed October 19, 2017.
11 Marlon M. Bailey, "Performance as Intravention: Ballroom Culture and the Politics of HIV/AIDS in Detroit," *Souls* 11, no. 3 (September 8, 2009): 255–257.
12 For a scholarly text that uses oral history see Ann Cvetkovich, *An Archive of Feelings: Trauma, Sexuality, and Lesbian Public Cultures* (Durham: Duke University Press, 2003). For examples of digital oral history projects see The AIDS Oral Histories, www.library.ucsf.edu/collections/archives/manuscripts/aids/oh, Regional Oral History Office, Berkeley, CA; HIV/AIDS Healthcare Providers Oral History Project, 2013–2014, http://discover.lib.umn.edu/cgi/f/findaid/findaid-idx?c=umfa;cc=umfa;rgn=main;view=text;didno=scrbt368; Jean-Nickolaus Tretter Collection in Gay, Lesbian, Bisexual and Transgender

Studies, University of Minnesota Libraries, Minnesota, MN; The Graying of AIDS, www.graying ofaids.org/; African American AIDS Activism Oral History Project, https://afamaidsoralhistory. wordpress.com/, Dan Royles; ACT UP Oral History Project, www.actuporalhistory.org/index1.html, In Their Own Words: NIH Researchers Recall the Early Years of AIDS, https://history.nih.gov/ NIHInOwnWords/index.html. All sources Accessed October 19, 2017.

13 A filmography of AIDS would require another essay. See, for example, Jean Carlomusto, *Sex in an Epidemic* (Outcast Films, 2010); David Weissman, *We Were Here* (2011); Jim Hubbard, *United in Anger: A History of ACT-UP* (2012); David France, *How to Survive a Plague* (MPI Home Video, 2013).

14 Vito Russo, "Why We Fight (Speech)," May 9, 1988, www.actupny.org/documents/whfight.html. Accessed October 19, 2017.

Further Reading

ACT UP/NY Women & AIDS Book Group. *Women, AIDS, and Activism*. Boston, MA: South End Press, 1999.

Bockting, Walter O., and Eric Avery. *Transgender Health and HIV Prevention: Needs Assessment Studies from Transgender Communities Across the United States*. Binghamton, NY: Haworth Medical Press, 2006.

Bost, Darius. "At the Club: Locating Early Black Gay AIDS Activism in Washington, D.C." *OCCASION* 8 (2015): 1–9.

Brier, Jennifer. *Infectious Ideas: U.S. Political Responses to the AIDS Crisis*. Chapel Hill: University of North Carolina Press, 2009.

———. "Reagan and AIDS." In *A Companion to Ronald Reagan*, ed. Andrew L. Johns. Chichester, West Sussex: Wiley Blackwell, 2015, 221–237.

Carroll, Tamar W. *Mobilizing New York: AIDS, Antipoverty, and Feminist Activism*. Chapel Hill, NC: University of North Carolina Press, 2015.

Cheng, Jih-Fei. "How to Survive: AIDS and Its Afterlives in Popular Media." *WSQ: Women's Studies Quarterly* 44, no. 1 (May 1, 2016): 73–92.

Cohen, Cathy J. *The Boundaries of Blackness: AIDS and the Breakdown of Black Politics*. Chicago: University of Chicago Press, 1999.

Cruz-Malavé, Arnaldo. *Queer Latino Testimonio, Keith Haring, and Juanito Xtravaganza: Hard Tails*. New York: Palgrave Macmillan, 2007.

Emmer, Pascal. "Talkin' 'Bout Meta-Generation: ACT UP History and Queer Futurity." *Quarterly Journal of Speech* 98, no. 1 (February 2012): 89–96.

Farajajé-Jones, Elias. "Fluid Desire: Race, HIV/AIDS, and Bisexual Politics." In *Bisexual Politics: Theories, Queries & Visions*, ed. Naomi Tucker, 119–130. New York: Haworth Press, 1995.

Geary, A. *Antiblack Racism and the AIDS Epidemic: State Intimacies*. New York: Palgrave Macmillan, 2014.

Gould, Deborah. *Moving Politics: Emotion and ACT UP's Fight Against AIDS*. Chicago: University of Chicago Press, 2009.

Hallas, Roger. *Reframing Bodies: AIDS, Bearing Witness, and the Queer Moving Image*. Durham: Duke University Press, 2009.

Juhasz, Alexandra. "VIDEO REMAINS Nostalgia, Technology, and Queer Archive Activism." *GLQ: A Journal of Lesbian and Gay Studies* 12, no. 2 (2006): 319–328.

McArthur, James B. "As the Tide Turns: The Changing HIV/AIDS Epidemic and the Criminalization of HIV Exposure." *Cornell Law Review* 94, no. 3 (2009): 707.

McKay, Richard A. "'Patient Zero': The Absence of a Patient's View of the Early North American AIDS Epidemic." *Bulletin of the History of Medicine* 88, no. 1 (Spring 2014): 161–194.

Meyer, Richard. "Rock Hudson's Body." In *Inside/Out: Lesbian Theories, Gay Theories*, ed. Diana Fuss, 259–288. New York: Routledge, 1991.

Patton, Cindy and Janice Kelly. *Making It: A Woman's Guide to Sex in the Age of AIDS*. Ithaca, NY: Firebrand Books, 1987.

Potts, Michelle C. "Regulatory Sites: Management, Confinement, and HIV/AIDS." In *Captive Genders: Trans Embodiment and the Prison Industrial Complex*, ed. Eric A. Stanley and Nat Smith, 99–111. Oakland: AK Press, 2011.

Race, Kane. "Reluctant Objects Sexual Pleasure as a Problem for HIV Biomedical Prevention." *GLQ: A Journal of Lesbian and Gay Studies* 22, no. 1 (January 2016): 1–31.

Ramirez-Valles, Jesus. *Compañeros: Latino Activists in the Face of AIDS*. Urbana: University of Illinois Press, 2011.

Rand, Erin J. "Gay Pride and Its Queer Discontents: ACT UP and the Political Deployment of Affect." *Quarterly Journal of Speech* 98, no. 1 (February 2012): 75–80.

Rodríguez, Juana María. *Queer Latinidad: Identity Practices, Discursive Spaces*. New York: NYU Press, 2003.

Rodríguez Rust, Paula C. "Bisexuality in HIV Research." In *Bisexuality in the United States: A Social Science Reader*, ed. Paula C. Rodríguez Rust, 355–402. New York: Columbia University Press, 2000.

Royles, Dan. " 'Don't We Die Too?:' The Political Culture of African American AIDS Activism." Ph.D. dissertation, Temple University, 2014.

Tiemeyer, Philip James. *Plane Queer: Labor, Sexuality, and AIDS in the History of Male Flight Attendants*. Berkeley: University of California Press, 2013.

Woubshet, Dagmawi. *The Calendar of Loss: Race, Sexuality, and Mourning in the Early Era of AIDS*. Baltimore: Johns Hopkins University Press, 2015.

Worobey, Michael. "1970s and 'Patient 0' HIV-1 Genomes Illuminate Early HIV/AIDS History in North America." *Nature* 539, no. 7627 (November 3, 2016): 98–101.

8

QUEER POLITICS IN NEOLIBERAL TIMES (1970–2010s)

Margot Weiss

Neoliberalism—as both economic theory and social or cultural formation—has had a profound effect on LGBT/queer cultures and politics. David Harvey defines neoliberalism as an economic theory that "proposes that human well-being can best be advanced by liberating individual entrepreneurial freedoms and skills within an institutional framework characterized by strong private property rights, free markets, and free trade."[1] Neoliberalism is also a cultural formation that produces and validates marketized understandings of the social world. As Wendy Brown argues, drawing on Michel Foucault's work on biopolitics and governmentality, neoliberalism is aimed at "extending and disseminating market values to all institutions and social action."[2] Neoliberalism offers "freedom" as the core political goal, and the market as the site where that freedom might be realized.

This vision has reshaped LGBT communities, debates, and social movements in the era after gay liberation. As neoliberal policies sought to privatize social services, foster consumer citizenship, and promote corporate welfare and urban redevelopment, LGBT sexual politics increasingly pitted "deserving" gay and lesbian people against "undeserving" others. Three constellations exemplify this trend: (1) the same-sex married couple vs. the "welfare queen," (2) the gay/lesbian consumer-citizen vs. the poor queer, and (3) the gay gentrifier vs. the "dangerous" other. Historicizing these oppositions reveals the intersections of sexuality, class, gender, race, and social policy that remain central to queer politics today in the aftermath of—if not after—neoliberalism.

Neoliberalism: Economics, Politics, Culture

Scholars have traced a pre-history of neoliberalism to the 1940s or even the 1920s, finding important intellectual precursors to neoliberalism proper in the attacks on Roosevelt's New Deal, the Public Works Administration, and the 1935 Social Security Act in the US; universal pensions, unemployment insurance, and the National Health Service in the UK; and on stock market and financial regulations in the name of property rights, economic rationality, and competition. Members of the Mount Pelerin Society, a neoliberal think tank founded by Friedrich August von Hayek in 1947, and the "Chicago Boys," especially Milton Friedman, formulated the core of the theory. These economists advanced a theory of the self-interested *homo economicus* (economic man) operating in a market "freed" from state control and regulation.

Neoliberal economic policy rose to dominance following the 1970s global economic crisis, characterized by rising unemployment, declining rates of profits, and inflation. Augusto Pinochet's 1973 coup in Chile, the 1979 election of Margaret Thatcher in the UK, and the 1980 election of Ronald Reagan in the US were also turns away from Keynesian state protections and market regulations. By the 1980s, with Latin American "structural adjustment," Thatcherism, and Reganomics in full swing, neoliberalism solidified its hold, resulting in policy reforms and austerity programs. In the US and UK, this led to the privatization and deregulation of public spaces and institutions (education, healthcare, social services); in the global South, neoliberalism took the form of programs that sought to "open up" markets for the free flow of capital. Recent anthropological studies of the global impact of neoliberalism have shown that "inequalities have risen sharply; most people are marginalized, dispossessed, and disenfranchised as public resources have been privatized, cities increasingly gentrified, social welfare programs reduced or slashed, and the rural and urban poor incorporated into market economies."[3]

Neoliberalism is a rapacious form of "accumulation by dispossession" characterized by the "corporatization, commodification, and privatization of hitherto public assets," predatory speculation and financialization, "crisis creation, management, and manipulation," and "state redistribution" of wealth upward, by privatizing social services and encouraging gentrification through tax codes and corporate welfare.[4] The growth of speculative, consumer-based, de-industrial markets in the global North is directly connected to global crises, precarity, and poverty in the global South, just as the rise of profiteering multinational corporations and service sector and low-paying just-in-time work has fostered a rising gap between rich and poor, owners and workers, in the United States.

Neoliberalism is an economic argument that the market should be freed from state regulation, resulting in social policies such as privatization and cuts in welfare, education, and healthcare. It is a political discourse that helps justify the resulting debt, fiscal crises, and the upward redistribution of wealth. And finally, neoliberalism is a hegemonic discourse—"the common-sense way many of us interpret, live in, and understand the world."[5] As such, it makes the ethical claim that individuals should be responsible, rational, "competitive," and "possessive" actors who make claims based on "consumer sovereignty."[6] For these reasons, neoliberalism as an organizing logic has had a profound impact on how everyone, including LGBT and queer people, understand and live out their political lives.

Neoliberalism and Queer Culture and Politics

Neoliberalism creates and relies on racial, gendered, and sexual inequality, but justifies this social inequality as a logical outcome of free choice, personal responsibility, and individualism. By redefining citizenship as ownership and freedom as freedom to consume, neoliberal economic policies have dismantled social welfare, enshrined a property-based right to privacy, and destroyed public sexual cultures accessible to poor, young, queer, and transgender communities of color. Building on the groundbreaking work of historians such as John D'Emilio, who linked gay identity to the rise of industrial capitalism, I focus on the ways that neoliberalism, in its relation to the culture of what Fredric Jameson has termed late capitalism, celebrates, endorses, and supports some aspects of sexuality, while at the same time limiting, policing, and punishing others.

As a rationality, neoliberalism has narrowed the vision of much LGBT political organizing to what Lisa Duggan calls "homonormativity": "a politics that does not contest dominant heteronormative assumptions and institutions but upholds and sustains them, while promising the possibility of a demobilized gay constituency and a privatized, depoliticized gay culture anchored in domesticity and consumption."[7] Mainstream gay advocacy organizations have pursued individual and family-based rights and turned away from liberationist or radical demands for dismantling oppressive systems or promoting sexual freedom or pleasure. We can see this vision reflected in the primary goals of the national movement through the 2010s: same-sex marriage and family recognition rights, market/cultural visibility, access to the military, and hate crime/safety legislation. The following three cases show how homonormativity has guided the mainstream LGBT rights movement for the past three decades.

Privatization of Social Services: Gay Marriage/The Welfare Queen

A February 15, 1976 *New York Times* article entitled " 'Welfare Queen' Becomes Issue in Reagan Campaign," began: "Few people realize it, but Linda Taylor, a 47-year-old Chicago welfare recipient, has become a major campaign issue in the New Hampshire Republican Presidential primary." The term "Welfare Queen" was popularized by Ronald Reagan in his 1976 stump speeches, where he used it to describe a poor black woman on welfare who was purportedly "cheating the system." The figure helped to rally support and justification for the massive cuts to welfare and social services that Reagan pursued. The "welfare queen" trafficked in older iconographies of poor black women's deviant sexuality that were reinvigorated after the 1965 Moynihan Report on the gendered and sexual "pathologies" of the black family. The Report depicted black single mothers as sites of "unrestrained sexual behavior"—and thus responsible for their own poverty. Relying on and reviving these imaginative links between race, poverty, and (sexual) pathology, the image of the "Welfare Queen" played a central role in portraying the poor as greedy, not needy. Harnessing sexual deviance to racialized poverty, the image helped shore up public support for the privatization and elimination of social services (in spite of the fact that most who needed welfare and child assistance were and are white).

This image continued to do its work in the post-Reagan era. The 1996 Personal Responsibility and Work Opportunity Reconciliation Act, for example, dramatically cut funding to basic safety net programs and ended "welfare as we know it," as Bill Clinton pledged. After public debate about welfare "abusers," the act replaced Aid to Families with Dependent Children with Temporary Assistance to Needy Families and required welfare recipients to take low-paying jobs to qualify for benefits (workfare). It also aimed to limit the number of children women on welfare could have, adding "family caps" to benefits and giving extra money to US states that reduced the number of "out-of-wedlock" births without increasing abortions. The Act also supported state abstinence-only education programs (that have roots in much longer eugenic histories of the sterilization and reproductive control of poor women of color). As Priya Kandaswamy argues, "Although the law had negative impacts on a wide array of women, support for the law was framed specifically as a means of disciplining sexually promiscuous, lazy black (and more recently Latina) 'welfare queens' who supposedly used government assistance to live outside the confines of both the labor market and the hetero-patriarchal family."[8] This history shows the connection between disciplining the racialized poor as sexually deviant and marshaling public consent for the neoliberal decimation of public assistance.

The pathologization of non-(hetero)normative racialized sexualities justifies a central component of neoliberal policy: limiting and privatizing welfare benefits. By propagating an image of the underserving (and hypersexual) welfare mother, and linking social support to normative sexuality, these acts endorsed anti-queer (and anti-feminist) policies such as abstinence until marriage, heteronormative marriage and family forms, and control over the reproductive futures of "undesirable" populations (poor people, indigenous people, people of color, queer people). As Cathy Cohen argues, "many of the roots of heteronormativity are in white supremacist ideologies which sought (and continue) to use the state and its regulation of sexuality, in particular through the institution of heterosexual marriage, to designate which individuals were truly 'fit' for full rights and privileges of citizenship."[9] Such arguments are ongoing: between 2005 and 2015, federal programs privatizing carework (within the family) and cutting state support for poor mothers and children provided $150 million a year to promote "healthy marriages" and "responsible fathers."

For many queer critics, because marriage promotion is one way that non-normative gender and sexuality—particularly the sexualities of black and poor women—is disciplined by the neoliberal state, the mainstream LGBT movement's emphasis on same-sex marriage was disappointing. Critics such as Michael Warner have long argued against state regulation in the form of marriage. In this most recent instantiation, the neoliberal withdrawal of public social support serves as an incentive to seek marriage as the source of care, support, and resource protection. As Cohen writes, "Same-sex marriage, far from ending 'marriage as we know it,' preserves a narrow system for the distribution of benefits that is tied to heteronormative understandings of the family. It allows the state to continue to shift its responsibility for the well being of its citizens to some private form we label the family."[10] In this context, the LGBT movement's emphasis on same-sex marriage must be viewed as the success of neoliberal policies that offer marriage as a privatized solution to peoples' needs for childcare, healthcare, economic stability, and social recognition.

In the 2015 US Supreme Court case granting same-sex couples the right to marry, the Court argued that the right to marry is foundational to individual autonomy, liberty, and personal choice; that marriage "fulfils yearnings for security, safe haven, and connection that express our common humanity"; and that marital status is the legitimate basis for both social recognition and material and state benefits, including inheritance and property rights, spousal privileges, medical decision-making, adoption rights, workers' compensation benefits, health insurance, and child custody and support benefits.[11] Justice Anthony Kennedy concludes the opinion: "No union is more profound than marriage, for it embodies the highest ideals of love, fidelity, devotion, sacrifice, and family. . . [The petitioners'] hope is not to be condemned to live in loneliness, excluded from one of civilization's oldest institutions. They ask for equal dignity in the eyes of the law."[12] Like other LGBT family-making strategies such as transracial and transnational adoption, new LGBT family rights are historically dependent on neoliberal transformations: the dismantling of social services, a shrinking social safety net, US migration and labor flows, and the racialized criminalization of poverty.[13] The call for the "dignity" of gay and lesbian marriage, like other pleas based on sexual respectability, depends on the regulation and policing of others—often the reproductive futurity of poor, queer, people of color. Such neoliberal family politics affirm the health and humanity of some, while helping to justify surveillance, exclusion, and poverty for others.[14]

The Pink Market: Queer Consumer Citizens/Queer Poverty

In May 1982, the *New York Times Magazine* ran an essay called "Tapping the Homosexual Market," in which Karen Stabiner reported that advertisers were now "wooing . . . the white, single, well-educated, well-paid man who happens to be homosexual." As Katherine Sender details, this new "pink market" was prompted by market research that seemed to point to the wealth of gay men and lesbians; in the early 1990s, Overlooked Opinions, a gay-marketing firm, claimed the American gay and lesbian market was worth $514 billion. Throughout the 1990s, gays and lesbians were described as ideal consumers: affluent, well-educated, fashionable, and "DINK" (double-income, no kids). As a 1995 article had it, "The gay and lesbian market is an untapped gold mine. Because gays are highly educated and usually have no dependants, they have high levels of disposable income. And because these consumers are disenfranchised from mainstream society, they are open to overtures from marketers."[15]

Recoding citizens as consumers, neoliberalism proffers privatized consumption as its model of citizenship and community. In a neoliberal world, "freedom is reduced to choice: choice of commodities, of lifeways, and, most of all, of identities" while politics is treated as a "personal trait or lifestyle choice. . . measured increasingly by the capacity to transact and consume."[16] The rise of the so-called "pink market" made gay men and lesbians visible as consumers and offered limited recognition to those who might "voice their politics through their spending."[17] In this form of consumer citizenship, LGBT politics aligns with market politics: good citizens, as David Evans notes, are those who express their identities and politics through the purchase of lifestyle commodities. The ever-expanding marketplace of such goods and services has transformed sexual identities and communities throughout the US. For these reasons, LGBT communities cannot be understood as oppositional to capitalism. Instead, capitalism "depend[s] on and generate[s] community," and communities—even alternative ones—can be "deployed to . . . facilitate the flow of capital."[18]

The growth of niche markets and consumer lifestyles is a boon for late capitalism. But it is less clear that the rise of the pink market has had positive effects for the majority of LGBT/queer people. Indeed, although marketers and the media paint gay men and sometimes lesbians as an affluent elite, research from at least the mid-1990s shows that this is a pernicious myth. As Amber Hollibaugh and Margot Weiss point out, research from 2013 revealed that bisexuals, lesbians, and gay men experience higher rates of poverty then heterosexuals. One in four bisexuals receive food stamps, more than one in five LGBT people who live alone report an income at or below the poverty level. In 2013, 2.4 million LGBT adults did not have enough money to feed themselves or their family. Poverty is compounded by sexism, racism, transphobia, disability, and other forms of structural oppression: people of color, trans people, and women—especially those who have a disability, live in rural regions, and are older—are much more likely to be poor. A 2011 study showed that trans people are four times more likely than the general population to live in poverty, and poverty rates among transgender people of color are particularly high—34 percent of black and 28 percent of Latina/o transgender people have household incomes of less than $10,000 per year. A lifetime of discrimination and criminalization renders LGBT people more vulnerable to the precarious conditions that face so many today struggling in the aftermath of neoliberal restructuring: living paycheck to paycheck, with limited opportunities to care adequately for oneself and one's kin, threatened by criminalized poverty and economic precarity.

The myth of gay affluence, which promotes the image of the acceptable gay consumer-citizen, blots from view the many LGBT people "who are manual workers, sex workers, unemployed, and imprisoned," queer and trans youth thrown out of their homes, homeless adults, and trans and queer poverty.[19] When LGBT people are only visible in the marketplace, non-white, non-middle-class, non-gender normative queer and trans people are shut out or rendered invisible; when LGBT politics is formulated around the desires of the consuming citizen, the neoliberal policies that keep so many LGBT/queer people precarious remain in place. The mainstream LGBT movement assists with this when it welcomes multinational corporations to sponsor pride parades or celebrates gay consumer or popular cultural achievements while ignoring the needs of the LGBT/queer poor and working-class people who make the rainbow paraphernalia and work in low-wage service or retail jobs and street economies in gay neighborhoods.[20] When LGBT activism has promoted the gay consumer-citizen at the cost of more radical and marginalized voices, it has sought political goals that benefit the wealthiest LGBT people at the cost of most.

3. Safe Spaces: Gay Gentrifiers/Dangerous Queers

In December 2010, the *New York Times* reported that "After 30 Years, Times Square Rebirth Is Complete." The project was a success. "Crime is down significantly from the days when pimps, prostitutes, drug addicts and dope pushers prowled Times Square and the Deuce, as that stretch of 42nd Street was known. The number of tourists is up 74 percent since 1993, to an estimated 36.5 million last year . . . Morgan Stanley, Allianz Global Investors, Viacom and Condé Nast now make their corporate homes there. . . . And while many billboards in Times Square were blank in 1979, today the area is a kaleidoscope of moving images depicting financial institutions, automakers and fashion houses, with the best spots on 1 Times Square's facade commanding as much as $4 million a year in rent." Tim Tompkins, president of the Times Square Alliance, told the *Times* that while "this place represents . . . the epitome of free-market capitalism . . . its transformation is due more to government intervention than just about any other development in the country." The upward state redistribution of resources in the form of tax incentives and corporate welfare that defines "free-market" neoliberalism has had profound effects on US LGBT life.

Begun in 1980, the Times Square 42nd Street Development Project follows similar paths to other US urban redevelopment projects.[21] The state condemned land parcels, evicting and razing businesses, and offered developers large property tax abatements and benefits such as zoning law changes to build new luxury skyscrapers and shopping malls. These transformations recreated the city as a landscape of consumption, orientated toward tourists and shoppers. Although gentrification in urban centers is not new, in the 1970s and 1980s neoliberal policies connected redevelopment to the privatization of other formerly public goods and services (education, healthcare, the arts, and even public parks). Newly privatized spaces of consumption drove out residents who could no longer afford to live where they worked. Rather than "gentrification," Martin Manalansan encourages us to use the phrase "neoliberal urban governance" to describe these processes, emphasizing that such transformations are not organic, but are orchestrated and enforced by the corporations and property owners who profit from them.[22]

The redevelopment of Times Square has resulted in the destruction of public sex cultures. Samuel Delany writes about the old Times Square—the sex workers, peep shows, and cruising places that redevelopment replaced with family- and tourist-friendly shopping experiences. Starting with the 1985 criminalization of bathhouses in New York City, Delany writes, "a notion of safety" ushered in safe sex, safe neighborhoods, safe cities, and safe (that is, committed and monogamous) relationships. "In the name of 'safety'" (or family values), developers, with city support, destroyed the publicly accessible institutions that supported unplanned and complex social and sexual encounters between different kinds of people—especially the cross-class and interracial intimacies that make for a thriving public sexual culture.[23] Delany's work makes clear that the "Disneyfication" of Times Square was not about safety, but about profit-making. In 1993, New York City began implementing more extensive "quality-of-life" interventions. Police targeted minor offenses such as jumping subway turnstiles, panhandling, and loitering. The next year, Mayor Rudolph Giuliani introduced new zoning policies to restrict strip clubs and erotic video stores and theaters to isolated nonresidential neighborhoods, prohibiting their proximity to schools, houses of worship, and other similar commercial establishments. By the end of the decade, Michael Warner warned, "a pall hangs over the public life of queers. . . . As in other US cities, sex publics in New York that have been built up over several decades—by the gay movement, by AIDS activism, and by countercultures of many different kinds—are now endangered by a new politics of privatization."[24]

The commodification of urban space meant that sexual cultures—including gay spaces— have been increasingly reduced to privatized spaces of consumption. Gay neighborhoods such as New York City's Village or San Francisco's Castro became tourist attractions and shopping/entertainment enclaves, capitalizing on the image of gay and lesbians as affluent, stylish consumers and taste-makers. Rather than representing vice or perversity as they had for most of the twentieth century, gays at the turn of the new millennium, David Bell and Jon Binnie argue, were increasingly "cast as model citizens of the urban renaissance, contributing towards the gentrification of commodifiable cosmopolitan residential and commercial areas."[25] At the same time, spaces for queers of color, queer youth, or poor queers—such as New York City's Chelsea piers—were razed and replaced with locked and gated parks and new condominium complexes. Redevelopment "is about fencing off unwanted colored [and queer] bodies," Manalansan writes, yet, rather than a target for intervention, it is celebrated by much of the LGBT press as "positive outcomes and developments for all queers."[26]

Like the rise of the same-sex marriage movement and the gay consumer-citizen, the reorientation of cities toward the wealthy obscures the queer poor people, street youth, people of color, people with disabilities, and trans people shut out from acceptable neoliberal citizenship. In cities across the US, LGBT activism since the 1980s has pitted the interests of white gay (and lesbian) middle-class residents/property-owners against young, queer and trans people of color, using "safety" as the language of power. In her history of gay and lesbian anti-violence activism, Christina Hanhardt shows how gay visibility and community has been used to justify the policing, targeting, and profiling of those assumed to be dangerous. In these imaginaries, wealthy gay consumers are good investors, cruising spaces and sexual zones should be privatized, and poor queer people, people of color, youth, trans people, and people with disabilities are rendered "risky," detrimental to "quality of life" and a potential threat to capital.

We therefore cannot look only at gains in "cultural visibility" for LGBT people to measure political and social progress. Historically, increased media visibility has been "directly connected to the criminalization of black people, trans people, people of color, and people doing sex work," Reina Gossett argues, because visibility projects tend to reinforce existing modes of sexual respectability.[27] This same dynamic exists today: the rise of media representations of trans women of color in 2014 and 2015, Gossett argues, corresponds to the highest recorded murder rates of those same women. LGBT campaigns for visibility—in the form of media visibility, marketing recognition, new gay-orientated business developments, or social recognition—have depended on the invisibility, criminalization, and abjection of queered others. As such, they have benefited from and reinforced neoliberal capitalist restructuring: the massive cuts in social programs (and their incomplete replacement by non-profit organizations shored up by corporate and major donor philanthropy), the privatization of public institutions and spaces, and the coercive policing of immigrant, racialized, and criminalized bodies that have occurred *alongside* the development of gay and lesbian commercial marketplaces and neighborhoods.

As with marriage rights and consumer citizenship, gay gentrification marks the triumph of the neoliberal distortion of gay liberation and social justice movements from the 1960s. As Duggan argues, in the era of New Homonormativity, " 'equality' becomes narrow, formal access to a few conservatizing institutions, 'freedom' becomes impunity for bigotry and vast inequalities in commercial life and civil society, the 'right to privacy' becomes domestic confinement, and democratic politics itself becomes something to be escaped . . . Welcome to the New World Order!"[28] Welcome to neoliberalism.

The Ends of Neoliberalism?

After the Great Recession of 2008, some scholars suggested that neoliberalism was over—that the deregulation, speculation, and free market policies that brought about this most recent crisis had been delegitimized. Most now agree that reports of its death were premature. Since neoliberalism has, for decades, transformed the way that the state creates and sustains new subjects and social relations best suited to new markets, the historical transformations that I detail in this essay—especially perhaps movement goals and visions—are not easily displaced.

Other scholars have argued that the language of freedom and choice so central to neoliberal ideology might be in retreat, or at least overwhelmed by a new emphasis on safety, security, and policing, especially after the events of 9/11. Susan Hyatt, for example, argues that "the idealized subject of neoliberal policy was the citizen-consumer who was 'responsibled' to make wise and prudent choices in the 'free market' of utilities and services, ranging from healthcare to schooling. In contrast, the idealized subject of the law-and-order state is now the citizen who both policies and agrees to be policed."[29] Still others argue that the carceral state—the explosive growth of the prison-industrial complex and new state security and surveillance apparatuses—is a continuation of, rather than a departure from, neoliberal policies.

In LGBT politics, the post 9/11 era marks a transition from homonormativity to what Jasbir Puar has called "homonationalism": the alignment of respectable LGBT citizen-subjects with the state and against other queered subjects, such as the terrorist, the criminal, the poor, and the undocumented, who face the harshest legal and extralegal techniques of the state and its related corporate interests.[30] As Karma Chávez argues, homonational logics that accept US state militarism as a prerequisite for national belonging are at work not only in campaigns such as the fight to repeal "Don't Ask, Don't Tell," but also in mainstream LGBT immigration politics. By prioritizing family reunification, such campaigns emphasized respectable, "deserving" same-sex bi-national families with higher income levels, allowing others to languish in militarized detention facilities; by supporting the DREAM Act, organizations accepted that conditional permanent residency would only extend to those youth who, among other criteria, possess "a clean criminal record and thus good moral standing" and attend either two years of college or serve at least two years in the military.[31] Another way homonationalism is pressed into the service of the state is through "pinkwashing," the use of gay-friendly images (such as tourist attractions or state support of same-sex marriage) to portray the state as tolerant and modern. In Israel and the US, even while hyper-securitized borders and an increasing surveillance-oriented state targets queered people for social death, pinkwashing perpetuates a civilizing narrative that justifies ongoing settler colonialism, occupation, and militarization in the name of anti-homophobia. These developments make use of and build upon neoliberal modes of extraction, securitization, and citizenship.

A final critique of neoliberalism concerns its utility as a concept. Some scholars, such as Catherine Kingfisher and Jeff Maskovsky, and John Clarke, have argued that "neoliberalism" has become a cant word, overused in scholarship that treats it as an abstract concept or actor in the world, rather than as a partial and unstable process. Others argue that "particularities and local categories and meanings" can be "erased when everything is subsumed under the framework of neoliberalism."[32] Still, there is a need for studies that take up neoliberalism not as a monolith, but as an assemblage, as "mobile calculative techniques of governing" in order to better understand divergent LGBT/queer projects and histories.[33]

These debates on the term itself reflect ongoing desires to better understand, historicize and critique the devastating effect global capitalism has had over the past forty years. In these projects, "neoliberalism" operates less as a fixed relation between the market, the state, and the subject, and more as a critique. Yet as we survey the impact neoliberal logics have had on the LGBT movement and queer culture since the 1970s, I think one of the greatest risks comes in neoliberalism's characteristic ability to reabsorb critique, recasting politics as freedom for the entrepreneurial self in the market. The absorption of social differences into new markets that I explored throughout this essay also plays out in the academy, where "politicized intellectual labor is simultaneously promoted and contained," perhaps especially in fields like queer studies.[34] In this context, we need to be especially mindful that our ideas risk being taken up, coopted and commodified. For neoliberalism describes not only the conditions that give rise to the sexual and economic politics that we seek to challenge but also to the social and political conditions of the contemporary US academy. This has included a restructuring of the academy in terms of the so-called "marketplace of ideas," the casualization of labor, and the privatization of education itself.

Even so, I find neoliberalism an essential concept for a project of historicizing queer sexual politics after the 1970s. The LGBT movement's focus on neoliberal goals—individual and family rights, formal legal equality, state protections, and market visibility—has, as Dean Spade argues, "come with enormous costs": missed opportunities for coalition and the alienation of many LGBT/queer people. Even more, the movement's turn toward "privatization, criminalization, and militarization have caused it to be incorporated into the neoliberal agenda in ways that not only ignore, but also directly disserve and further endanger and marginalize, those most vulnerable to regimes of homophobia and state violence."[35] A critique of neoliberalism in relation to LGBT communities and politics might help us avoid reinforcing the very systems that unevenly distribute life chances, security, and vulnerability. It would instead take account of the historical conditions that perpetuate queer and trans oppression today: histories of racialization and patriarchy, white supremacy, colonialism, state violence, and global capitalism.

For this reason, I want to end by pointing to the work of scholars and public intellectuals, activists and organizers who have and continue to fight against the rising global inequalities, dispossession, and precarity that goes by the name neoliberalism. I mean the left, feminist, and queer of color critique that I have drawn on throughout this essay that seeks to expand our knowledge of class and race as they intersect with sexuality and gender. And I also mean the ongoing political work of organizations aligned with liberationist, anti-capitalist, and justice projects that challenge the impact of the histories detailed in this essay—organizations such as Queers for Economic Justice, The Audre Lorde Project, FIERCE!, the Sylvia Rivera Law Project, Streetwise and Safe, Black and Pink, INCITE!, Against Equality, Communities United Against Violence, The Disability Justice Collective, Southerners on New Ground, Sex Work Outreach Project, Affinity, Gender JUST!, Critical Resistance, Project NIA, the Transformative Justice Law Project, and alliance movements such as #BlackLivesMatter.

Queer resistance to neoliberal sexual politics has been spearheaded by those most affected by these transformations: those who live in the intersections of economic precarity, racialized surveillance, and gender and sexual respectability politics; those whose lives are not protected by dignified marriage, respectable consumer citizenship, or streets made safe for property and profit. It is our task as cultural analysts to learn from these thinkers and activists, to defamiliarize what we have come to take for granted, so that we might move forward the vital work of understanding, confronting, and dismantling neoliberal logics.

Figure 8.1 Black Lives Matter disrupts the September 26, 2015 North Carolina Pride to call for solidarity with queer and gender nonconforming people of color, action against police brutality, and a recognition of the historical centrality of queer and trans people of color to LGBTQ liberation struggle.

Courtesy of Zaina Alsous.

Notes

1 David Harvey, *A Brief History of Neoliberalism* (Oxford: Oxford University Press, 2005), 2.
2 Wendy Brown, "Neoliberalism and the End of Liberal Democracy," in *Edgework: Critical Essays on Knowledge and Politics* (Princeton: Princeton University Press, 2005), 39–40.
3 Tejaswini Ganti, "Neoliberalism," *Annual Review of Anthropology* 43, no. 1 (2014): 94.
4 Harvey, *A Brief History of Neoliberalism*, 160–165.
5 Harvey, 3.
6 Aihwa Ong, *Neoliberalism as Exception: Mutations in Citizenship and Sovereignty* (Durham: Duke University Press, 2006), 11.
7 Lisa Duggan, *The Twilight of Equality? Neoliberalism, Cultural Politics, and the Attack on Democracy* (Boston: Beacon Press, 2003), 50.
8 Priya Kandaswamy, "State Austerity and the Racial Politics of Same-Sex Marriage in the US," *Sexualities* 11, no. 6 (2008): 707.
9 Cathy J. Cohen, "Punks, Bulldaggers, and Welfare Queens," *GLQ* 3 (1997): 453.
10 Cathy J. Cohen, "Obama, Neoliberalism, and the 2012 Election," *Souls* 14, no. 1–2 (2012): 22.
11 Syllabus to Obergefell. v. Hodges, 576 U.S. ___ (2015): 13, 17.
12 Obergefell. v. Hodges, 28.
13 Don Romesburg, "Where She Comes From: Locating Queer Transracial Adoption," *QED: A Journal in GLBTQ Worldmaking* 1, no. 3 (2014): 1–29.
14 For an exploration of the narrative of historical progress and its critique within queer US political history, see, in this volume, Marc Stein, "Law and Politics: 'Crooked and Perverse' Narratives of LGBT Progress."
15 Alexandra Chasin, *Selling Out: The Gay and Lesbian Movement Goes to Market* (New York: St. Martin's Press, 2000), 38.
16 John L. Comaroff and Jean Comaroff, "Criminal Justice, Cultural Justice: The Limits of Liberalism and the Pragmatics of Difference in the New South Africa," *American Ethnologist* 31, no. 2 (2004):

190; Jean Comaroff and John L Comaroff, "Millennial Capitalism: First Thoughts on a Second Coming," *Public Culture* 12, no. 2 (2000): 306.

17 David Bell and Jon Binnie, *The Sexual Citizen: Queer Politics and Beyond* (Malden, MA: Polity Blackwell Publishers, 2000), 6.

18 Miranda Joseph, *Against the Romance of Community* (Minneapolis: University of Minnesota Press, 2002), xxxi–ii. For the longer history of queer consumerism, see, in this volume, Stephen Vider, "Consumerism."

19 Rosemary Hennessy, *Profit and Pleasure: Sexual Identities in Late Capitalism* (New York: Routledge, 2000), 140–141.

20 In this volume, Sara Smith-Silverman's "Labor" chapter argues for a closer attention to class and work in US queer history.

21 See also, in this volume, Kwame Holmes, "The End of Queer Urban History?"

22 Martin F. Manalansan IV, "Race, Violence, and Neoliberal Spatial Politics in the Global City," *Social Text* 84–85 (2005): 154.

23 Samuel R. Delany, *Times Square Red, Times Square Blue* (New York: New York University Press, 1999), 121–122.

24 Michael Warner, *The Trouble with Normal: Sex, Politics and the Ethics of Queer Life* (New York: Free Press, 1999), 153. Also Lauren Berlant and Michael Warner, "Sex in Public," *Critical Inquiry* 24, no. 2 (1998): 547–566.

25 David Bell and Jon Binnie, "Authenticating Queer Space: Citizenship, Urbanism and Governance," *Urban Studies* 41, no. 9 (2004): 1815.

26 Manalansan, 151.

27 Jenny Marks, "Interview with Che and Reina Gossett," *Mask Magazine* 15, April 2015.

28 Duggan, *The Twilight of Equality?* 65–66.

29 Susan Brin Hyatt, "What Was Neoliberalism and What Comes Next? The Transformation of Citizenship in the Law-and-order State," *Policy worlds: Anthropology and the analysis of contemporary power* 14 (2011): 107.

30 See also, in this volume, Eithne Luibhéid, "Queer and Nation."

31 Karma R. Chávez, *Queer Migration Politics: Activist Rhetoric and Coalitional Possibilities* (Urbana: University of Illinois Press, 2013), 80.

32 Ganti, "Neoliberalism," 99.

33 Ong, *Neoliberalism as Exception*, 13.

34 Naomi Greyser and Margot Weiss, "Introduction: Left Intellectuals and the Neoliberal University," *American Quarterly* 64, no. 4 (2012): 790.

35 Dean Spade, *Normal Life: Administrative Violence, Critical Trans Politics, and the Limits of the Law.* (Brooklyn: South End Press 2011): 15.

Further Reading

Amar, Paul. *The Security Archipelago: Human-Security States, Sexuality Politics, and the End of Neoliberalism.* Duke University Press, 2013.

Badgett, M.V. Lee, *Money, Myths, and Change: The Economic Lives of Lesbians and Gay Men.* Chicago: University of Chicago Press, 2001.

Boyd, Nan Alamilla. "San Francisco's Castro District: From Gay Liberation to Tourist Destination." *Journal of Tourism and Cultural Change* 9, no. 3 (2011): 237–248.

Clarke, John. "Living With/in and Without Neo-liberalism." *Focaal* 2008, no. 51 (2008): 135–147.

Conrad, Ryan, ed. *Against Equality: Queer Revolution, Not Mere Inclusion.* Oakland: AK Press, 2014.

Dangerous Bedfellows, eds., *Policing Public Sex.* Boston: South End Press, 1996.

"Debate: Anthropology of Neoliberalism," *Social Anthropology* 20, nos. 1–3 (2012); 21, no. 1 (2013).

De Filippis, Joseph N. "Common Ground: The Queerness of Welfare Policy" *S&F Online: A New Queer Agenda* 10, no. 1–2 (2011).

D'Emilio, John. "Capitalism and Gay Identity." In *Powers of Desire: The Politics of Sexuality*, eds. Anne Snitow, Christine Stansell and Sharon Thompson, 100–113. New York: Monthly Review Press, 1983.

Eng, David L. *The Feeling of Kinship: Queer Liberalism and the Racialization of Intimacy.* Durham: Duke University Press, 2010.

Evans, David T. *Sexual Citizenship: the Material Construction of Sexualities.* New York: Routledge, 1993.

Ferguson, James. "The Uses of Neoliberalism." *Antipode* 41 (2010): 166–184.

Ferguson, Roderick A. *Aberrations in Black: Toward a Queer of Color Critique*. Minneapolis: University of Minnesota Press, 2004.

———. *The Reorder of Things: The University and Its Pedagogies of Minority Difference*. University of Minnesota Press, 2012.

Ferguson, Roderick A, and Grace Kyungwon Hong. "The Sexual and Racial Contradictions of Neoliberalism." *Journal of Homosexuality* 59, no. 7 (2012): 1057–1064.

Foucault, Michel. *The Birth of Biopolitics: Lectures at the Collège De France, 1978–79*. New York: Palgrave Macmillan, 2008.

Gane, Nicholas. "The Emergence of Neoliberalism: Thinking Through and Beyond Michel Foucault's Lectures on Biopolitics." *Theory, Culture & Society* 31, no. 4 (2014): 3–27.

Gluckman, Amy, and Betsy Reed. *Homo Economics: Capitalism, Community, and Lesbian and Gay Life*. New York: Routledge, 1997.

Hanhardt, Christina B. *Safe Space: Gay Neighborhood History and the Politics of Violence*. Durham: Duke University Press, 2013.

Haritaworn, Jin, Adi Kuntsman, and Silvia Posocco, eds. *Queer Necropolitics*. New York: Routledge, 2014.

Hollibaugh, Amber, and Margot Weiss. "Queer Precarity and the Myth of Gay Affluence." *New Labor Forum* 24, no. 3 (2015): 18–27.

Jameson, Fredric. *Postmodernism, Or, The Cultural Logic of Late Capitalism*. Durham: Duke University Press, 1991.

Jones, Daniel S., *Masters of the Universe: Hayek, Friedman, and the Birth of Neoliberal Politics*. Princeton: Princeton University Press, 2012.

Kingfisher, Catherine, and Jeff Maskovsky, eds. "The Limits of Neoliberalism," special issue of *Critique of Anthropology* 28, no. 2 (2008): 115–126.

Lemke, Thomas. "'The Birth of Bio-Politics': Michel Foucault's Lectures at the College De France on Neo-Liberal Governmentality." *Economy and Society* 30, no. 2 (2001): 190–207.

Lowe, Donald M. *The Body in Late-capitalist USA*. Durham: Duke University Press, 1995.

Luibhéid, Eithne, and Lionel Cantú Jr., eds. *Queer Migrations: Sexuality, U.S. Citizenship, and Border Crossings*. Minneapolis: University of Minnesota Press, 2005.

Maskovsky, Jeff. "Do We All 'Reek of the Commodity'? Consumption and the Erasure of Poverty in Lesbian and Gay Studies." In *Out in Theory: The Emergence of Lesbian and Gay Anthropology*, eds. Ellen Lewin and William L Leap. Urbana: University of Illinois Press, 2002.

Mink, Gwendolyn. *Whose Welfare?* Ithaca: Cornell University Press, 1999.

Mogul, Joey L., Andrea J. Ritchie, and Kay Whitlock. *Queer (In) justice: The Criminalization of LGBT People in the United States*. Boston: Beacon Press, 2011.

Mohanty, Chandra Talpade. "Transnational Feminist Crossings: On Neoliberalism and Radical Critique." *Signs* 38, no. 4 (2013): 967–991.

Nair, Yasmin. "Queer Immigrants, the Shackles of Love, and the Invisibility of the Prison Industrial Complex." In *Captive Genders: Trans Embodiment and the Prison Industrial Complex*, ed.s Nat Smith and Eric Stanley. Oakland: AK Press, 2011.

Pellegrini, Ann. "Consuming Lifestyle: Commodity Capitalism & Transformations in Gay Identity," In *Queer Globalizations: Citizenship & the Afterlife of Colonialism*. Ed. Arnaldo Cruz and Martin F. Manalansan. New York: New York University Press, 2002

Puar, Jasbir. *Terrorist Assemblages: Homonationalism in Queer Times*. Durham: Duke University Press, 2007.

———. "Rethinking Homonationalism." *International Journal of Middle East Studies* 45 (2013): 336–339.

Reddy, Chandan. *Freedom with Violence: Race, Sexuality, and the US State*. Durham: Duke University Press, 2011.

Richardson, Diane. "Sexuality and Citizenship." *Sociology* 32, no. 1 (1998): 83–100.

Roberts, Dorothy E. *Killing the Black Body: Race, Reproduction, and the Meaning of Liberty*. New York: Vintage Books, 1997.

Rofel, Lisa. *Desiring China: Experiments in Neoliberalism, Sexuality, and Public Culture*. Durham: Duke University Press, 2007.

Rose, Nikolas. *Powers of Freedom: Reframing Political Thought*. Cambridge: Cambridge University Press, 2007.

Sears, Alan. "Queer Anti-Capitalism: What's Left of Lesbian and Gay Liberation?" *Science & Society* 69, no. 1 (2005): 92–112.

Sender, Katherine. *Business, Not Politics: The Making of the Gay Market*. New York: Columbia University Press, 2004.

Smith, Anna Marie. *Welfare Reform and Sexual Regulation*. Cambridge: Cambridge University Press, 2007.

Spade, Dean. "Trans Politics on a Neoliberal Landscape," *Temple Political and Civil Rights Law Review* 18, no. 2 (2009): 353–373.

Weiss, Margot. "Gay Shame and BDSM Pride: Neoliberalism, Privacy and Sexual Politics." *Radical History Review* 100 (2008): 87–101.

——. *Techniques of Pleasure: BDSM and the Circuits of Sexuality*. Durham: Duke University Press, 2011.

Whitehead, Jaye Cee. *The Nuptial Deal: Same-sex Marriage and Neo-liberal Governance*. University of Chicago Press, 2011.

PART TWO

Spaces and Places

9

QUEER ARCHIVES

From Collections to Conceptual Framework

Kate Eichhorn

In the early twenty-first century, a persistent preoccupation with queer archives, queer archiving and what is sometimes simply referred to as *the queer archive* has resulted in the publication of dozens of books, edited collections and special issues of journals, as well as events ranging from conferences to exhibitions. The fact that archives appear in this volume alongside spaces and places as central as bodies and nations evidently speaks to their status in contemporary scholarship. Interestingly, much of the current scholarship on queer archives and archiving has been generated by scholars working outside the field of history (e.g., in media studies, cultural studies and sociology) and by queer artists and activists working on the borders of (or entirely outside) the academy. How might we account for this archival preoccupation?

In this essay I suggest that the queer preoccupation with archives cannot be fully explained in relation to the broader "archival turn" in critical theory that is often traced to the early works of Michel Foucault and the late works of Jacques Derrida being brought into English translation. Queer archives, both as sites of preservation and as a conceptual framework, have a specificity in lesbian, gay, bisexual, and transgender communities that is deeply entangled with these communities' historical circumstances, constraints, political aspirations and desires. It is also notable that the preoccupation with archives in gay, lesbian, bisexual and transgender communities long predates the "archival turn" more broadly. The queer turn towards the archive arguably happened in the late 1960s to early 1970s, not in the mid-1990s.

Above all else, I maintain that the queer preoccupation with archives, both real and imagined, is linked to the extrinsic value that queer people have come to attach to documents and artifacts of all kinds. After all, as much as queer archives are about preserving specific documents and artifacts, they are spaces where all the detritus of queer lives is imagined to gain a value that it was hitherto denied. Collected under the broader categories of gay, lesbian, bisexual, transgender and/or queer, documents and artifacts not only acquire a heightened degree of visibility (a visibility they may have never had in the first place) but also a heightened potential for signification. In queer archives, a photograph may function on a representational level (offering, for example, evidence of lesbian or gay sociality in another era), but it also may function as one object among many that has the potential to make certain histories possible. Moreover, documents and artifacts that may have not previously been read as queer may in turn be *queered* when placed in the context of a queer collection. It is this point of departure that I wish to take for understanding both the growth of queer archives since the 1970s and the attraction of *the queer archive* as a theoretical concept and curatorial trope among queer scholars, artists and activists since the 1990s.

Queer Collections: Private, Community and Institutional

Many of the largest and most important collections of queer materials in existence today started out as personal collections, often housed in the homes of individual gay, lesbian, bisexual and transgender collectors. The Lesbian Herstory Archives, which now occupies three stories of a brownstone in Brooklyn, first took shape in Joan Nestle and Deborah Edel's kitchen on the Upper West Side of New York City. The ONE National Gay and Lesbian Archives grew out of Jim Kepner's personal collection and was originally housed in his West Hollywood apartment. A large portion of the materials found in the Black Gay and Lesbian Archive Project, which is now housed at the New York Public Library's Schomburg Collection, were originally part of project director and archivist Steven Fullwood's personal collection. In addition, dozens of individual collections housed within larger queer collections—such as Cornell University's Human Sexuality Collection—exist today because individual LGBT individuals decided to start collecting their own documents and artifacts and those of their communities.

Queer collections not only frequently begin in the private sphere but also have often taken shape under the unique constraints of queer life. Many started out in the closet, so to speak, and originally functioned as sites of retreat for their collectors. Before online access to LGBT lives and support groups was available, a stash of lesbian pulps or gay porn magazines, often purchased and accumulated with great effort and risk, meant much more than the average stack of books or magazines. For obvious reasons, then, many of these collections, which may otherwise appear quite unremarkable, survived intact. As Ann Cvetkovich maintains, they often also bear the traces of the affects, and in some cases the traumas, that gave rise to their existence in the first place. The feeling that these stacks of papers and collections of photographs are somehow greater than their material worth—a shared recognition of their extrinsic value—is arguably what has historically driven the preservation impulse in queer communities and continues to do so.

While LGBT people were collecting the documentary traces of their lives and communities long before the rise of the modern LGBT rights movement, the migration of private collections into public institutions is part of the community's more recent history. In the United States, it is a history that belongs largely to a post-Stonewall Era. Indeed, it was in the context of gay liberation and lesbian feminist activism that public gay and lesbian archives started to appear. Three collections—the oldest and largest collections of LGBT materials in the United States today—are integral to understanding this history: the ONE Archives, the Lesbian Herstory Archives and Cornell University's Human Sexuality Collection. While there is little doubt that the development of research collections has been a shared vision for queer communities since the early 1970s, the content, mandate, location and funding of theses archives have taken myriad forms, often raised difficult ethical and political questions, and sometimes placed community and professional archivists at odds.[1]

The ONE Archives

The ONE Archives, officially known as the ONE National Gay & Lesbian Archives at University of Southern California, bills itself as the world's largest collection of LGBT materials. It is also the first known queer archive in the United States. In the 1940s, Jim Kepner started to collect gay materials, including newspaper clippings, books by well-known gay writers such as

Radclyffe Hall, and anything else he could find. After moving to Los Angeles, Kepner become an active member of the Mattachine Society and eventually a regular contributor to the *ONE Magazine*. Through his involvement, Kepner found himself at the center of early gay rights struggles and a *de facto* archivist of the early gay rights movement in the United States. While *ONE Magazine* eventually ceased publication, Kepner remained involved in activist and educational projects. In 1971, Kepner named his personal collection the Western Gay Archives. Increasingly, it started to function as an open archive, despite remaining in his apartment. It was only in 1979 that Kepner, largely using his own funds, moved the collection to a storefront space. The collection grew to 25,000 volumes under a new name, the National Gay Archives, and, later, the International Gay & Lesbian Archives. The archives spent over a decade at street level, where the materials were accessible to the community in a way that exceeds both the private space of the home and public space of a university library system. In the 1980s, the collections' store front location helped turn the archives into a hub of activity not only for archiving gay and lesbian history but also for other community-based endeavors. By the time of Kepner's death, the archives had negotiated the collection's transfer to the University of Southern California.

In many respects, the ONE Archives has had at least three lives. First, it was the impassioned private collecting project of an early gay activist who recognized the value and urgency of documenting his own history and history of the communities to which he belonged. Second, it became a publicly accessible center of community collecting and organizing—a catalyst for documentation and for change in the present. Finally, the collection arrived at its current destination—a university library where it exists in an institutional setting yet remains true to its roots by ensuring the collections it houses can be accessed by both academic researchers and a much broader spectrum of the community. Notably, the separate building in which the ONE Archives is housed on the University of Southern California campus was formally a frat house that had been shut down by the university. While the building's transition from frat house to LGBT archives is evidently ironic, it also appropriately means that the archives that started in Kepner's home have ultimately returned to an architectural structure originally designed for living. It is worth noting that the building's design also dictates somewhat atypical work practices for an archive (e.g., due to the nature of the space, staff frequently use the archive's central research space to process collections and as a result, work alongside visiting researchers).

The Lesbian Herstory Archives

While the Lesbian Herstory Archives (LHA) also started out in a private residence, it has ultimately followed a very different path. From the perspective of many archivists, the LHA's archival standards are far from exemplary. Videocassettes line the walls of the archive's working kitchen. Audiocassettes and records reside in a damp basement alongside banners, posters and other ephemera. To avoid privileging patrilineal authority, the collective's volunteer archivists alphabetize the books by authors' first names. Most photos are kept in albums and boxes in what appears to be a frighteningly disorganized storage cupboard located in the archive's dining room/office, just as they might be stored at a grandmother or great aunt's house. On the second floor, books, magazines and filing cabinets crowd two rooms. Personal fonds, some with detailed finding aids and some without, are crammed into boxes in a small windowless space. The house carries the distinct smell of rotting paper, especially on the second floor, but everything is lesbian and lesbians are clearly in charge. This has always been an integral part of the archive's principles.

The LHA states explicitly that the Archives' principles are "a radical departure from conventional archival practices." Their practices "are inclusive and non-institutional." Early on,

Figure 9.1 Longtime lesbian activism and Harlem Renaissance dancer Mabel Hampton (l) with
longtime archival coordinator Paula Grant (e. 1980s) at the Lesbian Herstory Archives,
which houses Hampton's collection.

Photo courtesy of the Lesbian Herstory Archives.

as Nestle acknowledge in her 1990 publication, "Will to Remember," "We realized that the
word 'archives' sounded formal and distancing to many of the women we wanted to reach
[and] we would have to dedicate many years to spreading the word about this new undertaking."[2] They did this by quite literally bringing the archives to the community, at times hauling
materials to churches, synagogues, bars and private homes, anywhere they were invited to speak.
As stated in the LHA mission, "All Lesbian women must have access to the Archives; no
academic, political, or sexual credentials will be required for use of the collection; race and
class must be no barrier for use or inclusion." Over the years, the archives' understanding of
who might be recognized as a lesbian woman has been contested, especially by the transgender
community, expanded, and remains open to revision, as new members bring their own
generational understandings of "lesbian" to bear. On a related note, the LHA maintains that
the archives "shall be housed within the community, not on an academic campus that is by
definition closed to many women." This, of course, explains why the LHA has maintained a
residential archive with a caretaker living onsite. In addition, the LHA has always sustained
a commitment to engaging in the "political struggles of all Lesbians." Related to this goal is a
commitment to ensuring that the archive will always been overseen by lesbians. Their mandate
explicitly states that "Archival skills shall be taught, one generation of Lesbians to another,
breaking the elitism of traditional archives" and that the "community should share in the work

of the Archives." The final and arguably most important aspect of the LHA's mandate is its funding structure. Funding, the mandate emphasizes, "shall be sought from within the communities the Archives serves, rather than from outside sources," and "The Archives will never be sold nor will its contents be divided."[3]

Thus, unlike most other large queer collections, which over time have exceeded their community mandates and been bequeathed to established university libraries or archives, the LHA's guiding principles have ensured that the collection has remained in the community.[4] Importantly, it has also remained immune to the pressures of outside funders. The LHA anticipated that with funding and institutional support come restrictions and compromises. Rejection of external funding has placed the onus on collective members to ensure that the archives continues to grow and preserve its holdings. It has also made certain types of projects, such as costly digital preservation projects, extremely challenging.

Yet the LHA stands as a remarkable testament to the persistence and innovation of the lesbian community.[5] The women who have been part of the collective have deployed a remarkable range of DIY approaches to archival labor that have in turn served as a template for other activist- and community-based collections around the world. Unlike many queer and feminist collections whose mandates have arguably been diluted by migrating from community to institutional spaces, the LHA has done more than preserve the everyday documents and artifacts of lesbians, they have preserved and maintained an early approach to queer community archiving that archives such as the ONE Archives have had to relinquish.

The Mariposa Collection/Cornell University's Human Sexuality Collection

In the 1970s, simultaneous to the inauguration of the Western Gay Archives and the early development of the LHA, the Mariposa Education and Research Foundation started to preserve materials related to gay liberation and, more broadly, human sexuality. Focusing on the American gay rights movement since the late 1940s, then-president of Mariposa Bruce Voeller envisioned an educational center that would serve researchers and activists alike. In 1988, the donation of the collection to Cornell's Rare and Manuscript Collections launched that university's Human Sexuality Collection.

The Mariposa Collection has somewhat different roots than Kepner's and Edel and Nestle's early collecting endeavors. Voeller, a biochemist by training, was involved in gay rights activism but his orientation was often focused on mainstream approaches of recognition, such as legal gains. As such, the collection does not have the same grassroots origins as many other major collections of LGBT materials. It was developed in and for a research institute. The collection holds a vast range of materials, including the papers of major LGBT organizations (e.g., National Gay and Lesbian Task Force (NGLTF), Parents, Families and Friends of Lesbians and Gays (PFLAG), Human Rights Campaign (HRC) and Gay and Lesbian Alliance Against Defamation (GLAAD).

While following a somewhat different history than many other LGBT archival collections, the importance of the Mariposa Collection's development cannot be underestimated. In many respects, the collection's location within a research institute solidified early on the importance of developing LGBT collections for research purposes. The legitimacy afforded to the collection by virtue of its affiliation with a research institute versus community center also had more far-reaching impacts (e.g., by making it easier for academic researchers to obtain travel grants to visit the collection). Most notably, of course, the collection's migration from the Mariposa Foundation to the Division of Rare and Manuscript Collections at the Cornell University Library in 1988 signaled the growing legitimacy of LGBT histories in the academy. The collection's establishment both was supported by the rise of queer studies and sexuality studies at the time and supported the continued growth of both of these fields in the late 1980s to 1990s.

Other Queer Archives and Queer Special Collections

Over the past two decades, the desire to establish stand-alone queer archives and to further develop queer collections in established archives has continued to grow. Newer collections range from smaller regional holdings, to dedicated collections in university archives, to digital projects. Many of these collections are listed in the Lesbian and Gay Archives Roundtable's *Lavender Legacies Guide.*

Some of these archives are identity-based, such as the Black Gay and Lesbian Archives housed at New York Public Library's Schomburg Collection in Harlem. That the Black Gay and Lesbian Archives exists reflects archivist Steven Fullwood's recognition of the fact that there were virtually no libraries or archives dedicated to the collection of black and queer materials. In Washington, the Latino GLBT History Project, another archival project started by an individual collector in a private home—in this case, in the home of José Gutierrez's—seeks to "collect, preserve and educate the public about the history, culture, heritage, arts, social and rich contributions of the Latino GLBT community in metropolitan Washington, D.C."[6] In 2004, the University of Michigan launched the National Transgender Archive and Library after acquiring the more than 1500 titles collected by Dallas Denny, the former editor of *Transgender Tapestry*.[7] Other collections have built up in relation to sexual subcultures more broadly defined. Albeit not entirely comprised of gay, lesbian, bisexual and transgender materials, by all intents and purposes the Leather Archives and Museum is a queer collection committed to preserving both the documents and artifacts of a wide range of sex subcultures.[8] In addition, many regional archives have developed over the past decade, including in areas with less well-documented and widely recognized histories. The Lesbian, Gay, Bisexual, Transgender, Queer Collection at the Indiana University South Bend Archives, for example, seeks to document queer life in a region broadly known as Michiana (a region that stretches across the Indiana and Michigan state borders).

Like many smaller regional collections, the collection at the Indiana University South Bend Archives may in fact be more aptly described as an oral history project with accompanying material documentation than an archival collection. To date, the collection holds nineteen oral histories alongside a small amount of related ephemera. Notably, the LGBT collection at the Indiana University South Bend Archives was also the result of a productive collaboration between community archivists and university archivists.[9] Oral histories are not only important to building up queer archives in regions were gay, lesbian, bisexual and transgender histories have historically existed on the margins but also, in some cases, in larger urban gay centers, such as San Francisco. When the GLBT History Museum in San Francisco's Castro neighborhood sought to launch an exhibit focusing on the lives of Asian Pacific Islanders (API), they discovered only 2 of the museum's 709 collections came from queer API donors. Oral histories were collected to help fill in a history that was absent from the broader collection. As a result, community members were also given an opportunity to become active agents in the collection building that is part of the museum and archive's established mandate.[10]

Perhaps one of the most significant queer collections to develop since the late 1990s is the ACT UP New York Collection at the New York Public Library. Comprised of over 234 boxes of materials—many of which have since been preserved on microfilm and/or digitized and made available online—the ACT UP Collection offers access to one of the most tumultuous chapters in queer US history. While the ONE Archives, LHA and Human Sexuality Collection represent eclectic collections comprised of myriad materials donated by individuals and organizations, the ACT UP Collection in many respects is a more traditional collection, insofar as it represents one organization's fonds. Yet, because of the number of people who circulated through ACT UP New York as volunteers, the collection is much more that the administrative memory of an organization. The collection contains letters and receipts and meeting minutes but also works by well-known artists, snippets of gossip and ephemera from hundreds of actions and protests. As part of the queer community's relatively recent history, the collection is also different in terms of its temporality. It is home to the words of many people who died much younger than they would have without the arrival of the AIDS epidemic in the 1980s, and of many people still active in queer struggles today.[11]

In many respects, the ACT UP New York Collection demonstrates how personal relationships and affects structure queer archives, even those that may, on the surface, appear to adhere to more traditional archival standards. As Marita Sturken suggests, however, archiving the ephemera of the AIDS epidemic also raises other challenges. As much as the crisis was a medical one, it was also a crisis of representation that resulted in a vast archive of materials. As Sturken observes, "The archives of the AIDS epidemic embody a set of contradictions: the work they contain was meant to be immediate, in the moment, on the street, and carried a particular kind of temporal meaning. The idea of an AIDS activist poster having historical value was not a part of its initial intention."[12] Indeed, the materials that were produced by AIDS activists were in fact typically produced to be easily and endlessly reproduced. As a result, what is being preserved in archives today are not, in most instances, precious one-of-a-kind documents but rather photocopies—in some cases, photocopies of photocopies of photocopies—materials that could be reproduced again in the present if there was still a reason to do so. The value of placing these materials in an archive, then, has less to do preserving fragile, one-of-kind documents and more to do with ensuring that the vast archive of materials connected to the movement remains united and as a result, in a position to carry forward the complex and at times contradictory story of the AIDS activist movement.

As the above examples illustrate, queer archives, broadly defined, have developed under very different conditions over time. While it may be tempting to suggest that the LHA is more vulnerable due to its decision to reject external funding and partnerships, the LHA's decision to remain independent and community driven has not, in fact, led to its demise. By contrast, there are also examples of smaller feminist and queer collections getting lost, to some extent, because they migrated from a private or community collection to an institutional archive. After all, while the individual papers of gay, lesbian, bisexual or transgender people are well preserved in many public and university archives, depending on how a collection is processed (e.g., whether or not an individual's queer identity is brought to the surface by the archivist writing the finding aid and more importantly how this identity is constructed in the finding aid), the queerness of the collection may or may not be preserved along with the papers. While this is arguably no longer the pressing concern it was in the past, at least when the LHA was founded in the early 1970s, it was still the case that a lesbian's papers donated to an established institution may be processed without the word lesbian ever being linked to the collection.

It is important to emphasize, however, that an institutional context does not necessarily preclude community access. Queer archives housed in public library systems or university archives are not necessarily divorced from their communities of origin. The ONE Archives, for example, continues to foster community access and collaboration through its exhibits and events, including exhibitions by contemporary artists whose work draws on materials from queer archives.

Queering the Archive

Alongside the development of stand-alone queer archives and queer collections, it is important to consider the impact of attempts to *queer* the archive and most notably to *queer* archival practices and standards. Admittedly, *queering* is a somewhat slippery term that has at times been taken for granted and at other moments been heavily contested both in and outside queer communities. Generally speaking, however, to queer something is now understood to signify either reading something as queer that has historically not been read as queer, or altering something to bring it into alignment with queer values and/or practices. Applied to the archive, queering has at least two implications.

First, queering happens when materials that may have historically not be been interpreted as relevant to queer lives are interpreted through a queer lens. This is the sort of queering involved in reading diaries or personal letters of cohabitating nineteenth-century spinsters (women in so-called "Boston marriages") as evidence of early forms of queer family.[13] This queering is also evident in attempts to read homosociality as eroticism into accounts of male soldiers huddled together in the trenches. Recovering queer moments and subjects that once could only be alluded to and not represented, and imagining the queer possibilities of lives in places where queerness may or may not have been present is by no means an uncontroversial practice nor one that transcends ethical considerations. The impetus to queer the historical record has proven important, but at times resulted in research more at home in the realm of fiction that history *per se*. Of course, salvaging queer fictions or semi-fictions is by no means necessarily problematic.

The archival inventions of queer artists such as Nina Levitt, Sharon Hayes and Andrea Geyer are important artistically and historically. For example, Levitt's 1991 photograph, *Submerged (for Alice Austen)*, reprints and partially erases an 1891 photograph of two female couples embracing, taken by early lesbian photographer Alice Austen.[14] In the process, Levitt asks us to consider what aspects of lesbian history are submerged, even when documented, as in Austen's original photograph. Similarly, Andrea Geyer, by redeploying archival photographs and texts, and Sharon Hayes, by putting the gestures, slogans and iconography of earlier eras of feminist and queer movements back into circulation, reveal the extent to which archives and archival documents have come to inform a queer archival imaginary.[15] Queering historical records has, among other things, played an integral role in foregrounding the extrinsic value of documents and artifacts in a context where material traces may function as evidence of both what was and what could have been or might still be.

Second, queering happens when archivists choose to intervene in established archival practices in an effort to open up new possibilities for LGBT materials to circulate and gain visibility. As Alana Kumbier emphasizes in *Ephemeral Material: Queering the Archive*, queering the archive can take place at the level of development, access or description. Most obviously, one might queer an archive by developing collections with queer content. This has been going on at NYU's Fales Library and Special Collections since the early 1990s, when the collection's longstanding director, Marvin Taylor, started to collect materials related to New York's downtown art scene. The Downtown Collection is not an explicitly queer collection, but since New York's downtown art scene has always been home to many queer artists, the collection's development created a home for many of their papers. The collection also exists in part because Taylor recognized—at the height of the AIDS epidemic—that the records of downtown artists were at risk of being lost: "One of the things I was doing was desperately trying to save a history of a place and people who at that point were dying. In some instances their papers were being thrown out."[16] Developing queer-related collections also changes institutional archives. Queer collections breed more queer collections. Taylor's work meant that the Fales Special Collection archives has, over time, become home to similar holdings. The Riot Grrrl Collection, which is also not an exclusively queer collection but a very queer collection nevertheless, was developed at Fales, in this case under the direction of senior archivist Lisa Darms, in part because by 2010, Fales was already known as a queer-oriented university archive. The presence of a queer collection in an archive might be said, then, to have a viral effect that in turn has an impact on who donates and on the types of materials donated over time.

One might also queer institutional archives from the inside by creating policies and procedures designed to accommodate queer records. Queer collections, donated by individuals, organizations, and loosely based collectives frequently entail especially complex negotiations (e.g., regarding access and privacy). An archivist's decision to come up with solutions to the problems posed by these queer collections can work to queer a traditional institutional archive by bringing about subsequent policy changes. At Barnard College, for example, librarian Jenna Freedman founded the Barnard Zine Collection, which has a mandate to collect zines by girls and women (cis- and transgender) with an emphasis on zines by women of color. While the collection does include an archive of zines (preserved in the college's archive), ensuring the collection is accessible is central to Freedman's mandate. As a result, she also maintains an open stacks collection in the library, which any student or member of the public can access. In addition, Freedman regularly has contact with the zine community, especially the queer and transgender zine community. As part of her professional work, she negotiates issues that many archivists and librarians would never imagine negotiating as part of their job (e.g., changing the authorship of a zine produced by a writer who has over time changed their gender affiliation and name). In short, just as gender and sexuality are fluid, so too are the policies that guide Freedman's feminist and queer zine collection at the Barnard Library.[17]

Finally, queering the archive can happen at the level of processing materials and authoring finding aids. As finding aids are increasingly digitized and made fully searchable using online search engines, the language used to describe individual records is more important than ever. What is and is not described can have a profound impact on whether or not a collection is accessed, by whom and for what intent. After all, when authoring a finding aid, describing something as a "Flyer, xeroxed" is not the same as describing something as a "Flyer for queer dungeon party, xeroxed." These decisions—often quite subjective—ultimately have a significant impact on the archival visibility of subjects, events and practices. In short, one can queer an archive by authoring a finding aid with the aim of rendering visible its queer content. Notably, despite assumptions that queer archives must be counter archives (archives that exist outside the constraints of formal institutions), there are many ways in which professional archivists queer their institutional archives at the level of development, processing and access. This work is often invisible, however, especially to people outside professional archival circles.

The Queer Archive as Theoretical and Curatorial Trope

Before the rise of queer theory and queer studies, lesbian, gay and sexuality archives and special collections had already been established across the United States and in several other countries (e.g., Canada, Germany and the United Kingdom). Individual and collective archiving endeavors arguably laid the groundwork for the rise of queer theory and queer studies in the 1980s and beyond. This is sometimes regrettably not given as much attention as it should in contemporary queer theoretical investigations of archives and archiving, where the archive has come to stand in for all kinds of things. Many archivists, charged with the often complex and laborious work of acquiring collections, negotiating collections' terms with donors and processing collections, maintain that the queer archive (referred to throughout this essay as *the queer archive*) that haunts queer theory and cultural production is not necessarily an archive *per se*. Still, as a conceptual framework, *the queer archive* has proven powerful and persistent.

Queer theory has arguably come to use the concept of the archive as shorthand for nearly any collection, any assemblage of fragmented thoughts, any curious assembly of queer memories or references culled from high and low culture. In *An Archive of Feelings*, Ann Cvetkovich adopts the concept of the archive as a way to bring together a vast array of objects of study, from texts and popular music to cinematic and visual artifacts. Laurent Berlant's *Queen of America* adopts the concept of the archive to stand in for a counter cultural canon of texts through which to rethink American life. In *In a Queer Time and Place*, Jack Halberstam refers to archives as a "a theory of cultural relevance, a construction of collective memory, and a complex record of queer activity." In *Cruising Utopia*, Jose Muñoz declares, "The archives is a fiction. Nobody knows that better than queers."[18] In the introduction to a special issue of the *Radical History Review* focusing on the subject of queer archives, co-editors Daniel Marshall, Kevin P. Murphy and Zeb Tortorici describe "the queer archive" as "evasive and dynamic," emphasizing that it has become "an exemplary space for academic, activist, and community contests over the proper or desirable boundaries of sex, gender, and knowledge."[19]

The queer archive has provided queer theorists with a way to rationalize bringing together often surprising and seemingly disparate objects of study. *The queer archive* has also come to stand in for something missing—a home, center, nation or stable notion of community. As Kumbier, a librarian who writes about archives, observes, despite the fact that these scholars may not always "engage conventional archives," we can nevertheless appreciate "how they draw our attention to the limits of existing archives."[20] One might then conclude that the concept of *the queer archive* does not necessarily work against the mandates of actual material archives. Indeed, Kumbier maintains this holds true on at least three important levels. First, theorists remind us that gay, lesbian, bisexual and transgender records often are especially eclectic and may include all sorts of ephemera traditionally excluded from archives (e.g., buttons, t-shirts and props used in political actions). Second, queer theory's preoccupation with archives has foregrounded the extent to which archives are structured by feelings and more specifically shared traumas. Finally, and perhaps most importantly, queer theorists have demonstrated the extent to which archives are structured by relationships (e.g., personal connections to donors) but also by the work of participant-archivists or archivists engaged in the passionate act of documenting their own community.[21] While many professional archivists remain hesitant to openly discuss how important relationships are to collection building, there is no question that many collections exist in archives simply because an archivist knew the papers existed or were at danger of being lost (as already noted, this was an impetus behind the Downtown Collection at Fales Library and Archives) or because someone with a collection happened to know an archivist and recognize the possibility that their papers may be of value to someone other than themselves.

Queer archives, queer collections housed in archives, and queering archives are all important. For queer history to be the rich and diverse field it is today, community and professional archivists have had to create and continue to make the collection and preservation of queer materials a priority. Indeed, one might make the argument that early queer archival endeavors—the work of community archivists like Jim Kepner, Joan Nestle, Deborah Edel and Bruce Voeller—were precisely what laid the groundwork for queer studies and sexuality studies in the late twentieth century. Queer theory, however, has arguably helped many of these earlier endeavors gain increased exposure and highlighted how queer archives work in the present.

Queer archives have done more than function in a formal way to preserve queer histories. Beyond preservation, queer archives, much like feminist archives, have at times functioned as clearinghouses—places to access information vital to addressing political and legal struggles in the present. Queer archives have also functioned as sites of community organizing. Finally, to speak of *the queer archive* is to speak of a collective history that exceeds the bounds of representation or preservation. It is to evoke all the excess, trauma, struggle, and passion that is synonymous with queer lives. Queer archives are places where the material residue of queer lives reside and spaces where future queer materialities not yet realized continue to be imagined.

Notes

1 See also, in this volume, Marcia Gallo, "Organizations."
2 Joan Nestle, "Will to Remember" *Feminist Theory* 34 (1990): 86–94.
3 "Principles," Lesbian Herstory Archives, www.lesbianherstoryarchives.org/history.html, accessed July 30, 2015.
4 Along with the Lesbian Herstory Archives, another large collection that has remained in community hands is the Gay, Lesbian, Bisexual, Transgender Historical Society in San Francisco.
5 For more on the particular opportunities and challenges of creating lesbian histories, see, in this volume, Julie R. Enszer, "Lesbian History: Spirals of Imagination, Marginalization, Creation and Erasure."
6 Latino GLBT History Project, www.latinoglbthistory.org/about-our-organization, accessed July 30, 2015.
7 Ashely Dinges, "Library Opens Transgendered Collection," *Michigan Daily*, March 26, 2004 www.michigandaily.com/content/library-opens-transgendered-collection. Accessed October 19, 2017.
8 Leather Archives & Museum, www.leatherarchives. org/home.html, accessed August 8, 2015.
9 For further discussion on this collection, see Katie Madonna Lee, Catherine Page-Vanore, Alison Stankrauff, "Partnership in Preservation of Rustbelt Queer History," *Archive Journal* 5 (Fall 2015), www.archivejournal.net/issue/5/archives-remixed/partnership-in-the-preservation-of-rustbelt-queer-history/. Accessed October 19, 2017.
10 For further discussion on this collection, see Don Romesburg, "Presenting the Queer Past: A Case for the GLBT History Museum," *Radical History Review* 120 (2014): 131–144.
11 See, in this volume, Jennifer Brier, "AIDS and Action (1980s–1990s)."
12 Marita Sturken, "AIDS Activist Legacies and the Gran Fury of the Past/Present," *E-Misferica* 9, no. 1/2 (2012), accessed July 30, 2015, http://hemisphericinstitute. org/hemi/en/e-misferica91/sturken#sthash.gIpMsRtQ.dpuf.
13 See, in this volume, Rachel Hope Cleves, "Revolutionary Sexualities and Early National Genders (1770s–1840s)."
14 For more, see Nina Levitt's work at www.ninalevitt.com/html/artwork/index.htm. Accessed October 19, 2017.
15 Also see Andrea Geyer and Sharon Hayes' collaborative publication, *History is Ours* (Berlin: Kehrer Verlag, 2010).
16 Marvin J. Taylor in conversation with Julia Ault, "Active Recollection," *The Whitney Museum*, http://whitney.org/file_columns/0005/5248/ault_taylor_final.pdf, accessed July 15, 2015.
17 See Kate Eichhorn, *The Archival Turn in Feminism* (Philadephia: Temple University Press, 2013).
18 Jack [Judith] Halberstam, *In a Queer Time and Place* (New York: New York University Press, 2005), 169–170; Jose Muñoz, *Cruising Utopia: The Then and There of Queer Futurity* (New York: New York University Press, 2009), 121.
19 Daniel Marshall, Kevin P. Murphy and Zeb Tortorici, "Editors' Introduction: Queering Archives: Historical Unravelings," *Radical History Review* 120 (2014): 1–2.
20 Alana Kumbier, *Ephemeral Material: Queering the Archive* (Sacramento: Litwin Books, 2014), 21.
21 Ibid., 22–23.

Further Reading

ACT UP New York Collection. http://archives.nypl.org/mss/10. Accessed July 30, 2015.
Berlant, Laurent. *The Queen of America Goes to Washington City: Essays on Sex and Citizenship.* Durham: Duke University Press, 1997.
Cvetkovich, Ann. *An Archive of Feelings.* Durham: Duke University Press, 2003.

Derrida, Jacques. *Archive Fever*. Chicago: University of Chicago Press, 1996.

Foucault, Michel. *Archaeology of Knowledge*. Translated by A.M. Sheridan Smith. New York: Pantheon Books, 1972.

Foucault, Michel. *The Order of Things*. New York: Pantheon Books, 1970.

Human Sexuality Collection. Cornell University. http://rmc.library.cornell.edu/HSC/. Accessed July 30, 2015.

LGBTQ Oral History Collaboratory. University of Toronto. http://lgbtqdigitalcollaboratory.org/. Accessed June 12, 2016.

ONE Archives. University of Southern California. http://one.usc.edu. Accessed July 30, 2015.

Society of American Archivists, Lesbian and Gay Archives Roundtable, Lavender Legacies Guide (1998, most recent version 2012). www2.archivists.org/groups/lesbian-and-gay-archives-roundtable-lagar/lavender-legacies-guide. Accessed October 19, 2017.

10

BODIES

David Serlin

In September 1945, just a month after Japan surrendered and World War II was declared officially over, the Cleveland Health Museum sponsored a contest to find the most "typical woman" in Ohio. According to historian Ian Carter, the contest followed in the wake of the Museum's purchase of two works of art, collaborations between sculptor Abram Belski and Robert Latou Dickinson, a well-known New York obstetrician, vice-president of Planned Parenthood, and amateur artist. Belski's sculptures, "Normman" and "Norma," were based on Dickinson's recording and averaging of the bodily measurements of fifteen thousand white men and women between the ages of 21 and 25 to determine the norms that exemplified the physical characteristics of "typical" Americans. The Cleveland Health Museum promised a $100 war bond to the Ohio woman whose measurements most closely approximated those of the Norma sculpture. There was no equivalent contest for men, perhaps owing to the desire not to scrutinize the bodies of the tens of thousands of disabled or traumatized veterans who were then undergoing rehabilitation and returning to civilian life. In late November 1945, after reviewing nearly four thousand entries, the Cleveland Health Museum announced that Martha Skidmore, a 23-year-old theater cashier and "former war worker," came closest to matching the sculpture's physical measurements. As the winner of the Norma Look-Alike Contest, Skidmore became a minor celebrity overnight.

For some, the Norma contest may appear in retrospect as an eccentric and ultimately benign celebration of the so-called "ordinary American" during the mid-twentieth century. Historians Anna Creadick and Sara Igo have discussed how the emergence of the "average Joe" (or Josephine), following on the heels of the mythological "forgotten man" of the Depression era, was politically meaningful to Americans following the defeat of Hitler, Mussolini, and Hirohito. In my book *Replaceable You*, I describe how terms like "typical" and "average" served as indexes of normalcy in a democratic nation that had vanquished race-conscious Nazis and authoritarian emperors, and predicted the ways that such terms would be associated with nationalistic values during the Cold War. Two decades later, a quirky nationalistic campaign such as the Norma contest would be forgotten and "overshadowed by the array of images of fashion models and pin-up girls put out by advertisers, the entertainment industry, and a burgeoning consumer culture" in the mid-1960s.[1] So how and why did Americans during the mid-1940s—the period of the so-called "Greatest Generation"—became so deeply invested in the "typical" body of a woman like Martha Skidmore?

Figure 10.1 Statue of "Norma," a 1943 artistic rendering by sculptor Abram Belski, based on eugenicist obstetrician-gynecologist Robert Latou Dickinson's ostensibly scientific rendering of the healthy "typical" American woman.

Courtesy of the Cleveland Museum of Natural History.

Any bodily ideal that seems to capture the zeitgeist is not exclusive to a single historical period; rather, it reflects many historical elements that precede it, which in turn influences the numerous historical elements that will follow it. Bodily ideals always carry trace elements of their past and always shape the arc of their future iterations. In this sense, Normman and Norma, and the statistical averages they allegedly represented, reflected some of the core complexities and tensions that characterized and sustained norms of race, class, gender, and sexuality during the first half of the twentieth century.

Normman and Norma, with their pretensions to classical sculpture and the enduring qualities of marble, were not all that dissimilar from the well-proportioned and physically normative male and female bodies that saturated early twentieth-century scientific and popular culture. They bear an eerie resemblance to the kinds of sculptures, photographs, and films of adult and child bodies exhibited at the Third International Eugenics Congress in 1932 at the American Museum of Natural History in New York City—an exhibition, as historian Devon Stillwell has shown, that promoted "better breeding" and the desirability of "fitter families" among future generations of Americans. The sculptures also resemble the kinds of stylized (and often deeply eroticized) male and female figures that were used, as historian Wolfgang Schivelbusch has explained, to crown both the massive public works projects initiated by President Franklin D. Roosevelt's New Deal during the second half of the 1930s and the monumental architectural projects initiated by Mussolini and Hitler across Italy and Germany. Indeed, Dickinson's involvement with Normman and Norma may have been inspired by his role as former president of the Euthanasia Society, an organization that, as historian Martin Pernick has detailed, was founded in 1938 to advocate "mercy killing" for children and adults born with disabilities. Euthanasia policies in US that destroyed bodies thought to violate acceptable norms resonate historically with euthanasia policies deployed against people with disabilities in Nazi Germany, part of a shared transnational sphere of racial science that disability studies scholars Sharon Snyder and David Mitchell have called the "eugenic Atlantic."[2] Examined in this light, the Norma Look-Alike competition is part of a genealogy of bodily norms and bodily differences that both preceded the contest and shaped the future.[3]

Conventional accounts of twentieth-century American history tells us that, with the arrival of the mainstream civil rights movement in the late 1950s and early 1960s, the bodies of young white women like Martha Skidmore that were exploited a decade earlier to crystallize norms of racial, economic, gendered, and sexual propriety—norms that were legally codified and socially sacrosanct, stipulating which bodies mattered more than others and where and how bodies could or could not circulate—began to see their privileged status called into question. Yet rather than rely on a simplistic binary of "before" and "after" the 1960s, it may be more productive to think about continuity between the past and the present and not merely presume that privileges accorded to bodies like Martha Skidmore's were revoked or that their idealized stature merely dissolved. Such presumptions make invisible or seemingly inconsequential the many decades of challenges to the status quo that took shape long before the civil rights era.

"The personal is political," for instance, the slogan associated with second-wave feminism of the late 1960s and early 1970s, was an effort to emphasize that all bodies, whether public or private, have politics. Yet such a slogan could have just as easily characterized the insights of Margaret Sanger, whose activism on behalf of poor and immigrant women seeking birth control and family planning during the 1910s and 1920s has shaped generations of reproductive rights advocates. Black Panther Stokely Carmichael's famous 1967 declaration, "if you put your filthy white hands on our beautiful black skin, we gonna [take care of business], period!" forms a genealogical conduit between the struggles of nineteenth-century abolitionists and anti-lynching activists like Harriet Jacobs and Ida B. Wells, and contemporary #BlackLivesMatter activists who, since 2013, have drawn attention to police brutality and mass incarceration of African Americans.[4] In a similar vein, an increasing number of scholars have endeavored to reclaim the stories of cross-dressers, sex workers, popular entertainers, immigrant laborers, and gender ambiguous and sexually nonnormative people we might today identify as transgender or inter-sex. These queer bodies, they argue, challenged or questioned norms long before the women's and sexual liberation movements of the 1960s.[5]

In *Replaceable You*, I discuss the lives of two such people: Gladys Bentley and Christine Jorgensen. Bentley was a black blues performer of Caribbean descent who, in the late 1920s, achieved notoriety as a bulldagger butch lesbian. In 1952, Bentley announced in an article for *Ebony* magazine entitled "I Am a Woman Again" that female hormone treatments had changed her body and her orientation to heterosexual and enabled her to become happily married to a man. Later during the same year, George Jorgensen, a white middle-class photographer of Danish descent, announced publicly that through female hormones and genital surgery she had become a woman named Christine. One US newspaper famously captured the story with the headline "Ex-GI Becomes Blonde Beauty." While seemingly unrelated, the stories of Bentley and Jorgensen share much in common. Gender and sexual norms of the 1950s, magnified by the politics of black respectability, demanded that a lesbian like Bentley recast her public reputation and identify publicly as a married heterosexual woman. Similarly, gender and racial norms for white women proscribed Jorgensen's behavior and demanded that Jorgensen affirm her female authenticity as part of her public reputation as a "typical American girl."

Bentley's and Jorgensen's efforts make clear that nothing is self-evident or natural about the category of the "typical"—except, perhaps, its compulsion to seem that way. For both Bentley and Jorgensen, medical technologies like hormone treatments and surgery brought their public profiles into closer alignment with the values associated with respectable middle-class American society, even if in retrospect their bodily queerness—whether in their avoidance of it, their embrace of it, or both—remains central to any retelling of their life stories. Thus, to mark someone or something as "typical" presumes a uniform lining-up of elements that are tacitly structured in opposition to that which is identified and defined as a deviation.

This is why the concept of "the typical" as it pertains to "the norm" is a calculated invention, since being typical, like being normal, must be idealized and sustained by an entire society. As a shared participatory fiction, the typical depends on the passively accepted and actively en-forced consent of a given society. For Bentley and Jorgensen, the cumulative pressures of living in the same historical moment indexed by bodies such as Martha Skidmore's was not an invitation to defy normative ideals and expectations. Rather, it was an opportunity for each of them to defy their own queerness on terms that made sense to themselves and the culture at large.

Perhaps what we identify as "the typical" and "the queer" are not diametrically opposed positions but, rather, ones that are inherently and dialectically linked. In *Epistemology of the Closet*, the literary critic Eve Kosofsky Sedgwick argued that heterosexuality, far from being simply the definition of "straight," requires a persistent policing of behavior or identity that is marked as *not* straight or non-heterosexual. But characterizing the non-normative properties or tendencies of a person or behavior is not in itself an affirmation of the normative. Rather, it merely exposes the binary opposition between that which is identified as "straight" and that which is identified as "queer," an opposition that is compulsively maintained because it is always perilously close to falling apart. Historians such as Jonathan Ned Katz and Alan Bray have taken up Sedgwick's challenge and applied it to familiar case histories in which the presumptive binary between heterosexual and homosexual ultimately fails to contain or even explain the queerness of ordinary bodies.

One could argue, for instance, that the great nineteenth-century American poet Walt Whitman was America's first queer theorist. Whitman's attention to the male body—both in his roles as a writer and as a nurse during the Civil War—aggressively celebrated the homoerotic tensions inherent in male-male social bonding, believing these tensions to be central to the American democratic experiment. Whitman's attention to and embrace of embodied nineteenth-century masculinities arguably set the tone for the numerous twentieth-century artists who followed in his wake. Graphic artist J.C. Leyendecker's advertising images during the 1910s and 1920s depict a suggestive world of furtive glances and shared smiles between "typical" military men and their working-class and white-collar counterparts. Artist Paul Cadmus lovingly expanded upon this world of images in the 1930s and 1940s with his depictions of flamboyant fairies picking up rough and muscular sailors. During the 1950s and 1960s, artists such as Kenneth Anger, Allen Ginsberg, Jack Smith, Andy Warhol, and Tom of Finland plumbed these depths even further by exploiting the queerness potential of heterosexual male iconography in their depictions of soldiers and sailors as well as police officers, construction workers, and motorcyclists.[6]

Similarly, recent debates over how to interpret the relationship between Abraham Lincoln and his roommate, Joshua Fry Speed—two bachelors who shared a bed for four years in the late 1830s—perfectly illustrates how historians are attempting to rethink earlier understandings of male social relations. As with Whitman's interpreters, the struggle to make meaning of Lincoln's and Speed's relationship as neither definitively heterosexual or homosexual but, rather, existing in a complex space in which people do things with their bodies and with the bodies of others that do not reflect how we organize our contemporary worldview, also reveals the need to protect the fragility of heterosexuality's claim to being a inviolable standard of Western culture. This has often led to historical reshufflings of what counts as standard, typical, or indeed normal. According to historian John Donald Gustav-Wrathall, during the late nineteenth and early twentieth centuries urban men (and, no doubt, urban women) who used the resources of a downtown YMCA (and YWCA) could experience "an embodied element: a delight in one another's physical proximity, an awareness of each other's bodies, a sort of excitement that overtook them at the prospect of spending time together."[7]

One would be hard pressed to rely upon the hetero/homo binary to explain these experiences at the YMCA. The binary's impoverished imagination also fails to account for the thriving culture of bachelor hotels described by historian Howard Chudacoff or the long-accepted tradition of "crushes" between women (within peer groups and across generations) at institutions of higher education, or the phenomenon of generations of unmarried women who cohabitated in so-called "Boston marriages" that historian Lillian Faderman famously detailed in her 1981 book, *Surpassing the Love of Men*. These histories illuminating the artifice of the hetero/homo binary are hidden in plain sight, invisible only to those that choose not to see them.[8]

But the queerness of the body, as something that resists binary categories of meaning, is not only articulated through the transgression of typical gender roles or sexual practices, such as those presented in medical textbooks or argued in legal cases, or through cultural representations, such as in photographs or sculptures. It is also located in the physical experience of having a body in the first place. Indeed, one could argue that desires and practices culturally marked as deviant or even taboo in certain historical moments—same-sex eroticism, for example—account for only a proportion of what constitutes bodily queerness across time and space. Within the institution of slavery, for instance, physical deformations of the black male and female body— marks and scar tissue from whips or manacles—exposed forms of subjugation often tied to sexual or gender exploitation, such the harrowing rape of a female slave.[9] Such practices just as often exceeded the terms of sexual exploitation, revealing other mechanisms of power, punishment, and humiliation suffered by the black body that African-American literary scholar Saidiya Hartman has fittingly characterized as "scenes of subjection." Bodies marked by war or industrial accidents (losing a limb or eye from battle or dangerous machinery), reproduction (stretch marks or surgical cuts from pregnancy), occupational experience (calluses from play-ing a musical instrument or wielding tools), or even enduring a childhood bout with illness (facial scars from a viral infection) produce surface differences on the physical body that exceed conventional explanatory powers of queerness but invite queer analysis. In this sense, the embodied experiences of previous generations, with all of their complex subjectivities, represents a lost Atlantis of queer history.

Since the body is, and remains, a perpetually contested site of meaning-making and attendant anxieties, a queer approach to US history should be committed to revealing the physical body in all of its delirious variety and infinitely queer manifestations. In the late 1980s, sociologists Susan Leigh Star and James Griesemer introduced the concept of the *boundary object*: that is, a site and an object against which the proximity and meaning of other sites and objects are measured. They argued that the boundaries that separate objects (both material and conceptual) are enormously plastic: a shoreline, for instance, typically marks the boundary between the land and the ocean. But at what point, exactly, does the beach end and the water begin? Most boundaries are permeable rather than precise, and yet boundaries have legal and material standing, affecting how we organize ideas that matter to us. Shorelines may be artificial constructions of nations and cartographers, but their contours profoundly shape how we think about concepts as diffuse as private and public, inside and outside, or inclusion and exclusion.

One could talk about queer bodies as boundary objects, since for centuries Americans have scrutinized, politicized, and policed bodies for reasons of convention and comprehensibility as well as for reasons of political and ideological power. From the first encounters between European explorers and Native American tribes to the latest headlines showing young black men wearing hoodies and transgender celebrities posing on magazine covers, discriminating and legislating bodily boundaries encourages people to mark their own identities through distinguishing them-selves from those marked as Other.

Before the modern era, bodily norms were organized around moral or religious approval, or else opprobrium, attached to physical appearances (e.g. being marked as a sinner because one had a congenital disfigurement) rather than to social identities (e.g. being marked as a sinner because one committed same-sex sexual acts). In particularly inflamed historical periods, embodied ways of being in the world serve as boundary objects. People with congenital disfigurements *become* people with disabilities, while those who participate in same-sex sexual acts *become* homosexuals. Americans with queer bodies often have been treated, and exploited, as boundary objects: not only as homosexuals (the boundary between straight and not-straight) or as people with disabilities (the boundary between "sickness" and "health" as fixed states of being) but as "mulattoes" (the boundary between racial categories), vagrants (the boundary between charity cases and cheats), circus performers (the boundary between the ordinary and the extraordinary), and intersex or trans (the boundary between gender "certainty" and gender "ambiguity").

Treating the body as a boundary object of modernity has roots in scientific innovations. Before the eighteenth century, distinctions between bodies were routinely made based on physical appearances—such as skin color or the shape of the head—that conformed to cultural tradition or religious convention. After the eighteenth century, however, the so-called "higher" senses such as vision and hearing were aligned with empiricism and rationality to produce the concept of *discrimination*, a privileged form of aesthetic judgment. Cultural critic Lennard J. Davis has shown how observation and comparison, the tools of scientific discrimination, were abetted by the rise of "objective" optical and mathematical instruments in helping to illuminate boundaries. The "bell curve," for example, first created by French mathematician Abraham de Moive in 1733, became a useful touchstone for understanding individuals and populations as either average, below average, or above average. By the 1860s, as Allan Sekula and Jay Dolmage have shown, the new technologies of the camera and the photographic archive had become "objective" tools for physicians, policy makers, and police departments in European cities. There they were used extensively to develop taxonomies of criminal "types": alcoholics, petty thieves, sexual deviants, prostitutes, and those deemed worthy of social rehabilitation.

By the late nineteenth century, many of these scientific practices were institutionalized in academic, clinical, and criminal settings across the US. Historian of science Jennifer Terry has identified the efforts by medical scientists to delineate the boundaries of bodily queerness using statistical data as "an American obsession." Under the watchful gaze of the microscope, the camera, and the X-ray machine, bodily differences became embodied social stigmas that were imagined as weaknesses to which the unhealthy flesh is heir. "Objective" metrics helped to shape the rise of evolutionary biology, phrenology (the pseudoscience of reading the human skull for telltale truths), and comparative anatomy at universities and scientific institutions. These, in turn, helped to shape the deployment of statistical and photographic technologies in the laboratory, the factory, the classroom, the clinic, and the asylum.[10]

What is offered as normal or deviant in these data is carefully choreographed, and is not so much a reflection of reality as it is a *production* of reality. It was the outcome of the influence of Carl Linnaeus, the eighteenth-century Swedish botanist and zoologist credited with establishing the first widely accepted protocols for classifying and categorizing plants, animals, and humans. Linnaeus and his adherents, as historian of science Londa Schiebinger has argued, used these various classification systems to explain the "natural" order of the Western world-view: they regarded breast milk and menstrual blood as evidence of women's "natural" primitive state, whereas hair distribution and broad foreheads were evidence of men's "natural" superior state, particularly for bearded men from Northern Europe. We should be careful not to treat such associations as laughable artifacts of the past. The idealized physiognomies of hirsute men from the Caucasus Mountains watch over every legislative act and demographic function since the nineteenth century that has deployed whiteness as a "natural" base line of civilization.

The importance of Linnaean taxonomies to tracing the history of queer bodies cannot be overestimated. On the one hand, the Linnaean system reinforced a liberal humanist vocabulary of dignity for recognizing and protecting bodily difference. One can see its influence on emancipation and universal suffrage discourse of the period, such as in African-American activist Sojourner Truth's 1851 declaration "Ain't I a woman?" As historian of medicine Susan Lederer has demonstrated, organizers of mid-nineteenth century abolitionist and early feminist suffrage movements devoted considerable energies to the establishment of the American Society for the Prevention of Cruelty to Animals, charted in 1869, which they saw intimately intertwined with preventing cruelty in animals' human counterparts. Claiming a right to bodily difference alongside humanistic rights would continue to resonate among disability rights and transgender and intersex rights activists well over a century later.

On the other hand, Linnaean taxonomies provided the basis for the scientific presentation and reception of queer bodies, many of whom were described as educational by businessmen such as famed circus promoter P.T. Barnum. Feder Jeftichew, known internationally as Jo-Jo the Dog-Faced Boy, and William Henry Johnson, known as Zip the Pinhead (or sometimes as What-Is-It?), were two mid-nineteenth-century sideshow performers who were promoted as "missing links" in the evolutionary development of humanity. Species-oriented metaphors, drawn from natural and industrial worlds to describe bodies with physical and cognitive difference—half-breeds, mongrels, she-males, Mongoloids, Oreos, hybrids, Heinz 57s—swelled exponentially as a result of taxonomic science. Such scientific evidence also provided endless rationales for producing legal and social boundaries. As historian Siobhan Somerville has shown, black bodies and homosexual bodies were imagined to exhibit similar characteristics since both inverted and mocked the "civilized" characteristics of Caucasian bodily norms. Their so-called primitive features—exaggerated genital development, poor or non-existent distribution of facial hair, under- or overactive endocrine glands—were used to prove the stability of Linnaean taxonomy (and, later, the rationality of eugenic logic).

The sustained connection between such bodily classifications and the struggle to articulate a national identity among the majority white American culture throughout the nineteenth century suggests that bodies served as boundary objects long before Normman and Norma arrived on the scene: from protecting white womanhood through interstate transportation laws, to containing native savagery through the Indian Removal Act, to curbing excessive immigration through racial profiling, to stigmatizing non-Christians, atheists, and socialists as blasphemous heathens, to characterizing the working classes as oversexed. By the early decades of the twentieth century, projects that promoted white, middle-class, heterosexual Christian civilization were naturalized within a climate that simultaneously celebrated the superior genetics of "old New England stock" while pitying the inferior genetics of atypical bodies. As literary historian Susan Schweik has shown, many US cities implemented "ugly laws," which applied existing vagrancy laws to prohibit the appearance of people with visible disabilities (many of whom were forced into begging and other forms of ritual humiliation for charity) on city streets.

Even while the popular culture at large was becoming more heterogeneous and heterosocial, reform groups and civic movements clung to a vision of an improved society in which bodies were segregated into separate spheres—white and non-white, male and female, children and adults, disabled and nondisabled, and all of those enmeshed in the interstices between. Political fears of the prospect of unwashed, delinquent hordes from East and South Asia and Eastern and Southern Europe diluting the quality of the American gene pool precipitated the passage of the Native Origins Act of 1924, which effectively shut down immigration to the United States until it was lifted 1965.[11] The desire to keep bodies from improperly mixing and mingling in heterogeneous public spaces informed heritage groups such as the Daughters of the American Revolution, which in 1937 successfully prevented the African-American opera singer Marian Anderson from performing in their auditorium. Their decision galvanized the first March on Washington, D.C. that year, inaugurating the tradition of hundreds of thousands of bodies on the Mall unified in protest for all future civil rights-inspired actions in the nation's capital.

In this sense, the Norma Look-Alike contest—which took place only eight years after Marian Anderson's appearance in Washington, D.C.—did not merely reflect prevailing codes of normativity. The contest *created* the boundaries of normativity, both those of racial superiority (what ethnic studies scholar George Lipsitz has called "the possessive investment in whiteness") or the ideals of physical perfection (what literary scholar Robert McRuer has called "compulsory ablebodiedness"). Understanding how such practices exposed the tacit investment in norms usually made invisible by culture makes it possible to understand how, under particular conditions, the actions of a disparate range of individuals and institutions—from scientists and public health officials to political leaders, educators and even entertainers—can cohere into ideological alignment.[12]

In the 1970s, the philosopher Michel Foucault argued that the appeal of statistical data as objectively neutral resides in its alleged capacity to reveal something about the "truths" of our bodies, characters, or even our souls. This is how those data hold that appeal, and ultimately exercise their authority over us. The instrumental use of statistics to make categorical distinctions between what is normal and what is abnormal is what Foucault called *biopolitics*: a government's use of the variabilities of human biology, such as reproductive capacity, physical ability, aptitude for military service, physical endurance, disease susceptibility, and mortality rates. This is why, Foucault argued, since the eighteenth century, political leaders, military organizations, police bureaus, and financial and insurance companies have compiled mountains of data for the purposes of predicting, legislating, and shaping everything from birth and mortality rates and labor productivity to social behavior and educational aptitude. Such data are the raw materials that become transformed into *biopower*, which can be used to justify the exigencies of police force, military engagement, or political decision-making. Methods of biopower continue to shape the work of public health officials, advertising executives, insurance actuaries, nutritionists, and social media entrepreneurs—all of whom rely upon the rhetoric of statistical "neutrality" in the collection, storage, and use of our bio-data.

By casting a critical gaze toward typical and atypical bodies that putatively mark boundaries, we deflect what is genuinely queer about efforts to collect, store, and use statistical data in the first place. During the World War I for example, the US Army's focus on measuring, quantifying, and comparing male bodies for recruitment and training included testing the resistance, or lack thereof, of a male recruit's sphincter muscle.[13] A tight, uncompromised anus free of any signs of "unnatural" sexual activity aligned the idea of healthy male body to the idea of a healthy nation—a syllogistic leap that provides historical evidence of America's unresolved biopolitical obsession with queerness. At approximately the same historical moment, pageants and beauty contests organized for babies, adolescent girls, and whole families at country fairs extolled the virtues of "better breeding," a concept translated from livestock and agriculture, for the nation as a whole. Such contests are dialectically linked to the Supreme Court's decision in *Buck v. Bell* (1927), which argued that the right of institutions to sterilize women deemed "unfit" to be mothers—especially the physically or cognitively disabled, who were seen as public charges—should be constitutionally protected.

Buck v. Bell is an exemplary case study of the ways that law can harness biopolitics to become an instrument of biopower. But one could argue that the coexistence of *Buck v. Bell* and beauty pageants in the same historical moment also provides evidence of a queer biopolitics at work. The eugenics movement not only punished atypical bodies; it also focused elaborate attention on adorable white babies and pretty white girls. Such practices normalized the erotic tensions involved in scrutinizing the bodies of young white women, ostensibly to prove their "natural" superiority, all the while disavowing the legacies of Linnaean taxonomy and the historical specter of eugenics. The unresolved erotic character of such practices of normalization remains a recurring theme in twentieth-century queer history. After 1945, for instance, most Americans deliberately and vocally turned their backs on anything redolent of the excesses of racial science, especially after the horrific lessons of Hiroshima and Nagasaki and the revelations of the Nazi concentration camps. But efforts to discriminate against bodies as a form of competitive or hierarchical practice has continued apace. Beauty pageants of all kinds, shorn of their eugenic associations with "better breeding," continued to be woven into and deeply cherished by our national culture. Americans continue to attend country fairs, submit their children to the public gaze, and bask in the glow of whiteness as a privileged form of racial affiliation.

In retrospect, Normman and Norma, should be regarded as essential symbols of mid-twentieth-century American biopower, nourished by the legacies of eugenics. They serve as mirror surfaces through which one could see aspirations to a particular kind of normal or typical status perpetually reflected. The bodily attention inherent in these comparative practices—which are deliberately, incessantly, compulsively heterosexual as well as racial—turned the categorization and separation of healthy bodies from unhealthy ones into biopolitical examples for the national interest. The "typical," or that which was used to stand in for the typical, is always a biopolitical project that disavows its own queerness. And that which is perceived as typical is never a constant, despite the best efforts of scientists, legislators, and moralists to make it seem so. In 1944, for example, the US federal government enacted major pieces of legislation, including the Servicemen's Readjustment Act of 1944 (better known as the G.I. Bill). Historian Margot Canaday has argued that the G.I. Bill fundamentally transformed American culture by tilting it toward what she calls a "straight state": a white, middle-class, heterosexual norm rewarded with government-sponsored resources such as free education, subsidized mortgages, and generous employment opportunities exclusively designed to support straight veterans and their heterosexual family units.

Yet the G.I. Bill was inaugurated during precisely the same period in which researchers like Frank Beach, Alfred Kinsey, William Masters and Virginia Johnson, and Lewis Terman were overturning the stability of heterosexual norms.[14] In his interviews with twenty thousand informants, Kinsey discovered that a sizeable number who identified as heterosexual had had a wide variety of sexual encounters, many resulting in orgasm, with a same-sex partner and even sometimes with a partner of a different species. Bioethicist Peter Singer recounts that Kinsey "found that 8 percent of males and 3.5 percent of females stated that they had, at some time, had a sexual encounter with an animal. Among men living in rural areas, the figure shot up to 50 percent."[15]

Kinsey's headline-grabbing revelations about American sexuality—published in 1948 and 1953—suggested, too, that the boundaries of white, middle-class heterosexuality coexisted alongside multiple forms of sexual variation that were not contained by the statistical but in fact laid bare its irreconcilable internal contradictions and inconsistencies. Likewise, through their extensive case studies, Masters and Johnson provided evidence that any claims to the "norms" of sexual response (let alone those of sexual identity) were fictions intended to proscribe sexual behaviors and attitudes rather than reflect their multiple and complex expressions. With the emergence of the women's and gay liberation movements of the 1960s and 1970s, the work of Kinsey and Masters and Johnson, as Donna Drucker and Michael Pettit have noted, would be marshaled to confront legal, psychiatric, and religious prohibitions against gender and sexual diversity in state and federal law.

Recognition of the inherent queerness of all bodies, some have argued, has been lost in struggles by LGBT organizations to promote social respectability, political legitimacy, and, in some cases, legal expediency—in, for example, the fight to legalize same-sex marriage or to allow openly gay, lesbian, bisexual, and transgender Americans to serve in the armed forces. Even among disability rights advocates, praise for the Americans with Disabilities Act of 1990 has been accompanied by queer criticism. Benefits and protections for gender-nonnormative and trans bodies, for instance, were explicitly excluded from the ADA, marking it as a piece of successful but compromised federal legislation. Some critics argue that queer bodies have been straightened out in the process of making political strides.

Looking at the proliferation of queer bodies across numerous historical periods in US history, however, reveals that the struggle to define queerness either in terms of acts or identities ignores the fundamental and extraordinarily mutable status of the body itself. Certain forms of bodily queerness are transformed by circumstance and convention: veterans with PTSD and "wounded warriors," for instance, occupy privileged positions in the social hierarchy of disabled bodies, even if they are also routinely exploited to instill values of normative masculinity and give silent assent to aggressive militarism. Meanwhile, some cultural practices that normalize and even make invisible the queerness of bodily assessment and discrimination remain under the radar. Pageants for young women and babies that emerged in the popular culture of eugenics continue on in the form of reality television series such as *America's Next Top Model* and *Toddlers and Tiaras*. Whereas having the typical American body in the early twentieth century meant affirming one's proximity to a racialized or gendered norm, in the early twenty-first century many contemporary Americans invest enormous effort and money in transforming their own bodies in order to transcend the typical, or else to re-inscribe the "typical" with new standards. Bleaching skin and straightening hair, using high-tech exercise equipment, undergoing cosmetic procedures, and using steroids to build muscle (and shrink genitals) are compensatory strategies intended to beat the odds of what Freud once called "anatomical destiny."

The queer American body requires more than an intersectional analysis of the familiar analytical categories of race, class, gender, sexuality, and citizenship. It also demands that we investigate less familiar aspects of embodied experience. Like queerness, the normative is never a boundary object with fixed properties. It is always fragile and evanescent while also in a state of becoming. That which is claimed as normative—the contemporary affectation for particular kinds of behaviors, shapes, and surfaces that mark one as "normal"—is never a universal against which difference is measured across history. Whether it is being enforced from without or applied to one's self from within, it is always a ruse, a fiction, a beauty contest with no winners.

Notes

1 Jacqueline Urla and Alan C. Swedlund, "Measuring Up to Barbie: Ideals of the Feminine Body in Popular Culture," in Nancy Cook, ed., *Gender Relations in Global Perspective: Essential Readings* (Toronto: Canadian Scholars' Press, 2007), 140.

2 Sharon Snyder and David Mitchell, *Cultural Locations of Disability* (Chicago: University of Chicago Press, 2006), esp. Chapter 3.

3 For the longer queer history of medicalization, see, in this volume, Katie Batza, "Sickness and Wellness."

4 Stokely Carmichael, speech given at Garfield High School, Seattle, Washington, April 19, 1967, available at www.aavw.org/special_features/speeches_speech_carmichael01.html. Accessed September 28, 2015.

5 For the longer history of trans, see, in this volume, Finn Enke, "Transgender History (and Otherwise Approaches to Queer Embodiment."

6 Catherine Davies, *Whitman's Queer Children: America's Homosexual Epics* (New York: Bloomsbury Academic, 2012); Eric Jefferson Segal, "Realizing Whiteness in U.S. Visual Culture: The Popular Illustration of J.C. Leyendecker, Norman Rockwell, and the *Saturday Evening Post*, 1917–1945" (Ph.D. dissertation, UCLA, 2002); Lincoln Kirstein, *Paul Cadmus* (New York: Pomegranate Press, 1992); Juan A. Suarez, *Bike Boys, Drag Queens, and Superstars: Avant-Garde, Mass Culture, and Gay Identities in the 1960s* (Bloomington: Indiana University Press, 1996); Micha Ramakers, *Dirty Pictures: Tom of Finland, Masculinity, and Homosexuality* (New York: St. Martin's Press, 2000).

7 John Donald Gustav-Wrathall, *Take the Young Stranger By the Hand: Same Sex Relations and the YMCA* (Chicago: University of Chicago Press, 1998), 57.

8 For more on the history of Boston Marriages in the nineteenth century, see, in this volume, Rachel Hope Cleves, "Revolutionary Sexualities and Early National Genders (1770s–1840s)" and Elizabeth Clement and Bean Velocci, "Modern Sexuality in Modern Times (1880s–1930s)."

9 For more on the queer history of slavery, see, in this volume, Clare Sears, "Centering Slavery in Nineteenth-Century Queer History (1800s–1890s)."

10 See also, in this volume, Elizabeth Clement and Beans Velocci, "Modern Sexuality in Modern Times," and Batza, "Sickness and Wellness."

11 For further elaboration of how production of the nation shapes queer history, see, in this volume, Eithne Luibhéid, "Queer and Nation."

12 In 1984, anthropologist Gayle Rubin coined the phrase "the charmed circle of sex" to characterize the privilege given to some sexual practices (such as serial monogamy and missionary-style intercourse). With the onset of the AIDS crisis, social conservatives drew boundaries around the "charmed circle" in order to stigmatize sex- and drug-sexual acts that were identified as vectors of HIV transmission.

One could draw a parallel between the rhetorical use of the "charmed circle" to contain and punish queer acts and the use of statistics to contain and punish queer bodies. Gayle Rubin, "Thinking Sex: Notes for a Radical Theory of the Politics of Sexuality" (1984) in *Deviations: A Gayle Rubin Reader* (Durham: Duke University Press, 2011), 137–181.

13 See David Serlin, "Crippling Masculinity: Queerness and Disability in US Military Culture, 1800–1945," *GLQ* 9, nos. 1–2 (2003): 162.

14 For a more general queer history of the postwar era, see, in this volume, Amanda Littauer, "Sexual Minorities at the Apex of Heteronormativity (1940s–1965)."

15 Peter Singer, "Heavy Petting" (2001), available at www.egs.edu/faculty/peter-singer/articles/heavy-petting/ Accessed December 22, 2017.

Further Reading

Bray, Alan. *The Friend*. Chicago: University of Chicago Press, 2006.

Briggs, Laura. *Reproducing Empire: Rae, Sex, Science, and U.S. Imperialism in Puerto Rico*. Berkeley: University of California Press, 2003.

Canaday, Margot. *The Straight State: Sexuality and Citizenship in Twentieth-Century America*. Princeton: Princeton University Press, 2011.

Carter, Julian. *The Heart of Whiteness: Normal Sexuality and Race in America, 1880–1940*. Durham: Duke University Press, 2007.

Chudacoff, Howard. *The Age of the Bachelor*. Princeton: Princeton University Press, 2000.

Creadick, Anna G. *Perfectly Average: The Pursuit of Normality in Postwar America*. Amherst: University of Massachusetts Press, 2010.

Davis, Lennard J. *Enforcing Normalcy: Disability, Deafness, and the Body*. London: Verso, 1995.

Dolmage, Jay. "Framing Disability, Developing Race: Photography as Eugenic Technology," *Enculturation: A Journal of Rhetoric, Writing, and Culture* (March 11, 2014), available at http://enculturation.net/framing disability. Accessed September 28, 2015.

Drucker, Donna. *The Classification of Sex: Alfred Kinsey and the Organization of Knowledge*. Pittsburgh: University of Pittsburgh Press, 2014.

Faderman, Lillian. *Surpassing the Love of Men: Romantic Friendship and Love Between Women from the Renaissance to the Present*. New York: HarperCollins, 2001 [1981].

Foucault, Michel. *The Birth of Biopolitics: Lectures at the Collège de France, 1978–1979*. New York: Picador, 2010.

Hartman, Saidiya. *Scenes of Subjection: Terror, Slavery, and Self-Making in Nineteenth-Century America*. New York: Oxford University Press, 1997.

Igo, Sara. *The Averaged American: Surveys, Citizens, and the Making of a Mass Public*. Cambridge: Harvard University Press, 2008.

Katz, Jonathan Ned. *The Invention of Heterosexuality*. Chicago: University of Chicago Press, 2007.

Lederer, Susan. *Subjected to Science: Human Experimentation in America Before the Second World War*. Baltimore: Johns Hopkins University Press, 1995.

Lipsitz, George. *The Possessive Investment in Whiteness: How White People Profit from Identity Politics*. Philadelphia: Temple University Press, 2006.

McRuer, Robert. "Introduction: Compulsory Able-Bodiedness and Queer/Disabled Existence." In *Crip Theory: Cultural Signs of Queerness and Disability*. New York: NYU Press, 2006.

Pernick, Martin. *The Black Stork: Eugenics and the Death of "Defective" Babies in American Medicine and Motion Pictures Since 1915*. New York: Oxford University Press, 1999.

Pettit, Michael. "The Queer Life of a Lab Rat," *History of Psychology* 15, no. 3 (2012): 217–227.

Schiebinger, Londa. *Nature's Body: Gender in the Making of Modern Science*. Boston: Beacon Press, 1993.

Schivelbusch, Wolfgang. *Three New Deals: Reflections on Roosevelt's America, Mussolini's Italy, and Hitler's Germany, 1933–1939*. New York: Picador, 2007.

Schweik, Susan. *The Ugly Laws: Disability in Public*. New York: NYU Press, 2009.

Sedgwick, Eve Kosofsky. *Epistemology of the Closet*. Berkeley: University of California Press, 2008 [1990].

Sekula, Allan. "The Body and the Archive," *October* 39 (Winter 1986): 3–64.

Serlin, David. *Replaceable You: Engineering the American Body in Postwar America*. Chicago: University of Chicago Press, 2004.

Somerville, Siobhan. *Queering the Color Line: Race and the Invention of Homosexuality in American Culture*. Durham: Duke University Press, 2000.

Starr, Susan and James Griesemer. "Institutional Ecology, 'Translations,' and Boundary Objects: Amateurs and Professionals in Berkeley's Museum of Vertebrate Zoology, 1907–39," *Social Studies of Science* 19, no. 3 (August 1989): 387–420.

Stillwell, Devon. "Eugenics Visualized: The Exhibit of the Third International Congress of Eugenics, 1932," *Bulletin of the History of Medicine* 86, no. 2 (Summer 2012): 205–236.

Terry, Jennifer. *An American Obsession: Science Medicine, and Homosexuality in Modern Society.* Chicago: University of Chicago Press, 1999.

11

ORGANIZATIONS

Marcia M. Gallo

Since the mid-twentieth century, queer people and our allies have created thousands of organizations that have helped change the cultural and physical landscape of America. Starting with a few brave folks in Chicago in the 1920s who asserted that sexual rights are human rights, lesbians, gay men, bisexuals, transgender, and queer people (LGBTQ) established a plethora of associations, centers, sites and institutions in a bold determination to find and provide community where, before, it did not officially exist. Whether the need was for basic survival or a desire to construct entities that would establish our existence and prove our value, LGBTQ activists have built ephemeral and long-lasting structures of affiliation and affirmation. From archives and historical societies to athletic competitions and campus-based groups; from religious entities to political campaigns; and from community service organizations to activist networks, LGBTQ peoples and our allies have come together to provide social, political, recreational, intellectual, professional, and philanthropic resources. We fought isolation and exclusion; we also recognized that pleasure is as crucial as pain in advancing social change.

We did so amid massive shifts in American society. As scholars have noted, during the decades in which the LGBTQ movement grew, US policies and political cultures moved from a dominant New Deal liberalism of the 1930s through the 1960s that recognized government's responsibility to redress some of its people's longstanding inequalities into, by the 1970s through today, the increasingly rabid privatizations of neoliberalism, which marginalize some forms of diversity while profiting from others. LGBTQ local and national organizations are products of their times and sometimes have embraced surprising bedfellows in their quest for social acceptance and political victories.

This chapter highlights some of the ways in which LGBTQ peoples have formed and sustained social or political groups and how historians and other scholars have described them. The central argument is that LGBTQ organizations, as varied and complicated as their members, have navigated with remarkable resiliency and creativity the historical times through which they developed. By grouping their activities into specific time periods, we can highlight how LGBTQ groups reflected the realities of their historical eras as they worked to transform stigmatized individuals into cohesive communities and collectively altered the status quo.

The second focus for this essay is the study of LGBTQ organizing, which has been a queer historical project since the late 1970s and early 1980s. The histories of our organizations engage scholars because they not only provide a record of our efforts but also give us a way to evaluate the messy constructions of, and monumental contradictions within, queer America. Given the enveloping silences surrounding LGBTQ lives until the late twentieth century, activists and scholars since then have prioritized historical reclamation efforts to ensure future generations will have access to our stories, our victories, and our challenges.

The histories of organized LGBTQ efforts vividly demonstrate that we were and are myriad peoples with multiple identifications and realities that have never have fit neatly into static categories. Connection can provide important social and psychological benefits. Recent research on black lesbians by the Zuna Institute reinforces the idea that "identity development can be positively influenced by group affiliations. Support groups or organizations that encompass multiple parts of a person's identity help to foster greater self-esteem."[1] Yet community differences are reflected in experience as well as an imbalance in the distribution of social, political, and economic resources. This disproportionality of attention and assets has fallen most heavily upon nonwhite LGBTQ peoples throughout the movement's history, hindering it from achieving its full potential as a multifaceted force for social justice.

"Friendship and Freedom"—The 1920s and 1930s[2]

As esteemed historian, medical researcher, and sexual minorities advocate Vern Bullough writes, "Gays and lesbians had difficulty going public."[3] Despite the example of European groups who were forming a homosexual emancipation movement in the late nineteenth and early twentieth centuries, Henry Gerber's efforts represent the first such attempt in the United States. Gerber was born in Bavaria, Germany on June 29, 1892 and immigrated with his family in 1913, settling in Chicago. He served in the US Army during World War I; while stationed in Germany he learned of groups such as Magnus Hirschfeld's Scientific-Humanitarian Community in Berlin. On his return to Chicago, Gerber started The Society for Human Rights (SHR), the first known US gay rights organization, in 1924. Gerber and a small group of friends, including John Graves, an African American preacher, hoped to reach others like themselves by publishing a newsletter entitled *Friendship and Freedom*. A year later, their new organization disbanded after the wife of an officer of SHR reported her husband's homosexual activities to a social worker. That led to the involvement of the local police. Gerber's apartment was searched and all materials pertaining to SHR were confiscated, as well as his personal diaries. He endured three court trials and, despite being acquitted, lost his job and left Chicago for New York, where his later efforts to organize gay men were unsuccessful. However, Gerber maintained a personal correspondence club for gay men during the 1930s that developed into a national network. He continued to support nascent gay organizing for the rest of his life.[4]

Although Gerber died in 1972, he is remembered today in part because activists gave his name (along with Chicago radical attorney Pearl Hart) to one of the oldest LGBTQ archives in the United States. The Gerber/Hart Library and Archives was founded in 1981 and reflects one of the strengths of the organizing done by activists in the recent past: ensuring the preservation and promotion of LGBTQ people's papers, photographs, and other personal items. As is true of most of the queer archives that have been established since the 1980s, Gerber/Hart's reach exceeds the bounds of place. It also stands as an example of the LGBTQ movement's longstanding desire to reclaim the stories of those who have been "hidden from history."[5]

In addition to his writings on Gerber, Vern Bullough, with his wife Bonnie, were responsible for bringing to light an early lesbian research effort. In the mid-1970s they received an unfinished manuscript by a member of Bullough's extended family that explored lesbianism in Salt Lake City, Utah during the 1920s and 1930s. It was a description of one lesbian's life, those of her partners (one of whom was Bonnie's mother) and two dozen lesbian friends. During the First

World War, Bonnie's mother had met the author of the manuscript, "M.B." (Mildred Berryman). Berryman gathered data from friends and colleagues for nearly twenty years, in a survey that aimed to establish the respectability of the members of her community. Most of the white and middle-class respondents had been born into Mormon homes. They rejected any taint of pathology in themselves or their friends. The manuscript testifies to the discreet lesbian social groups and networks that formed in parts of the country not normally recognized as significant sites of lesbian and gay life. Decades before the first small groups of "homophile" activists would begin organizing on the West Coast by creating private social spaces as well as political discussions, in Salt Lake City and numerous other small towns and cities throughout America lesbians and gay men created their own social and support systems. It would take the seismic shifts in American life brought about by World War II to provide opportunities for moving beyond informal groups to bona fide gay and lesbian organizations.

The Homosexual Minority—The 1940s and 1950s[6]

World War II mobilized people of all genders and races throughout the US and overseas, brought about new demands for civil rights, and brought new levels of classification and scrutiny of sexuality. In 1941, the Committee for the Study of Sex Variants published one of the first comprehensive studies of homosexual behavior. That same year, the military began stepping up its official removal of those suspected or convicted of homosexuality, issuing tens of thousands of Section 8 discharges that kept service members from receiving postwar benefits, yet aided the organizing activities of the postwar period. As Allan Bérubé argues, this shared experience of oppression, in the context of expanded opportunities for homosocial congregation, inspired new organizations in the postwar era. One of the first gay groups to organize postwar was the Veteran's Benevolent Association, formed in 1945 in New York by leaders who refused to be apologetic about their homosexuality. It provided counseling as well as social activities such as dances and parties for its members.

The Veteran's Benevolent Association was followed in 1948 by a Los Angeles organization started by an interracial couple, Merton L. Bird and W. Dorr Legg: the Knights of the Clocks. In addition to being the first gay group to affirmatively "promote fellowship and understanding between homosexuals themselves, specifically between other races and Negroes, as well as to offer its members aid in securing employment and suitable housing," as scholar Michael Bronski notes, the Knights also can be credited with ushering in the era of "homophile" reliance on arcane organizational names. For the next few years the Knights of the Clocks provided counseling, referrals, and hosted social events.[7]

Two other organizations were founded in the early 1950s in Los Angeles: the Mattachine Society (1950) and ONE, Inc. (1953). With few exceptions, most Mattachine organizers were middle-class white men. ONE, Inc., which was started primarily to support a new gay magazine, had a multiracial board at its inception. Soon the Daughters of Bilitis (1955), often referred to as DOB, began in San Francisco as a secret social club for lesbians. DOB's founders included two interracial couples. In 1976 and 1983, respectively, gay historians Jonathan Ned Katz and John D'Emilio established these groups' significance to modern gay political history. Subsequently, numerous historians—notably Nan Alamilla Boyd, Margot Canaday, Daniel Hurewitz, C. Todd White, and myself—have produced scholarship that explores the intersections among pre- and postwar artistic, social, and activist endeavors, as well as the growing classification systems used by the US government, all of which aided the development of the LGBTQ movement.

Mattachine, ONE, and DOB utilized organizational names drawn from obscure references to showcase their focus on same-sex desire while shielding their members from unwanted discovery by hostile outsiders. The possible consequences of affiliation made many women and men wary, as the 1950s ushered in a period of tightening scrutiny of, and punishment for, real or suspected gender, sexual, or political deviance. While the organizations' leaders had diverse political perspectives, all three predominantly pursued liberal approaches to social inclusion, education, and civil rights that reflected the dominant social and political conformism of the era. Homophile groups also developed bylaws and other official documents so that they could receive state recognition as nonprofit organizations. As scholars Leila Rupp and David Churchill have shown, they provided activists with nascent networks of members and supporters in cities across America as well as internationally.

They also often collaborated through the end of the 1950s and into the 1960s despite some conflicts among them, which included sexist attitudes and behaviors on the part of the men and divergent political perspectives among all of them. Mattachine and DOB prioritized establishing chapters in cities throughout the US and thus helped the movement spread; in some places they shared office space. ONE, Inc. established an Institute in 1956 that sponsored educational programs at which members of Mattachine and DOB, as well as interested members of the public, participated. All three shared a commitment to visibility and to reaching new members, the leaders of other organizations, and the public.

A main strategy was publishing. *ONE* was the first ongoing, regularly published gay magazine in the US, followed by the *Mattachine Review* in 1955 and the DOB's *The Ladder* in 1956. As Craig Loftin, Martin Meeker, and I demonstrate, these publications expanded the reach and the impact of the new movement, introducing its goals and its leaders to America. In doing so they built on such short-lived efforts as the newsletter *Vice Versa*, started in Los Angeles in 1947 by the pseudonymous Lisa Ben, who later joined DOB and became one of the homophile movement's favorite performers.

Coming Out—The 1960s and 1970s[8]

The cover of *The Ladder*'s March 1964 issue broke new ground for the movement. For the first time, the words "A Lesbian Review" were included on the front cover of an ongoing, popularly available American magazine that could be purchased at bookstores and newsstands. Two years later, the magazine again made history when it featured a cover photo of Ernestine "Eckstein," an African American lesbian who used a pseudonym in her work as vice president of DOB's New York chapter. The issue also featured her involvement in homophile activism, the civil rights movement, and her ideas about how to move both forward. "Eckstein" urged DOB to engage in picketing and litigation, referencing strategies used effectively by the National Association for the Advancement of Colored People (NAACP).[9] Both overt inclusion of the word "lesbian" and the portrait of a nonwhite civil rights activist on the magazine's cover signaled significant changes in the gay movement's strategies of visibility and affiliation.[10]

The 1960s saw the movement's emphasis shift to demanding access to all sectors of American society while also working with mainstream liberal institutions. As scholars have noted, small but growing groups of lesbians, gay men and their allies used social and recreational activities as well as publications, public meetings, conferences, and protests to publicly insist that they were sexual minorities deserving of basic civil rights, years before the Stonewall riots of June 1969. They adapted lessons learned from other social and political movements of the time, especially the black civil rights movement, to craft a more militant network for change. They challenged America to recognize that "Homosexuals Are American Citizens Too," in the words of one early picket sign at Independence Hall in Philadelphia, where from 1965 to 1969 homophiles held annual July 4 public protests. They also organized themselves into regional and national coalitions and created hundreds of new organizations.

In the early to mid-1960s, the now-national Mattachine and DOB continued to encourage the development of local chapters in a number of cities, such as Chicago, where, as Timothy Stewart-Winter describes, the chapter had several false starts before finding its footing. In Philadelphia, where, as Marc Stein details, remarkable organizing occurred across gender, despite many challenges. In San Francisco, Columbian American performer and political candidate Jose Sarria's League for Civil Education was founded in 1962, as was the gay and lesbian Tavern Guild, organized to fight ongoing police harassment at the local bars. By the mid-1960s there were enough homophile and gay organizations to support the founding of the first gay coalition, NACHO (North American Conference of Homophile Organizations), which began meeting in 1965. By 1967, the first Student Homophile League was founded at Columbia University in New York.

From liberal ministers and sympathetic psychologists to bar owners, from athletes and drag queens to street kids, the gay movement and its allies broadened their reach in the 1960s and 1970s. In Philadelphia, the Janus Society began in 1964 and started publishing *DRUM* magazine; that same year, in San Francisco, SIR (Society for Individual Rights) established

Figure 11.1 In the early 1960s, neighbors gather at Barbara Gittings' apartment in Philadelphia to help the New York Chapter of the Daughters of Bilitis send out a mailing.
Courtesy of the New York Public Library.

itself as a more radical alternative to existing homophile organizations. Within a few years, they would create what would become the nation's first gay community center. As Joey Plaster details, in 1966, Vanguard was organized by and for gay street youth in San Francisco's Tenderloin district. Religious coalitions such as the Council on Religion and the Homosexual in San Francisco (1964) helped bring gay people and supportive ministers into activist networks that condemned police brutality, racism, and poverty.

Finally, as Susan Stryker describes, those advocating rights, recognition, affinity, and/or revolution related to gender diversity also organized throughout the 1960s. In some ways, the efforts of Virginia Prince and Sylvia Rivera might be understood as bookends to this process. In 1960, Prince founded the first known group for transvestites, the Foundation for Personality Expression, which also published *Transvestia*. Immediately following the 1969 Stonewall Inn riots in New York, Latino/a activist Sylvia Rivera and African American organizer Marsha Johnson created STAR, the Street Transvestite Action Revolutionaries, so as to include in the growing movement the young hustlers and street people who helped fuel the fight against repression, bigotry, and greed that Stonewall represented at that time.

The 1970s saw an explosion of LGBT organizing. Building on the activist ethos of the era as well as the 1950s and 1960s foundations, radical and reform-oriented gays, bisexuals, lesbians, and transgender people formed the Gay Liberation Front (1969) and Radicalesbians (1970) as well as the Gay Activists Alliance (1970), which inspired the creation of even more local groups. One was the Gay and Lesbian Activist Alliance in Washington, D.C. (1971), which today, according to OutHistory.org, is "the oldest continuously active gay rights organization" in the United States.[11] From Affirmation (LGBT Mormons) to the Metropolitan Community Church and the Sisters of Perpetual Indulgence, one of the triumphs of the 1970s was the movement's ability not only to organize itself into myriad upstanding as well as freewheeling groups—cultural, social, religious, and political—but also to effectively defend the gains it was just beginning to realize.

In the process of creating new organizations, activists began to diversify. As historian Vicki Eaklor notes, "Race (and class) could be divisive among GLBT people, especially when white privilege was ignored or dismissed by whites." She emphasizes that nonwhite peoples often came together first as caucuses within larger groups but then broke off to form their own organizations. "Lesbian and gay Chicanos in Los Angeles, for example, met in Unidos, founded in 1970. In San Francisco Randy Burns and Barbara Cameron, with ten others, formed Gay American Indians in 1975 and the network grew quickly to include nations all over the country."[12] Black and Latina lesbians created the Salsa Soul Sisters in New York in 1974, the first such organization in the country; by the end of the 1970s, the National Coalition of Black Lesbians and Gays organized a National Third World Lesbian and Gay Conference to coincide with the first National March on Washington for Lesbian and Gay Rights. The groundbreaking black feminist lesbian organization Combahee River Collective produced a signature 1977 Statement that premiered intersectional analysis as essential to social justice and left an enduring influence on activist theories within and beyond the LGBTQ movement.

Other important intellectual inroads were made as well: in 1970 the American Library Association's Task Force on Gay Liberation, now known as the GLBT Round Table, was launched; the Gay Academic Union was founded in 1973. Through community-based gay history projects begun in cities such as Chicago, San Francisco, Los Angeles, and New York, the growing movement ensured that individual and organizational stories and ephemera would be gathered and preserved for future generations.

Personally and politically, the movement also expanded to advocate for basic rights. Lesbian mothers in Seattle organized a National Defense Fund and started publishing *Mom's Apple Pie* in 1974, spurred by a growing number of custody disputes. The National Gay Task Force (today the National LGBTQ Task Force) held its first organizing meetings in New York in 1973 to develop strategies for advocacy on national policy issues affecting gay people, as did Lambda Legal Defense and Education Fund, modeled on the ACLU as well as the NAACP.

By the late 1970s, the rise in anti-gay animus and, sometimes, violence—literally on the streets and rhetorically at the ballot box—required the young movement to grow up fast.

In Sickness and In Health—The 1980s and 1990s

It is impossible to write a history of LGBTQ organizations in the 1980s and 1990s without acknowledging the legendary groups created in response to the AIDS epidemic. Much as World War II marked a departure from previous efforts to bring lesbian, gay, bisexual, and transgender people into community, the firestorm of fear, illness, death and extraordinary acts of love and social change associated with the Acquired Immune Deficiency Syndrome crisis represents a dividing line between organizing "before" and "after."[13]

In the frightening early years of the AIDS crisis, "homosexuality" again was equated with "disease" amid a growing reactionary political climate, which began after activists and researchers successfully lobbied the American Psychiatric Association to drop homosexuality from its categories of mental illness in 1973. Gay men and their allies, both those who were infected and those who were not, became active on their own behalf; by the end of 1981, in San Francisco and New York, new groups were launched to deal with the disease: the Kaposi's Sarcoma Research and Education Foundation (later the San Francisco AIDS Foundation) and Gay Men's Health Crisis (GMHC), which quickly became the largest AIDS organization in the nation.

Federal, state, and municipal interventions generally could not keep up with the spread of the new disease (even lagging in creating prevention efforts aimed at distinguishing between casual personal contact, which did not spread HIV, the virus that caused AIDS, and the exchange of bodily fluids, which did). Incredibly, President Ronald Reagan did not address the epidemic until 1987 despite the deaths of over 4,000 Americans by that time. Clearly, community organizing was essential to reaching various constituencies. As historian Martin Duberman notes, "By 1985, New York's Health Department had still not developed AIDS prevention material in Spanish, though it was the city's second language. Late in that year, with the formation of the Hispanic AIDS Forum and the New York chapter of the Minority Task Force, an opportunity seemed at hand for cooperative efforts to do more in reaching minority communities ... By the end of 1985, more than twenty thousand cases of AIDS had been reported in the United States—with a startling 50 percent of them African American."[14]

Historian Jennifer Brier has considered the influence of feminism on AIDS and on the 1980s more broadly, noting that lesbian activists' experiences in the women's health movement helped frame how they discussed, described, and fought for resources as the epidemic unfolded. Disparities in available resources were unmistakably marked not only by gender and sexuality but also by race, class, and the growing poverty of the early neoliberal period. These issues would only increase as promising drugs to manage the disease became available in the mid-1990s; access to health care, especially for women, poor people, and people of color, became an imperative for progressives in the LGBTQ movement. Further, lesbians took on AIDS-related caretaking and activism, in spite of the ongoing sexism of many gay men and slow official recognition of women with HIV/AIDS. As one example, the San Diego-based Blood Sisters, who donated blood for people with AIDS after the federal government banned men who had sex with other men from being blood donors.

The slow official response to the disease led also to the creation of legendary groups such as PWA San Francisco in 1983, the first organization created by and for people with AIDS, and the AIDS Coalition To Unleash Power (ACT UP), founded in New York in 1987. During this same period, the National Coalition of Black Gays (later the National Coalition of Black Lesbians and Gays) was formed with a broad agenda that included AIDS but was not defined by it. Their renaming themselves to explicitly include lesbians represents another hallmark of organizational shifts in the 1980s and 1990s—pushes to become more expansive and diverse. American Indian Gays and Lesbians, which formed in 1987, held a transnational conference one year later that adopted the term "two-spirit" to reference gender-crossing in Native cultures. Other examples of LGBT people of color organizing in the 1980s include the National Association of Black and White Men Together, which had numerous local affiliates during the 1980s; the National Latina/o Lesbian and Gay Organization (LLEGO) as well as the Asian Pacific Lesbian Network were founded in 1987. There also were new political groups for bisexuals, such as BiPOL in San Francisco (1983). Some new trans groups formed as well, despite heavy losses from AIDS, such as FTM (later renamed FTM International).

In its mass mobilizations, the movement also made efforts to be more inclusive and politically progressive. These efforts can be seen in the demands of the 1987 March on Washington for Lesbian and Gay Rights, which for the first time linked gay and lesbian liberation to activism against racism, sexism, and anti-Semitism as well as demanding an end to South African apartheid. The March organizers reached out to key civil rights spokespeople such as United Farm Workers leader Cesar Chavez and the Rainbow Coalition's Rev. Jesse Jackson. These were significant cross-movement interventions, especially given the devastating news from the US Supreme Court in 1986, which upheld state sodomy laws in its ruling in *Bowers v. Hardwick*. Also emerging from the March, in part due to the unwillingness of organizers to include bisexuals in the official name, came a flurry of activity that led to the first-ever National Bisexual Conference in 1990 and the subsequent creation of BiNet, the oldest national bisexual organization in the United States.

The 1990s started with the establishment of the first university-based research center in the United States, the Center for Lesbian and Gay Studies (now the Center for LGBTQ Studies), founded by historian and playwright Martin Duberman at the City University of New York Graduate Center in 1991. It also heralded the presidential election of William J. Clinton in 1992, which promised positive advances at the federal level, such as a willingness to consult national gay and lesbian leaders on a number of issues including ending discrimination against gays and lesbians serving in the military. Clinton also appointed the first openly lesbian or gay federal official, Roberta Achtenberg, who became Assistant Secretary of the US Department of Housing and Urban Development in 1993.[15] These efforts of the new administration—the first Democratic one in twelve years—did not offset the devastating impact of its 1993 "compromise" regarding military service, which was a policy that served to institutionalize secrecy and surveillance known as "Don't Ask, Don't Tell." In addition, state measures such as Colorado's Amendment 2, passed by voters in 1992, intended to dismantle anti-discrimination laws on the basis of sexual identity. Challenges to this measure worked their way through the federal court system and were resolved by the high court in 1996 in the case of *Romer v. Evans*.

The first part of the decade also saw a number of gay mobilizations. The third March on Washington, held in 1993 and this time titled "for Lesbian, Gay, and Bi Equal Rights and Liberation," marked the movement's efforts to mesh its liberal and radical wings; it mobilized half a million people and received significant media coverage. It also inspired the creation of at least two new events and organizations, the National Coming Out Day Project and the

Dyke March, started by the newly formed group Lesbian Avengers, to coincide with annual Pride festivities. These parades and festivals commemorating the Stonewall riots, organized by local groups, became increasingly important sites for LGBTQ activism throughout the end of the twentieth century. They continued to spread to cities and towns across the country in the twenty-first century, expanding the scope—and tempering the militancy—of previous commemorations of the 1969 riots. The twenty-fifth anniversary of Stonewall in 1994 was organized in classic LGBTQ style with a huge national celebration, complete with more radical countermarches to protest the exclusion of transgender people and politics from the "official" event. In a new twist, it was promoted heavily not only by LGBTQ organizations but also by the City of New York, which recognized the economic benefits of gay tourism, a growing boom to some cities and resort areas throughout the end of the century.

Such benefits were not yet apparent with regard to an increasingly visible LGBTQ anti-discrimination issue, that of same-sex marriage. Although the 1987 March had included a mass wedding/protest at the Internal Revenue Service headquarters in Washington, D.C., and a few cases were decided in state courts during the 1980s and 1990s, the issue did not become a major focus for the movement until the 1990s. The growing awareness of the fragility of lesbian and gay relationships vis-à-vis state or federal sanctions became glaringly apparent both during the AIDS crisis and through the publicity given such tragic situations as the Sharon Kowalski case, in which a 1983 car accident severely disabled Kowalski, yet familial as well as official homophobia kept her lover and partner Sharon Thompson from being named her guardian for nearly a decade.

To no one's surprise, growing visibility did not necessarily translate into safety in this period. Publicity surrounding increasing violence against gay people also was a hallmark of the 1990s, when activists' efforts to include anti-gay bias within definitions of "hate crimes" were successful despite internal movement challenges to and questions about the wisdom of embracing such criminal justice strategies. Horrific crimes such as the 1993 murder of Brandon Teena in rural Nebraska accelerated transgender organization and activism, leading to extensive media coverage. Five years later, the 1998 murder of Wyoming student Matthew Shepard exploded on the airwaves. In addition to publicly opposing the imposition of the death penalty for one of his killers, Shepard's parents created a foundation in his name to advocate for LGBTQ rights and services for queer youth.

The history of this recent past and the corresponding efforts of lesbians, gay men, bisexuals, transgender, queer people and their allies to create organizational vehicles for securing a modicum of personal and political protection also leads us to 1996. That year, the US Supreme Court's ruling in *Romer v. Evans* marked the first positive federal court decision for LGBTQ rights as it invalidated discriminatory anti-gay laws at state and municipal levels, where many of the movement's legal advances were taking place in this period. However, at the same time, the Congress passed the Defense of Marriage Act, which denied federal protection for same-sex marriage. These decisions mark an end-point of sorts for twentieth century LGBTQ activism and the proliferation of organizations that resulted. They also signal some of the significant efforts that continued into the twenty-first.

Queer and Homonormative America—The 2000s

In *Rethinking the Gay and Lesbian Movement*, historian Marc Stein records the reclamation of the word "queer" and its transformation from insult to radical emblem. He noted the creation of the activist group Queer Nation in New York in 1990 to engage in direct action challenging hetero- and homo-normativity. Stein observed that the term "queer" at that time meant different things depending on its usage and audience; it since has become a shorthand of sorts for all of those who consider themselves lesbian, gay, bisexual, transgender and/or allied peoples who defy gender and sexual conventions.[16]

Although still controversial in some circles, the use of "queer" opens up the possibilities of multiple coalition partners and a variety of involvements in various campaigns. Organizations such as Queers for Economic Justice (2002–2012) have done just such work with the concept of "queer." However, the general utility of "queer" as an organizational marker of anti-normativity and alliance across the margins seems less persistent. A quick Google search reveals very few groups in 2014 whose name includes "queer" without appending it to "lesbian, gay, bisexual, and transgender." With the rising tide of pro-same-sex marriage laws at both state and federal levels, which signify for some members of our communities the ultimate in assimilationism for LGBTQ people, queerness could be seen as all the more important as a way to distinguish between liberal and radical perspectives for organizing gender and sexual minorities to advance social justice. At the same time, organizations doing more radical and anti-normative work have opted for other kinds of names, gesturing toward queerness but also suggesting more specific aims, such as Gay Shame, Against Equality, FIERCE!, and the Sylvia Rivera Law Project.

As scholar Don Romesburg writes, "Critical perspectives grounded in queer theory have problematized the rise of a marriage-and-kids-focused LGBT national movement since the 1990s. They often characterize this within a neoliberal shift from downward to upward redistribution of rights and resources that led the movements for many marginalized peoples away from liberationist views toward 'individual rights' equality concepts." Many scholars and activists have argued that the fight for equal rights pioneered by homophile activists in the 1950s was radicalized by gay, lesbian, bi, and trans liberationists in the 1970s but then narrowed by national LGBT organizations at the end of the twentieth century. Fueled by wealthy donors, many of whom prioritized inclusion rather than transformation, the mainstream LGBT movement increasingly promoted an equality agenda that "promises that once access to marriage, family, the military, and employment nondiscrimination are secured, 'good' gays will retreat into normative aspirations of domesticity, consumption, and nationalism."[17] While there is no debate that basic rights and fair treatment should be assured to all people in the United States, the national LGBT movement's primary focus on securing access to mainstream institutions has too often pushed aside or left out the pressing concerns of the most marginalized members of our communities. Such "homonormativity" comes at a high price: it not only minimizes the ongoing need for radical changes in American social norms and institutions but also fits neatly into the overarching ideology of privatization and individualism that now dominates our lives.

Despite the extraordinary gains of the last century, sexual minorities still remain vulnerable.[18] Although in 2003 the Supreme Court declared, in the case of *Lawrence v. Texas*, that state sodomy laws that criminalized adult private consensual sex violated constitutional rights to privacy, the decision did not end debates over what is or is not considered acceptable sexuality. In addition, rarely is it noted that the invasion of privacy at issue in the *Lawrence* case involved an interracial couple who were arrested at the home of one of them, the white man, after a neighbor called police to report a "suspicious person" nearby. The particularities of which sexually nonconforming people are likely to be targeted by law enforcement or government agents continue to be influenced by other factors, such as race, class, age, and appearance, as was true in Henry Gerber's day.

Further, the impressive breakthroughs of the twenty-first century—from extensive media visibility and access to governmental and corporate employment to legal victories such as Supreme Court rulings striking down bans on military service and upholding marriage rights—must be balanced by the fact that currently only twenty-two states and the District of Columbia have any laws protecting people against discrimination based on sexual orientation, gender identity, and/or gender expression. While our activism has helped many of us to achieve an unprecedented level of acceptance and inclusion within our families and communities, the benefits do not flow evenly to everyone. Race, class, gender, citizenship status, and ability too often still separate us. There is much more to be done to ensure that such barriers to true equality are removed. As this essay's brief review of LGBTQ organizing and organizations shows, collective efforts to create change for *all* LGBTQ people and our allies will take time, vision, and determination. Such efforts are well worth the investment.

Notes

1 Francine Ramsey, Dr. Marjorie J. Hill, and Cassondra Kellam, "Black Lesbians Matter," Zuna Institute, Sacramento CA July 2010 www.zunainstitute.org. Accessed February 23, 2015.

2 For more general queer history of the era, see, in this volume, Elizabeth Clement and Beans Velocci, "Modern Sexuality in Modern Times (1880s–1930s)."

3 Vern Bullough, "When Did the Gay Rights Movement Begin?" History News Network, April 5, 2005, http://historynewsnetwork.org/article/11316. Accessed March 14, 2015.

4 Henry Gerber, Chicago Gay and Lesbian Hall of Fame, 1992, www.glhalloffame.org. Accessed March 13, 2015.

5 The phrase "hidden from history" references the title of a significant early gay history anthology: Martin Bauml Duberman, Martha Vicinus, and George Chauncey, Jr., eds., *Hidden from History: Reclaiming the Gay & Lesbian Past* (New York: New American Library/Penguin, 1989).

6 For more general queer history of this era, see, in this volume, Amanda Littauer, "Sexual Minorities at the Apex of Heteronormativity (1940s–1965)."

7 Michael Bronski, *A Queer History of the United States* (Boston: Beacon Press, 2011): 176–177.

8 For more general queer history of this era, see, in this volume, Whitney Strub, "Gay Liberation (1960s–1970s)."

9 Marcia M. Gallo, "Introduction, An Interpretation and Document Archive—The *Ladder*: A Lesbian Review," *Women and Social Movements* 14, no. 2 (September 2010): 10.

10 For more on the efforts of the DOB and others to construct a lesbian history, see, in this volume, Julie Enszer, "Lesbian Histories: Spirals of Imagination, Marginalization, Creation, and Erasure."

11 Exhibit, "Gay and Lesbian Activist Alliance of Washington, D.C., 1971–2010," *OutHistory.org*. Accessed March 13, 2015.

12 Vicki L. Eaklor, *Queer America: A People's GLBT History of the 20th Century* (New York: The New Press, 2008), 123–124; 132–135, 148–151.

13 For more focused discussions on the themes of health and AIDS, see the chapters in this volume by Katie Batza and Jennifer Brier, respectively.

14 Martin Duberman, *Hold Tight Gently: Michael Callen, Essex Hemphill, and the Battlefield of AIDS* (New York: The New Press, 2014), 119–120.

15 Achtenberg had been a member of the San Francisco Board of Supervisors and was former director of the National Center for Lesbian Rights, founded in 1977 by attorney Donna J. Hitchens as the Lesbian Rights Project of Equal Rights Advocates, a feminist law firm.

16 Marc Stein, *Rethinking the Gay and Lesbian Movement* (New York: Routledge, 2012): 184–85.

17 Don Romesburg, "Where She Comes From: Locating Queer Transracial Adoption," *QED: A Journal in GLBTQ Worldmaking*, 1, no. 3 (Fall 2014): 18–19. See also Margot Weiss's essay, "Queer Politics in Neoliberal Times," in this collection.

18 For a longer analysis of the question of "progress" in queer history, see, in this volume, Marc Stein, "Law and Politics: 'Crooked and Perverse' Narratives of LGBT Progress."

Further Reading

Bérubé, Allan. *Coming Out Under Fire: The History of Gay Men and Women in World War Two.* New York: The Free Press, 1990.

Brier, Jennifer. *Infectious Ideas: U.S. Political Responses to the AIDS Crisis.* Chapel Hill: University of North Carolina Press, 2009.

Boyd, Nan Alamilla. *Wide-Open Town: A History of Queer San Francisco to 1965*. Berkeley: University of California Press, 2003.

Bullough, Vern, ed. *Before Stonewall: Activists for Gay and Lesbian Rights in Historical Context*. Philadelphia: Harrington Park Press/Haworth Press, 2002.

Bullough, Vern and Bonnie Bullough. "Lesbianism in the 1920s and 1930s: A Newfound Study." *Signs: Journal of Women in Culture and Society* 2, no. 4 (1977): 895–904.

Canady, Margot. *The Straight State: Sexuality and Citizenship in Twentieth-Century America*. Princeton: Princeton University Press, 2009.

Churchill, David S. "Transnationalism and Homophile Political Culture in the Postwar Decades." *GLQ* 15, no. 1 (2008): 31–66.

Combahee River Collective. "Combahee River Collective Statement." *The Black Activist* 1 (2013 [1977]): 57–66.

D'Emilio, John. "Cycles of Change, Questions of Strategy: The Gay and Lesbian Movement After Fifty Years." In *The World Turned: Essays on Gay History, Politics, and Culture*, 85–88. Durham: Duke University Press, 2002.

——. *Sexual Politics, Sexual Communities: The Making of a Homosexual Minority in the United States, 1940–1970*. Chicago: University of Chicago Press, 1983.

Enke, Finn. *Finding the Movement: Sexuality, Contested Space, and Feminist Activism*. Durham: Duke University Press, 2007.

Gallo, Marcia M. *Different Daughters: A History of the Daughters of Bilitis and the Rise of the Lesbian Rights Movement*. New York: Carroll & Graf, 2006; Berkeley: Seal Press, 2007.

Hurewitz, Daniel. *Bohemian Los Angeles and the Making of Modern Politics*. Berkeley: University of California Press, 2007.

Katz, Jonathan Ned. *Gay American History*. New York: Avon Books, 1976.

Loftin, Craig. *Letters to ONE: Gay and Lesbian Voices from the 1950s and 1960s*. Albany: SUNY Press, 2012.

Meeker, Martin. *Contacts Desired: Gay and Lesbian Communications and Community, 1940s–1970s*. Chicago: University of Chicago Press, 2006.

Mumford, Kevin J. "The Trouble with Gay Rights: Race and the Politics of Sexual Orientation in Philadelphia, 1969–1982." *Journal of American History* 98, no. 1 (2011): 49–72.

Plaster, Joey. "Imagined Conversations and Activist Lineages: Public Histories of Queer Homeless Youth Organizing and the Policing of Public Space in San Francisco's Tenderloin, 1960s and Present." *Radical History Review* 113 (2012): 99–109.

Rupp, Leila J. "The Persistence of Transnational Organizing: The Case of the Homophile Movement." *American Historical Review* 116, no. 4 (2011): 1014–1039.

Smith, Barbara. *The Truth that Never Hurts: Writings on Race, Gender and Freedom*. New Brunswick: Rutgers University Press, 2000.

Stein, Marc. *City of Sisterly and Brotherly Loves: Lesbian and Gay Philadelphia, 1945–1972*. Philadelphia: Temple University Press, 2004.

Stewart-Winter, Timothy. *Queer Clout: Chicago and the Rise of Gay Politics*. Philadelphia: Temple University Press, 2016.

Stryker, Susan. *Transgender History*. Berkeley: Seal Press, 2008.

Takahashi, Saori, review of Jane Ward, "Respectably Queer: Diversity Culture in LGBT Activist Organizations." *Spaces for Difference: An Interdisciplinary Journal* 2, no. 2 (2011): 31–34.

White, C. Todd. *Pre-Gay L.A.: A Social History of the Movement for Homosexual Rights*. Champaign: University of Illinois Press, 2009.

12

THE END OF QUEER URBAN HISTORY?

Kwame Holmes

In 2001, the Brookings Institution told a beleaguered Washington, D.C. city council they needed to jump-start property ownership in the nation's capital. Lawmakers were offered two options. The "family strategy" promised to attract a robust "middle class" population of "teachers, law enforcement officers, nurses and other . . . professional, technical, and clerical workers" by subsidizing single family homeownership and reforming public schools. The "adult" strategy focused on drawing childless, unmarried high-income residents into a Washington that boasted strong "cultural amenities, restaurants, nightlife, and racial, ethnic and income diversity."[1] Nowhere is the "adults" strategy more evident than in the redevelopment of the Navy Yard into the riverfront home of the Washington Nationals. The success of the "adults" oriented strategy in Washington should give historians of urban queerness pause. For most of the previous century urban planners were committed to resisting their cities' attraction to unmarried adults.

During and after World War II, city leaders added urban planning to their arsenal of tactics against the deleterious influence of the broadly unattached; unmarried women, homeless and homosexual men and sex workers. Yet in twenty-first-century Washington, not only were single adults identified as welcome additions to the city's tax rolls, but the redevelopment of the Navy Yard displaced a commercial district that had served Washington's gay men, and which other queer populations had made their own. One of a half-dozen gay bars forced to close during the construction of Nationals Park was Follies, owned by former call boy Marty Crowetz (whose former clients included a federal judge and more than a few congressman).[2] In a gay commercial zone designed to serve the interests of elite white gay men, Crowetz's working-class identity made space for black, white and latinx drag performers and hustlers who frequented his bar. Follies' closure spoke to a material loss of territory for economically and sexually marginal communities, all in the name of making a national capital for "adults."

Had Brookings released their report 20 years earlier, it is likely they would have avoided terms as cavalier as "adult." As historian Whitney Strub notes, in the early 1980s, at the height of the influence of the Moral Majority, Washington's most visible "adult" oriented businesses were pornography theaters, X-rated book stores and illicit massage parlors nestled within African American and gay associated neighborhoods. Today, not only has Washington embraced an adult development strategy, its implementation has displaced one form of queerness—porn theaters and gay bars—for another—singleness and childlessness. Similar trends have made every major city around the globe equal-measures tolerant to sexual difference and prohibitively expensive to all but the wealthiest potential residents, be they gay or straight.

All of this leaves US queer urban history in a bit of a bind. In addition to uncovering the stories of sexual minorities who survived less accepting times, the field has contributed to our understanding of urban leisure, policing, planning, politics and economics. As Julie Abraham notes in *Metropolitan Lovers*, homosexuality's illegibility has directed our collective conceptualization of twentieth century cities as mysterious, titillating and deadly. "To condemn" or "embrace homosexuality" she writes, is to "condemn" or "embrace the city."[3] But the dis-aggregation of singleness, childlessness and transience from contemporary conceptions of the "urban deviant" or queer, begs important questions about the continued utility of homo-sexuality as a symbolic anchor for historical investigations into urban political economy. Has queer urban history come to an end?

Spoiler alert, this essay responds in the negative. Still, the predominate conception of queer within American historiography is too tethered to LGBT identity to assemble an easy case for the relevance of queer urban history. Does "queer" refer to a constituency? We know from George Chauncey's *Gay New York* that white gay men in interwar cities first used the term to refer to homosexuals who retained a masculine gender presentation. Yet masculine white gay men are precisely those queers who, in spite of verifiable evidence, are most often read as a boon to a twenty-first-century city's economic fortune.[4] Black feminist political scientist Cathy Cohen offers guidance by expanding the realm of the normative and arguing for a theory of queer that is "inclusive of all those who stand on the outside of. . .state-sanctioned white middle and upper-class heterosexuality."[5] Borrowing from Cohen, Roderick Ferguson and a now significant black feminist/queer literature, I contend that "queer" speaks to a historical object's disruptive relation to normativity. While the primary metaphors for "normal" and "deviant" are drawn from sexual and reproductive imagery, many intersecting forces of meaning-making, such as racialization, class, and adherence to or deviance from "good" urban citizenship, hold sway as well.[6] Framing queer as a dynamically mutually constitutive other, determined in compliment to the shifting pole of "normalcy," defers any claims that cities "are" (or "are not") normative. A more expansive understanding of queer opens up an opportunity to rethink the field's foundational assumptions.

This framing requires us to reassess the body of scholarship currently categorized as "queer urban history," which is a literature primarily concerned with LGBT-identified sexual minorities. Here, I mark as relevant any scholarship that gives significant attention to the experience of *sexual minorities* (those whose sexual behavior or identity fell outside the bounds of what predominate political and cultural rhetorics defined as normal) or that centers the *regulation of sexuality* as a protagonist in histories of urban political economy. Deploying a large net incorporates a slate of books published before "queer" became an institutionalized category of analysis within American history. In keeping with the post-structuralist origins of queer theory, this essay sets aside scholarly intent and draws in relevant works from the broad array of multicultural social history. An expansive application of queer to urban historiography reveals that women and gender history, as well as feminist and black feminist studies, provide the intellectual architecture for LGBTQ urban history.

Given my ambitious disciplinary scope, I've written a kind of historiographical synthesis. The analysis centers author interventions, to tell the queer history of three distinct historical periods. "Development and Desire in the Gilded Age-Progressive Era" covers queer populations and queer urban geographies from the end of the Civil War through the New Deal.[7] These years were defined by unprecedented human mobility as millions of migrants entered the nation's large and mid-size cities, which presented a challenge to traditional sexual mores and institutions. "Infiltration and Opportunity before Stonewall" reads through historians' investigations into the primacy of concealment, covertness and subterfuge, to the regulation of urban LGBT people at the height of Cold War America. Finally, in "The Cost of Visibility" I engage with scholarship on the post-Stonewall queer city to see how historians have explained the emergence of "gay and lesbian" normativity and the persistence of marginalization of non-homonormative urban populations.

Development and Desire in the Gilded Age-Progressive Era

The Gilded Age-Progressive Era (1877–1929) democratized desire in the United States.[8] Between 1870 and 1900, nearly 12 million Asians, Latin Americans, black Caribbeans and Europeans migrated to the United States. This massive movement of people not only uncorked new modes of sexuality, but empowered sexuality as a constitutive force in American culture and political economy. Queer urban history is so ubiquitous that each of these constituencies are represented in foundational or forthcoming urban histories. In Nayan Shah's social history of Asian immigrants in turn-of-the-century San Francisco, *Contagious Divides: Epidemics and Race in San Francisco's Chinatown*, he describes queer domesticity as a "variety of erotic ties and social affiliations that counters normative expectations . . . of respectable middle-class, heterosexual marriage," from "female headed household networks to [male] workers' bunkhouses and opium dens."[9] Shah understands municipal health reform as an effort to discipline Chinese migrants into normative gender and sexual roles, and unearths migrants clever strategies for maintaining "queer" Chinese cultural traditions through dissemblance and popular culture. Shah's work is essential for understanding the political impulse towards normativity within the American city.

Other texts have more closely analyzed the relationship between migration and homosexual sex. There is now a significant popular and academic literature on men and women's deviant sexuality in the modern migrant city. Taken together, their work illuminates distinct gendered and racial paths migrants took to experimentation, and even commitment to same-sexuality and/or marginalized sexual community. Indeed, the literature on queer urbanization in mid-Atlantic and Midwestern cities is so significant, it is necessary to further divide the field along gender lines.

As Tim Gilfoyle and George Chauncey demonstrate, unattached bachelors began congregating in major cities during the early national period. Peter Boag and Frank Tobias Higbie suggest how nineteenth-century gender imbalance in frontier towns and in urban "sporting life" encouraged the proliferation of illicit homosocial spaces where same-sexuality posed little challenge to men's access to "manhood" provided their sexual role was penetrative, and their demeanor rough and tumble. By contrast, the emergence of the modern city at the turn of the twentieth century was more characterized by a marked increase in unmarried or "adrift" women in urban populations. Julie Abraham's analysis of the sublimated sexual imperatives driving Jane Addams' reform movement offers a useful frame for centering women's history to the history of queer urbanity in the Progressive Era. There, Abraham argues that settlement reflected a maternal lesbian intervention against the deprivations of urban poverty. Addams never identified as a "mannish-woman" or female "invert," but her vision for the settlement movement emphasized the importance of women "loving on each other" in what Abraham calls "combination."

Women's social historians were the first to craft methods to unearth evidence of "deviant" sexuality as byproduct of urban poverty. In *Women Adrift: Independent Wage Earners in Chicago, 1880–1930* Joanne Meyerowitz combines census and immigration data from industrial cities with records left by reform workers in the Chicago settlement house movement to make sense of women's intimate home lives in the turn of the century metropolis. There, she found that women's survival strategies made same-sex affection, broadly defined, more likely as migrant women pooled financial and emotional resources, sharing household expenses and bedrooms in unforgiving industrial cities. Meyerowitz found queer female alternative domesticities beyond the wealthy and professional-class "Boston marriages" of some high-status women in the era.

Queer women, of course, do not only live indoors. Lillian Faderman's *Odd Girl and Twilight Lovers* locates queer women whose exhibitionist approach to the 1920s roped them into headline grabbing scandals or into the clutches of the criminal justice system. Indeed, lesbians were most visible to the state, and by proxy historians, when caught up in informal or criminalized economies. Police reports and sociological investigations most readily apprehend lesbian desire among women going through some form of personal crisis. Similar archives have allowed historians access into stories of sex work, a vast labor sector that is a constituency of queer urban history.

Meyerowitz and Faderman's contemporaries in women's labor history and black women's history reveal that regardless of sexual orientation, women's sexuality was fraught terrain in the Gilded and Progressive city; particularly as migration and technological change allowed women new access to compartmentalized urban public spheres. Much of this scholarship reveals that, but for rare exceptions, class ambition and racial anxiety collided with most urban women's impulse towards sexual experimentation, of any type. In *Cheap Amusements*, Kathy Peiss found that urban dance halls, carousels, and movies opened opportunities for women to exert sexual agency, but that the commercialization of women's autonomy commodified "an ideology . . . that fused notions of female autonomy and pleasure with heterosexual relationships and consumerism."[10]

Hazel Carby's influential article, "Policing the Black Woman's Body in an Urban Context," reads black and white women's reform activism in New York through the lens of black feminist theories of respectability politics. She establishes that black women's urbanization inspired a moral panic—or as she writes, "a series of responses from institutions and individuals that identified the behavior of these migrating women as a social and political problem . . . that had to be rectified order to restore a moral order." Carby also shows how the institutionalization of charity empowered middle-class white and black women to discipline the moral attitudes and behaviors of working-class black women.[11] Ruth Alexander's *The 'Girl Problem'* and Mary Odem's *Delinquent Daughters* approached the politicization of women's sexual autonomy through the lens of a parallel moral panic; middle class concern with juvenile crime. Odem's investigations into juvenile court made clear that working class families were willing to use the criminal justice system to regulate young women's behavior.[12] Cheryl Hicks' *Talk With You Like a Woman* further complicated Odem's intervention by demonstrating how the court system proved to be the sector of state power African Americans could most reliably wield in their communities and families. Black women's sexuality became an object of concern and political organizing.

Throughout the Progressive Era, brothels, speakeasies, flat parties, and the jail house were the most visible urban institutions that made space for women's queer sexualities, as historians such as Alecia Long and Elizabeth Clement describe. Gendered embargoes around finance credit, and women's relatively weak purchasing power made it difficult for them to establish commercial spaces that did not respond to male sexual desire. As Nan Boyd points out in *Wide Open Town*, lesbian commercial spaces were rare in major cities prior to the 1920s, and even then, were scant in relation to spaces available to homosexual men. For black women, racialization already limited the scope of black institutional territory, forcing recorded evidence of sexual agency to the most marginal urban geographies. In *I've Got to Make My Livin': Black Women's Sex Work in Turn-of-the-Century Chicago*, Cynthia Blair illuminates the labor conditions that demanded black women's participation in professional courtesanship. Misogynoir left working class black women with the option of domestic work, where they might be vulnerable to unwanted sexual advances, or the informal economy, which included participation in policy games, bootlegging and prostitution.

Somewhat like lesbians and gay men in the Progressive Era, sex workers moved in and out of non-normative behaviors, depending on their immediate economic conditions. Cheryl Hicks' *Talk With Me Like a Woman* advances Carby's interest in the regulation of black women's gender and sexuality and locates archival evidence of black lesbianism within the city's criminal justice system. Sociological investigations into women's same-sex behavior in Rikers Island show researchers searching for evidence to confirm black women were more likely to be "inverts." In turn, as black migrant communities gained greater access to the court system, Harlem elites used criminal prosecution as a form of moral reform, keeping black women's gender and sexual expression in line. Indeed, if we highlight the regulation of gender and sexuality in queer histories, then the vast literature of black intra-community sexual regulation must be taught as urban queer history alongside works featuring LGBT subjects.[13]

As women's urban historians, starting in the 1980s, advanced early twentieth-century queer urban historiography with social history methods, scholarship on queer urban men and masculinity emerged in dialogue with the turn towards cultural studies in the early 1990s, by scholars such as Gail Bederman and George Chauncey. Queer men's urban history was more likely to also draw upon Foucauldian analyses of discursive emergence and Butler's feminist phenomenology in order to periodize the categorization of "the homosexual" (or queer) and the "heterosexual" (or normative) prior to World War II. In Chauncey's *Gay New York*, diverse male sexual taxonomies of fairies, wolves, punks, normals, and queers emerged horizontally, in languages and activities ranging from the verbal to the sartorial. To substantiate his claim that "the gay world" was vibrant and well known prior to World War II, Chauncey overlaid journalistic coverage of urban perversion with sexology research and the private diaries and letters of middle-class gay men who traveled throughout the city's many same-sex friendly geographies.

Chauncey's interest in discursive and performative infrastructures of homosexuality influenced several books concerned with the fluid boundaries of "manhood" in the modern city. Progressive city "manhood" could be maintained, provided a gentleman assumed the penetrative role in sexual behavior and provided that homosocial recreation refused the prying eyes of women reformers. Kevin Mumford's *Interzones* took up the subject of interracial sexuality as a potential limit to male sexual authority within the city. White men's ability to travel from middle class neighborhoods into liminal "interzones" gave them access to men and women's bodies across the color line, even as anxiety about black penetration of white women advanced federal legislation and anti-black pogroms. Kevin T. Murphy engaged these questions within political history, arguing that political leaders in Progressive Era New York distanced themselves from the "political hermaphrodites" who supported women's reform agenda and associated themselves with the virile masculinity of working-class men.

Chad Heap's *Slumming* complicated these notions by arguing that men were not the only ones who accessed the power of normativity in opposition to a constitutive other. Indeed, his social and cultural history of slumming revealed that as the Progressive Era became the 1920s, the growth of heterosocial entertainment made it possible for white women to sample a buffet of urban deviance, including the allure of black male heterosexuality.[14] *Slumming* also reveals the extent to which sexual deviance became racialized by the end of the Progressive Era. As southern and eastern European immigrants graduated from neighborhoods within what University of Chicago sociologist Robert Park called the urban "deterioration zone," African Americans replaced them and inherited not only their dwellings, but the association between poverty, vice and homosexuality. This dynamic is taken into serious account in Julio Capo's book *Welcome to Fairy Land*, a history of queer Miami prior to 1940.

Defined by demographic mobility that brought millions of laboring migrants from rural farms to urban factories and the unprecedented gender, ethnic and racial diversification of cities, the Gilded Age-Progressive Era gave birth to the nation's first modern sexual subjects and moral crises. In these years, new sexual opportunities were directly tied to the compartmentalization of urban geography and new avenues for spatial and moral boundary crossings. Historians should most often identify queerness as a state of liminality, where the borders of sexual identities, systems and geographies were in constant flux. Nowhere was this truer than in cities that underwent dynamic transformation.

Opportunity and Infiltration before Stonewall

World War II and its aftermath ushered in a new era in American urban sexual subcultures.[15] As Clayton Howard explains, federal investment in white suburban homeownership expanded the reach of metropolitan areas and, in turn, organized a suburban–urban divide in the nation's sexual geography. As Nick Syrett notes, postwar national investment in suburbs opened opportunities for white-collar men with car ownership and business travel to find extramarital same-sex liaisons while "on the road." Those same forces, though, placed distance between white queer suburban youth and cities, which helped construct racially specific imaginaries of the rural-to-urban coming out narrative that took hold as postwar youth came of age in the 1960s and 1970s.[16] Simultaneously, hundreds of thousands of gay men and lesbians took advantage of travel opportunities presented by military service. Deposited into coastal cities, queer veterans—particularly those disorderly discharged from the armed forces–launched the homophile movement, the first national gay community service and political organizations.[17] In these organizations, gay political and personal identity were crafted with the city in mind and heart, solidifying into the pavement of Los Angeles, San Francisco, Chicago, Philadelphia, D.C., Miami and New York. As the nation's sexual geography became more explicitly rigid, sexual minorities and regulators alike conceived of sexual behavior and identity in increasingly binary terms. One way to make sense of these developments is to think about the postwar years as defined by queer opportunities amid national anxieties about queer infiltration.

Historiographically, this complicates our efforts to capture a queer urban history. Read together, studies of homosexual, sex work and slumming subcultures in Progressive Era cities reveal inner city vice districts as intersectional, playing host to overlapping queer communities. Moving into the literature on the racialization of suburban development and urban renewal from the 1940s through the 1960s, though, metropolitan development was designed, in part, to racially manage regional populations as postwar liberalism placed mounting cultural pressure against explicit segregationism.[18] In this context, for many white Americans, to protect one's home was to protect it from infiltration from racial and sexual minorities.[19] Within cities, "tough," "family men" mayors used police power and eminent domain to root out sexually irresponsible homosexuals and public housing residents. Urban clean-up efforts took two predominate forms, aggressive anti-gay policing and urban renewal.

There is a much larger body of queer historical literature examining the former strategy. Estelle Freedman and George Chauncey established templates for examining anti-gay policing in this era through their histories of postwar sex crime panics. For both, sensationalist coverage of gruesome sexual crimes against women and children became rationales for new medicalized discourse that diagnosed homosexuals as monsters incapable for controlling their hidden desires. Research on the sex crime panic reveals a fundamental shift in how homosexuality was represented within urban media outlets between the inter and postwar years. Gone was the interplay between sensation and censure. Medicalized readings of homosexuals and of cities themselves raised the stakes of sexually normative landscapes, and municipal police departments responded in kind.

Local studies such as Marc Stein's *City of Brotherly and Sisterly Loves*, Chris Agee's *The Streets of San Francisco*, and Timothy Stewart-Winter's *Queer Clout* offer unique interpretations of anti-gay policing in these years. Stein identifies police departments' awareness of shifting trends in gay male desire, as the Philadelphia police sent attractive men into popular cruising areas to entrap gay men in public lewdness or solicitation charges. Agee discusses the practice of "gayola" wherein police agents would shakedown gay bar owners for protection money, and how a scandal related to this practice led to police reform in that city. Stewart-Winter focuses on widespread raids conducted against gay bars in Chicago as an ongoing check against gay power well into the 1970s. Indeed, gay bar raids were among the more popular form of anti-gay policing, creating an atmosphere of insecurity in one of the few spaces gay people could call their own.

Urban renewal also produced an assault on the queer urban poor, broadly defined. The 1953 *Bowers v. Chapman* decision expanded federal, state and municipal governments' ability to engineer urban landscapes to their liking, and they took aim at neighborhoods "blighted" by vice and single motherhood. Queer studies has not tended to include the significant history of welfare rights into our histories, but nearly all of the major monographs on urban welfare rights movements argue that the 1965 Moynihan Report—itself the culmination of decades of sociological work—stigmatized poor women's sexuality and reproduction outside of marriage.[20] Kevin Mumford's work reveals the way sociological and social psychological research identified homosexuality as a by-product of "broken families." Similarly, urban planners condemned and redeveloped urban residential corridors in a vain effort to attract the married middle class back into the city. Some LGBT urban historians have directly approached these questions. Stein's far-reaching text engages the controversy over naming the Walt Whitman bridge, illuminating how easy it was for urban Americans to define themselves in relation to urban architecture. Josh Sides' *Erotic City* details the mutual evolution of pro-growth planning and anti-gay crusades in San Francisco. My own work on Washington, D.C. reveals that wiping out sexual deviance, particularly within African American neighborhoods, was a contributing factor to the political will for urban renewal in the nation's capital. The transition within federal anti-poverty policy towards active reform of the individual increased attention on the homosexual as a constituent of the urban crisis. Christina Hanhardt and Martin Meeker's work reveals that gays and lesbians, where visible, were targeted by more therapeutic urban technocracy as well.

However paranoiac, anxiety about homosexual infiltration reflected, in part, white gays and lesbians' ability to make slow in-roads into elite urban social and artistic circles in these years. Racial privilege did not guarantee white gays and lesbians could overcome the downward pressure their sexuality placed on their economic or personal ambitions. Rather, it made possible a range of improvisations that generated unique subcultures all around the country. In *Cherry Grove/Fire Island: Sixty Years in America's First Gay and Lesbian Town*, Esther Newton describes patterns of gay cooperative renting and home ownership within elite New York beach towns that allowed working-class gays, many of them artists, to move and shake among the holidaying hoi polloi. Meanwhile, upstate in Buffalo, Elizabeth Kennedy and Madeline Davis used oral history methodologies to describe a world of working-class butches and femmes mixing across racial divisions that hardened over time.

These years also witnessed the germination of the modern gay rights political movement, setting the terms for its evolution as a constituent of urban development through the present moment. It is important to distinguish between organizational histories of gay political movements that were located within the city, and works that take the urban character of gay politics as a primary subject. In the former category, we can include an enormous range of scholarship, nearly every institutional history in popular or academic realms. Daniel Hurewitz's history of early homophile organizing in Los Angeles and Marcia Gallo's history of the Daughters of Bilitis illuminate the centrality of cities, and in the case of Hurewitz, a single neighborhood, to fostering notions of self-conscious sexual identity necessary for politicization. Genny Beemyn and David Johnson's work on homophile activism in Washington places the otherwise sleepy capital city on the map of LGBT history. Indeed, the Mattachine Society of Washington's picketing of the federal government in 1965 could be called the first "national" mobilization of LGBT politics in US history.

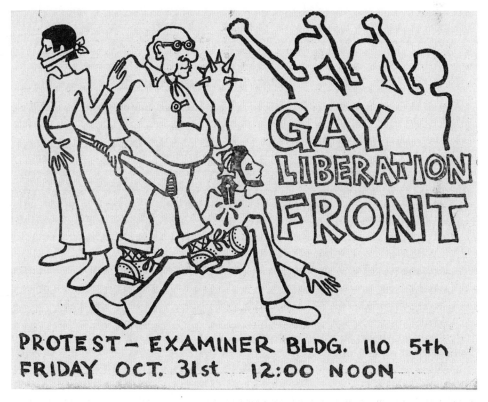

Figure 12.1 Committee for Homosexual Freedom/Gay Liberation Front flier, San Francisco, 1969, invoking, as Emily Hobson notes in *Lavender and Red: Liberation and Solidary in the Gay and Lesbian Left* (Berkeley: University of California Press, 2016), the white male establishment's threat through militarism, media, and policing to urban black and gay liberation.
Courtesy of the GLBT Historical Society.

White gay men and lesbian's partial access to white landscapes expanded racialized distinctions within urban LGBTQ communities. As Marlon Ross makes clear in "Beyond the Closet as Raceless Paradigm," gay identity became predicated upon material and imagined mobility from rural and suburban to urban, a migratory pattern that was less meaningful for African Americans in hyper-segregated cities during the 1960s and 1970s. For most urban African Americans in postwar America, new public housing construction, highway development and radicalized redlining limited their access to the kinds of mobility that made LGBT community-making possible. In turn, the politicization of sexuality manifested differently within black urban areas. As Thaddeus Russel discovered, inner-city black communities readily consumed sexual non-normativity in the entertainment sphere, shifting rightward on the matter when the civil rights movement demanded a morally pure black body politic. Through the story of Prophet Jones, Detroit's most famous charismatic preacher with a penchant for same-sex desire, Tim Retzloff reveals that black communities were occasionally immune to national trends in anti-gay hysteria, supporting the religious figure despite his arrest for sexual solicitation.

If Gilded/Progressive America was defined by an ongoing liminality, the binary logic of the Cold War consolidated all moral authority on the side of narrowly defined economic and national security interests. Binaries proliferated, establishing suburban–urban and heterosexual–homosexual divides. The increased knowability of homosexuality and lesbianism in these years cast urban sexual difference as a threat to public safety and national security. Yet gay and lesbian activists and business owners, particularly those who could secure a proximity to middle-class whiteness and respectability, began to make inroads into legitimacy as urban citizens.

The Problem of Visibility since Stonewall

With good reason, queer studies scholars have pushed back against the Stonewall myth.[21] From the moment a collection of black, latinx and white drag queens, sex workers and gay men resisted police encroachment into the Stonewall Inn, the Stonewall Riot became a rallying cry for gay urban activisms that—at times—lacked the racial and economic diversity displayed in the riot itself. Nonetheless, Stonewall symbolized a process that, by the turn of the twenty-first century, would disaggregate gay urbanity from queerness. As gay populations concentrated in neighborhoods such as the Castro, Lakeview or DuPont Circle, activists replicated political strategies honed by urban minority constituencies since the Progressive Era, promoting gay populations as essential to the city's future. Historians have only begun to write about these years, but some trends have emerged.[22]

Several new gay urban social histories combine diligent archival work with oral histories to mark similarities and variation between gay and African American or women's activist histories since Stonewall. Stewart-Winter's *Queer Clout* frames gay activisms as part of an ongoing diversification of machine politics in Chicago and other major cities. By forging alliances with African Americans, gay activists aided and took advantage of a leftward turn in the cultural politics of the city during the 1970s and 1980s. As cities passed open housing and anti-discrimination law, gay activists joined those efforts and in Washington, Miami-Dade, St. Paul Minnesota, Philadelphia, San Francisco, Boston and New York, could expand those ordinances to include sexual orientation protections.[23] Perhaps most importantly, this work illustrates the ways white gay men gained literal ownership over gay space—squeezing out the influence of organized crime—and symbolic ownership over the brand of the "gay ghetto." Urban women's historians such as Anne Valk and Georgina Hickey, along with queer geographers such as Jen Jack Giesking, have documented the challenges lesbians and second-wave feminists faced in making gay-friendly cities as amenable to unmarried women. Women's relative disinterest in creating profitable community spaces gave them less political capital than movements financed by gay male club owners. Steeped in social history, these scholars emphasize the struggle sexual minorities face against the state. Still more work needs to be conducted on the impact of a resurgent moral majority in the late 1970s and early 1980s, and a public indifferent to the HIV-AIDS epidemic in the 1980s on urban LGBT politics and identity.[24]

Simultaneously, a cadre of urban cultural studies scholars deploy gay politics as one of many public discourses contributing to the aggressive neoliberalization of urban life.[25] Michael Warner's *The Trouble with Normal* and Sam Delaney's *Times Square Red, Times Square Blue* unpack the Koch and Dinkins adminstration's efforts to sanitize New York's Time Square, clearing the land of sexual minorities in favor of "family friendly" commercial development. Christina Hanhardt's *Safe Space* traces LGBT anti-violence politics in tandem with criminological thought about the origins and consequence of inner-city crime. If gay urban social histories are primarily concerned with tracing gay population's relationship to the state, cultural queer urban studies take the imperatives of capital as an institution that shapes sexual regulation. In Hanhardt, for example, the visibility differential between white gay male and women of color anti-violence politics is determined by each constituency's relationship with purchasing power, speculative fantasies of land investors, and middle-class consumers.

Indeed, queer urban studies of the post-Stonewall period reveal that queer people exist on a Kinsey scale measuring proximity to racial and economic normativity. Work by Martin Manalansan, Carlos Decena and Horacio Roque Ramirez illuminates how transnational labor migration continues to bring queer immigrant populations into cities. There they must navigate and remake the incentives for migrant populations to pool resources, this time through heterosexual marriage. Independent black gay movements, as much informed by women of color feminism and black nationalism as by the gay liberation front, began to emerge in the late 1970s in the Bay Area, Chicago, Detroit, DC, Newark, Baltimore, New York and Atlanta.[26] In turn though, the Black Power movement expanded the reach of patriarchy in the black community, framing gender normativity as an inheritance white society denied black communities. As Kevin Mumford, E Patrick Johnson and Daniel Martin document, Black Power institutions were also sites of intense gender regulation and hyper masculinity. As a result, non-heterosexual African Americans were more likely to travel within worlds of tight gender and sexual supervision, engaging in furtive sexual contacts and disavowing gay identity. Indeed, for queer communities of color, visibility could be a source of angst. As I argue elsewhere, political rhetoric by queers of color—when associated with sites of urban decline—has been used by pro-growth politicians to rationalize aggressive displacement of the queer space through urban redevelopment and gentrification.

Conclusion: Reclaiming the Queer City

While preparing this essay, I perused the 2015 edition of the American Values Atlas (AVA), an interactive map of American political and religious belief covering four US regions, 50 states and over 30 metropolitan areas. Though public support for same-sex marriage and anti-LGBT discrimination law has grown significantly in the last two decades, I expected the Atlas to show that national support for LGBT rights was anchored in our largest cities. From the 1970s to the 2010s, the dialectical politicization of sexual freedom and conservatism has mapped this divide onto partisan electoral politics, producing isolated blue oases for LGBT survival amid the yawning red clay of "flyover country." But this is no longer the case. Whether in

San Francisco, which topped the nation in support for LGBT rights at 81 percent or in Houston, which recorded a low of 67 percent support for the same, the AVA found that urban attitudes towards LGBT rights mirrored those held by the state as a whole.

The erasure of a rural-urban divide on LGBT issues signals a series of major transitions in American political and cultural history. For most of the modern period, American cities have been more hospitable to LGBTQ populations than rural or suburban areas. In turn, "the city" has served as a potent site of national imagination, helpfully exhibiting the constitutive other who shores up the normative borders of "the suburbs." But the advancement of LGBT acceptance outside of major metropolitan areas has decreased national dependence on fantasies of urban perversion. In turn, LGBTQ people no longer concentrate in enclaves once understood as gay ghettos. Nor can they. As global real estate investment continues to flood the nation's largest cities, LGBTQ people, like all metropolitan residents, are regionally sorted by class. The AVA survey tells us the process is all but complete.

The declining influence of the suburban-rural Moral Majority in recent years has also coincided with the dilution of urban institutions designed to serve the unique needs of LGBT populations. Indeed, most gay urban territory only remains legible through marketing collaborations between city hall and entrepreneurs seeking the progressive dollar in neighborhoods such as the Castro or Dupont Circle or Boystown. These developments will require LGBTQ historians to ask new questions about the queer urban past, illuminating stories that historicize liminality, fluidity and disidentification along with the personal and political adventures of sexual minorities. Otherwise, to focus on queer as a coherent demographic is to cling to a no-longer usable past, a queer history whose final chapter is closed.

Notes

1 Carol O'Cleireacain and Alice M. Rivlin, "Envisioning a Future Washington," Brookings Greater Washington Research Program, Brookings Institute, June 2012, 1–2.
2 Marty Crowetz Oral History interview available by request at the Rainbow History Project.
3 Julie Abraham, *Metropolitan Lovers: The Homosexuality of Cities* (Minneapolis: University of Minnesota Press, 2009), xiv–xv.
4 The mythology surrounding white gay male upward pressure on land value was first circulated in gay and non-gay periodicals in the late 1970s and advanced by Manuel Castells' *The City and the Grassroots*. Castells' claims are little more than hearsay, relying upon the word of real estate agents and non-scientific surveys of gay residential patterns. In *Gay Politics, Urban Politics* Robert Bailey notes that high levels of gay residency correlate both with high vacancy and occupancy rates, a variance that precludes drawing strong conclusions about the relationship between gay residency and rental prices or land values. Nonetheless, narratives of gay gentrification have graduated to a kind of common sense, most famously circulated in Richard Florida's *The Rise of the Creative Class*.
5 Cathy J. Cohen, "Punks, Bulldaggers, and Welfare Queens: The Radical Potential of Queer Politics?" *GLQ* 3, no. 4 (1998): 441.
6 This literature, exemplified by Rod Ferguson's 2003 book *Aberrations in Black: Toward a Queer of Color Critique*, prefigures blackness and sexual deviance as mutually constitutive. Black feminist historians such as Jennifer Morgan have affirmed such theories. See her *Laboring Women Reproduction and Gender in New World Slavery*.
7 Here I am referring to periodization that identifies the Gilded Age-Progressive Era as periods with decidedly different ethos, despite sharing the years between the end of the Civil War and the Great Depression.
8 For more generally on this era, see, in this volume, Elizabeth Clement and Beans Velocci, "Modern Sexuality in Modern Times (1880s–1930s)."
9 Nayan Shah, *Contagious Divides: Epidemics and Race in San Francisco's Chinatown* (Berkeley: University of California Press, 2001) 13, 78.
10 Kathy Lee Peiss, *Cheap Amusements: Working Women and Leisure in Turn-of-the-Century New York* (Philadelphia: Temple University Press, 1986), 114.

11 Hazel V. Carby, "Policing the Black Woman's Body in an Urban Context" *Critical Inquiry* 18, no. 4 (Summer 1992): 740.

12 Also see Regina G. Kunzel, *Fallen Women, Problem Girls: Unmarried Mothers and the Professionalization of Social Work, 1890–1945* (New Haven: Yale University Press, 1995); Marian J. Morton, *And Sin No More: Social Policy and Unwed Mothers in Cleveland, 1855–1990* (Columbus: Ohio State University Press, 1993). On the politicization of juvenile sexuality see, Peter C. Baldwin, "'Nocturnal Habits and Dark Wisdom': The American Response to Children in the Streets at Night, 1880–1930." *Journal of Social History* 35, no. 3 (2002): 593–611; Stephen Robertson, "Age of Consent Law and the Making of Modern Childhood in New York City, 1886–1921," *Journal of Social History* 35, no. 4 (2002): 781–98.

13 See, for example, LaShawn Harris, Sex *Workers, Psychics, and Numbers Runners: Black Women in New York City's Underground Economy* (Urbana: University of Illinois Press, 2016); Cookie Woolner, "'Woman Slain in Queer Love Brawl': African American Women, Same-Sex Desire, and Violence in the Urban North, 1920–1929," *Journal of African American History* 100, no. 3 (2015): 406–427.

14 Scholarship from Don Romesburg has similarly pushed us to include men and boys into histories of sex work. Don Romesburg, "'Wouldn't a Boy Do?' Placing Early-Twentieth-Century Male Youth Sex Work into Histories of Sexuality." *Journal of the History of Sexuality* 18, no. 3 (2009): 367–392.

15 For more generally on the queer history of this period, see, in this volume, Amanda Littauer, "Sexual Minorities at the Apex of Heteronormativity (1940s-1965)."

16 See, especially, Kath Weston, "Get Thee to a Big City: Sexual Imaginary and the Great Gay Migration," *GLQ: A Journal of Lesbian and Gay Studies* 2, no. 3 (1995): 253–277.

17 John D'Emilio's 1984 classic *Sexual Politics, Sexual Communities* detailed how stepped up anti-gay policing helped urban gay men and lesbians begin to organize as a political minority in the postwar homophile movement. For more on the development of LGBT organizations, see, in this volume, Marcia M. Gallo, "Organizations."

18 See, especially, David Freund, *Colored Property* (Chicago: University of Chicago Press, 2010); George Lipsitz, *How Racism Takes Place* (Philadelphia: Temple University Press, 2011); Wendell E. Pritchett, *Robert Clifton Weaver and the American City: The Life and Times of an Urban Reformer* (Chicago: University of Chicago Press, 2008); Kevin M. Kruse, *White Flight: Atlanta and the Making of the Modern American South* (University of Princeton Press, 2007).

19 The Cold War added geopolitical import to local concerns around the establishment and protection of normativity. Communism's seemingly exhaustive ability to infiltrate any level of federal or local government, to worm its way into popular culture, rationalized aggressive regulation of the public sphere, and the private lives of all Americans. See, for example, John D'Emilio, "The Homosexual Menace: The Politics of Sexuality in Cold War America," in *Passion and Power: Sexuality in History*, ed. Kathy Peiss and Christina Simmons (Philadelphia: Temple University Press, 1989), 226–240; Alan Nadel, *Containment Culture: American Narrative, Postmodernism, and the Atomic Age* (Durham: Duke University Press, 1995).

20 See, especially, Anne M. Valk, *Radical Sisters: Second-Wave Feminism and Black Liberation in Washington, D.C* (Urbana: University of Illinois Press, 2008); Felicia Kornbluh, *The Battle for Welfare Rights: Politics and Poverty in Modern America* (Philadelphia: University of Pennsylvania Press, 2007); Annelise Orleck, *Storming Caesar's Palace: Black Mother's Fought Their Own War on Poverty* (Boston: Beacon Press, 2005); Rhonda Y. Williams, *The Politics of Public Housing: Black Women's Struggles Against Urban Inequality* (Oxford: Oxford University Press, 2004); Dorothy E Roberts, *Killing the Black Body: Race, Reproduction, and the Meaning of Liberty* (New York: Pantheon Books, 1997).

21 See, especially, Elizabeth A. Armstrong and Suzanna M. Crage, "Movements and Memory: The Making of the Stonewall Myth," *American Sociological Review* 71, no. 5 (2006): 724–751; Martin F. Manalansan, "In the Shadows of Stonewall: Examining Gay Transnational Politics and the Diasporic Dilemma," *GLQ* 2, no. 4 (1995): 425–438.

22 For a more general queer history of the 1970s and gay liberation, see, in this volume, Whitney Strub, "Gay Liberation (1963–1980)."

23 See, for example, Kevin J. Mumford, "The Trouble with Gay Rights: Race and the Politics of Sexual Orientation in Philadelphia, 1969–1982," *Journal of American History* 98, no. 1 (2011): 49–72.

24 For more on AIDS in the context of queer US history, see, in this volume, Jennifer Brier, "AIDS and Action (1980–1990s)."

25 For one attempt to historicize the queer US neoliberal era, see, in this volume, Margot Weiss, "Queer Politics in Neoliberal Times (1970–2010s)."

26 Much of the scholarship on these cities is forthcoming. Also see Darnell L. Moore et al., "A Community's Response to the Problem of Invisibility: The Queer Newark Oral History Project," *QED: A Journal in GLBTQ Worldmaking* 1, no. 2 (2014): 1–14; Kevin Mumford, *Not Straight, Not White: Black Gay Men from the March on Washington to the AIDS Crisis* (Chapel Hill: The University of North Carolina Press, 2016).

Further Reading

Agee, Christopher. *The Streets of San Francisco: Policing and the Creation of a Cosmopolitan Liberal Politics, 1950–1972*. Chicago: University of Chicago Press, 2014.

Alexander, Ruth. *The Girl Problem: Female Sexual Delinquency in New York, 1900–1930*. Ithaca: Cornell University Press, 1995.

Bailey, Robert C. *Gay Politics, Urban Politics: Identity and Economics in the Urban Setting*. New York: Columbia University Press, 1998.

Bederman, Gail. *Manliness and Civilization: A Cultural History of Gender and Race in the United States, 1880–1917*. Chicago: University of Chicago Press, 1996.

Beemyn, Genny. *A Queer Capital: A History of Gay Life in Washington D.C.* New York: Routledge, 2014.

Blair, Cynthia M. *I've Got to Make My Livin': Black Women's Sex Work in Turn-of-the-Century Chicago*. Chicago: University of Chicago Press, 2010.

Boag, Peter. *Same-Sex Affairs: Constructing and Controlling Homosexuality in the Pacific Northwest*. Berkeley: University of California Press, 2003.

Boyd, Nan Alamilla. *Wide-Open Town: A History of Queer San Francisco to 1965*. Berkeley: University of California Press, 2003.

Capo, Julio. *Welcome to Fairyland: Queer Miami before 1940*. Chapel Hill: University of North Carolina Press, 2017.

Castells, Manuel. *The City and the Grassroots*. Berkeley: University of California Press, 1983.

Chauncey, George. *Gay New York: Gender, Urban Culture and the Making of the Gay Male World, 1890–1940*. New York: Basic Books, 1994.

——. "The Postwar Sex Crime Panic." *True Stories from the American Past*, ed. William Graebner, 160–178. New York: McGraw-Hill, 1993.

Clement, Elizabeth A. *Love for Sale: Courting, Treating, and Prostitution in New York City, 1900–1945*. Chapel Hill: University of North Carolina Press, 2000.

Decena, Carlos Ulises. *Tacit Subjects: Belonging and Same-Sex Desire among Dominican Immigrant Men*. Durham: Duke University Press, 2011.

Delaney, Samuel R. *Times Square Red, Times Square Blue*. New York: New York University Press, 1999.

D'Emilio, John. *Sexual Politics, Sexual Communities: The Making of a Homosexual Minority in the United States, 1940–1970*. Chicago: University of Chicago Press, 1983.

Faderman, Lillian. *Odd Girls and Twilight Lovers: A History of Lesbian Life in Twentieth-Century America*. New York: Columbia University Press, 1991.

Ferguson, Roderick. *Aberrations in Black: Toward a Queer of Color Critique*. Minneapolis: University of Minnesota Press, 2003.

Florida, Richard. *The Rise of the Creative Class*. New York: Basic Books, 2002.

Freedman, Estelle. "'Uncontrolled Desires': The Response to the Sexual Psychopath, 1920–1960." *Journal of American History* 74, no. 1 (1987): 83–106.

Gallo, Marcia. *Different Daughters: A History of the Daughters of Bilitis and the Rise of the Lesbian Rights Movement*. Berkeley: Seal Press, 2006.

Gilfoyle, Timothy J. *City of Eros: New York City, Prostitution, and the Commercialization of Sex, 1790–1920*. New York: W. W. Norton & Company, 1994.

Gieseking, Jen Jack. "Crossing over into Neighborhoods of the Body: Urban Territories, Borders and Lesbian-Queer Bodies in New York City" *Area* 48, no. 3 (September 2016): 262–270.

Ha, Kim Chi. "Is a Gay Strip Club Too Close to Nationals Park for D.C.'s Comfort?" Washington City Paper, July 2, 2010, www.washingtoncitypaper.com/news/article/13039176/is-a-gay-strip-club-too-close-to-nationals-park. Accessed October 13, 2016.

Hanhardt, Christina. *Safe Space: Gay Neighborhood History and the Politics of Violence*. Durham: Duke University Press, 2013.

Heap, Chad. *Slumming: Sexual and Racial Encounters in American Nightlife, 1885–1940*. Chicago: University of Chicago Press, 2010.

Higbie, Frank Tobias. *Indispensable Outcasts: Hobo Workers and Community in the American Midwest, 1880–1930*. Urbana: University of Illinois Press, 2003.

Hickey, Georgina. "The Geography of Pornography: Neighborhood Feminism and the Battle against 'Dirty Bookstores' in Minneapolis." *Frontiers: A Journal of Women Studies* 32, no. 1 (May 2011): 125–151.

Hicks, Cheryl. *Talk with You Like a Woman: African American Women, Justice, and Reform in New York, 1890–1935*. Chapel Hill: University of North Carolina Press, 2010.

Holmes, Kwame. "What's the T: Gossip and the Production of Black Gay Social History." *Radical History Review* 2015, no. 122 (2015): 55–69.

Howard, Clayton. "Building a 'Family-Friendly' Metropolis: Sexuality, the State, and Postwar Housing Policy." *Journal of Urban History* 39, no. 5 (2013): 933–955.

Howard, John. "The Library, the Park, and the Pervert: Public Space and Homosexual Encounter in Post-World War II Atlanta." *Radical History Review* 1995, no. 62 (1995): 166–187.

Hurewtiz, Daniel. *Bohemian Los Angeles: and the Making of Modern Politics*. Berkeley: University of California Press, 2007.

Johnson, David K. "'Homosexual Citizens': Washington's Gay Community Confronts the Civil Service." *Washington History* 6, no. 2 (Fall/Winter: 1994/1995): 44–63.

Johnson, E. Patrick. *Appropriating Blackness: Performance and the Politics of Authenticity*. Durham: Duke University Press, 2003.

Kennedy, Elizabeth and Madeline Davis. *Boots of Leather, Slippers of Gold: The History of a Lesbian Community*. New York: Penguin Books, 1994.

Long, Alecia P. *The Great Southern Babylon: Sex, Race, and Respectability in New Orleans, 1865–1920*. Louisiana: Louisiana State University Press, 2005.

Manalansan IV, Martin F. *Global Divas: Filipino Gay Men in the Diaspora*. Durham: Duke University Press Books, 2003.

Martin, Daniel. "'Lift Up Yr Self!' Reinterpreting Amiri Baraka (Leroi Jones), Black Power, and the Uplift Tradition." *Journal of American History* 93, no. 1 (2006): 91–116.

May, Elaine Tyler. *Homeward Bound: American Families in the Cold War Era*. New York: Basic Books, 1988.

Meeker, Martin. "The Queerly Disadvantaged and the Making of San Francisco's War on Poverty, 1961–1967." *Pacific Historical Review* 81, no. 1 (February 2012): 21–59.

Meyerowitz, Joanne. *Women Adrift: Independent Wage Earners in Chicago, 1880–1930*. Chicago: University of Chicago Press, 1988.

Morgan, Jennifer. *Laboring Women Reproduction and Gender in New World Slavery*. Philadelphia: University of Pennsylvania Press, 1996.

Mumford, Kevin J. *Interzones: Black/White Sex Districts in Chicago and New York in the Early Twentieth Century*. New York: Columbia University Press, 1997.

——. "Untangling Pathology: The Moynihan Report and Homosexual Damage, 1965–1975." *Journal of Policy History* 24, no. 1 (January 2012): 53–73.

——. *Not Straight, Not White: Black Gay Men from the March on Washington to the AIDS Crisis*. Chapel Hill: University of North Carolina Press, 2016.

Murphy, Kevin P. *Political Manhood: Red Bloods, Mollycoddles, and the Politics of Progressive Era Reform*. New York: Columbia University Press, 2008.

Newton, Esther. *Cherry Grove/Fire Island: Sixty Years in America's First Gay and Lesbian Town*. Boston: Beacon Press, 1993.

Odem, Mary. *Delinquent Daughters: Protecting and Policing Adolescent Female Sexuality in the United States, 1885–1920*. Chapel Hill: University of North Carolina Press, 1995.

Putney, Clifford. *Muscular Christianity: Manhood and Sports in Protestant America, 1880–1920*. Cambridge: Harvard University Press, 2003.

Retzloff, Tim. "'Seer or Queer?' Postwar Fascination with Detroit's Prophet Jones." *GLQ* 8, no. 3 (2002): 271–296.

Roque Ramírez, Horacio N. "In Transnational Distance: Translocal Gay Immigrant Salvadoran Lives in Los Angeles." *Diálogo Magazine* 12, Center for Latino Research, DuPaul University (Summer 2009): 6–12.

Ross, Marlon B. "Beyond the Closet as Raceless Paradigm." In *Black Queer Studies: A Critical Anthology*, ed. E. Patrick Johnson and Mae Henderson, 161–189. Durham, NC: Duke University Press, 2005.

Russell, Thaddeus. "The Color of Discipline: Civil Rights and Black Sexuality." *American Quarterly* 60, no. 1 (2008): 101–128.

Sides, Josh. *Erotic City: Sexual Revolutions and the Making of Modern San Francisco*. New York: Oxford University Press, 2011.

Stein, Marc. *City of Sisterly and Brotherly Loves: Lesbian and Gay Philadelphia, 1945–1972*. Chicago: University of Chicago Press, 2000.

Stewart-Winter, Timothy. *Queer Clout: Chicago and the Rise of Gay Politics*. Philadelphia: University of Pennsylvania Press, 2016.

Strub, Whitney. *Perversion for Profit: The Politics of Pornography and the Rise of the New Right*. New York: Columbia University Press, 2013.

Summers, Martin. *Manliness and Its Discontents: The Black Middle Class and the Transformation of Masculinity, 1900–1930*. Chapel Hill: The University of North Carolina Press, 2004.

Valk, Anne M. *Radical Sisters: Second-Wave Feminism and Black Liberation in Washington, D.C.* Urbana: University of Illinois Press, 2008.

Warner, Michael. *The Trouble with Normal: Sex, Politics, and the Ethics of Queer Life*. Cambridge: Harvard University Press, 1999.

Whitman, Carl. *A Gay Manifesto*. New York: Red Butterfly, 1970.

13

RURAL

Pippa Holloway and Elizabeth Catte

In 2014, the US Department of Agriculture undertook the "LGBT Rural Summit Series," the agency's first ever outreach to LGBT individuals living in rural areas. In a total of five meetings across the country, participants discussed the unique needs of the rural LGBT community and learned about federal programs designed to support LGBT rural people and families. This outreach program indicates a growing realization that the historical development and contemporary expression of LGBT identity is not solely urban. Both scholarship and popular culture have tended to either ignore rural queer lives or characterize them as being marked by secrecy, discrimination, and violence. Americans across the political spectrum often incorrectly generalize rural populations with whiteness, conservatism, and anti-gay Christian values. In reality, as queer geographers Jon Binnie and Gil Valentine note, the central relevant characteristic of the rural is simply low population density; a secondary characteristic is predominately agricultural economy. People in rural places might be indigenous or migrants. While many may associate the rural United States with whiteness, this association is neither historically nor presently true. Rural populations include Native Americans (especially those on reservations), Hispanics (migrant and/or settled), and African Americans. Rural people have had varied experiences and beliefs, and rural areas have offered distinctive opportunities for gender and sexual diversity throughout US history.

This chapter has two goals. First, it examines scholarship on the particular ways that rural locations supported or limited individuals engaged in non-normative gender and sexual practices, as well lesbian, gay, bisexual, and trans* identities and communities. What kinds of queer lives have been possible and impossible in rural areas over the course of US history? How have rural contexts shaped the emergence of LGBT identities and queer subjectivities? Second, the chapter explores the idea of the rural in shaping understandings of LGBT identities and queer sexuality. How has the rural/urban binary helped to construct sexual identities? How has the figure of the rural informed, supported, or challenged non-normative genders and sexualities?[1]

Within historical scholarship a tendency to shortchange rural experiences is due in part to the fact some of the earliest works in the field investigated the urban communities of which the first LGBT historians were themselves a part. This led to a model of LGBT community formation that emphasized urbanization and industrialization. John D'Emilio's pioneering 1983 article "Capitalism and Gay Identity" suggested that in order for gay identities to develop, individuals had to detach from the family economy by moving to cities and surviving without opposite-sex spouses and offspring. In other words, only in times and places where heterosexual families were no longer essential to subsistence could same-sex desires turn into queer lives and identities.

This focus has led to what Jack Halberstam has dubbed "metronormativity," namely that "most theories of homosexuality within the twentieth century assume that gay culture . . . has a special relationship to urban life." This assumption results in the normalization of certain white, upper- and middle-class queer identities and produces truths about gay life in cities that elide the vast diversity of LGBT experience. Furthermore, metronormativity supposes that the full, satisfied, and safe expression of a queer sexual self is an urban phenomenon, and so burdens non-metropolitan queers with negative fictions of the rural world. Halberstam determines that metronormativity relies on spectacles of rural violence, such as the 1993 murder of Nebraskan Brandon Teena, to dismiss the potential for a legible queer existence outside of cities. Halberstam suggests, rather, that Teena's particular kind of masculine identity might have only been possible in a rural locale.[2] The term "metronormative" has a long genealogy, arguably beginning with Alfred Kinsey's 1948 study *Sexual Behavior in the Human Male*. Kinsey found high rural incidences of homosexuality, particularly in the West. This, he wrote, "contradicts the theory that homosexuality in itself is an urban product." Kinsey concluded that such behaviors were part of a long tradition that was "probably common among pioneers and outdoor men in general."[3] Historically, there have been many queer worlds within the rural.

Sexual Practices in the Colonial Era

In rural locations during the first two centuries of US history, individuals formed same-sex sexual relationships, enacted desires, and transgressed gender identities in diverse ways. The United States, after all, began as a thinly populated rural nation in a historical period that preceded the articulation of homosexual or trans★ identities. Sexuality in colonial rural geographies mirrored the intersectional nature of early American life. American colonists experienced sexuality in deeply gendered and racialized ways, and individuals frequently reconfigured their understanding of sexuality to reflect the way gender and racial hierarchies worked in their worlds. In some cases, this resulted in attempts by those with power to regulate the sexualities of those assigned to a lower class, while at the same time exploiting their own license to thwart gender norms and "proper" expressions of sexuality.[4]

Court records of sodomy trials document colonial rural queer lives and practices. As legal historian William Eskridge argues, sodomy charges were particularly common in the American colonies in the seventeenth-century, likely because of the influence of religious ideologies, particularly Puritan, on both sex and the legal system. The legal category of sodomy was not exclusively same-sex, however, capturing a wide range of non-reproductive sexual activities. In addition to male-male intercourse, crimes against nature included bestiality. Punishment for these sexual offenses included execution, whipping, castration, and lesser punishments such as fines and ostracism. Over the colonial period, convictions and punishments for such crimes declined, so that by the time of the early republic most new states had abolished the death penalty for sodomy.

Before there were categories such as "homosexuals" or even "sodomites" in urban areas, people in diverse American locations believed that some men could be identified by their predilection for same-sex acts. Richard Godbeer's work on colonial New England suggests that rural locations offer evidence that some community members "posited an ongoing erotic predilection that transcended the acts themselves." Citizens of rural communities, where cooperation and community were necessary for survival were, further, more likely to view the actions of their neighbors in context. This differentiated local and rural reactions to sodomy from those of predominately urban theological and legal authorities, who only recognized immoral acts.[5] This is not to say that rural communities were universally more tolerant; in other instances rural courts recommended harsher punishments for sexual deviance, as Doron S. Ben-Atar and Richard Brown point out in their examination of prosecutions for bestiality at the close of the eighteenth century. Seeking to understand why two elderly men in rural New England were sentenced to death for this crime when executions for bestiality ceased over a century earlier, they conclude that local elites participated in a "nostalgic spasm" of Puritanism in the face of growing trends of cosmopolitan liberalism. Taken as a whole, though, this scholarship underscores the extent to which reactions to sexual and gender deviance reflected tensions between rural/traditional worlds and urban/modern ones.

The binary systems of sex and gender that rural colonists often embraced were at odds with the gender diversity colonists encountered among Native people in the Americas and the Caribbean. European explorers commented on non-normative gender expressions in a number of Native American societies. Individuals living in such roles—today called "Two-Spirit"—were tolerated and sometimes even celebrated in their communities, though the practice varied from culture to culture. For example, in 1536 a Spanish explorer named Alvar Núñez Cabeza de Vaca crossing through the coasts of Louisiana and Texas reported: "I saw a wicked behavior (*diablura*), and it is that I saw one man married (*casado*) to another, and these are effeminate, impotent men (*unos hombres amarionados impotents*). And they go about covered like women, and they perform the tasks of women, and they do not use a bow, and they carry very great loads."[6] The American colonial enterprise was violent, and this violence could have a sexual component. Anglo and Spanish colonizers made gender-diverse Native Americans particular targets for such assaults. Deborah Miranda uses the term "gendercide" to describe the "coordinated plan of destruction" enacted against third gender Native individuals at the hands of Spanish colonizers in California.[7] While Spanish colonizers used many forms of violence against indigenous populations, Miranda has shown that perpetrators often singled out third gender individuals in ways that demonstrated a deep abhorrence for their gender identities while simultaneously attempting to force compliance with the mission system of governance.

Richard Trexler asserts that such violence should be placed alongside other forms of sexual violence central to the colonial project, including acts of abuse by white men and women toward slaves. In a society where citizenship was reserved for white, propertied men, not only was violence against the rest of the population rarely punished, it was formative the social order. At the micro level, the existence of the plantation household was predicated on the violence—either practiced or threatened—against slaves. Violence was not the exclusive provenance of men. As Thavolia Glymph details, plantation mistresses—celebrated in popular culture as refined ladies—engaged in assaults on enslaved people as well. More scholarship might explore the roles of same-sex sexual violence as well as the complex tangle of same-sex desire and eroticism in spaces such as slave markets and plantation households. In the rural seventeenth- and eighteenth-century context, sexual and racial deviance were often linked in law and practice. Kirsten Fischer writes that in colonial North Carolina, courts afforded men the privilege of suing another for slanderous sexual remarks. Slander often involved sexual acts with an animal, sexual acts with another man, or sexual acts with a "Negro" or "Mulatto." Because accusations of sodomy lowered one's social status and implied that one had lost control over one's body, they were linked to emasculation and passivity as core traits of "blackness." Sodomy, she explains, "symbolically combined aspect of femininity and blackness in ways that blurred the distinction between white men and black men."[8]

In the Colonial Era and Early Republic, rural sexual practices were entrenched in the building of a social order that privileged landed white Euro-American culture. Close physical and emotional contact between classes, races and genders marked the beginning of attempts to regulate sexual practices in law and society, a process that would become more complicated in the next century with widespread migration to other rural spaces in the American frontier and beyond.

Nineteenth-Century Emergence of Queer Identities

Over the course of the nineteenth century, the United States transformed into an urban nation. People living in rural areas became a minority by 1920. As rural and urban lives diverged, rural areas began to offer particular and unique opportunities for queer identities. Individuals in rural areas took advantage of the changing economy and new geographic terrains to find new ways to support themselves outside the bounds of heterosexual marriage and family. In rural environments, community often shaped queer identities and practice.

The story of Charity Bryant and Sylvia Drake in early nineteenth-century New England offers an example of a marriage-like arrangement between rural women. Bryant and Drake shared a home and business for over forty years. Rachel Hope Cleves's *Charity and Sylvia: A Same-Sex Marriage in Early America* concludes that their status and recognition, similar to that of a married couple, was made possible by their life in a rural community that prioritized maintaining social relations for the "general benefit" of the local populace. In an environment where survival was difficult, individuals relied on each other and their community to a large degree. The two women shared food with neighbors, boarded individuals who needed homes, loaned and borrowed money, and tended the sick. Rural life thus presented particular space and advantages for these two women. Their relationship was an "open secret"; while the nature of their bond was not discussed, neither was it completely ignored. While Sylvia's family in particular seemed to have some misgivings about her refusal to marry and her long-term partnership with Charity, they maintained contact with the couple. The potential of rural economies to foster queer lives and relationalities challenges the dominant historical perspective on the relationship between industrial capitalism and LGBT subjectivities. The story of Charity and Sylvia suggests that localized household production offered female same-sex couples opportunities for financial independence and social status that they lost to the spread of low-wage industries. While the city could offer men and women anonymity, Charity and Sylvia flourished because their community accepted their relationship as a mirror of an antebellum marriage. Cleves suggests that women "of Charity and Sylvia's generation spoke far more often of their desire to retire together to a little cottage in the countryside, than of their urge to move together to the city."[9]

Rural environments offered other opportunities for same-sex sexual practices and gender diversity that cities could not. Individuals living in rural same-sex environments such as mining and lumber camps and boarding schools had particular opportunities for sexual intimacy. In addition, the ability to shed one's personal history through migration, particularly in the rural West and Midwest, offered opportunities for individuals to change genders. Peter Boag's *Re-Dressing America's Frontier Past* suggests that on the frontier a surprisingly large number of people lived and dressed outside of their birth-assigned sex, and some moved west to take advantage of the relative freedom for such transgressions afforded there.

A central goal for Boag's work is to explain the erasure of this population from memories of the West and the resulting association of rural areas with heterosexuality and normative gender roles. As fears of the "New Women," sexual inverts, immigration, and racial degeneracy pervaded the nation, the increasingly popular work of sexologists identified cities as the source of social disorder. Indeed, by the late nineteenth and early twentieth century, identities based on sexual and gender deviance appeared in urban areas. In turn, the western frontier was reconceptualized from a place of bawdy gender transgression to a sanctum of American exceptionalism where a virile manhood prevailed. The national definition of whiteness depended on a particular narrative of the frontier—one in which the reality of sexual and gender diversity in this space had been obscured. Boag explains that in this context, the only recognition of male-to-female cross dressing was marshaled as evidence of the inadequacy of masculinities racialized as non-white.[10]

As urban cultures became culturally dominant in the United States, rural space and people became valorized as pure, unspoiled, and closer to nature. The "primitive" aspect of Native American sexual and gender practices became significant to their contemporary meaning in Euro-American culture. Michael Bronsky has argued that racist understandings of "primitive" sexualities helped establish the dichotomy between normal and abnormal desires. White "fantasies of native people" had by the nineteenth century "evolved to become foundational to how American culture was to conceptualize male-male relationships." In other words, imagined aspects of Native American gender and sexual practices gave non-normative sexualities a cultural significance to people of Anglo-European ancestry who examined them in the nineteenth century.[11]

Moreover, the opening of the frontier also brought new, racialized understandings of sexuality that came to bear on the organization of the boundaries between normative and non-normative gender and sexuality. Works by Clare Sears and Nayan Shah examine cross-racial attitudes and practices in the context of Chinese, South Asian, and Filipino migration to the western United States from the mid-eighteen to mid-twentieth centuries. These authors concur with previous scholarship that argues that the American frontier created possibilities for queer populations, but also detail the many ways queer practices were or were not assimilated into white Euro-American culture.

Twentieth-Century Communities and Networks

In the twentieth century the association of sexual desires with identity was key to the formation of queer subjectivities and communities. While written sources, generated both by LGBT individuals and by state officials charged with regulation and surveillance, give historians insights into growing urban communities, a relative lack of sources about rural queers presents the potential for their exclusion from the historical narrative. Rural individuals who engaged in same-sex sexual or gender diverse practices were less likely to consider themselves part of a queer community and often did not participate in the political organization and struggles for change that dominate archival records. Still, historians are seeking out different archives and modes of analysis to bring modern rural queer subjects to the fore.

Colin Johnson, in particular, has shown how rural settings made possible expressions of gender and sexuality that could be considered risky or deviant in other contexts. The New Deal's Civilian Conservation Corps (CCC) camps are a striking example of how rural space becomes queer space. From 1933 to 1942, between 2.5 and 3 million young men aged eighteen to twenty-three called one of the CCC's 1,400 camps home. According to Johnson, camps represented liminal spaces "on the thresholds between the country and the city, between poverty and financial stability," and "between adolescence and adulthood." The federal government intended the relief work program to regenerate both the mind and body of men defeated by the Depression, and daily life in a CCC camp focused on intensely physical conservation work and male camaraderie. The isolated rural setting and homosocial environment allowed men to exercise what Johnson calls "a certain leeway to depart from gender and sexual convention."[12] Drag performance, male beauty revues, and body-building competitions were not uncommon forms of entertainment, and camp commanders often interpreted participation in these events as a sign of healthy morale. Although sexual encounters between men likely occurred with regularity at CCC camps, discharges for sexual offenses were rare. Margot Canaday has argued that while this was an intentional strategy to shore up the reputation of the CCC as a moral program, a failure to discipline queer behavior opened up "radical possibilities" for the young men who lived there.[13] Johnson concurs, and finds in CCC camps a challenge to the wider argument within the history of sexuality that queer behavior among men "was driven underground" in the 1930s. Rather, he suggests, queer sexuality was driven "into the woods."[14]

The visibility and tolerance of rural queer male culture suggests that rural geography blurred the boundaries between personal and community space in ways that shaped same-sex desire and identity construction. In the postwar rural South, John Howard finds that men built queer lives based on "circulation rather than congregation" in a "place-based, sustained, urban gay enclave." While rural areas lacked community spaces found in cities, they sustained queer networks, points of connection, and places of fleeting contact. These networks might have served erotic desires, but they also had social ends, whereby individuals exchanged information and support.[15]

Queer women formed less visible but equally critical networks through organizations such as the Daughters of Bilitis and the Cambridge Lesbian Liberation group. Heather Murray has shown that the process of therapeutic letter writing was particularly important in the 1970s for women in rural communities removed from urban gay liberationist culture. Daniel Rivers finds that lesbian mothers in rural areas fought isolation and accessed legal help for custody battles by writing to the Lesbian Mothers National Defense Fund.

Building on the idea of networking and correspondence that linked rural and urban queer lives, Nick Syrett's study of communities of gay men in the "midcentury Midwest" identifies men who travelled around the region and maintained active correspondences with each other. Men planned visits, exchanged information, and shared contacts. Rather than a linear path from rural to urban, these men moved in circuits or circles, often returning to their point of origin. He concludes that men in small towns and the rural Midwest did not build gay lives based on physical proximity with each other and distance from their families. Rather, their gay world was based on mobility. Mobility was also a critical aspect of life for female impersonators at midcentury who earned a living performing at small venues across the country. As Don Romesburg has shown, female impersonators such as Rae Bourbon navigated "a host of contested meanings about rurality, nature, sexuality, gender, modernity, technology, and commercialized leisure" that often saw these performers seek "queer networking across spaces and regions."[16]

In some cases, a movement *to* as opposed to *from* rural geographies allowed queer individuals to embrace or explore their sexual identities. Scott Herring asserts that rural enclaves have offered spaces where migrants could separate themselves from the dominance of heteronormativity and develop uniquely queer identities. Communes of radical faeries, intentional queer communities, the women's land movement, and womyn's music festivals are all examples of rural places where LGBT individuals sought freedom in rural areas. The journal *RFD: A Country Journal for Gay Men Everywhere* has celebrated and supported communities of rural queer men since 1974. Some lesbians, too, went "back to the land," forming communities for those who chose to live in rural areas and music festivals for those who opted to just visit. *Lesbian Connection* magazine, also founded in 1974, supported networks among rural lesbians through its reader-generated content, while also distributing a list of "Contact Dykes" in rural areas and small

Figure 13.1 Cover of rural gay magazine *RFD* (Fall 1975), which continues to be in production in
2017.

Courtesy of the GLBT Historical Society.

towns. The largest women's music festival—the Michigan Womyn's Music Festival—was held 1975–2015 in Oceana County, Michigan. When the festival was in full gear, it was the largest town in the county. Herring has labeled the new political aesthetic of rural life "queer anti-urbanism." LGBT lives outside of cities are as "vibrant, diverse, and plentiful as any urban-based sexual culture" but rural queers are a radical force that challenges the normalizing identities that come from privileging the urban.[17]

Some LGBT people migrated temporarily to rural vacation retreats. These communities formed in what Esther Newton called "protective isolation," which served as a way to imagine a queer future. On Fire Island in New York, Newton argues, the "lack of civilization" allowed metropolitan gay and lesbian individuals to form a "social identity based on homoeroticism and gender dissidence" to an extent not possible in urban areas. The rural economies may have also aided acceptance of queer communities. Because gay and lesbian individuals invested significant capital in the community, many of the heterosexual families who lived year-round in Cherry Grove ignored expressions of sexualities "on the other side of the law."[18]

The movement of LGBT people to rural areas was aided by a long literary tradition of conceptualizing the rural as wild and untamed. Rural geographies appear in literature as places unburdened by rigid social orders that often encourage expression of queer sexuality by placing the protagonist in the way of welcome temptation or by promising safety from prying eyes. In Gore Vidal's *The City and the Pillar*, the protagonist Jim experiences a gay sexual awakening on a camping trip with his best friend, while Sally Gearhart's *The Wanderground: Stories of the Hill Women* is an example of ecofeminism that presents women living in the wildness, completely in tune with nature. Collectively, such works highlight the importance of what David Bell and Gill Valentine called the "mythic, Edenic place in the gay imaginary."[19]

Some queer rural communities, activists, and writers have examined and embraced what they believe to be Native American spiritual and sexual practices. Tolerance for gender variation in Native American societies has been seen as evidence that intolerance of gays, lesbians, and trans★ people is a product of modern western culture. To some, Native American cultures of the past function as an idyll in which respect and spiritual value for sexual and gender diversity reigned.

That popular imaginary has been challenged by the scholarship of Trexler and Ramón Gutiérrez, who argues that the "lives of the berdache were lives of humiliation and endless work, not of celebration and veneration."[20] Scott Lauria Morgensen shows that a claimed connection to Native traditions offered—and still offers—an alternative narrative for the move to rural land by urban white people. Radical faeries who understood and endorsed critiques of settler colonialism's dispossession of indigenous people could differentiate themselves from such settlers by asserting that their sexuality and commitment to the rural gave them a "sacred affinity" with Native Americans.[21]

For Native Americans, acknowledging Two-Spirit traditions has become a means of empowerment as this movement has developed since gay- and lesbian-identified Native Americans began formally organizing in the 1970s. Many on rural reservations have embraced Two-Spirit identities and cultural practices to connect queerness with traditions and to build connections with other Two-Spirit individuals across Indian country. As Brian Joseph Gilley explains, this is not always seamless. Competing demands from broader queer, trans★, and Native communities make the Two-Spirit individual's sense of belonging vulnerable to disruption.[22]

The contradiction of seeing oneself both *within* and *outside* of communities has a distinct resonance in rural geographies. While some rural queer people have historically found this disconnect empowering, for others it has carried a profound sense of alienation and loss. In the 1980s, not only did rural individuals contract HIV/AIDS, but the disease also forced some men who had migrated into gay urban life to return back to rural communities for extended care. In the early years of the epidemic, several authors attempted to describe the impact of AIDS on Appalachia and document the experiences of people with AIDS in rural communities. The most significant is Abraham Verghese's memoir about his work as a doctor in Johnson City, Tennessee. Verghese describes the shape of the AIDS epidemic in a small town where young gay men returned home to die, still-closeted men became infected by anonymous encounters, and a small number of heterosexual men and women contracted AIDS from contaminated blood transfusions. Some died alone, in exile, but many were surrounded by loving family members. In some cases, those who cared for people with AIDS led efforts to open rural communities to acceptance of LGBT individuals. His depiction stands in contrast to a 1994 article by Jeffrey Fleishman entitled "Appalachia Mean, Lonely Place for People to Die with AIDS." Fleishman wrote that "In Appalachia, there is no meaner or lonelier way to die than by AIDS." In an analysis of such representations, Mary Anglin argues that the latter followed a standard media trope of such stories, that due to rural backwardness and inhumanity, gay men with AIDS died in isolation, shunned by their communities, families, and even medical professionals.

A growing awareness of the paucity of historical sources about queer lives in the rural South has sparked efforts to fill this gap with oral history projects and archival collections. For example, in 2005, Carol Burch-Brown donated a significant collection of oral history interviews and photographs to the Smithsonian, which documented the culture of a rural West Virginian gay bar called The Shamrock. Titling her project "It's Reigning Queens in Appalachia," Burch-Brown explores how proprietor "Miss Helen" maintained a thriving gay sanctuary in the heart of Appalachia for 37 years, from 1964 to her death in 2001. Other examples include the Queer Appalachia Oral History Project at the Lonnie B. Nunn Center for Oral History at the University of Kentucky and the online project "COUNTRY QUEERS: A Multimedia Oral History Project Documenting the Diverse Experiences of Rural and Smalltown LGBTQI folks in the U.S.A."

Conclusion

This chapter has explored how LGBT practices took unique forms in rural areas and asked why rural spaces have been generative of queer identities across US history. At the same time, it has demonstrated ways that the rural/urban dichotomy has functioned in the popular imagination to construct binary systems of gender and sexual identity while also offering opportunities to subvert these binaries. To consider the idea of "rural" without reference to the specificities of region is, necessarily, a relatively ahistorical project. Collapsing diverse non-urban regions under the label "rural" without recognizing their regional distinctiveness is, after all, an approach that is fundamentally at odds with historical methodologies, which rigorously explore and define specific spatial and temporal contexts.

The problematic nature of this undertaking is perhaps most stark in the modern era. For example, Appalachia was and is a rural region unlike others and occupies an unparalleled place in the American imagination.[23] In the 1960s and 1970s, representations of Appalachian hypersexuality transformed from innocent to sinister, a transformation most commonly seen in James Dickey's 1970 novel *Deliverance* and subsequent 1972 film. Does *Deliverance* perpetuate stereotypes specific to Appalachia or all rural America? What is the relationship between gay liberation as an organized movement and a literary fascination with rural sexual deviance? As Carissa Massey explains, "Appalachian bodies reflect many kinds of anxieties centering on whiteness, class, and gender and at this moment in history that anxiety shifted to the heterosexual body."[24] Cultural shifts that threaten masculinity, such as organized gay liberation, mirror the literal threats of rape and bestiality in *Deliverance* faced by encroaching city-slickers in Appalachia. But it is also possible to argue that *Deliverance* evokes the threat and perversity of many kinds of rural peoples. The circulation of derogatory images of all rural peoples often depends on exaggerating aspects of degenerate sexuality.

More recent films have demonstrated how rural America is generative of queer sexualities while also asserting that queer sexualities are a positive force in these areas. The film *Goodbye Gauley Mountain* follows two "ecosexuals in love" who deploy their sexuality as part of their activism against mountain-top removal. Starring former porn star, sexologist, and performance artist Annie Sprinkle and her partner, professor and artist Elizabeth Stephens, *Goodbye Gauley Mountain*, was shown at the first Appalachian Queer Film Festival, which took place in 2014 in Lewisburg, West Virginia. Queer films with rural themes often explore the intersectional nature of queer rural life and feature common rural issues such as environmental activism, arts, and music, as well as social problems associated with rural areas. In a recent interview, the organizers of the Appalachian Queer Film Festival described their work as a way to reach out to two marginalized groups—Appalachians and LGBTQ individuals—who would benefit from recognizing similarities in their historical experiences. Organizer Tim Ward commented, "We want to challenge the perception folks have that West Virginians are backwards, toothless hillbillies . . . There's a thriving LGBTQ community here. Tolerance and acceptance are not hiding under a rock."[25]

The introductory chapter of *Queer Twin Cities*, an oral history-driven analysis of gay life in Minneapolis and St. Paul, begins by describing a scene from Gus Van Sant's film *Milk* that caused controversy in the Twin Cities queer community. During the scene in question a young Harvey Milk, on his way to becoming the first openly gay elected politician in California, advises a desperate and depressed gay teen from Minnesota to escape on the first bus to San Francisco. The audience encounters the same teen later in the film, transformed into a liberated gay activist in Los Angeles. As Jennifer Pierce writes, "The film's use of the 'boy from Minnesota' to position cities like San Francisco as cosmopolitan sites of salvation in a national geography marked by intolerance, fear, and repression continues to circulate in our own time."[26]

Urban environments remain the sites where gay identity coalesced first and most profoundly around collective political demands, but the study of rural communities suggests a more longstanding blurring of act-based expressions of sexuality, identity-based terminology, and definitions of community itself. As such, queer rural history highlights what David Halperin calls "the definitional uncertainty about what homosexuality itself really is."[27] Indeed, the study of queer rural history finds individuals who both challenge and celebrate our shifting ideas of what it means and meant to be authentically LGBT across space and time. Queer rural lives represent a diverse range of experiences, from the radical to the repressive. The identities that rural queers embody are highly contextual and malleable. Their histories thwart metronormative assumptions that flatten the possibilities of rural queer life into a generalized script of estrangement and eventual escape.

Notes

1 The most thorough historical work exploring queer rural issues, and one to which this article owes key insights, is Colin Johnson, *Just Queer Folks: Gender and Sexuality in Rural America* (Philadelphia: Temple University Press, 2013). Another important overview that offers a legal perspective is Bud W. Jerke, "Queer Ruralism," *Harvard Journal of Law and Gender* 34 (2011): 260–312.

2 Jack Halberstam, *In a Queer Time and Place: Transgender Bodies, Subcultural Lives* (New York: NYU Press, 2005), esp. 35. A key antecedent is Kath Weston, "Get Thee To a Big City: Sexual Imaginary and the Great Gay Migration," *GLQ: A Journal of Lesbian and Gay Studies* 2, no. 33 (1995): 253–277

3 Alfred Kinsey, Wardell B. Pomeroy, Clyde E. Martin, *Sexual Behavior in the Human Male* (Philadelphia: W.B. Saunders, 1948), 457.

4 For a more extensive detailing of Early American queer history, see the chapters by Richard Godbeer and Rachel Hope Cleves in this book.

5 Richard Godbeer, "The Cry of Sodom': Discourse, Intercourse, and Desire in Colonial New England," in *Long Before Stonewall: Histories of Same-Sex Sexuality in Early America*, ed. Thomas A. Foster (New York: New York University Press, 2007), 100.

6 Ramón A. Gutiérrez, "Warfare, Homosexuality, and Gender Status Among American Indian Men in the Southwest," in *Long Before Stonewall*, 21.

7 Deborah Miranda, "Extermination of the *Joyas*: Gendercide in Spanish California," *GLQ: A Journal of Lesbian and Gay Studies* 16, no. 1–2 (2010): 260.

8 Kirsten Fischer, *Suspect Relations: Sex, Race, Resistance in Colonial North Carolina* (Ithaca: Cornell University Press, 2002), 145–147.

9 Rachel Hope Cleves, *Charity and Sylvia: A Same-Sex Marriage in Early America* (New York: Oxford University Press, 2014), xiii. See also Rachel Hope Cleves, " 'What, Another Female Husband?': The Prehistory of Same-Sex Marriage in America," *Journal of American History* 101, no. 4 (March 2015): 19–43.

10 For more on this era, see, in this volume, Clare Sears, "Centering Slavery in Nineteenth-Century Queer History."

11 Michael Bronski, *A Queer History of the United States* (Boston, MA: Beacon Press, 2011), 25.

12 Johnson, 130, 140.

13 Margot Canaday, *The Straight State: Sexuality and Citizenship in Twentieth-Century America* (Princeton: Princeton University Press), 94, 119.

14 Johnson, 130.

15 John Howard, *Men Like That: A Southern Queer History* (Chicago: University of Chicago Press, 1999), xiv.

16 Don Romesburg, "Camping Out with Ray Bourbon: Female Impersonators and Queer Dread of Wide Open Spaces," originally in *Reconstruction* 7.2 (2007), available on-line at www.academia.edu/6237933/Camping_Out_with_Ray_Bourbon_Female_Impersonators_and_Queer_Dread_of_Wide-Open_Spaces. Accessed 30 April 2015.

17 Herring, Scott. "Out of the Closets, into the Woods: *RFD, Country Women*, and the Post- Stonewall Emergence of Queer Anti-Urbanism." *American Quarterly* 59 (2007): 341–372; Scott Herring, *Another Country: Queer Anti-Urbanism* (New York University Press, 2010), 6.

18 Esther Newton, *Cherry Grove, Fire Island: Sixty Years in America's First Gay and Lesbian Community* (Boston: Beacon Press, 1993), 40, 22.

19 David Bell and Gill Valentine, "Queer Country: Rural Lesbian and Gay Lives," *Journal of Rural Studies* 11, no. 2 (1995): 114.

20 Ramón A. Gutiérrez, "Warfare, Homosexuality, and Gender Status Among American Indian Men in the Southwest," in *Long Before Stonewall*, 19–31.

21 Scott Lauria Morgensen, "Arrival at Home: Radical Faerie Configurations of Sexuality and Place," *GLQ: A Journal of Lesbian and Gay Studies* 15, no. 1 (2009): 77.

22 For another discussion of the ways in which two-spirit Native Americans have historically struggled to assert presence and persistence, see, in this volume, Nayan Shah, "Queer of Color Estrangement and Belonging."

23 Ronald Eller famously described Appalachia as "Always part of the mythical South, Appalachia continues to languish backstage in the American drama, still dressed, in the popular mind at least, in the garments of backwardness, violence, poverty, and hopelessness once associated with the South as a whole." See Ronald Eller "Foreword," in *Back Talk from Appalachia: Confronting Stereotypes*, eds. Dwight B. Billings, Gurney Norman and Katherine Ledford (Lexington: University of Kentucky Press, 2001), xi.

24 Carissa Massey, "Appalachian Stereotypes: Cultural History, Gender, and Sexual Rhetoric," *Journal of Appalachian Studies* 13, no.1/2 (Spring/Fall 2007): 133.

25 Erica Lies, "Looking Back at the Screen: The First Annual Appalachian Queer Film Festival," *The Hairpin*, 25 November 2014, available online at http://thehairpin.com/2014/11/looking-back-at-the-screen-the-first-annual-appalachian-queer-film-festival. Accessed 13 March 2015.

26 Jennifer L. Pierce, "Introduction: Queer Twin Cities," in *Queer Twin Cities*, ed. Twin Cities GLBT Oral History Project (Minneapolis: University of Minnesota Press, 2010), xi.

27 David Halperin, "How to do the History of Male Homosexuality," *GLQ: A Journal of Gay and Lesbian Studies* 6, no. 1 (2000): 89.

Further Reading

Anglin, Mary K. "Stories of AIDS in Appalachia." In *Back Talk from Appalachia: Confronting Stereotypes*, eds. Dwight B. Billings, Gurney Norman and Katherine Ledford, 267–283. Lexington: University of Kentucky Press, 2001.

Ben-Atar, Doron S. and Richard D. Brown. *Taming Lust: Crimes Against Nature in the Early Republic*. Philadelphia: University of Pennsylvania Press, 2014.

Binnie, Jon and Gill Valentine. "Geographies of Sexuality—A Review of Progress." *Progress in Human Geography* 23, no. 2 (1999): 175–187.

Boag, Peter. *Re-Dressing America's Frontier Past*. Berkeley: University of California Press, 2012.

"COUNTRY QUEERS: A Multimedia Oral History Project Documenting the Diverse Experiences of Rural and Smalltown LGBTQI folks in the U.S.A." http://countryqueers.com/. Accessed October 22, 2017.

D'Emilio, John. "Capitalism and Gay Identity." In *Making Trouble: Essays on Gay History, Politics, and the University*, 3–16. New York: Routledge, 1992.

Dickey, James. *Deliverance*. Boston: Houghton Mifflin, 1970.

Driskill, Qwo-Li, Chris Finley, Brian Joseph Gilley, and Scott Lauria Morgensen, eds. *Queer Indigenous Studies: Critical Interventions in Theory, Politics, and Literature*. Tucson: University of Arizona Press, 2011.

Eskridge, William. *Dishonorable Passions: Sodomy Laws in America, 1861–2003*. New York: Viking, 2008.

Gearhart, Sally. *The Wanderground: Stories of the Hill Women*. Boston: Alyson Publications, 1984.

Gilley, Brian Joseph. *Becoming Two-Spirit: Gay Identity and Social Acceptance in Indian Country*. Lincoln: University of Nebraska Press, 2006.

Glymph, Thavolia. *Out of the House of Bondage: the Transformation of the Plantation Household*. New York: Cambridge University Press, 2008.

Jacobs, Sue-Ellen, Wesley Thomas, and Sabine Lang, eds. *Two-Spirit People: Native American Gender Identity, Sexuality, and Spirituality*. Urbana: University of Illinois Press, 1997.

Johnson, Colin. *Just Queer Folks: Gender and Sexuality in Rural America*. Philadelphia: Temple University Press, 2013.

Murray, Heather. "This is 1975, Not 1875: Despair and Longings in Women's Letters to Cambridge Lesbian Liberation and Daughters of Bilitis Counselor Julie Lee in the 1970s." *Journal of the History of Sexuality* 23, no. 1 (January 2014): 96–122.

Queer Appalachia Oral History Project. QUAPP001. Louie B Nunn Center for Oral History, University of Kentucky, Lexington, Kentucky.

Rivers, Daniel Winunwe. *Radical Relations: Lesbian Mothers, Gay Fathers and their Children in the United States Since World War II*. Chapel Hill: University of North Carolina Press, 2013.

Sears, Clare. "All that Glitters: Trans-ing California's Gold Rush Migrations." *GLQ: A Journal of Lesbian and Gay Studies* 14, no. 2–3 (2008): 383–402.

Seidman, Steven. "Identity Politics in a 'Postmodern' Gay Culture: Some Historical and Conceptual Notes." In *Fear of a Queer Planet*, ed. Michael Warner, 105–142. Minneapolis: University of Minnesota Press, 1993.

Shah, Nayan. "Race-ing Sex." *Frontiers: A Journal of Women Studies* 35, no. 1 (2014): 26–36.

Shamrock Bar Collection. NMAH.AC.0857. National Archives Center, Smithsonian Museum of American History, Washington, DC.

Syrett, Nicholas. "Mobility, Circulation, and Correspondence: Queer White Men in the Midcentury Midwest." *GLQ: A Journal of Lesbian and Gay Studies* 20, nos. 1–2 (2014): 75–94.

———. "A Busman's Holiday in the Not-So-Lonely Crowd: Business Culture, Epistolary Networks, and Itinerant Homosexuality in Mid-Twentieth Century America." *Journal of the History of Sexuality* 21, no. 1 (2012): 121–140.

Trexler, Richard C. *Sex and Conquest: Gendered Violence, Political Order, and the European Conquest of the Americas*. New York: Cornell University Press, 1995.

Verghese, Abraham. *My Own Country: A Doctor's Story of a Town and Its People During the Age of AIDS*. New York: Vintage Books, 1994.

Vidal, Gore. *The City and the Pillar*. New York: EP Dutton, 1948.

14

QUEER AND NATION

Eithne Luibhéid

"Queer" and "US nation" have co-produced one another in a continually shifting dynamic. Like a double helix, they operate as "two strands that wind around each other like a twisting ladder."[1] In order to illustrate how queer and nation intertwine to co-produce one another, this essay explores major processes through which the United States became the nation-state it is today, and shows how those processes interconnect with queers, queerness, and queering.[2]

Defining the Terms

"Queer" is a term with varied meanings. Siobhan Somerville describes how "queer" tends to be used in two seemingly contradictory ways: as an umbrella term for LGBT people, and conversely "as a term that calls into question the stability of any categories of identity."[3] Trans and Bi Studies scholars suggest that queer has often functioned as a synonym for lesbian and gay people, rather than as a category that meaningfully engages either trans or bi lives and theories, and has often problematized sexuality, but less often normative binary gender systems. Nonetheless, queer, trans, and bi studies and activisms have often traveled in tandem, informing and engaging one another.[4] Queer/trans of color scholarship and activisms further make clear that sexual and gender norms are inextricable from racialization and class processes— and from geopolitical inequalities. Thus, "at its most capacious," queer denotes individuals and communities that identify, or have been identified and treated by others, as non-normatively sexual and/or gendered, in ways that articulate racial, class, and geopolitical hierarchies.[5]

"Queer" is also an adjective and verb. It refers to the ways that systems of power "queer" populations, including people who may not self-identify as LGBTQ, resulting in discrimination, dispossession, violence, and death—and how queered populations variously respond, ranging from assimilation to demanding revolution.

The term "nation" is similarly polysemic. Nations are frequently understood as long-standing and timeless, based around people who "naturally" share something in common (whether culture, language, history, religion, or biological descent—which often gets problematically framed as "race"). The modern nation, and the current global order comprised by unequally positioned nation states, emerged through processes of imperialism and global capitalism. Benedict Anderson suggests that nations are both inherently limited and sovereign "imagined political communities.[6] Postcolonial scholars have significantly criticized Anderson's Eurocentric and teleological model of how nation formation has occurred across colonized time and space, but his core conceptualization of the nation remains widely accepted.

Nations are often spoken of as interchangeable with states, but it is important to differentiate between them, while acknowledging their interconnections. Grewal and Kaplan suggest that "a state can be seen as the political and bureaucratic institutions, practices, and policies that govern a given territory and population."[7] Thus, states materialize national imaginaries in ways that are ongoing and contested. Some imagined nations are not (yet) associated with state forms. Nation- and state-making processes entail forms of pedagogy and performance that seek to "capture" people's identifications and orient them toward particular imaginaries, life trajectories, and norms.[8]

Citizenship is one key mechanism through which these processes occur, and is another complex, multi-dimensional, and contested concept. At one level, citizenship is simply one's juridical status. At another level, "citizenship is a relationship among strangers who learn to feel it as a common identity based on shared historical, legal, or familial connection to a geo-political space."[9] Institutions and ideologies continually work to create that sense of connection. Citizenship is also a matter of everyday experiences and practical action. It is imagined or experienced as a promise—of happiness, protection, access to rights, conditions of possibility—that is often at odds with the realities of lived inequalities. As Lauren Berlant sums up, "US citizenship may best be thought of as an intricate scene where competing forces, definitions, and geographies of freedom and liberty are lived concurrently."[10]

Nations, states, and citizenries need to be reproduced, ideologically and materially.[11] This reproductive mandate opens possibilities for diverse queer, feminist, anti-racist, anti-colonial, and anti-capitalist critiques. For example, M. Jacqui Alexander argues that heteropatriarchy—a term by which she indicates that racism, (hetero)sexism, capitalist exploitation, and imperialism intersect—has been central to the formation and reproduction of nations, states and citizenries.[12] Her argument suggests rich possibilities for analyzing major processes entailed in US nation building and the co-production of queerness. These processes include the colonization of the Americas, slavery and expanding capitalism, empire, and the growth of the bureaucratic state (including immigration management and the creation and rollback of the welfare state).

Colonization of the Americas

The fundamental interrelationalities between gender, sexual, racial, colonial, and class categories and processes are amply demonstrated by the history of colonization of the Americas. Native Studies scholars have shown that sexual and gender violence and terror were fundamental to colonization, and the institutionalization of white supremacy. Tribes had sexual and gender systems that differed significantly from those of the colonists, including allowing for more flexible gender roles and identities, and varied sexual practices. Scott Morgensen describes how "colonists interpreted diverse practices of gender and sexuality as signs of a general primativity among Native peoples," which became the basis for engaging in and justifying land theft, genocide, and/or forcible relocation.[13] Colonists particularly projected sodomy as stigma onto Native men, while constructing Native women as lacking modesty and not properly under male control, and deeming those who did not adhere to binary gender roles as abominations. Effectively, most colonists "framed Native peoples as queer populations marked for death."[14]

Death was not only physical, though for millions it was just that; as Andrea Smith describes, "the goal of colonialism is not just to kill colonized people, but to destroy their sense of being people. It is through sexual violence that a colonizing group attempts to render a colonized group inherently rapable, their lands inherently invadable, and their resources inherently extractable."[15] Death and destruction also entailed efforts to forcibly assimilate survivors into white, heteronormative logics and structures, including sending children to white-run, often highly abusive boarding schools. Morgensen argues that colonization established the basis for all modern sexualities and genders in the Americas, including the modern "queer." Therefore, non-Native queer peoples and movements must actively challenge settler colonialism as both a legacy and ongoing process, including in terms of how it shapes modern queerness, or remain complicit in its terrorizing histories.[16]

This colonial history highlights key interconnections between the US nation and queerness: that nation, state, and citizen formation processes were (and are) violent; the processes worked through and recreated distinctions of gender, sexuality, race, and economics that are associated with sanctioned inequalities; the processes produced populations who were marked for ongoing colonization, disposability or death, and, at the same time, articulated norms and values that had to be anxiously policed and constantly enforced; the processes pathologized particular intimacies and sexualities while seeking to promote sanctioned intimacies and sexualities that served dominant interests; and people variously reacted to and negotiated these forms of violence.[17]

Slavery

Racialized slavery was also fundamental to the formation of the modern US nation-state. The colonies that became the United States made African-descended people slaveable—property that could be exploited and exchanged. This expanded even as the United States claimed to be grounded in freedom and democracy. Gender and sexual logics were central to the institutionalization, justification, and workings of the slave system. The stereotype of the sexually promiscuous African was a key anchor for racialized thinking. Colonial ideologies and the US slave system posited that only by being placed under the control of white masters could Africans be disciplined and retrained into appropriate gender, sexual, and civilizational norms. Yet the system depended on a violent erotics in which the sexual abuse and rape of enslaved women became sanctioned and routine aspects of political, economic, social and psychic domination. Moreover, these practices produced children who, by law, acquired their mothers' rather than fathers' status, thereby increasing property and profit for the slave-owning class. Slave women were also subjected to painful medical experimentation to further the development of gynecology.[18]

Enslaved people were characterized as hypersexual beings who needed to be placed under white control. They were not permitted to participate in the institutions that secured heteronormativity as a function of whiteness: they could not legally marry (though many formed unions that they fought to sustain), partners and offspring could be sold away at will, and children were the property of the master. These experiences speak to the ways that African-descended people were "queered" by the nation and capital—denied opportunities to participate in valued social institutions and norms, then abused and exploited because they did not and could not.[19]

Scholarship about African/American and Black experiences in the Americas significantly expands our understanding of the connections between nation, queerness, and violence that is colonialist, racialized, gendered, sexualized, and economic. For example, Omise'eke Natasha Tinsley characterizes as "queer" the relationships that emerged among enslaved people during the middle passage when ships carried them to be sold in distant lands:

> [R]egardless of whether intimate sexual contact took place between enslaved Africans in the Atlantic or after landing, relationships between shipmates read as queer relationships. *Queer* not in the sense of a "gay" or same-sex loving identity waiting

to be excavated from the ocean floor but as a praxis of resistance. *Queer* in the sense of marking disruption to the violence of normative order and powerfully so: connecting in ways that commodified flesh was never supposed to, loving your own kind when your kind was supposed to cease to exist, forging interpersonal connections that counteract imperial desires for Africans' living deaths.[20]

Tinsley also reads the Atlantic Ocean as queer: a watery, erotic body that contains, carries, and queerly refracts the bodies of drowned Africans, linking the middle passage to contemporary histories of migrants drowning at sea in the face of global apartheid enacted through immigration systems. In Tinsley's deft hands, the Black Atlantic also becomes a rubric through which to engage in queer analysis. Tinsley's scholarship speaks to the ways African-descended people were queered by, and engaged in queer-resistant projects in the context of, a slave system that was critical to the US nation, yet constituted globally.

With the abolition of slavery, whites found new ways to maintain white supremacy through racialized gender and sexual terror, including by lynching Black men and the continued rape and sexual abuse of black women. Economic, political and spatial segregation was steadily institutionalized, accompanied by laws against intermarriage, and economic measures designed to force Black women, men and children into menial, exploitative, and dead-end employment.[21] Gender and sexual logics continued to be used as tools for anti-Black racism and terror. Aliyya Abdur-Rahman describes how sociological discourses and government policies still construct African Americans as "a debased, impoverished, dysfunctional nation of butchy black women and sissified black men" in order to justify continued anti-Black racism, the abdication of responsibility for addressing entrenched poverty and unemployment, and the roll-back of the welfare state combined with the massive expansion of the prison industrial complex.[22]

Scholarship on African American histories opens up rich possibilities for rethinking the relationship between queer and nation. As Cathy Cohen describes, "queer politics has often been built around a simple dichotomy between those deemed queer and those deemed heterosexual." This dichotomy does not address the ways that "heteronormativity interacts with institutional racism, patriarchy and class exploitation to define us in numerous ways as marginal and oppressed."[23] Cohen, Tinsley and other scholars conceive queer broadly: not only women-loving women, men-loving men, and gender non-conforming people but also, for example, "punks, bulldaggers, and welfare queens," the "drag-queen prostitute," or "the gang-raped black girl, the infantilized black man, the pedophile, the unwed teenage mother, the extra-terrestrial, the castrated victim of lynching, the gun-toting revolutionary, the victim of domestic violence, the religious fanatic, the incest survivor, the lynch mob, the slave."[24] While broadening our concepts of queer as an analytical tool, these scholars never minimize the importance of same-gender erotics and non-normative gender identities and practices. Rather, they take pains to recover and revalue those histories, too.

Empire

The colonization of the Americas, the enslavement of Africans, and the sexual logics interconnected with racial, gender, and economic violence that secured these processes all provided templates on which expanding nineteenth-century US imperialism was built. For example, Nerissa Balce argues that the imagery of other countries as "virgin" territory occupied by "savages"—a judgment based on gender, sexual, and sumptuary practices that differed from those demanded by racialized heteropatriarchy—fueled American settler colonialism across the Southwest and was then used to justify and naturalize conquest overseas.

During the nineteenth century, the United States forcibly acquired substantial amounts of land from Mexico, which became the basis for a continually contested territorial border. As Gloria Anzaldúa describes, "the US Mexico border *es una herida abierta* where the Third World grates up against the first and bleeds. And before a scab forms, it hemorrhages again, the life-blood of two worlds merging to form a third country—a border culture."[25] This border culture is inhabited by those who reveal the violence that is required to sustain normalizing lines: "the squint-eyed, the perverse, the queer, the troublesome, the mongrel, the mulatto, the half-breed, the half dead; in short, those who cross over, pass over, or go through the confines of the 'normal.' "[26] Scholars have richly explored borders as queer spaces and entailing queering processes, which queers traverse, yet that differentiate among queers in ways that both undo and remake multiple hierarchies. For example, scholars have shown that cross-dressing in the West and Southwest during the nineteenth century was common, and entailed negotiating multiple social hierarchies. Yet, the extent and varied meanings of cross-dressing became significantly forgotten because of two converging processes: the popularization of Frederick Jackson Turner's myth of the closing of the frontier, and the emergence of the modern sex/gender system. In this context, male-to-female cross-dressing, in particular, became associated with non-Anglo cultures and communities, which "rendered America's frontier past not only a white place and time, but a heterosexual one as well" in the mainstream imagination.[27]

In the late nineteenth and early twentieth centuries, conquest also included the acquisition of the Philippines, Puerto Rico, Hawaii, Guam, and Samoa as well as the invasion and occupation of numerous countries throughout the Caribbean, Latin America, Asia and the Pacific. Imperial ideas about race in this era were linked to emerging theories of sexology. Sexology drew on scientific racism to delineate concepts of sexual deviance and normalcy, and to link these to racial imaginaries and projects, including empire. Consequently, "sex in the colonies was never a private act that was irrelevant to empire."[28] Rather, colonial administrators and military leaders sought to regulate sexuality and gender in ways that reflected and preserved white male power and prestige, while ensuring white female domesticity. Amy Kaplan shows that gendered and racialized ideologies of "domesticity" developed in tandem with imperial encounters, and "the discourse of domesticity negotiate[d] the borders of an increasingly expanding empire and divided nation."[29]

Imperial regulation of sexuality also involved the subordination of colonized people. These efforts materialized and legitimized multiple forms of violence and inequality in the colonies. US colonizers attempted to transform the sexual and gender norms and practices of colonized peoples. While this allowed "imperialists to claim that empire was benevolent and that it improved the lives of colonized populations . . . imperialist interventions in sexuality could also enforce local patriarchies, stigmatize alternative sexualities, and serve as instruments of imperial control over colonized peoples."[30] These efforts materialized and legitimized multiple forms of violence and inequality in the colonies, but at the same time revealed that whiteness was deemed vulnerable to becoming undone or undermined, including through unsanctioned forms of sex that "threatened to corrupt the entire [white] 'race' and called into question the superiority of the colonizing power."[31]

Territorial and overseas expansion; growing industrial capitalism and urbanization; expanding state-making; and shifts in the human sciences—it was in the context of these changes that, in the latter part of the nineteenth century, sexologists offered divergent explanations of homosexuality and gender diversity. Many nineteenth- and early-twentieth-century experts understood same-sex desires and gender diversity not through the contemporary lenses of "sexual

Figure 14.1 Founding flier to form Gay American Indians, the first LGBT/Two-Spirit indigenous
 organization, 1975, San Francisco.
Courtesy of GLBT Historical Society.

orientation" or "gender identity" but as matters of "gender inversion" (a tendency to embody
the characteristics associated with the so-called "opposite sex"). As Siobhan Somerville describes,
sexologists and others also drew on scientific racism when conceptualizing homosexuality,
generating beliefs that homosexuality reflected bodily weakness, degeneracy, and primitivism.[32]
Emma Pérez suggests that US scientific understandings of homosexuality were connected with
efforts to delineate a stable territorial national border with Mexico. Thus, the production of

"the homosexual" was inextricably connected with anxieties about, and efforts to recreate, stable boundaries of empire, gender, race, nation, and class. This underscores that these categories are not simply analogous, but rather, mutually constitutive, in shifting ways that connect to wider social, economic, and cultural relations and struggles.[33]

Along with the delineation of "the homosexual," there occurred the production of "the heterosexual." As Julian Carter describes, at the turn of the twentieth century it was widely believed that whites were "biologically and culturally superior to all other people," and that the "steady development of civilization to ever higher levels could not be separated from the sexual health [and practices] of native born whites."[34] Thus, the anxious efforts to delineate homosexuality were inextricable from the consolidation, dissemination, and efforts to reproduce white marital heterosexuality as the unmarked "normal." Heteronormativity became a socially constructed and enforced standard that linked an idealized racialized, bipolar gendered, middle-class, and marital heterosexuality to nationalism. Based on this standard, men-loving men, women-loving women, and a wide range of other non-normatively sexualized and gendered persons would become singled out, and subjected to regulation, punishment, and dispossession. For example, local vice squads, courts, and licensing boards vigorously regulated people who challenged gender and sexual norms, doing so in ways that interacted with racial, ethnic, and class segregation (thereby contributing to materially and ideologically producing specific concepts of queerness and deviancy).

Over time, expanding eugenic policies sought not only to encourage marriage and child-bearing that bred "superior" citizens among the white middle class, but also to reduce childbearing among the "unfit"—communities of color, immigrant communities, the poor, those with physical or mental disabilities, and those deemed criminal or immoral. Laws increasingly forbade marriage across racial lines, or by those deemed to be "genetically defective." Programs of coercive sterilization were implemented, while "eugenicists opposed social programs designed to improve the living conditions of the poor" because that interfered with the "natural" elimination of the "unfit."[35] Within the context of empire, borders, and borderlands, these all became techniques through which to constitute, regulate, and reiterate the national body—and to purge, punish, or pathologize those people who did not approximate its aims.[36]

Immigration

The transformations wrought by the US nation-state's acquisition of the Southwest, other imperialisms and expanding capitalism around the world generated increased migration. Consequently, by the end of the nineteenth century, immigration administration was nationalized under the federal (rather than state) government. Because immigration policies reproduced the national population and mediated national/global interfaces, controlling immigration became an increasingly important means to express and materialize racialized, heteropatriarchal national sovereignty.

The link between immigration control and national sovereignty was enabled by the expansion of the bureaucratic state. Officials needed ways to unambiguously establish who did and did not belong to the nation state, and to sift among non-citizens so as to either bar or admit them. Technologies such as photography and fingerprinting, which developed in the context of empire and the rise of the human sciences, enabled these differentiations. The processes did not necessarily reflect identities that migrants already "had." Rather, they divided up and classified populations in changing ways in relation to state-making projects.[37] Over time, immigration control expanded to include state capacity for tracking immigrants after entry, and an increasingly complex deportation apparatus.

Those whom officials deemed transgressive of dominant sexual or gender norms became steadily barred from admission to the United States; these exclusions thoroughly articulated racial and economic ones. For example, the 1875 Page Law, which mandated the exclusion of Asian women who were thought to be coming to the United States for "lewd and immoral purposes," marked the beginning of this restrictive federal regime. Working-class Chinese women were particularly affected, since immigration officials presumed that they were all entering the United States to work in the sex industry, and tried to exclude them accordingly. The Page Law provided the blueprint through which the US immigration system became transformed into an apparatus for regulating sexuality in relation to shifting gender, racial, ethnic, class, and geopolitical anxieties.[38]

Following the Page Law, restrictive immigration legislation multiplied. Chinese migrants were barred on racial grounds in 1882, and by 1924, all Asians (except Filipinos, who were US nationals because of colonization) were barred. Southern and Eastern European arrivals were greatly reduced while preference was given to Northern and Western Europeans. Mexicans and those from other Western Hemisphere nations were regulated in ways that made them available as cheap labor when needed, after which they were summarily deported or repatriated. Class restrictions multiplied, including bans on contract laborers and those deemed liable to become public charges. Gender also shaped admission. By the early twentieth century, women experienced great difficulties entering the United States unless they came under the "protection" of a male who seemed "respectable" and could provide support. Bans on polygamists, prostitutes, and immoral women, which thoroughly articulated racial and class fears and hierarchies, were added. Those whose bodies and identities challenged gender norms were liable to be barred or excluded. From these intersecting restrictions, a preference for (and materialization of what counted as) heteropatriarchal family steadily emerged.[39]

What followed was a century of immigration policies and practices meant to bolster what Margot Canaday has dubbed the "straight state."[40] In 1917, those deemed by officials to be "constitutional psychopathic inferiors," a category that included but extended beyond LGBT people, became barred from entering the United States. During the "Lavender Scare," when the Cold War panic over communism became linked to widespread fears of homosexuality, the 1952 McCarren Walter Immigration Act recodified the ban on those perceived as lesbian, gay, or gender non-normative, this time on the grounds of "psychopathic personality." In 1965, when immigration law underwent another sweeping revision, "sexual deviates" became banned. In 1987, those who tested positive for HIV were banned (until the ban was repealed in 2010). In 1990, the ban on lesbian and gay immigrants was repealed. Still, access to migration was not realistically enabled, since immigration preferences remained normed around white, middle-class, and cisgender heterosexuality. In 1996, the Defense of Marriage Act codified marriage as a relationship between a man and a woman, thus cementing until 2013 the impossibility of same-sex couple migration, and generating highly contradictory policies toward couples where one or both persons were trans.

The immigration service's efforts to identify and exclude or deport sexually and gender transgressive people were never simply a matter of identifying those who already "were" LGBTQ, in some sort of essentialist way. Rather, efforts to identify and exclude or deport revealed the ways that the immigration service was centrally involved in the changing production of sexual and gender categories that only partly mapped onto people's self-identifications or experiences. For self-identified queers who felt forced to hide and for those who were perceived by officials as queer even when they did not view themselves that way, such shifts in law had devastating consequences. These immigration service policies and practices thoroughly articulated colonial racial, economic, and geopolitical logics.

Overall, migration controls have provided a literal means to try to produce a white, heteronormative nation-state and citizenry—and a locus for challenge and struggle against those norms. While migrants have most obviously been affected, citizens are affected, too, since discriminatory migration controls articulate, affirm, and reconstitute inequalities among the citizenry. Migration controls have actively produced and shaped the meaning of sexuality and gender categories and hierarchies, linking them to broader processes of citizenship, nation-making, and empire. At the same time, migrants are never just victims; even under the most challenging circumstances, they make choices and take actions. Moreover, migrants have substantially contributed to, transformed, and enriched US queer, trans, subaltern, and resistant communities and cultures in ways that have yet to be fully analyzed. Their presence reflects larger transnational flows and mediating structures of power that shape gender, sexual, racial, and economic logics at local, national, and transnational scales.[41]

Modern Queers and the Nation-State

Colonization, slavery, capitalism, empire, immigration, state expansion, and changing knowledge regimes: modern queer cultures, communities, and movements would emerge from these processes.[42] Their emergence was aided by the growth of urban "gay worlds"—networks of institutions and spaces created by those "who recognized their erotic attraction to members of their own sex."[43] As Colin Johnson discusses, people also participated in diverse, same-sex and gender non-conforming acts, intimacies, and cultures across small towns and in rural America. They were deeply affected by and found ways to survive pervasive hostility, violence, and discrimination in every institution. World War II proved to be a watershed, mobilizing millions to leave home and serve in gender- and race-segregated environments. At the end of the war, many settled in major urban areas, contributing to growing queer communities and cultures. Yet, the post-war emphasis on white domesticity, combined with McCarthyism's association of homosexuality with Communism, resulted in witch-hunts, job losses, arrest, incarceration, or institutionalization for untold numbers of people. The 1950s also saw the birth of the homophile movement, which sought gay and lesbian inclusion within the US nation's citizenship norms.

Historians have variously periodized twentieth-century gay, lesbian, trans, and queer resistance, organizing, and efforts to transform their status within the nation-state—that is, the meaning of their citizenship. For example, George Chauncey describes after World War II both escalation in policing and growing, diverse resistance; gay liberationist projects after the Stonewall riot of 1969; "retrenchment and resurgence" in the 1980s and early 1990s in the context of AIDS and the growth of a well-funded and organized right wing; and significant transformations in the late 1990s and at the turn of the millennium.[44] Other historians have employed other analytic lenses and periodizations. These LGBTQ histories have overlapped with, borrowed from, and contributed to civil rights, women's rights, welfare rights, indigenous sovereignty, reproductive justice, anti-war, anti-imperialism, queer of color, women of color, immigrants' rights, prison abolition, and other movements, including because these issues were not easily separable in the lives of many who were involved.[45]

LGBTQ groups not only engaged the terms of citizenship; they also reimagined nation. Jill Johnson's *Lesbian Nation: The Feminist Solution* inspired thousands of (mostly white) women to experiment with lesbian separatism including in housing, food provision, and credit unions, and inspiring groups such as the Van Dykes (who, as their name suggests, were dykes who lived in a roving van). Queer Nation, founded in 1990 by HIV/AIDS activists from ACT UP, sought to occupy and resignify hegemonic public spaces, often through forms of consumption that dramatized and challenged "how thoroughly the local experience of the body is framed by laws, politics, and social customs regulating sexuality."[46] Cherríe Moraga published her vision of Queer Atzlán as a decolonized, non-sexist, and non-homophobic homeland for Chican@ people of all persuasions. Queer and two-spirit members of Native nations articulated models of nation that are "decolonizing and critical of heteropatriarchy."[47] A "Black Nations/ Queer Nations" conference held in 1995 created networks and infrastructure for theorizing and engaging Black queer nations and diasporas.

These citizenship and nationalist struggles have brought about change but also revealed the contradictions of citizenship: as promising inclusion but effectively producing a spectrum of differentiations and hierarchies. In the United States, this process has been inseparable from expanding neoliberalism since the 1970s.[48] As Lisa Duggan explains, neoliberalism is characterized by valorization and essentialization of the market, and efforts to extend market logics into ever-growing spheres of human life through the dual logics of privatization and personal responsibility. While neoliberalism is presented as neutral, technical, and separate from politics and culture, in reality it works through—and reconfigures—historic inequalities of gender, sexuality, race, class, and geopolitics, while at the same time seeking to depoliticize struggles organized on these bases. Neoliberalism's effects are particularly evident in the radical roll-back of the welfare state, the exponential increase in the prison industrial complex, and growing wealth and wage gaps. In this context, mainstream LGBT politics became focused around access to marriage and the right to serve openly in the military—with notable success. Most spectacularly, the Supreme Court ruled in June 2015 that same sex couples have the right to marry nationwide. Since marriage and the military are cornerstones of US nation-making processes, ideologies, and intimacies, changes in these domains signal critical shifts in the relationship of LGBT people to the nation as an imagined, political community.

Critics are concerned that these changes reflect homonormativity, which Duggan defines as "a politics that does not contest dominant heteronormative assumptions and institutions, but upholds and sustains them, while promising the possibility of a demobilized gay constituency and a privatized, depoliticized gay culture anchored in domesticity and consumption."[49] The fact that gay men and lesbians who are white, middle-class, citizen, and gender normative have most benefitted from these changes has raised critical questions about how to make sense of formations of power that "increasingly speak the language of women's, gay, and transgender rights," yet operate in ways that foster "ascendancies" for some of these groups while consigning others to abandonment, disposal, and death.[50]

In the context of US engagement in sustained wars abroad, combined with the so-called war or terror "at home" (as the nation is now commonly described), Jasbir Puar coined the term homonationalism to capture a range of intersecting developments.[51] These include that certain privileged US gay men and lesbians have become incorporated into US militarized nationalism— and become useful figures through which the US nation presents itself globally as "exceptionally tolerant" of sexual diversity, while painting other nation-states as "exceptionally homophobic" in order to legitimize military intervention, coercive donor sanctions, and colonialist discourses and practices, even while leaving its own practices of violence and abuse unaddressed, and ignoring the perspectives and priorities of queer organizers in these other countries.[52]

Various LGBT NGOs based in the United States but operating internationally have adopted similarly troubling strategies and discourses, generating intense debate about alternatives for crafting global solidarities. Thus, the "transnational turn" in LGBTQ studies (and politics) announced by Elizabeth Povinelli and George Chauncey in 1999, has taken off exponentially and is evident in innovative activisms and scholarships on queer migration, queer diaspora, queer tourism, queer asylum, global queers, global LGBTQ rights, and much more. These works explore ways that queers and nations interconnect and diverge at different scales, and in various configurations of power, inequality, and resistance. They certainly demonstrate that "national" sexual cultures are inextricably formed in the interplay between national and transnational, in the context of histories of imperialism and global capitalism.

Conclusion

"Queer" and "US nation" have continually coproduced one another in shifting, contested, and changing ways that articulate hierarchies at local, regional, national, transnational, and imperial scales. The terms' interrelationship involves histories of violence, dispossession, dislocation, and subjugation—and dreams, visions, imaginaries, possibilities, and transformations—that future scholarship and activism will continue to explore.

Notes

1 "Structure of the Double Helix," GeneEd Web, http://geneed.nlm.nih.gov/topic_subtopic.php?tid= 15&sid=16. Accessed November 27, 2016.
2 See also, in this volume, Emily K. Hobson, "Thinking Transnationally, Thinking Queer."
3 Siobhan Somerville, "Queer," in *Keywords for American Cultural Studies*, ed. Bruce Burgett and Glenn Hendler (New York: New York University Press, 2007), 187.
4 Heather Love, "Queer," *TSQ* 1 nos. 1–2 (May 2014): 172–176.
5 Love, "Queer," 174.
6 Benedict Anderson, *Imagined Communities: Reflections on the Origins and Spread of Nationalism* (London: Verso, 1983), 5–7.
7 Inderpal Grewal and Caren Kaplan, *An Introduction to Women's Studies: Gender in a Transnational World*, 2nd ed. (Boston: McGraw Hill, 2006), 151.
8 On pedagogy, performance, and nation, see Homi K. Bhabha, "DissemiNation: Time, Narrative, and the Margins of the Modern Nation," in *Nation and Narration*, ed. Homi K. Bhabha (New York; Routledge, 1990), 291–322. On processes of orienting people toward particular national futures, see Sara Ahmed, *The Promise of Happiness* (Durham: Duke University Press, 2010).
9 Lauren Berlant, "Citizenship," in *Keywords for American Cultural Studies*, 2nd edition, ed. Bruce Burgett and Glenn Hendler (New York: New York University Press, 2014), 41.
10 Berlant, "Citizenship," 42.
11 Alys Weinbaum, "Nation," in *Keywords for American Cultural Studies*, 2nd edition, ed. Bruce Burgett and Glenn Hendler (New York: New York University Press, 2014), 180.
12 M. Jacqui Alexander, "Erotic Autonomy as a Politics of Decolonization," in ed. Alexander and Mohanty, *Feminist Genealogies, Colonial Legacies, Democratic Futures* (New York: Routledge, 1997), 63–100.
13 Scott Morgensen, "Settler Homonationalism: Theorizing Settler Colonialism Within Queer Modernities," *GLQ* 16 no.1–2 (2010): 106.
14 Morgensen, "Settler Homonationalism,"106.
15 Andrea Smith, "Queer Theory and Native Studies: The Heteronormativity of Colonialism," in *Queer Indigenous Studies*, ed. Qwo-Li Driskill, Chris Finley, Brian Joseph Gilley, and Scott Luria Morgensen (Tucson: University of Arizona Press, 2011), 59.
16 Morgensen, "Settler Homonationalism," 124.
17 For more on queer early American indigenous struggles with colonization, see, in this, volume, Richard Godbeer, "Colonial North America (1600s–1700s)," Clare Sears, "Centering Slavery in Nineteenth-Century Queer History," and Andrea Ritchie and Kay Whitlock, "Criminalization and Legalization."
18 Dorothy Roberts, *Killing the Black Body: Race, Reproduction, and the Meaning of Liberty* (New York: Vintage Books, 1998).
19 See also, in this volume, Sears, "Centering Slavery in Nineteenth-Century History."
20 Omise'eke Natasha Tinsley, "Black Atlantic, Queer Atlantic: Queer Imaginings of the Middle Passage," *GLQ* 14, nos. 2–3 (2008): 199.

21 For critical discussion about the ways that the Freedman's Bureau promoted compulsory heterosexuality and normative marriage, see Mattie Richardson, "No More Secrets, No More Lies: African American History and Compulsory Heterosexuality," *Journal of Women's History* 15, no. 3 (Autumn 2003): 63–76; Priya Kandaswamy, "The Obligations of Freedom and the Limits of Legal Equality," *Southwestern Law Review* 41, no. 2 (2012): 265–274.

22 Aliyya Abdur-Rahman, *Against the Closet: Black Political Longing and the Erotics of Race* (Durham: Duke University Press, 2012), 15.

23 Cathy Cohen, "Punks, Bulldaggers and Welfare Queens," in *Black Queer Studies: A Critical Anthology*, ed. E. Patrick Johnson and Mae G. Henderson (Durham, NC: Duke University Press, 2005), 24, 31.

24 Cohen, "Punks," 47; Roderick Ferguson, *Aberrations in Black: Toward A Queer of Color Critique* (Minneapolis: University of Minnesota Press, 2004), 1; Abdur-Rahman, *Against the Closet*, 6.

25 Gloria Anzaldúa, *Borderlands: La Frontera* (San Francisco: Spinsters/Aunt Lute, 1987), 3.

26 Ibid, 3.

27 Peter Boag, *Re-Dressing America's Frontier Past* (Berkeley: University of California Press, 2011), 7.

28 Mytheli Sreenivas, "Sexuality and Modern Imperialism," in *A Global History of Sexuality*, ed. Robert Buffington, Eithne Luibhéid, and Donna Guy (Chichester: Wiley Blackwell, 2014), 58.

29 Amy Kaplan, "Manifest Domesticity," *American Literature* 70, no.3 (September 1998): 585.

30 Sreenivas, "Sexuality and Modern Imperialism, 76. For discussion of how empire has been used to reconsolidate US norms of whiteness (yet has threatened to undo these norms, too), see Matthew Frye Jacobson, *Whiteness of a Different Color* (Cambridge: Harvard University Press, 1998), especially chapter 6.

31 Sreenivas, "Sexuality and Modern Imperialism," 69.

32 Siobhan Somerville, *Queering The Color Line: Race and the Invention of Homosexuality in American Culture* (Durham: Duke University Press, 2000).

33 For the longer queer history of medicalization and racialization, see, in this volume, Katie Batza, "Sickness and Wellness."

34 Julian Carter, *The Heart of Whiteness* (Durham, NC: Duke University Press, 2007), 7.

35 Roberts, *Killing the Black Body*, 65.

36 See also, in this volume, David Serlin, "Bodies."

37 Eithne Luibhéid, "Immigration," in *Keywords for American Cultural Studies*, ed. Bruce Burgett and Glenn Hendler (New York: New York University Press, 2014), 125–129.

38 Eithne Luibhéid, "Introduction," in *Queer Migrations: Sexuality, US Citizenship, and Border Crossings* ed. Eithne Luibhéid and Lionel Cantu (Minneapolis: University of Minnesota Press, 2005), 5.

39 Eithne Luibhéid, *Entry Denied: Controlling Sexuality at the Border* (Minneapolis: University of Minnesota Press, 2002); Luibhéid, "Introduction."

40 Margot Canaday, *The Straight State: Sexuality and Citizenship in Twentieth Century America* (Princeton: University of Princeton Press, 2011).

41 E.g. see Martin F. Manalansan IV, *Global Divas: Filipino Gay Men in the Diaspora* (Durham: Duke University Press, 2003); Carlos Decena, *Tacit Subjects: Belonging and Same-Sex Desire Among Dominican Immigrant Men* (Durham: Duke University Press, 2011).

42 See especially, in this volume, Nayan Shah, "Queer of Color Estrangement and Belonging."

43 George Chauncey, *Gay New York: Gender, Urban Culture and the Making of the Gay Male World, 1890–1940*, Basic Books, 1995), 7; John D'Emilio, *Sexual Politics, Sexual Communities* (Chicago: University of Chicago Press, 1983), 11.

44 George Chauncey, *Why Marriage?* (New York: Basic Books, 2004), 23–58.

45 See Audre Lorde, "I Am Your Sister: Black Women Organizing Across Sexualities," in *A Burst of Light* (New York: Firebrand Books, 1988), for an eloquent articulation of this point.

46 Lauren Berlant and Elizabeth Freeman, "Queer Nationality," in Berlant, *The Queen of America Goes to Washington City. Essays on Sex and Citizenship* (Durham, NC: Duke University Press, 1997), 148.

47 Chris Finley, "Decolonizing the Queer Native Body (and Recovering the Native Bull-Dyke)," in *Queer Indigenous Studies*, ed. Qwo-Li Driskill, Chris Finley, Brian Joseph Gilley, and Scott Luria Morgensen (Tucson: University of Arizona Press, 2011), 40.

48 For more on the queer history of US neoliberalism, see in this volume, Margot Weiss, "Queer Politics in Neoliberal Times (1970–2016)."

49 Lisa Duggan, *The Twilight of Equality?* (Boston: Beacon Press, 2003), 50.

50 Jin Haritaworn, Adi Kuntsman, and Silvia Posocco, "Introduction," in *Queer Necropolitics* eds. Haritaworn, Kuntsman and Posocco (New York: Routledge, 2014), 1, 2.

51 Jasbir Puar, *Terrorist Assemblages: Homonationalism in Queer Times* (Durham, NC: Duke University Press, 2007), 4, 9–10.
52 For discussion of how nation-states deploy discourses about queer people for purposes of state- and nation-making within global contexts, see Cynthia Weber, *Queer International Relations*. Oxford: Oxford University Press, 2016.

Further Reading

Alexander, M. Jacqui. *Pedagogies of Crossing: Meditations on Feminism, Sexual Politics, Memory, and the Sacred.* Durham: Duke University Press, 2006.

Anzaldúa, Gloria. *Borderlands: La Frontera.* San Francisco: Spinsters/Aunt Lute, 1987.

Balce, Nerissa. *Body Parts of Empire: Visual Abjection, Filipino Images, and the American Archive.* Anne Arbor: University of Michigan Press, 2016.

Berlant, Lauren. *The Queen of America Goes to Washington City: Essays on Sex and Citizenship.* Durham: Duke University Press, 1997.

Canaday, Margot. *The Straight State: Sexuality and Citizenship in Twentieth Century America.* Princeton: University of Princeton Press, 2011.

Chávez, Karma. *Queer Migration Politics: Activist Rhetoric and Coalitional Possibilities.* Urbana: University of Illinois Press, 2013.

Decena, Carlos. *Tacit Subjects: Belonging and Same-Sex Desire Among Dominican Immigrant Men.* Durham: Duke University Press, 2011.

D'Emilio, John. *Sexual Politics, Sexual Communities,* 2nd edition. Chicago: University of Chicago Press, 1998.

Holland, Sharon. *The Erotic Life of Racism.* Durham: Duke University Press, 2012.

Johnson, Colin R. *Just Queer Folks: Gender and Sexuality in Rural America.* Philadelphia: Temple University Press, 2013.

Johnson, E. Patrick and Mae G. Henderson, eds. *Black Queer Studies: A Critical Anthology.* Durham: Duke University Press, 2005.

Luibhéid, Eithne. *Entry Denied: Controlling Sexuality at the Border.* Minneapolis: University of Minnesota Press, 2002.

Luibhéid, Eithne and Lionel Cantú Jr., eds. *Queer Migrations: Sexuality, US Citizenship, and Border Crossings.* Minneapolis: University of Minnesota Press, 2005.

Manalansan, Martin F. IV. *Global Divas: Filipino Gay Men in the Diaspora.* Durham: Duke University Press, 2003.

Moraga, Cherríe. "Queer Atzlan: The Reformation of Chicano Tribe." In *The Last Generation*, 145–174. Boston: South End Press, 1993.

Morgensen, Scott. *Spaces Between Us: Queer Settler Colonialism and Indigenous Decolonization.* Minneapolis: University of Minnesota Press, 2011.

Pérez, Emma. "Queering the Borderlands: The Challenges of Excavating the Invisible and Unheard." *Frontiers* 24, nos.2–3 (2003): 122–131.

Povinelli, Elizabeth and George Chauncey. "Thinking Sexuality Transnationally." GLQ 5, no. 4 (1999): 439–450.

Puar, Jasbir K. *Terrorist Assemblages: Homonationalism in Queer Times.* Durham: Duke University Press, 2007.

Shah, Nayan. *Stranger Intimacy: Contesting Race, Sexuality and the Law in the North American West.* Berkeley: University of California Press, 2011.

Somerville, Siobhan. *Queering the Color Line: Race and the Invention of Homosexuality in American Culture.* Durham: Duke University Press, 2000.

Stein, Marc. "'Birthplace of the Nation': Imagining Lesbian and Gay Communities in Philadelphia, 1969–70." In *Creating a Place for Ourselves*, ed. Brett Beemyn, 253–288. New York: Routledge, 1997.

Stern, Alexandra. *Eugenic Nation: Faults and Frontiers of Better Breeding in Modern America.* Berkeley: University of California Press, 2005.

West, Isaac. *Transforming Citizenships: Transgender Articulations of the Law.* New York: New York University Press, 2014.

15

THINKING TRANSNATIONALLY, THINKING QUEER

Emily K. Hobson

Where and when is the transnational, and what does it have to do with queer history in the United States? Transnational history is less a topic than a method. It fits somewhat awkwardly, yet appropriately, into this volume's section on "Spaces and Places" as it refers not to specific locations but to a type of cartography.[1] The transnational describes networks and circuits that move across national borders and that make the construction of national borders and ideologies visible. Key transnational networks in US history include the Atlantic world, the African diaspora, the French, Spanish, and Mexican borderlands, and the Pacific Rim. Transnational ties also operate through militarism and globalization, structures integral to the growth of US power across the twentieth century and especially since World War II. Despite such wide-ranging geographies, some of the most productive transnational histories are local, asking how specific crossroads reveal or constitute larger formations. Others trace either hegemonic or oppositional cultural politics. Most centrally, as Joanne Meyerowitz puts it, "transnational histories question the nation as the default unit of analysis and remind us of the artificiality and permeability of political borders."[2] Gayatri Gopinath's point that diaspora is often imagined as a false copy of the nation, while queerness is treated as a false copy of heterosexuality, suggests that transnational scholarship offers a means to queer the nation and the containers in which we do history.[3]

Transnational history has developed in close formation with histories of sexuality over the last few decades. Links between the fields have flourished since the 1990s through analyses of what anthropologist Ann Laura Stoler terms the "intimacies of empire," initially attending primarily to interracial heterosexuality between Europeans or Euro-Americans and colonial subjects. Queer history builds on this scholarship not only by attending to same-sex and gender-transgressive "intimacies," but also by asking how multiple forms of sexual deviancy and gender difference have been placed outside racial, colonial, and national boundaries.

This essay explores three key areas of study that are central to transnational analyses of queer US history and that reveal how sexuality and gender have been imbricated within norms of race, class, global difference, and citizenship. These three areas are the racialized epistemologies of sexuality and gender created in and through colonialism and empire; the construction of sexual citizenship; and transnational LGBTQ activism since World War II. The first two of these topics have received fairly extensive scholarly attention, while the last has been less explored but holds notable possibilities for further research.

Transnational histories stand in direct opposition to transcultural or transhistorical claims that universalize across space or time; rather, they contextualize and denaturalize modern nation-states. This sets the transnational in productive but tense relationship with early colonial histories, which trace the epistemologies that brought later nation-states as well as ongoing settler colonialism into being. Scholars of queer history carry a particular imperative to consider how colonial archives have shaped perceptions of Native or indigenous genders and sexualities.

A key argument revolves around *berdache*, a term that both colonists and past scholars used to describe people in traditional Native societies who had bodies designated male but who performed feminine gender or sexual roles. The term entered anthropology and history directly from colonial records. In the 1970s, writers of gay and lesbian history began to adapt the concept for new and more celebratory accounts, reversing narratives of sin and social degradation in favor of tolerance and spiritual power. The contemporary scholar Scott Lauria Morgensen critiques this genealogy in queer studies, and seeking to distinguish non-indigenous from indigenous systems of knowledge, refers to the term as the "the colonial object berdache."

Crucially, the word *berdache* derived from the Arabic *bradaj*, a term for male prostitutes that Spanish, French, and English observers first began to use in Orientalist observations of Arab and Muslim cultures. Spanish colonists and missionaries adapted this concept—earlier used to demarcate enemies in the Iberian Peninsula and Africa—to legitimize war against Native people in the Americas and to construct a colonial state. Indeed, as Tracy Brown demonstrates in her study of Spanish-Pueblo relations in New Mexico, Spanish colonial authorities prosecuted sodomy as a sin particularly evident in the New World. Further, Spanish, French, and English colonists constructed a shared discourse of *berdache* that elided differences among Native people. While some tribes accorded respected roles to same-sex sexuality and gender transgression, others defined them through exploitation and violence. Additionally, for many, gender transgression was principally social rather than sexual. *Berdache* lumped together differing practices into one category and emphasized homosexuality as the most central concern.

The discourse of *berdache* also shaped nation-to-nation relations between Native and European or Euro-American people. Gunlög Fur examines relationships between the Delaware (Lenape), the Iroquois, and English colonists in Pennsylvania on the eve of the American Revolution. The Iroquois termed the Delaware "a nation of women," meaning by this that the Delaware were weak, fell under Iroquois protection, and owed the Iroquois loyalty. The characterization was a hostile one, but may have also evidenced the latitude that existed for women's leadership and male effeminacy in Delaware society. The Pennsylvania government used the Iroquois' characterization of the Delaware to benefit their own takeover of Delaware land. Fur contends that, as a result, growing numbers of Native people came to view effeminacy and women's authority as signs of dishonor.[4]

As settler colonialism propelled state building, the US state used the logic of *berdache* as a sign of Native passivity and primitivism that could be remedied only through assimilation into individualized property ownership, citizenship, and nuclear family settlement. Through war, the reservation system, boarding schools, and heteronormative property and citizenship law, the United States worked to control Native peoples' gender and family systems in order to naturalize its own national myths and power. US queer history and histories of sexuality would benefit greatly from further research into these forms of regulation, not only within the United States, but also as they circulated across the Americas and in Australia, South Africa, and elsewhere.

Against the history of *berdache*, contemporary Native activists have created the term Two-Spirit. Both *berdache* and Two-Spirit are transnational terms, but they operate in very different ways; the concept of Two-Spirit is not a celebratory replacement of *berdache* and does not propose inherent indigenous tolerance or a universal queer past. Rather, Two-Spirit is purposefully anticolonial and contemporary. It describes a wide range of same-sex and gender-nonconforming Native identities—some of them linked to traditional roles and others not, but all open to pantribal exchange, redefinition, and inclusion of women and others in designated female bodies. Two-Spirit highlights the importance of recognizing the genealogies of the language that structure historical accounts. It also demands of queer history a sustained engagement with Native sovereignty, guidance for which can be found in the work of Joanne Barker, Qwo-Li Driskill, J. Kēhaulani Kauanui, and Mark Rifkin, among others.[5]

The circulation of science and print culture across the Atlantic World offers another site for analyzing racialized epistemologies of sexuality and gender. Significantly, popular knowledge of same-sex and gender-transgressive behavior grew in tandem with white male sexual privilege. In her history of the category of intersex in early America and the United States, Elizabeth Reis shows that colonists understood the so-called "hermaphrodite" as a woman with a clitoris large enough to penetrate other women, and that they believed such bodies were especially common among African, South Asian, and Caribbean people. Shifting to law, Clare Lyons observes that residents of eighteenth and early nineteenth century Philadelphia were eager readers of English, French, and other European publications about punishment of sexual deviance, including newspaper accounts of molly houses and sodomy trials in London. Yet Philadelphia's courts rarely prosecuted same-sex behavior. Lyons attributes this difference to structures of race and class, arguing that latitude for same-sex behaviour encouraged white male unity against black men and all women.

Scholarship on racialized imaginaries of sexual and gender difference in the colonial period and early United States offers a prehistory to the more explicit delineation of sexual citizenship that began to take shape in the mid-to-late nineteenth century. As Roderick Ferguson argues, in the late nineteenth and early twentieth centuries the US political economy and its cultures of imperialism combined to construct a linked set of racially and sexually "perverse" geographies, including the "premodern" Mexican home, "deviant" Chinatowns, and African American "vice" districts.[6] While ostensibly domestic, such spaces and hierarchies upheld conceptions of global difference. Indeed, they defined Asian and Latino/a people as perpetual foreigners while linking that exclusion to anti-black racism maintained through sexual norms. Laws, policies, and prosecutions regulating sexuality centered most heavily on people of color and migrants, codifying divisions between deviant and normal that would underlie the mid-twentieth century development of a heterosexual/homosexual binary in citizenship policy.

Histories of sexual citizenship typically begin with Chinese Exclusion, which began at a federal level with the 1875 Page Law restricting the entry of Chinese women. Over its six decades of enforcement (1882–1943), Chinese Exclusion limited migrants' long-term settlement in favor of movements back and forth across the Pacific. Immigration restrictions worked to create, and Alien Land and anti-miscegenation laws to maintain, a gender-imbalanced "bachelor" society among Asian men. Meanwhile, Anglo representations described Chinatowns as sites of disease, prostitution, and rumored same-sex relations. Discourses of Asian deviance, which defined women as exploited and submissive and men as exploitative and effeminate, fueled US and European imperialism and constructed working-class white masculinity along with white feminism. Clare Sears contends that Chinese Exclusion also furthered legal and cultural restrictions against cross-dressing, tying transgender history to the boundaries of race and nation.

An intriguing site for further queer histories of Chinese Exclusion lies in San Francisco's early twentieth century "rescue homes." Though reformers created these institutions to pull Chinese women and girls out of prostitution, they soon functioned largely as shelters from coerced domestic service, and secondarily as sites of immigrant detention and foster care. Yet publications about rescue homes obscured this complexity in favor of narratives of white women's protection. In practice as well as in representation, the sites fostered unequal but strong ties between Anglo and Asian women: one Chinese resident became the lifelong assistant to (and was eventually buried beside) Donaldina Cameron, the well-known "Matron" of the San Francisco Presbyterian Mission Home. White women posed in Chinese women's attire to represent their reform work and wore Western men's clothing to participate in "slumming tours" in Chinatown. Chinatown "rescue homes" call out for further study as sites that staged female homosociality on the grounds of missionary feminism and national and racial exclusion.[7]

Moving beyond Chinese Exclusion, Pablo Mitchell shows that colonial relations in the US Southwest shaped the formation of sexual citizenship and what Margot Canaday has termed the "straight state." Mitchell examines the regulation of gendered comportment and sexual behavior in the schools, courtrooms, marriage law, medicine, religious practices, and consumer culture of late nineteenth and early twentieth century New Mexico. Through this investigation, he reveals how the formation of sexual categories intersected with those of race. In order to justify the territory's drive to statehood, Anglos regulated Hispano sexual practice by ascribing non-normative gender to Pueblo Indians and promiscuity to black people. Anglos, and more tenuously Hispanos, aligned themselves with a nationalist whiteness through discourses of the ideal home. Mitchell expands transnational analyses of sexual modernity by arguing that "a defining feature of modern America, its imperialistic adventure with Latin America, may have roots in New Mexico" and its regulation of sexuality.[8]

In dynamic conversation with Mitchell's analysis of law and courts, Nayan Shah's *Stranger Intimacy* shows that sodomy prosecutions in the early twentieth century US and Canadian Northwest constructed South Asian migrants as dangerously foreign. These prosecutions tipped the scale toward anti-Asian restriction by defining South Asian men as prone to sodomy with white men and boys and thus as threatening white and national honor. Ultimately, Shah argues, "The presumed propensity of vagrants and racialized foreigners to sodomy anticipated the consolidation of the dangerous figure of the 'male homosexual pervert' as the dominant threat to the development of normal masculinity."[9] This account expands Margot Canaday's analysis of how discourses of vagrancy and economic dependency structured the containment of homosexuality in early twentieth century US immigration enforcement and the New Deal.

The boundaries of US sexual citizenship solidified most clearly in the aftermath of World War II and through the Cold War. Joanne Meyerowitz argues that as the United States turned away from overt racial exclusion and towards liberal civil rights, it replaced explicit racial discrimination with a discourse of sexual normativity. As the late Peggy Pascoe observed, this discourse gained power in part because it was couched in color-blind guise. By the mid-twentieth century, the US government enacted explicitly anti-homosexual discrimination that defined gay men, lesbians, and bisexuals as less than fully American. Such exclusion targeted native-born whites as well as immigrants and people of color. But heteronormativity continued to converge with structural racism through frameworks of "illegitimacy," criminality, and the supposed "pathology" of poor black families.[10]

Small wonder that as medicine opened up possibilities for transsexuality, these options remained tightly constrained by racial, gender, and citizenship norms. David Serlin and Susan Stryker show that the transsexual celebrity Christine Jorgensen gained global fame only to the extent that she fit narrow scripts of heterosexual romance, whiteness, and US militarism as well as binary sex and gender. The career of Rae Bourbon, a transsexual performer in the US–Mexico borderlands, underscores these limits. Don Romesburg argues that although Bourbon's racial and gender fluidity attracted audiences in the 1930s and 1940s, in later decades Bourbon faced harsher policing and restricted social mobility.

Sexual limits on "American" belonging became particularly evident in US immigration policy after World War II. Eithne Luibhéid and Siobhan Somerville explain how racialized Cold War logics structured the Immigration and Nationality (McCarran-Walter) Act, which excluded homosexual immigrants from 1952 to 1990. Cold War priorities also remained central as the state began to dismantle McCarran-Walter. As Susana Peña and Julio Capó, Jr. demonstrate, the presence of gay, transgender, bisexual, and lesbian migrants in the 1980 Mariel boatlift from Cuba pushed the United States to ease McCarran-Walter's exclusions and to recognize anti-gay persecution as a basis for refugee claims. Yet, as Jennifer Brier has detailed, Cold War interests drove the exclusion of HIV-positive migrants that began in 1987 and the US's selective attention to global HIV/AIDS care.[11] Alissa Solomon shows that today, the rhetoric of national security continues to structure exclusions of transgender migrants and their sexual abuse in detention.

Scholars of sexual citizenship focused only on the United States, no matter how transnational their accounting of migration or of borderlands, have yet to explain why anti-homosexual exclusion became widespread across so many disparate sites following World War II—in nation-states that were variously communist, socialist, capitalist, democratic, and fascist. We need multi-sited research to explain why such exclusions solidified in so many places in the same period and what transnational dynamics shaped this pattern. Moving into more recent history, Nan Alamilla Boyd suggests that histories of gay tourism and consumerism might account for the transnational expansion of marriage equality, while Nicholas Syrett's history of a wealthy white gay couple's land takeovers in mid-twentieth-century Hawai'i points towards a long history of "pinkwashing," or the use of narratives of sexual freedom to divert attention from settler colonialism. The simultaneous development of pinkwashing and of transformations in sexual citizenship demands further accounting.

A final major area of study for transnational queer US history revolves around LGBTQ activism from World War II through the present. Although relatively underdeveloped, trans-national histories of LGBTQ activism are growing, especially in relation to the homophile movement; to gay liberation, lesbian feminism, and the gay and lesbian left; and to queer of color organizing. This work benefits from cultural studies scholarship, including that by Jasbir Puar on homonationalism; Gayatri Gopinath on queer diasporic public cultures; and accounts by Martin Manalansan, Susana Peña, Horacio N. Roque Ramírez, and others of how queer migrants to the United States navigate the nationalist and developmentalist lenses through which they are regulated and seen. Relatedly, Maylei Blackwell's concept of "translenguaje" articulates how LGBTQ activists can remake transnational exchange by "translating, reworking, and contesting meaning" from Global South to North.[12] Such theoretical tools and ethnographic accounts provide invaluable entry points for historical work, even as it remains incumbent upon historians to track change over time in transnational queer activism.

David Churchill has described postwar homophile activists as constructing a Cold War "liberal internationalism, an attempt to both normalize and historicize homosexual persons and bring them into the shelter and normative embrace of modern legal citizenship." Through a careful reading of US homophile periodicals, he shows that US activists exchanged ideas with contemporaries in Europe, followed European news, and organized formal tours to Europe, North Africa, and Asia. But while US activists described Europe as a site of everyday life, tourism, and law reform, they viewed the rest of the world through an anthropological gaze, using accounts of primitivism to represent homosexuality as simultaneously transcultural, trans-historical, and subject to modernization. Further, "European homophiles emphasized the deep cultural legacy of same-sex sexuality, pointing to the classical period" to mark their distance from gender transgression, sex work, and street- and bar-based queer cultures. Churchill argues that homophile activists shared a developmentalist view of themselves and the world: "lesbians and gay men in Los Angeles, Paris, Rome, and Sydney argued that they were entitled to legal standing and all the privileges of modern civil and human rights, while continuing to distinguish and separate themselves from their supposedly more primitive brethren."[13] How did such rhetoric interact with homophile activists' citation of the black freedom struggle as a model for their own cause? Did what Churchill terms "liberal internationalism" encourage homophiles to view sexuality and race as analogous rather than intersecting?[14]

In contrast to the homophile movement's Cold War liberalism, late 1960s and 1970s gay liberation and lesbian feminism found catalysts in the New Left and Third World Left.[15] These influences pushed activists to imagine internationalist links between sexual liberation and anti-imperialism. Gay liberation and lesbian feminism grew not only in the United States but also across Latin America, in Canada and Australia, and throughout Western and parts of Eastern Europe. Gay and, to a lesser extent, lesbian radical publications circulated between countries; US gay liberation newspapers printed reports from their peers in Argentina, Mexico, and Britain, and they covered anti-gay repression in both socialist and right-wing states, as by comparing Castro's Cuba to the military dictatorship in Brazil. As Ian Lekus has shown, gay and lesbian radicals contended with expressions of anti-gay hostility and hypermasculinity that circulated transnationally throughout the left. In my own work, I have argued that US gay radicals valorized effeminacy by linking it to draft resistance and anti-imperialism, while US lesbian feminists crafted a politics of collective self-defense that they expressed through idealized images of revolutionary Vietnamese, Cuban, and black women and through support for the revolutionary underground.

By the late 1970s and 1980s, another form of transnational gay, lesbian, and bisexual activism emerged through the Central American solidarity movement. The solidarity movement as a whole was presumptively straight, but gay, lesbian, and bisexual radicals became prominent within it, propelled by identification with Central Americans as fellow targets of Reagan and the global right. Lesbian, gay, and bisexual activists not only joined larger anti-intervention groups but also formed specifically lesbian and gay solidarity organizations. As my work shows, this activism gained special strength in the San Francisco Bay Area, where Central American immigrant, refugee, and Latina/o communities overlapped with multiracial queer and radical organizing. In Nicaragua, gay and lesbian activists drew on transnational solidarity networks to develop their own AIDS program and to push the Sandinista Revolution toward lesbian and gay inclusion. In the United States, Central American solidarity intersected with Latina/o queer organizing and women of color feminisms, and it also trained hundreds of activists in the direct action tactics that they would use to challenge the political crisis of AIDS.

Across the late Cold War, activists crafted transnational networks of both liberal and leftist sexual politics. In broad terms, liberals pursued goals of inclusion and rights, while leftists articulated liberationist and socialist-feminist visions. Liberal efforts have gained more attention from scholars, including through critical assessments of globalization and neoliberalism; leftist politics warrant further study, but should not be imagined as innocent of imposition across global difference. In her study of the 1980s Mexican lesbian and gay movement, Lucy Grinnell shows that activists' opposition to the Mexican state's policies of austerity and "moral renovation" drove their participation in networks of Central American solidarity and the International Gay Association (IGA, later ILGA). But US-based lesbian feminists, including radical Latina women, objected when Mexican gay and lesbian activists prioritized Latin American networks over agendas shared with those in the US.[16]

Figure 15.1 Third World Gay Caucus, here marching in the 1977 San Francisco Gay and Lesbian
Freedom Day parade, sought to build community and coalition across diasporic
communities of color.
Photograph by Marie Ueda, Courtesy of the GLBT Historical Society.

Other important transnational exchanges across the 1970s and 1980s include those across
the northern border and around the Anglophone world. Gay and lesbian activists in Canada
protested the US New Right, while the Toronto-based magazine *Body Politic* shared readership
and politics with the Boston-based *Gay Community News*. Similarly, US and British activists
sustained dialogue on the threats of Reagan and Thatcher, and many gay and lesbian leftists
in the United States looked to their British peers for guidance in socialist-feminist critique.[17]
Other rich sites for research lie in the links between the global anti-apartheid movement and
LGBTQ organizing; in the transnational visions of the religious right; and in HIV/AIDS. It
remains crucial for historians to account for the transnational dimensions of the epidemic, in
particular the relationship of HIV/AIDS activism to the neoliberal replacement of the state by
non-governmental organizations (NGOs).

As a field invested in shifting, mobile boundaries, US queer history has gained a good deal
from transnational analysis and can only be enriched further. While not all historical topics are
transnational, we strengthen any research project when we consider what transnational currents
or points of connection may apply. As a way of thinking, of conducting research, and of situating
ourselves as scholars in relation to broader fields, transnational history enables us to investigate
changes both within and beyond the nation, to contest the limits of nationalism as a frame,
and to make our historical imagination a little more queer.

Notes

1 See also, in this volume, Eithne Luibhéid, "Queer and Nation."
2 Joanne Meyerowitz, "Transnational Sex and US History," *American Historical Review* 114, no. 5 (December 2009): 1273.
3 Reflecting this, this essay resists the conflation of the United States with "America," approaching the Americas in hemispheric terms and using "American" only to describe borderlands spaces and to name histories prior to the establishment of the United States.
4 See also, in this volume, Richard Godbeer, "Colonial North America (1600s–1700s)" and Rachel Hope Cleves, "Revolutionary Sexualities and Early National Genders (1770s–1840s)."
5 See also, in this volume, Nayah Shah, "Queer of Color Estrangement and Belonging."
6 Roderick A. Ferguson, *Aberrations in Black: Toward a Queer of Color Critique* (Minneapolis: University of Minnesota Press, 2003), 13–14.
7 Rescue home narratives include Pacific Presbyterian Publishing Company, *Dragon stories: The bowl of powfah, The hundredth maiden, naratives* [sic] *of the rescues and romances of Chinese slave girls* (Oakland: Pacific Presbyterian Publishing Company, 1908); and Jessie Juliet Knox, *In the house of the Tiger* (New York: Eaton and Maine, 1911). On the relationship between Donaldina Cameron and her assistant, see Judy Yung, *Unbound Feet: A Social History of Chinese Women in San Francisco* (Berkeley: University of California Press, 1995), 40.
8 Pablo Mitchell, *Coyote Nation: Sexuality, Race, and Conquest in Modernizing New Mexico, 1880–1920* (Chicago: University of Chicago Press, 2005), 178.
9 Nayan Shah, *Stranger Intimacy: Contesting Race, Sexuality, and Law in the North American West* (Berkeley: University of California Press), 151.
10 For a more extensive discussion of queer of color analysis as central to urban history, see, in this volume, Kwame Holmes, "The End of Queer Urban History?"
11 For a larger discussion of AIDS in queer US history, see, in this volume, Jennifer Brier, "AIDS and Action (1980s–1990s)."
12 Maylei Blackwell, "Translenguas: Mapping the Possibilities and Challenges of Transnational Women's Organizing Across Geographies of Difference," in *Translocalities/Translocalidades: Feminist Politics of Translation in the Latin/a Americas*, ed. Sonia E. Alvarez et al. (Durham: Duke University Press, 2014), 299–300.
13 David Churchill, "Transnationalism and Homophile Political Culture in the Postwar Decades," *GLQ: Gay and Lesbian Quarterly* 15, no. 1 (2009): 33, 43, 57.
14 For more on queer organizational history, see, in this volume, Marcia Gallo, "Organizations."
15 For a more general queer history of this era, see, in this volume, Whitney Strub, "Gay Liberation (1963–1980)."
16 See also Migdalia Reyes, "The Latin American and Caribbean Feminist/Lesbian Encuentros: Crossing the Bridge of Our Diverse Identities," in *This Bridge We Call Home: Radical Visions for Transformation*, ed. Gloria Anzaldúa and Analouise Keating (New York: Routledge, 2002), 463–470.
17 For one example, see Marc Stein, "Sexual Politics in the Era of Reagan and Thatcher: Marc Stein in Conversation with Jeffrey Weeks," *Notches: (Re)marks on the History of Sexuality*, February 10, 2015, www.notchesblog.com. Accessed October 20, 2017. The mid-1980s efforts of Lesbians and Gays Support the Miners, a London-based group organized in solidarity with the UK miners' strike, bears striking resemblance to Central American solidarity work in the United States.

Further Reading

Barker, Joanne, ed. *Critically Sovereign: Indigenous Gender, Sexuality, and Feminist Studies*. Durham: Duke University Press, 2017.
Boyd, Nan Alamilla. "Sex and Tourism: The Economic Implications of the Gay Marriage Movement." *Radical History Review* 100 (Winter 2008): 223–234.
Brier, Jennifer. "The Immigrant Infection: Images of Race, Nation, and Contagion in the Public Debates on AIDS and Immigration." In *Modern American Queer History*, edited by Allida M. Black, 253–270. Philadelphia: Temple University Press, 2001.
Brier, Jennifer. *Infectious Ideas: U.S. Political Responses to the AIDS Crisis*. Chapel Hill: University of North Carolina Press, 2011.

Briggs, Laura, Gladys McCormick and J.T. Way. "Transnationalism: A Category of Analysis." *American Quarterly* 60, no. 3 (September 2008): 625–648.

Brown, Tracy. "'Abominable Sin' in Colonial New Mexico: Spanish and Pueblo Perceptions of Same-Sex Sexuality." In *Long Before Stonewall: Histories of Same-Sex Sexuality in Early America*, ed. Thomas Foster, 51–77. New York: New York University Press, 2007.

Canaday, Margot. *The Straight State: Sexuality and Citizenship in Twentieth-Century America*. Princeton: Princeton University Press, 2011.

Canaday, Margot. "Thinking Sex in the Transnational Turn: An Introduction." *American Historical Review* 114, no. 5 (December 2009): 1250–1257.

Cantú Jr., Lionel and Nancy A. Naples and Salvador Vidal-Ortiz, eds. *The Sexuality of Migration: Border Crossings and Mexican Immigrant Men*. New York: New York University Press, 2009.

Capó Jr., Julio. "Queering Mariel: Mediating Cold War Foreign Policy and U.S. Citizenship Among Cuba's Homosexual Exile Community, 1978–1994." *Journal of American Ethnic History* 29, no. 4 (Summer 2010): 78–106.

Driskill, Qwo-Li, Chris Finley, Brian Joseph Gilley, and Scott Lauria Morgensen, eds. *Queer Indigenous Studies: Critical Interventions in Theory, Politics, and Literature*. Tucson: University of Arizona Press, 2011.

Foster, Thomas, ed. *Long Before Stonewall: Histories of Same-Sex Sexuality in Early America*. New York: New York University Press, 2007.

Fur, Gunlög. *A Nation of Women: Gender and Colonial Encounters Among the Delaware Indians*. Philadelphia: University of Pennsylvania Press, 2009.

Gopinath, Gayatri. *Impossible Desires: Queer Diasporas and South Asian Public Cultures*. Durham: Duke University Press, 2005.

Gordon, Linda. "Internal Colonialism and Gender." In *Haunted by Empire: Geographies of Intimacy in North American History*, edited by Ann Laura Stoler, 427–451. Durham: Duke University Press, 2006.

Grinnell, Lucy. "'Intolerable Subjects': Moralizing Politics, Economic Austerity, and Lesbian and Gay Activism in Mexico City, 1982–85." *Radical History Review* 112 (Winter 2012): 89–99.

Hobson, Emily K. *Lavender and Red: Liberation and Solidarity in the Gay and Lesbian Left*. Berkeley: University of California Press, 2016.

Hobson, Emily K. "'Si Nicaragua Venció': Lesbian and Gay Solidarity with the Revolution." *Journal of Transnational American Studies* 4, no. 2 (Fall 2012): 1–26.

Kauanui, J. Kēhaulani. *Hawaiian Blood: Colonialism and the Politics of Sovereignty and Indigeneity*. Durham: Duke University Press, 2008.

Lekus, Ian K. "Queer Harvests: Homosexuality, the U.S. New Left, and the Venceremos Brigades to Cuba." *Radical History Review* 89 (Spring 2004): 57–91.

Luibhéid, Eithne. *Entry Denied: Controlling Sexuality at the Border*. Minneapolis: University of Minnesota Press, 2002.

Luibhéid, Eithne and Lionel Cantú Jr., eds. *Queer Migrations: Sexuality, U.S. Citizenship, and Border Crossings*. Minneapolis: University of Minnesota Press, 2005.

Lyons, Clare A. *Sex Among the Rabble: An Intimate History of Gender and Power in the Age of Revolution, Philadelphia, 1730–1830*. Chapel Hill: University of North Carolina Press, 2006.

Manalansan IV, Martin F. *Global Divas: Filipino Gay Men in the Diaspora*. Durham: Duke University Press, 2003.

Manalansan IV, Martin F. "In the Shadows of Stonewall: Examining Gay Transnational Politics and the Transnational Dilemma." *GLQ* 2 (1995): 425–438.

Morgensen, Scott Lauria. *Spaces Between Us: Queer Settler Colonialism and Indigenous Decolonization*. Minneapolis: University of Minnesota Press, 2011.

Pascoe, Peggy. *What Comes Naturally: Miscegenation Law and the Making of Race in America*. New York: Oxford University Press, 2009.

Peña, Susana. *¡Oye Loca! From the Mariel Boatlift to Gay Cuban Miami*. Minneapolis: University of Minnesota Press, 2013.

Puar, Jasbir. *Terrorist Assemblages: Homonationalism in Queer Times*. Durham: Duke University Press, 2007.

Reis, Elizabeth. *Bodies in Doubt: An American History of Intersex*. Baltimore: Johns Hopkins University Press, 2012.

Reddy, Chandan. *Freedom with Violence: Race, Sexuality, and the US State*. Durham: Duke University Press, 2011.

Rifkin, Mark. *When Did Indians Become Straight? Kinship, the History of Sexuality, and Native Sovereignty*. Oxford: Oxford University Press, 2011.

Romesburg, Don. "Longevity and Limits in Rae Bourbon's Life in Motion." In *Transgender Migrations: The Bodies, Borders, and Politics of Transition*, edited by Trystan T. Cotton, 119–135. New York: Routledge, 2012.

Roque Ramírez, Horacio N. "Claiming Queer Cultural Citizenship: Gay Latino (Im)Migrant Acts in San Francisco." In *Queer Migrations: Sexuality, U.S. Citizenship, and Border Crossings*, edited by Eithne Luibhéid and Lionel Cantú, Jr., 161–188. Minneapolis: University of Minnesota Press, 2005.

Rupp, Leila J. "The Persistence of Transnational Organizing: The Case of the Homophile Movement." *American Historical Review* (October 2011): 1014–1039.

Sears, Clare. *Arresting Dress: Cross-Dressing, Law, and Fascination in Nineteenth-Century San Francisco*. Durham: Duke University Press, 2015.

Serlin, David Harley. "Christine Jorgensen and the Cold War Closet." *Radical History Review* 62 (1995): 136–165.

Shah, Nayan. *Contagious Divides: Epidemics and Race in San Francisco's Chinatown*. Berkeley: University of California Press, 2001.

Solomon, Alissa. "Trans/Migrant: Christina Madrazo's All-American Story." In *Queer Migrations: Sexuality, U.S. Citizenship, and Border Crossings*, edited by Eithne Luibhéid and Lionel Cantú, Jr., 3–29. Minneapolis: University of Minnesota Press, 2005.

Somerville, Siobhan. "Sexual Aliens and the Racialized State: A Queer Reading of the 1952 U.S. Immigration and Nationality Act." In *Queer Migrations: Sexuality, U.S. Citizenship, and Border Crossings*, edited by Eithne Luibhéid and Lionel Cantú, Jr., 75–91. Minneapolis: University of Minnesota Press, 2005.

Stein, Marc. "All the Immigrants Are Straight, All the Homosexuals Are Citizens, But Some of Us Are Queer Aliens: Genealogies of Legal Strategy in Boutilier v. INS." *Journal of American Ethnic History* 29, no. 4 (Summer 2010): 45–77.

Stoler, Ann Laura, ed. *Haunted by Empire: Geographies of Intimacy in North American History*. Durham: Duke University Press, 2006.

Stryker, Susan. "We Who Are Sexy: Christine Jorgensen's Transsexual Whiteness in the Postcolonial Philippines." *Social Semiotics* 19, no. 1 (March 2009): 79–91.

Syrett, Nicholas L. "'Lord of a Hawaiian Island': Robert and John Gregg Allerton, Queerness, and the Erasure of Colonization in Kaua'i." *Pacific Historical Review* 82, no. 3 (2013): 396–427.

PART THREE

Themes

16

LANGUAGE, ACTS, AND IDENTITY IN LGBT HISTORY

Jen Manion

More than other fields in LGBT studies, history has been wrapped up in dynamic contestation with philosopher Michel Foucault's claim that a modern schema defining sexual desire and behavior as something innate—akin to an "identity"—emerged in the late-nineteenth century.[1] In earlier periods, then, people who engaged in same-sex sexual "acts" were not designated "homosexual." So for decades, scholars have relied on the "acts-vs-identities" paradigm to teach students that our contemporary understanding of sexual orientation had a beginning. While literary scholars criticize historians for their overreliance and/or misinterpretation of Foucault's claim about periodization, historians have "tested" his thesis, producing dozens of path-breaking social and cultural histories of the pre-twentieth century in the process. Histories of this earlier period have boldly documented a great diversity of approaches to sexual desires, acts, identities, and communities. As such, historians of the queer past have demonstrated how multiple and even competing systems were used to make meaning of friendship, intimacy, and sex between people of the same sex. Most significantly, the scholarship has shown how a community's judgment of a relationship was influenced by other aspects, including the age, race, class, and status of the individuals involved, as well as the norms, values, and needs of the community within which they lived.[2]

Consider historian Rachel Hope Cleves' recent scholarship on an intimate relationship between two women in the early decades of the nineteenth century. Charity and Sylvia fell in love, worked together, set up a household and the rest—as they say—is herstory. They chose each other over any (and every) man and never feigned otherwise. The author's assertion that the relationship between Charity and Sylvia was sexual is buttressed by abundant evidence of Charity's sexual prowess with women throughout her life, along with specific, intimate writings between the two lifelong partners. By characterizing their relationship as a marriage, Cleves surely sought to offer it a legitimation that, in today's era of legalized same-sex marriage, appeals to a readership hungry to see historical precedents. To call their relationship a "marriage," however, also minimizes the hardships and uncertainty of becoming oneself, finding love and building a relationship within a society, community, and family that scarcely understood them and were not really supportive of their love or life. What Charity and Sylvia might also suggest is how "marriage," as metaphor, legality, or practice, can only do so much for queer people—then or now—in facing the precarity of their lives. Most importantly, though, Cleves' scholarship broke through the centuries-long silence/erasure of the possibility of an intimate, sexual relationship between women in early nineteenth-century America.[3]

For men, this barrier was broken decades ago when Richard Godbeer published his field-defining essay in the *William and Mary Quarterly* about two seventeenth- and eighteenth-century New England sodomy trials. Though neither case documented a longstanding loving intimate relationship, both showed that neighbors understood those charged with initiating sodomy with other men as not simply "acting" on a fleeting desire but rather having sustained preferences for sex with men throughout their lives, even having a "proclivity" for it. More recent scholarship by Charles Upchurch and Anna Clark on England in the early decades of the nineteenth century indicates that there was at least a small group of upper-class men organized to reform the sodomy law in the 1820s and 1830s, building their arguments around an "identity" category, and arguing their feelings were both inborn and natural.

We still are, of course, a community in need of a past. As Jonathan Ned Katz has repeatedly reminded us, while scholars in the academy often write as if understanding the history of sexuality was an idea imagined by Foucault alone atop a French hilltop, the 1960s and 1970s saw the explosion of angry, vibrant, and organized movements of LGBT people (though not yet utilizing that acronym) determined to fight the stigmatization and discrimination they faced on a daily basis.[4] One important piece of this movement was finding their place in the past. No one could have predicted the path-breaking import nor lasting relevance of Jonathan Ned Katz's volume *Gay American History: Lesbians and Gay Men in the U.S.A*, which quite literally and audaciously established several foundational paradigms of the field.[5] While most of the sections were labeled thematically (such as "Treatment" or "Resistance") two identity groups received their own chapters—"Passing Women" and "Native American/s Gay Americans." In an ambitious effort to include the widest range of people involved with sexual or gender disruption as well as a commitment to expanding a source base beyond sodomy records of white men, Katz simplified and distorted the meanings of the subjects falling into these chapters. Given hindsight's perfection, we can now see the limits of such categorizations.[6]

For instance, consider Deborah Sampson. I have been inspired by and burdened with Deborah Sampson as a forebear for as long as I can remember—from the first time I cracked open Katz's groundbreaking book at the Philadelphia Lesbian and Gay History Archives. Deborah Sampson was born in December 1760, assumed the name Robert Shurtliff and enlisted in the Continental Army in May 20, 1782. Sampson fought in the American Revolution until they were discharged October 25, 1783. Sampson went on to work on their aunt and uncle's farm in Sharon, Massachusetts and soon after married a farmer named Benjamin Gannett, Jr. They had three kids by 1790. Sampson received back pay from the Massachusetts legislature in 1792 for an "extraordinary instance of female heroism." They collaborated with school teacher and writer Herman Mann on a semi-fictional biography *The Female Marine* (1797). Sampson went on a speaking tour in 1802–1803 and was finally awarded a pension in 1805.[7] All of this earned Sampson a place in the traditional US history narrative that privileges soldiers, wars, and presidents over everyday life and regular people. Katz established Sampson as an important figure in the history of sexuality by listing them as the first entry in his "Passing Women" section. We know nothing of Sampson's gender identity, *per se*, and one wonders if they would even have made the cut for inclusion in the early canon of gay history based on their short-lived gender crossing alone. It seems that the tantalizing passages of intimacies with other women featured in the fictionalized biography are what later made their case irresistible to activists looking to claim a lesbian and gay past.

Katz's analysis of the category of "passing women" was binary yet nuanced. "While the adoption of the costume of the 'opposite' sex is certainly important in these passing women's lives, their adoption of the occupation, vocabulary, tone of voice, gesture, walk, sports, and aspirations of the "other" sex are equally significant," he wrote:

> To appreciate the full complexity of these lives, the concept of transvestism or cross-dressing needs to be supplemented by such concepts as cross-working and cross-speaking. If such terms seem odd, it is because they emphasize what is ordinarily taken for granted as given and eternal—the historically and socially determined sexual division of labor and sex polarization of American society.

Katz's engagement with the concept of gender identity bares striking resemblance to contemporary usage within transgender studies and communities:

> In trying to understand the character and meaning of these lives, we must note that the distinction between biologically determined gender and socially defined "masculinity" and "femininity" is basic. The concept of *gender identity* may also be useful, although difficult to apply, as it refers to both physical gender and socially conditioned psychological identification, and may, if carelessly used, convey all the traditional, politically loaded assumptions about "masculinity" and "femininity." It is also useful to distinguish analytically between *sexual* attraction, whatever its object, character, or origin, and the desire to dress, *pass*, and *work* as the "opposite" sex.[8]

Katz also drew from the emergent concept of gender identity within psychoanalysis, coined by Robert J. Stoller in the 1960s to describe "one's sense of being a member of a particular sex" distinct from sexual identity as well as sex roles.[9]

Even though "passing women" have occupied this rich and storied place in the public imagination for a long time, people still struggle to know what to make of them and how to write about them.[10] Accounts of people living between or across genders or assuming an identity, status, or persona typically reserved for those assigned a different sex at birth are well-known to historians. People designated female who presented as men to fight in the military, work at sea, flee a bad situation at home or find a long-lost lover have been well-documented in eighteenth and nineteenth century memoirs, narratives, court records, and newspapers. In the 1980s and 1990s, gender crossers—more than many other groups from the early period—were given great meaning as feminists and lesbians singled them out as our historical predecessors and linked them to contemporary political movements. These strong women who flouted convention and challenged gender roles, taking what they wanted, whether it was freedom, opportunity, or even the love of a woman, became important role models for both feminist and the lesbian and gay rights movements.[11] In more recent years, this same group—though still long dead—has been fashioned to assume a new role in American life as gender warriors for our transgender rights movement.[12] Scholars without intellectual or political investments in gender studies, feminism, or LGBT rights have done little better in understanding these figures on their own terms, instead offering utilitarian explanations rooted in the historic limitations of women's economic and geographic mobility, to the exclusion of gendered and sexual dynamics entirely.

People with quite varied experiences of thwarting gender or sexual norms were declared "passing women" including those described during their time with the word "female" as a

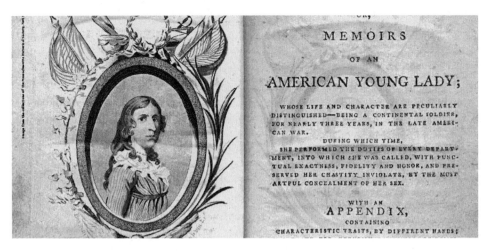

Figure 16.1 Frontispiece of an engraved portrait of Deborah Sampson and title page of Herman Mann's fictionalized *The Female Review: or, Memoirs of an American Young Lady; whose Life and Character are Peculiarly Distinguished–Being a Continental Soldier, for Nearly Three Years, in the Late American War* (Dedham, MA: Nathaniel and Benjamin Heaton, 1797).

Courtesy of the Massachusetts Historical Society.

modifier of some occupation or role typically assumed by a man, such as female soldier, female husband, female hunter, female marine, etc. Other language used to describe them throughout the nineteenth century included "curious," "aberration," "amazon," and "problem." Historians have long used the category "cross-dresser" as a catch-all for a wide range of people who crossed genders.[13] There are several issues with this designation. It is reductive, minimizing a dangerous, multifaceted, and sometimes life-long process of being affirmed as a man by others into the seemingly simple act of dressing oneself in another's clothes. It glosses over the numerous other behaviors that were expected of men and indeed were key to passing, from romantic relationships with women to drinking and smoking.

When I first learned of Sampson in the 1990s, I had little interest in separating fact from fiction. I instantly identified with certain aspects of their life, ignored the other parts that didn't interest me, and embraced Shurtleff/Sampson as a forbearer for gender and sexual transgressions. By graduate school, however, I learned better. This historic person who stood as a place holder for strong women, gender transgression, and even lesbianism was woven neatly into a progressive narrative of settler colonialism and the formation of a nation-state anchored in and defined by the enslavement of African Americans. Sampson's normative exceptionalism seemed to preclude the existence of other more radical gender crossers who might identify with history's losers in this struggle for freedom, property, and citizenship. Sampson always seemed so easily contained, never contributing much to history beyond a celebration of war and independence. Rather, they demonstrated that even those constituted outside of citizenship could help build and advance the systems that defined their own exclusion.

★ ★ ★

Like many early activists who came before me, I too turned to the past for role models, to understand myself, and to find context for the fight against homophobia. Learning about the history of people "like me" was of great personal and political urgency. One of the first things I read was Marc Stein's dissertation on the lesbian and gay movement in Philadelphia in the 1950s and 60s.[14] I learned of the "annual reminders" in which a group of activists marched in front of Independence Hall every fourth of July from 1965 to 1969. They held signs that said "15 MILLION HOMOSEXUAL AMERICANS ASK FOR EQUALITY, OPPORTUNITY, DIGNITY" while dressed in gender conforming professional attire, promoting a politics of respectability. They had everything to gain because gay people had no rights, but they also had everything to lose: their jobs, their relationships, their lives. As I struggled with the rejection of friends and family and adjusted to the strange looks and indignities that came along with living an openly queer life, I told myself over and over "If they could do it, you can do it." When it comes to inclusion of LGBT people and communities in history, the stakes have always been very high for me.

The prospects for a lesbian past, however, have always been marked by a methods problem, anchored in the difficulties of separating sex, gender, and sexuality—a task made nearly impossible by sexology itself. Carroll Smith-Rosenberg examined this dimension of early sexology in her 1985 essay on "The New Woman and the Androgyne" writing:

> Krafft-Ebing did not focus on the sexual behavior of the women he categorized as lesbian but, rather, on their social behavior and physical appearance. In every case study, Krafft-Ebing linked lesbianism to the rejection of conventional female roles, to cross-dressing, and to "masculine" physiological traits.

She went on to argue the constitutive role of class in determining not only which women were proper lesbian subjects for sexologists (note: bourgeois and educated women need not apply—no toaster ovens for them) but also how this same group eschewed cross-dressing or as I prefer to call it, gender crossing. Of this early period she concluded:

> Thus far, however, nothing in these male medical discussions of lesbianism referred directly to the lives and loves of such bourgeois and educated women as Sarah Orne Jewett, Jane Addams, Vida Scudder, or M. Carey Thomas. These women praised the feminine qualities of the women they loved; they certainly did not practice cross-dressing. None of them reported feeling that a male soul inhabited her female body.[15]

The figure of the lesbian has always raised questions about gender identity (did she think she was a man or a woman or something else entirely?) as well as gender expression (why did she look or act "like a man?"). This work revealed how the category of "lesbian" itself was historically bound by prevailing views of women's role in society, her right to a political voice, education, or financial independence and culturally bound by gender norms that were highly raced and classed.[16]

The fact remains that gender and sexuality are conceptually and historically bound together in many understandings of lesbianism. Transgender studies offers a different set of questions that can illuminate not only transgender but also lesbian histories. For instance, we can expand our view of a relevant past by asking the following questions: What motivated people to push, blur, or cross the line that distinguished men from women? How did legal, medical, and religious authorities respond to such individual efforts? What language was used to describe such people in the past and how best might we characterize them today?

Pioneering transgender historians Leslie Feinberg and Susan Stryker both argue for the use of a broad umbrella when studying the past. Feinberg described transgender as "an umbrella term to include everyone who challenges the boundaries of sex and gender" while Stryker calls for use of the term to describe a political experience of challenging gender norms and moving away from the gender associated with one's assigned sex.[17] Accounts of gender crossings that were once awkwardly and often without substantial evidence deemed lesbian are in fact an amazing archive for a broader approach to the history of sexuality and gender. Moving away from a search for people who neatly fit into identitarian categories toward analysis of structures that enable or restrict a wide range of gender or sexual variance offers tremendous promise for historians. Rather than erase "lesbians" from history or assert transgender subjectivity on someone long dead, this approach offers tremendous pay off for a more accurate and nuanced understanding of the past—including evidence of lives of people who challenged gender and sexual norms of their time.

Increasingly, scholars are moving from sexuality back to gender as a critical departure point for interrogating a queer past. Greta LeFleur emphasizes the wide variety of terms used to describe gender in the eighteenth century including, "macroclitorides, sapphists, tribades, amazons, female husbands, molies, bachelors, macaronis, viragos, fops, tommies, effeminate men, petit-maitres, unsex'd females and masculine women, to name only a few."[18] As I have shown in a digital exhibit for Outhistory.org, nineteenth-century newspapers and magazines feature stories of children and adults alike who refused to conform to expectations, describing them with such terms as girl-boy, boy-girl, male-girl, tom-boy to name a few.[19] The nineteenth century is marked by a drastic reduction in the possibilities for gender variance in the United States, an increasingly binary approach to such fluidity, and by the later decades, increasing hostility.

Literary scholars have laid the groundwork for this reinvigorated approach to early histories of gender and sexuality. In a 1994 essay, Martha Vicinus reflected on how shifting methodologies and assumptions transformed what we thought we knew, writing:

> Our current models all privilege either the visibly marked mannish women or the self-identified lesbian; romantic friendships, once the leading example of a lesbian past, are now either reconfigured in terms to fit these categories or labeled asexual. We seem to accept only what is seen and what is said as evidence.[20]

She proposed that we embrace the "not said" and the "not seen" as we aim to write lesbian history. Building on this, Valerie Traub offers a definition of a method called "queer historicism":

> Rather than practice "queer theory as that which challenges all categorization," I believe there remain ample reasons to practice a queer historicism dedicated to showing *how* categories, however mythic, phantasmic, and incoherent, *came to be* . . . this is not a historicism that creates categories of identity or presumes their inevitability; it is one that seeks to explain such categories' constitutive, pervasive, and persistent force."[21]

This is the approach LaFleur takes in her study of Deborah Sampson. She calls for a broader reading of *The Female Marine* beyond our own obsession with Sampson's gender and sexuality. Instead, she considers the significance of co-author Herman Mann's deployment of "the natural science of botany as a means of discussing sexual difference" while simultaneously insisting "that no taxonomy yet exists that adequately characterizes the 'species' of love between them."[22]

Similarly, in *The Sexuality of History*, Susan Lanser demonstrates how not being able to "really" know if or how two women had sex has always been a defining feature of representations of "sapphic" love in the early modern period and that such accounts were signposts for modernity.

Rejecting decades of frustration about the limitations historical methods have plac
ability to "know" identities or acts for sure, these scholars tear apart and make meanin
obstructions.

This conceptual view can also be extended to questions of gender identity, gender expression,
and/or sexual intimacies in transgender, gender-crossing, and passing narratives. Not being able
to "know" how someone who lived as a man felt about their gender identity, expression, or
role has always been a part of the telling of accounts and histories of transgender expressions,
experiences, and lives in the distant past. We have yet to fully historicize the use of this rhetorical
device and its role in making both lesbian and transgender history impossible. By letting go of
the idea that "lesbian" is an essential ahistoric cross-cultural category, however, and embracing
"transgender" as an analytical concept, we will at least get closer to the truth about women
who loved women, people assigned female sex at birth who lived as men and loved women,
and those of indeterminate gender identity who passed and lived as men.[23]

There is no perfect language for such an approach. While the problems with "passing women"
are clear, the alternatives are all complicated. I have consciously used the phrase "passing
as men" in several publications (see "Further Reading") because that was one thing I could
confidently say. I am not entirely satisfied with this approach. "Passing" is more widely understood in the context of race and it privileges normative gender expressions that are anchored
in whiteness. Moreover, it undermines the legitimacy or authenticity of the subject to which
it refers, because it implies that passing is less than real. Finally, it erases any mention of one's
status as at least having been born (and possibly still identifying as) a woman. Each new turn
of phrase seems to introduce a new set of problems.

Emphasizing who a person becomes instead of where they began makes sense in this political
and intellectual moment. In practice, we affirm the gender one is regardless of where one was.
We embrace the possibility of "movement" and "change" in regard to our gender and sexuality. No one simply is a gender—we are all always in the process of becoming, as Judith Butler
would say, a gender that is continually gaining its meaning from others. The intellectual question
that lingers, however, is why scholars are so comfortable labeling everything and anything
"queer" but refuse "transgender" as anachronistic or inappropriate in the absence of evidence
of an individually articulated gender identity?

If the parameters for defining homosexuality and gender diversity in the eighteenth or
nineteenth centuries are fuzzy, contested, and intentionally obscured, historians of the twentieth
century face a different set of challenges in charting the origins of modern gay, lesbian, bisexual,
and transgender identities and communities. This transition was delineated years ago by John
D'Emilio, who called for a distinction between homosexual "behavior" and gay "identity" in
challenging the activist impulse to claim an ahistorical lesbian or gay identity. D'Emilio argued
that the emergence of gay identity was linked to capitalism. "The expansion of capital and the
spread of wage labor have effected a profound transformation in the structure and functions
of the nuclear family, the ideology of family life, and the meaning of heterosexual relations,"
he wrote. "It is these changes in the family that are most directly linked to the appearance of
a collective gay life."[24] Of course, that collective gay life was not accessible to everyone. If it
was true, as D'Emilio argued that "Capitalism has created the material conditions for homosexual desire to express itself as a central component of some individuals' lives," it was also
true that these material conditions were vastly different for communities by race, class, gender,
and region.[25] The idea that gay, lesbian, possibly bisexual, and even transsexual identities were
fixed by the mid-twentieth century once seemed like a sign of progress—that the community
had arrived and that one's sexuality and gender identity were core aspects of one's identity.
Subsequent research has revealed a more complicated narrative, demonstrating the wide range

[handwritten margin note: Confusion of language + gender]

xperiences, lives, genders, and sexualities left them on the margins of the

set of exclusions has been partly addressed by the queer turn in LGBT ed the focus away from a narrowly conceived group of subjects to broader ons about normativity, deviance, alienation, and belonging—especially ommunities of color, who were often excluded from earlier work. Nayan irts how South Asian migrant workers in California built community, family, ther in a hostile, punishing environment—what he calls "stranger intimacy." es, "migratory work and transportation crossroads produced environments ality, but it was the appetite for passionate engagement, the determination to smash alienation, and the desire for visceral solidarity that created both fleeing and enduring friendships."[26] Shah positions these communities as vibrant and dynamic site of queerness because they "sustained the social dynamics of mixing and non-normative sexualities emerge through the different kinds of 'queer domesticity' that counter, contest, upset, and challenge normative expectations and practices."[27] State and federal governing officials were invested in regulating social, domestic, and sexual practices deemed non-normative and unacceptable. As Margot Canaday and Peggy Pascoe have argued, the significance and implication of these regulatory functions only come into focus when we leave the archives of the so-called "gay community" and take a broader view of the relationship between the state and the "family."

Scholarship on the carceral state has also challenged the privileging of LGBT identities in favor of broader examination of the conditions in which modern concepts of sexuality were defined. Regina Kunzel shows how important sex between men in prison was in shaping scholarly and scientific knowledge about sexual desire and behavior more broadly. A state-controlled social space long neglected by scholars aiming to wrest gay identity from the negative association with anti-sodomy laws has actually held the key to shattering the longstanding myth that those who engaged in "situational" homosexual acts were distinct from those who freely and deliberately embraced a gay identity. Kunzel reveals just how foolhardy these assumptions were in a careful demonstration of the mutually constitutive relationships between gay social and sexual norms in the "free" world and those behind prison walls. My research shows how responses to men having sex with other men shaped major policy decisions regarding the organization of penitentiaries—including the reliance on solitary confinement—in the 1820s. Other scholarship in carceral studies shows the exclusions that result when lines are drawn around "gay" neighborhoods and "gay" issues. Often, the most vulnerable LGBTQ people—especially queer and trans youth, the homeless, and poor communities of color—get left on the outside. Christina Handhart has shown how calls for "safe space" by gay community leaders can have devastating effects on communities of color disproportionately targeted by the police. A queer of color theoretical approach—one that centers communities of color while also deconstructing systems that define belonging, normativity, and privilege—is our key to understanding the full reach and impact of the carceral state.

While the "queer" turn decentered specific lesbian, gay, bisexual, or transgender subjectivities and identities within the history of sexuality, it is just the latest challenge. Feminist and critical race theorists of intersectionality showed us long ago how language limits what we look for, what we are able to see, and what we think we know when we study the past. Queer people of color continue to document the multiple and persistent erasures of Native American, African American, Asian American, and Latino/a communities, people, and experiences in histories of LGBTQ America. Consider the late Horacio Ramirez's work on mid-to-late-twentieth-century Latino/a communities, charting the insufficiency of "gay" or "bisexual" to do the work of historical and historiographic identity intersectionality. Ramirez argued, that:

even in the field of cultural history, presumably less stuffy than intellectual or political history, most people who actually lived this history were missing from the narratives. Even more unfairly, I thought, their lives rarely provided the interpretive frames shaping those narratives themselves.[28]

In his work on the formation of the Gay Latino Alliance in San Francisco, Ramirez challenged the longstanding practice of centering "queer sexual desires" in histories of the LGBTQ community, instead showing that "race and ethnicity are indispensable" to the work.[29] Ramirez further called out the Anglo- and Euro- centricity of the widely used "catch-all" acronym LGBT, arguing for its reliance on "public politicized identity" categories and exclusion of other terms that are more commonly used in non-white or non-European communities.[30] The promise of inclusion offered by "LGBT" and even "Queer" is ripe with contradictions and scarcely realized.[31]

These issues are not new. Even the earliest scholarship in the field of LGBT history noted the distinctions between those who engaged in homosexual acts and those who embraced a gay identity. George Chauncey's insights about the role that gender played in giving meaning to same sex acts between a diverse group of men in early twentieth century New York still stand as one of the most interesting findings in the history of sexuality. Recognizing and understanding these distinctions—between sex and gender, between gender and sexuality, between normativity and deviance, between those who embrace a transgender identity and those who otherwise flout gender conventions, between those who embrace a gay identity and those who have gay sex—will always be an important task of the historian. Yet these binaries—shorthand ways of signaling difference—will always obscure more than they illuminate. Transgender critique and methods are the key to future LGBTQ studies, enabling scholars to theorize and document nuance, uncertainty, instability, transience, marginality, permeability, and states of in-between, so that we might find our way to a more inclusive, dynamic, and truthful LGBTQ past.[32]

Notes

1 Michel Foucault, *History of Sexuality Volume I: An Introduction*, trans. Robert Hurley (New York: Pantheon Books, 1978).

2 For further discussion of disparity in early American communities' responses to same-sex relations, see, in this volume, Richard Godbeer, "Colonial North America (1500s–1700s)" and Rachel Cleves, "Revolutionary Sexualities and Early National Genders (1770s–1840s)."

3 See also, in this volume, Cleves, "Revolutionary Sexualities and Early National Genders (1770s-1840s)".

4 Jonathan Ned Katz, *The Invention of Heterosexuality* (New York: Dutton, 1995), 10.

5 Jonathan Ned Katz, *Gay American History: Lesbians and Gay Men in the U.S.A.: A Documentary* (New York: Crowell, 1976). Also see Jonathan Ned Katz, *Gay/Lesbian Almanac: A New Documentary* (New York: Harper & Row, 1983).

6 See also in this volume the discussion of Katz's book and its categories in Don Romesburg, "Introduction: Just a Moment or Momentous?"

7 Alfred F. Young, *Masquerade: The Life and Times of Deborah Sampson, Continental Soldier* (New York: Knopf, 2004), 10–11.

8 Katz, *Gay American History*, 210–211.

9 Joanne Meyerowitz, *How Sex Changed: A History of Transsexuality in the United States* (Cambridge: Harvard University Press, 2002), 115.

10 Emily Skidmore has written a very compelling analysis of another one of Katz's "passing women" Ralph Kerwineo. Despite embracing Kerwineo as a man and using male pronouns throughout, Skidmore emphasizes his "queer" body. Emily Skidmore, "Ralph Kerwineo's Queer Body: Narrating the Scales of Social Membership in the Early Twentieth Century," *GLQ: A Journal of Lesbian and Gay Studies* 20, no. 1–2 (2014): 141–166.

11 See, for example, Lilian Faderman, *Surpassing the Love of Men: Romantic Friendship and Love Between Women from the Renaissance to the Present* (New York: William Morrow, 1981), 58–60; 93–94.

12 Leslie Feinberg, *Transgender Warriors: Making History from Joan of Arc to Rupaul* (Boston: Beacon, 1996); Martha Vicinus, ed., *Lesbian Subjects: A Feminist Studies Reader* (Bloomington: Indiana University Press, 1996); Leila Rupp, *Sapphistries: A Global History of Love Between Women* (New York: New York University Press, 2009). For one reflection on this development, see Emma Donohue, "Doing Lesbian History, Then and Now," *Historical Reflections/Reflexions Historiques*, 33, no. 1 Eighteenth-Century Homosexuality in Global Perspective (2007): 15–22.

13 See, for example, Peter Boag, *Re-Dressing America's Frontier Past* (Berkeley: University of California Press, 2012).

14 The dissertation was the basis for the book, Marc Stein, *City of Sisterly and Brotherly Love: Lesbian and Gay Philadelphia, 1945–1972* (Chicago: University of Chicago, 2000).

15 Carroll Smith-Rosenberg, "The New Woman as Androgyne," *Disorderly Conduct: Visions of Gender in Victorian America* (New York: Oxford University Press, 1985), 271, 273–274.

16 See also, in this volume, Julie Enszer, "Lesbian History: Spirals of Imagination, Marginalization, Creation, and Erasure."

17 Feinberg, *Transgender Warriors*, x; Susan Stryker, *Transgender History* (Berkeley: Seal Press, 2008), 24.

18 Greta LaFleur, "Sex and 'Unsex': Histories of Gender Trouble in Eighteenth-Century North America," *Early American Studies*, 12, no. 3 (Fall 2014): 489.

19 Jen Manion, "Transgender Children in Antebellum America," *outhistory.org*, http://outhistory.org/exhibits/show/transgenderchildrenantebellum. Accessed December 16, 2016.

20 Martha Vicinus, "Lesbian History: All Theory and No Facts or All Facts and No Theory?" *Radical History Review* 90 (Fall 1994): 58.

21 Valerie Traub, *Thinking Sex with the Early Moderns* (Philadelphia: University of Pennsylvania Press, 2015), 81.

22 Greta L. LaFleur, "Precipitous Sensations: Herman Mann's *The Female Review (1797)*, Botanical Sexuality, and the Challenge of Queer Historiography, *Early American Literature* 48, no. 1 (2013): 99, 111.

23 For analysis of the historic function of the category of "lesbian" as a tool that suppresses transgender identity and belonging, see Nan Alamilla Boyd, "The Materiality of Gender," *Journal of Lesbian Studies* 3, no. 3 (1999) pp. 73–81.

24 John D'Emilio, "Capitalism and Gay Identity," in *The Lesbian and Gay Studies Reader*, ed. Henry Abelove, Michele Aina Barale, David M. Halperin (New York: Routledge, 1993), 469.

25 D'Emilio, "Capitalism and Gay Identity," 474.

26 Nayan Shah, *Stranger Intimacy: Contesting Race, Sexuality and the Law in the North American West* (Berkeley: University of California, 2012), 55.

27 Nayan Shah, "Race-ing Sex," *Frontiers: A Journal of Women's Studies*, 35, no.1 (2014): 28. See also, in this volume, Shah's chapter, "Queer of Color Estrangement and Belonging."

28 Horacio N. Roque Ramírez, "My Community, My History, My Practice," *Oral History Review* 29, no. 2 (Summer/Fall 2002): 88.

29 Horacio N. Roque Ramírez, " 'That's My Place!': Negotiating Racial, Sexual, and Gender Politics in San Francisco's Gay Latino Alliance, 1975–1983," *Journal of History of Sexuality* 12, no. 2 (April 2003): 227.

30 Horacio N. Roque Ramírez, "Introduction: Homoerotic, Lesbian, and Gay Ethnic and Immigrant Histories," *Journal of American Ethnic History*, 29, no. 4 (Summer 2010): 7.

31 In her chapter for this volume, "Bisexual History: Let's Not Bijack Another Century," Loraine Hutchins makes a related point about the ways that bisexual erasure plagues much "gay and lesbian," "LGBT" and "queer" historiography.

32 For more on trans method and queer history, see in this volume Finn Enke, "Transgender History (and Otherwise Approaches)."

Further Reading

Boyd, Nan Alamilla and Horacio N. Roque Ramírez, eds. *Bodies of Evidence: The Practice of Queer Oral History*. New York: Oxford University Press, 2012.

Butler, Judith. *Undoing Gender*. New York: Routledge, 2004.

Canaday, Margot. *The Straight State: Sexuality and Citizenship in Twentieth-Century America*. Princeton: Princeton University Press, 2009.

Chauncey, George. *Gay New York: Gender, Urban Culture, and the Making of the Gay Male World, 1890–1940.* New York: Basic Books, 1994.

Clark, Anna. "Ann Lister's Construction of Lesbian Identity." *Journal of the History of Sexuality* 7, no. 1 (July 1996): 23–50.

Duggan, Lisa. *Sapphic Slashers: Sex, Violence, and American Modernity.* Durham: Duke University Press, 2001.

Enke, Finn. *Finding the Movement: Sexuality, Contested Space, and Feminist Activism.* Durham: Duke University, 2007.

Feinberg, Leslie. *Stone Butch Blues.* Ithaca, NY: Firebrand Books, 1993.

Foster, Thomas, ed. *Long Before Stonewall: Histories of Same-Sex Sexuality in Early America.* New York: New York University Press, 2007.

Foucault, Michel. *History of Sexuality Volume I: An Introduction,* trans. Robert Hurley. New York: Pantheon Books, 1978.

Griffin, Farah Jasmine, ed. *Beloved Sisters and Loving Friends: Letters from Rebecca Primus of Royal Oak, Maryland, and Addie Brown of Hartford, Connecticut, 1854–1868.* New York: Knopf, 1999.

Halberstam, J. Jack. *Female Masculinity.* Duke University, 1998.

Hanhardt, Christina B. *Safe Space: Gay Neighborhood History and the Politics of Violence.* Duke University Press, 2013.

Kennedy, Elizabeth Lapovsky and Madeline D. Davis. *Boots of Leather, Slippers of Gold: The History of a Lesbian Community.* New York: Routledge, 1993.

Kunzel, Regina. *Criminal Intimacies: Prison and the Uneven History of Modern American Sexuality.* Chicago: University of Chicago Press, 2008.

Lanser, Susan S. *The Sexuality of History: Modernity and the Sapphic, 1565–1830.* Chicago: University of Chicago, 2014.

Love, Heather. *Feeling Backward: Loss and the Politics of Queer History.* Cambridge: Harvard University Press, 2007.

Manion, Jen. *Liberty's Prisoners: Carceral Culture in Early America.* Philadelphia: University of Pennsylvania, 2015.

Manion, Jen. "The Queer History of Passing as a Man in Early Pennsylvania." *Pennsylvania Legacies, LGBTQ History* 16, no. 2 (Spring 2016): 6–11.

Manion, Jen. "Gender Expression in Antebellum America: Accessing the Privileges and Freedoms of White Men." In *U.S. Women's History: Untangling the Threads of Sisterhood,* Leslie Brown, Jacqueline Castledine, and Anne Valk, eds. 127–146. New Brunswick, NJ: Rutgers University, 2017.

Mogul, Joey L., Andrea J. Ritchie, Kay Whitlock. *Queer (In)justice: The Criminalization of LGBT People in the United States* (Boston: Beacon, 2012).

Mumford, Kevin. *Not Straight, Not White: Black Gay Men from the March on Washington to the AIDS Crisis.* University of North Carolina, 2016.

Pascoe, Peggy. *What Comes Naturally: Miscegention Law and the Making of Race in America.* New York: Oxford University Press, 2010.

Spade, Dean. *Normal Life: Administrative Violence, Critical Trans Politics, and the Limits of Law* (Durham, NC: Duke University Press, 2011).

Stryker, Susan and Aren Z. Aizura, eds. *The Transgender Studies Reader 2* (New York, NY: Routledge, 2013).

Stryker, Susan and Stephen Whittle, eds. *The Transgender Studies Reader* (New York, NY: Routledge, 2006).

Upchurch, Charles. "The Consequences of Dating Don Leon." In *Queer Difficulty in Art and Poetry: Re-thinking the Sexed Body in Verse and Visual Culture,* Christopher Reed and Jongwoo Kim, eds. New York: Routledge, 2017.

17

TRANSGENDER HISTORY (AND OTHERWISE APPROACHES TO QUEER EMBODIMENT)

Finn Enke

The first time I taught a transgender history course (2007, "Trans/Gender in Historical Perspective"), a local news editor contacted me about "innovative courses" at the state university where I teach. She began the interview with the question, "but transgender is so new; how could there possibly be enough material for an entire history course?" Perhaps this was a skillful way of eliciting a story-worthy response, but the journalist's surprise was genuine when I told her that the challenge is figuring out how to organize several millennia of human gender inquiry in a single global and transnational course.[1] Historians know that sex is not simply dimorphic and that gender has in no place or time been culturally uniform or stable. Yet we have been pressed to develop methods and analytical frameworks that allow us to analyze gender complexity in contextually appropriate ways. While queer history often positions transgender as an outlier or idiosyncratic topic, many scholars have developed a growing awareness that gender has always been more complex and salient than we have even begun to articulate. In other words, we have been bumping into a pervasive transgender history all along.

The queer academic placement of trans history as a special (rather than integral) topic might rest on the belief that trans history is or should be limited to those who identify as transgender.[2] Trans history, however, reaches outside of contemporary identitarian concepts. Marginalization also stems from a relentless tendency to privilege birth-assigned sex when interpreting queerness; needless to say, a great deal of trans and gender-rich history has been subsumed within LGBQ attachments.[3] I am not here referring to a taxonomic debate about whether historical figures should be considered lesbian, queer men, passing, or transgender. Transgender history demands far more theoretically and analytically nuanced questions. Most queer history continues to take presumed birth-assigned sex as determinative or "real" embodiment. It is thus possible for scholars of queerness to largely ignore trans theories, methodologies, and vocabularies as they frame even the most complexly gendered phenomena in terms of sexuality. Put simply, despite queer history's refusal of identitarian confinement, a great deal of it seems nonetheless attached to presumed genital status. In contrast, trans history seeks to undo that admittedly sticky assignment

224

by prioritizing analysis of gender not as genital status or archetype, but as architecture. Seen this way, the purview of queer history has always been animated by transness, or embodiment that begs more attention to the human creation of significant gender articulations, taxonomies, vocabularies and instabilities.

Transgender history now exists as a distinct field with a history, and it is about as old as queer history. Transgender history has come into its own through many mechanisms, including the development of methodological lenses that more explicitly refuse assumptions of sex/gender stability or transparency; the proliferation of transgender history books and readers that gather trans-relevant primary sources; a rapidly growing historiography that incorporates trans analysis of gender production; the elaboration of transgender history courses; the establishment of massive "brick and mortar" as well as digital trans archives; the professionalization of the field through special issues in history journals such as *Radical History Review* and *Early American Studies*; historians' solid presence on the editorial board of *Transgender Studies Quarterly*; and state-of-the-field panels at major association conferences such as the Organization of American Historians, the American Historical Association, the American Studies Association, and the Berkshire Conference on the History of Women.

Simultaneously, because transgender history has never been limited to an identitarian search, the field has also "come into its own" by opening up a vast range of possibility not easily identifiable through a canon of either primary or secondary sources. Unlike many academic subfields, transgender history is more apt to include virtually anything as relevant rather than assume that other subfields have little to offer.

In this essay, I reflect on the major goals and problems that generate transgender history, while highlighting examples of secondary scholarship that refute the relegation of trans to a special or marginal topic within queer history and US history. I begin by discussing in broad strokes the conceptual terrain of transgender history, then engage historiographically with historical findings, critical methodologies, and theoretical frameworks that expand the scope and imagination of trans and queer history. In particular, contexts and periods not rooted in universalizing modern concepts of male-female sex and gender binaries suggest that a trans-inflected analysis necessarily begins by suspending assumptions about how and what gender means, how and what bodies mean, and the significance of both.

Queer and trans histories share a drive to engage the multiplicity of ways that humans have infused bodies with meanings. Trans history further cautions that even as we might place an infinite number of histories under the loose rubric of *trans*, we can not assume that sex/gender systems and expressions in one time and place are either continuous or discontinuous with those articulated in any other context. Our method is heuristic rather than strictly comparative, designed to open diverse epistemologies rather than foreclose them. Queer, gender, and trans histories have shown that concepts of embodiment are contingent, gaining significance in relation to multiple contingent formations such as gender, sex, race, dis/ability, age, nation, economic and legal status. In short, queer American history already contains more than ample reason to center gender and trans history.

Two of the most common narratives about the growth of transgender history are infused with paradoxically marginalizing projections of "progress" and "incorporation." Both narratives frame this maturation in terms of a "transition from a social movement to a discipline," as trans theorist Sandy Stone put it.[4] The first suggests that the field matured from an identitarian search for transgender people in the past to a more methodologically contextualized and theoretically complex approach to gender diversity. The trajectory viewed this way articulates an increased social vision and also an increased academic value. While this sounds positive, it undermines the complexity of early work in the field; this simultaneously suggests that transgender history

Figure 17.1 "Clownfish History," 2016. Among clownfish, if the female of a pair dies, the male of the pair will transform into a female in order to reproduce with surviving male offspring. Zoologists have estimated that nearly half of all beings in the animal kingdom change gender or occupy multiple genders simultaneously. K–12 schools have sometimes faced pushback when teaching students such content as a way of contextualizing gender diversity in U.S. history and contemporary society.

Courtesy of Finn Enke.

did not exist prior to the emergence of scholarship rooted in contemporary queer and trans vocabularies and theories.

A second marginalizing narrative suggests that *transgender* started as a potentially revolutionary social movement, entered academia with little capital but significant subversive potential, and recently earned legitimacy at the cost of losing its critical edge. It is with unease that many view the field's increased success and commodification within an inherently hierarchical institution; many ask if we are selling our radical potential before we have begun to challenge the status quo on a deep level. While this radical critique emerges from a deep distrust of dominant social institutions and from a deep commitment to transformative justice, it shares with the first narrative an oversimplification of the past and present of the field.

From the outset, gender and queer historiography has inclined toward undoing its own sex/gender foundations. When history of sexuality and gender emerged as fields in the 1970s, historians were already asking, "Can we name the subject of our inquiry? When looking at the past, what do we look for? What counts as evidence?" Always haunting and occasionally supplanting any desired queer past is the need to acknowledge that across place and time, we may not even know sex and gender when we see it, or if something that looks like gender and sex might have been something else altogether. These theoretically, methodologically and politically sophisticated questions have driven the scholarship for nearly five decades. When we can see *trans* as integral to the emergence of the history of sexuality and gender, we must acknowledge that transgender history has been a much messier thing that *all along* has moved us in *multiple* directions simultaneously. Rather than debating who got where first or better, or valorizing the most-queer over the not-queer-enough, we will gain much more by grappling with the trans and gender complexity of early work as well as paradigm-shifting recent work. We might ask, for example, why works such as Kennedy and Davis' *Boots of Leather, Slippers of Gold*, or Chauncey's *Gay New York* are routinely regarded as history of sexuality and not as transgender history despite the explicit gender complexity articulated by the subjects within each work.[5]

Transgender history thus marks as problematic a persistent tendency to privilege a very particular narrative about the emergence of modern concepts of sex, gender and sexuality, and to place nearly all of this as the province of queer history and history of sexuality rather than being simultaneously understood as gender/transgender history. Early scholarship in the history of sexuality showed that modern identitarian concepts and vocabularies of sex, gender and sexuality arose from a trajectory that began in late nineteenth-century Europe and the United States. This scholarship highlights, in part, how sexuality came to be understood apart from gender expression; it joined mid-to-late twentieth-century trends in medicine, psychiatry, and dominant-culture social activism that worked to disentangle sexual identity from gender identity or more precisely, gay from transgender. On this foundation, a great deal of scholarship perceived sexual and gender diversity and named it "sexuality." Assuming sex/gender dimorphism, it failed to analyze queer phenomena as *also* a trans/gender story. As queer history—under the influence of queer of color, transnational, de-colonial, and trans critique—increasingly recognizes that the taxonomical distinction between sexuality and gender is itself an historically-rooted cultural construction in the service of attachment to modern sexual identity, it might find that a new taxonomy of the field of queer might be in order. We will find, at the same time, that the queer archive of trans history is vast.[6]

Histories of the emergence of transgender defined by gender-crossing have piggy-backed on histories of the distinction between sex, sexuality and gender while attending to the instability and contingency of this distinction itself. Much as trans-ness is currently anchored to (even as it steps away from) birth-assigned sex, the subject of transgender history first appeared as a figure articulating unconventional gender understood in relation to the presumed body (sex) underneath. To be sure, trans histories confirm that people have always exceeded the social expectations typically accorded to particular body types, and they have elaborated sexual and gender diversity in ways that enhance and problematize the concept of transgender. Still, it has also been necessary to establish that transgender *is* a culturally specific social category; that is, there is a *history* of transgender as a twentieth-century US phenomenon and its roots in a particular cultural (not universal) epistemology. Works such as JoAnne Meyerowitz's *How Sex Changed*, Susan Stryker's *Transgender History*, and David Valentine's *Imagining Transgender* all provide ways to understand the emergence of transgender as a modern category of being. While *How Sex Changed* focuses on the confluence of medicine and popular culture in the constitution of the category transsexual, *Transgender History* focuses on realms of activism and engagements with medicine, social movements, and community formation. *Imagining Transgender* reveals subcultural sex/gender taxonomies and epistemologies that challenge the universal application of transgender, and simultaneously shows the institutionalization of transgender as a category of white middle-class dominance.

Transgender histories have necessarily theorized our subject itself, that is, what we are looking for and how we know it when we see it, given that we move across temporal, cultural, linguistic and geographic parameters including the "pre-historical." As KJ Rawson has argued, the archive of transgender history is far from settled and in fact the notion of archive only highlights the limitations of any single approach to trans. Transgender history might include expressions of "cross gender" existence or gender fluidities, gender non-normativities as they were contextually understood, and/or elaborations of nonbinary or instable gender histories and the meanings they were accorded in their context.[7] Originating largely within British and North American imperial and settler-colonial contexts, the institutionalization of "transgender"—like "queer"—trucks in globalizing normativities and hierarchies.[8] History's greatest potential for critical engagement may thus come from those arenas that have not been automatically or institutionally recognized as "transgender," offering lenses that fundamentally challenge queer history or more self-evidently "transgender" history paradigms.

Trans history is creating findings, methods, and theoretical frameworks that move us beyond binary oppositions often posed between transgender/not transgender, essentialist/constructionist, and local/global. Trans history suggests the salience of contextually specific and fluid gender, sex, and trans analysis. For example, Clare Sears's *Arresting Dress: Cross-Dressing, Law, and Fascination in Nineteenth Century San Francisco* uses a *transing* method to analyze the nineteenth-century legal and social production of cross-dressing as a practice with diverse meanings and outcomes. Sears is not interested in answering whether and how some people might or might not have been transgender, but, rather, considers gendering practices within a nexus of efforts to distinguish race and nationality, class, age, and occupation in the ordering of public spaces. Sears interrogates the boundary between normative and non-normative by homing in on the regulation of and fascination with multiple forms of gendering dress practices.

Sears thus includes not only "problem bodies" in the "wrong places" (those that come under legal scrutiny), but also those that cross-dress in the right places without censure. In these ways, Sears highlights disparate and contradictory meanings and effects of cross-dressing practices without making claims about the identities of those who engage them.

In addition to their inherent trans-disciplinarity, trans historical methods also may reconceptualize history as they sustain analysis of gender, race, and other aspects of social embodiment—particularly those figured through binary oppositions. Historian Simon D. Elin Fisher, for example, offers new ways to understand the enormous significance of the work of Civil Rights activist Pauli Murray, by bringing to the fore Murray's trans-of-color analysis of, and resistance to, Jim Crow. While prior historians have analyzed Murray's critique of Jim/Jane Crow as an early articulation of intersectional feminism, Fisher newly analyzes Murray's early navigations of gender and racial norms through close examination of Murray's experiences as a person whose racial appearance and gender expression confounded dominant black/white and female/male binaries. Fisher convincingly argues that Murray's desire for gender self-definition (specifically, Murray's efforts to achieve masculine/male embodiment) was intimately connected with Murray's theoretical analysis of Jim/Jane Crow, as Murray's trans experience as well as biracial experience gave Murray "a distinct perspective on systemic operations of subjectification."[9] Murray's perspective enters into the early Civil Rights movement in ways that have thus far been vastly underestimated. Giving attention to Murray's multiple transing perspectives, we not only newly appreciate the importance of Murray's work, but we may also more deeply understand the constitution, performance, and significance of gender in the early Civil Rights movement.

Concerned as it is with embodiments, transgender history might also proceed with an orientation toward the ways social processes historically enable and disable beings. Critical theorist and disability studies scholar Ellen Samuels, for example, has convincingly shown that efforts to make race, gender, and class scientifically verifiable and legally necessary identities in the United States has in so many instances relied on notions of ability and disability. In *Fantasies of Identification: Disability, Gender, Race*, Samuels analyzes nineteenth- and twentieth-century national and biopolitical imperatives to establish people's "legal identity." Fantasies that scientific empirical methods of bodily scrutiny can determine the truth or falsity of people's social performances, Samuels argues, have naturalized the concept of legal identity. Each instance to certify identity (through finger-printing, blood quantum rubrics, DNA testing, and so forth) ultimately fails in the face of the instability of categories of race, gender, sex, and ability. Samuels concludes that concepts of disability animate every effort to codify and "biocertify" race, gender, and sex. In the face of biocertification (a term Samuels coined), bodies are constituted through and also pass in and out of legal statuses as they move across administratively organized spaces, and they are complexly enabled and disabled by the fantasy that they are certifiable at all. Such analysis illuminates the multiple crossings and categorical instabilities that are at the heart of transgender history.

Transgender history, with its examination of categorization and boundary-making, has placed a strong emphasis on transnational dimensions, circulations, and morphings of modern concepts of transgender. Many works reveal the flaws and limitations of a colonizing and US-centric perspective. Even in an anthology such as the *Routledge History of Queer America*, then, we might pause before the delimitation of our queer focus to the United States.[10] Afsaneh Najmabadi's *Professing Selves: Transsexuality and Same-Sex Desire in Contemporary Iran*, for example, convincingly explains why the "western" distinction drawn between sex, gender, and sexuality not only does not hold up in the Iranian context, but in fact might be so situated and contingent that it hampers our ability to ask contextually appropriate questions. Najmabadi shows that in Iran, a single concept, *jins*, linguistically and culturally conflates sex and gender identifications, desires, and practices. Moreover, Iranian law distinguishes between homosexuals and transsexuals (homosexual activity is illegal; transsexuality is legal and state subsized). She argues that Iranian psychology, law, Islamic doctrine, and activism, "instead of constructing an impassible border" between same-sex desire and cross-gender identification, and between homosexuals and transsexuals, have created a process that offers "a safe passage between categories." This nebulous interzone crucially makes life possible for some non-normative people. As Najmabadi discusses at length the challenges of "translation," the work as a whole clearly demonstrates the vast differences and disjunctures between epistemological frameworks.[11] It is hard, following

Najmabadi's analysis, to take an exclusively US-based queer history as anything other than wishful thinking. More usefully, it can offer queer scholars good sparks for breaking out of limited paradigms.

Scholars working within decolonial, settler colonial, and indigenous studies extend this critique still more directly. They remind us that the meanings and enforcements of gender did not spring from a neutral intellectual and medical foundation. Rather, the modern and largely dimorphic sex–gender–sexuality rubric was derived specifically from contexts of colonial domination of indigenous populations, a transnational slave trade and the importation/exportation of slaves and servants, and transnational migration, national boundary-making, genocide, and increasing incarceration of people of color. If such contexts are the dominant epistemological foundation for thinking sex and gender, we need not only rigorous post-modern and deconstructivist theorizations, but also decolonial ways of knowing in order to trans gender and queer history.

The goal is not to claim indigeneity or the global south as particularly trans or queer— whatever that might mean. Nor is it to use indigeneity in the service of a desire to claim that "earlier" peoples honored gender diversity (a highly problematic and colonizing gloss to say the least). Rather, it is to acknowledge, as the special *Decolonizing the Transgender Imaginary* issue of *TSQ: Transgender Studies Quarterly* and other works do, that other epistemologies have always existed. Ignoring or delegitimating them perpetuates global asymmetries and violence. Transgender histories are challenged not only by linguistic, categorical and ontological diversity, but also by academic structures that privilege certain performances of knowledge and intellectual property. Transforming history in the face of settler-colonialism and cultural and linguistic changes over centuries, contemporary indigenous scholars offer methods for understanding gender diversity in the past and also re-engaging linguistic evolution in the present. Necessarily, scholars of decolonial projects thus suggest different modes of listening and storytelling. They seek and use indigenous taxonomies while acknowledging that contemporary indigenous people navigate "dissonant paradigms"[12] as well as "trauma caused by language loss." Qwo-Li Driskill, for example, analyses contemporary linguistic practices within the Cherokee nation in order to theorize the term "Two Spirit" and its potential utility and failure within Cherokee meaning-making systems.[13]

Deborah Miranda, in contrast, reads against the grain archival materials produced by Spanish missionaries to California. "Unfiltered Indian voices" do not exist in the archival record because the contest of colonization as well as indigenous practices of oral rather than written histories, inhibited production or collection of textual traces. Finding one short handwritten field note that feels "like a petroglyph," Miranda is drawn into and pulls together many different and layered stories to highlight aspects of California Indian sex/gender expression and meaning during the eighteenth century.[14] While all historians should be trained to interpret their sources contextually and with a mind to the bias of their producers, settler colonial critique demands that we acknowledge that our entire modern sex/gender system was founded in part on the destruction of indigenous epistemologies and the simultaneous erasure of the fact that indigenous North Americans *continue* to make meaning within and apart from dominant systems of gender, sexuality, spirituality, property ownership, and law. This leaves queer and trans historians with the critical work of reframing our epistemological roots in terms of their emergence within contexts of settler colonialism, as the work of Scott Morgenson notably does.

Additional challenges to the twentieth-century paradigms of transgender come from historians analyzing gender during periods prior to sex/gender modernity. For example, the *Journal of Early American Studies* offered a special issue, *Beyond the Binary: Critical Approaches to Sex and Gender*, that explicitly resists uniform terminologies in favor of offering various methodological and analytical approaches to interpreting early American contexts of gender that exceed modernist binary models. The collection lightly suspends twenty-first-century US understandings of gender that are differentiated from a concept of "biological sex," while asking whether and to what extent a notion of gender "as a self-conscious technology of self-representation" existed during the early American period.[15] Noting that "in studies of the history of race and the history of colonialism, scholars tend to automatically think about gender in multifaceted and relational terms," Greta LaFleur encourages further theorization of gender's contingencies with other formations such as race, slavery, economies, geographies and so forth. Crucially for transing early American history, LaFleur finds that "a vast vocabulary for describing both sex behavioral and gender variation among organic life forms (plants and animals, including humans) existed" in eighteenth-century Britain and its colonies, including North America.

Historians of all periods, whether working in "queer" history or not, might disabuse themselves of the assumption that gender was not a signifying concept in some earlier time; neither was it in any way simple or binary. LaFleur notes that "some eighteenth-century cultural notions about the proper meaning, discipline, or performativity of gender share significant ideological terrain with some of the fundamental assertions of the contingency and mutability of gender" that twentieth-century feminist and queer theorists have advanced. Yet importantly, LaFleur cautions against assuming that gender in other contexts is easily translatable into contemporary queer or transgender understandings. Instead, LaFleur calls for a deeper theorization of genderings, allowing the possibility of "similarities as distinct from continuities."[16]

Engaging both transgender theory and settler colonial perspectives in early American religious contexts, Scott Larson complicates the notion of gender-crossing and offers an example of one way "gender was challenged 'before' transgender." Arguing that "being 'no longer male and female'" could be the result of "radical religious experience," Larson analyzes discourses surrounding the "Publick Universal Friend," also known as Jemima Wilkinson of Cumberland, Rhode Island, who died in 1776 and was resurrected as a genderless spirit with a new name. Publick Universal Friend, according to Larson, consciously "defied the line between living and dead, body and spirit, divine and human, male and female" by intentionally "mixing worldly signifiers" such as use of dress, behavior, and use of genderless language. Rather than assuming the meanings of various performances and signifiers, Larson delves into the context of religious and theological dispute and settler colonialism in order to better understand how the ways that the Friend and Friend's followers challenged gender, social subjectivity and embodiment were constituted.[17] Yet Larson is quick to remind us that followers used genderless language for the Friend "not as a commitment to new ideas about gender in the abstract, but as a theological practice and a statement of faith." Equally important, the Friend is not to be understood as a human person, but a "reanimated tabernacle of flesh inhabited by God's spirit." In grappling with this history, Larson points toward trans methodologies that effectively shatter both the binary presumption on which transgender rests, and also the individualized subjectivity on which identity-based analyses rest.

If neither "gender crossing" nor transgender are the right descriptors in contexts that might not be organized by a stable binary, transgender history has also challenged the framework of a "binary" and the assumption that certain kinds of figures or performances challenged or "went beyond" a supposedly hegemonic binary sex/gender system. Emphasizing the plasticity of gender, for example, Sean Trainor analyzes the touring career of Madame Josephine Clofullia, a prominently bearded lady, during the 1850s. Trainor finds that while a cultural and medical elite questioned Clofullia's womanhood due to "biological" ambiguity, few others seemed to find her beard or other physical aspects challenging or confounding to their interpellation of her as a woman. Most people apparently placed greater emphasis on her behavior and sensibility than her physical appearance.[18] Knowing that gender—however we see fit to define that term—is produced with class, race, ability, and so forth, this and other histories serve as useful reminders to queer and trans historians that we cannot rely on assumptions of crossing, non-normativity, or abjection when looking for or defining the subject of our inquiry. What we find, instead, is that even within any given sector of a culture, people are understanding bodies, sexes and genders in multiple and sometimes contradictory ways simultaneously. We might also ask whether queerness necessarily revolves around signs of success or abjection in relation to a set of norms we have yet to adequately nuance.

Just as historians should not arrive at any consensus about the definition or purview of what counts as transgender history, we critically keep in mind that few if any histories or individuals can be said to exist *apart from* transgender. We can approach this challenge both historically and theoretically. Historically speaking, we might reconsider the transness within communities that defined themselves according to more available or more highly prioritized subjectivities. Marlon Bailey offers one of the most significant examples, showing how within black queer ball culture throughout the twentieth century and into the present, elaborate lexicons and explicit articulation of gender diversity and signification have existed under shifting and evolving definitions of community as black and gay or queer. Scholars such as E. Patrick Johnson, Martin Manalansan, and Cathy Cohen, similarly, have long drawn attention to highly significant gender complexity within many queer of color taxonomies in the United States.

A strong case can also be made for redefining both the feminist and the gay and lesbian liberation movements of the 1960s–1970s in light of the formative and integral presence of trans people within those movements. While it is common to talk of those movements as trans-exclusive, doing so is historically inaccurate and perpetuates a definition of feminist and gayness as that which is not trans. Historical evidence suggests that feminism and gayness were always already trans both in that trans people were among those who generated the movements and subcultures, and also in that gender diversity was complexly understood and central to the ways the movements articulated themselves.[19]

Theorizing transgender in history necessarily raises the possibility of theorizing non-transgender in history. First comes the knowledge that we cannot assume "unmarked" people or communities were not trans. Any trans/not trans binary proves untenable and efforts to fix either side only reveal the seepage within the constructs themselves. And yet, if the construct of trans by any definition seems slippery, the construct of not-trans is—by its status as normative—taken to be far less slippery. To be sure, the determinative value of birth-assigned sex or genital status becomes sticky because it resists theorization. As queer, feminist, and critical race theorists have argued, normativity is defined or granted by successful passing that looks like absence, or the achievement of an unmarked status. Historians are compelled to prove trans-ness, never to prove or define non-transness, which seems to go without saying until we historicize this, too.

David Valentine offers one route toward theorizing non-transsexuality—and more specifically, the agency or choice to embrace a non-transsexual identity—that begins by historicizing contemporary non-transsexuality in terms of its relation to sex reassignment surgery (and even more specifically, genital surgery). Valentine finds that many queers and feminists assert support of trans people, but assert their non-trans identities by articulating alienation from trans surgeries. In contrast to whiteness, heterosexuality, and masculinity, naturalized forms of privilege that all have shifting but long pedigrees, this kind of non-transsexuality has only been possible since the 1950s or so. Yet, Valentine argues, non-transsexuality *is* a "subject position," and it should be "understood as the product of agentive action." Critiquing contemporary queer and feminist discourses that distance themselves from trans body modification, Valentine demands that "feminist and queer non-transsexuals . . . consider what it means to do the work of being non-transsexual, because refusing to do so naturalizes the very sexed and gendered bodies and power relations most queer theorists and feminists are at pains to denaturalize."[20] Valentine's call offers one possible historicization of transsexuality/non-transsexuality, and also a useful theorization of the stabilizing labors on which non-transsexuality depends. This should further encourage queer historians to a deeper gender analysis that neither exceptionalizes nor erases transgenderings in favor of concepts such as "same sex" and "sexuality."

Trans methodologies and analyses also compel us to continually question which *parts* matter. This is a relative of the question, "what are we looking for?" Transgender history demonstrates how sex/gender is situational and signified in numerous ways that derive their significance within simultaneous racialization and dis/ablization. We still necessarily must confront the question of which significations—which parts—may be slippery and malleable, and which parts are so sticky that we believe them to be transhistorical and even universal. Inherent within trans, by definition, is a dialectic between assignment into a social category of sex/gender and rejection of, or moving away from, that assignment. Historians should interrogate the motivations for trans-ing categories, and keep in mind aspects of epistemology and subjectivity that are not simply psychoanalytic but deeply historical.

A trans lens and method requires that we take care not to homogenize variations in gender arrangements across time and space; we can pay critical attention to historical vocabularies and epistemologies in order to discern the range of gender in each context. Keeping in mind that gender itself is not a transhistorical or transcultural concept and thus holding the term lightly, we might even ask, does trans history have to be about gender at all? Does it have to be about humans, or, as Mel Chen, M. Dale Booth, and Joan Roughgarden have demonstrated, might it be also about nonhuman being and objects? In short, trans studies scholars have analyzed sex/gender variation and contingent embodiments, all the while elaborating what we might mean by *trans* as a lens and as a method that necessarily generates critical theories for thinking across and through categorical, temporal, and spatial boundaries and frameworks.

This may always be a political project as well. Human recognition and citizenship the world over seems to depend on occupying a legally recognized or conferred sex/gender status, as does the ability to cross administrative borders. Sex/gender is currently such a ubiquitous and seemingly transnational (universal?) administrative category that it is hard to imagine otherwise. Yet different regimes of gender definition collide at national and temporal borders that are often violently maintained and that turn bodies into exchangeable commodities. At the very least, we must be aware of the ways that the search to find, define, and document transgender history inevitably touches on the violences and exclusions wrought by administrative categories as well as historical ones. Given the sheer innovation and will through which gender diverse people have lived, however, we cannot simply document these violences. What is trans if not an invitation to imagine otherwise?

Notes

1 Epistemological interest in sex/gender diversity and category crossing has been documented throughout human history in most parts of the world.
2 Briefly, transgender is often boxed within a narrow definition as "cross-gender" behavior or identity that specifically depends on the modern articulation of gender as distinct from perceived birth-assigned sex, and/or on a set of differentiated (usually dimorphic and binary) sexes and genders that one can "cross" and embrace as an ontological truth of personhood.

3 Founding history of sexuality works exemplify this slippage. Jonathan Ned Katz includes a special section on gender-crossing individuals in the impressive collection, *Gay American History: Lesbians and Gay Men in the U.S.A.* (New York: Thomas Crowell, 1976). Editors make no distinction between gay, lesbian, and gender-crossing figures in Martin B. Duberman, Martha Vicinus and George Chauncey, Jr., eds., *Hidden from History: Reclaiming the Gay and Lesbian Past* (New York: New American Library, 1989). Later surveys continue the trend well after transgender history offered distinct analytical tools for engaging gender diversity. More recent examples include Leila Rupp, *A Desired Past: A Short History of Same-Sex Love in America* (Chicago: University of Chicago Press, 1999) and Thomas A. Foster, *Long Before Stonewall: Histories of Same-Sex Sexuality in Early America* (New York: New York University Press, 2007). Still more recently, transgender may be specifically named in title but only marginally in content as in, for example, Leila Rupp and Susan K. Freeman, eds., *Understanding and Teaching U.S. Lesbian, Gay, Bisexual and Transgender History* (Madison: University of Wisconsin Press, 2014.)

4 Sandy Stone, "Guerilla." *TSQ* 1, nos. 1–2 (May 2014): 94.

5 See this chapter's further reading list for many works that helped establish gender analysis of things queer in the United States. See also Jen Manion's discussion in "Language, Acts, and Identity in LGBT Histories" in this volume.

6 On the queer history archives, see, in this volume, Kate Eichhorn, "Queer Archives: From Collections to Conceptual Framework."

7 Works that theorize the purview of transgender history include Mary Weismantel, "Toward a Transgender Archaeology: A Queer Rampage Through Prehistory," in *Transgender Studies Reader* Vol. 2, ed. Susan Stryker and Aren Z. Aizura (New York: Routledge, 2013), 319–335; Richard LaFortune Anguksuar, "A Postcolonial Colonial Perspective on Western [Mis]Conceptions of the Cosmos and the Restoration of Indegnous Taxonomies" in Sue-Ellen Jacobs, Wesley Thomas and Sabine Lang, *Two-Spirit People: Native American Gender Identity, Sexuality, and Spirituality* (Urbana: University of Illinois, 1997), 217–223; Genny Beemyn, "Transforming the Curriculum: The Inclusion of the Experiences of Trans People," in Leila Rupp and Susan Freeman, eds, *Understanding the Teaching U.S. Lesbian, Gay, Bisexual and Transgender History* (Madison: University of Wisconsin Press, 2014); and Evan Towle and Lynn Morgan, Romancing the Transgender Native: Rethinking the Use of the 'Third Gender' Concept," *GLQ* 8, no. 4 (2002): 469–497.

8 See, for example, Amanda Lock-Swarr, *Sex in Transition: Remaking Gender and Race in South Africa* (Albany: SUNY Press, 2012); Aniruddha Dutta and Raina Roy, "Decolonizing Transgender in India: Some Reflections," *TSQ* 1, no. 3 (August 2014): 320–337; C. Riley Snorton and Jin Haritaworn, "Trans Necropolitics: A Transnational Reflection on Violence, Death, and the Trans of Color Afterlife" in Stryker and Aizura eds, *The Transgender Studies Reader* vol. 2 (New York: Routledge: 2013), 66–76; Susan Stryker, "Kaming Mga Talyada (We Who Are Sexy): The Transsexual Whiteness of Christine Jorgensen in the (Post)Colonial Philippines" *Social Semiotics* 19, no. 1(2009): 79–91.

9 Simon D. Elin Fisher, "Pauli Murray's Peter Panic: Perspectives from the Margins of Gender and Race in Jim Crow America." *TSQ* 3, nos. 3–4 (2016): 100. Don Romesburg also directly engages binary interpretations in his history of a figure who seemed to subvert most forms of subjectification in "Longevity and Limits in Rae Bourbon's Life in Motion," in Trystan Cotton, ed, *Transgender Migrations* (New York: Routledge, 2011): 119–135.

10 Several other chapters in this volume similarly push "queer America" toward the transnational as a necessary methodology, including Eithne Luibhéid's "Nation," Emily Hobson's "Transnational Circuits," and Nayan Shah's "Queer of Color Estrangement and Belonging."

11 Afsaneh Najmabadi, *Professing Selves: Transsexuality and Same-Sex Desire in Contemporary Iran* (Durham: Duke University Press, 2014), 4.

12 Anguksuar (Richard La Fortune), "A Postcolonial Colonial Perspective on Western [Mis]Conceptions of the Cosmos and the Restoration of Indigenous Taxonomies" in Lang, Thomas, Jacobs, *Two Spirit People*, 217–222.

13 Qwo-Li Driskill, "D4Y D3C (Asegi Ayeti) Cherokee Two-Spirit People Reimagining Nation" in Qwo-Li Driskill et al eds., *Queer Indigenous Studies: Critical Interventions in Theory, Politics, and Literature* (Tucson: University of Arizona Press, 2011), 97–111. See also Saylesh Wesley, "Twin-Spirited Woman: Sts'iyoye smestiyexw slha:li" *TSQ* 1. No. 3 (August 2014): 338–351; Wesley Thomas, "Navajo Cultural Conceptions of Gender and Sexuality" in Jacobs, Thomas and Lang eds, *Two Spirit People* (156–173).

14 Deborah A. Miranda, "Extermination of the Joyas: Gendercide in Spanish California," *GLQ: A Journal of Lesbian and Gay Studies* 16, no. 1–2 (2010): 255.

15 Greta LaFleur, "Sex and 'Unsex': Histories of Gender Trouble in Eighteenth-Century North America," *Early American Studies* 12, no. 3 (Fall 2014): 470.

16 LaFleur, 471–473.

17 Scott Larson, "Indescribable Being: Theological Performances of Genderlessness in the Society of the Publick Universal Friend, 1776–181," *Early American Studies* 12, no. 3 (Fall 2014): 578.

18 Sean Trainor, "Fair Bosom/Black Beard: Facial Hair, Gender Determination and the Strange Career of Madame Clofullia, 'Bearded Lady,'" *Early American Studies* 1, no. 3 (Fall 2014): 548–575.

19 Finn Enke, "Sticky Assignments: Trans-temporality and the Historio-Graphic Securitization of Sex" Rutgers University, March 14, 2013. See also, Tim Retzloff, "Eliding Trans Latino/a Queer Experience in U.S. LGBT History: Jose Sarria and Sylvia Rivera Reexamined," *Centro Journal* 19, no. 1 (2007): 140–161.

20 David Valentine, "Sue E. Generous: Toward a Theory of Non-Transexuality," *Feminist Studies* 38, no. 1 (Spring 2012): 187.

Further Reading

Aizura, Aren, Trystan Cotton, Carsten Balzar/Carla LaGata, Marcia Ochoa, and Salvador Vidal-Ortiz, eds. *Decolonizing the Transgender Imaginary*, a special issue of *TSQ: Transgender Studies Quarterly* 1, no. 3 (August 2014).

Anzaldúa, Gloria. *Borderlands/La Frontera: The New Mestiza*. San Francisco: Aunt Lute, 1987.

Bailey, Marlon. *Butch Queens Up in Pumps: Gender, Performance and Ballroom Culture in Detroit*. Ann Arbor: University of Michigan, 2013.

Boag, Peter. *Re-Dressing America's Frontier Past*. Berkeley: University of California Press, 2011.

Booth, M. Dale. "Locating a Tranimal Past: A Review Essay of Tranimalities and Tranimacies in Scholarship." *TSQ* 2, no. 2 (2015): 353–358.

Bornstein, Kate. *Gender Outlaw: On Men, Women, and the Rest of Us*. New York: Routledge, 1994.

Butler, Judith. *Gender Trouble: Feminism and the Subversion of Identity*. New York: Routledge, 1990.

Chauncey, George. *Gay New York: Gender, Urban Culture, and the Making of the Gay Male World, 1890–1940*. New York: Harper Collins, 1994.

Chen, Mel. *Animacies: Biopolitics, Racial Mattering, and Queer Affect*. Durham: Duke University Press, 2012.

Cohen, Cathy. "Punks, Bulldaggers, and Welfare Queens: The Radical Potential of Queer Politics?" In *Queer Black Studies: A Critical Anthology*, eds. E. Patrick Johnson and Mae G. Henderson, 21–50. Durham: Duke University Press, 2005.

Feinberg, Leslie. *Stone Butch Blues*. Ithaca: Firebrand, 1993.

Halberstam, Judith/Jack. *Female Masculinity*. Durham: Duke University Press, 1998.

Jacobs, Sue Ellen, Wesley Thomas, and Sabine Lang, eds. *Two Spirit People: Native American Gender Identity, Sexuality and Spirituality*. Urbana: University of Illinois, 1997.

Johnson, E. Patrick. *Sweet Tea: Black Gay Men of the South*. Chapel Hill: University of North Carolina Press, 2008.

Kennedy, Elizabeth and Madeleine Davis. *Boots of Leather, Slippers of Gold: The History of a Lesbian Community*. New York: Routledge, 1993.

Manalansan, Martin. *Global Divas: Filipino Gay Men in the Diaspora*. Durham: Duke University, 2003.

Meyerowitz, JoAnn. "A History of 'Gender.'" *American Historical Review* 113, no. 5 (December 2008): 1346–56.

Meyerowitz, JoAnn. *How Sex Changed: A History of Transsexuality in the United States*. Cambridge: Harvard University Press, 2002.

Morgensen, Scott. *The Spaces Between Us: Queer Settler Colonialism and Indigenous Decolonization*. Minneapolis: University of Minnesota, 2011.

Prosser, Jay. *Second Skins: The Body Narratives of Transsexuality*. New York: Columbia University Press, 1998.

Rawson, KJ. "Archive This! Queer(ing) Archival Practices." In *Practicing Research in Writing Studies: Reflections on Ethically Responsible Research*, eds. Katy Powell and Pam Takayoshi, 237–250. New York: Hampton Press 2012.

Roughgarden, Joan. *Evolution's Rainbow: Diversity, Gender, and Sexuality in Nature and People*. Berkeley: University of California, 2004.

Rubin, Gayle. "The Traffic in Women: Notes on the 'Political Economy' of Sex." In *Deviations: A Gayle Rubin Reader*, 33–65. Durham: Duke University Press, 2011 [1975].

Rubin, Gayle. "Thinking Sex: Notes for a Radical Theory of the Politics of Sexuality." In *Deviations: A Gayle Rubin Reader*, 137–180. Durham: Duke University Press, 2011 [1984].

Rubin, Gayle. "Of Catamites and Kings: Reflections on Butch, Gender, and Boundaries." In *Deviations: A Gayle Rubin Reader*, 241–253. Durham: Duke University Press, 2011.

Stone, Sandy. "The Empire Strikes Back: A Posttranssexual Manifesto." In *Body Guards: The Cultural Politics of Gender Ambiguity*, eds. Julia Epstein and Kristina Straub, 280–304. New York: Routledge, 1991.

Samuels, Ellen. *Fantasies of Identification: Disability, Gender, Race*. New York: New York University Press, 2014.

Sears, Clare. *Arresting Dress: Cross-Dressing, Law, and Fascination in Nineteenth-Century San Francisco*. Durham: Duke University Press, 2015.

Stryker, Susan. *Transgender History*. Berkeley: Seal Press, 2008.

Valentine, David. *Imagining Transgender: Ethnography of a Category*. Durham: Duke University Press, 2007.

Vicinus, Martha. " 'They Wonder to Which Sex I Belong': The Historical Roots of the Modern Lesbian Identity." *Feminist Studies* 18, no. 3 (Fall 1992): 467–497.

Williams, Cristan. "Radical Inclusion: Recounting the Trans Inclusive History of Radical Feminism." *TSQ* 3, nos. 1–2 (2016): 254–258.

18

LESBIAN HISTORY

Spirals of Imagination, Marginalization, and Creation

Julie R. Enszer

Do lesbians have a history? In the mid-twentieth century, prior to a developed movement for lesbian rights, Jeannette Howard Foster and Barbara Grier asked themselves this question. Foster was trained as a librarian, Grier was an autodidact. These women stalked libraries and bookstores, answering questions invented from their own needs and desires. Unauthorized and untrained in the conventions of historiography, Foster and Grier created a community-based and extraordinarily influential foundation for the ever-expanding field of lesbian history. Subsequent radical liberation movements of the 1960s and 1970s sparked authorization for new histories. As women's history, women's studies, LGBT history, and the history of sexuality emerged as formal historical studies, each field enabled lesbian history to occupy newly authorized spaces. Central to these evolving histories initially was the question: What is a lesbian? Early scholarship by literary historians including Caroll Smith-Rosenberg, Lillian Faderman, and Martha Vicinus straddled multiple modes of historical inquiry to expand the definitions of lesbian and remove it from psychiatric and criminal frames. Today, scholarly lesbian history emerges from multiple academic locations: sociology, literature, history, women's studies, American studies, performance studies and more. Community-based writers, activists, archivists, and librarians also continue to write lesbian histories. Compared to the intellectual environment that Foster and Grier encountered, readers today can find an array of materials.

While there are multiple meaningful engagements with lesbian histories, erasure and marginalization continue to challenge their production and preservation. The expansion of disciplines and sub-fields creates fecund environments but also presents challenges. The common language and intellectual genealogies of a discipline can be lost in the overlapping inter- and transdisciplinary work that characterizes contemporary lesbian scholarship on the past. In addition, proliferating queer and trans★ identities, while offering exciting possibilities, can also situate lesbian identity as singularly anachronistic and antagonistic. Flashpoints of conflict, such as skirmishes between trans★ activists and some of the lesbian-feminist activists at the Michigan Womyn's Music Festival for the past quarter century, can flatten complex and overlapping histories of identity formation and community. Finally, the politics of preserving the raw materials of history—papers, archives, and other ephemera—too often prioritize white male cisgender archives, marginalizing lesbian histories. Despite these challenges, lesbian history continues to evolve as a dynamic and vital field.

Unauthorized Lesbian Histories

You walked alone, full of laughter, you bathed bare bellied. You say you have lost
all recollection of it, remember! You say there are not words to describe it; you
say it does not exist. But remember! Make an effort to remember! or failing that,
invent.

Monique Wittig, Les Guérillères *(Boston: Beacon Press, 1969, 1985), 89*

Throughout the twentieth century, lesbians, individually and communally, have been concerned
with preserving a lesbian past. The circulation of Sappho's writing and life story is one example.
As Yopie Prins documents, Sappho's work was widely translated and read in Victorian England.
Circulation of translations of Sappho combined with sexologists' preoccupations about homosexuality subsequently framed early twentieth-century desires for lesbian histories. In Paris, Renee
Vivien and Natalie Barney viewed Sappho as a foremother. The work of French writer and
trickster Pierre Louÿs in *Les Chasons de Bilitis*, a text engaged with Sapphic fragments as well
as archeological and literary dialogues about Sappho, also appealed to Vivien and Barney. Using
literary history, Vivien and Barney created an imagined world that celebrated lesbian lives and
loves. Thirty years later, as historian Marcia Gallo notes, lesbians in the United States used
Louÿs's Bilitis to name the first lesbian organization, the Daughters of Bilitis. Early lesbians'
affection for Sappho and her knock-off Bilitis demonstrate the desire for a past as an imaginative
tool to create a present.

Mid-century, Jeannette Howard Foster constructed a literary history of lesbians. Her 1956
self-published book, *Sex Variant Women in Literature*, reviews a broad array of literature from
antiquity to the present. Foster begins with Sappho and includes the Hebrew story of Ruth
and Naomi as well as other ancient texts. She also discusses literature by Algernon Charles
Swinburne, Louise Labé, Adah Isaacs Menken, Michael Field, Emily Dickinson and others.
Engaging biographical information to identify lesbian authors, Foster decoded themes, imagery,
and biographical narrations consonant with lesbianism. Foster primarily focused on thematic
portrayals of lesbianism; she was as content to read portrayals of lesbianism by men, heterosexual and homosexual, as those by women. In *Sex Variant Women in Literature*, Foster yokes
together literary work and themes for readers to encounter as lesbian, and teaches readers,
imagined to be both lesbians and enlightened others, to read as lesbians.

The distribution of Foster's 1956 edition was limited. Rejected by dozens of commercial
publishers, Foster eventually self-published it with Vantage Press with a press run of 3,500.
Of those 3,500 copies, "Vantage sold nearly eleven hundred copies" and sold "unbound pages
to British publisher Frederick Muller, Ltd., in 1958" for a British edition.[1] The book had a
resurgence in the 1970s and 1980s during the Women's Liberation Movement. A 1975 edition
by Diana Press, made with the original plates from the 1956 edition, sold 2,272 copies (probably
on an original press run of 2,500) and earned Foster $1,383.72 in total royalties.[2] As I explain
in "The Whole Naked Truth of Our Lives," this edition doubled the initial audience of
the book and was a modest success for the press. More importantly, the Diana Press edition
of *Sex Variant Women in Literature* reached lesbian readers. The women's movement enabled
Diana Press and the lesbian-feminist press more broadly to build audiences of lesbian
readers marketing directly to them through newsletters, newspapers, and community events.
Sex Variant Women in Literature continued its life in the 1980s through Naiad Press; in 1984,
Barbara Grier reissued it. *Sex Variant Women* defined lesbian literature and offered a literary
history of lesbians. For a half a century, this book offered a sustained *yes* to the question:
Do lesbians have a history?

Figure 18.1 Lesbian librarian and literary pioneer Jeannette Howard Foster (seated, center), author of the foundational study *Sex Variant Women in Literature* (1956), with lesbian-feminist Naiad Press publishers Barbara Grier and Donna McBride and an unidentified friend, c. 1970s.
Photo courtesy of Lesbian Herstory Archives.

Foster's work inspired Barbara Grier. Grier was a prodigious book reviewer for *The Ladder*, the journal of the Daughters of Bilitis. Through her column "Lesbiana," Grier continued Foster's work as a literary critic and historian. She positioned a number of literary works as lesbian, including the first poetry collection by Mary Oliver, who did not come out until the next century.[3] Through her reviews, Grier carefully directed readers to work where they could find Sapphic love, affection, and emotions. Given the lack of women who openly identified as lesbians, Grier, like Foster, treated representations of lesbianism by heterosexual men and women with equal time, attention, and enthusiasm. Grier writes of Boris Todrin and his poem "Hate Song," "It is hard to be enthusiastic over someone who obviously wrote in hatred . . . This is the story of one man's loss of his wife to another woman. It is very effective poetry though certainly negative in its approach." James Wright's poems "Sappho" and "Erinna to Sappho" earn Grier's appraisal of "unusually intuitive, coming as they do from a male author's pen."[4] Grier's reading practices were concordant with the desires of her readers during the 1960s. Like Foster, Grier demonstrates how to analyze literature for lesbian themes, desires, and images. Also like Foster, Grier delighted in identifying writers as lesbian when she could.

Grier was not the only one interested in lesbian history within *The Ladder*. When the periodical began publishing in 1956, writers and editors filled its pages with stories about lesbians of yore. Like our fascination today with reality television and celebrity gossip, lesbians from the 1950s onward speculated about the sexual orientation of famous and infamous people. As the Women's Liberation Movement alighted with journals, newspapers, and other small press productions, attention to lesbians in history grew. *The Furies*, a newspaper published from 1971–1973, contains articles about Emily Dickinson as a lesbian and about Gertrude, the lesbian queen of Sweden.[5] Real or imaginatively created, the desire for a past, a heritage, a lineage, is a theme of lesbian communities during the twentieth century as expressed in books, journals, newspapers, and magazines produced primarily outside formally authorized histories.

While authorized lesbian histories begin to emerge in the late 1970s, one significant community history was published in 1984 by Judy Grahn, a poet and theorist enmeshed in early lesbian and feminist communities in the San Francisco Bay Area. *Another Mother Tongue* is a concatenation of histories: cultural history, autobiography (often written as intimate conversations with Grahn's first lover Von), and a synthetic history of feminism and lesbian-feminism. Grahn's history reflects her belief that culture "gives any group of people distinction and dignity."[6] Her political commitments as a lesbian-feminist led her to call for lesbians and gay men to embrace a multicultural and multiracial history and culture. *Another Mother Tongue* was a popular success, appealing to a wide range of common readers. It won the 1985 Gay Book Award of the American Library Association. Historians rarely engage *Another Mother Tongue* and Grahn's subsequent work on menstruation and matriarchy, yet these books function as important imaginative and literary contributions. As historical documents, they demonstrate how unauthorized historians uncover lesbian history.

Like Foster's and Grier's work, Grahn's *Another Mother Tongue* is an originary history crafted with the intention of explaining origins of a people or an idea. Originary histories are often popular histories. They have a material function for activists, recreational readers, and engaged citizens: they support an imaginary within communities that sustains in times of challenge. Formally authorized historians of sexuality largely eschew originary histories in favor of what Michel Foucault calls "genealogical histories."[7] Genealogical histories map disparities and fields of change, rejecting points of origin. Yet, Foucault's dispassionate declension of origins would not have cut through the archive fever of Grahn, Grier, and Foster. They demonstrate what Jacques Derrida calls "an irrepressible desire to return to the origin, a homesickness, a nostalgia for the return to the most archaic place of absolute commencement."[8] Both originary histories and genealogical histories affirm the epistemological position that lesbian communities have a past that can be traced and recounted—a notion accepted today but once contested, even dismissed. Using the archives available to them, Grahn, Grier, and Foster created early lesbian histories that reflected the needs and desires of their communities. As unauthorized historians, they defined archives for lesbian histories, told stories that created communities, and informed subsequent histories.

Authorized Lesbian Histories

> To be what you are is one thing, to be what you want, now that's something else.
> *Ferron, "Sunken City," Phantom Center (1990)*

Authorized lesbian histories emerged in the late 1970s. Written by formally educated scholars often working within academia, authorized histories have developed primarily at the confluence of three sub-disciplines: women's history, LGBT history, and the history of sexuality. If unauthorized lesbian historians wrote histories that lesbians wanted to read, authorized historians uncovered new worlds of lesbians and lesbian life; they wrote histories expanding possibilities for lesbians.

Women's history and the formation of women's studies as a discipline was significant for lesbian histories. Carroll Smith-Rosenberg's 1975 article, "The Female World of Love and Ritual," inaugurated a lively conversation over the next two decades about the question: What is a lesbian? Smith-Rosenberg argued that "sexual and emotional impulses are part of a continuum or spectrum of affect gradations strongly effected by cultural norms and arrangement, a continuum influenced in part by observed and thus learned behavior."[9] Lesbian poets Adrienne Rich and Audre Lorde amplified this idea of a lesbian continuum in their work.

Smith-Rosenberg's work draws on letters between women. Textual analysis shaped many early, authorized lesbian histories. Other influential early lesbian literary histories joined Smith-Rosenberg's work, including Faderman's *Surpassing the Love of Men* (1981), a cultural history of love and friendship between women extending 500 years, and *Odd Girls and Twilight Lovers* (1990), a history of lesbianism in the United States during the twentieth century. These were joined by Bonnie Zimmerman's *The Safe Sea of Women* (1990), an examination of how lesbian literature expresses lesbian politics, and Terry Castle's *The Apparitional Lesbian* (1993), an exploration of the invisibility of lesbians in history and literature. The connection between literary history and lesbian history emerged through both the defined archives and the disciplinary locations open to lesbians as an object of study.

In a 1992 overview article on lesbian history, Martha Vicinus asserts, "Lesbian desire is everywhere, even as it may be nowhere. Put bluntly, we lack any general agreement about what constitutes a lesbian."[10] Still, Vicinus identifies three prevailing models for thinking about lesbians and lesbians in history: retrieval and reconstruction of lesbian and lesbian communities, exploration of "major paradigmatic models" of lesbian behavior (butch-femme and romantic friendships), and questions of when and under what conditions modern lesbian identity emerged.[11] These continue to be important models extended and influenced by LGBT history and the history of sexuality.

In equal measures as women's history, LGBT history influences lesbian history. British historian Jeffrey Weeks located the origin of homosexuality in nineteenth-century sexology in *Coming Out: Homosexual Politics in Britain from the Nineteenth Century to the Present* (1977). Weeks explored the contingencies of history that produced homosexuality, lesbian and gay behavior, and lesbian and gay identities. John D'Emilio's seminal 1983 essay, "Capitalism and Gay Identity," and book, *Sexual Politics, Sexual Communities* (1983), traced the way that modern gay and lesbian identity emerged out of tensions in US capitalist development across the nineteenth and early twentieth centuries, taking shape in the post-World War II era with the homophile movement. D'Emilio asserts that lesbians and gay men have not always existed. They are in the modern formations "a product of history, and have come into existence in a specific historical era."[12] This social constructionist framework shaped subsequent decades of LGBT history. Early scholarship by D'Emilio and Weeks drew attention to the question: historically, what are the different manifestations of homosexuality—behavior, identity, sexual practices—and how do we understand them?

LGBT histories take up questions of how and under what conditions lesbian, gay, bisexual, and transgender (or other specific sexually and gender diverse) identities emerged and, more specifically, how LGBT communities formed. Building on D'Emilio's work throughout the 1990s and 2000s were a series of books examining histories of lesbian and gay communities in particular geographical locations. Books centrally considering lesbians include Elizabeth Kennedy and Madeline Davis's *Boots of Leather, Slippers of Gold*, Genny Beemyn's anthology *Creating a Place for Ourselves*, Marc Stein's *City of Sisterly and Brotherly Loves: Lesbian and Gay Philadelphia, 1945–1972*, Nan Alamilla Boyd's *Wide-open Town: A History of Queer San Francisco to 1965*, and Stephanie Gilmore's *Groundswell: Grassroots Feminist Activism in Postwar America*. Kennedy and Davis used oral histories to narrate a complex and nuanced history of working-class lesbian communities in Buffalo with particular to attention to butch-femme relationships and bar culture during the pre-Stonewall era. Roey Thorpe's work on lesbians in Detroit during the same era, included in Beemyn's collection, further decenters coastal narratives of lesbian identity.

Stein and Boyd trace cross-gender coalition work and the emergence of gay and lesbian formations. Boyd also uncovers how lesbian visibility emerges in public culture including lesbian neighborhoods in the 1950s, which evolved through entertainment tourism. Gilmore's history of the National Organization of Women (NOW) examines the different ways lesbian identity influenced various NOW chapters. Forthcoming work by La Shonda Mims extends these inquiries into underexamined geographies by exploring southern lesbian life.

The history of sexuality more broadly also contributes to LGBT history. Published in 1988, D'Emilio and Estelle B. Freedman's *Intimate Matters: A History of Sexuality in America* solidified the field of the history of sexuality as central to the study of the US past. *Intimate Matters*, deeply informed by feminist approaches to historical interpretation, provides an interpretive framework for thinking about the history of sexuality in the United States, from the early days of the American colonies to the present. Its scope and approach shapes projects such as Nancy Cott's *Public Vows: A History of Marriage and the Nation*, which explores the interconnections between governmental and legal regulation of marriage, constructions of ideas about love and monogamy, and negotiations between public and private in relationship to marriage and intimate partnerships. Leila J. Rupp's *A Desired Past: A Short History of Same-Sex Love in America* traces understandings about same-sex love from early American sources through the world of romantic friendships, industrialization, a more coherent identity of "invert," and finally to the identities of lesbian as deployed during the Women's Liberation Movement. Jennifer Terry's *An American Obsession*, Margot Canaday's *The Straight State*, and Amanda Littauer's *Bad Girls* are further examples of a genealogical approach to the LGBT past that recognize the specificity of lesbian history. Terry examines discursive formations of science and medicine, and how these discourses accrete meaning to homosexuality between the 1860s and the 1980s. Canaday traces how US policy changes in the twentieth century in immigration, welfare, and the military regulate homosexuality and gender in ways that have specific implications for women understood by the state as lesbian. Littauer explores women's defiance of sexual conventions in the post-World War II period, transgressing heteronormativity and disciplinary gender norms. These histories explore how lesbian sexuality is expressed and enforced under different historical conditions. More than twenty years since Vicinus' mapping of the field, new developments in LGBT history and the history of sexuality contribute vital insights about the impacts on lesbian lives of the state, politics, and culture.

Biography is another important genre for the exploration of lesbian lives. Rachel Hope Cleves' recent *Charity and Sylvia*, for example, examines how women constructed relationships in early America. Biography is a particularly effective way to understand the contingencies and complexities of lesbian lives. Some biographies illuminate the lives of conventionally famous women while exploring the nuances of same-sex friendships and intimacies, as Blanche Weisen Cook did in the biography of Eleanor Roosevelt, and Martha Nell Smith did in her work on Emily Dickinson. Others explore the lives of open lesbians, as Alexis de Veaux has with Audre Lorde and Joanne Passet has with Jeannette Howard Foster and Barbara Grier. Biography can also illuminate the constraints of gender binaries, as in Diane Middlebrook's *Suits Me: The Double Life of Billy Tipton*. By exploring complex intersections of race and sexuality in *Doctor Mom Chung of the Fair-Haired Bastards: The Life of a Wartime Celebrity*, Judy Wu excavates the challenges of life history in relation to gender binaries. Biography also can examine broad cultural and social movements. In the biography of Miriam Van Waters, Estelle Freedman illuminates the role of lesbians in social reform and prison reform movements of the early twentieth century. Similarly, in *Intertwined Lives*, a dual biography of Ruth Benedict and Margaret Mead, Lois Banner explores how the anthropologists worked for racial and sexual equality during a period of publicly entrenched racism and xenophobia. Autobiography, infused with fiction and mythology, provides important imaginative narratives of lesbian and bisexual women's lives. Audre Lorde's *Zami: A New Spelling of My Name* gives voice to the lesbian *bildungsroman* of a Caribbean immigrant; Daisy Hernández's *A Cup of Water Under My Bed* explores the intersection of race and class with bisexual identity and politics; Leslie Feinberg's novel *Stone Butch Blues* renders the identities of transgender and butch women. Biographies and autobiographies express how women live their lives as lesbian, queer, same-gender loving, and a host of other expressions of sexuality and gender.

Literary texts continue to provide an important archive for historians and the basis for trenchant theoretical engagements. Susan Lanser's *The Sexuality of History: Modernity and the Sapphic, 1565–1830*, for example, considers how erotic representations of lesbians map to broad cultural concerns. Kathryn Kent's *Making Girls into Women: American Women's Writing and the Rise of Lesbian Identity* examines modern lesbian identity as rooted in white, middle-class women's culture and its focus on the mother as a figure of disciplinary intimacy. Lisa Duggan's *Sapphic Slashers* explores the late nineteenth- and early twentieth-century emergence of a public lesbian through the real life and fictional trope of the "lesbian love murder." Duggan's, Lanser's, and Kent's work, which could not have been created without the imbrication of historical and literary archives and methods, highlights the vexed histories of public lesbian figures and identities.

The early 1990s turn to queer theory prompted new and exciting engagements in lesbian histories. Scholars such as Linda Garber, Theresa de Lauretis and Elizabeth Grosz emphasized the shared histories and intellectual stakes of situating queer theory in relationship to feminist theory. Attentions from scholars such as Judith/Jack Halberstam and Nan Alamilla Boyd pivoted the identity of lesbian from its imbrication with feminism to an imbrication with gay male, queer, and trans★ communal formations. In *Female Masculinities*, Halberstam contextualizes masculine-of-center queer women, historically disarticulating masculinity from an inevitable link to birth-assigned male-bodied identities. Halberstam's *In A Queer Time and Place* explores the intersections and tensions among lesbian, queer, and trans cultural and historical production, focusing on the stakes of biography, temporality, and memory. Boyd's "Bodies in Motion" similarly considers tensions within lesbian and transgender identity formations, particularly how they reproduce nationalism. One principal effect of this queering of lesbian history has been the contestation of any coherence in the constitution of lesbian historiography as distinct from other historiographies centered on sexuality and gender. As trans★ studies develops as a field in its own right, scholars question the notion that there is an evident or apparent way to distinguish lesbian from trans★ history. Most recently, a 2016 "Trans/Feminisms" issue of *TSQ: Transgender Studies Quarterly* includes articles by Susan Stryker, Talia Beetcher, Emma Heaney, and Cristan Williams that elaborate the contested and intertwined relationships among histories of lesbian-feminism, lesbian communities and identities, and trans★ histories, identities, and communities.

Although literary studies are significant, lesbian histories always have emanated from multiple intellectual formations, emphasizing the interdisciplinary nature of lesbian histories and the role of history within the broader rubric of lesbian studies. In *Sex and Sensibility: Stories of a Lesbian Generation*, sociologist Arlene Stein conducted ethnographic interviews to explore the terrain of lesbian identity and its changes between the 1970s and the 1990s, capturing a particularly significant era in lesbian history. Sara Warner's *Acts of Gaiety* uses the disciplinary tools of performance studies to reconsider multiple sites of lesbian political actions from the 1970s through the 2000s as rooted in pleasure and gaiety. Many critics have flattened—wrongly— lesbian feminism in the 1970s and 1980s as an archaic era of white privilege, anti-trans politics and anti-sex culture. Interdisciplinary histories that rely upon oral histories and other primary sources from the people involved offer an urgent corrective. Joining Stein and Warner,

Christina Hanhardt's *Safe Space: Gay Neighborhoods and the Politics of Violence* examines how the production of gay neighborhoods simultaneously marginalizes poor people and people of color—and how different queer community formations challenged this dynamic. Daniel Winunwe Rivers' *Radical Relations: Lesbian Mothers, Gay Fathers, and Their Children in the United States since World War II* explores the co-constitutive dynamics of lesbians' and gay men's desire to create families in hostile legal and political environments.[13] Kristen Hogan's *The Feminist Bookstore Movement: Lesbian Antiracism and Feminist Accountability* recounts lesbian contributions to anti-racist practices and transnational coalitional work through the bookstore movement. Faderman's *The Gay Revolution* traces a robust narrative of this period as well. These histories testify to the complexity and dynamism of the 1970s and 1980s, as well as its resonance and relevance today.

Recently, inquiries into transnational, borderland, and critical race studies suggest new directions for lesbian history.[14] Leila Rupp's *Sapphistries: The Global History of Love Between Women* explores a synthetic history of lesbians around the world, asserting the presence of lesbian and trans sexuality and desire in an array of global locations. Ruth Morgan and Saskia Wieringa's collaborative ethnographic scholarship with women from multiple national contexts documents lesbian cultures, practices, affinities, and histories across the African continent. Gloria Wekker examines women's sexual cultures, including love and desire for other women, in the Afro-Surinamese diaspora. Gayatri Gopinath engages the concept of diaspora to produce "queer female diasporic subjectivity" as a critical tool to understand transnational lesbian histories and identities. Eithne Luibhéid, Katie L. Acosta, Emma Pérez, and Fatima El-Tayeb excavate how lesbian and queer identities cross borders. Luibhéid's *Entry Denied* explores the tensions related to sexuality since the nineteenth century as people have crossed US borders, particularly detailing the risks of "looking like a lesbian" in the post-World War II era. Acosta argues that although lesbians create "imagined communities" as they migrate, the borderlands are still riddled with inequalities and tensions. Pérez argues for a decolonial imagination to challenge these inequalities. El-Tayeb considers how queer Muslims in Europe reshape queerness and challenge hegemonic narratives of coming out.

In the US context, critical race scholars continue many conversations initiated by woman of color theorists, including Cherríe Moraga, Gloria Anzaldúa, and Audre Lorde. Siobhan Somerville's *Queering the Color Line: Race and the Invention of Homosexuality in American Culture* considers the links between race and homosexuality from the late nineteenth century through the 1930s in the US. Rachel Afi Quinn traces how the work of Audre Lorde travels among lesbians in the Dominican Republic. Maria Lugones and Jacqui Alexander demonstrate the importance of a transnational lens for further understanding power and colonialism in queer histories. New theoretical lenses, methods, and archives offered by transnational, border, and critical race studies make visible different lesbian communities and various forms of identities. These new scholarly directions expose broader structures of power and privilege in history—and in the material world.

Lesbian Spirals

Straddling multiple academic formations presents challenges to lesbian history. How can lesbians stay in focus? In women's history, scholars can struggle to keep a focus on lesbians and sexuality; similarly, in LGBT history, more archival information about gay men can challenge scholars interested in focusing on lesbians, requiring more creatively constructed archives; transgender histories can complicate secure understandings of what constitutes a lesbian past. Likewise, histories of sexuality can shift the focus away from lesbians toward wider and/or more specific constructions of sexuality and gender. Rather than understanding these various tensions as threats to lesbian history, however, these vibrant, multiple locations should be understood as generative to lesbian history, offering twists and turns along the spiral of its creation.[15]

Imagination always has been key to lesbian histories, but archives—the raw materials of history—are vital.[16] Ann Cvetkovich, linking archival theory and affect theory, argues for an archive of lesbian feelings and the publics they construct as a strategy to make lesbian lives visible and universal. Cvetkovich's book prompted an "archival turn" in queer studies—a curious phrasing for historians already embedded in the archives. Two lesbian archives in the US, the Lesbian Herstory Archives (LHA) in Brooklyn and the June L. Mazer Archives in Los Angeles, promote the collection of materials about lesbian lives. Their work is supported by other institutional feminist and LGBT archives. Joan Nestle describes the LHA:

> Forty years later, the uniqueness of the LHA still stands: its grassroots base; its refusal of governmental funds; its demystifying of the archives profession; its determination to keep *lesbian* as the all-inclusive noun; the collective ownership of its building, which functions as a community cultural center, funded through small donations from many; its collective structure where consensus still rules—thus the building, the means of organization, its lesbian centeredness, makes the LHA its own kind of artifact.[17]

Preserving materials by and about lesbians is important to ensure that these materials and the women who created them are not lost to future histories. Recent scholarship on lesbian archives is rich and capacious, including Nestle's reflections on the LHA, McKinney's analysis of visual images and the LHA, Chenier's analysis of oral histories of Canadian lesbians, Heather Love's *Feeling Backward*, Jaime Cantrell and Amy Stone's edited collection, *Out of the Closet, Into the Archive*, and two issues of *Sinister Wisdom* highlighting Southern lesbian-feminist oral histories. These archival engagements demonstrate how authorized and unauthorized historians continue to capture and preserve lesbian histories.

With a nod to odd bedfellows Halberstam's *In a Queer Time and Place* and Starhawk's *The Spiral Dance*, lesbian histories can be appreciated as spirals of stories about lesbians. Halberstam configures queer time and space existing "at least in part, in opposition to the institutions of family, heterosexual, and reproduction." Starhawk accounts for a double spiral, "whirling into being and whirling out again." Brought together, these two aspects of the spiral of lesbian histories continually rework and reimagine knowledge about lesbian lives, past and present. To answer the main question, then, "What is a lesbian?", lesbian histories offer origin stories and genealogies. They crystalize communities of lesbians and contest coherence. They isolate incidents of power and moments of oppression even as they contextualize lesbian lives and broader societal trends. Lesbian histories draw from multiple communities of scholars and activists—authorized and unauthorized—in order to innovate, inspire, and create praxis in the present. In the process, lesbian histories offer new historiographic theories and methodologies. Most importantly, they tell stories.

Do lesbians have a history? Most definitely. Or rather, lesbians do not have *a history*, we have *many histories*. The telling and preserving of these histories is an ongoing series of collaborative projects. Promoting and supporting the communal stakes among writers and readers of lesbian histories is crucial. Resisting erasure of lesbians within history and within archives challenges the constant threat of marginalization. A persistent desire to tell more stories ensures that lesbian histories are—and continue to be—multiplicitous and polyvocal.

Notes

1 Joanne Passet, *Sex Variant Woman: The Life of Jeannette Howard Foster* (New York: Da Capo Press, 2008), 193, 195.
2 Coletta Reid's records on the book indicate that in February 1978, Diana Press had 150 additional copies of the book in stock. File Drawer One, Diana Press Papers, June Mazer Lesbian Archives.
3 Oliver acknowledged her partner, Molly Malone Cook, when she won the National Book Award in 1992 (Sue Russell, "Mary Oliver: The Poet & the Persona," *Harvard Gay and Lesbian Review* (Fall 1997), 21) but she did not publish work discussing her partnership with Cook until in the early 2000s.
4 Grier, "Poetry of Lesbiana," Undated copy from Lesbian Herstory Archives.
5 All issues of The Furies are available online through the Rainbow History Project. The Furies, Inc., "The Furies, Goddesses of Vengeance: a new lesbian/feminist monthly magazine," *Rainbow History Project Digital Collections*, accessed March 19, 2016, http://rainbowhistory.omeka.net/items/show/4938056. Accessed October 21, 2017.
6 Judy Grahn, *Another Mother Tongue* (Boston, Beacon Press, 1984), xiii.
7 Michel Foucault, "Nietszche, Genealogy, History," *The Essential Foucault: Selections from Essential Works of Foucault, 1954–1984*, ed. Paul Rabinow and Nikolas Rose (New York: The New Press, 2003), 353.
8 Jacques Derrida, *Archive Fever: A Freudian Impression* (Chicago: University of Chicago Press, 1998), 91.
9 Carroll Smith-Rosenberg, "The Female World of Love and Ritual: Relations between Women in Nineteenth-Century America," *Signs* 1, no. 1 (Autumn 1975): 29. For another discussion of the importance of Smith-Rosenberg's article to queer history see, in this volume, Don Romesburg, "Introduction: Having a Moment Four Decades in the Making."
10 Martha Vicinus, " 'They Wonder to Which Sex I Belong'; The Historical Roots of the Modern Lesbian Identity," *Feminist Studies* 18, no. 3 (1992): 468.
11 Linda Garber revisited this paradigm and introduced the idea of lesbian historical fiction extending these models in "Claiming Lesbian History: The Romance Between Fact and Fiction," *Journal of Lesbian Studies* 19 (January 2015): 129–149.
12 John D'Emilio, "Capitalism and Gay Identity," *Powers of Desire: The Politics of Sexuality*, ed. Ann Snitow, Christine Stansell, and Sharon Thompson (New York: Monthly Review Press, 1983), 102.
13 See also, in this volume, Daniel Rivers, "Families."
14 For a broader discussion of the transnational in queer history, see, in this volume, Emily Hobson, "Thinking Transnationally, Thinking Queer."
15 For a more extended discussion of these tensions, see, in this volume, Jen Manion, "Language, Acts, and Identity in LGBT History."
16 For more on the queer history of archives, see, in this volume, Kate Eichhorn, "Queer Archives: From Collections to Conceptual Framework."
17 Joan Nestle, "Who Were We to Do Such a Thing? Grassroots Necessities, Grassroots Dreaming: The LHA in Its Early Years," *Radical History Review* 122 (May 2015): 236.

Further Reading

Acosta, Katie L. "Lesbianas in the Borderlands: Shifting Identities and Imagined Communities." *Gender & Society* 22, no. 5 (October 2008): 639–659.
Alexander, M. Jacqui. *Pedagogies of Crossing: Meditations on Feminism, Sexual Politics, Memory, and the Sacred.* Durham: Duke University Press, 2005.
Anzaldúa, Gloria. *Borderlands/La Frontera: The New Mestiza.* San Francisco: Spinsters/Aunt Lute, 1987.
Anzaldúa, Gloria, ed. *Making Face, Making Soul/Haciendo Caras: Creative and Critical Perspectives by Feminists of Color.* San Francisco: Aunt Lute Books, 1995.
Banner, Lois. *Intertwined Lives: Margaret Mead, Ruth Benedict, and Their Circle.* New York: Knopf, 2003.
Beemyn, Brett. *Creating a Place for Ourselves.* New York: Routledge, 1997.
Boyd, Nan. *Wide-Open Town: A History of Queer San Francisco to 1965.* Berkeley: University of California Press, 2003.
Boyd, Nan. "Bodies in Motion: Lesbian and Transsexual Histories," in *A Queer World: The Center for Lesbian and Gay Studies Reader*, Martin Duberman, ed., 134–152. New York: New York University Press, 1997.

Canaday, Margot. *The Straight State: Sexuality and Citizenship in Twentieth-Century America*. Princeton: Princeton University Press, 2009.

Castle, Terry. *The Apparitional Lesbian: Female Homosexuality and Modern Culture*. New York: Columbia University Press, 1993.

Cleves, Rachel Hope. *Charity and Sylvia: A Same-Sex Marriage in Early America*. New York: Oxford University Press, 2014.

Cook, Blanche Weisen. *Eleanor Roosevelt: Volume One 1884–1933*. New York: Viking, 1992.

Cook, Blanche Weisen. *Eleanor Roosevelt: Volume 2, The Defining Years, 1933–1938*. New York: Viking, 1999.

Cott, Nancy F. *Public Vows: A History of Marriage and the Nation*. Cambridge, MA: Harvard University Press, 2000.

Cvetkovich, Ann. *An Archive of Feelings: Trauma, Sexuality, and Lesbian Public Cultures*. Durham: Duke University Press, 2003.

De Lauretis, Teresa. *The Practice of Love: Lesbian Sexuality and Perverse Desire*. Bloomington: Indiana University Press, 1994.

DeLauretis, Teresa. "The Essence of the Triangle Or, Taking the Risk of Essentialism Seriously: Feminist Theory in Italy, the U.S., and Britain." *Differences: A Journal of Feminist Cultural Studies* 1 (1989): 3–37.

D'Emilio, John. *Sexual Politics, Sexual Communities: The Making of a Homosexual Minority in the United States, 1940–1970*. Chicago: University of Chicago Press, 1983.

D'Emilio, John, and Estelle B. Freedman. *Intimate Matters: A History of Sexuality in America*. New York: Harper & Row, 1988.

De Veaux, Alexis. *Warrior Poet: A Biography of Audre Lorde*. New York: W.W. Norton, 2004.

Duggan, Lisa. *Sapphic Slashers: Sex, Violence, and American Modernity*. Durham: Duke University Press, 2000.

El-Tayeb, Fatima. "'Gays who Cannot Properly Be Gay': Queer Muslims in the Neoliberal European City." *European Journal of Women's Studies* 19, no. 1 (2002): 79–95.

Enszer, Julie R. "The Whole Naked Truth of Our Lives: Lesbian Feminist Print Culture from 1969 through 1989." PhD diss, University of Maryland, 2013.

Faderman, Lillian, ed. *Chloe Plus Olivia: An Anthology of Lesbian Literature from the Seventeenth Century to the Present*. New York: Viking, 1994.

Faderman, Lillian. *The Gay Revolution*. New York: Simon & Schuster, 2015.

Faderman, Lillian. *Odd Girls and Twilight Lovers: A History of Lesbian Life in Twentieth-Century America*. New York: Columbia University Press, 1991.

Faderman, Lillian. *Surpassing the Love of Men: Romantic Friendship and Love Between Women from the Renaissance to the Present*. 1st ed. New York: Morrow, 1981.

Feinberg, Leslie. *Stone Butch Blues*. Ithaca, NY: Firebrand Books, 1993.

Foster, Jeannette Howard. *Sex Variant Women in Literature*. New York: Vantage Press, 1956; Baltimore: Diana Press, 1975; Tallahassee, FL: Naiad Press, 1985.

Foucault, Michel. "Nietszche, Genealogy, History," in *The Essential Foucault: Selections from Essential Works of Foucault, 1954–1984*, eds. Paul Rabinow and Nikolas Rose. New York: The New Press, 2003.

Freedman, Estelle. *Maternal Justice: Miriam Van Waters and the Female Reform Tradition*. Chicago: University of Chicago Press, 1996.

Gallo, Marcia. *Different Daughters: A History of the Daughters of Bilitis and the Rise of the Lesbian Rights Movement*. New York: Carroll & Graf, 2006.

Garber, Linda. *Identity Poetics: Race, Class, and the Lesbian-Feminist Roots of Queer Theory*. New York: Columbia University Press, 2001.

Gilmore, Stephanie. *Groundswell: Grassroots Feminist Activism in Postwar America*. New York: Routledge, 2012.

Gopinath, Gayatri. *Impossible Desires: Queer Diasporas and South Asian Public Cultures*. Durham: Duke University Press, 2005.

Grahn, Judy. *Another Mother Tongue: Gay Words, Gay Worlds*. Boston, MA: Beacon Press, 1984.

Grahn, Judy. *Blood, Bread, and Roses: How Menstruation Created the World*. Boston: Beacon Press, 1993.

Grahn, Judy. *The Highest Apple: Sappho and the Lesbian Poetic Tradition*. San Francisco, CA: Spinsters, Ink, 1985

Grier, Barbara. *Lesbiana: Book Reviews from the Ladder, 1966–1972*. Reno: Naiad Press, 1976.

Grier, Barbara. *The Lesbian in Literature*. 3rd ed. Tallahassee: Naiad Press, 1981.

Grosz, Elizabeth. "The Labors of Love," in *Feminism Meets Queer Theory*, eds. Elizabeth Weed and Naomi Schor, 292–314. Bloomington: Indiana University Press, 1997.

Halberstam, Judith. *In a Queer Time and Place: Transgender Bodies, Subcultural Lives*. New York: New York University Press, 2005.

Halberstam, Judith. *Female Masculinity*. Durham: Duke University Press, 1998.

Hanhardt, Christina B. *Safe Space: Gay Neighborhood History and the Politics of Violence*. Durham: Duke University Press, 2013.

Heaney, Emma. "Women-Identified Women: Trans Women in 1970s Lesbian Feminist Organizing." Special Issue on Trans/Feminisms. *TSQ: Transgender Studies Quarterly* 3, no. 1/2 (2016): 137–145.

Hernández, Daisy. *A Cup of Water Under My Bed*. Boston: Beacon Press, 2015.

Howard, John. *Men Like That: A Southern Queer History*. Chicago: University of Chicago Press, 2001.

Katz, Jonathan. *Gay American History: Lesbians and Gay Men in the U.S.A.: A Documentary*. New York: Crowell, 1976.

Kennedy, Elizabeth Lapovsky, and Madeline D. Davis. *Boots of Leather, Slippers of Gold: The History of a Lesbian Community*. New York: Routledge, 1993.

Kent, Kathryn R. *Making Girls into Women: American Women's Writing and the Rise of Lesbian Identity*. Durham: Duke University Press, 2002.

Lanser, Susan. *The Sexuality of History: Modernity and the Sapphic, 1565–1830*. Chicago: University of Chicago Press, 2014.

Littauer, Amanda H. *Bad Girls: Young Women, Sex, and Rebellion before the Sixties*. Chapel Hill: University of North Carolina Press, 2015.

Lorde, Audre. *A Burst of Light: Essays*. Ithaca: Firebrand Books, 1988.

Lorde, Audre. *Sister Outsider: Essays and Speeches*. Berkeley: Crossing Press, 1984.

Lorde, Audre *Zami: A New Spelling of My Name*. Trumansburg, NY: Crossing Press, 1982.

Love, Heather. *Feeling Backward: Loss and the Politics of Queer History*. Cambridge, MA: Harvard University Press, 2007.

Luibhéid, Eithne, and Lionel Cantú, eds. *Queer Migrations: Sexuality, U.S. Citizenship, and Border Crossings*. Minneapolis, MN: University of Minnesota Press, 2005.

Middlebrook, Diane. *Suits Me: The Double Life of Billy Tipton*. New York: Houghton Mifflin, 1998.

Mims, La Shonda. "Lesbian History in Charlotte and Atlanta." PhD diss, University of Georgia, 2012.

Moraga, Cherríe L. *A Xicana Codex of Changing Consciousness: Writings, 2000–2010*. Durham, NC: Duke University Press Books, 2011.

Moraga, Cherrie. *Loving in the War Years: Lo Que Nunca Paso Por Sus Labios*. Cambridge: South End Press, 2000.

Moraga, Cherríe, and Gloria Anzaldúa, eds. *This Bridge Called My Back: Writings by Radical Women of Color*. New York: Kitchen Table, Women of Color Press, 1983.

Passet, Joanne Ellen. *Sex Variant Woman: The Life of Jeannette Howard Foster*. Cambridge, MA: Da Capo Press, 2008.

Passet, Joanne Ellen. *Indomitable: The Life of Barbara Grier*. Tallahassee, FL: Bella Books, 2016.

Prins, Yopie. *Victorian Sappho*. Princeton, NJ: Princeton University Press, 1999.

Quinn, Rachel Afi. "This Bridge Called the Internet: Black Lesbian Feminist Activism in Santo Domingo" in *Transatlantic Feminisms: Women and Gender Studies in Africa and the Diaspora*, eds., Rodriguez, Cheryl R., Dzodzi Tsikata, and Akosua Adomako Ampofo, 25–44. Lexington Books, 2015.

Rich, Adrienne. *On Lies Secrets, and Silence*. New York: W. W. Norton, 1979.

Rich, Adrienne. *Blood, Bread, and Poetry: Selected Prose 1979–1985*. Reissue edition. W. W. Norton & Company, 1994.

Rivers, Daniel Winunwe. *Radical Relations: Lesbian Mothers, Gay Fathers, and Their Children in the United States since World War II*. Chapel Hill: University of North Carolina Press, 2015.

Rubin, Gayle. *Deviations: A Gayle Rubin Reader*. Durham: Duke University Press, 2011.

Rupp, Leila J. *A Desired Past: A Short History of Same-Sex Love in America*. Chicago: University of Chicago Press, 1999.

Rupp, Leila J. *Sapphistries: A Global History of Love between Women*. New York: New York University Press, 2009.

Smith, Martha Nell. *Rowing in Eden: Rereading Emily Dickinson*. Austin: University of Texas, 1992.

Smith-Rosenberg, Carroll. "The Female World of Love and Ritual: Relations between Women in Nineteenth-Century America." *Signs* 1, no.1 (1975): 1–29.

Somerville, Siobhan. *Queering the Color Line: Race and the Invention of Homosexuality in American Culture*. Durham: Duke University Press, 2000.

Starhawk. *The Spiral Dance: A Rebirth of the Ancient Religion of the Great Goddess.* New York: HarperOne, 1989.

Stein, Arlene. *Sex and Sensibility: Stories of a Lesbian Generation.* Berkeley: University of California Press, 1997.

Stein, Marc. *City of Sisterly and Brotherly Loves: Lesbian and Gay Philadelphia, 1945–1972.* Philadelphia: Temple University Press, 2004.

Stone, Amy L, and Jaime Cantrell. *Out of the Closet, into the Archives: Researching Sexual Histories.* Albany: SUNY Press, 2015.

Stryker, Susan and Talia M. Bettcher. "Introduction: Trans/Feminisms." Special Issue on Trans/Feminisms. *TSQ: Transgender Studies Quarterly* 3, no. 1/2 (2016): 5–14.

Terry, Jennifer. *An American Obsession: Science, Medicine, and Homosexuality in Modern Society.* University of Chicago Press, 1999.

Thorpe, Roey. "The Changing Face of Lesbian Bars in Detroit, 1938–1965," in *Creating a Place for Ourselves,* ed. Brett Beemyn. New York: Routledge, 1997.

Vicinus, Martha. *Intimate Friends: Women Who Loved Women, 1778–1928.* Chicago: University of Chicago Press, 2004.

Warner, Sara. *Acts of Gaiety: LGBT Performance and the Politics of Pleasure.* Ann Arbor: University of Michigan Press, 2012.

Weed, Elizabeth, and Naomi Schor. *Feminism Meets Queer Theory.* Bloomington, IN: Indiana University Press, 1997.

Weeks, Jeffrey. *Coming out: Homosexual Politics in Britain from the Nineteenth Century to the Present.* London; New York: Quartet Books, 1977.

Wekker, Gloria. *The Politics of Passion: Women's Sexual Culture in the Afro-Surinamese Diaspora.* Columbia University Press, 2006.

Wieringa, Saskia, and Ruth Morgan. *Tommy Boys, Lesbian Men and Ancestral Wives.* Johannesburg: Jacana, 2005.

Williams, Cristan. "Radical Inclusion: Recounting the Trans Inclusive History of Radical Feminism." Special Issue on Trans/Feminisms. *TSQ: Transgender Studies Quarterly* 3, no. 1/2 (2016): 254–258.

Wu, Judy Tzu-chun. *Doctor Mom Chung of the Fair-Haired Bastards: The Life of a Wartime Celebrity.* Berkeley: University of California Press, 2005.

Zimmerman, Bonnie, ed. *Lesbian Histories and Cultures: An Encyclopedia.* New York: Garland Publishers, 2000.

Zimmerman, Bonnie. *The Safe Sea of Women: Lesbian Fiction, 1969–1989.* Boston, Mass: Beacon Press, 1990.

19

BISEXUAL HISTORY

Let's Not Bijack Another Century

Loraine Hutchins

> When the gay theologians tell us that our forefather David must have been a homosexual because he loved Saul's son Jonathan 'as his own soul' they frequently forget to tell us that he also had no less than eight wives and assorted concubines . . . and he is not the only bisexual this has happened to . . . [O]f history's hijacked bisexuals[,] 'bijacked' might be an appropriate term.
>
> *Rachel Haggen-Holt and Sarah Haggen-Holt[1]*

People loving more than one gender are often claimed by a monosexual paradigm that assumes the focus of their attraction as *either* heterosexual or homosexual, rather than as multiple. As gay, lesbian, queer and arguably trans histories/identities have gained attention in recent years, monosexist assumptions continue to burden bisexual history. This erasure of people's complex desires, feelings, and experiences renders bisexuals invisible, perpetuates the telling of only partial stories, and stifles innovative ways of interpreting the past. This silencing is perpetuated in classrooms across this country, in historical scholarship and analysis, even in so-called LGBT (or queer) history. The bisexual part of the history is loudly absent.[2]

As Haggen-Holts' quote leading the essay highlights, the most obvious form of erasure is the historical *mis*labeling of people known to have attraction to more than one gender. From reading most LGBT history texts it would be understandable for one not to know, for instance, that some of the key leaders of the Stonewall uprising and the Pride celebrations it engendered, such as Sylvia Rivera and Brenda Howard, had significant erotic relationships with more than one gender and/or identified as bi.[3] One would not learn that the first student homophile group in the United States, founded at Columbia University in 1968, was started by a bisexually identified man, or that bisexuals David Lourea and Cynthia Slater were key leaders of the earliest public health response to AIDS.[4] As journalist Eliel Cruz documents, gay and mainstream media repeatedly mislabeled as gay Robyn Ochs, one of the leaders in the marriage equality movement and part of the first same-sex couple to marry in Massachusetts. Ochs is a popular and nationally known bi speaker. African American activist, poet, and essayist June Jordan wrote openly about being bisexual, yet her bisexuality and its political importance are often erased or glossed over. Even her official bio on her posthumous website hails her participation in "the gay and lesbian rights movement," but nothing about her bi identity and related activism.

Indeed, many of those who loved more than one gender throughout the centuries of Western civilization—Sappho, Hans Christian Andersen, Shakespeare, Edna St. Vincent Millay, Virginia Woolf, James Baldwin, Margaret Mead, Eleanor Roosevelt, Victoria Woodhull, Billie Holiday, Oscar Wilde, John Maynard Keynes, Freddie Mercury, Katherine Hepburn, Mae West, Walt Whitman, Leonard Bernstein, Maya Angelou, Alice Walker, the list goes on and on—have been labeled gay or straight when neither is a full characterization of their loves and lives.

Erasure goes beyond mislabeling of bisexual people in history. In 2000, legal scholar Kenji Yoshino's groundbreaking essay, "The Epistemic Contract of Bisexual Erasure," argued that self-identified heterosexuals and gays and lesbians share overlapping interests in the erasure of bisexuality that has lead them into unseeing, or downplaying, the recognition of bisexuality. At the moment of contact with bisexuality, many scholars render bisexuality invisible or marginal because it makes monosexual orientations and binary sex/gender categories more coherent and, thus, more straightforward as objects of study. Unchallenged, the violence, misrecognition, and inaccuracies that come from such "epistemic contracts" remains invisible. Both for the viability of bisexual people and for more nuanced scholarship, Yoshino calls for the contestation of such erasures.

How does historical scholarship contribute to this contemporary dilemma? What are the historical reasons for the persistence of contemporary bisexual erasure in epistemic contracts? It has doubtless been historically important both to establish the validity of and make visible same-sex relations and to expose how what Adrienne Rich terms "compulsory heterosexuality" has historically hidden and subordinated homoerotic affinities. Gay liberation and feminism's second wave raised these issues decades ago.[5] Much ink has been spilled in feminist scholarship and LGBT/Queer studies on how binaries necessarily construct hierarchies of stronger/weaker opposing poles. Yet the discipline of history remains largely stuck in the either/or binary of gay or straight at the cost of streamlining bisexuality out of existence. Rejecting one lie (heteronormativity) by adding another (mononormativity) fails to recognize the entirety of people's relationships, identities, experiences, and thus fails as accurate historical documentation. To tell the whole story, we must first understand how bisexual erasure's roots in western sexology shapes approaches to queer history. We also must interrogate why this eclipsing continues. Finally, we need to examine the costs of bijacking history for the culture as a whole. For teachers and scholars to make bisexualities visible, a re-examination of the definitions that perpetuate this erasure must occur.

Bisexual Erasure's Roots in Western Sexuality Research

Historically, the word *bisexual* has multiple, contradictory meanings. Across 150 years, scientists and academics have used *bisexual* to mean everything from intersex (formerly hermaphrodite, i.e. a being possessing biologically aspects of more than one sex) to someone attracted to more than one sex and/or gender. Prior to the late nineteenth century, sexology did not divide humanity into homosexual and heterosexual categories, nor did individuals particularly conceptualize themselves through orientation labels related to sexuality's medicalization. It was, however, quite clear what fell inside the bounds of acceptability and not. As Jonathan Ned Katz details, discourse on identities and labels that emerged in the late 1800s as the new discipline of sexology developed coined terms such as *homosexuality*, *heterosexuality*, and, to a lesser extent, *bisexuality* and was a significant step forward. It allowed for the recognition of sexual orientation and desire, separate from a given and fixed gender identity (where men were assumed to be identified and defined as male, by their anatomy, at birth, and only attracted to women, and vice versa). *Heterosexuality*, however, did not originally mean someone attracted to a different sex. It wasn't used to label people who fit the social norm, or majority, as the word is used today. Rather, it described people labeled as highly sexed, those *not* interested in settling down and creating family. *Homosexuality* conflated gender inversion with same-sex attraction, presuming that any relationship has to contain one *playing* the man and one *playing* the woman; a function of essentialist views of sex and gender. This use of homosexuality described same-sex attraction as a deviant characteristic of human behavior and pathologized those labels of such types as unnatural, confused, and/or gender-reversed.[6]

Sexologists around the same time period in Europe coined *bisexual* to mean what we now call intersex, that is, people with some degree of male and female physiology, babies born with physical attributes of more than one sex. However, this definition, relating to external genital anatomy viewed at birth, says nothing about to whom the child will be attracted. Children who appeared hermaphroditic were considered to be developmentally arrested. Similarly, Freud and other psychoanalytical sexologists also believed that those attracted to more than one gender were more child-like, and could remain arrested in a phase that others would "grow out of." The majority of early twentieth-century sexologists adopted Freud's infantile and/or "primitive" polymorphous perversity theories, thus assuming bisexuality was more related to undifferentiated desire and pleasure. They contrasted this with the supposedly more mature, focused desire which found its orientation in clear object choice toward males or females, only.

As historian Steven Angelides explains, both intersex and polymorphous perversity models of "bisexuality" paint this orientation as "less evolved," stuck in an evolutionary past of Darwinian "primordial hermaphroditism." This construct infantilizes everyone but heterosexual white men.

> [B]lacks, women, children and homosexuals were thought to be the effect of an unsuccessful evolution, closer to, or retaining many more elements of, the originary (pre-historic) bisexuality of the human race and individual embryo. . . . Within this framework, therefore, the axes of race, age, gender, and sexuality were defined and aligned by their very *relation* to bisexuality.[7]

Angelides argues that since the late 1800s, mixed physiological and psychic "bases" for bisexuality provided the axis to establish the "opposite" camps of homosexual and heterosexual. This is important. Although often eclipsed/erased/dismissed, bisexuality serves as the unacknowledged axis supporting the binary of supposedly exclusive same and other-sexed attractions. It also implies that the parallel ("same" or "opposite") attraction requires binary maleness and female-ness instead of a spectrum of genders. As Kate Millet, another bi second-wave feminist often mislabeled as lesbian, famously said, "homosexuality was invented by a straight world dealing with its own bisexuality," and therefore heterosexuality needs homosexuality, so-called, to reassure itself that it is the norm, by defining the "Other" as the "abnormal" opposite.[8] The illusion that there is no (authentic and/or mature) middle ground is essential to maintain these hierarchical, binary frameworks of orientation and gender. Even today, early sexology's marginalization of bisexuality unfortunately still serves, Angelides asserts, as "the defining mark of Gay and Lesbian history writing," with a "methodological reliance on an identity paradigm that requires a distinction between sexual behavior and identity."[9] Few queer historians have fully grappled with the implications of Angelides's scholarship for the way of seeing sexuality and gender categories, identities, behaviors, cultures, politics, and dynamics.

How Bisexual Erasure Continues

Although mid-twentieth-century researcher Alfred Kinsey is often described as the sexologist who substantiated the prevalence of homosexuals in the US population, he eschewed dividing people into identity categories, preferring to simply catalogue his subjects' various sexual behaviors. Kinsey famously said, "the world is not divided into sheep and goats," yet in much queer history writing, when same-sex activity occurs as part of a bisexual context it often vanishes into *hetero* or *homo* activity, classification, or identification, as when same-sex sexual expression gets rounded up to "homosexual acts."[10] This languaging erases bisexual people from history and lumps any same-sex sexual activity into the homosexual category.[11]

There is a curious historical incuriousness about how *LGBT* originated as the acronym for our mass movement. The usual textbook narrative explains that "the gay liberation movement" became the "gay and lesbian rights movement" once women insisted upon it. Less well narrated is how L/G became LGB and how LGB added T. Not only did women insist on both bi feminism and bisexual inclusion in an expansive women-loving-women feminism in the 1970s, bisexual and transgender men and women in the 1980s demanded recognition within student-led groups on campuses and the AIDS care and protest movements. These culminated in mobilizing for more expansive visions, demands, and names for the 1987 National March on Washington for Lesbian and Gay Rights and the 1993 March on Washington for Lesbian, Gay, and Bi Equal Rights and Liberation.[12] The LGBT acronym was forged from the crucible of inter-generational, inter-racial, inter-gender, cross-regional/geographics/demographics organizing that became more and more imperative as the right wing backlash against all sexual and gender minorities intensified, and the so-called culture wars and Reagan Revolution wore on. The acronym flourished in the coalition politics of the 1990s and has been sustained through the early twenty-first century.[13] It works better than any other as an expansive marking of our interrelated struggles and passions. New generations increasingly understand that articulating the intersections of gender and orientation beyond binary limits are necessary to describe even basic reality.[14]

Although there has not (yet?) been a "Queer" March on Washington, there has definitely been a move to skip over the contradictions involved in resolving the binaries by just painting everything outside heteronormativity as "queer." Though the Q is useful and important, the changed terminology can, potentially, sidestep the fundamental binary trouble a truly bi-aware historical narrative and method would require. The term's confusion comes up in current history-writing and textbook glossary nomenclatures that similarly redefine bisexuality inherently as queer fluidity. We cannot "queer" our way out of this dilemma without committing bi erasure and callous disregard of the process.

When we are ignorant of and/or dismiss bi historic facts and interpretations, history itself suffers. One example is the way the historic significance of the 1984 presidential campaign is reported. Various historians cite news articles from the time that mention 150,000 people marching in the streets of San Francisco to encourage the Democrats to strengthen their support for gay and lesbian rights.[15] Left out is the key role in the event played by people such as publicly identified bisexual Alan Rockway. Especially since there was no field of bisexual history at the time, Rockway gets identified as gay by default. Rockway, a psychologist, in 1976 developed what is believed to be the first-ever undergraduate level course on bisexuality in the US, at Sonoma State University. He mobilized public opposition to Anita Bryant's 1977 Save The Children campaign in Florida, co-authored the first successful gay rights ordinance put to public vote in Dade County, Florida, and co-organized the related "gaycott" of Florida Orange Juice. In 1984, after he had moved back to California, Rockway helped co-found

BiPOL in San Francisco and worked to get bi activist Lani Ka'ahumanu onto the Democratic convention stage as a potential nominee for US vice president. The plan was to use the allotted fifteen minutes every vice-presidential nominee got onstage at the convention to talk about bisexual, lesbian, and gay family issues, the ERA, and demand AIDS research funding. Lesbian and gay march organizers intentionally excluded bi activists. BiPOL had previously secured the march's end site for their own rally, though, thus scoring a victory for bi visibility.[16]

Even John D'Emilio and Estelle Freedman's pathbreaking 1988 survey *Intimate Matters* only nods to bisexuality in its AIDS chapter. D'Emilio and Freeman's third edition, published in 2012, ends with the chapter, "Politics and Personal Life at the Turn of the Century," which should certainly highlight the role of the bisexual political movement from the 1970s through the 1990s. Instead, it discusses "the reconfiguration of the gay and lesbian movement" and neglects bi activism. The mention of a 1992 voter-approved anti-gay ballot measure in Colorado does not explain that it was historically significant for being the first of its kind to single out bisexuals alongside gay men and lesbians. What is doubly confusing in this book, like many similar texts, is that it alternates between using "LGBT" and "lesbian and gay," often with no recognition of the stakes in using one over the other. On one page "the agenda of the LGBT movement" is mentioned, followed on the very next page by the sentence, "Family was another important arena where gay men and lesbians pressed for recognition." In this slippage, bi and trans people suddenly didn't have families, or work within the LGBT family rights movement, which, of course, they did and do. An even more egregious example of bi erasure occurs in discussing Matthew Shepard's murder, saying, "the targeted killings of gay

Figure 19.1 BiPOL founding organizer Lani Ka'ahumanu wields her "Bi-Phobia Shield" as she marches with her contingent in the 1984 Lesbian and Gay Freedom Day Parade.

Photo by Arlene Krantz, courtesy of GLBT Historical Society.

men, lesbians, and transgender men and women continued in the new century."[17] Bisexuals escaped killing? Historical erasure haunts even our deaths.

Michael Bronski's *A Queer History of the US* is another history survey that sidesteps a fully bi-inclusive historical method and narrative. For example, Bronski notes that Emma Goldman and other turn-of-the-century radicals "established public reputations as sexually adventurous women with both males and females," but frames it in terms of "heterosexual and homosexual" relations.[18] Like Lillian Faderman before him (whom he cites), he stops short of exploring how leading bi lives informed radicals' politics. Such accounts highlight only the same-sex aspects of people's relations as significant. This is not about using the "right labels" for historical figures, but rather more fully understanding how gender variance, gender/sex roles expansion, sexual fluidity, a multiplicity of desires, and the variety of relationships and family forms matter to historical actors.

Bronski makes similar erasive commentaries in describing "lesbians and gay men in WWII," which presumably is a shorthand for both identity and practice, as well as postwar Beat culture, about which he writes that "heterosexual Beats such as Kerouac and Neal Cassady also had sex with men."[19] Were they "heterosexual?" Were they even "straight-identified?" While they were not "bisexual-identified," either, a bisexual historical analysis would have deepened Bronski's exploration of Beat sexuality. We must examine how middle grounds have been produced in different times and contexts. This requires historians of sexuality to resist easy slippages into either "lesbians and gay men" as a descriptor of all those engaging in same-sex sexual activity or, for that matter, using "homosexuality" as the blanket descriptor for that activity. Do either of these approaches accurately account for those relations and activities in their context with other activities and identifications across genders by the same actors? Queer history demands precision about so many other aspects of sexuality—why does a bisexual method and narrative so rarely make it to the page?

It is frustrating how close some historians come to getting beyond the binary confines of the limited, inadequate gay/straight paradigm, even going so far as to be tentatively inclusive in their narratives of the past, yet still fall short of fully conceptualizing bisexual movement history as it actually happened. In *Rethinking the Gay and Lesbian Movement*, for instance, Stein stresses that in reviewing "the last seven decades of gay and lesbian history" it is important to not myopically focus only on LG identities, but rather shine the light on the much larger group who exhibit same-sex behaviors. Like many LGBT historians, he asks "why movements represent some constituencies better than others," and ventures that we "can reflect on how the movement has influenced and been influenced by sexual desires, acts, identities, and communities." He urges readers to think historically, to "explore how activists have understood same-sex sexuality as a fixed orientation or a minority, a universal potential in everyone, or both." He asks whether the movement has been concerned "primarily with sexual freedom for everyone or the interests of gays and lesbians specifically." These are all great points. But then he says, "We can compare gay and lesbian political organizing to parallel and intersecting efforts to organize adulterers, cohabitants, crossdressers, fornicators, masturbators, polyamorists, polygamists, pornographers, prostitutes, sadomasochists, sodomites, transgenders, and transsexuals."[20] In this expansively "queer" list, how do bisexuals and the organizing they have done throughout these decades not make the cut? This is simply erasure.

Notably, Stein then directly asks, "Why not refer to the movement as 'bisexual' as well?" He asserts that it would be worse to use "bisexual" alongside "gay and lesbian," because it could "constrain" the more inclusive meanings of those latter terms as "incorporating everyone who is sexually attracted to people of the same sex, regardless of whether they also have cross-sex attractions." He concludes that he's going to use gay and lesbian "expansively" in his book and reserve the term "bisexual" only "for moments when bisexuality became a subject of debate and discussion."[21] Debate and discussion by whom? Using the problematics of our provisional language as a rationale for overlooking a sustained bisexual historical method intersectionally with lesbian and gay—or queer—method means downplaying the organizing that bisexuals have been doing since the 1950s.

In some ways, Stein's decision to title his book *Rethinking the Gay and Lesbian Movement* and to refer to the movement as "gay and lesbian" throughout is not so much a problem of what is most historically accurate for the main period he examines—certainly before the late 1980s, many, particularly those who were not bisexual, in the movement called it "gay and lesbian" or "lesbian and gay." Rather, such a naming is a problem because of what its usage conceals, which is that there has been bisexual participation and shaping of the movement at every stage. Stein's decision to use "gay and lesbian" is especially frustrating because he does, indeed, address bisexuality throughout, from its early sexological usage as intersexuality and/or sexual in-betweenness, to the ways homophile, gay liberation, and lesbian feminist concepts and terminology sought to either exclude or embrace bisexual people and freedoms. At various points he also describes briefly bisexual-specific movement building from the 1970s through the 1990s.[22]

Yet the effects of Stein's usage of "gay and lesbian" as the main label results in disappearing bisexuals from spaces where they were active and visible. Stein writes, for example, that in "the 1970s and 1980s the number of gay and lesbian groups on college and university campuses expanded."[23] This would have been a perfect place to note how from the mid-1980s on there was a significant change in those groups' membership, self-definitions and chosen titles that included substantial efforts to include the word "bisexual" and, at times, the word "transgender" as well. As he mentions in his earlier book on Philadelphia, one of the earliest gay liberation student dances, held at Temple University in 1970, was expressly open to "bisexuals, homosexuals, liberated straights, lesbians and male gays, blacks, whites."[24] Yet in *Rethinking*, this vital aspect of student organizing is left untold, so the exclusivity of the categories of "gay" and "lesbian" remain functionally intact, against historical reality and the archive. Similarly, in *Rethinking*'s section on AIDS, while he acknowledges a 1980s protest of the television show *Midnight Caller* for its biphobia AIDS hysteria, he omits the fact that out HIV-positive bisexual men in San Francisco, New York, and other cities were some of the first educators who created early safer sex protocols and manuals for public health practitioners.[25]

Stein's work here includes bisexuality and bisexuals yet, in its overarching language use of "gay and lesbian," creates slippages into bi erasure. These obscure significant contributions to the movement by bisexual people, who, in the context of AIDS, died fighting to be recognized and to save lives. I single out Stein here not to suggest that as a historian he is particularly egregious in his bi erasure—quite the contrary. Rather, I do so to show how vexing the challenge is to get bisexual incorporation right analytically and consistently in work that principally gets conceived as limited to "gay and lesbian" only.

I challenge other queer historians to, first, realize that "queer" has *not* supplanted bi, historically (that is too lazy and inaccurate), and, second, examine their own scholarship in terms of how effectively they have conceptualized and described bisexuals, bisexuality, and bi organizing, culturally and politically. They should ask themselves, if they have not done so thoroughly and well, then why not?

Why Bi Erasure Continues

Since it has become customary to skip over bisexuality in favor of the more capacious identity label and historiographic descriptor of "queer," it is important that any chapter on bi erasure address this issue directly. Queer has been seized upon as a label because of its ambiguity and flexibility against normativity. However, it must be acknowledged that this is not the only reason it is used. Because bisexuality remains over-sexualized, objectified, trivialized, and retrograde, queer historians have tossed out "bisexual" in favor of "queer" even as they have held on to "lesbian and gay" or "LGBT" alongside it. A lot of people have tried to argue that labels such as queer make bi unnecessary in the writing of history. I beg to differ. We have not interrogated this dilemma enough nor evaluated how to dismantle it and prevent its continuing.

Biphobia and bi stigma in the present inform the ways in which the queer past gets described and known. Even bisexually identified people have internalized a lot of biphobia. The intensity of this stigma and marginalization is finally beginning to be substantiated in psychological literature. Disproportionate numbers of bisexual people suffer from drug addiction, suicidal ideation, unemployment, sexual assault, poverty, and many other challenges due to the costs of stigmatization in the dominant binary. New research increasingly shows that bisexuals are *more* likely than lesbians and gays to be closeted and un-accepted, *more* likely to suffer from negative stereotypes about who they are and how they live their lives.[26] I call upon historians of the queer past to reflect upon and take accountability for their complicity in this, whether conscious or unconscious. Calculating the collateral damage of erasure is a thankless and exhausting task, not to mention a re-traumatizing one. Consciously ignoring the fullness of people's real lives and loves to make a temporary political point is idiomatically bijacking. As a society, we still have not truly unpacked why we're stuck in these binary backwaters. The younger generation is moving forward, whether we come along or not. Will our histories be theirs? If, as Yoshino argues, "the number of bisexuals is greater than or comparable to the number of homosexuals," then "erasure occurs because the two dominant sexual orientation groups–self-identified straights and self-identified gays–have shared investments in that erasure.'[27] How can historians divest themselves from this erasure?

Several decades of using the LGBT acronym have us teaching from LGBT/Queer 101 texts that talk about "same-sex sexuality and/or gender nonconformity."[28] It's a huge step forward. Re-examining history in light of these insights has been a key part of it. Celebrate! Okay, now what are the next steps? True human sexual liberation is about this and more. What's the more? Queer historians talk about this in terms of how "LGBT" history focuses too much on confronting homophobia, without getting to its roots in heteronormativity, sort of like white liberals who confront racial prejudices and biases (the symptoms manifest in the racist system) without ever wrestling with the elements of white privilege, structural and institutionalized racism and the roots of white supremacy. But in this backlash age of conservative values masquerading as neoliberal redemption (let's accept marriage as is, with a few extra apps), we're not going to get very far because we've lost the radical roots of queer liberation to begin with.

As long as queer studies leap-frogs over the multiplicities of contradictions B/T presents it will not uncover the deep foundational level where oppression is rooted. Now emerging more visibly, the fluid, non-binary spectrums of erotic identities present the next generation of scholars with key critical challenges that have been largely unaddressed to date. Bi, poly, pan, and trans shake up assumptions about gender, for all of us conditioned in a cis- and monosexually obsessed culture the way it is currently structured.[29] Power relations between the sexes have to change, they just have to: feminists (bisexual and otherwise) have been saying this, gay men, lesbians, bisexuals, and trans people know it. If humans are easily attracted to more than one gender, if humans often, and perhaps increasingly, experience gender itself more fluidly, what does this say about our homo/hetero and female/male lenses on the past?

Gender is key, yes. But not in only the ways that genderqueer dispensing-with and beyond-gender advocates are rightfully demanding. The questions bisexualities raise about gender are different than the questions same-sex desire or gender-transition alone raise. They are deeply intersectional, and so must be addressed, analytically and historically, simultaneously. Talking about same-sex relationships and gender variance, especially in relation to each other, as some of the newer LGBT 101 textbooks do, is great. Still, we haven't yet learned to talk comfortably about both/and, about how *both* of these concepts—loving our own and allowing gender expression freedom, are related to each other and can only root and grow and thrive in a *larger* healthy culture of sexual and gender diversities. These two concepts—orientation diversity and gender diversity—must be part and parcel of a program for erotic liberation, for sex-positive education, for judicial and public policy guidelines that support all the ways that humans love and make healthy families, communities, cultures, societies.

Still Bi After All These Years . . .

"Bisexual Men should be put in concentration camps.
Showered with gas."
REALLY?
Ibrahim Abdurrahman Farajajé, in Recognize: The Voices of Bisexual Men[30]

This is *not* a quote from the distant past. In fact, Farajajé pulled this trolling attack on bi men from recent social media. Though it obviously gestures to the horrors of the Holocaust, it is a haunting and frightening reminder of how that history stays alive. In 2015, the American Institute on Bisexuality created the Still Bi campaign, featuring celebrities and ordinary people who appear, with photographs and brief statements, under the logo, "Still Bi," precisely to counteract the belief that bisexuality is merely a phase or something to be rounded up (down?) to gay or straight. Organizers and scholars in the bi movement have also claimed their place at the table in more and more venues: at White House roundtables on federal policy recommendations, academic and activist conferences focused on LGBTQ issues, and leading "unlearning biphobia" and "bi 101" trainings to national, state and local LGBTQ-oriented organizations, such as GLAAD, the Trevor Project, HRC and the National LGBTQ Taskforce.[31]

Despite these developments, longstanding structural and systemic issues persist. The bulk of philanthropic LGBT donations still go to projects serving middle-class white gay cisgender men, even while research data shows that they are the minority in the LGBTQ community. Similarly, the bulk of LGBTQ textbooks and more advanced studies still have a significant bi erasure problem. Not all legislative and policy regulations accurately reflect the needs of bisexual, fluid, pan, and poly people even when they have improved in serving the needs of gay/lesbian, and sometimes transgender, populations. It is a work in progress. This is a time of uncertainty. How might queer historians take up this task in their own scholarship and teaching? It remains for the next generation to guide the course of inclusion in the widest possible way. Fingers and toes all crossed, this individual, still bi after all these years, will never stop longing for more bi history chronicling. Will you do your part?

Notes

1 *Living It Out: A Survival Guide for Lesbian, Gay and Bisexual Christians and Their Friends, Families and Churches* (London: Canterbury Press, 2009), 27.

2 See, for example, Gerard Koskovich's recent lamentation that as of 2016, no Ph.D. history dissertations focusing "entirely or substantially on the history of bisexuality" had been completed in the US, and that "compared to homophile, gay-liberation, and lesbian-feminist cultures, bisexual publics may have taken less interest in using history as a political and cultural tool—or bisexual organizers may have faced more obstacles in uncovering historical evidence and in producing and transmitting historical knowledge." "The History of Queer History: One Hundred Years of the Search for the Share Heritage," *LGBTQ America: A Theme Study of Lesbian, Gay, Bisexual, Transgender, and Queer History*, ed. Megan E. Springate (Washington, DC: National Park Foundation, 2016), 04-35, 04-37. One recent corrective to this is Loraine Hutchins, "Making Bisexuals Visible," LGBTQ America: A Theme Study of Lesbian, Gay, Bisexual, Transgender, and Queer History, ed. Megan E. Springate (Washington, DC: National Park Foundation, 2016), 08-1-08-33.

3 Lani Ka'ahumanu and Loraine Hutchins, "New 25th Anniversary Introduction," *Bi Any Other Name: Bisexual People Speak Out*, rev. ed. (New York: Riverdale Press, 2015), 17.

4 Bob Martin (also called Stephen Donaldson or Donny the Punk) started the Columbia homophile group. He was having an affair with lesbian activist Martha Shelley, as documented in her October 12, 2003 interview with Kelly Anderson on file (Tape 2, 29) at the Sophia Smith Collection, Voices of Feminism Oral History Project, Smith College, Northampton, MA. Lourea and Slater, active in San Francisco's leather community before their deaths from AIDS-related causes, can be found at Faith Cheltenham, "The Bisexual History of HIV/AIDS, In Photos," LGBT Health Link, http://blog.lgbthealthlink.org/2015/01/29/the-bisexual-history-of-hivaids-in-photos. Accessed April 16, 2016.

5 For more on this period in queer history, see, in this volume, Whitney Strub, "Gay Liberation (1963–1980)."

6 For more that generally contextualizes sexology in relation to queer history of the era, see, in this volume, Elizabeth Clement and Beans Velocci, "Modern Sexuality in Modern Times (1880s–1930s)." For the longer history of the medicalization of queer sexualities and diverse genders, see, in this volume, Katie Batza, "Sickness and Wellness."

7 Stephen Angelides, *The History of Bisexuality* (Chicago: University of Chicago Press, 2001), 131.

8 Kate Millet, *Flying* (Champaign: University of Illinois Press, 2000 [1974]), 97.

9 Angelides, 6.

10 Alfred Kinsey et al., *Sexual Behavior in the Human Male* (Philadelphia: W.B. Saunders Co., 1948), 639.

11 Although there have been recent efforts in social science to expand beyond the gay/lesbian labeling confines for describing same-sex activity, these efforts have often bent themselves into pretzel shapes to avoid labeling bisexual behavior as bisexual. See Jane Ward's research on "dude sex" refined into her recent book, *Not Gay: Sex Between Straight White Men* (New York: New York University Press, 2015) and Tom Waidzunas, *The Straight Line: How the Fringe Science of Ex-Gay Therapy Reoriented Sexuality* (Minneapolis: University of Minnesota Press, 2015).

12 There was a heated debate the night the title of the 1993 march was chosen, with bisexual and transgender activists supporting each other to include B and T in the title. Transgender people were refused inclusion and bisexual activists were told the title could include the "Bi" word only, not the full spelling of "bisexual," which was considered "too sexual." From oral histories shared with the author by bi representatives at the meeting.

13 Emily Zak, "LGBPTQQIIAA—How We Got Here From Gay," Ms. Magazine blog, October 1, 2013, http://msmagazine.com/blog/2013/10/01/lgbpttqqiiaa-how-we-got-here-from-gay/. Accessed October 22, 2017. Marc Stein, *Rethinking the Gay and Lesbian Movement* (New York: Routledge, 2012), 6–7, 182–188, also details this evolution in naming.

14 For more on the politics and consequences of naming, see, in this volume, Jen Manion, "Language, Acts, and Identity in LGBT History."

15 For example, Stein, 175.

16 This history was recently detailed in the exhibit "Biconic Flashpoints: 4 Decades of Bay Area Bisexual Politics," GLBT History Museum, San Francisco, 2014, and further information about Rockway gathered from author's interview with Lani Ka'ahumanu, March 17, 2016.

17 John D'Emilio and Estelle Freedman, *Intimate Matters: A History of Sexuality in America*, 3rd ed. (Chicago: University of Chicago Press, 2012) 373, 375.

18 Michael Bronski, *A Queer History of the United States* (Boston: Beacon Press, 2012), 121, 151.

19 Bronski, 200.

20 Stein, 4.

21 Stein, 6.
22 Stein, 25, 28, 50, 84, 97, 122, 152. In his earlier study on Philadelphia, Stein similarly uses "lesbian and gay" to describe the city's movement and culture from the 1940s through the 1970s, which facilitates a kind of bisexual erasure, even as he incorporates more of the "b" between the covers. He takes care, for example, to note where the local homophile groups debated bisexual inclusion, where lesbian bar and political culture policed men's and women's bisexuality, and where some called for bisexual women's self-determination in the lesbian-feminist movement. Stein also names key movement actors as bisexual, countering their presumed enfolding into "lesbian and gay." Marc Stein, *City of Sisterly and Brotherly Loves: Lesbian and Gay Philadelphia, 1945–1972* (Chicago: University of Chicago Press, 2000), 98, 193, 198, 264, 338.
23 Marc Stein, *Rethinking the Gay and Lesbian Movement*, 201, 206.
24 Stein, *City of Sisterly and Brotherly Loves*, 328. For more on student group organizing around bisexuality, see Loraine Hutchins, "Making Bisexuals Visible," in *LGBTQ America: A Theme Study of Lesbian, Gay, Bisexual, Transgender, and Queer History*, ed. Megan E. Springate (Washington, DC: National Park Foundation and the National Park Service, 2016).
25 Stein, *Rethinking the Lesbian and Gay Past*, 150.
26 In public health, psychology, and sociology, these citations have been piling up in recent years. See the excellent slideshow at BiNet USA's website (www.binetusa.org Accessed October 22, 2017) and the summary in Bi Any Other Name's introduction to the 25th anniversary edition.
27 Kenji Yoshino, "The Epistemic COntarct of Bisexual Erasure" (200), Faculty Scholarship Series, paper 4384, http://digitalcommons.law.yale.edu/fss_papers/4384, 363.
28 This phrase is regularly used in *Finding Out: An Introduction to LGBT Studies*, the LGBT Studies 101 text by Michelle Gibson, Jonathan Alexander, and Deborah Meem (Thousand Oaks, CA: Sage Publications, 2013), but it is also used in a variety of other texts.
29 For more on a trans analytic and method for history, see, in this volume, Finn Enke, "Transgender History (and Otherwise Approaches to Queer Embodiment."
30 "Fictions of Purity," *Recognize: The Voices of Bisexual Men*, ed. Robyn Ochs and H. Sharif Williams (Boston: Bisexual Resource Center, 2014), 146.
31 Such trainings with predominately G/L-led organizations are not new. I have been involved with such efforts for about a quarter century, ever since 1993 when a delegation of us national bi leaders first met with the board of directors of the then National Gay and Lesbian Task Force (now the National LGBTQ Task Force). Resistance to real bi expansion and inclusion is deeply entrenched. Many subsequent meetings and repeated iterations have sometimes resulted in reports on bi youth (HRC) and bi health (the Task Force), or bi 101 manuals (HRC, GLAAD). Still, egregious phrases such as "gay and transgender" persist in LGBTQ organizational communications and are thus perpetuated to the general public.

Further Reading

Beemyn, Genny [Brett]. "The New Negro Renaissance, A Bisexual Renaissance: The Lives and Works of Angelia Weld Grimke and Bruce Nugent." In *Modern American Queer History*, 36–48. Philadelphia: Temple University Press, 2001.
——. "The Silence Is Broken: A History of the First Lesbian, Gay, and Bisexual College Student Groups." *Journal of the History of Sexuality* 12, no. 2 (2003): 205–223.
——. "Bisexuality, Bisexuals, and Bisexual Movements." In *LGBT: The Encyclopedia of Lesbian, Gay, Bisexual, and Transgender History*, ed. Marc Stein, 141–144. New York: Charles Scribners and Sons, 2003.
——. "Bisexual Movements." GLBTQ: An Online Encyclopedia, 2004. Archived at www.glbtqarchive.com. Accessed October 22, 2017.
BiNet USA. "A Brief History of the Bisexual Movement." c. 2006. www.binetusa.org/bihistory2.html. Accessed July 11, 2016.
Blow, Charles M. *Fire Shut Up in My Bones*. New York: Mariner Books. 2015.
Colker, Laura. *Hybrid: Bisexuals, Multiracials, and Other Misfits Under American Law*. New York: New York University Press, 1996.
Cruz, Eliel. "When Bisexual People Get Left Out of Marriage." *The Advocate*, August 26, 2014, www.advocate.com/bisexuality/2014/08/26/when-bisexual-people-get-left-out-marriage. Accessed October 21, 2017.

Donaldson, Stephen. "The Bisexual Movement's Beginnings in the 70s: A Personal Retrospective." In *Bisexual Politics: Theories, Queries and Visions*, ed. Naomi Tucker, 31–45. New York: Harrington Park Press, 1995.

Eisner, Shiri. *Bi: Notes for A Bisexual Revolution*. Berkeley: Seal Press. 2013.

Faderman, Lillian. *Odd Girls and Twilight Lovers: A History of Lesbian Life in Twentieth-Century America*. New York: Penguin Books, 1992.

Fox, Ronald. *Current Research on Bisexuality*. New York: Routledge, 2004.

Hall, Donald E. and Jagose, Annamarie, eds. *The Routledge Queer Studies Reader*. New York: Routledge, 2013.

Hemmings, Clare. *Bisexual Spaces: A Geography of Sexuality and Gender*. New York: Routledge, 2002.

Hutchins, Loraine. "Making Bisexuals Visible." In *LGBTQ America: A Theme Study of Lesbian, Gay, Bisexual, Transgender, and Queer History*, ed. Megan E. Springate. Washington, DC: National Park Foundation and the National Park Service, 2016.

Jordan, June. "A New Politics of Bisexuality." In *Technical Difficulties: African-American Notes on the State of the Union*. New York: Vintage, 1994.

Katz, Jonathan Ned. *The Invention of Heterosexuality*. Chicago: University of Chicago Press, 2007.

Lovaas, Karen E., Elia, John P., and Yep, Gust A. *LGBT Studies and Queer Theory: New Conflicts, Collaborations, and Contested Terrain*. New York: Harrington Park Press, 2006.

MacDowell, Lachlan. "Historicizing Contemporary Bisexuality." *Journal of Bisexuality* 9 (2009): 3–15.

Marcus, Nancy. "Bridging Bisexual Erasure in LGBT Rights Discourse and Litigation." *Michigan Journal of Gender and Law* 22, no. 2. (2015): 291–305.

Monro, Surya. *Bisexuality: Identities, Politics and Theories*. New York: Palgrave Macmillan. 2013.

Munro, Suyra, Hines, Sally, and Osborne, Antony. "Is Bisexuality Invisible? A Review of Sexualities Scholarship, 1970–2015." *Sociological Review* (2017): 1–19.

Pallotta-Chiarolli, Maria. *Border Sexualities, Border Families in Schools*. Lanham, MD: Rowman and Littlefield, 2008.

Rich, Adrienne. "Compulsory Heterosexuality and Lesbian Existence." *Signs* 5, no. 4 (1980): 661–660.

Rupp, Leila J. and Freeman, Susan K, eds. *Understanding and Teaching U.S. Lesbian, Gay, Bisexual, and Transgender History*. Madison: University of Wisconsin Press, 2014.

Rust, Paula C. *Bisexuality and the Challenge to Lesbian Politics: Sex, Loyalty and Revolution*. New York: New York University Press, 1995.

Rust, Paula C. Rodriguez. *Bisexuality in the United States: A Social Science Reader*. New York: Columbia University Press, 1999.

Schneiderman, Jason, ed. *Queer: A Reader for Writers*. New York: Oxford University Press. 2016.

Serano, Julia. *Excluded: Making Queer and Feminist Movements More Inclusive*. San Francisco: Seal Press. 2013.

Stimpson, Catharine R. and Herdt, Gilbert, eds. *Critical Terms for the Study of Gender*. Chicago: University of Chicago Press, 2014.

Storr, Merl. *Bisexuality: A Critical Reader*. New York: Routledge. 1999.

Suresha, Ron, ed. *Bisexual Perspectives on the Life and Work of Alfred C. Kinsey*. New York: Routledge, 2010.

Ulrich, Lindasusan. *Bisexual Invisibility: Impacts and Recommendations*. San Francisco: San Francisco Human Rights Commission LGBT Advisory Committee, 2011.

Wiegman, Robyn. *Object Lessons*. Durham: Duke University Press, 2012.

Yoshino, Kenji. "The Epistemic Contract of Bisexual Erasure". Faculty Scholarship Series. Paper 4384. 2000. http://digitalcommons.law.yale.edu/fss_papers/4384. Accessed October 23, 2017.

20

QUEER OF COLOR ESTRANGEMENT AND BELONGING

Nayan Shah

A conventional history of sexual diversity and gender identity in the United States emphasizes a progressive narrative moving from obscurity to identity, from isolation to community, and from fear to liberty.[1] Both personally and structurally, gender variant and sexually non-normative people experience alienation, exclusion and violence. In the *American Heritage Dictionary*, to estrange is an active process of forcible dislocation that removes people from "an accustomed place or set of associations." It sours the grounds of shared membership by sowing feelings of hostility, distrust, and indifference.[2] In North America, estrangement has, historically, been a systemic and group condition that has been particularly divided along racial and ethnic fault lines. For those gender variant and sexually non-normative people marked by nonwhite racialization, estrangement has long been aggravated, persistent and intensified.

In 1990, black gay poet and activist Essex Hemphill claimed he could "be gay in only a few cities in this country, but I'm Black everywhere I go."[3] Where interpersonal estrangement operates doubly as both forcible dislocations from one's birth family/community and from normative social conventions, queer people of color must create new resources and networks in order to navigate the hypervisibility of race and the situational invisibility of sexual desire, activity, relationality, and identity. While the experience can be felt as isolated and particular, systemic force accumulates and operates through the broad power towards targeted groups.

The history of sexuality and gender in the United States is inextricably bound to the history of racialization. Conquest, slavery, voluntary migration, segregation, exclusion, stratification, detention and the struggles to challenge disparity, inequity and subordination have shaped erotics, reproduction, identity and kinship across four centuries. This context of exclusion, violence and inequity has shaped the experiences of Indigenous, African, Latino and Asian peoples, and the durability of these racialized categories.

Estrangement operates through several technologies: colonial and imperial knowledge formation; state policing, incarceration and extralegal violence; subordination, exclusion and normalization. While these technologies have produced terrible conditions under which racialized people have been made to struggle, they have also produced grounds for, and strategies of, survival and belonging. Appreciating the operations of estrangement, its changing contexts, and the conditions though which is has produced forms of belonging and endurance opens up alternative ways of understanding the queer past. The technology of colonial and imperial knowledge production has been a transnational process of systemic cataloguing and organizing of mores, practices and embodiments of gender and sexual diversity into relentless hierarchies. Invidious comparison and contrasts by race, nation and geography developed out of the European encounter and conquest and, in the nineteenth and twentieth centuries, intensified into systemic and scientific organization. Processes of racialized and sexual classification pathologized bodies, cultures, and practices of racially subordinated peoples by unfavorably contrasting them with modern heteronormative Western European/white society. This corpus of visual, textual and sensory representations of sexual difference contributed to the fomenting and perpetuating of racial fantasies. These racialized knowledge systems heightened sex surveillance, policing, and punitive judgment of nonwhite peoples in ways that undergirded policy and governance. These, in turn, contributed to the ways in which indigenous peoples were dispossessed of land and contributed to the withholding of care or protection from African Americans, Asian Americans and Latino/as.[4]

Conquest, trade and enslavement were the contexts for the production of colonial knowledge in North America from the first moments of encounter. As Evan B. Towle and Lynn Marie Morgan explain, European colonization by English Protestants, French Catholics and Spanish Catholics led to the racialization of indigenous peoples in the Americas. Colonizers responded with revulsion and violence to everyday indigenous sexual relations, bodily comportment, dress and nudity. Mark Rifkin, Maurice Kenny, and Qwo-Li Driscoll describe how the ferocity of the violence, punitive humiliation and public shaming that defined behavior as lewd, immoral and shameful puzzled and frightened Native peoples. The processes of Christian conversion and colonial control uprooted and regulated Native peoples' sexuality, marriage, bodily comportment and lifeways. Deborah Miranda explains how Spanish missionaries and soldiers were threatened by the "abomination" of third-gender *joyas*, who blended male and female genders, and engaged in gendercide by violently exterminating, punishing and shaming *joyas*, and severing their spiritual and communal roles in California-indigenous communities. In the late twentieth century, the modern pan-Indian two-spirit movement's strategies of "archival reconstruction" have challenged the technologies of colonial knowledge production and reclaimed indigenous knowledge and practices to restore *joya* spiritual and social roles in indigenous communities.

Similarly, from the fifteenth to the mid-nineteenth century, enslaved Africans experienced sexual assault, denigration and terror as part of the pervasive structure of white domination and control.[5] As Aliyyah I. Abdur-Rahman details, these violences were justified by knowledge production based in mythologies of lascivious black sexuality and the need for colonial control and management of African peoples in North America. These, in turn, validated white extralegal violence and the continuation of rape and sexual assault, sexualized humiliation and pervasive violence in the struggles over emancipation and freedom during the late nineteenth and early twentieth centuries. An example of the scope of extralegal violence and the precarious application of justice was the Memphis Riots of 1866 and its aftermath. A former slave, Frances Thompson, was raped by a group of white men during the riots as part of broader systemic rape and violence visited upon black women and children. In a courageous move in the antebellum South, which denied that black women's sexual violation by white men could ever be considered rape, Thompson testified to a congressional committee investigating the riots, helping to call attention to the ongoing sexual exploitation of black women by white men. However, her testimony and that of other black women who had been raped in the riots was later discredited when it was discovered that Thompson had been born male-bodied. Here, as Hannah

Rosen explains, an audience already eager to disavow white sexual violence against black women found a ready cause for dismissal by declaring the impossibility of white male rape of a black man dressed as a woman.

Such struggles for African peoples in the US conjoined the technology of colonial knowledge production with the second technology of estrangement, namely the force of heightened policing, state incarceration, and the tacit encouragement of extralegal violence on people of color.[6] The repertoire of policing, extralegal violence and incarceration extended from black and indigenous peoples to racialized immigrants. Drawing upon colonial representations that suspected racialized men and women as prone to immoral behavior and criminal activity fueled fears of the dangers of interracial association. Policing deployed visual scrutiny and the geographical concentration of racialized locations to track mobility and activity. As I explore in *Stranger Intimacy*, in the early twentieth century, "foreign" and racialized migrants, tramps, and hoboes were subject to heightened police surveillance and arrests for vagrancy, disreputable assault, and sodomy. Moreover, Peter Boag emphasizes the cross-class relations and variations in rural and urban experience in the Pacific Northwest that hardened white middle-class and white and European immigrant working-class concerns about male sexual license. At the same time, these racializing relations served to consolidate modern heterosexual and homosexual sexual identities.

Starting in the late nineteenth century and intensifying in the early twentieth, the scrutiny over disreputable and immoral sex, and fears of sexual trafficking also heightened and targeted immigration and border policing of Asian and Latino/a women and men, as both Grace Pena Delgado and Eithne Luibhéid show. Police and border patrol also tacitly and explicitly ignored white mob violence through lynching, driving out campaigns, harassment and humiliation. Often, sexualized rationales were deployed to justify extralegal violence of racialized groups. Extra-legal assault, murder, robbery, and rape frequently went unchecked by police, and victims were denied legal prosecution or fair hearing in a judicial system exclusively populated with white men, and where testimony from Asian, Latinos, black and Native people was either denied or denigrated.

The third technology of estrangement, subordination and exclusion, relied upon legal, political and economic policies as well as knowledge production to enforce and extend exploitative racialization and its reach into diverse sexualities and genders.[7] The racialization of immigrants from Asia, the Middle East and Latin America drew upon strategies of labor exploitation and legal strategies of exclusion. The extension of segregation regimes required innovative bureaucratic and legal strategies, including denial of land tenancy, work contracts, political participation and citizenship status. From the nineteenth to mid-twentieth centuries, claiming that Asian and Latin American migration to the US were pernicious threats to democratic politics, economic distributions, and social morality justified the withholding of economic power and political representation.

Scholars such as David Eng, Frank Chin, Paul Chan, Richard Fung, Gina Marchetti, and Elaine Kim have critically interpreted the lurid and sensationalist imagery of Asian American bachelor "vice" to understand broader patterns of sexualized and gendered race-making that buttressed racial antipathy and segregation. Racial caricatures of effeminate men and treacherous women as well as subservient women that circulated in nineteenth- and twentieth-century media reinforced the perception of the "Oriental" race as gender atypical, sexually non-normative, and bereft of sexual agency. As Clare Sears demonstrates, US white men's deployment of cross-gender dress practices dovetailed with anti-immigrant politics, specifically through racializing, feminizing discourses that targeted Chinese residents for exclusion from the nation. Judy Wu shows how the "compulsory condition of 'deviance'" among the early generation of Asian Americans "indexes more than 'racial victimization'.'" It also produced the "opportunity for non-normative sexual exploration." Cultural representations of "Oriental" exoticism and vice "encouraged experimenteation and attraction across racial boundaries."[8]

The spaces, institutions, and practices that sustained social dynamics of mixing and non-normative sexualities emerged through different kinds of "queer domesticity" that counter, contest, upset, and challenge normative expectations and practices. Notwithstanding the alternative socialities generated, these queer domesticities and erotics also trafficked in a complex array of gender, class, age and race hierarchies and disparities.[9] Racially differentiating and then denying civic and legal protections to Native, African, Latino and Asian Americans contributed to the unchecked exploitation of laborers and reinforced a cartel of white supremacy. As I argue in *Stranger Intimacy*, this not only redistributed contingent and precarious membership/citizenship, it foreclosed upon most possibilities for interracial sociality—erotic or otherwise—that were egalitarian or at least not saturated with exploitation. As processes of estrangement hardened into color lines, intimacies between strangers as cross-cultural association diminished.

Strategies of Survival and Belonging

While the technologies of estrangement have produced a long history of violence to person-hood, relationality, and intimacy, they have never been totalizing. Estrangement has also inspired strategies of survival, coping, and belonging. Repertoires of possibility in claiming both privacy and publicity have created adhesiveness, refuge, and support in a hostile world.

A key class-differentiated strategy of survival for queer people was the practice of respect-ability and dissemblance. This drew upon and referenced dominant moral codes about bodily comportment, discretion, and self-control in sexual expression, mannerism, and practice. In order to succeed, others had to recognize one's respectability, which enabled one's discretion. For people of color, poor, and working-class people, and those who transgressed gender norms, such tactics were therefore more precarious than for those queer people whose bodies, mannerisms, and comportment cleaved more closely to the normative. Put another way, actualizing respectability required a discretion that, in turn, required successful claims to privacy.

Respectability strategies, including discretion, privacy, and the performance of conventional and respected gender roles, thus made up the materiality of class formations that served as a form of protection against unwanted attention. In the mid- and late nineteenth century, some free African Americans enjoyed, as did many members of the dominant society, the ideology and practice of separate spheres for women and men, which fostered the development of romantic and sometimes erotic same-sex friendships.[10] A glimpse of such a relationship in the black community is provided by the correspondence between two Connecticut freeborn women, domestic servant Addie Brown and schoolteacher Rebecca Primus, in the 1860s. Brown's preserved letters describe an intensely emotional and physical intimacy. Their families and friends supported their intimate friendship. However, to maintain social respectability, they were still expected to marry, as both women did reluctantly. As Farah Jasmine Griffin and Karen Brown assert, the two women positioned their committed and erotic love along a continuum of relationality that included courtships and marriages to men.

Queer biographies have offered unique case studies that demonstrate the complexities of navigating exoticism and experimentations with diverse gender and sexual subjectivities, as well as interracial same-sex romantic and friendship ties. Much of this scholarship challenges the presumption that human erotic desires and activities can be neatly distinguished as either heterosexual or homosexual, that desires and acts are consistent and static over life course, or that the bodies and intimacies involved can be easily fit into the gender binary. Amy Sueyoshi's recent biography of the poet Yone Noguchi emphasizes the mobility and complexity of race and national difference in erotic attraction and sexual desire over life's course, in Noguchi's affairs with white men and women. Sueyoshi reveals the expression of personal fantasies, frustrated intimacies, and sexual relations in conflict with social and cultural norms. She asserts that Noguchi found himself compelled—by white desires to orientialize him, a quest to belong in the intensely xenophobic US of the late nineteenth and early twentieth century, and changing laws and norms about interracial relationships—into a mixture of queer associations with men and women. Judy Wu's biography of Chinese-American doctor Margaret Chung similarly examines the range of emotional ties and romantic possibilities with women and men, and Chung's decisions to create a social and kinship network outside of respectable marriage. Wu addresses Chung's early- to mid-twentieth-century experiences of gender variance, erotic relations, and struggles to create and define kinship, household, and families of choice. Tolerance of gender and sexual variance could vary dramatically across scales of urban neighborhood, region, and nation, as Emily Skidmore examines in her exploration of the early-twentieth-century controversy over mixed race Ralph Kerwineo's female embodiment and marriage to a Polish immigrant woman. Their partnership had greater tolerance in their Milwaukee neighborhood, which respected Kerwineo's successful performance as masculine provider and South American immigrant. By contrast, the sensationalizing national press heightened his black and Native identities as related to Kerwineo's supposed gender deception and sexual seduction of innocent white women.

Beyond respectability and privacy, though, people of color claimed queer belonging through the strategic claiming and use of public space and commercial entertainment. In the late nineteenth and early twentieth centuries, US commercial entertainment and urban-rural migrant labor circulation fostered a variety of intensive, transitory and flexible interracial encounters and relationships.[11] Homosocial bunking and boarding houses, opium dens, gambling houses, and restaurants, and dating cultures, new urban amusements of cafes, cinemas, and arcades, all produced their own intimacies. Filipino, Japanese and Mexican men's participation in taxi-dance hall culture, and the social and political consequences has been the focal point for a rich array of studies. Scholars such as Linda Maram and Rhacel Parrenas have explored the race, gender performance, and romance in these working-class heterosocial and homosocial cultures. Strategies of suturing diverse people into belonging, familiarity, and affiliation based on shared public and commercial space sustained multi-racial encounter, meeting, and circulation. Over time, intensified policing of public "immoral sex" or illegal activity between men and between men and women prevented alternative socialities from functioning.

By the mid-twentieth century, this unevenly produced a divide between sexual and racially heterogenous meeting. This, in turn, helped to usher in the racialization of the white, heteronormative settled family world as the normative space of association. As John D'Emilio has shown, this normative social and political world was a precarious and shadowy site for interracial same-sex intimacy. Even in interracial pacifist and civil rights organizations in the 1950s and 1960s, black social justice organizer Bayard Rustin's arrests for sex with men in Pasadena and New York made it challenging for him to assume visible political leadership. The intense anti-gay climate of the era pushed him from the spotlight into behind-the-scenes roles in nonviolent direct action organizing in peace and civil rights movements.

Beginning in the 1910s and extending into the 1960s, though, new connections developed in urban interracial and cross-class entertainment cultures that featured and sustained and promoted sexual and gender diversity in the 1910s to 1940s. Scholars such as Hazel Carby, Chad Heap, Nan Boyd, and Angela Davis have detailed the nightclubs, female impersonation

Figure 20.1 Jiro Onuma (center), Akira Kakiuchi (right), and friend posing at Moriyama Studio in San
  Francisco's Japantown (c.1930s). Onuma lived a life as a working-class Nikkei gentleman
  bachelor and lover of men. His collection at the GLBT Historical Society contains the only
  known documentation of LGBT survivors of US internment of Japanese-Americans in
  World War II concentration camps.

Courtesy of GLBT Historical Society.

shows, blues and jazz clubs, speakeasies, rent parties, and hotel encounters in New York, Chicago,
St. Louis, Philadelphia Detroit, Los Angeles and San Francisco that created what Eric Garber
has dubbed "a spectacle of color." The black ball culture from the 1920s through the 1950s
also produced both communities of gender and sexual diversity and racialized spectacles for a
white audience.[12]

Roey Thorpe examines how African American lesbians living in the urban Northeast and
Midwest in the 1930s and 1960s socialized in house parties held in apartments and homes in
black communities. Communicated by word of mouth and financed by paying a cover fee at
the door, these house parties were opportunities to socialize with friends, dance, drink, and
eat home-cooked food despite race and gender segregation. White lesbian bars were often

alienating or notoriously racist. Few women generally had the capital or connections to own bars or acquire liquor licenses, and lesbian bars carried the risk of public exposure, police harassment and harassment from heterosexual men. Often interpersonal bias and structural estrangement thus led white lesbians to exclude black women or tacitly make them unwelcome. Bypassing the humiliation of racist gay bars and the general interdiction on same-sex public dancing, Black women often travelled between midwestern cities to attend parties and socialize. By the 1970s some of these informal hosted parties became business ventures.

From the 1980s through the 2000s, a widespread presumption in secular, urban, and progressive lesbian, gay, bisexual, and transgender communities held that traditional mores and conservative religious beliefs produced more antigay, biphobic, and antitrans antipathy in racial minority, ethnic and diasporic communities than in white, middle-class, US-born ones. The higher political and public visibility of predominantly white gay and lesbian urban communities, correspondingly, heightened a perception within communities of color of queer sexual and gender identities as contagious "white diseases." Furthermore, the general societal and specific gay subcultural climates of white superiority made it difficult for nonwhite racialized subjects to speak of homophobic violence in their communities. Queer of color critique offers a diagnostic of the power relations producing both these perceptions and their conditions, marking them as consequences of excess, contradiction and subversion of the uneven processes of normalization for communities of color and LGBT people.

Roderick A. Ferguson defines queer of color analysis as an interrogation of social formations as the intersections of race, gender, sexuality, and class, with particular interest in how those formations correspond with and diverge from nationalist ideals and practices. Queer of color analysis is a heterogeneous enterprise made up of women of color feminism, materialist analysis, poststructuralist theory, and queer critique. Genealogies of queer of color theory finds its roots in radical feminism in the 1970s and 1980s, AIDS and related experiences of loss during the 1980s and 1990s, and critical responses to racism and erasure in queer theory and the heterosexual dominance in ethnic studies scholarship from the 1970s through the present.[13] In the early twenty-first century, a critical mass of queer of color scholars began investigating the ways in which gender and sexuality figure in empire, global economic structures, immigration, citizenship, prisons, social welfare.[14]

Heteronormativity and homonormativity are central dilemmas for queer of color critique. They both traffic in strategies of discretion, respectability and survival that produce racialized and classed others against which to secure their normativity. The formation of a heteronormative middle-class zone of privacy required the support of an elaborate network of state regulations, judicial rulings, and police powers, and defined its survival against the "prejudicial exclusion of others from the rights of association or bodily autonomy."[15] Privacy is a class privilege that manages labor, polices space and produces privileged access to mobility, autonomy, and protection. Organized around exclusive habitation, it does the work of the idealized and contained nuclear family even as it conceals the domestic labor of working-class women and men who make such "private" households viable.

The intensification of the policing of the public space has long disproportionately impacted poor and brown queer people. This occurred in the nineteenth-century reforms to "clean up" urban streets to make them "safe" for white, middle-class women and children, then in the early twentieth-century production of segregated vice, entertainment districts, and housing, and again in the white flight suburbanization of the mid-twentieth century. In the late twentieth century, this intensification was exemplified by, for example, the refashioning of places such as Times Square as "family-friendly" as well as the flourishing of police-approved (or at least tolerated) gay ghettos. Each justified middle-class demand for comfort in public space and sought to minimize the unexpected encounter or confrontation. Policing produced the semblance of safety by pathologizing nonnormative persons and criminalizing certain social practices in ways disproportionately surveilled and prosecuted within a racialized system. The protection of white, heteronormative family society from the disordered, dangerous, and aberrantly gendered and sexed links up with local and state government harassment of Latino/as, Asian Americans, African Americans, and immigrants. The concept of normativity has been deployed as an anti-democratic tactic to restrain the viability of the border intimacies forged by heterogeneous association as well as sharply curtails access to resources, support and safety.

Another dimension of the racialized consequences of heteronormativity and discretion is the emergence of "down low" in contemporary media and popular culture to show how these portrayals reinforce troubling perceptions of black working-class sexualities. Both Jeffrey McCune and C. Riley Snorton advance how black sexuality is marked by hyper visibility and confinement, spectacle and speculation. "Down low" links blackness and queerness in the popular imagination and is just one example of how media and popular culture surveil and police black sexuality.

Lisa Duggan defines the term homonormativity as "a politics that does not contest dominant heteronormative assumptions and institutions, but upholds and sustains them, while promising the possibility of a demobilized gay constituency and a privatized, depoliticized gay culture anchored in domesticity and consumption."[16] Homonormativity is a claim for class security and privilege, tenuously joined to self-protection as well as recourse to state protection and resources. Because homonormativity holds out for some gay and lesbian subject-citizens the promise of equality, with the related reward of assimilation into aspirational models of the middle-class nuclear family, it shores up many of the founding assumptions of heteronormativity. Homonormativity's pervasive narrative of racial progress, inclusion, and color-blind meritocracy is premised upon unexamined assumptions of the respectable, propertied, family household as the model for national assimilation.[17] For the most normative among us, liberal societies provide a capacious embrace of tolerance. Homonormative liberalism goes further, and extends rights-based legitimacy and avenues for redress, but often this is only accessible to LGBT people who personify its normative demands. As Roderick Ferguson and Amy Villarejo have shown, homonormativity was summoned as the comparative racialized rebuke to the disreputable and deviant, and also to suppress radical alternatives and alliances that challenged dominant systems of property, privilege and propriety. As Susan Stryker contends, the suppression and obscuring of complex alliances forged by gender and sexual variant and people of color distorts historical memory and understanding of solidarities against police harassment and violence.[18]

Because heteronormativity and homonormativity reward belonging based in sameness and/or similarity, they foster assimilation for some against the punitive marginalization of others, but not democratic affinity across difference. Paradoxically, "strangerhood" is a crucial ingredient for the public meeting, reinvigorating unexpected, uncomfortable, and heterogeneous encounters. As Samuel Delaney has shown, unconventional yet widespread sociability reveals neglected models for democratic livelihood and distributions of ideas, resources and social well-being. The exchanges between strangers of feelings, beliefs, ideas, actions, and erotics have the capacity to renew and create anew ethical, political and social formations of civic living and participation. Such formations do not give membership priority to the individual subject birthed in the bourgeois family, but, rather, to affinities based in alternative models for relationality and belonging. These affinities can even be produced through the family. David Eng, Don Romesburg, and Shelly Park have underscored how the conflicting histories of US transracial and transnational adoption, and the growing criminalization of low-income women and families of color have produced the complex emergence of what Don Romesburg calls the "queer transracial families." Negotiating gendered dynamics of parenting and the imperatives of the consumerist privatized family, these multiply raced queer families experiment with kinship, belonging and difference.[19]

The affective intersections of race and sexuality that connects individuals to collective social movements is evidenced in the emergence of people of color LGBT identity, organization, cultural and political expression from the 1970s to the present. In the 1980s and 1990s, racial and ethnic identity organizing emerged as a counterweight to marginalization and erasure by white dominant lesbian, gay, and feminist organizations and movements, as Horacio Roque-Ramirez, Kevin Mumford, and Finn Enke have detailed. Cathy Cohen has strenuously argued that lesbian and gay respectability politics and especially queer activism, if not strenuously interrogated, can come at the expense of making alliances with the wide range of queer and disreputable and devalued subjects requiring justice. Christina Handhardt and Timothy Stewart Winter have, similarly, demonstrated how in the 1970s and 1980s urban white gay communities shook off the burden of routine police harassment and responded to anti-gay violence with calls for intensified policing, alienating the fragile alliances they had forged with Black, Latino and Asian activists.

The 1970s to 1990s ushered in an era of creative, performative, and public expression by black, Native, Latina/o, and Asian feminist, lesbian, queer, gay, bisexual, and transgender artists. This robust activity on the streets, in theaters and bars, bookstores, galleries, community centers, and film festivals had a transformative impact on what Lauren Berlant and Michael Warner have conceptualized as "queer worldmaking." Through queer worldmaking, "artful exhibition, street activism and practices of everyday" have produced inventive and fragile counterpublics that emerge through many mediums, such as dance, spoken word, poetry, and performance. These counterpublics depend on "parasitic and fugitive elaboration through gossip, dance clubs, softball leagues, and . . . print-mediated left culture."[20] An example of these world-making counterpublics is the 1980s and 1990s transformation by queer people of color of what had begun as 1920s black ballroom culture into the contemporary ballroom scene. The social, linguistic and performance vernaculars elaborated in Jennie Livingston's documentary of New York balls in *Paris is Burning* (1991) gave life—figuratively and literally—to future generations, as detailed in Marlon Bailey's ethnography of ballroom culture in Detroit.

Within queer of color worldmaking, gossip has been a particularly generative means of unofficially sharing information, perspectives, and warnings, as well as policing the behavior of others. For black and brown people, queer gossip actively resists visibility, recognition, and institutionalization, all of which are key strategies of modern identity politics. Instead, it demonstrates a response to Black sexual minorities' vexed relationship to a politics of visibility. Kwame Holmes argues that rather than a formal resistance, black gay gossip produces a "political framework that actively disidentifies with the liberatory potential of historical and political incorporation."[21] It engages with concepts of "fugitivity" or "taking flight" that are signature idioms of black diasporic culture. Black studies scholarship on fugitivity explores the dimensions and consequences of a person who is fleeing from persecution and intolerable circumstances, and in the process creating transitory, elusive relations and refuges, both metaphorically and materially, from carceral and captivity systems of which slavery and the prison are the enduring historical manifestations.

Both transnational ties and struggles with racial antipathy and attraction have shaped the contemporary history of diasporic LGBT community and identity. Complex racial, linguistic, and national differences continue to shape dissident sexual and gender identities and relations, and the possibilities of community and alliance. As Chandan Reddy, Timothy Randazzo and Juana Rodriguez have shown, the precarious grounds on which sexual and gender persecution refugee asylum claims have been made require the controversial presumption that US sexual modernity provides unequivocal protections for "gay rights" while other countries are backwards and oppressive. This obscures enduring struggles over sexualized and gendered targeting and violence in the US, often at the hands of the state, as well as the challenges of pervasive pejorative US-centered representations of racialized gender and sexuality.[22]

There are profound complexities in the ways Latina/o and Asian migrants navigate developing social solidarities and demands for cultural and political belonging in the US. As Martin Manalansan has shown, Filipino diasporic queer communities of the past several decades have creatively adapted queer indigenous terms such as *Bakla* by fusing them with elements of Western metropolitan gay identity. In so doing, Filipino migrants have produced new ecologies of dissident gender and sexual identities as they navigate racialized US urban and transnational geographies. Similarly, diasporic cultures since the late 1980s refashioned *Tóngzhì*, which originated as Communist Party vernacular Chinese for "comrade," to refer to dissident genders and sexualities in mainland China, Taiwan, Hong Kong and the Chinese diaspora in the US and elsewhere. Its usage directs a "politics beyond the homo-hetero duality" that integrates "the sexual into the social."[23] Each of these resists an easy enfolding of diasporic queer people of color into a US white-dominant identity framing as "LGBT."

Performance studies scholars have offered analytical strategies that recognize the challenge of assumption of universality and homogeneity in LGBT history. E. Patrick Johnson uses "Quare" as a mutation of queer that emphasizes practices, behaviors and bodies that are odd or slightly off kilter, and its usage originates through transgenerational African American vernacular. "Quare" specifically speaks to the embodied, lived experiences of queer people of color and embraces intersectional identities, relations and locations, in a process similar to José Esteban Muñoz's concept of "disidentification," which "scrambles and reconstructs" encoded meaning and exposes "universalizing and exclusionary" mechanisms. Both "quare" and dis-identification use this recognition "as raw material for representing a disempowered politics or positionality that has been rendered unthinkable by the dominant culture."[24]

To make possible the unthinkable involves reckoning with the legacies of racial exclusion and violence and critically engaging with how the technologies of estrangement of colonial and imperial knowledge formation, policing, subordination and exclusion and normalization persist in ignoring and devaluing variation and divergence in human life, relations and society. Through the convergences of women of color feminisms, transnational feminisms, and de-colonial critique, Michael Hames Garcia, Roderick Ferguson, and Grace Hong emphasize an understanding of interrelated analysis of race, sexuality, gender, and capitalism, and insist that practices of resistance to the sexual violence of colonialism and racial domination should be the starting point in queer historical analysis. Charting alternative genealogies and epistem-ologies of dissident and variant sexualities and genders requires overcoming the forms of narrative and knowledge production that have justified colonial power for centuries. The breadth of fugitive and generative practices of world-making emerges through imagining and performance, pursuing memory and archival traces, and through rituals, embodiments and lifeways.

Today, we live within a queer of color present that fiercely commits to practices of alterna-tive worldmaking, drawing on the past for inspiration. Simultaneously, we are haunted by the historical forces of racialization, colonialism, and capital that saturate the experiences of estrangement in our bodies, gender expressions, and passions. Queer Dreamers and Black Lives Matter activists emphasize enduring historical legacies of racialized and sexualized brutality in contemporary struggles to fight police violence and criminalization of black and brown people and undocumented immigrants. Drawing upon strategies of public defiance and disclosure, and yet mindful of the risks, queer of color activists are connecting protests over racist and anti-trans and queer denigration with struggles for justice, freedom to exercise the liberty of mobility and bodily expression, and demanding respect for collective and individual worth. The aim of violence can be brutally direct, as the horrifying 2016 massacre at the Pulse night club in Orlando demonstrates. The gathering of Puerto Rican, Latino, and people of color queer and trans people into this tenuous refuge highlighted the hunger for community spaces and how the sensations of dancing, music and festive world-making could be so viciously shattered. Still, and always, the rallying of LGBT and national, and even international, mourning and support reveals how LGBT people of color have amplified the demand for our dignity, safety and the fullness of our lives.

Notes

1 For a critical exploration of the progress narrative, see, in this volume, Marc Stein, " 'Crooked and Perverse': Narratives of LGBT Progress."
2 *American Heritage Dictionary of the English Language*, Fifth Ed. (New York: Houghton Mifflin Harcourt Publishing Company, 2011).
3 Essex Hemphill, interview by Chuck Tarver, "Untied Inspiration," *Network*, December 1990, www.qrd.org/qrd/www/culture/black/essex/blessings.html. Accessed October 23, 2017.
4 See also, in this volume, Emily Hobson, "Thinking Transnationally, Thinking Queer."
5 For a queer history of slavery, see, in this volume, Clare Sears, "Centering Slavery in Nineteeth-Century History (1800s–1890s)."
6 On the long history of US criminalization for queer people, especially of color, see, in this volume, Andrea Ritchie and Kay Whitlock, "Criminalization and Legalization."
7 For the longer queer history of US nationalism, see, in this volume, Eithne Luibhéid, "Queer and Nation."
8 Judy Wu, "Asian American History and Racialized Compulsory Deviance," *Journal of Women's History* 15, no 3 (2003): 60.
9 For a greater elaboration of this point, see Nayan Shah, "Policing Privacy, Migrants and the Limits of Freedom," *Social Text* 84–85 (Fall/Winter 2005): 275–284; Nayan Shah, "Between 'Oriental Depravity and Natural Degenerates': Spatial Borderlands and the Making of Ordinary Americans," *American Quarterly* (September 2005): 703–725.
10 On the history of romantic friendships in the eighteenth and nineteenth centuries, see, in this volume, Rachel Hope Cleves, "Revolutionary Sexualities and Early National Genders (1770s–1840s)" and Clare Sears, "Centering Slavery in Nineteenth-Century History."
11 For a general context for late nineteenth and early twentieth-century queer history, see, in this volume, Elizabeth Clement and Beans Velocci, "Modern Sexuality in Modern Times (1880s–1930s)."
12 For the longer queer history of race and urbanization, see, in this volume, Kwame Holmes, "The End of Queer Urban History?"
13 For more on the queer history of AIDS, see, in this volume, Jennifer Brier, "AIDS and Action (1980–1990s)."
14 A key text marking this shift for queer studies was the "What's Queer about Queer Studies Now?" special double issue edited by David Eng, Judith Halberstam, and José Esteban Muñoz for *Social Text* 84–85 (2005).
15 Michael Warner, *The Trouble with Normal: Sex, Politics, and the Ethics of Queer Life* (Cambridge: Harvard University Press, 1999), 175.
16 Lisa Duggan, *Twilight of Equality? Neoliberalism, Cultural Politics, and the Attack on Democracy* (Boston: Beacon Press, 2003), 179.
17 For a queer history of US neoliberalism, see, in this volume, Margot Weiss, "Queer Neoliberal Times (1970–2010s)."
18 See also, in this volume, Finn Enke, "Transgender History (and Otherwise Approaches to Embodiment."
19 In this volume, for more on the queer history of consumerism, see Stephen Vider, "Consumerism"; for the longer queer history of families, see Daniel Rivers, "Families."
20 Lauren Berlant and Michael Warner, "Sex in Public," *Critical Inquiry* 24, no. 2 (1998): 558.

21 Kwame Holmes, "What's the Tea: Gossip and the Production of Black Gay Social History," *Radical History Review* 122 (May 2015): 55–69.
22 See also, in this volume, Emily K. Hobson, "Thinking Transnationally, Thinking Queer."
23 Chou Wah-shan, *Tongzhi: Politics of Same-Sex Eroticism in Chinese Societies* (Binghamton, NY: Haworth Press, 2000), 2.
24 José Esteban Muñoz, *Disidentifications: Queers of Color and the Performance of Politics* (Minneapolis: University of Minnestoa Press, 1999), 31.

Further Reading

Abdur-Rahman, Aliyyah I. "'The Strangest Freaks of Despotism': Queer Sexuality in Antebellum African American Slave Narratives." *African American Review* 40, no. 2 (Summer 2006): 223–237.

Asian Women United of California, ed. *Making Waves: An Anthology of Writings by and about Asian America Women*. Boston: Beacon Press, 1989.

Boag, Peter. *Same Sex Affairs: Constructing and Controlling Homosexuality in the Pacific Northwest*. Berkeley: University of California Press, 2003.

Cantú, Lionel. *The Sexuality of Migration: Border Crossings and Mexican Immigrant Men*. New York: New York University Press, 2009.

Capó Jr., Julio. "Gay bars were supposed to be safe spaces. But they often weren't." *Washington Post*, June 14, 2016, www.washingtonpost.com/posteverything/wp/2016/06/14/gay-bars-were-supposed-to-be-safe-spaces-but-they-often-werent/. Accessed July 28, 2016.

Carby, Hazel. "'It Jus Be's Dat Way Sometime': The Sexual Politics of Women's Blues." *Radical America* 20, no. 4 (1986): 9–24.

Chavez, Ernesto. "'Ramon is not one of these': Race and Sexuality in the Construction of Silent Film Actor Ramón Novarro's Star Image." *Journal of the History of Sexuality* 20, no. 3 (September 2011): 520–544.

Cohen, Cathy J. "Punks, Bulldaggers, and Welfare Queens: The Radical Potential of Queer Politics?" *GLQ* 3, no. 4 (1997): 437–465.

Davis, Angela Y. *Blues Legacies and Black Feminism: Gertrude "Ma" Rainey, Bessie Smith, and Billie Holiday*. New York: Vintage, 1999.

Delgado, Grace Pena. "Border Control and Sexual Policing: White Slavery and Prostitution along the US–Mexico Borderlands, 1903–1910." *Western Historical Quarterly* 43, no. 2 (Summer 2012): 157–178.

D'Emilio, John. *Lost Prophet: The Life and Times of Bayard Rustin*. New York: Free Press, 2003.

Driskill, Qwo-Li. "Stolen From Our Bodies: First Nations Two-Spirits/Queers and the Journey to a Sovereign Erotic." *Studies in American Indian Literature* 16, no. 2 (2004): 50–64.

Eng, David. *Racial Castration: Managing Masculinity in Asian America*. Durham: Duke University Press, 2001.

Enke, Finn. "Smuggling Sex through the Gates." *American Quarterly* 55, no. 4 (December 2003): 635–667.

Fajardo, Kale Bantigue, "Queering and Transing the Great Lakes: Filipino/a Tomboy Masculinites and Manhoods Across the Great Lakes." *GLQ* 20, nos. 1–2 (2014): 115–140.

Ferguson, Roderick A. *Aberrations in Black: Toward A Queer of Color Critique* (Minneapolis: University of Minnesota Press, 2003).

——. "Race-ing Homonormativity: Citizenship, Sociology, and Gay Identity." *Black Queer Studies: A Critical Anthology*, eds. E. Patrick Johnson and Mae G. Henderson, 52–67. Durham: Duke University Press, 2005.

Foster, Thomas A. "The Sexual Abuse of Black Men Under American Slavery." *Journal of the History of Sexuality* 20, no. 3 (September 2011): 445–464.

Fung, Richard. "Looking for My Penis: The Eroticized Asian in Gay Video Porn." *Q & A: Queer in Asian America*, eds. Alice Hom and David Eng. Philadelphia: Temple University Press, 1998.

Garber, Eric. "A Spectacle in Color: The Lesbian and Gay Subculture of Jazz Age Harlem." In *Hidden from History: Reclaiming the Gay and Lesbian Past*, ed. Martin Duberman, Martha Vicinus, and George Chauncey Jr., 318–331. New York: Meridian, 1989.

Griffin, Farah Jasmine. *Beloved Sisters and Loving Friends: Letters from Rebecca Primus of Royal Oak, Maryland, and Addie Brown of Hartford, Connecticut, 1854–1868*. New York: One World/Ballantine, 2001.

Hames-García, Michael and Ernesto Javier Martínez, eds. *Gay Latino Studies: A Reader*. Durham: Duke University Press, 2011.

Hames-García, Michael, ed. Dossier: Jotería Studies Special Issue of *Aztlan: A Journal of Chicano Studies* 38, no.1 (Spring 2014): 135–160.

Hanhardt, Christina B. *Safe Space: Gay Neighborhood History and the Politics of Violence*. Durham: Duke University Press, 2013.

Hansen, Karen V. "'No Kisses Like Yours': An Erotic Friendship Between Two African American Women During the Mid-Nineteenth Century." *Gender and History* 7, no. 2 (1995): 153–182.

Heap, Chad. *Slumming: Sexual and Racial Encounters in American Nightlife, 1885–1940*. Chicago: University of Chicago, 2009.

Hicks, Cheryl, *Talk with You Like a Woman: African American Women, Justice and Reform in New York, 1890–1935*. Chapel Hill: University of North Carolina Press, 2010.

Hoang, Nguyen Tan. *A View from the Bottom: Asian American Masculinity and Sexual Representation*. Durham: Duke University Press, 2014.

Hong, Grace Kyungwon. *Strange Affinities: The Gender and Sexual Politics of Comparative Racialization*. Durham: Duke University Press, 2011.

Johnson, E. Patrick. "'Quare' Studies Or (Almost) Everything I Know About Queer Studies I Learned From My Grandmother." *Text and Performance Quarterly* 21, no. 1 (January 2001): 1–25.

Kenny, Maurice. "Tinselled Bucks: An Historical Study in Indian Homosexuality." In *Gay Roots: Twenty Years of Gay Sunshine, An Anthology of Gay History, Sex, Politics and Culture*, ed. Winston Leyland, 113–23. San Francisco: Gay Sunshine Press, 1991.

Kim, Elaine. *Slaying the Dragon*. Berkeley: Asian Women United of California, 2011.

——. "Such Opposite Creatures: Men and Women in Asian American Literature." *Michigan Quarterly Review* 29, no. 1 (Winter 1990): 68–93.

Kunzel, Regina. *Criminal Intimacy: Prison and the Uneven History of Modern Sexuality*. Chicago: University of Chicago Press, 2008.

Leonard, Kevin. "Containing 'Perversion': African Americans and Same Sex Desire in Cold War Los Angeles." *Journal of the History of Sexuality* 20, no 3 (September 2011): 545–567.

Luibhéid, Eithne. *Entry Denied: Controlling Sexuality at the Border*. Minnesota: University of Minnesota Press, 2002.

Manalansan, Martin. *Global Divas: Filipino Gay Men in the Diaspora*. Durham: Duke University Press, 2003.

——. "Queer Intersections: Sexuality and Gender in Migration Studies." *International Migration Review* 40, no. 1 (February 2006): 224–249.

Marchetti, Gina. *Romance and the "Yellow Peril": Race, Sex, and Discursive Strategies in Hollywood Fiction*. Berkeley: University of California Press, 1993.

McCune, Jeffrey. *Sexual Discretion, Black Masculinity and the Politics of Passing*. Chicago: University of Chicago Press, 2014.

Meyer, Leisa D. "Strange Love: Searching for Sexual Subjectivities in Black Print Popular Culture during the 1950s." *Feminist Studies* 38, no. 3 (Fall 2012): 625–657.

Miller-Young, Mireille. *The Feminist Porn Book: The Politics of Producing Pleasure*. New York: Feminist Press, 2013.

Miranda, Deborah A. "Extermination of the Joyas: Gendercide in the Spanish Americas." GLQ 16, nos. 1–2 (2010): 253–284.

Mitchell, Michelle. "Silences Broken, Silences Kept: Gender and Sexuality in African-American History." *Gender and History* 11, no. 3 (November 1999): 433–444.

Moraga, Cherrie. "Queer Aztlan: The Reformation of the Chicano Tribe." In *Latino/a Thought: Culture Politics and Society*, eds. Francisco Vasquez and Rodolfo Torres, 258–274. Lanham, MD: Rowman and Littlefield, 2002.

Mumford, Kevin. "The Trouble with Gay Rights: Race and the Politics of Sexual Orientation in Philadelphia, 1969–1982. *Journal of American History* 98, no. 2 (2011): 49–72.

——. *Not Straight, Not White: Black Gay Men from the March on Washington to the AIDS Crisis* (Durham: Duke University Press, 2016).

Muñoz, José Esteban. *Cruising Utopia: The Then and There of Queer Futurity*. New York: New York University Press, 2009.

Park, Shelly M. "Queer Orphans and their Neoliberal Saviors: Racialized Intimacy in Adoption." In *Mothering Queerly, Queering Motherhood: Resisting Monomaternalism in Adoptive, Lesbian, Blended and Polygamous Families*, 85–118. Albany: SUNY Press, 2013.

Perez, Emma. "Queering the Borderlands: The Challenges of Excavating the Invisible and Unheard." *Frontiers: A Journal of Women Studies* 24, nos. 2/3 (2003): 122–131.

Randazzo, Timothy J. "Social and Legal Barriers: Sexual Orientation and Asylum in the United States." In *Queer Migrations: Sexuality, US Citizenship, and Border Crossings*, eds. Eithne Luibhéid and Lionel Cantú, 30–60. Minneapolis: University of Minnesota Press, 2005.

Reddy, Chandan. "Asian Diasporas, Neoliberalism, and Family: Reviewing the Case for Homosexual Asylum in the Context of Family Rights." *Social Text* 23 (2005): 101–119.

Rifkin, Mark. *When Did Indians Become Straight?: Kinship, The History of Sexuality, and Native Sovereignty.* New York: Oxford University Press, 2011.

Rodriguez, Juana Maria. *Queer Latinidad: Identity Practices, Discursive Spaces.* New York: New York University Press, 2003.

——. *Sexual Futures, Queer Gestures and other Latina Longings.* New York: New York University Press, 2014.

Romesburg, Don. "Where She Comes From: Locating Queer Transracial Adoption." *QED: A Journal in GLBTQ Worldmaking* 1, no. 3 (Fall 2014): 1–29.

Roque-Ramirez, Horacio, " 'That's My Place!': Negotiating Racial, Sexual and Gender Politics in San Francisco's Gay Latino Alliance 1975–1983." *Journal of the History of Sexuality* 12, no. 2 (2003): 224–58.

Rosen, Hannah. " 'Not That Sort of Women': Race, Gender, and Violence During the Memphis Riot of 1866." In *Sex, Love, Race: Crossing Boundaries in North American History*, ed. Martha Hodes, 267–293. New York: New York University Press, 1998.

Sears, Clare. *Arresting Dress: Cross-Dressing, Law, and Fascination in Nineteenth-Century San Francisco.* Durham: Duke University Press, 2014.

Shah, Nayan. *Stranger Intimacy: Contesting Race, Sexuality and the Law in the North American West.* Berkeley: University of California Press, 2011.

Snorton, C. Riley. *Nobody Is Supposed to Know: Black Sexuality on the Down Low.* Minneapolis: University of Minnesota Press, 2014.

Solomon, Alisa. "Trans/migrant: Christina Madrazo's All-American Story." In *Queer Migrations: Sexuality, US Citizenship, and Border Crossings*, eds. Eithne Luibhéid and Lionel Cantú, 3–29. Minneapolis: University of Minnesota Press, 2005.

Stewart-Winter, Timothy. *Queer Clout: Chicago and the Rise of Gay Politics.* Philadelphia: University of Pennsylvania Press, 2016.

Stryker, Susan. "Transgender History, Homonormativity and Disciplinarity." *Radical History Review* 100 (Winter 2008): 145–157.

Sueyoshi, Amy. *Queer Compulsions: Race, Nation, and Sexuality in the Affairs of Yone Noguchi.* Honolulu: University of Hawai'i Press, 2012.

Torres, Lourdes. "Compañeras in the Middle: Toward a History of Latina Lesbian Organizing in Chicago" *GLQ* 20, nos. 1–2 (2014): 41–74.

Towle, Evan B. and Lynn Marie Morgan. "Romancing the Transgender Native: Rethinking the Use of the 'Third Gender' Concept." *GLQ* 8, no. 4 (2002): 469–497.

Villarejo, Amy. "Tarrying with the Normative: Queer Theory and Black History." *Social Text* 84–85 (Fall–Winter 2005): 69–84.

Wu, Judy Tzu-Chun. *Doctor Mom Chung of the Fair-Haired Bastards: The Life of a Wartime Celebrity.* Berkeley: University of California Press, 2005.

21

FAMILIES

Daniel Rivers

For many Americans, the idea of LGBT parents is a relatively recent concept. It was not until the mid-1980s, when the US media started reporting on the use of insemination and surrogate mothering relationships by lesbians, gay men, and bisexuals in same-sex couples, that widespread discussion of gay and lesbian families with children appeared in United States culture. The popular media portrayed the participants in this "lesbian 'gay-by' boom" as the forerunners of a novel type of family, made possible only through the advent of new technologies.[1] As I assert in my 2013 book, *Radical Relations*, this popular narrative completely obscures the fact that self-identified gay men and lesbians have been raising children since at least World War II.

A history of gay and lesbian parents and their children expands our view of LGBT history in general and offers new perspectives on the historical functioning of the American family as a site of both regulation and resistance. These stories are part of a history that acknowledges the power of the family to act as a hegemonic boundary that separates "fit" citizens from "unfit" ones by restricting and policing family formation. Scholarship in Native American, African-American, immigrant, and women's history has shown how the family has served as a regulatory structure to police non-white, working-class communities. Historically, an important aspect of policing the family in the United States has been the operation of two linked cultural assumptions: that families are by definition heterosexual, excluding gay, lesbian, and bisexual parenting relationships; and inversely, that same-sex relationships are by definition childless. The long history of self-identified lesbians, gay men, and bisexuals raising children since at least World War II contradicts these ideological beliefs. In the 1950s and 1960s, lesbian and gay parents raised children in hiding and in the relative safety of bohemian neighborhoods. In the 1970s, lesbian, gay, and bisexual parents and their children started organizing on their own behalf, declaring their presence in opposition to prevailing heterosexist notions of family. This activism, and the legacy of the families that came before it, played a large role in moving familial, domestic, and marital rights to the center of the modern LGBT freedom struggle by the first decades of the twenty-first century.

Historical depictions of gay men, lesbians, bisexuals, and transgender people as unfit parents intersect with those that pathologize parents of color, poor families, and single women. Campaigns against minorities in US legal and political systems often begin with a description of a pathological family, unhealthy to children and to the very stability of society itself. In her work on miscegenation law in the West, Peggy Pascoe explicitly compares the racist social parameters reinforced by miscegenation law with the denial of the right of marriage to same-sex couples in the United States. Other work on the historical operation of the marital institution by Nancy Cott stresses the ways in which marriage has acted as a social, economic, racial, and political boundary and compares these historical processes with the gay and lesbian struggle for domestic civil liberties. The study of LGBT parents and their children can complement these reevaluations of the history of the American family. The regulation, and threats of regulation, that have undermined the stability of lesbian and gay childrearing arrangements are part of a basic symbolic function of the American family to limit social access and support boundaries built on race, class, gender, and sexual identity. Despite state, social pressures and religious biases, sexual and gender minorities have raised children, created families, and, more recently, compelled a more expansive understanding of family that recognizes them.[2]

The stories of LGBT parents and their children can significantly broaden our historical perspective on queer history in the contexts of the World War II and both the repression and dynamism of the 1950s. A demographic shift accompanying the end of World War II left port cities such as New York, San Francisco, and Los Angeles with newly enriched queer communities. Gay men, lesbians, and bisexuals encountered same-sex communities in barracks and motor pools, often as they themselves came into consciousness of their same-sex attractions. At war's end, instead of returning home, these women and men remained in the cities where they disembarked, or joined up with other like-minded veterans before settling down. The postwar history of queer communities in the 1950s is a complex one characterized by both dynamic change and severe repression that resulted from increased visibility. Many LGBT historians have written on the persecution of sexual minorities during the McCarthy era. Organizations were purged of "sex deviants" as gay men, lesbians, and bisexuals were likened to child molesters and communists. LGBT people faced increased scrutiny from psychological "experts" and isolation from a mandated white, middle-class, nuclear family model, and were subject to forced incarceration and brutal treatment. In both the South and the North, a revived anti-homosexual fervor led to arrests and raids. These experiences and social forces were shaped by race and racism, as well. A white supremacist, anti-communist homophobia attacked both the African-American and LGBT civil rights movements in ways that intersected and rendered queer people of color highly vulnerable and subject to police harassment.[3]

All of these factors influenced the lives of gay and lesbian parents and their children in the immediate postwar period. Like so many other men and women, some parents left their homes in the heartland for the coast and newfound labor opportunities. Most had children from heterosexual marriages, but others had always identified with queer community. All LGBT parents found themselves raising children in a hostile postwar society in which same-sex relationships were both increasingly visible and increasingly policed. Same-sex desire was seen as deeply pathological, gender diversity was highly suspect, and the notion that someone could be both a parent and homosexual, bisexual, or gender-diverse was fundamentally understood as a contradiction in terms. Some were caught in raids on working-class gay and lesbian bars and forced to lie to authorities about their sexuality in order to keep their children. Even simply being seen in queer spaces by the wrong people could cost queer parents both their children and their jobs. Vera Martin, who would later work as a black lesbian feminist organizer in Los Angeles, was terrified of this threat in the late 1950s when she ventured out to lesbian bars with her Japanese-American lover, Kay. The couple would often make sure they were accompanied by gay male friends with whom they could pose as heterosexual couples if necessary. Martin knew that both she and Kay, as lesbian mothers of color with children from previous heterosexual marriages, were in constant danger of losing their children. She also feared for her job with the city, which was an important part of her ability to provide for her children.[4]

As early as the mid-1950s the homophile movement of early lesbian and gay civil rights organizations had already begun discussing parenting.[5] Related announcements and reader correspondence appeared in the very first national lesbian periodical. The initial issue of *The Ladder* (October 1956), a publication of the Daughters of Bilitis (DOB), featured an article expressing surprise at how many "women are raising children in a deviant [same-sex] relationship" and stated that men were "undertaking this responsibility too." A subsequent article reported that "anything which strays from the sincere feeling or true values can be said to be deviant and there very definitely can be deviant heterosexuals as well as deviant homophiles . . . Love and security overshadow almost all other factors." DOB co-founders Del Martin and Phyllis Lyon remembered that there were many lesbian mothers in the organization in these early years, but they rarely publicized this out of fear that these women would lose their children.[6] Men in homophile organizations and social networks were also discussing same-sex parental rights by the 1960s. In 1964, eleven male homophile organizations expressed their views on same-sex marriage and whether homosexuals should be allowed to adopt children. In the five surviving statements, some groups were concerned that it was too soon to be demanding marital and familial rights, while others supported claiming these rights.[7] At the same time, gay and bisexual fathers who were aware of homophile organizations took refuge in their existence. Men who were in marriages with women wrote of being too afraid of discovery to go into gay bars and expressed gratitude for the connection that the homophile organizations gave them. One married man from Corvalis, Oregon, stopped into the offices of the San Francisco chapter of the Mattachine Society in April of 1962 and spoke of the "tremendous lift" it gave him, although he did not feel he could subscribe to *The Mattachine Review* out of fear of the risks to his family.[8] One man, a "vice-president of a local firm," who wrote to *The Ladder* from Washington D.C. identified himself as "the father of four children," and added that "only the objects of my desires know of my penchant."[9]

Many men and women lived double lives in this era. Will Whiting, who began identifying as gay in the service during World War II, was lovers for years, "every Monday," with a married man who had a wife and a daughter.[10] Andrew Weiler also began to realize his attraction for men in the service. However, after World War II he went to college and courted his future wife for four years in the late forties. He remembers talking to another man in school who was gay and upset about it because he wanted a family. Weiler admitted that he felt the same way, and the young man recommended therapy. Weiler married in 1950, eventually having five children with his wife, to whom he stayed married for eighteen years. Living in Los Angeles, Weiler also met men in the bathhouses. Eventually his wife left him, and he moved to San Francisco, where he was an active member of the gay community in the early 1980s.[11]

Many self-identified lesbians with children were also in marriages to men and were concerned with the impact of their lesbian identities on their roles as mothers. As one writer in *The Ladder* explained: "Sometimes she marries before she has reached complete understanding of herself and perhaps a child complicates the situation."[12] One woman, interviewed by her lesbian daughter in 1975, recalled having her first sexual relationship with a good friend in the mid-1950s. "When I look back on it, it was very 'closety.' We were both married. We really cared for one another, but she wanted the security of her home—even though she couldn't stand . . . her husband." In the early 1960s, this woman had been placed in a psychiatric institution by her husband and given electro-shock treatment.[13] For many women, coming into consciousness of their lesbianism while also becoming wives and mothers left them extremely vulnerable.

Lesbian mothers also raised children in the increasingly defiant and visible cultural spaces of working-class butch-fem communities. Blue Lunden, who in 1954 would give birth to her daughter Linda, began associating with butch-fem lesbian culture in the French Quarter at fifteen. By that age, Blue had been in and out of the local House of the Good Shepherd, where she had her first girlfriends. Her poor Irish and Cajun family disowned her at seventeen when she was caught in a massive raid on a New Orleans lesbian bar, the Golden Rod, and the local paper published her picture. The following year, Blue got pregnant after sleeping with a man for the first time, for money. In 1955, Blue gave Linda up in an informal adoption to a heterosexual couple, motivated by the belief that she could not be a good mother and a lesbian at the same time, and moved to New York City. Four years later, she returned to New Orleans to reclaim her daughter, bringing Linda back to New York and raising her in the white, Puerto-Rican, and black lesbian communities of the East Village in the early 1960s. Linda and Blue would eventually walk hand-in-hand in the first annual commemoration of the Stonewall Riots, the Christopher Liberation Day Parade of 1970 in New York City.[14]

By the early 1970s, gay fathers and lesbian mothers were regularly losing custody, visitation, and full parental rights across the country. The custody cases reveal links between racism, sexism, and homophobia in the denial of custody to lesbian mothers of color, as well as the structure of general prohibition on same-sex parenting. Though custody courts were local and relatively autonomous, judges gave remarkably similar reasons for denying parental rights. These marked fundamental elements of their own prejudices, which mirrored those of society and social science at the time, including the anxiety that lesbian mothers or gay fathers would sexually molest their children or perform sexual acts in front of them, and that the children of gay men and lesbians would experience gender difficulties, become homosexual themselves, or face stigma because of their parents.[15]

The idea that homosexuality is dangerous to children was a prominent and important part of the institutionalized homophobia at work in the custody cases common from 1967 to 1985.[16] In 1967, in Sacramento, California, Doris Nadler lost custody of her two children because she was a lesbian. In a hearing, Nadler was berated with questions that underlined the notion of sexual danger to the children and the assumed pathology of same-sex relationships. "Well, let me ask you," the public defender representing Mr. Nadler said, referring to an instance of lesbianism he had questioned Mrs. Nadler about, "where were the children? Were they in your home?" This line of questioning continued for some time, developing into a precise inquiry into how much time the plaintiff and her partner Sally spent together in the company of the children. "All right," the public defender continued, after questioning Doris Nadler about her living arrangements, "Did you ever kiss Sally in front of the children?" She replied, "no." He also asked, "Have you ever made the statement that the children should be exposed to both ways of life, meaning heterosexual and homosexual?" Doris Nadler replied, "Absolutely not." Nadler was later aggressively questioned by both her ex-husband's attorney and the presiding judge, Judge Joseph Babich, about her sexual practices and was forced to give names of women she had known.[17] Some parents were ostracized from their children for decades while others were only allowed to visit them on the condition that they not be in the presence of any other gay person, even their partner. Visitation rights were usually granted only under the condition that the parent waive their constitutional rights of association.[18]

By the mid-1980s, however, a growing number of states began awarding custody or visitation to gay and lesbian parents. These victories took place only in certain regions of the country and involved a preponderance of working- and middle-class white families, and so do not reflect the difficulties faced by poor and nonwhite lesbian, gay, and bisexual parents. Nonetheless, a change did begin to occur, and the numbers of custody cases involving previous heterosexual marriage began to drop. The change in the legal culture surrounding same-sex parenting was the result of a struggle that was as much about the definition of family as it was about sexuality.[19]

These shifts were also connected to the formation of lesbian mother and gay father networks nationwide. Many of the earliest lesbian mother groups grew out of lesbian feminist communities in the 1970s. The first ongoing group in the United States was the Lesbian Mothers Union (LMU). One of the co-founders of the group was DOB co-founder Del Martin, who had raised a daughter with her partner, Phyllis Lyon, in the 1950s. In June 1971, Martin, Lyon, and a group of women at a gay women's conference in Los Angeles decided to form the lesbian mother organization to publicize the lack of child care at lesbian gatherings, mothers' sense of isolation within the lesbian community, and the persecution of lesbian mothers in the custody courts. The women expressed fears they shared concerning their ex-husbands and a society that saw them as unfit mothers simply because they were lesbians. Two of the mothers reported that they lived "in constant fear that their ex-husbands will learn they are lesbians and take away their children." News of the formation of the LMU spread through feminist and gay liberation magazines, including *Mother, Sisters, The Advocate, The Bay Area Reporter* and *The Ladder*. The account in *Mother* cited "more than 36 women" in the LMU. In the early 1970s, the LMU demanded that the San Francisco Family Agency recognize the struggles of lesbian mothers and gay fathers, raised funds for attorney and expert witness fees for lesbians involved in custody disputes, and held social gatherings.[20]

In Seattle, the Lesbian Mother's National Defense Fund (LMNDF) emerged in 1974. It became the nation's most productive and well-known clearinghouse for information on lesbian mother custody struggles. The LMNDF was founded by twelve women after Geraldine Cole and Lois Thetford met and began talking about the need to form an organization to assist lesbian mothers in custody battles. Neither Cole nor Thetford were themselves immediately under threat of losing their children to ex-spouses, and remembered feeling a debt to women who could not be as open as they could be as lesbian mothers. The twelve founders of the LMNDF including Joan Pittell, Karen Burr, Pam Keeley, and Gail Hethcote, were also politicized by the difficult case fought by a local lesbian couple, Nancy Driber and Marilyn Koop, who both fought for custody of children they had from previous heterosexual marriages. Throughout the 1970s and 1980s, the LMNDF published *Mom's Apple Pie*, a nationally distributed periodical that focused on lesbian mother custody cases and activism.[21]

In 1976 in New York, Carole Morton and others founded Dykes and Tykes, a multi-racial, lesbian feminist group that would become the most prominent East Coast lesbian mother activist group. It developed an intersectional political perspective that saw the family as a site of racist, homophobic, patriarchal, and classed hegemonies in need of deep transformation. Dykes and Tykes' member Audre Lorde expressed this vision in her essay about raising her son, "Man-Child, A Black Lesbian Feminist Response."[22] Dykes and Tykes was in coalition with a broad range of activist groups and a complex reproductive justice movement that connected the struggles of poor women, women of color, and lesbian mothers. The group set up social events to help members find other lesbian mothers in the community, and increasingly took part in advocating for lesbian mothers fighting custody cases. In 1978, Dykes and Tykes and the National Lawyers Guild set up a summer lesbian custody legal workshop that led to the founding of the Dykes and Tykes Legal Custody Center.

Lesbian mother groups were connected to each other and a larger network of lesbian feminist communities across the country. Karen Burr of the LMNDF wrote Del Martin and told her that the Washington group had formed. Similarly, Carole Morton, who knew Martin in the late 1960s, when Morton was a member of DOB New York and New Jersey chapters, wrote to Del Martin when she founded Dykes and Tykes in 1976.[23] Lesbian mother groups also connected networks of sympathetic attorneys and expert witnesses to help lesbian mothers in custody trials and to provide social space for lesbian mothers and their children. By the late

Figure 21.1 The "Dykes and Tykes" float at the 1978 Christopher Street Liberation Day March in New York City drew awareness to the existence of lesbian parents and their children.
Courtesy of the Lesbian Herstory Archives.

1970s, lesbian mother groups had formed in Seattle, Toronto, Los Angeles, Cambridge, San Francisco, Oakland, CA, Chicago, Boston, Austin, Philadelphia, Ann Arbor, Dallas, Denver, Minnesota, Providence, New Haven, Cincinnati, New York City, and St. Louis.[24]

By the early 1980s, gay father groups were also forming across the United States. A radical politics of gay fatherhood had been connected to gay liberation, and groups concerned with gay fatherhood were founded in counterculture, gay liberation communities in San Francisco, New York, Washington D.C., and Detroit. The first gay father group was founded in San Francisco in 1975.[25] However, as more men migrated to gay enclaves such as the Castro in San Francisco, Greenwich Village in New York, and West Hollywood in Los Angeles, these migrations tempered and moderated the revolutionary gay liberationist ethic that had previously been prevalent in these spaces.[26] By the late 1970s and early 1980s, many men who joined gay father groups came from middle-class heterosexual marriages, and by the mid-1980s, most gay father groups were largely made up of middle-class, white professional men. By then, gay father groups existed in San Francisco, Boston, Los Angeles, New York, Philadelphia, Chicago, San Diego, Seattle, Cleveland, and Boston.[27]

Gay father groups helped men who were struggling to come out about their same-sex sexuality from within heterosexual marriages. Whereas married gay fathers in the 1950s and 1960s had few options, these groups gave men going through this often alienating and terrifying transition support and community. John McClung, who came from a conservative Mennonite community, remembered sitting outside the Gay Community Center in Los Angeles in 1984, gathering up the nerve to go in and find an advertised Gay Fathers of Los Angeles meeting.

Once inside, McClung met other gay fathers in the group who gave him advice on community gatherings and custody concerns. Meetings were often very emotional. Andrew Hallum, who attended Gay Fathers of Los Angeles meetings in the early 1980s, remembered meetings as intimate places where men would spontaneously break out crying, overwhelmed with the fears of losing their children as a result of coming out about their same-sex sexuality.[28] Like lesbian mother groups, gay father groups supported their members who were involved in custody cases, raising funds and gathering political support when cases were being fought. San Francisco Bay Area Gay Fathers set up an emergency fund for members who were facing the high cost of legal fees.[29]

Still, in lesbian and gay parent groups, bisexual parents faced invisibility.[30] Many individuals in gay father and lesbian mother groups were involved in lesbian-feminist and gay liberation cultures that, despite an ethos of sexual freedom, often in practice encouraged people to see themselves and "come out" as exclusively lesbian or gay. In this environment, parental activists who thought of themselves as bisexual sometimes chose not to publicly disclose it. Billy S. Jones-Hennin, a bisexual African-American man who was at the center of Washington D.C. gay men of color activism and who founded a group for gay parents in the mid-1970s, remembered that he felt too vulnerable to identify as bisexual and chose instead to identify as a gay father and activist.[31]

Most gay father groups came from different political perspectives than lesbian feminist ones. They did not embrace multi-issue politics aside from finding abstract inspiration in the history of other groups gaining civil rights in America. But they did argue defiantly that gay fathers could be fit parents and that their families were strong. As groups with more income and faith in the electoral system than lesbian feminists, they often forged what I call a "gay family politics of respectability" as a powerful counter narrative to the resurgent anti-gay "family values" politics of the New Right. In 1985, Bill Jones, president of San Francisco Bay Area Gay Fathers (SFBAGF), argued that the gay fathers contingent in the Freedom Day parade made "a powerful political statement, with our numbers, our clean-cut look, and most of all with the wonderful faces of our kids who look happy and well-cared for." Jones contrasts this with the "sleaziness of overdone drag queens." For some members, gay fatherhood represented a politics of normalcy and assimilation that asserted the fitness of gay fathers and provided a political counterpoint to the growing backlash against gay, lesbian, and bisexual civil rights.[32]

By the 1980s, individual gay father groups were often part of a nationwide umbrella organization, Gay Fathers Coalition International. This organization was founded in October of 1979 at the National March on Washington for Lesbian and Gay Rights by members of gay father groups in Philadelphia, New York, and Washington D.C. One month after its founding, the organization would also include groups in San Francisco, Los Angeles, Cleveland, Baltimore, and Toronto. By 1986, the group, then renamed the Gay and Lesbian Parents Coalition International (GLPCI), had affiliated groups across the country and was in dialogue with mainstream lesbian and gay activist organizations such as the National Gay and Lesbian Task Force and the Lambda Legal Defense Fund. Throughout the 1980s and 1990s, GLPCI would continue to grow and would play a major role in driving a focus on gay and lesbian parental, domestic, and marital rights in the modern LGBT freedom struggle.[33]

By the late 1980s, the AIDS epidemic hit gay father groups, some of which faced the death of 50–80 percent of their membership from 1983 to 1990. In interviews, Bill Jones remembered years of memorials as deaths destroyed the gay father community of San Francisco. John McClung, sobbing, indicated similar numbers by showing me a rolodex he kept with back-facing cards indicating a GFLA member's death.[34] As Estelle Freedman has noted, the often brutal disenfranchisement of gay male couples, with or without children, when one partner was dying from HIV/AIDS, brought on by the lack of legal recognition for same-sex relationships, became a focus in the 1980s. Along with the organizing of lesbian mothers and gay fathers, the lack of legal rights that allowed people to be ostracized from their partners as they were dying drove a new focus on domestic, parental, and marital rights.[35]

Lesbian mother activism and gay father organizing of the 1970s and 1980s contributed to a growing awareness of the need for same-sex parental and domestic rights. The Lesbian Rights Project, which would later become the National Center for Lesbian Rights (NCLR), was founded in 1977 in part out of the lesbian feminist organizing of lesbian mothers. By the late 1980s, attorneys focused on lesbian and gay family law, such as Paula Ettelbrick, were working with NCLR, Lambda Legal, and the National Gay and Lesbian Task Force (NGLTF), each of which had inaugurated a specific program on lesbian and gay family rights. At the same time, individuals in these groups, especially Ivy Young, who headed the NGLTF's Lesbian and Gay Families Project, were joining with veterans of the gay father movement to call for municipal and state domestic partnership laws.[36] This activist network was energized in 1993 when the Hawaii Supreme Court, in a surprise decision, ruled that banning same-sex marriage was unconstitutional under the Hawaiian state constitution. Quickly, the political momentum that rested on the persistence of decades of non-heterosexual parents helped drive the movement for same-sex marriage. Evidence of this continuing influence can be seen in the prominent place given to same-sex parents and their children in twenty-first century movements for marriage equality.

Membership of many parental organizations shifted from men and women who had come out within heterosexual marriages to those who had children after embracing a lesbian, gay, bisexual, and/or trans identity. These "gayby boom" families were often created through insemination, surrogacy, and adoption, sometimes in non-nuclear groups of LGBT co-parents brought together as family by friendship and romantic intimacy. Although some adoption agencies had tacitly placed teenagers with openly gay adoptive fathers, prospective gay and lesbian parents also faced intense discrimination, and it was not until the early 1980s that gay men and lesbians began adopting children openly. Wayne Steinman and Sal Iacullo jointly adopted their daughter Hope in New York in 1988. That same year, Steinman helped found Center Kids, an organization based out of the Lesbian and Gay Community Services Center in New York and created to give support to lesbians and gay men who wanted to have children.[37]

By the late 1970s, grassroots lesbian insemination networks had developed in New York, Boston, Oakland, Seattle, California, and Burlington, Vermont. These networks emerged from lesbian feminist communities and often used gay men as donors with the assistance of lesbian feminist parental activists who acted as go-betweens. Maidi Nickele, who became pregnant through insemination herself in 1980, helped lesbians in Seattle get pregnant with the help of gay male donors. Nickele remembered that from 1980 to 1986, she assisted in around 40 inseminations, of which roughly half resulted in births. By the mid-1980s, lesbian couples were increasingly utilizing donor insemination to have children, although they faced discrimination from doctors, sperm banks, and family judges.[38]

In the 1990s and beyond, LGBT parents and their children could draw on an increasing number of resources and organizations. The children of same-sex households began organizing in their own right, with the formation of Children of Lesbians and Gays Everywhere (COLAGE) in 1989 from a group of children within GLPCI.[39] In sharp contrast to the lives of same-sex households who had raised their children underground in the 1950s and 1960s, these families enjoyed a growing number of LGBT family-specific children's books, summer camps, and social groups.[40]

The long history of lesbian mothers, gay fathers and their children demonstrates important ways in which sexuality, gender, and the family have long been intertwined in American society. Further study of bisexual and transgender parents is needed to deepen and nuance our understanding of these connections as they have changed over time. The twin assumptions that the family is by definition heterosexual and that queerness is by definition a childless state has left LGBT families invisible and vulnerable for decades. Their own persistence and struggle gradually challenged these assumptions and helped shape the focus on domestic, familial, and marital rights that has been a priority of the contemporary LGBT freedom struggle.

Notes

1 For examples, see Kris Hundley, "The Lesbian Baby Boom," *Springfield (Massachusetts) Valley Advocate*, February 15, 1988; Charles Laurence, "Baby Boom Among US Lesbians," *The Daily Telegraph*, February 21, 1989; Deborah Bradley, "Gays, Lesbians Becoming Parents Through Alternative Insemination," *The Buffalo News*, July 30, 1995, final edition; "Lesbian Couples Opt For Babies," *The San Diego Union-Tribune*, November 8, 1993.

2 My book (Daniel Rivers, *Radical Relations: Lesbian Mothers, Gay Fathers, and Their Children in the United States since World War II*, Chapel Hill, NC: University of North Carolina Press, 2013) begins to do this work, but my focus was on parents who identified as lesbian and gay. Much work remains to uncover the history of bisexual and transgender parents. Such scholarship will deepen our knowledge of the complex ways in which the history of all queer parents intersect and diverge.

3 For a general postwar queer history, see, in this volume, Amanda Littauer, "Sexual Minorities at the Apex of Heteronormativity (1940–1965)."

4 Rivers, *Radical Relations*, 25–27.

5 For queer organizational history, see, in this volume, Marcia Gallo, "Organizations."

6 "Raising Children in A Deviant Relationship," *The Ladder*, October 1956, 9; "Relationship Not So 'Deviant' If Child Has Love and Security," *The Ladder*, April 1957, 8–11; Del Martin and Phyllis Lyon, interview with author, San Francisco, CA, February 17, 2006.

7 Discussions of these organization statements are in the September, October, and November issues of *Atheneum Review*, Newsletter Collection (Legal Size), Gay, Lesbian, Bisexual and Transgender Historical Society (hereafter GLBTHS), San Francisco, CA.

8 Letters dated April 23, 1962 and May 9, 1963, box 4, file 4, Donald Stewart Lucas Papers, GLBTHS.

9 "Readers Respond," *The Ladder* 1, no. 9 (June 1957): 29.

10 Keith Vacha and Cassie Damewood ed., *Quiet Fire: Memoirs of Older Gay Men* (Trumansburg, NY: The Crossing Press, 1985), 63.

11 Vacha and Damewood, ed., *Quiet Fire*, 96–110.

12 Nancy Osbourne, "One Facet of Fear," *The Ladder* 1, no. 9 (June 1957):6.

13 "Mother and Daughter," transcript of a taped interview. *Madness Network News*, 3, no. 6, (February 1975): 22–26.

14 Rivers, *Radical Relations*, 39–40.

15 Ibid., 59–67.

16 For the long history of LGBT criminalization, see, in this volume, Andrea Ritchie and Kay Whitlock, "Criminalization and Legalization."

17 Lyon/Martin Papers, box 124, folder 18. GLBTHS.

18 Rivers, *Radical Relations*, 57–67.

19 Ibid., 74–79.

20 Martin and Lyon interview with author; Judith Anderson, "Motherhood and the Gay Woman" in *San Francisco Chronicle*, 23 October 1971; "Lesbian Moms Court for Kids" in *The Berkeley Barb*, February 4, 1972; Del Martin, "Lesbian Mother's Union: Women Unite at L.A. Conference," *Mother* (Stanford, CA) 1, no. 3 (August 1971): 1; Rivers, *Radical Relations*, 84, 94, 105; *Lesbian Mothers Union Newsletter* 1, January 1972, box 124, folder 2 and folder 1, box 126, Lyon/Martin Papers, GLBTHS.

21 I am eternally grateful to Jenny Sayward, who allowed me to photograph the entire 14 boxes of this publication she had archived in her garage and for her willingness to share her own story of custody struggle as a lesbian mother with me. LMNDF Files, digital copy in author's possession; Jenny Sayward, interview with author, Edmonds, WA, July 18, 2006.

22 Dykes and Tykes Newsletters, Dykes and Tykes (Org. and Legal Custody Ctr.), Organizational Files, Lesbian Herstory Archives, Brooklyn, NY.

23 Communication in 1974 between Martin and Burr in the LMNDF Files; July 1974 from Burr to Martin in folder 1, box 124, Lyon/Martin Papers, GLBTHS; letter from Carole Morton to Del Martin dated 4/19/1976, folder 19, box 124, Lyon/Martin Papers, GLBTHS.

24 On Seattle, New York, the San Francisco Bay Area, Philadelphia, Denver, Dallas, and Ann Arbor, see Rivers, *Radical Relations*, 80–110; on Toronto, see correspondence between the LMNDF and both Jeanne Lovsted and Francie Wyland, LMNDF Files; on Los Angeles, see "Lesbian Mother Group Forming," *The Lesbian Tide*, July 197: 5 and material in folder 5, box 126, see Lyon/Martin Papers, GLBTHS; on Cambridge, see "Lesbian Mothers' Conference," *Mom's Apple Pie*, August 1978; on Oakland, Chicago, Austin, and Boston, see letter dated 17 November 1976 from the LMNDF to editors of *Northwest Passage* in LMNDF Files; on Providence, New Haven, and Cincinnati, see copy of "NGTF Gay Support Packet" in folder 5, box 126, Lyon/Martin Papers, GLBTHS; on St. Louis, see *Moonstorm*, June 1979: 14.

25 Rivers, *Radical Relations*, 111–121.

26 For the broader history of gay liberation and lesbian feminism, see, in this volume, Whitney Strub, "Gay Liberation (1963–1980)."

27 For the San Francisco Bay Area, see "San Francisco Bay Area Gay Fathers, Newsletter Files, GLBTHS, San Francisco, CA; on Los Angeles, see "Gay Fathers of Los Angeles," Subject Files, One Institute and Archives, University of Southern California, Los Angeles, CA; on New York, see "Gay Fathers Forum of New York," Subject Files, One Institute and Archives, University of Southern California, Los Angeles, CA; for Chicago, San Diego, Boston, and Cleveland, see material in the International Gay Information Center collection at the New York Public Library; information on Seattle group in LMNDF Files; on Philadelphia, see "Gay Fathers of Greater Philadelphia," Subject Files, John J. Wilcox Archives, William Way LGBT Community Center, Philadelphia, PA.

28 John McClung, interview with author, Apple Valley, CA, May 22, 2003; Andrew Hallum, interview with author, Lynden, WA, June 27, 2003.

29 Rivers, *Radical Relations*, 131.

30 For the particular challenge of bisexual history, see, in this volume, Loraine Hutchins, "Bisexual History: Let's Not Bijack Another Century."

31 Billy S. Jones-Hennin, interview with author, Washington, D.C., June 29, 2012; Catherine Gunther, "Gay Dads and Gay Moms: The Parents Are Alright," *City Paper: Baltimore's Biweekly Newspaper*, July 13, 1979. See also "Growing Up With A Bisexual Dad: Billy & Peaches Jones," in *Bi Any Other Name: Bisexual People Speak Out*, Loraine Hutchins and Lani Kaahumanu, eds. (Boston: Alyson Publications, 1991): 159–166.

32 Bill Jones, "President's Message," San Francisco Bay Area Gay Fathers Newsletter, June 1985, 3. San Francisco Bay Area Gay Fathers folder, GLBTHS; Rivers, *Radical Relations*, 121–130.

33 Rivers, *Radical Relations*, 135–138.

34 Bill Jones, interview with author, Sausalito, CA, May 19, 2004; John McClung, interview with author, Apple Valley, CA, May 22nd, 2003; Rivers, *Radical Relations*, 133–135.

35 Estelle Freedman, *Feminism, Sexuality, and Politics: Essays by Estelle B. Freedman* (Chapel Hill: University of North Carolina Press, 2006), 192. See also, in this volume, Jennifer Brier, "AIDS and Action (1980–1990s)."

36 Rivers, *Radical Relations*, 193–197.

37 Ibid., 173–206.

38 Ibid., 169–170; 173–206.

39 COLAGE records, 1982–2000, GLBTHS.

40 Rivers, *Radical Relations*, 203–206.

Further Reading

Ball, Carlos. *Same Sex Marriage and Children: A Tale of History, Social Science, and Law.* New York: Oxford University Press, 2014.

Beemyn, Ginny. *A Queer Capital: A History of Gay Life in Washington D.C.* New York: Routledge, 2015.

Berube, Allan. *Coming Out Under Fire: The History of Gay Men and Women in World War Two.* New York: Free Press, 1990.

Briggs, Laura. *Somebody's Children: The Politics of Transracial and Transnational Adoption*. Durham, NC: Duke University Press, 2012.

Coontz, Stephanie. *The Way We Never Were: American Families and the Nostalgia Trap*. Basic Books, 1992.

Cott, Nancy. *Public Vows: A History of Marriage and the Nation*. Cambridge, MA: Harvard University Press, 2000.

D'Emilio, John. *Sexual Politics, Sexual Communities: The Making of a Homosexual Minority in the United States, 1940–1970*. Chicago: University of Chicago Press, 1983.

D'Emilio, John. *Lost Prophet: The Life and Times of Bayard Rustin*. New York: Free Press, 2003.

Flynn, Taylor. "The Ties That (Don't) Bind: Transgender Family Law and the Unmaking of Families." In *Transgender Rights*, eds. Paisley Currah, Richard Juang, and Shannon Prince Minter, 32–50. Minneapolis: University of Minnesota Press, 2006.

Gordon, Linda. *Heroes of Their Own Lives: The Politics and History of Family Violence*. New York: Viking, 1988.

Gutterman, Lauren Jay. " 'The House on the Borderland': Lesbian Desire, Marriage, and the Household, 1950–1979." *Journal of Social History* 46, no. 1 (Fall 2012): 1–22.

——. "Another Enemy Within: Lesbian Wives, or the Hidden Threat to the Nuclear Family in Postwar America." *Gender & History* 24, no. 1 (August 2012): 475–501.

Jensen, Joan. "Native American Women and Agriculture: A Seneca Case Study." In *Unequal Sisters: A Multicultural Reader in U.S. Women's History*, eds., Ellen DuBois and Vicki Ruiz. New York: Routledge, 1990.

Kennedy, Elizabeth Lapovsky and Madeline Davis. *Boots of Leather, Slippers of Gold: The History of a Lesbian Community*. New York: Routledge, 1993.

Lefkovitz, Alison. " 'The Peculiar Anomaly': Same-Sex Infidelity in Postwar Divorce Courts." *Law and History Review* 33, no. 3 (August 2015): 665–701.

Lewin, Ellen. *Lesbian Mothers: Accounts of Gender in American Culture*. Ithaca, NY: Cornell University Press, 1993.

Lorde, Audre. "Man-Child: A Black Lesbian Feminist's Response." In *Sister Outsider: Essays and Speeches*. Berkeley, CA: The Crossing Press, 1984.

May, Elaine Tyler. *Homeward Bound: American Families in the Cold War Era*. Basic Books, 1988.

McGuire, Danielle. *At the Dark End of the Street: Black Women, Rape, and Resistance—A New History of the Civil Rights Movement from Rosa Parks to the Rise of Black Power*. New York: Random House, 2010.

Meyer, Leisa. *Creating GI Jane: Sexuality and Power in the Women's Army Corps during World War II*. New York: Columbia University Press, 1998.

Notches Editorial Board. "The Obergefell Syllabus: Historicizing Same-Sex Marriage in the United States." *NOTCHES: (re)marks on the history of sexuality*, June 27, 2015, http://notchesblog.com/2015/06/27/the-obergefell-syllabus-historicizing-same-sex-marriage-in-the-united-states/. Accessed July 19, 2016.

Pascoe, Peggy. *What Comes Naturally: Miscegenation Law and the Making of Race in America*. New York: Oxford University Press, 2009.

Pleck, Elizabeth H. *Not Just Roommates: Cohabitation after the Sexual Revolution*. Chicago: The University of Chicago Press, 2012.

Polikoff, Nancy. *Beyond (Straight and Gay) Marriage: Valuing All Families under the Law*. Boston: Beacon Press, 2008.

Rivers, Daniel. *Radical Relations: Lesbian Mothers, Gay Fathers, and Their Children in the United States since World War II*. Chapel Hill, N.C.: The University of North Carolina Press, 2013.

Roberts, Dorothy. *Killing the Black Body: Race, Reproduction, and the Meaning of Liberty*. New York: Vintage Books, 1998.

Robson, Ruthann. "Reinscribing Normality? The Law and Politics of Transgender Marriage." In *Transgender Studies Reader 2*, eds. Susan Stryker and Aren Aizura, 623–629. New York: Routledge, 2013.

Romesburg, Don. "Where She Comes From: Locating Queer Transracial Adoption," *QED: A Journal in GLBTQ Worldmaking* 1, no. 3: 1–29.

Solinger, Rickie. *Wake up Little Susie: Single Pregnancy and Race before Roe v. Wade*. New York: Routledge, 1992.

Self, Robert. *All in the Family: The Realignment of American Democracy since the 1960s*. New York: Hill and Wang, 2013.

22

SICKNESS AND WELLNESS

Katie Batza

Sickness and wellness are malleable political constructs as well as physical and mental realities that have shaped sexual and gender minorities' experiences since at least the late nineteenth century.[1] Deployed by mainstream medicine and utilized by sexual and gender minorities, discourses of sickness and wellness have fueled, reinforced, and challenged ideals of sexuality and gender, particularly as they have intersected with perceptions of race, class, ability, morality, and citizenship. Debates over what constitutes sickness and/or wellness have shaped sexual and gender minorities' identity formation, community building, and political activism.

Pathologization has had significant and complex medical effects beyond labeling often otherwise healthy individuals as sick. In addition to the obvious burdens of being "treated" for one's supposed deviancy, the threat of diagnosis and treatment has discouraged many individuals from seeking out necessary medical help. Pathological classification provided medical legitimacy for the expanding criminalization and discrimination of sexual minorities and gender transgressors. Throughout the twentieth century, officials regularly justified legal injustice or violence by citing medical pathology. Effects fell most heavily upon racial minorities, the working class, immigrants, and people with disabilities. For much of the twentieth century, most homosexuals feared diagnosis, as it ushered in the threat of persecution, job loss, and social ostracism. In short, by proclaiming sexual and gender difference as pathological, doctors ensured that sexual and gender minorities had a much greater chance of becoming ill, criminalized, and economically weak.

Vast changes in medicine, society, and politics have propelled and informed shifting and contentious interactions between mainstream medicine and sexual and gender minorities. This essay identifies four thematic periods tracking the dynamic historical interaction between health, politics, and medicalized social norms. The first, spanning from the 1880s to the 1940s, marked the period of pathologization in which doctors classified, diagnosed, and stigmatized sexual and gender non-conformity. Medical experts created the identities and diagnoses of homosexuality, "sexual inversion," and "transvestitism" and affixed them to people rather than behaviors. These identities then dovetailed with contemporary social norms and legal practices that ostracized sexual and gender minorities. The second period, from the 1940s to the late 1960s, witnessed a slow political awakening of sexual and gender minorities, a creation of minority communities, a shift in medical interpretations of gender and sexual "deviance" away from hereditary and moral weaknesses toward molecular science and hormones, and a tremendous expansion of psychoanalytic "therapies." From the late 1960s to 1980, the third period, sexual and gender minorities challenged mainstream medical authority, recast the sickness narrative for their own political and medical needs, and overturned long-standing medical classifications of homosexuality and gender non-conformity. Beginning in 1981, gender and sexual minorities struggled to adapt empowering definitions of sickness and wellness in the face of AIDS, reliance on mainstream medicine, and growing discrimination.

Becoming Pathologized: 1880–1950

Prior to the late nineteenth century, society generally understood homosexuality and gender non-conformity as activities rather than core identities. Such acts or behaviors could warrant varying degrees of social sanction or criminalization, depending on the nature of the transgression and the race, class, and nationality of the transgressor. In the final decades of the 1800s, regulating sexuality and gender became both a medical *and* legal endeavor for the first time. The popularity of life science taxonomy, social Darwinism, and eugenics propelled the first consequential intersection of medicine and homosexual and gender non-conforming behaviors. Doctors created "deviant" identity categories and assigned subjects to them, with related suggestions for treatment, cure, and/or punishment. Almost simultaneously, some of those that shared significant oppressions resulting from their new "pathology" began speaking back to the experts and imagining the possibility of community building among others similarly categorized.[2]

US experts followed the initial European psychiatrists and sexologists (practitioners of the new field dedicated to the study of sex) who began creating sexual taxonomies. Psychiatrist Carl Westphal, in an 1870 publication, became one of the first to medically document same-sex attraction and sex, labeling it "contrary sexual feeling."[3] Psychiatrist and sexologist Robert Krafft-Ebing, in his 1887 *Psychopathia sexualis: Eine klinisch-forensische Studie* (*Sexual Psychopathy: A Clinical-Forensic Study*), classified same-sex desire as "psychosexual inversion," an example of "perverted sexual drive."[4] British physician Havelock Ellis added to the growing field of sexology through his important text *Sexual Inversion*, first published in German in 1896 and the first medical textbook in English on the topic in 1897. By the early 1900s, doctor Magnus Hirschfeld had created a complex sexual taxonomy comprised of 64 possible types of sexual expression including "Transvestit," a term he coined for people who wore clothing not conforming to their assigned gender.[5] In 1892, James Kiernan was the first in the United States to use the terms heterosexual and homosexual. As Bert Hansen and Jonathan Ned Katz have detailed, he went on to argue sexual impulse (a mixture of biological attraction and psychological development) resulted in homosexuality. Historians Don Romesburg and Julian Carter detail how sexologists in the United States understood homosexuality as a somewhat natural phase of sexual growth and development that needed to be moved through quickly and without guilt if "normal" gender, racial, and sexual hierarchies were to remain intact.

Though their work became the basis of many discriminatory medical and legal practices, initially European doctors focused on observing, documenting, and understanding difference, often, historian Harry Oosterhuis notes, with an eye toward building a more accepting society. Ivan Crozier asserts that Kiernan sought to decriminalize homosexuality in the United States through his sexological research and legal work. Regardless of their intended effect, these works clearly illustrate the important role scientific classification and investigation played in this post-Darwinian period. These sexological taxonomies often complemented the popular theories of eugenics in ways that harmed gender, sexual, and racial minorities during this period. Inspired in part by Darwin's theory of evolution, the eugenics movement focused medical attention on creating the "fittest" humans through genetic trait analysis, strategic procreation, and occasionally, sterilization. These scientific studies labeled sexual inversion and transvestitism medical anomalies and classified them as medical illnesses, moral weaknesses, or forms of psychological arrested development.

While doctors documented cases of "sexual inversion" and "transvestism" among almost entirely white and European populations, these and other forms of sexual "perversion" also factored heavily in US-based pathologizing of sexual and gender minorities, racial minorities, immigrants, the poor, and people with disabilities. Margot Canaday, Siobahn Somerville, and Regina Kunzel detail how law, medicine, and social norms classified these groups as perverse throughout the twentieth century, paving the way for injustices ranging from colonization to mass incarceration. Within the broader social and medical context, early sexologists tagged these groups, along with sexual and gender minorities, as having less desirable traits, though some did so in an effort to foster acceptance. In short, the moment sexual inversion and transvestism became part of the scientific lexicon, they also legitimized social stigma against sexual inverts and transvestites.

The early decades of the 1900s also saw the rise of Sigmund Freud's influential theories of psychosexual development and psychoanalysis. While removed from eugenics, Freud's theories similarly created many medical and social hurdles for gender and sexual minorities. Like many of the early sexologists, he did not intend to pathologize homosexuality but his successors argued that same-sex attraction and gender non-conformity resulted from stunted psychological growth, regressions, and neuroses. Consequently, psychoanalysis reinforced the pathologizing of sexual and gender minorities, and then further stigmatized them as not only anomalous but also as psychologically underdeveloped. Both psychoanalysts and later practitioners of aversion therapy (a treatment developed by Philadelphia-based doctor Joseph Wolpe in the mid-twentieth century to avert homosexual attraction) went a step further by suggesting that intensive treatments could potentially cure individuals of these neuroses. In effect, they portrayed those who resisted treatment as either content in their illness or beyond rehabilitation.

Fueled by some of the most popular science of the early twentieth century, discourses of sexual inversion and transvestitism quickly became important tools for exclusion, discrimination, and, at times, incarceration. The creation of the medico-legal "sexual psychopath" concept that led, as Estelle Freeman and Tamara Rice Lave have shown, to the indeterminate sentencing of many homosexuals to psychiatric institutions during the middle decades of the twentieth century in the United States, certainly serves as an extreme example. The quotidian and often insidious usages of these classifications are, in a way, more telling of the true consequences of the pathology affixed to these groups. As Canaday argues, immigration officials, motivated by nativism, xenophobia, and racism, found sexual pathology a useful tool to deny entry to unwanted immigrants that did not easily fit into the other disqualifying categories, thus reinforcing racial, class, sexual, and gender norms already operating within the country. Police, prosecutors, judges, and disapproving family members, able to portray sexual and gender minorities as criminal, mentally ill, or simply menacing under existing sexual psychopath laws, also used these medical diagnoses to justify their incarceration of "deviants" either in prisons or asylums, sometimes with indeterminate sentences. In these settings, those in positions of power easily ascribed sexual deviancy to support and enforce social norms and ideals around race, nation of origin, ability, and class. Furthermore, those in power typically ascribed or prescribed gender and sexual minority status from above rather than the minorities themselves creating and claiming it. However, some, such as Ralph Werther (aka Earl Lind and Jennie June) and Alan Hart did embrace their minority status, published early critiques of the medical and legal mistreatment of homosexuals and gender non-conformers, and countered their social ostracism with chronicles of their lives and communities.

Becoming Medicalized: 1940–1970

Increasingly punitive social and legal responses to those classified as homosexuals and transvestites of the mid-twentieth-century fueled and echoed science and medicine's growing emphasis on "treatment."[6] Treatments for homosexuality, a term widely used among medical professionals by the mid-twentieth century that could capture everything from occasional same-sex sexual desire or activity ("tendencies") to active bisexuality and/or exclusive same-sex relationships and identity, included psychoanalysis, hospitalization, hormone therapy and hormonal castration. Electro-shock therapy and lobotomy were also popular treatments from the 1940s through the 1960s. Conflating other social stigmas and forms of "deviance," doctors considered nonwhite, working class, disabled, and poor homosexuals as typically more deviant than middle- and upper-class white homosexuals and thus treated them with more punitive rather than rehabilitative treatments. The works of Eithne Luibhéid, Margot Canaday, Regina Kunzel, Siobahn Somerville, and many others illuminate these disparities. Lesbians across nearly all social strata, though still classified as deviant, garnered less attention from both the medical and legal realms, as they benefitted from a wider range of accepted sexual norms and less policing. Many middle- and upper-class homosexuals who could afford it and believed doctors could cure them of the illness that caused their ostracism from society sought out these treatments, psychoanalysis specifically, only to suffer from the mental, physical, and social consequences when they failed, as historian Martin Duberman documents in his moving memoir, *Cures: A Gay Man's Odyssey*. As a result, this period fostered significant distrust of medicine and psychiatrists, in particular, among homosexuals and bisexuals.

World War II hastened the medicalization of sexual "deviance" as doctors used psychological evaluations and physical inspection to cull homosexuals from the ranks of newly enlisted men and, to a lesser degree, women. Allan Bérubé's work illustrates how while some doctors, such as Henry Stack Sullivan, argued against labeling homosexuals as ill and disqualifying them from military service, it became common practice during recruitment throughout the war.[7] For those who evaded detection during inspection, though, gender-segregated environments such as the military or female-majority factory floors provided opportunities for those with same-sex desire to build communities.

After the war, sexologist Alfred Kinsey's two books, *Sexual Behavior in the Human Male* (1948) and *Sexual Behavior in the Human Female* (1953), illustrated naturally occurring sexual diversity to a greater extent and to a larger audience than any previous study of gender and sexual variance in the United States. Kinsey was criticized for his methods, findings, scale (which offered a 1–6 rating of sexual attraction from fully heterosexual to fully homosexual), and misunderstood claim that 10 percent of the population was homosexual. Yet, as Janice Irvine details, his work provided sexual and gender minorities validation and acceptance, a rarity from the scientific world. With the exception of Kinsey's reports and the public discussions about sexuality they briefly inspired, the postwar period witnessed increasing use of scientific beliefs to police and pathologize gender and sexual minorities.

While the political consequences of medicine proved overwhelmingly negative for gender and sexual minorities during the first half of the twentieth century, medical innovations offered new possibilities for some of those originally classified as transvestites. The mid-twentieth century brought surgical and pharmacological advancements that complicated such people's relationship to treatment and doctors. In 1951, Christine Jorgensen became the first American widely known to have sex-reassignment surgery. The procedure, conducted in Denmark, consisted of two surgeries and hormone replacement therapy. Jorgensen's celebrity return to the United States in early 1952 symbolized a moment of both new possibilities and increased medicalization for gender non-conforming people. On the one hand, doctors in the United States became more aware of, and comfortable with, the use of hormone replacement therapy, while a handful of doctors learned the sex reassignment surgery procedures from their European counterparts. On the other hand, doctors set up significant hurdles between these treatments and the patients who wanted them, including required diagnoses and more incremental "treatments" (though often more socially noticeable and stigmatized) than hormone therapy or surgery.[8] These requirements would shift over the course of the twentieth century as treatments and classifications varied; however, for those wanting to change their bodies to be more aligned with their gender presentation, some official diagnosis of a mental illness remained a constant prerequisite. In this way, doctors became gatekeepers to desired treatments as well as arbiters of pathology. Furthermore, a newly rigid medical perspective equated any gender non-conformity with a desire for sex reassignment, leaving little room for gender non-conformity as a constant state or identity.

The first edition of the Diagnostic Statistical Manual (DSM), a manual listing the medical criteria for, and classification of, all mental disorders, appeared in 1952 and built upon the early work of sexologists and psychiatrists to pathologize homosexuality and gender non-conformity. Agreed upon by the American Psychiatric Association as a shared language, this manual and the disorders it detailed became a significant obstacle for gender and sexual minorities, as it proclaimed homosexuality as well as myriad gender-related behaviors as sicknesses in a new and official way. Others sought out doctors and medical intervention as they opened doors to possible hormone therapy or sex reassignment surgery. As Henry Minton asserts, throughout the 1950s and 60s, gender and sexual minorities struggled with the medical, social, and political realities of these notions of sickness and pathology, which both ostracized them from mainstream society and provided shared experiences that unified them as outcasts.

Becoming Politicized: 1960–1980

In early political activism among sexual and gender minorities in the United States, medical classification and the concomitant stigma and persecution took center stage.[9] Founded in 1951, the Mattachine Society, the first modern rights organization for homosexuals ("homophiles" as they called themselves), engaged with their "sickness" by largely accepting the label but pushing against the consequences often resulting from it. The lesbian-focused Daughters of Bilitis started in 1955 and employed a similar strategy of tepid acceptance of medical pathologization while fighting for greater rights. These organizations, which came to include local chapters in many cities by the end of the 1950s, produced newsletters discussing their "sickness" with psychiatrists while simultaneously organizing protests against job discrimination, particularly within the government, on the basis of their homosexuality. John D'Emilio, Marcia Gallo, and Martin Meeker each explore the political tactics of illness deployed by these early activists.

The mid-1960s saw a significant recasting of the sickness narrative by the younger members of the Mattachine Society and Daughters of Bilitis. Frustrated by the ineffectiveness of accepting the "pathological" label in their fight for rights, and propelled by the other social movements around them, some within these organizations rejected the label of sickness entirely and framed their struggle as one for civil rights denied to an oppressed group. This new perspective of illness echoed similar conversations within the civil rights movement, but also in the work of psychologist Evelyn Hooker. Her 1957 paper "The Adjustment of the Male Overt Homosexual" picked up where Kinsey's research had left off, tracking not just the prevalence and behaviors of homosexuality but also its correlation to mental health, arguing that there was no correlation between homosexuality and mental illness.[10] The ideological rift within the homophile groups ultimately resulted in the 1969 founding in New York City of the Gay Liberation Front, a new co-ed organization that challenged the innate sickness of homosexuals. This shift in political strategy from accepting sickness labels to rejecting and redefining them coincided with a larger swing toward more militant and liberation-focused political activism among the younger generation of gays and lesbians of the late 1960s and early 1970s.

Undercutting and rewriting scripts of sickness and wellness became the bedrock for social relationships, politics, and medicine in the gay liberation era.[11] Previously, political groups and activism had provided sanctuary and support to homosexuals as they grappled with an "innate" sickness that had been ascribed to them by doctors, legal arbiters, and society. In the gay liberation era, identity was self-determined and sparked activism that emanated out from the idea that gay men, lesbians, and bisexuals were not inherently sick, but rather made sick by a society that discriminated against them.

Trans individuals also experienced a significant political and medical landscape shift during the 1960s and 1970s. Millionaire philanthropist and transman Reed Erickson, through his Erickson Educational Foundation, personally bankrolled researcher Harry Benjamin's *The Transsexual Phenomenon* (1966), which, in turn, inspired clinical research programs on transsexualism to open at major medical research universities across the country. The Center for

Figure 22.1 Volunteers staff the first gay caucus booth at the American Public Health Association's meeting in 1975. Founded by Walter Lear, the APHA's gay caucus was one of the first of any professional medical association. It furthered LGBT issues within the profession and improved LGBT public health. Within a decade, nearly all major medical professional organizations had a similar caucus.

Image taken by Walter Lear and gifted to author as part of oral interview.

Special Problems, a clinic that provided counseling, medical, and social services specifically for transsexuals, opened in San Francisco in 1967, offering supportive services for a wide range of trans people for the first time.[12] Amid this new supportive, if still problematic, landscape, some trans individuals found easier access to a path to self-realization through hormone therapies and surgery, where before there had been only dead-ends and ostracism.

While trans health and activism during this period turned toward the possibilities offered by medicalization, the notion of coming out, arguably the essence of gay liberation, hinged upon blocking medicalization.[13] It demanded that individuals view their sexual identity as worthy of celebration and reject medical treatment that pathologized that identity. Moreover, it challenged those to whom they came out to reconsider the existing social and medical stereotypes of the sexual "deviant." Sexual liberation and experimentation also refuted the shame and negativity long ascribed to homosexuality by medicine and society. Gay liberation politics characterized the sexual liaisons of previous decades as fear- and guilt-filled and juxtaposed those with a forward-thinking sexual politics focused on pleasure, love, and community. Even though many trans communities embraced the politics and ethos of gay liberation, the trans community's embrace of medicalization and treatments led to their marginalization and pathologization by many within the larger lesbian and gay communities, a concept explored by Susan Stryker's works.

The political reframing of sickness and health required a move beyond individual acts toward social services created for and by gays, lesbians, and bisexuals. When the Los Angeles Gay Community Services Center opened in 1971, its founders framed the services offered there as an organized response to "oppression sickness," a concept they invented and which showcases the dramatic recasting of health and sickness that epitomized this period. Oppression Sickness encompassed issues such as job loss, violence, depression, substance abuse, isolation, homelessness, medical malpractice, and self-destructive behaviors that stemmed from societal homophobia.[14]

This new framing of health served numerous purposes. First, it allowed gay men, lesbians, and bisexuals a way to understand their experiences without accepting the pathology forced upon them by medicine and society. Second, oppression sickness altered their relationship to sickness so that they could discuss and address medical ailments common in their communities without assuming the pathology of deviants. Finally, it pushed beyond the rigid boundaries of a medical understanding of health and illness, blurring the lines between medical and political issues. Questioning the authority of those that labeled gays and lesbians sick became a political act with medical implications; oppression sickness conflated health and liberation. The perspectives of politicized health revealed homophobia, patriarchy, racism and white ethnocentrism as symptoms of the same sickness that infected people. While the term oppression sickness was unique to gay activists in Los Angeles, many social services appearing at this time within and beyond the community embraced the concept's spirit, such as the S.T.A.R. House, a shelter for homeless LGBT youth and drag queens founded in 1970 in New York.

The shifting political and medical geography of sexuality and gender of the 1970s also emboldened gay and lesbian doctors, medical professionals, and activists to challenge mainstream medicine's approach to homosexuality as pathology. Their fight to remove homosexuality from the DSM-II was perhaps the most dramatic and consequential example of medical political activism of this period. In *Homosexuality and American Psychiatry*, historian Ronald Bayer describes how protestors, including psychiatrists, at the 1973 American Psychiatric Association's (APA) annual meeting wore paper bags over their heads to ensure anonymity and demanded that homosexuality be removed from the manual. The protest, along with shifting social norms and new scientific understandings of the formation of sexual identity, successfully pushed the

APA to remove homosexuality from the DSM-II that year. However, many diagnoses problematic for gender minorities remained.

While removing the diagnosis from the DSM-II was a vital step for gays, lesbians, and bisexuals reclaiming their health, the impact of treating homosexuality as a pathological illness extended far beyond the realm of psychiatry. While every adult demographic, except for lesbians, between ages 18–45 during this time period experienced venereal disease in epidemic proportions, gay men were unique in that venereal diseases among them were often diagnosed at much later and more severe stages. This resulted from gay and bisexual men avoiding medical attention for as long as possible due to their distrust and fear of doctors. Furthermore, even when gay and bisexual men went to doctors and disclosed their sexual practices, few doctors knew how venereal disease presented in men who had sex with men—a dire consequence of medical training that focused on homosexuality as an illness rather than on the illnesses homosexuals might contract. Consequently, treatment and recovery cost more money, time, and resources.

Because of their avoidance of regular medical care, gay men, lesbians, and, although less studied, likely bisexuals, experienced higher incidence of a wide array of illnesses, or were often sicker upon diagnosis than the rest of the population. From weight-gain and substance abuse to late-stage diagnoses of cancer, medicine's classification of homosexuality and bisexuality as pathological all but ensured a lower quality of life and reduced the likelihood of complete health. Even when not hindered by their own fear or their doctors' ignorance, many met outright discrimination as doctors refused service or extorted huge fees for discretion. Lesbians wanting to become mothers remained barred from buying frozen sperm as sperm banks refused to sell to lesbians or single women.[15] Removing homosexuality from the DSM did nothing to address these realities just as it did nothing for gender minorities.

Gaining access to greater health and restoring at least some trust in medicine for LGBT people required a multi-faceted approach that called upon medical professionals, researchers, and community members. Throughout the 1970s, gay, lesbian, and bisexual medical professionals created caucuses within almost every national medical professional organization in the country, where they built professional networks, encouraged research, filled gaps in medical training on gay, lesbian, and bisexual health, and formed new relationships with the larger LGBT communities. They hoped to increase the chances that gay men, lesbians, and bisexuals would find new acceptance and quality care in their doctors' offices. Along these same lines, individual gay, lesbian, and bisexual medical professionals teamed up with community activists and social service agencies to provide health care. In cities across the country, new clinics and services offered gay venereal disease testing, gynecological care, and therapy. Medical researchers of this period also addressed the dearth of research on gay, lesbian, bisexual, and transsexual health and medical needs. By the early 1980s, dozens of clinics specifically for gays and lesbians peppered the country, gay caucuses existed in every major professional medical organization, and lesbians could buy frozen sperm from a non-discriminatory feminist sperm bank. In 1976, nurse and sex therapist Maggi Rubenstein founded the Bisexual Center in San Francisco, which actively provided counseling, referrals, and support. On the other hand, the hard fought legal and medical influence won by liberal doctors who favored offering gender reassignment therapies and surgeries in the 1970s waned in the conservative 1980s as many major university-based clinics providing transgender services closed, replaced by more profit-driven private doctors and clinics.[16]

While the developments of the 1970s were unprecedented in their scope and approaches to how both medical professionals and sexual minorities understood homosexuality in relation to health and sickness, many remained left out of the new health narrative. Most of the activists, doctors, and organizations that emerged out of this time conflated gayness (and lesbian-ness) with whiteness in ways that left many lesbians, gays, and bisexuals of color unaffected by the

significant change in quality or access to healthcare. As medical definitions continued to differentiate gender non-conformity from homosexuality, and as gay and lesbian communities sought
greater political power and legitimacy in mainstream society, gay and lesbian health activists
often abandoned gender minorities and the specific needs of bisexuals. Furthermore, beyond
the newly created gay-friendly medical spaces, many gay men and lesbians still encountered
homophobia and ignorance on the part of individual doctors. Progress to fight bias and provide education remained slow and tedious. Lastly, though challenged more than ever before,
homophobia in the workplace, mainstream politics, and legal venues remained fairly intact despite
the official removal of pathology from homosexuality. The health challenges posed by the 1980s
highlighted and accentuated all of these shortcomings in the 1970s health gains.

Sickness Re-inscribed: 1981–2010

The emergence of a virus in 1981 meant that, once again, homosexuality became deeply
entangled with illness and pathology in the eyes of medical professionals and in mainstream
society—a quick end to the hard-fought, short-lived period in which homosexuals appeared
to be gaining legitimacy as "well" individuals. The first reports of what would later be called
AIDS appeared in June 1981 in the Centers for Disease Control's *Morbidity and Mortality Weekly
Report (MMWR)*, describing a rare cancer, Kaposi's Sarcoma, in 11 homosexual men.[17] That
initial bulletin, and hundreds of news stories that would follow as the epidemic took form,
linked what would become known as HIV/AIDS to gays in consequently catastrophic ways.
The new disease was so enmeshed with homosexuality that from the outset health professionals
initially named it Gay Related Immune Deficiency (GRID) in early 1982. A few months later,
the name changed to Acquired Immune Deficiency Syndrome (AIDS) in response to protest
from gay activists, who argued GRID was both inaccurate and stigmatizing for gay men. Naming
the disease captured the politics and struggle that became characteristic of the epidemic.

The political consequences of relating AIDS to homosexuality and bisexuality in the
medical and popular imaginary played out in three problematic ways. First, those looking
for a rationale to discriminate against gay and bisexual men either blamed them for AIDS or
framed the scourge of AIDS as a sort of moral and medical referendum of homosexual behavior. From this perspective, the early epidemic most impacted those who "brought it upon
themselves," excusing a slow response and unprecedented discrimination. Consequently, those
suffering from HIV/AIDS in the 1980s faced a stark medical reality in which treatments were
slow to develop and often just as deadly as the virus. In addition, fear of the disease teamed
up with homophobia and the shrinking welfare state under the Reagan administration. Gay
and bisexual people with HIV/AIDS often also dealt with job loss, homelessness, denial of
access to public services (including hospitals), and rejection from family and society. Within
the growing political conservatism and cultural emphasis on heterosexuality and morality of
the 1980s that became synonymous with the rise of the New Right, mainstream society
used the diagnosis and specter of AIDS and its close association with homosexuality to
legitimize anti-gay discrimination.

Second, the medical and political realities of the early AIDS crisis caused the gay community
to rearticulate their whiteness and middle-class status in an effort to present themselves as more
"worthy" of state and medical intervention.[18] By highlighting their whiteness and class, gay
men crafted a tragic narrative around the AIDS epidemic that relied as much upon structural
racism and classism within mainstream America as it did upon the ferocity of the virus. While
this tactic may have resulted in greater support and political leverage (though to what extent
is debatable) it further alienated people of color from "gay" spaces and communities.[19]

Third, the association of homosexuality and bisexuality with AIDS, the incredible stigma around AIDS that resulted, and the deployment of whiteness within the gay community all combined to negatively impact those beyond the "gay community" who were at risk of getting HIV/AIDS, particularly people of color. Communities of color, already facing enough discrimination and stigma on the basis of their race, and often class, sought to avoid further stigma or social and medical pathology by marginalizing people of color with AIDS and ignoring the extent of it within their communities. Similarly, public health professionals, doctors, and researchers insistent upon understanding AIDS as a disease affecting mostly homosexuals, were slow to respond as the virus became increasingly prevalent in heterosexual communities of color. Both the association and stigma of AIDS and homosexuality fueled the spread of the epidemic among populations that did not consider themselves homosexual. Meanwhile, gay and bisexual people of color faced racism in the gay community and often homophobia in their racial communities in ways that informed their education about HIV/AIDS, the services available to them (which were often church-based), and the assumptions made about how they transmitted the virus. As Cathy Cohen argues, these factors combined to ensure that homosexually transmitted HIV/AIDS had greater stigma in communities of color while simultaneously disproportionately affecting them.

Beyond these political consequences of medicine linking homosexuality to AIDS, the use of the epidemic as a political tool and movement among gay men, lesbians, bisexuals, and transgender people also marks an important reiteration of the relationship between health, sickness, and sexual politics. Without legal protection and frustrated with the pace of a medical response, gay and bisexual men turned the tragedy of the AIDS epidemic into a largely political movement. Echoing the efforts of activists from just a decade earlier who framed their health struggle as a political one against "oppression sickness," LGBT health activists of the AIDS era fought the epidemic on many political fronts while also providing care to one another. As scientists identified the HIV virus and gained understanding of how AIDS spread and developed, gay, bisexual, and lesbian activists explored and educated the public on political dimensions of the epidemic. They achieved this through providing services to those infected, education to others in the community, and protesting government officials, medical agencies, and those they believed profited from the ineffective and slow medical response. From their vantage point, AIDS was a deadly and fast-moving illness, but it was also a symptom of a society and politics that embraced homophobia and fostered discrimination.

AIDS highlighted existing structural violence. Over the course of the 1980s, and particularly in the direct action and advocacy group ACT-UP (AIDS Coalition to Unleash Power), this narrative became more inclusive of racial, gender, and economic diversity, folding anti-racist and anti-capitalist rhetoric and politics into their critique of the handling of the AIDS crisis. While unique in its scope and gravity, the early AIDS epidemic, with its political framing of illness, the challenge to medical authority, and the resistance to consequences of medically imposed and socially reinforced stigma, echoed themes common to the history of health and sickness in relation to sex, sexuality, and gender in the twentieth century.[20]

The struggles over wellness and sickness continue in the twenty-first century, as trans identified people won a major victory in decoupling their gender expression from pathology with the removal of Gender Identity Disorder (GID) from the DSM-V in 2012. By replacing GID with Gender Dysphoria, the American Psychiatric Association sought to de-stigmatize and de-pathologize trans experiences, while also attempting to provide a diagnosis that would compel insurance companies to cover hormone treatments and surgeries for those who wanted them. While hormones and surgery remain out of reach for many, this terminology shift highlights again the powerful relationship between pathology and stigma, and the political implications of sickness and health. The American Institute of Bisexuality, founded by Dr. Fritz Klein in 1998, has hastened bisexuality's move toward the front of LGBT health activism by exploring the consequences of stigma and omission of bisexuality from both mainstream and LGBTQ health services.[21] The pushback against "gay conversion" therapy, including the 2012 California law banning the practice, and the controversy surrounding the 2016 Republican Party Platform's support of such therapies, showcases the interconnectedness of pathology and politics.

Sickness and wellness as medical and political constructs have played pivotal roles in twentieth-century LGBTQ history as they have been deployed by medicine, the state, society, and by members of the LGBTQ communities. During the more than century-long period in which medicine and sexual and gender minorities have had a formal relationship, these terms served as both the basis for structural violence and the tools of agency; they defined identities and communities both from the top-down and the bottom-up. Shaping and reflecting social norms around race, class, ability, and nationality alongside gender and sexuality, the concepts of wellness and sickness provide an important and unique lens into LGBTQ history.

Notes

1 I use "gender and sexual minorities" to provide consistent terms throughout the chapter, though terminology for gender and sexual minorities changed across time and space from 1880–2015.

2 For more on this queer history of this era, see, in this volume, Elizabeth Clement and Beans Velocci, "Modern Sexuality in Modern Times (1880s–1930s.)"

3 Carl Westphal, *Die Konträre Sexualempfindung: Symptom eines neuropathologischen (psychopathischen) Zustandes* in: Archiv für Psychiatrie und Nervenkrankheiten, (Berlin, 1870), 2, 73–108.

4 Richard von Krafft-Ebing, *Psychopathia Sexualis: Eine Klinish-Forensische Studie*, (Stuttgart: Ferdinand Enke, 1887), 226–228.

5 Magnus Hirschfeld, *Die Homosexualität Des Mannes Und Des Weibes*, (Berlin: L. Marcus, 1914), 31.

6 For more on the queer context of the postwar era, see, in this volume, Amanda Littauer, "Sexual Minorities at the Apex of Heteronormativity (1940s–1965)."

7 Allan Bérubé, *Coming out under Fire: The History of Gay Men and Women in World War Two* (New York: Free Press, 1990), 9–11. The ways that Sullivan's personal life, which included a same-sex relationship with another man for several decades, relates to his work, has been the subject of multiple studies. See, for example, Peter Hegarty, "Harry Stack Sullivan and His Chums: Archive Fever in American Psychiatry?" *History of the Human Sciences* 18, no. 3 (2005): 35–53; Mary J. Belchner, "The Gay Harry Stack Sullivan: Interactions between His Life, Clinical Work, and Theory," *Contemporary Psychoanalysis* 41, no. 1 (2005): 1–19.

8 Toby Beauchamps' important new research charts various strategies used by trans individuals to assert agency in their treatments and bodies through acquiring hormones in other ways.

9 For queer US organizational history, see, in this volume, Marcia Gallo, "Organizations."

10 Evelyn Hooker, "The Adjustment of the Male Overt Homosexual," *Journal of Projective Techniques* 21, no. 1 (1957): 18–31. For more on Hooker, see *Changing Our Minds: The Story of Dr. Evelyn Hooker*, DVD, dir. Richard Schmiechen (San Francisco: Frameline, 1991).

11 For more on the gay liberation era, see, in this volume, Whitney Strub, "Gay Liberation (1963–1980)."

12 Susan Stryker, *Transgender History* (San Francisco: Seal Press, 2008), 79–80.

13 For specific ways in which trans history differs from queer history, see, in this volume, Finn Enke, "Transgender History (and Otherwise Approaches to Embodiment.)"

14 Author's interview with Donald Kilhefner, October 31, 2007.

15 For more on the history of LGBT families, see, in this volume, Daniel Rivers, "Families."

16 Joanne Meyerowitz, *How Sex Changed: A History of Transsexuality in the United States* (Cambridge: Harvard University Press), 208–75.

17 A.E. Friedman-Kien et al., "Kaposis Sarcoma and Pneumocystis Pneumonia among Homosexual Men—New York City and California," *MMWR. Morbidity and Mortality Weekly Report* 30, no. 25 (1981): 305–8.

18 Jennifer Brier, *Infectious Ideas: U.S. Political Responses to the AIDS Crisis* (Chapel Hill: University of North Carolina Press, 2009), 6. See also, in this volume, her chapter on "AIDS and Action."
19 See also, in this volume, Nayan Shah, "Queer of Color Estrangement and Belonging."
20 For more on the context of AIDS in LGBT history, see Jennifer Brier's chapter in this volume, "AIDS and Action (1980s–1990s)."
21 Bisexual health disparities persist today. See, for example, Marshall Miller et al., *Bisexual Health: An Introduction and Model Practices for HIV/STI Prevention Programming* (New York: National Gay and Lesbian Task Force Policy Institute, the Fenway Institute at Fenway Community Health, and BiNet USA, 2007).

Further Reading

Bayer, Ronald. *Homosexuality and American Psychiatry: The Politics of Diagnosis*. Princeton: Princeton University Press, 1987.
———. *Private Acts, Social Consequences: AIDS and the Politics of Public Health*. New Brunswick, N.J.: Rutgers University Press, 1991.
Berstein, Elizabeth and Laurie Schaffner, eds. *Regulating Sex: The Politics of Intimacy and Identity*. New York: Routledge, 2005.
Bérubé, Allan. *Coming Out Under Fire: The History of Gay Men and Women in World War Two*. New York: Free Press, 1990.
Black, Allida, ed. *Modern American Queer History*. Philadelphia: Temple University Press, 2001.
Brandt, Allan. *No Magic Bullet: A Social History of Venereal Disease in the United States in 1880*. New York: Oxford University Press, 1985.
Canaday, Margot. *The Straight State: Sexuality and Citizenship in Twentieth Century America*. Princeton: Princeton University Press, 2009.
Carter, Julian. *The Heart of Whiteness: Normal Sexuality and Race in America, 1880–1940*. Durham: Duke University Press, 2007.
Cohen, Cathy. *The Boundaries of Blackness: AIDS and the Breakdown of Black Politics*. Chicago: University of Chicago Press, 1999.
Crozier, Ivan. "James Kiernan and the Responsible Pervert." *International Journal of Law and Psychiatry* 25, no. 4 (2002): 331–350.
Dittmer, John. *The Good Doctors: The Medical Committee for Human Rights and the Struggle for Social Justice Health Care*. New York: Bloomsbury Press, 2009.
Drescher, Jack and Joseph Merlino. *American Psychiatry and Homosexuality: An Oral History*. New York: Harrington Park Press, 2007.
Ellis, Havelock. *Sexual Inversion: Studies in the Psychology of Sex*. Philadelphia: F.A. Davis Co., 1901.
Foucault, Michel. *The Birth of the Clinic: An Archaeology of Medical Perception*. New York: Pantheon Books, 1973.
———. *The History of Sexuality*. New York: Vintage Books, 1988.
Freedman, Estelle. "'Uncontrolled Desires': The Response to the Sexual Psychopath, 1920–1960." *Journal of American History* 74, no. 1 (1987): 83–106.
Gallo, Marcia. *Different Daughters: A History of the Daughters of Bilitis and the Rise of the Lesbian Rights Movement*. San Francisco: Seal Press, 2006.
Hanhardt, Christina. *Safe Space: Gay Neighborhood History and the Politics of Violence*. Durham: Duke University Press, 2013.
Hansen, Bert. "American Physicians' 'Discovery' of Homosexuals, 1880–1900: A New Diagnosis in a Changing Society." In *Framing Disease: Studies in Cultural History*, ed. C. E. Rosenberg, 104–133. New Brunswick, NJ: Rutgers University Press, 1992.
Hart, Alan. *In the Lives of Men*. New York: W.W. Norton and Company, 1937.
Hoffman, Lily. *The Politics of Knowledge: Activist Movements in Medicine and Planning*. Albany: State University of New York Press, 1989.
Irvine, Janice M. *Disorders of Desire: Sexuality and Gender in Modern American History*, rev. and expanded ed. Philadelphia: Temple University Press, 2005.
Johnson, David K. *The Lavender Scare: The Cold War Persecution of Gays and Lesbians in the Federal Government*. Chicago: University of Chicago Press, 2004.
Katz, Jonathan Ned. *The Invention of Homosexuality*. Chicago: University of Chicago Press, 2007.

Kinsey, Alfred, et al. *Sexual Beahvior in the Human Male*. Philadeplhia: W.B. Saunders Co., 1948.

———. *Sexual Behavior in the Human Female*. Bloomington: Indiana University Press, 1953.

Kunzel, Regina. *Criminal Intimacy: Prison and the Uneven History of Modern Sexuality*. Chicago: University of Chicago Press, 2008.

Lave, Tamara R. "Only Yesterday: The Rise and Fall of Twentieth Century Sexual Psychopath Laws." *Louisiana Law Review* 69, no. 3 (2009): 549–592.

Luibhéid, Eithne. *Entry Denied: Controlling Sexuality at the Border*. Minneapolis: University of Minnesota Press, 2002.

Meeker, Martin. "Behind the Mask of Respectability: Reconsidering the Mattachine Society and Male Homophile Practice, 1950s and 1960s." *Journal of the History of Sexuality* 10, no. 1 (2001): 78–116.

Minton, Henry. *Departing from Deviance: A History of Homosexual Rights and Emancipatory Science in America*. Chicago: University of Chicago Press, 2001.

Nelson, Alonda. *Body and Soul: The Black Panther Party and the Fight against Medical Discrimination*. Minneapolis: University of Minnesota Press, 2011.

Oosterhuis, Harry. *Stepchildren of Nature: Krafft-Ebing, Psychiatry, and the Making of Sexual Identity*. Chicago: University of Chicago Press, 2000.

Patton, Cindy. *Inventing AIDS*. New York: Routledge, 1990.

———. *Sex and Germs: The Politics of AIDS*. Boston: South End Press, 1985.

Pfeffer, Naomi. *The Stork and the Syringe: A Political History of Reproductive Medicine*. Cambridge: Polity Press, 1993.

Rofes, Eric. *Dry Bones Breathe: Gay Men Creating Post-AIDS Identities and Cultures*. New York: Haworth Press, 1998.

Romesburg, Don. "The Tightrope of Normalcy: Homosexuality, Developmental Citizenship, and American Adolescence, 1890–1940." *Journal of Historical Sociology* 21, no. 4 (2008): 417–442.

Somerville, Siobahn. *Queering the Color Line: Race and the Invention of Homosexuality*. Durham: Duke University Press, 2000.

Stryker, Susan and Stephen Whittle, eds. *The Transgender Studies Reader*. New York: Routledge, 2006.

Stryker, Susan and Aren Aizura, eds. *The Transgender Studies Reader 2*. New York: Routledge, 2013.

Terry, Jennifer. *An American Obsession: Science, Medicine, and Homosexuality in Modern Society*. Chicago: University of Chicago Press, 1999.

Werther, Ralph (pseud.) and Alfred W. Herzog. *Autobiography of an Androgyne*. New York: Medico-Legal Journal, 1918.

———. *The Female-Impersonators: A Sequel to the Autobiography of an Androgyne and an Account of Some of the Author's Experiences During His Six Years' Career as Instinctive Female-Impersonator in New York's Underworld*. New York: Medico-Legal Journal, 1921.

23

CRIMINALIZATION AND LEGALIZATION[1]

Andrea J. Ritchie and Kay Whitlock

The evolution of criminalization of lesbian, gay, bisexual, transgender and queer (LGBTQ) people in the United States neither began with the enactment of sodomy laws nor ended when the Supreme Court struck them down, nor, for that matter, when the court affirmed the right to marriage equality in 2015. It begins from the first European contact and continues through the present, and throughout US history LGBTQ and gender nonconforming people of color have been both its main targets and at the forefront of movements challenging it.

Long before modern LGBTQ identities, colonizers projected "deviant" sexualities onto Indigenous peoples, enslaved Africans, and immigrants of color. Such projections were integral to the dehumanization required by logics of colonization, genocide, enslavement, and exclusion, effectively criminalizing and excluding entire populations on the basis of actual or perceived deviation from nonprocreative sexualities and rigid binary, hierarchical notions of gender. Less than a century after Columbus first landed, Dominican cleric Bernardino de Minaya described Indigenous peoples as "idolatrous, libidinous," people who "commit sodomy." As historian Byrne Fone notes "sodomy . . . very often became a useful pretext for demonizing—and eliminating—those whose real crime was to possess what Europeans desired."[2]

Imposition of the gender binary was also essential to the establishment of the US nation state on Indigenous land. Although Indigenous societies are widely reported to have allowed for a range of gender identities and expressions, Native Studies scholars Andrea Smith and Paula Gunn Allen argue the construction of gender hierarchies and their violent, sexualized enforcement were central and essential to the colonization of this continent, rather than a mere side effect of the importation, imposition, and evolution of European cultures and moralities.[3] As Scott Lauria Morgenson details, accounts of missionaries and colonists are replete with alternately voyeuristic and derogatory references to Indigenous individuals described as "men" who take on the appearance, mannerisms, duties, and roles of "women," and who are simultaneously described or assumed to be engaging in sexual conduct with members of the "same" sex. Tales of "women" who dressed and acted as "men" while concealing their "true" nature, often accompanied by derisive descriptions of sexual relations with women, were also recorded, albeit far less frequently. Policing and punishment of perceived sexual and gender deviance among Indigenous peoples—what Deborah Miranda terms "gendercide"—was often explicit and harsh, an intentional eradication of anyone who departed from European conventions of gender and sexuality, and a tool to terrorize entire Indigenous populations. By the late nineteenth and twentieth centuries, it extended into the administrative systems established to police and punish Indigenous peoples through laws, schools, and religion.

Deviant sexualities were similarly ascribed to Africans as justification for the colonization of Africa, the transatlantic slave trade, and chattel slavery. As legal scholar Dorothy Roberts notes, "[e]ven before the African slave trade began, Europeans explained the need to control Africans by mythologizing the voracious 'sexual appetites' of Blacks."[4] Scientific racism, projecting physical differences as representations of racialized sexualities, including the notion that African women possessed "over developed clitori" enabling them to have sex with other women, played a significant role in justifying European domination of sub-Saharan Africa.[5] Perceptions of sexual deviance traveled with enslaved Africans. Historian Richard Trexler cites one source that claims that "infection" from Africa was in part responsible for what colonists perceived as the prevalence of "sodomy" in the Americas.[6] Such gendered and sexuality-based constructions of race persist, and have always driven policing and punishment of African-descended people in the United States.[7] Criminalization of racialized individuals and peoples deemed sexually and gender-nonconforming was thus integral to the colonial project, and it is against this backdrop that sodomy laws were enacted and enforced.

Sodomy Laws and Gender Policing in Early America[8]

Sodomy laws, ultimately struck down by the Supreme Court, are often perceived as relics of puritanical times and the primary mechanism of criminalization of homosexuality, particularly of gay and bisexual men. However, sodomy laws were just one mechanism among many through which sexual and gender nonconformity were criminalized across the centuries. Each American colony made sodomy and buggery capital crimes. Although many more people were known to have relationships with or engage in non-procreative sexual encounters, William Eskridge finds fewer than ten documented executions for buggery/sodomy—including bestiality—in the seventeenth century, and still fewer in the hundred years that followed. Men charged with bestiality were the most likely candidates for trial and execution. Beyond bestiality, sodomy prosecutions involved largely nonconsensual sexual relationships or encounters. Even within this realm, those charged tended to be those who, as historian Thomas Foster asserts, engaged in behavior that upset "orderly hierarchies of race, age, and status among men." While both black and white men accused of sodomy faced possible execution, imposition of a death sentence appears to have been more likely for black men. As Foster notes, "Of the three men accused of sodomy in the Massachusetts Superior Court—a black servant, a white servant, and a [white] gentleman—only the black servant was executed." [9] In 1646, Jan Creoli, a man described only as "a negro," was executed—choked to death and then "burnt to ashes"—for what was described as his second sodomy offense in the Dutch colony of New Netherland. Manuel Congo, the ten-year old black boy who was allegedly sodomized by Creoli, was also sentenced to death by being tied to a stake, flogged, and burned.[10] Sodomy laws were not only used to punish same sex relations—they were also instrumental in enforcing racialized sexual hierarchies. For instance, in 1712, a black man named Mingo (also known as "Cocho") was convicted of the charge of forcible buggery of his white employer's young teenage daughter and sentenced to be hanged.[11]

Influential white men enjoyed more protections, even when they were widely known to coerce unwilling subordinates, including indentured servants and younger men of lesser standing. In Windsor, Connecticut, Nicholas Sension, wealthy and married, was accorded three chances over thirty years to reform his behavior before facing formal charges. Finally, in 1677,

Sension appeared in General Court on charges of sodomy lodged by one of Sension's indentured servants. Legal proceedings were only initiated when, as Richard Godbeer explains, "the social disruption brought about by Sension's advances seemed to outweigh his worth as a citizen." Finally convicted of the non-capital offense of attempted sodomy, Sension was sentenced to whipping, public shaming, disenfranchisement, and placement of his estate in bond to ensure good behavior.[12] However, white men were not wholly exempt from capital convictions. In 1624 in Virginia Colony, Richard Cornish, a ship's captain, was found guilty of buggery involving a sexual attack on his (white) indentured servant and sentenced to death. The execution produced no justice for the servant, whom the court ordered to secure another master "who would then compensate the government for the costs of prosecuting and executing Cornish. In effect [the servant's] labor helped defray the cost of his master's execution."[13]

Punishment of female sexual and gender nonconformity often proceeded along different paths. While the harsh policing of Native and enslaved African-descended women rarely required formal legal proceedings, the "deviant" sexualities of poor white women, free women of color, and immigrant women of low status and financial means were generally punished under laws prohibiting fornication, prostitution, vagrancy, disorderly conduct, and "lewd, lascivious, and unseemly" behavior. In two recorded instances, white women appear to have been charged with same-sex sexual offenses: in 1642, in the Massachusetts Bay Colony, a servant, Elizabeth Johnson, was sentenced to whipping and a fine; seven years later, two women from Plymouth Colony were charged with engaging in "leude behavior."[14] While well-to-do white women might be charged with fornication or adultery, few actually appeared in court—their punishment was more often privatized and addressed through confinement in places away from public view.

Eventually, the death penalty for sodomy was abolished, first in Pennsylvania, where it was replaced with graduated punishments of whipping, hard labor, and forfeiture. These practices continued to evolve into newer forms of discipline. As Jen Manion details in *Liberty's Prisoners: Carceral Culture in Early America*, ideas about race, gender, and sexuality "were central driving roles in the transformation of punishment." States of "unfreedom"—enslavement, indentured servitude, penalties for purported wrongdoing, and even the attribution of wrongdoing—were defined and transformed in tandem. White women, for example, did not face the same presumption of criminality—or the same institutional assumptions regarding possibilities for their successful reform and rehabilitation—as black women. The intersectional manipulation and policing of these norms inexorably shaped the new system of discipline and reform.[15]

Penitentiaries, precursors to modern-day prisons, came into existence in the United States at the end of the eighteenth century as a reform motivated by growing abhorrence of corporal and capital punishment and appalling jail conditions. Their stated purpose was to rehabilitate "criminals" and deter crime by sentencing those convicted of offenses to isolation from unwholesome influences, inculcation with appropriate moral and spiritual values, hard labor, and repentance.[16] Over time, penitentiaries became the most common form of punishment for those convicted of violating sodomy laws and other laws regulating sexual and "deviant" behavior.

Nineteenth and Early Twentieth Century: Policing Gender, Sexuality, and National Identity[17]

Historian Margot Canady argues that as the modern US nation state developed, contested sex and gender norms structured various state arenas, helped to shape the public imagination, and distributed rights and recognition. Pathologizing successive waves of immigrants to the newly formed United States, for example, was constitutive of the criminalization of sexual and gender nonconformity. In the mid-nineteenth and early twentieth centuries, the process quickly extended from Northern and Southern European immigrants to migrants from Asia and Latin America, in service of building a gendered, white, and heteronormative national identity, excluding undesirables, and maintaining classed power relations. As Eithne Luibhéid details, from the time the first federal immigration law was enacted in 1875, immigration control was a site for the regulation of sexuality. Officials often used prohibitions on entry for "lewd and immoral purposes" and of individuals labeled with psychiatric conditions or deemed "likely to become public charges" to police gender and sexual nonconformity at the borders.[18]

At the local and state level, the policing of sex and gender in service of nation building is readily apparent in the policing of gender diversity. Along with sexual acts deemed deviant, deviation from gender norms served as a basis of criminalization during and beyond the colonial period. The first recorded law targeting gender nonconformity was a 1696 Massachusetts statute banning cross-dressing, "intended to curb the possibility of same-sex sexual encounters."[19] Legal scholar I. Bennett Capers describes the proliferation of "sumptuary laws" banning cross-dressing during the Civil War and Reconstruction eras that supplemented and replaced laws proscribing enslaved people and people of lower classes from wearing clothing associated with those of ruling classes.[20] Clare Sears traces cross-dressing laws in 45 cities in over 21 states during the latter part of the nineteenth and early twentieth centuries, periods also marked by demands for women's political and economic equality, and the literal right to wear pants, as well as the emergence of lesbian and gay subcultures in larger cities. These prohibitions were often found within broader indecency laws targeting "lewd" conduct and prostitution, "one part of a broader legal matrix centrally concerned with the boundaries of race, sex, citizenship and city space."[21] San Francisco's law carried a penalty of up to six months in jail, deportation for non-citizens, and eventually, potential psychiatric institutionalization. According to Sears, such laws were explicitly intended to both regulate racialized boundaries of gender and "construct a gender-normative nation," as part of a larger project of imposing a moral order in municipalities in order to make them safe for "good" white middle- and upper-class citizens by excluding gender "outlaws" from public spaces. Even where not enforced and ultimately struck down, the existence of cross-dressing laws through the late twentieth century branded gender nonconforming individuals—and particularly people of color and low-income people—as embodiments of "disorder," and "fraud," leading to continuing criminalization by other means.

The deployment of deeply raced notions of gender and sexuality in service of nation building is evident. For instance, Clare Sears details how both Asian men and women were perceived as "problem bodies" manifesting gender nonconformity in both appearance and behavior.[22] Nayan Shah highlights ways in which South Asian men who came to the United States in the early twentieth century were framed as "importers of 'unnatural' sexual practices and pernicious morality."[23] Phrases such as "Hindu sodomites" and "disgusting Oriental depravity" were commonplace. These projections were mobilized as justifications for surveillance within the United States and exclusion from it. For instance, in central California, police turned an especially harsh gaze on consensual sexual encounters between older foreign migrant men and younger, white "American" men, using vagrancy sweeps and charges of prostitution, public disturbance, "lewdness," and property offenses to punish migrants deemed to be "polluting" the nation with "deviant" sexualities.[24]

Luibhéid describes how categories of lesbian, "prostitute" and "immoral women" are used to "produce particular visions of the US nation and citizenry" rooted in "racialized, class-differentiated forms of patriarchy," emphasizing how the "immigration-control system has historically disciplined lesbians. . .by denying them entry." This was the case for Sarah Harb

Quiroz, a mother, domestic worker and lawful US permanent resident stopped at the US/ Mexico border because a US immigration officer with a reputation for detecting "sexual deviates" perceived her to be a lesbian based on her appearance. Quiroz was subjected to deportation proceedings in which government interrogators hammered at her sexual life, and her employer testified that she wore "trousers and a shirt when she came to work, and that her hair was cut shorter than some other women's."[25] Ultimately, Quiroz was deported, though she had been legally present in the United States and harmed no one. Through exclusion, criminalization, and deportation, executed through bars to entry as well as mobilization of criminalizing archetypes against entire populations of immigrants, a heteronormative, gender conforming and intrinsically white national identity was thus constructed and enforced.

Post-World War II

The post-war era is perhaps the most well-known period in which sodomy, anti-cross-dressing, vagrancy, sedition, lewd conduct and prostitution laws were deployed to criminalize LGBTQ people.[26] Historian John D'Emilio describes the chilling atmosphere of the 1950s, in which a zealous "hunt for homosexuals and lesbians" fixed queers in the public mind as dangerous moral "perverts". At every level of government and in many businesses, complex systems of tests, standards, and regulations were implemented to uproot the imaginary threat, and police forces throughout the country were given "a free rein in harassment." [27] Nan Alamilla Boyd chronicles the ways in which military police, liquor control authorities, and local law enforcement collaborated to mark places and people for routine raids, arrests, convictions, and court-martial both in San Francisco and across the country. The practice of publishing names of those arrested in raids constituted, in Allan Bérubé's words, a "war on homosexuals," in which patrons were subjected not only to fines, police brutality, and imprisonment, but also divorce, loss of child custody, loss of employment, beatings and murders, isolation, humiliation, and suicide.[28] Increasing enforcement of prostitution laws during the post-war era also caught LGBTQ people in its net. Police departments increasingly cracked down on lesbian gathering places, charging lesbians under anti-prostitution laws regardless of whether they were trading sex. Both Joan Nestle and Nan Boyd describe lesbian involvement in the sex trades, police conflation of cross-dressing among women with prostitution, and shared experiences of raids and survival. Mack Friedman similarly chronicles the mounting policing of young gay and transgender "hustlers" on the streets from Los Angeles to New York as part of nationwide efforts to stamp out "vice" and restore "wholesome" society. For many queers, the atmosphere of threat pervaded every aspect of their lives.

From the late 1940s into the early 1960s, the Cold War phrase "security threat" was code for many groups and individuals whose lives, political beliefs, and work were considered a presumptive challenge to the status quo—including "homosexuals." Closeted by necessity, lesbians, gay men, and bisexuals were presumed not only to be morally compromised, but also especially susceptible to sexual seduction and extortion by enemy agents. The virulent homophobia that accompanied the rise of McCarthyism led many state legislatures to pass new laws against gay bars, leading to the arrests of thousands every year in some cities. Anti-gay purges by local, state, and federal government agencies were inextricably entwined with the hunt for Communists and other allegedly dangerous subversives in schools and universities, publishing, film, and broadcast industries, and countless other public and private institutions.

David K. Johnson's *The Lavender Scare* reveals the chillingly systemic nature of efforts to eliminate queer people from government service as part of a larger agenda of repression.

I'LL GO, BUT NOT QUIETLY!   AND AWAY WE GO

Figure 23.1 On July 20, 1956, the Los Angeles Police Department arrested comic performer Rae
Bourbon for "impersonating a woman" onstage, despite the performer's claim of having
undergone a gender reassignment procedure in Mexico several months prior. Bourbon
turned photographs of the arrest into promotion on a comedy album, *Hollywood Exposé*,
as featured above. Bourbon's life was dogged by the law, and the performer later died
while incarcerated.
Don Romesburg personal collection.

As James A. Schnur and Stacey Braukman both detail, in the wake of the *Brown v. Board of
Education* rulings in 1954, Florida's politicians established the Florida Legislative Investigative
Committee (FLIC). FLIC initially sought to destabilize the Florida affiliate of the National
Association for the Advancement of Colored People (NAACP) by falsely linking its members
to Communist subversion. Unable to prove its allegations, FLIC selected a new target: alleged
homosexuals who could be linked both to Communist subversion and "race agitation." An
initial witch hunt on the University of Florida for "sexual deviancy" ensnared a growing number
of students and teachers before spreading to Florida Agricultural and Mechanical University
(FAMU), a historically black college. Black educators at other institutions were hounded with
questions about homosexuality and other possible criminal activity; some had their teaching
licenses revoked. Investigators also pressed female prison informants incarcerated for "crimes
against nature" to implicate female K-12 teachers alleged to be "recruiting" young students.
Finally, the Committee's own excesses triggered its dissolution in 1965.

Beyond big city bar raids and political witch-hunts, smaller towns experienced outbreaks of anti-homosexual hysteria demonizing gay men as child predators. The fear was fueled by what historian Estelle Freedman calls the "incorporation of the sexual psychopath into American criminal law" amid the phenomenon of "sex-crime panics" that harnessed sensational media coverage, leveraging popular fear of violent rape and sexual murder of children into brutal and unjust carceral crusades.[29] The search for clear ways to diagnose and preemptively identify child sexual abusers began taking root in the late nineteenth and early twentieth centuries, amid growing determination to ferret out the "born criminals"(including queers) in society by means of eugenic evaluation and psychiatric determination.[30] The medical construction of the "sexual psychopath" carried significant symbolic weight: a violent, hypersexual, usually male, sexual criminal unable to control his impulses: the archetypal sex fiend and pervert. Already understood to be sexually deviant, homosexual men were also framed as inherently violent child molesters. The concept of mental illness merged seamlessly into the criminalizing process. Between 1935 and 1965, the rapid proliferation of federal, state, and local sex crime commissions and laws ensured that a person convicted as a sexual psychopath could be incarcerated in a psychiatric institution for an indefinite period of time. Almost any sexual offense—including sodomy and indecent exposure—could trigger the diagnosis.[31]

Against this backdrop, a little-known "sex crime scandal" erupted in 1955 in Sioux City, Iowa. A boy and a girl were sexually assaulted and brutally murdered in two separate incidents. Fueled by sensational media coverage, a frenzy of outrage and panic ensued. Under intense political pressure to solve the murders, police arrested the most readily available "sexual deviates" in the area, 22 white men—including a dance teacher, three men who operated hair salons, two cosmetology students, and a department-store window dresser—identified primarily through police sting operations in which the men were coerced into "naming names" of other homosexuals. Journalist Neil Miller emphasizes: "These men had nothing to do with those crimes; the authorities never claimed they did."[32] Threatened with felony sodomy charges and lengthy sentences, the men pled guilty to lesser charges of conspiracy to commit sodomy or, in one case, "lewd and lascivious" acts with a minor (who may or may not have existed). Prosecutors asked courts to utilize a state law to declare them all to be criminal psychopaths. Twenty of the men were sentenced to indefinite confinement in a locked ward in a mental hospital. They remained there for months until, one by one, lives shattered, they were quietly released.

Freedom of speech was curtailed by laws that criminalized many forms of LGBTQ communication in this era. Even after a successful 1958 US Supreme Court ruling in *ONE, Inc. v. Olesen* providing that representation of the subject of homosexuality was not necessarily, in and of itself, obscene, many erotic and expressive representations of same-sex sexuality and gender diversity continued to be considered criminal. Historian Susan Stryker details how Virginia Prince, founder of one of the first transgender publications, was prosecuted in 1960 for distributing obscenity through the mail, ostensibly based on her sexually explicit letters to a correspondent. After a public trial, she was sentenced to five years' probation (later reduced to one), during which she was not to "cross-dress" in public or use the mail for "indecent purposes." In 1964, two publishers of "dirty books" including transgender themed publications were convicted of federal charges stemming from shipping books across state lines and sentenced to 40 years in prison.[33]

Resistance

Despite the intense repression of the post-war period—or perhaps because of it—resistance to the regulation and criminalization of sexuality and gender nonconformity was growing apace, setting the stage for the more visible resistance and nascent movements of the 1960s and 1970s. Resistance to criminalization has, of course, existed since its inception—from the persistence of Indigenous people who refused to conform to violently imposed strictures of gender and sexuality, to the courtroom protestations of people arrested for violating cross-dressing laws, to insistence on the right to assembly, expression and association. Stonewall was not even the first point of mass resistance to bar raids or police harassment. In May 1959, to name one example, gay men and transgender women, primarily black and Latina/o, resisted police harassment at Cooper's Donuts, a popular Los Angeles gathering place. Fed up with daily demands for identification and arrests for prostitution, vagrancy, and loitering, sparked by another nightly round up of patrons, customers began throwing donuts at the police, leading to street fighting and arrests.[34]

Under the shadow of McCarthyism, two of the first homophile organizations, the Mattachine Society (founded in 1950) and Daughters of Bilitis (DOB, founded in 1955) challenged marginalization and exclusion of lesbians and gay men. By the 1950s and early 1960s, they were protesting bar raids and police harassment—one of Mattachine's first actions was a protest of the 1952 arrest of one of its members for "lewd and dissolute behavior."[35] DOB framed its protest in the framework of civil rights, championing the constitutional rights of freedom of assembly, while Mattachine argued that gay bars served a worthy purpose by minimizing entrapment raids and policing of public spaces.[36]

Those with no choice but to exist in public spaces were also organizing. Between 1965 and 1970, a group of homeless gay and trans youth in San Francisco, many of whom traded sex, came together as Vanguard, "an organization of, by, and for the kids on the streets," to fight police harassment and abuse, as well as discrimination by businesses, through organizing, publications and direct action.[37] Vanguard played an instrumental role in sparking the 1966 Compton's Cafeteria riot, where "drag queens" and gay "hustlers" fought back when police tried to arrest them for doing nothing more than being out. As Stryker points out, the Compton's uprising was prompted not only by discrimination by restaurant owners but ongoing police harassment, and physical and sexual violence toward transgender women, many of whom were engaged in street-based sex work.[38] By the late 1960s, frequent police raids, harassment and brutality across the country were meeting with increasing resistance. This period also saw uprisings in Watts, Detroit, Chicago, Newark and dozens of other cities, in many cases sparked by incidents of widespread racial profiling and abuse of people of color by police.

It was against this backdrop that, in the early morning of June 28, 1969, a routine raid of the Stonewall Inn in New York City became a flashpoint of mounting resistance. Claiming to be enforcing liquor laws, police, striking patrons with billy clubs, spewing homophobic abuse, began violently making arrests. Led by "drag queens" and "butch lesbians," who, contrary to popular representations, were primarily people of color, patrons, joined by "street people," began yelling "Gay Power!", throwing shoes, coins, and bricks at the officers. Over the next several nights, police and queers clashed repeatedly in the streets of the West Village.[39] The Stonewall Uprising, which has been mythically cast as "birthplace" of the modern US LGBT rights movement, was one of many catalysts in the era. In the weeks that followed, activists formed the Gay Liberation Front, inspired by contemporaneous movements such as the women's liberation movement, the Black Panther Party and the Young Lords.[40]

Spontaneous resistance to police raids on gay bars and bathhouses blossomed in the ensuing decade, as did more formal legal strategies. As a result, raids and harassment decreased in many major cities. Yet, particularly where establishments serving LGBTQ people of color were concerned, they continued largely uninterrupted and persist today. For instance, on September 29, 1982, over 20 uniformed NYPD officers raided Blue's, a black lesbian and gay working-class bar. Activists reported:

[t]his raid was not for the purpose of arrest or mere harassment, but was a violently racist, homophobic attack. . . . The bar was wrecked: bottles smashed, sound equipment destroyed. The Black gay men and lesbians at the bar were savagely beaten: blood spattered the walls and dried in pools on the floor . . . At one point a cop threw a handful of bullets saying, "These are fag suppositories. Next time I'll put 'em up your ass."

Flyers noted that the raid came at a time when two popular local lesbian bars had lost their liquor licenses and "street transvestites and transsexuals" in Greenwich Village faced growing harassment.[41] Lesbian historian Joan Nestle also described police attacks on black lesbians in Washington Square Park, and renewed arrests of "men wearing women's clothing" on Long Island. Framing these incidents as "part of increasing right-wing violence and police abuse directed at black, Latina/o, Asian and Native peoples, women, unionists, undocumented workers and political activists," activists placed them within a larger analysis of state violence, stating "[y]our race, class, sex and sexual identification all affect how police treat you."[42] The Blues raid sparked demands for national attention to police violence against LGBTQ people of color at a congressional hearing in Brooklyn. The Anti-Police Abuse Coalition formed to organize rapid response to police violence and build alliances among communities targeted by police.[43]

Solidarity with criminalized and incarcerated LGBTQ people—and political prisoners—was at its height during this period. As documented by Regina Kunzel and publicized by transgender activist and filmmaker Reina Gossett, the march commemorating the first anniversary of the Stonewall Uprising ended at the Women's House of Detention, where members of the Black Panther party were being held, with chants of "Free Our Sisters! Free Ourselves!"[44] Stonewall leaders Sylvia Rivera and Marsha P. Johnson organized as Street Transvestite Action Revolutionaries (STAR) to ensure the survival, and fight criminalization, of transgender street-based youth. In 1971, the Trans Liberation Newsletter called for abolition of all cross-dressing laws and immediate release of all people in psychiatric facilities or prison for "transvestism or transsexualism."[45] During the 1970s and 80s, the Prisoner Project of Boston's *Gay Community News* published letters and columns from LGBT prisoners and articles on prison-related issues, facilitated correspondence with queer prisoners, provided prisoners with books and free subscriptions, and, along with what was then known as the National Gay Task Force, successfully sued for prisoners' right to receive gay publications.[46] Unfortunately, in the decades to come, as the leadership of mainstream organizations consolidated among primarily middle-class white LGB people, the focus began to shift toward achieving formal legal equality, and away from a broader resistance to state violence.

Contemporary US Legalization—and Ongoing Criminalization

In a virulently homophobic opinion, the US Supreme Court in 1986 decided *Bowers v. Hardwick*, reaffirming the legal premise for discrimination and criminalization by upholding the constitutionality of anti-gay sodomy laws. As legal scholars Robert Jacobson and Sarah Geraghty detail, while state sodomy laws were only selectively enforced, they had a lasting, stigmatizing impact, often justifying other forms of legal discrimination in employment, housing and family court. Even where they were struck down before *Lawrence*, sodomy convictions for consensual same-sex acts forced many to register as sex offenders.

AIDS provided an additional pretext for criminalization. In early days of the epidemic, political leaders, including some in the LGBTQ movement, invoked the specter of bathhouses teeming with AIDS-infected gay men to justify police raids aimed at shutting establishments down.

This, in turn, contributed to a resurgence of police violence.[47] According to Priscilla Alexander, the epidemic was also used to justify increased policing of prostitution, both queer and hetero-sexual. Police response to mounting direct actions in the context of the AIDS crisis became increasingly harsh and homophobic, and laws criminalizing HIV transmission began to proliferate, based on the limited scientific understanding of HIV at the time, many of which remain on the books to this day.

Even as states quietly began to repeal sodomy laws in the late 1970s—by 1979, twenty states' laws were struck down or eliminated—discriminatory enforcement of "lewd conduct" statutes against gay men and prostitution laws against lesbian and trans women escalated in the 1980s and 1990s. To cite just a few examples, an 18-month undercover operation entrapped 540 men at a single rest stop in New Jersey in the late 1980s.[48] Close to 2000 gay men a year were arrested for "lewd conduct" in Los Angeles between 1997 and 1999. In San Antonio, Texas, over 900 men were arrested between 1999 and 2001, and the *San Antonio Express* printed the names of individuals arrested, stopping only after one outed man committed suicide. Hundreds more were caught up in Michigan State Troopers' decade-long "bag a fag" operation targeting truck stops across the state. Massachusetts State Troopers engaged in a similar operation until it was brought to a halt by a lawsuit filed by GLAD (Gay & Lesbian Advocates & Defenders).[49]

Despite the elimination of homosexuality as a psychiatric illness in 1973, the advent of sex offender registries in the early 1990s signaled a new pathologization and branding of LGBTQ people acting on their sexuality at an early age as mentally deranged, sexually deviant bodies. A 2009 study concluded that LGBT youth are "disproportionately charged with and adju-dicated for sex offenses in cases that the system typically overlooks when heterosexual youth are involved. Even in cases involving nonsexual offenses, courts sometimes order LGBT youth to submit to...sex offender treatment programs based merely on their sexual orientation or gender identity." Individuals convicted of sodomy, particularly involving an individual under the age of 18, whether consensual or not, are still required to register as sex offenders in many states.[50]

In the midst of shifting regulation of queer sexualities and gender identities, the late 1990s and early 2000s also saw a resurgence of queer leadership in broader police accountability movements, as well as a burgeoning movement calling for prison abolition.

Simultaneously, the bulk of resources of emerging mainstream LGBTQ organizations were poured into achieving legal equality—and specifically the right to marry—relegating struggles against policing and mass incarceration to relative invisibility. Critical trans studies scholar Dean Spade chronicles a similar trajectory among groups advocating on behalf of trans people—for the right to medical treatment, name changes, and non-discrimination, leaving behind low-income and trans people of color who could access few of these benefits and continued to be criminalized through actual or perceived engagement in survival economies and racialized, gendered policing of poverty.

In 2003, the US Supreme Court struck down the Texas sodomy law that explicitly criminalized same-sex sexual conduct in *Lawrence vs. Texas*. But the legal arguments and court reasoning focusing on the right to privacy left critical areas open to continued criminaliza-tion, including public sex, commercial sex, and sex among minors. The result was a dramatic resurgence in undercover police stings targeting gay men for "lewd conduct" arrests in public restrooms and parks. While "lewd conduct" arrests have declined in some cities as a result of organizing efforts, legal challenges, and declining law enforcement resources, the impact on gay men of color and immigrant gay men continues to be devastating. A rash of arrests of young men of color in the bathrooms of New York City's Port Authority in 2014 demon-strates that lewd conduct enforcement continues to serve as a site of ongoing criminalization.[51]

"Lewd" conduct enforcement falls within the larger constellation of "broken windows" policing, which targets perceived "disorder" through selective enforcement of minor and vague offenses, rooted in age-old vagrancy laws, which prohibit an expanding spectrum of activities, including standing ("loitering"), sleeping, drinking, urinating, making noise, and approaching strangers. By criminalizing otherwise lawful activities in public spaces, police have virtually unlimited tools to stop, ticket, and arrest increasing numbers of people, most notably youth of color, people believed to be involved in street-based sex trade, and homeless people, including, disproportionately, LGBTQ people.

From the beginning, a monolithic construction of "gays," undifferentiated along lines of race, class, gender, and gender conformity, amplified the false belief that all gay people faced identical threats to their wellbeing and produced devastating effects for multiply marginalized queers. In *Safe Space: Gay Neighborhood History and the Politics of Violence*, Christina B. Hanhardt charts decades of destructive racial, gender, and economic impacts produced by neoliberal urban "safety and revitalization" strategies that emphasize policing, privatization, and gentrification. Bringing policing into LGBTQ spaces and communities, she asserts, has led to safety for the most normative among us while putting the rest of us at greater risk of criminalization.

During this period, regulation and exclusion of queers at the borders similarly shifted from overt criminalization to more subtle forms, often having the same effect for marginalized members of LGBTQ communities. In 1990 the bar against immigration by "homosexuals" finally fell—leaving standing bans on immigration of HIV+ people and people who have "engaged in prostitution." While the HIV ban was removed in 2010, the prostitution ban remains in place to this day, effectively barring entry to countless LGBTQ people who, by choice, circumstance, or coercion have engaged in prostitution prior to entry in the United States.

Criminalization of Violence Against LGBTQ People

Beginning in the 1980s, heightened attention to violence against LGBTQ people produced demands for intensified policing and harsher punishments, resulting in passage of hate crime laws and other statutes intended to offer LGBTQ people protections against intimate partner and family violence. In 2009, the Local Law Enforcement Enhancement Act (LLEEA), also known as the Matthew Shepard and James Byrd, Jr. Hate Crimes Prevention Act, authorized the Department of Justice to assist, or, where local authorities are unwilling or unable, take the lead, in state and local investigations and prosecutions of offenses in which sexual orientation or gender identity are motivating factors. In March 2013, President Barack Obama signed into law a reauthorization of the Violence Against Women Act inclusive of protections and funding to serve LGBTQ survivors of intimate partner and family violence. By that same year, 30 states and the District of Columbia had a hate crime law that included sexual orientation alone or both sexual orientation and gender identity as "protected" status categories.

Paradoxically, criminal legal responses to homophobic, transphobic and interpersonal violence serve as one of the primary sites of criminalization of LGBTQ people, including survivors of violence, who are also at heightened risk for harassment and abuse by responding police. Anti-violence advocates across the country consistently report that law enforcement officers routinely profile transgender, gender nonconforming, or more "masculine" people, people of color, immigrants, people with no or limited English proficiency, young people, and working-class and homeless people as the perpetrator of violence or abuser in any given situation, leading to frequent false arrests and police abuse of LGBTQ people targeted for violence.[52] By the late 1990s and early 2000s, progressive queer critiques of hate crime and related laws began to appear, arguing that laws intended to offer increased protections to LGBTQ survivors of violence actually intensified abusive policing and prison practices targeting LGBTQ people, and particularly LGBTQ people of color.[53]

At the same time, as historian Regina Kunzel points out, the reality—or perception—of widespread sex among prisoners held in same-sex facilities has driven intensive policing and punishment of sexual and gender nonconformity within prison walls since their inception.[54] The passage of the federal Prison Rape Elimination Act of 2003 (PREA) was driven in part by the notion of prisons as intrinsically queer spaces—characterized by violent, victimizing, corrupting, and predatory sexuality. Organizations such as Black and Pink, made up of and advocating on behalf of LGBTQ prisoners, note that PREA has produced intensified surveillance, policing and punishment of queer sexualities—and queer survivors of violence—in prisons.

Conclusion

While the history of queer America is often framed as a story of decriminalization and "legalization" of LGBTQ acts and identities, ultimately the evolution of criminalization is far more complex, featuring a shift from punishments and proscriptions explicitly targeting individuals, populations, and sexual practices deemed "deviant" to enforcement of laws of general application—including laws intended to protect LGBTQ people—to the same ends.[55] Criminalization of people and populations deemed sexually and gender nonconforming has always served the interests of establishing and maintaining structural relations of power along the lines of race, gender, class and nation. As a result, the effects of decriminalization and legalization have been most felt among more privileged segments of LGBTQ communities, leaving people of color, low income and homeless LGBTQ people and LGBTQ immigrants to continue to bear the brunt of ongoing policing, punishment and exclusions.

The early twenty-first century has been marked by renewed examination of the role and racial impacts of policing, criminalization, and mass incarceration, prompted by the record-breaking incarceration of over 2 million people, exertion of criminal legal control over an additional 5–7 million annually, and detention and deportation of millions more, all overwhelmingly Black and Brown, as well as a mounting death toll of Black and Brown people at the hands of police. As a result of the leadership of Black LGBTQ organizers on the ground in communities such as Ferguson, New York City, and Chicago, among the founders and leaders of the #BlackLivesMatter movement, and among the many authors of the broader movement policy platform, the Vision for Black Lives, and of the increasing involvement of national, regional, and local LGBTQ organizations, challenging criminalization of LGBTQ people has never been more present within conversations about the larger meanings of policing, crime and safety. It remains to be seen whether increased visibility will translate into deeper solidarity and a fully integrated analysis of the operation of policing of gender and sexuality within larger systems of racialized and poverty-based criminalization and structural violence. An end to criminalization of LGBTQ people will require an end to race, gender, and class-based policing and punishment. Anything less will simply be another evolution in how criminalization is carried out against those on the margins.

Notes

1 Parts of this chapter have been adapted and expanded from sections of Joey L. Mogul, Andrea J. Ritchie, and Kay Whitlock, *Queer (In)Justice: The Criminalization of LGBT People in the United States* (Boston: Beacon Press, 2011).

2 Andrea Smith, *Conquest: Sexual Violence and American Indian Genocide* (Cambridge: South End Press, 2005), 10; Byrne Fone, *Homophobia: A History* (New York: Metropolitan Books, 2000), 320–321, 326.

3 Smith, *Conquest*, 1, 8.

4 Dorothy E. Roberts, "Rape, Violence, and Women's Autonomy," *Chicago-Kent Law Review*, 69 (1993), 359, 365–367.

5 Sander L. Gilman, "Black Bodies, White Bodies: Toward an Iconography of Female Sexuality in Late Nineteenth Century Art, Medicine, and Literature," *Critical Inquiry* 12 (Autumn 1985): 218.

6 Richard C. Trexler, *Sex and Conquest: Gendered Violence, Political Order, and the European Conquest of the Americas* (Ithaca: Cornell University Press, 1995), 5.

7 For the queer history of US slavery, see, in this volume, Clare Sears, "Centering Slavery in Nineteenth-Century Queer History."

8 For more on Early American history of criminalization of gender and sexuality, see in this volume Richard Godbeer's "Colonial North America" and Rachel Hope Cleves' "Revolutionary Sexualities and Early National Genders."

9 Thomas Foster, *Sex and the Eighteenth-Century Man: Massachusetts and the History of Sexuality in America* (Boston: Beacon Press, 2006), 156–157, 160.

10 Jonathan Ned Katz, *Gay/Lesbian Almanac* (New York: Harper and Row, 1983), 90.

11 Foster, *Sex and the Eighteenth-Century Man*, 158; Elizabeth Bouvier, Head of Archives, Massachusetts Supreme Judicial Court, email correspondence with a co-author (Whitlock), April 9, 2009.

12 Richard Godbeer, *Sexual Revolution in Early America* (Baltimore: Johns Hopkins University Press, 2002), 45–50.

13 Katz, *Gay/Lesbian Almanac*, 69–70.

14 Godbeer, *Sexual Revolution*, 105–107.

15 Jen Manion, *Liberty's Prisoners: Carceral Control in Early America*, (Philadelphia: University of Pennsylvania Press, 2015), 5, 8–9.

16 Angela Y. Davis, *Are Prisons Obsolete?* (New York: Seven Stories Press, 2003), 40–59; Brenda V. Smith, "Prison and Punishment: Rethinking Prison Sex: Self-Expression and Safety," *Columbia Journal Gender and Law* 15 (2006): 185, 196–197.

17 For a more extensive discussion of this issue, see in this volume "Queer and Nation" by Eithne Luibhéid.

18 Eithne Luibhéid, *Entry Denied: Controlling Sexuality at the Border* (Minneapolis: University of Minnesota Press, 2002), x–xii.

19 Michael Bronski, *A Queer History of the United States* (Boston: Beacon Press 2011), 13.

20 I. Bennett Capers, "Cross Dressing and the Criminal," *Yale Journal of Law and the Humanities* 10 (2008): 8–9.

21 Clare Sears, *Arresting Dress: Cross-Dressing, Law, and Fascination in Nineteenth-Century San Francisco* (Durham: Duke University Press, 2015), 10.

22 Sears, *Arresting Dress*, 121–133.

23 Nayan Shah, "Between "Oriental Depravity" and "Natural Degenerates": Spatial Borderlands and the Making of Ordinary Americans," *American Quarterly* 57 (September 2005): 704. See also, in this volume, Nayan Shah, "Queer of Color Estrangement and Belonging."

24 Nayan Shah, *Stranger Intimacy: Contesting Race, Sexuality and the Law in the North American West* (Berkeley: University of California Press, 2011), 141–144.

25 Luibhéid, *Entry Denied*, 81, 77–101, 207.

26 For the broader queer history of the postwar era, see, in this volume, Amanda Littauer, "Sexual Minorities at the Apex of Heteronormativity (1940s–1965)."

27 John D'Emilio, *Sexual Politics, Sexual Communities: The Making of a Homosexual Minority in the United States, 1940–1970*, 2nd ed. (Chicago: The University of Chicago Press, 1998), 40–53.

28 Allan Berubé, "The History of Gay Bathhouses," in *Policing Public Sex*, ed., Dangerous Bedfellows (Cambridge: South End Press, 1996), 210, 214–215.

29 Estelle Freedman, "Uncontrolled Desires: The Response to the Sexual Psychopath, 1920–1960," in *Feminism, Sexuality, & Politics* (Chapel Hill: The University of North Carolina Press, 2006), 121–139.

30 For a useful overview of eugenics, the social construction of criminality, and structural violence, see Kay Whitlock and Michael A. Bronski, *Considering Hate: Violence, Goodness and Justice in American Culture and Politics* (Boston: Beacon Press, 2015), 20–30.

31 For the longer history of queer medicalization, see, in this volume, Katie Batza, "Sickness and Wellness."

32 Neil Miller, *Sex-Crime Panic: A Journey to the Paranoid Heart of the 1950s* (Los Angeles: Alyson Books, 2009), xvii.

33 Susan Stryker, *Transgender History* (Berkeley: Seal Press, 2008), 50–54.

34 Stryker, *Transgender History*, 60–61.

35 Michael Bronski, *A Queer History of the United States*, 180.

36 D'Emilio, *Sexual Politics, Sexual Communities*, 108–111. See also, in this volume, Marcia Gallo, "Organizations."

37 Stryker, *Transgender History*, 72–73; Jennifer Worley, "Street Power and the Claiming of Public Space: San Francisco's 'Vanguard' and pre-Stonewall Queer Radicalism," in *Captive Genders: Trans Embodiment and the Prison Industrial Complex* (San Francisco: AK Press, 2011).

38 Stryker, *Transgender History*, 67.

39 Leigh W. Rutledge, *The Gay Decades: From Stonewall to the Present: The People and Events that Shaped Gay Lives* (New York: Penguin, 1992), 3.

40 For the broader queer history of the gay liberation era, see, in this volume, Whitney Strub, "Gay Liberation (1963–1980)."

41 Mogul et al., 54.

42 *Fight Police Abuse! Remember Blues!* flyer, undated (c. 1984), Lesbian Herstory Archives, New York City.

43 Che Gossett, Reina Gossett, and AJ Lewis, "Reclaiming Our Lineage: Organized Queer, Gender-Nonconforming, and Transgender Resistance to Police Violence," *Scholar and Feminist Online* 10.1–2 (Fall 2011/Spring 2012). See also Regina Kunzel, "Lessons in Being Gay: Queer Encounters in Gay and Lesbian Prison Activism," *Radical History Review* 100 (Winter 2008): 14.

44 Che Gossett et al., "Reclaiming Our Lineage" and Regina Kunzel, *Criminal Intimacy: Prison and the Uneven History of Modern Sexuality* (Chicago: University of Chicago Press, 2010), 191.

45 Stryker, *Transgender History*, 96–97.

46 Interview with Amy B. Hoffman by co-author Whitlock, September 23, 2009; Urvashi Vaid, *Virtual Equality: The Mainstreaming of Gay and Lesbian Liberation* (New York: Anchor, 1995), 70–72.

47 Dangerous Bedfellows, eds., *Policing Public Sex*, xi, 30, 36; Berubé, "The History of Gay Bathhouses," 207.

48 R. Esposito and C. Wright, "Widow Prompted Rest Stop Stings, Marie Lombardi Threatened to Remove Coach's Memorabilia," *Newsday*, March 2, 1990, 8.

49 Amnesty International, *Stonewalled: Police Abuse and Misconduct Against Lesbian, Gay, Bisexual and Transgender People in the United States*, (2005), 22, 23, 24, 27, 28.

50 Katayoon Majd, Jody Marksamer, and Catolyn Reyes, *Hidden Injustice: Lesbian, Gay, Bisexual and Transgender Youth in Juvenile Courts* (San Francisco: Legal Services for Children, National Center for Lesbian Rights, National Juvenile Justice Center, 2009), 3; Washington College of Law Fifty State Survey of Adult Sex Offender Registration Requirements, NIC/WCL Project on Addressing Prison Rape (2010), available at: www.wcl.american.edu/endsilence/documents/FiftyStateSurveyofAdultSex OffenderRegistrationStatutes_November2010Update.pdf. Accessed October 24, 2017.

51 National Coalition of Anti-Violence Programs, "Anti-Lesbian, Gay, Bisexual, and Transgender Violence in 2007 (New York: NCAVP, 2008), 18. Amnesty, *Stonewalled*, 26–29; Joseph Goldstein, "Lawyers Challenge Lewdness Arrests at Port Authority Bus Terminal," *New York Times*, October 7, 2014. For the long queer urban history of racialization, see, in this volume, Kwame Holmes, "The End of Queer Urban History?"

52 National Coalition of Anti-Violence Programs, 2015 *Report on Lesbian, Gay, Bisexual, Transgender, Queer, and HIV-Affected Hate Violence* (New York: NCAVP, 2016); Amnesty, *Stonewalled*, 85–87.

53 For a useful summary of growing progressive queer critiques of hate crime laws, see Mogul, et al., *Queer (In)Justice*, 118–140. See also Against Equality, summary of queer hate crime law challenges, www.againstequality.org/about/prison/. Accessed February 9, 2016.

54 Kunzel, *Criminal Intimacy*, 2, 8–9.

55 For an exploration and critique of the limits of "progress" as a narrative for US LGBT legal and political history, see in this volume, Marc Stein, " 'How Crooked and Perverse': Constructing and Deconstructing 'Progress' in LGBT Law and Politics."

Further Reading

Agee, Christopher. *The Streets of San Francisco: Policing and the Creation of Cosmopolitan Liberal Politics 1950–1972*. Chicago: University of Chicago Press, 2014.

Alexander, Priscilla. "Bathhouses and Brothels: Symbolic Sites in Discourse and Practice." In *Policing Public Sex*, ed., Dangerous Bedfellows. Cambridge: South End Press, 1996.

Boyd, Nan Alamilla. *Wide Open Town: A History of Queer San Francisco to 1965*. Berkeley: University of California Press, 2003.

Boyd, Susan C. *From Witches to Crack Moms: Women, Drug Law and Policy*. Durham: Carolina Academic Press, 2004.

Braukman, Stacey. "'Nothing Else Matters but Sex': Cold War Narratives of Deviance and the Search for Lesbian Teachers in Florida, 1959–1963." *Feminist Studies* 27. No. 3 (Autumn 2001): 553–575.

Eskridge, William. *Dishonorable Passions: Sodomy Laws in America, 1861–2003*. New York: Viking, 2008.

Friedman, Mack. *Strapped for Cash: A History of American Hustler Culture*. Los Angeles: Alyson Publications, 2003.

Geraghty, Sarah. "Conversation: Residency Restrictions on Sex Offenders: Challenging the Banishment of Registered Sex Offenders from the State of Georgia: A Practitioner's Perspective." *Harvard Civil Right-Civil Liberties Law Review* 513 (2007): 513–529.

Gilman, Sander L. "Black Bodies, White Bodies: Toward an Iconography of Female Sexuality in Late Nineteenth-Century Art, Medicine, and Literature." *Critical Inquiry* 12 (Autumn 1985): 204–242.

Hanhardt, Christina B. *Safe Space: Gay Neighborhood History and the Politics of Violence*. Durham: Duke University Press, 2013.

Johnson, David K. *The Lavender Scare: The Cold War Persecution of Gays and Lesbians in the Federal Government*. Chicago: The University of Chicago Press, 2004.

Kandaswamy, Priya. "Gendering Racial Formation." In *Racial Formation in the Twenty-First Century*, Daniel Martinez HoSang, Oneka LaBennett and Laura Pulido, eds. Berkeley: University of California Press, 2012.

Jacobson, Robert L. "'Megan's Law': Reinforcing Old Patterns of Anti-Gay Police Harassment." *Georgetown Law Journal* 87 (1999): 2440–53.

Leslie, Christopher. "Creating Criminals: The Injuries Inflicted by 'Unenforced' Sodomy Laws." *Harvard Civil Right-Civil Liberties Law Review Harvard Civil Right-Civil Liberties Law Review* 35 (2000): 103–181.

Massad, Joseph A. *Desiring Arabs*. Chicago: University of Chicago Press, 2007.

Oaks, Robert. "'Things Fearful to Name:' Sodomy and Buggery in Seventeenth-Century New England" *Journal of Social History* 12 (Winter 1978): 268–281.

Miranda, Deborah A. "Extermination of the Joyas: Gendercide in Spanish California." *GLQ* 16, nos. 1–2 (2010): 252–284.

Manion, Jen. *Liberty's Prisoners: Carceral Culture in Early America*. Philadelphia: University of Pennsylvania Press, 2015.

Morgensen, Scott Lauria. *Spaces Between Us: Queer Settler Colonialism and Indigenous Decolonization*. Minneapolis: University of Minneapolis Press, 2011.

Nestle, Joan. *A Restricted Country*. Ithaca, New York: Firebrand Books, 1987.

Robson, Ruthann. *Lesbian (Out)law: Survival Under the Rule of Law*. Ann Arbor: Firebrand Books, 1992.

Schnur, James A. "Closet Crusaders: The Johns Committee and Homophobia, 1956–1965." In *Carryin' On: In the Lesbian and Gay South*, ed. John Howard, 132–164. New York: New York University Press, 1997.

Somerville, Siobhan B. *Queering the Color Line: Race and the Invention of Homosexuality in American Culture*. Durham: Duke University Press, 2000.

Spade, Dean. *Normal Life: Administrative Violence, Critical Trans Politics, and the Limits of Law*, revised and expanded ed. Durham: Duke University Press, 2015 [2011].

Stanley, Eric/a and Nat Smith, eds. *Captive Genders: Trans Embodiment and the Prison Industrial Complex*. Oakland: AK Press, 2011.

Whitlock, Kay and Michael Bronski. *Considering Hate: Violence, Goodness, and Justice in American Culture and Politics*. Boston: Beacon Press, 2015.

Young, Vernetta and Zoe Spencer. "Multiple Jeopardy: The Impact of Race, Gender, and Slavery on the Punishment of Women in Antebellum America." In *Race, Gender and Punishment: From Colonialism to the War on Terror*, ed. Mary Bosworth and Jeanne Flavin, 65–76. New Brunswick: Rutgers University Press, 2007.

24

LAW AND POLITICS

"Crooked and Perverse" Narratives of LGBT Progress

Marc Stein

There are compelling reasons to narrate the history of US lesbian, gay, bisexual, and transgender (LGBT) law and politics as a chronicle of progress. Philosophers of history, however, have long questioned the tendency to think about past and present in these terms. In 1931, Herbert Butterfield's *The Whig Interpretation of History* referred to "how crooked and perverse the ways of progress are, with what willfulness and waste it twists and turns, and takes anything but the straight track to its goal." In 1946, R. G. Collingwood's *The Idea of History* declared:

> The conception of a 'law of progress', by which the course of history is so governed that successive forms of human activity exhibit each an improvement on the last, is . . .a mere confusion of thought. . . . The old dogma of a single historical progress leading to the present and the modern dogma of historical cycles . . . are thus mere projections of the historian's ignorance upon the screen of the past.

Decades later, Michel Foucault's *The History of Sexuality* reworked these insights to challenge the notion that the history of sexuality is best conceptualized as a story of progress from "repression" to "liberation."[1] Yet narratives of progress continue to exert a powerful hold on popular historical imaginations in general, ideas about the history of sexuality and gender more specifically, and conceptions of US LGBT law and politics in particular.

The first half of this essay offers an inventory of arguments that support the notion that there has been long-term historical progress in US LGBT law and politics. The second half contests this idea. While the essay does not resolve the conflict between these two positions, it challenges those who make uncritical assumptions about LGBT progress and those who disdain or dismiss the points of their opponents in these debates.

One of the most convincing arguments in favor of a narrative of US LGBT legal progress focuses on the decriminalization of same-sex sex acts, a subject explored by Jonathan Ned Katz, Richard Godbeer, William Eskridge, and Stephen Robertson. Sodomy and buggery (generally interpreted to mean anal intercourse, sometimes applied to oral sex, and disproportionately used to police same-sex sex) were capital offenses in most European colonies in North America. In these jurisdictions, a small but significant number of people were executed for committing same-sex sex acts during the seventeenth and eighteenth centuries. Sodomy law reform began in 1682, when Pennsylvania eliminated its death penalty for sodomy. This "holy experiment" lasted eighteen years for "negroes" and thirty-six for everyone else, but in 1786, after the United States achieved independence from Great Britain, Pennsylvania more permanently ended capital punishment for sodomy.[2] One by one, other states followed Pennsylvania's lead until the final three, North Carolina, South Carolina, and Arkansas, did so in 1868–1873, a rarely noted aspect of Reconstruction era law reform.[3] Over the next century, most states further reduced their penalties for sodomy, buggery, and "crimes against nature" until Illinois in 1961 and Connecticut in 1969 became the first to decriminalize private same-sex sex by consenting adults. Influenced by LGBT political mobilization after the Stonewall riots of 1969, twenty states decriminalized sodomy in the 1970s; three more did so in the 1980s; and the US Supreme Court struck down as unconstitutional the final fourteen state sodomy laws in 2003.[4]

The history of laws against cross-dressing, which has been studied by Kathleen Brown, Eskridge, Joanne Meyerowitz, Susan Stryker, and Clare Sears, also seems to align with a progress narrative. Europe's North American colonies harshly penalized certain types of cross-dressing, sometimes through spectacles of public humiliation and often in the context of broader prohibitions on deception and disguise. In the 1840s and 1850s, several cities followed the lead of Columbus, Ohio, in passing more specific bans on cross-dressing; twenty-five, including Chicago and San Francisco, did so by the end of the nineteenth century. Additional cities, including Detroit, Miami, and San Diego, joined them in the first seven decades of the twentieth; others continued to rely on laws against deception and disguise. The penalties faced by nineteenth- and twentieth-century cross-dressers included imprisonment and institutionalization. For laws against cross-dressing, the key reform decades were the 1970s and 1980s, when LGBT activism, feminist mobilization, and new fashion trends reduced support for these bans. Many restrictions on cross-dressing were repealed by city governments or invalidated by courts; others became moot when local authorities stopped enforcing them.

When we consider police practices more broadly, there are additional reasons to highlight LGBT progress. Policing has been investigated at the national level by John D'Emilio and Eskridge and at local and regional levels in my work on Philadelphia and the work of Elizabeth Kennedy and Madeline Davis on Buffalo, Esther Newton on Fire Island, George Chauncey on New York City, Sharon Ullman on Long Beach, John Howard on Mississippi, Nan Alamilla Boyd on San Francisco, Peter Boag on the Pacific Northwest, and more recent authors on a broad range of locations. Local authorities had expansive powers to enforce sex and gender laws in the colonial and antebellum eras. In the second half of the nineteenth century and the first seven decades of the twentieth, gender and sexual "deviants" arguably lived in a police state where law enforcement officials had tremendous legal and extralegal power to abuse, arrest, attack, and imprison them. Gender and sexual policing was especially intense in sites that had reputations for attracting people interested in same-sex sex or cross-dressing, including bars, clubs, bathhouses, bathrooms, parks, and theaters. People of color, immigrants, poor people, and gender transgressors were distinctly vulnerable. According to the best estimates, from the late nineteenth century through the 1960s the police annually arrested thousands and perhaps tens of thousands of people for violating laws against same-sex sex, cross-dressing, and crimes linked to these offenses, such as disorderly conduct, indecency, lewdness, solicitation, and vagrancy. Each year, they also extorted, raided, and closed hundreds or thousands of businesses frequented by LGBT people. Here, too, the critical transition seemingly occurred in the late 1960s and early 1970s, when LGBT lobbying, litigation, and demonstrations led to major declines in gender and sexual policing. In a striking sign of change, by the early twenty-first century many police departments were recruiting LGBT officers.[5]

At the federal level, five major policy arenas provide evidence of LGBT progress.[6] Liberalization arguably occurred first in obscenity law, which had long been used to censor LGBT speech and expression. As Eskridge has shown, in the nineteenth century many states and cities, beginning with Illinois in 1845 and Cincinnati in 1849, passed laws against obscene publications and immoral plays. Soon the federal government got involved. In 1873, Congress passed the Comstock Act, which prohibited the mailing of obscene materials. This inspired further federal, state, and local laws against sexual speech and expression. My work and the work of Whitney Strub explores the major changes in sexual censorship that occurred in the 1950s and 1960s, when the US Supreme Court narrowed the constitutionally permissible def- -inition of obscenity. In 1958 and 1962, the Supreme Court ruled that a homophile movement periodical and a male physique magazine were not obscene. These developments contributed significantly to the growth of LGBT magazines, newspapers, literature, and film.

Liberalization at the federal level next occurred in civil service rules and regulations, a subject examined by D'Emilio, Eskridge, and David Johnson. The US government long required its workers to meet moral standards, but in 1953 President Eisenhower issued an executive order excluding "sexual perverts" from federal jobs. In the 1940s, 1950s, and 1960s, more than 5000 workers lost their jobs because of these policies. Thousands more were rejected as job applicants and countless others were more quietly dismissed or excluded because of anti-LGBT animus. In this case, the most significant changes occurred in the late 1960s and 1970s, when lobbying and litigation convinced the US Civil Service Commission to modify and then end its ban on the employment of homosexuals. A few decades later, the Equal Employment Opportunity Commission (EEOC) added further protections. In 2012, it ruled that the 1964 Civil Rights Act prohibited federal government employment discrimination based on gender identity. Three years later, the EEOC ruled that the Civil Rights Act's ban on employment discrimination based on sex applied to sexual orientation discrimination.[7]

Civil service reform was followed by changes in immigration law. My work and the studies of Eskridge, Eithne Luibhéid, and Margot Canaday have explored this process, which began in the late nineteenth and early twentieth centuries, when Congress passed statutes that targeted individuals who had been convicted of crimes of "moral turpitude" and those who were "constitutional psychopathic inferiors." Congress then banned the immigration of persons "afflicted with psychopathic personality" in 1952 and "sexual deviates" in 1965. These provisions and others, including those that targeted individuals likely to become "public charges," were applied to people suspected of engaging in same-sex sex or transgressing conventional genders. Hundreds and perhaps thousands were excluded or deported on these bases until the late 1970s, when the Public Health Service announced that since it no longer viewed homosexuality as a mental illness it would no longer provide the medical certificates required to exclude or deport aliens based on homosexuality. Shortly thereafter the Immigration and Naturalization Service announced that aliens would not be questioned about their sexual orientation but would be excluded or deported if they openly affirmed their homosexuality. The culmination of progress in LGBT immigration law seemingly occurred in 1990, when Congress repealed the ban on immigrants with "psychopathic personalities" and "sexual deviations."

The fourth federal policy arena in which there is compelling evidence of LGBT progress is military policy, which has been examined by D'Emilio, Allan Bérubé, Leisa Meyer, Eskridge, and Canaday. In 1778, when the Continental Army first court-martialed soldiers for engaging in same-sex sex, the US military inaugurated more than two centuries of sodomy prosecutions. Congress affirmed the military's ban on sodomy in 1920; shortly thereafter new regulations provided for the rejection of recruits based on "sexual perversion," "sexual psychopathy," and bodies that exhibited signs of the "opposite sex." In 1941, just before the United States entered World War II, the military barred the enlistment of homosexuals, though this was impossible to enforce. After the war, the Veterans Administration announced that individuals discharged because of homosexuality were ineligible for veterans' benefits. In the 1960s, the military deemed transsexuals ineligible for enlistment. From 1940 to 1970, there were more than 50,000 discharges based on allegations of homosexuality. In contrast to the policy arenas discussed above, military policy continued to be strongly anti-LGBT in the 1970s and 1980s, when more than 25,000 anti-homosexual discharges occurred. In 1993, however, Congress adopted the "don't ask, don't tell" policy, under which the military would not question service members about their sexual orientation and individuals could continue to serve if they did not disclose their homosexuality. Thousands were discharged under this policy until Congress repealed the ban on gay and lesbian service members in 2011. Four years later the Defense Department announced that it was lifting its ban on transgender service members.[8]

The fifth federal policy arena where there is evidence to support a narrative of progress is marriage recognition, which can be linked to broader progress in family law at local, state, and national levels. As the work of Daniel Rivers, Rachel Cleves, and others has shown, people who engaged in same-sex sex or transgressed binary genders formed intimate relationships, participated in commitment rituals, birthed and raised children, and established families across US history.[9] Until the 1970s, however, local, state, and national governments refused to recognize the legitimacy and legality of same-sex sexual partnerships and only accepted marriages if they involved one person classified as male at birth and one classified as female at birth. They also discriminated against LGBT people in parental custody and legal guardianship decisions and declined to permit them to adopt children or serve as foster parents. In a society that provided thousands of benefits, billions of dollars, and tremendous cultural capital to people who married and parented legally, these restrictions had major ramifications.

In the late twentieth century, much of this began to change. In the 1970s, openly LGBT parents began to win parental custody cases, successfully arguing for their rights and for the best interests of their children. Many states began to permit LGBT people to adopt children and serve as foster parents. By the 1980s the combined effects of LGBT political mobilization and assisted reproduction technologies were contributing to a LGBT baby boom. By 2016 LGBT people could adopt and foster in most US jurisdictions and same-sex second parent adoptions were common. Meanwhile, in the 1970s same-sex couples began to appeal to the courts for marriage rights and in 1976 New Jersey became the first state to knowingly permit a transsexual to marry in their post-operative sex. In the 1980s, businesses such as the *Village Voice* and municipalities such as Berkeley and West Hollywood led the way in extending domestic partner benefits to the same-sex spouses of their employees; by the early twenty-first century thousands of employers did so. After decades of LGBT efforts to win government recognition for their intimate relationships, Massachusetts became the first to recognize same-sex marriages in 2003–2004. More states followed suit and in 2013 the Supreme Court overturned the 1996 Defense of Marriage Act, which had denied federal recognition of same-sex marriages. Two years later, the Supreme Court invalidated the remaining state bans on same-sex marriage.[10]

The narrative of LGBT progress becomes even more compelling when we consider evidence suggesting that the state has gone from being an enemy to a friend of LGBT rights. Before the 1970s, LGBT activists generally focused on reducing the state's role in policing gender and sexuality. As these goals began to be achieved, they increasingly envisioned positive roles for the state, as my work and the work of Eskridge and Ellen Andersen have demonstrated.

In 1972, Ann Arbor and East Lansing led the way in banning public employment discrimination based on sexual orientation. Pennsylvania became the first state to do so in 1975. In the same year, Minneapolis was the first city to ban discrimination based on gender identity in employment, housing, and public accommodations; in 1993 Minnesota was the first state to do so. By 2016, twenty-two states had passed sexual orientation antidiscrimination laws; twenty had passed gender identity antidiscrimination laws; and more than 140 cities and counties had passed antidiscrimination laws that covered sexual orientation and gender identity.

Additional positive roles for the state emerged in the form of hate crime laws, which provide enhanced penalties when crimes are motivated by animus toward a protected class, and laws addressing LGBT issues in public schools. In 1984, California became the first state to reference sexual orientation in hate crime legislation; in 2016 thirty states did so. In 1990, Washington, D.C., became the first US jurisdiction to reference gender identity in a hate crime law; in 2016 seventeen states did so. In 2009, Congress amended the federal hate crime law to cover crimes motivated by animus based on sexual orientation or gender identity. Two years later California became the first state to mandate the teaching of LGBT history in public schools. By 2016 there were restrictions on anti-LGBT school bullying in twenty-one states.[11]

Progress also seems to be evident in government approaches to sex/gender classifications. As Meyerowitz and Stryker explain, through much of US history local, state, and federal authorities refused to allow individuals to change their sex/gender designations on official government documents, including birth certificates and drivers' licenses. Influenced by trans visibility and activism in the 1950s and 1960s, Illinois, Arizona, and Louisiana were among the first states to permit these changes. Nine more states did so in the 1970s and eight followed their lead in the 1980s. In the early 2010s, the State Department, Veterans Health Administration, and Social Security Administration began allowing individuals to update their sex/gender designation without evidence of sex reassignment surgery. By 2016, all states permitted changes of sex on drivers' licenses and most allowed changes of sex on birth certificates.[12]

One final set of reasons to believe in the narrative of LGBT progress relates to political parties, elections, and appointments, which have been examined in my work and that of Robert Bailey and David Rayside. As Kevin Murphy's scholarship on the Progressive Era illustrates, before the 1970s it was common for US politicians to cast aspersions on their opponents by implicitly or explicitly suggesting that their inversions and perversions rendered them unfit for office. Before the 1970s, no major political party supported LGBT rights; no openly LGBT political candidate won an election; no openly LGBT person was appointed to a political office; and no openly LGBT person was elected or appointed to serve as a judge. In the 1940s, 1950s, and 1960s, LGBT activists began to participate in electoral politics and in several instances they influenced the outcome of local races. In the 1970s, they began to form gay and lesbian Democratic Party clubs, won election to serve as delegates to Democratic Party conventions, garnered support for their rights in Democratic Party platforms, and were increasingly recognized as part of the Democratic electoral coalition. In the 1980s, LGBT activists began to form Log Cabin Republican Party clubs and organize receptions at Republican conventions; over the next few decades several prominent Republicans came out as gay. As they increased their involvement in party politics, LGBT candidates began to win elections. In the 1970s, openly gay and lesbian candidates won election to the city councils of Ann Arbor, Madison, and San Francisco and the state legislatures of Massachusetts and Minnesota. Openly bisexual candidates began to win local and state elections in the 1990s, and openly trans candidates in the 2000s. Openly gay candidates began to win elections to the US House in the 1980s; lesbian and bisexual successes followed in the 1990s and 2010s. The first openly lesbian U.S. Senator was elected in 2012 and the first openly bisexual governor was elected in 2016. By 2016, there were more than 100 openly LGBT judges and more than 500 openly LGBT elected officials in the United States; these include mayors, governors, and members of the US House and Senate.

The evidence of LGBT progress in law and politics, across all of the areas discussed above, is substantial. Why, then, do some scholars and activists challenge these narratives? I do not refer here to those who oppose LGBT empowerment or deny that increased recognition of LGBT rights should be regarded as progress. I refer instead to those who question the notion that progress has occurred and offer other arguments against narratives of progress. One reason is that there is compelling evidence of deep, profound, and ongoing limitations on LGBT freedom and equality. This does not mean that progress has not occurred, but it cautions us about premature celebrations that might deter and defer additional progress.

One set of limitations relates to laws that police sex and gender. The Supreme Court invalidated state sodomy statutes in 2003, for instance, but as of 2016 twelve states had not repealed their sodomy laws. The continued existence of these bans expresses symbolic opposition to same-sex sex and also has more tangible consequences. Prisoners, minors and their partners, sex workers and their clients, and people who have public sex can be and still are prosecuted for engaging in same-sex sex. Many jurisdictions require people convicted of sodomy before 2003 to register as sex offenders. US immigration law discriminates against people convicted of same-sex sex offenses in other countries. State and local authorities continue to use laws against disorderly conduct, indecency, lewdness, solicitation, and vagrancy to police LGBT cultures. Many cities have not repealed their anti-cross-dressing laws and as recently as 2007 (in Delcambre, Louisiana) some have passed new ones. Several states have recently passed anti-trans "bathroom bills."[13]

Limitations on progress in police practices have been demonstrated in studies by David Serlin, Timothy Stewart-Winter, Christina Hanhardt, and me. Since the 1980s, for example, there have been fewer police raids on, and government closures of, bathhouses frequented by people who enjoy same-sex sex, but this is partly because many were forced to close based on false assertions about public health during the early years of the AIDS crisis. Public sex and sex for money continue to be intensively policed, as was evident in the Department of Homeland Security's 2015 Rentboy.com arrests. The same-sex sexual activities of teenagers, seniors, people with disabilities, and people with sexually transmitted diseases may be more aggressively policed in the twenty-first century than they were previously. Some police departments now hire and recruit LGBT people, but many do not; many do not respond appropriately to crimes against LGBT people; and many engage in abusive, discriminatory, and violent practices against LGBT people of color, LGBT poor people, and trans people.[14]

There have also been limits on LGBT progress in federal law and politics. As Strub and I emphasize, for example, the Supreme Court may have adopted stricter definitions of obscenity in the 1950s and 1960s, but it continues to hold that the First Amendment does not apply to obscenity. Since the 1950s, the Court has consistently accepted the use of double standards in the regulation of obscenity. In the 1960s, it adopted special rules for materials aimed at "sexual deviants" and in the 1980s it endorsed special protection for materials that provoked "normal, healthy sexual desires." In the 1970s, the Court revised its rules to permit the use of restrictive local standards in policing obscenity and upheld the aggressive use of zoning regulations to limit the locations of sex businesses. Later in the 1980s, when the Federal Bureau of Prisons announced that it would allow inmates to have access to sexually explicit publications, it retained its ban on homoerotic materials. In the 1980s, 1990s, and 2000s, the Centers for Disease Control, National Endowment for the Arts, National Endowment for the Humanities, and other federal agencies vetoed funding for projects because of LGBT content. Congress authorized these actions and the Supreme Court upheld them. In the 2000s and 2010s, the emergence of new technologies seems to have led to an escalation in the policing of sexual communication by minors.

LGBT progress has also been limited in relation to civil service rules and regulations, immigration laws and procedures, and military policies and practices. As my work makes clear, the Civil Service Commission may have ended the federal government's ban on the employment of homosexuals in the 1970s, but for decades it made exceptions for the Central Intelligence Agency, Federal Bureau of Investigation, and National Security Agency. Congress may have repealed its ban on LGBT immigrants in 1990, but around the same time it authorized exclusion and deportation for immigrants with HIV/AIDS, a policy not rescinded until 2010. The US asylum and refugee system may now be open to claims about anti-LGBT persecution in foreign countries, but many who make such claims find it impossible to meet the system's requirements. Moreover, the rules often require individuals to claim coherent and core identities that are at odds with their experiences and preferences. The process also typically expects applicants to denounce their countries and cultures of origin. In relation to the military, the United States ended its service ban on LGBT people, but the Trump administration is attempting to reimpose a trans one. Ongoing anti-LGBT abuse, harassment, and violence occurs in the armed forces.[15]

While many limitations on LGBT progress in family law were removed by the Supreme Court's 2015 rejection of state laws banning same-sex marriage, others persist. As of 2018, it is not clear whether government workers will be permitted to invoke their religious beliefs to justify not serving LGBT people who want to adopt, foster, or marry, and whether private businesses that serve the public will be permitted to not serve LGBT people. More than twenty states currently have religious exemption laws that apply in one or more of these situations. LGBT people continue to report bias, prejudice, and discrimination in local and state adoption, assisted reproduction, day care, and foster care systems.[16]

As for the more positive roles that governments can play, there is still no federal law that bans discrimination based on sexual orientation or gender identity in employment, housing, or public accommodations. As of 2016, discrimination based on sexual orientation is legal in thirty states; discrimination based on gender identity (unless interpreted as a form of sex discrimination) is legal in thirty-two. In these contexts, federal and state courts generally have applied minimum scrutiny in cases that address discrimination based on sexual orientation or gender identity. Twenty states do not have hate crime laws that address anti-LGB animus; thirty-three do not address anti-T animus. Several do not permit changes of sex on birth certificates; many make it difficult to make such changes.[17]

Limitations on LGBT progress are also evident when we consider political parties, elections, and appointments. One of the two major US political parties—the one that controls all three branches of the federal government and most state governments in 2017 and 2018—consistently opposes LGBT rights. The Supreme Court may reverse its recent LGBT rights decisions if a justice who supports LGBT rights is replaced by one who does not. The number of state legislative seats held by openly LGBT individuals declined after the 2014 elections and declined again after the 2016 elections. In 2016, only 1 percent of US Senators, 1.4 percent of US Representatives, 1.1 percent of federal judges, and 2 percent of US governors are openly LGB. None is openly T. There has never been a US President, Vice President, Cabinet member, or Supreme Court justice who is openly LGBT.[18]

By now, some readers may be thinking: "Sure, there are limitations on LGBT progress, but that does prove that progress has not occurred. It just shows that we need more of it." Critics of progress narratives, however, highlight other reasons to question the scope of LGBT legal and political advances. First, the multitude and magnitude of exceptions and anomalies, noted by Eskridge, Stryker, Rivers, and others, belie the achievement of progress. In the 1970s and 1980s, for example, Virginia increased its maximum penalty for sodomy from three to five years. Cincinnati passed a new ordinance against cross-dressing. Florida banned adoptions by homosexuals. Massachusetts limited the ability of same-sex couples to serve as foster parents. New Hampshire barred gays and lesbians from adopting or fostering. Anti-discrimination laws were repealed in Boulder, Dade County, Eugene, St. Paul, Wichita, and other jurisdictions. In the 1990s and 2000s, the number of states with constitutional bans on same-sex marriage increased from zero to thirty.[19]

Second, there have been local variations. For more than a decade, same-sex marriages were recognized in some but not other states. For more than four decades, discrimination based on sexual orientation and gender identity in employment, housing, and public accommodations has been illegal in some jurisdictions and legal in others. As of 2016, LGBT people hold elected state government positions in thirty-nine states but no such positions in eleven.[20]

Third, progress varies greatly based on race, gender, class, (dis)ability, and other factors. As Luibhéid, Nayan Shah, Pablo Mitchell, and others have demonstrated, people of color, poor people, and immigrants have been disproportionately vulnerable to gender and sexual policing.[21] Those who do not have documented US citizenship have experienced distinct forms of punishment when accused of breaking laws against gender and sex—exclusion at the border, incarceration without due process, and deportation from the United States. Meyer and Rivers show that lesbians have faced intense forms of gender and sexual policing in the US military and in parental custody cases. Hanhardt and Genny Beemyn note that local police have targeted genderqueer people in general and trans sex workers in particular; at the same time, they have been distinctly non-responsive to violence against trans people. Holly Anne Wade and others have shown that LGBT people with disabilities have experienced major challenges when asserting their rights to select their caretakers and guardians, establish partnerships and marriages, experience intimacy and pleasure, and otherwise make decisions about their lives.

Fourth, as the work of Gayle Rubin would lead us to expect, there has been far more progress when LGBT people have fought for rights that are aligned with dominant US values than when they have fought for rights that are not. In the last half-century, LGBT people have been relatively successful in fighting for privacy, marital, and reproductive rights, but not when fighting for rights related to public sex, promiscuity, and prostitution. For decades, LGBT victories in immigration and military policy rested on the notion of "don't ask, don't tell": LGBT immigrants gained freedom from exclusion and deportation and US military service members gained freedom from discharge if they did not speak openly and publicly about their LGBT affiliations and affinities. In the same period, the federal government recognized LGBT rights of speech and expression, but denied government funding for projects that exercised those rights. Another way of interpreting this evidence is to say that the price of progress in the private sphere was the entrenchment of inequality in the public sphere.

Fifth, LGBT legal and political advances in the United States do not compare favorably to the progress that has been achieved in other countries. As Rayside and others have shown, many countries decriminalized same-sex sex and permitted LGBT people to serve openly in their militaries before the United States did. More than fifteen legally recognized same-sex marriages before the United States did. Many have banned sexual orientation and gender identity discrimination in employment, housing, and public accommodations. The United States has criticized countries that do not protect and recognize LGBT rights, but it has not been a world leader in sexual and gender rights.[22]

Defenders of progress narratives might respond by saying: "Sure, there have been exceptions, anomalies, variations, and lags, but none of this means that there has not been progress. As the case of same-sex marriage demonstrates, there may have been short-term setbacks, but long-term progress. We should criticize the disproportionate gender and sexual policing experienced by people of color, poor people, immigrants, trans people, and people with disabilities, but each of these groups has experienced positive change. Progress does not necessarily have to be linear. Zigs have been corrected by zags."

Whether or not this is true, there are more fundamental challenges to narratives of LGBT legal and political progress. First, if we broaden our chronological and geographical parameters and consider the history of North America before and after Europeans invaded the continent, which has been done by Sue-Ellen Jacobs, Wesley Thomas, Sabine Lang, Will Roscoe, and Tracy Brown, the story of progress over the last five hundred years arguably has to be super-seded by a narrative of declension that has taken more than five hundred years to reverse. Though some scholars question the generally accepted notion that most Native American cultures tolerated and respected people who had "two spirits" (male and female) and people who engaged in same-sex sex, many certainly did and there is little evidence to suggest that pre- or post-contact Native Americans treated same-sex sex or gender-crossing behaviors as criminal offenses deserving of capital punishment, long-term incarceration, or other legal penalties. From this perspective, recent reforms are better described as restoring the legal situation that prevailed before Europeans conquered North America. This may be progress, but progress that can be situated within a longer historical framework that acknowledges declension.

Second, evidence from early Americanists such as Godbeer and Cleves and the broadly synthetic work of Eskridge seems to suggest that the legal and political treatment of same-sex sex and gender transgression was comparatively lenient before the late nineteenth century and comparatively harsh from the late nineteenth century to the 1960s.[23] While it is true, for instance, that many European colonies and early US states authorized harsh punishment for sodomy and buggery, arrests and convictions under these laws were rare. In the last few decades of the nineteenth century and the first seven decades of the twentieth, laws against sex and gender multiplied. The Comstock Act introduced new restrictions on obscenity. Sodomy laws were rewritten and reinterpreted to criminalize oral sex. States adopted laws against disorderly conduct, public indecency, lewd conduct, and sexual solicitation. Congress enacted immigration restrictions that targeted gender and sexual "deviates." Post-Prohibition liquor control regulations had negative consequences for LGBT bars and clubs. The US military adopted explicit restrictions on LGBT enlistment and retention. "Perverts" were purged and barred from government jobs. Arrest statistics in many jurisdictions suggest an escalation of, not a reduction in, anti-LGBT policing before the 1970s.

This in turn relates to a third fundamental challenge to narratives of LGBT progress. As Canaday makes clear, the growth of the state in the twentieth century increased its capacity to police gender and sex. The regulation of sex and gender, for example, grew with the expansion of local police forces in the late nineteenth and early twentieth centuries. Anti-LGBT immigration restriction increased when the federal government assumed greater responsibility for border control in the same period. Restrictions on gays and lesbians in the military escalated with the emergence of modernized enlistment policies and procedures during World War II. The ban on homosexuals in federal government jobs was enabled by decades of civil service reform and the growth of civil service bureaucracies. More recently, increased government surveillance of sexual communication has been made possible by technological advances and the expansion of government powers during the "War on Terror."

These arguments offer strong challenges to the notion of long-term LGBT political and legal progress, but it is significant that most of them do not apply to the recent past. Defenders of LGBT progress narratives might grant many of these points and still insist on the achievement

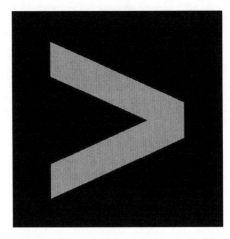

Figure 24.1 Against Equality logo, 2009. The collective formed to dislodge the centrality of equality
           rhetoric and challenge demands for LGBT inclusion in the institutions of marriage, the
           military, and the prison-industrial complex. The logo's ">" design and colors disrupt
           the more widely disseminated "=" branding of the Human Rights Campaign, a powerful
           national LGBT rights organization with moderate and integrationist politics.
www.againstequality.org.

of substantial progress over the last several decades. For this period, critics of progress narratives
offer an additional set of challenges.

One set of arguments is rooted in patterns of post-reform repression. Bérubé's work shows
that during World War II psychiatric reformers persuaded US military officials to adopt progressive new screening and rehabilitation policies, which they understood to be comparatively
lenient, but the results proved to be harshly punitive for LGBT people. Estelle Freedman argues
that post-war reformers hoped that new sexual psychopath laws would promote treatment
rather than punishment, but in many cases these led to increased incarceration for sex offenders.
In the 1960s, Illinois became the first state to decriminalize sodomy, but Stewart-Winter notes
that the state also adopted repressive new liquor control regulations that were used against LGBT
bars, and that Chicago authorities subsequently increased their policing of LGBT public sex.
Eskridge's work demonstrates that in 1969, when Kansas became the first state to decriminalize
cross-sex sodomy, it became the first to simultaneously criminalize same-sex sodomy; seven
more states did this in the 1970s and 1980s. Most states that repealed their sodomy laws in the
1960s, 1970s, and 1980s passed new laws against soliciting and loitering to solicit sodomy. Police
in some locations used these and other laws to increase their arrests of LGBT people. After
the US Congress repealed its ban on the immigration of "sexual deviates" in 1990, it passed
a new ban on the immigration of people with HIV/AIDS. From 1994 to 2001, the number
of military service members discharged under "Don't Ask, Don't Tell" increased in all but one
year. As examples of post-reform repression accumulate, critics of progress narratives have argued
persuasively for broader and deeper analysis of the dynamics of reform.

Troubling patterns are evident in these developments. For instance, if the price of progress
in the private sphere has been the entrenchment of inequality in the public sphere, it may have
become more difficult to dislodge structural forms of inequality.[24] If increased freedom of
expression in private homes, private bars, and other private spaces has been accompanied by
increased policing in public streets, public parks, and other public accommodations, should the

results be characterized as progress? If immigration restriction based on sexual orientation and gender identity has been replaced by immigration restriction based on disease and disability, has there been progress? An especially revealing example of this dynamic has emerged as some public and private employers that formerly granted domestic partner benefits to their employees (LGBT and not) because of legal restrictions on same-sex marriage have announced plans to end non-marital domestic partner benefits now that same-sex marriage is legal. In this case, progress for married LGBT people is coming at the expense of benefits for unmarried domestic partners (LGBT and not).[25] Moreover, if one believes that the state should get out of the business of recognizing and legitimizing marital relationships, there are reasons to worry about anything that might increase participation in and support for state-based marriage. If one believes that marital status should not influence access to immigration rights, health care, higher education, and other rights and benefits, there are reasons to be concerned about the possibility that the legalization of same-sex marriage might decrease support for open borders, health care for all, and universal education. If one believes that the institution of legal marriage is fundamentally at odds with the principles of sexual freedom, there are reasons to think that achieving the freedom to marry may damage those who seek freedom from marriage.

This relates to arguments about whether "progress" is the best way to characterize the history of the LGBT movement. Some believe that the grassroots mass mobilization that was characteristic of the movement in the late 1960s and early 1970s was superseded by more national, more top-down, and less democratic political mobilization in the late 1970s and early 1980s. The pattern arguably repeated itself with the rise of radical AIDS activism in the late 1980s, followed by the movement's increased bureaucratization and institutionalization in the post-1980s era. There are also claims that the LGBT movement in the 1970s was more committed to political alliances with other disenfranchised groups and social justice struggles (against police violence, institutionalized racism, and structural sexism) than it has been since that time. Closely linked to this is the notion that the movement has lost its radical politics, moving away from the broad commitments to social transformation that were characteristic of gay liberation, lesbian feminism, and radical AIDS activism and focusing instead on social inclusion in normative and respectable institutions like the military, marriage, and the family. For some critics, LGBT incorporation into Democratic Party politics has made it more difficult to offer radical challenges to party politics; LGBT incorporation into city economies has made it more difficult to offer radical challenges to economic inequality; and LGBT incorporation into city planning and regional tourism has made it more difficult to offer radical challenges to urban gentrification.

Some also argue that as the movement has increasingly accepted the sexual and gender frameworks that society seems to favor (including binary divisions between homosexuality and heterosexuality, between maleness and femaleness, and between masculinity and femininity), it has weakened its ability to argue against these frameworks. From all of these perspectives, the movement has lost more than it has gained.

This last point is related to the notion that much of the progress achieved by the LGBT movement has been based on essentialist conceptions of sex, gender, and sexuality that have hindered more profound freedom, equality, and justice. If the movement has often succeeded by insisting that one is "born" gay or lesbian and that one's sexual orientation and gender identity are fixed and unchanging, where does that leave those who think about their sexualities and genders as matters of choice, desire, and preference? While LGBT activists have tended to reject the notion that they are trying to convert and seduce new recruits, they have also tended to distance themselves from radical efforts to liberate everyone's desires to engage in same-sex sex and transgress gender norms. Insofar as the US political and legal systems typically require minority groups to argue against discrimination and argue for representation by articulating their demands in the language of identity politics, the LGBT movement has seemingly achieved "progress" by avoiding the language of universal queerness.

A final set of arguments builds on the points raised above about race, class, gender, and (dis)ability, but looks beyond LGBT politics and law to consider other developments that may intersect with and override the LGBT progress that has been achieved. Many LGBT Native Americans, Native Alaskans, Native Hawaiians, African Americans, Asian Americans, Latinos/ Latinas, and Puerto Ricans might situate LGBT progress in relation to five hundred years of colonialism, genocide, imperialism, nativism, racism, segregation, and slavery. As for more recent developments, what does it mean that LGBT people have gained civil rights protections in a period marked by new efforts to curtail and constrain the application and enforcement of civil rights laws? What does it mean that LGBT people have gained increased political representation in an era that is witnessing new challenges to voting rights and new efforts to use legislative redistricting to reduce minority representation? What does it mean to win long-fought battles against anti-LGBT immigration restriction in a period marked by new efforts to police the country's borders, expel non-citizens, and undermine birthright citizenship? What does it mean to gain freedom from certain types of gender and sexual policing in an era when critics of racialized police practices have had to remind us that "black lives matter"? What does it mean to achieve reduced incarceration for some types of gender and sexual crimes in a period marked by mass incarceration? And what does LGBT legal and political "progress" mean in relation to the rise in economic inequality, homelessness, and poverty that has seemingly accompanied all of this "progress"?

Herbert Butterfield did not have US LGBT history in mind when he wrote in 1931 of "how crooked and perverse the ways of progress are." In the early twenty-first century, however, US LGBT legal and political history may be a particularly good subject for considering the advantages and disadvantages of historical narratives that make arguments and assumptions about progress. From a variety of perspectives, the fact of US LGBT legal and political progress seems apparent, especially when the last several decades are considered. This essay has tried to offer some of the best arguments to support these narratives of progress, but it has also introduced some of the best challenge to these narratives. Significantly, the essay was drafted before the 2016 US elections, which featured competing narratives about national progress and decline, but it was completed after the elections, when confidence and optimism about the future of LGBT legal and political progress quickly dissipated.

In one of the final paragraphs of *The Idea of History*, R. G. Collingwood, the other critic of progress narratives whose words were quoted at the beginning of this essay, wrote, "Progress is possible. Whether it has actually occurred, and where and when and in what ways, are questions for historical thought to answer." Here and elsewhere Collingwood made it clear that he was not opposed to all progress narratives, just uncritical and untested ones.[26] As I hope this essay has shown, debates and discussions about progress in general and LGBT progress in particular would benefit if we were willing to ask a series of difficult questions, including "progress for whom" and "progress toward what." In relation to the former, it is possible that there has been progress for some LGBT people but a lack of progress or even regression for others. In relation to the latter, it is possible that there has been progress toward certain types of LGBT rights and freedoms, but a lack of progress or even regression toward others. Ultimately the greatest paradox of LGBT "progress" might be the "perverse" possibility that the recognition and acceptance of LGBT rights and freedoms has been accompanied by a strengthening of the borders and boundaries that divide people based on sex, gender, and sexuality.

Notes

1 Herbert Butterfield, *The Whig Interpretation of History* (1931; New York: Norton, 1965), 16; R. G. Collingwood, *The Idea of History* (1946; New York: Oxford University Press, 1956), 323, 328; Michel Foucault, *The History of Sexuality: An Introduction* (New York: Random House, 1978).

2 The Religious Society of Friends (Quakers) referred to their Pennsylvania colony as a "holy experiment."

3 For more on the queer history of colonial and early national America, see, in this volume, Richard Godbeer, "Colonial North America (1600s–1700s)" and Rachel Hope Cleves, "Revolutionary Sexualities and Early Modern Genders (1770s–1840s)."

4 For an extended history of queer criminalization, see, in this volume, Andrea Ritchie and Kay Whitlock, "Criminalization and Legalization."

5 On recent developments, see "Recruitment and Outreach," Out to Protect, www.comingoutfrom behindthebadge.com/organizations/recruitment-outreach. Accessed January 24, 2016.

6 For an earlier review of "progress" in law and politics, see Marc Stein, *Rethinking the Gay and Lesbian Movement* (New York: Routledge, 2012). For status reports, see Movement Advancement Project, "Equality Maps," www.lgbtmap.org/equality-maps. Accessed August 13, 2016.

7 On recent developments, see Noam Scheiber, "U.S. Agency Rules for Gays in Workplace Discrimination," *New York Times*, July 18, 2015, B1. For more on US queer labor history, see, in this volume, Sara Smith-Silverman, "Labor."

8 On recent developments, see Matthew Rosenberg, "Pentagon Moves to Allow Transgender People to Serve Openly in the Military," *New York Times*, July 14, 2015, A14.

9 For more on the queer history of family in the twentieth century, see, in this volume, Daniel Rivers, "Families."

10 On recent developments, see Adam Liptak, " 'Equal Dignity': 5–4 Ruling Makes Same-Sex Marriage a Right Nationwide," *New York Times*, June 27, 2015, A1, A11.

11 On developments in California, see Don Romesburg, Leila J. Rupp, and David Donahue, eds, *Making the Framework FAIR: California History-Social Science Framework Proposed LGBT Revisions Related to the FAIR Act* (San Francisco: Committee on Lesbian, Gay, Bisexual and Transgender History, 2014).

12 On recent developments, see Sunnivie Brydum, "Social Security Removes Surgical Requirement for Gender Marker Change," *Advocate*, June 14, 2013, www.advocate.com/politics/transgender/2013/06/14/social-security-removes-surgical-requirement-gender-marker-change. Accessed August 12, 2015; Lambda Legal, "Changing Birth Certificate Sex Designations: State-By-State Guidelines," February 3, 2013, www.lambdalegal.org/know-your-rights/transgender/changing-birth-certificate-sex-designations. Accessed August 12, 2015.

13 Christopher Coble, "Do Sodomy Laws Still Exist?" http://blogs.findlaw.com/blotter/2015/09/do-sodomy-laws-still-exist.html. Accessed January 24, 2016; "Arresting Dress: A Timeline of Anti-Cross-Dressing Laws in the United States," *PBS Newshour*, May 31, 2015, www.pbs.org/newshour/updates/arresting-dress-timeline-anti-cross-dressing-laws-u-s/. Accessed August 12, 2015. See also, in this volume, Ritchie and Whitlock, "Criminalization and Legalization."

14 Stephanie Clifford, "Escort Site Is Said to Promote Prostitution," *New York Times*, August 26, 2015, A17; Sacha M. Coupet and Ellen Marcus, ed., *Children, Sexuality and the Law* (New York: New York University Press, 2015); National Center on Elder Abuse, "Research Brief: Mistreatment of LGBT Elders," 2014, www.lgbtagingcenter.org/resources/pdfs/ResearchBrief_LGBT_Elders_508web.pdf. Accessed August 26, 2015; Holly Anne Wade, "Discrimination, Sexuality and People with Significant Disabilities: Issues of Access and the Right to Sexual Expression in the United States," *Disability Studies Quarterly* 22, no. 4 (Fall 2002): 9–27; Centers for Disease Control and Prevention, "HIV Specific Criminal Laws," www.cdc.gov/hiv/policies/law/states/exposure.html. Accessed July 25, 2015; National Coalition of Anti-Violence Programs, "2014 Report on LGBTQ and HIV-Affected Hate Violence," www.avp.org/resources/avp-resources/405. Accessed January 24, 2016.

15 Equal Employment Opportunity Commission, "Facts about Discrimination in Federal Government Employment," www.eeoc.gov/federal/otherprotections.cfm. Accessed July 24, 2015; Deborah A. Morgan, "Not Gay Enough for the Government: Racial and Sexual Stereotypes in Sexual Orientation Asylum Cases," *Law and Sexuality* 15 (2006): 135–162; Service Women's Action Network, "Rape, Sexual Assault and Sexual Harassment in the Military," July 2012, http://servicewomen.org/wp-content/uploads/2012/10/Final-RSASH-10.8.2012.pdf. Accessed July 24, 2015. See also, in this volume, Eithne Luibhéid, "Queer and Nation."

16 Morgan Lee and Jeremy Weber, "Here's What Supreme Court Says about Same-Sex Marriage and Religious Freedom," *Christianity Today*, June 26, 2015, www.christianitytoday.com/gleanings/2015/june/supreme-court-states-cant-ban-same-sex-marriage.html. Accessed August 12, 2015; Movement Advancement Project, "Equality Maps."

17 See Movement Advancement Project, "Equality Maps"; Lambda Legal, "Changing Birth Certificate Sex Designations: State-By-State Guidelines."

18 The Senator is Tammy Baldwin. The House members are Jared Polis, David Cicilline, Sean Patrick Maloney, Mark Takano, Mark Pocan, and Krysten Sinema. The governor is Kate Brown. See also Movement Advancement Project, "Equality Maps."

19 Pew Research Center, "Same-Sex Marriage: State by State," June 26, 2015, www.pewforum.org/2015/06/26/same-sex-marriage-state-by-state/ Accessed August 18, 2015.

20 Pew Research Center, "Same-Sex Marriage"; Movement Advancement Project, "Equality Maps."

21 See also, in this volume, Nayah Shah, "Queer of Color Estrangement and Belonging."

22 Aengus Carroll, *State-Sponsored Homophobia: A World Survey of Laws* (Geneva: International Lesbian, Gay, Bisexual, Trans and Intersex Association, 2016).

23 See, in this volume, the first four chapters covering the colonial period through the nineteenth century.

24 For a queer history of the 1970s to the present through the frame of neoliberalism, see, in this volume, Margot Weiss, "Queer Neoliberal Times (1970–2010s)."

25 Tara Siegel Bernard, "With Marriage a Right, Domestic Partner Benefits Come into Question," *New York Times*, June 29, 2015, A11.

26 Collingwood, *The Idea of History*, 333.

Further Reading

Agee, Christopher Lowen. *The Streets of San Francisco: Policing and the Creation of a Cosmopolitan Liberal Politics, 1950–1972*. Chicago: University of Chicago Press, 2014.

Andersen, Ellen Ann. *Out of the Closets and into the Courts*. Ann Arbor: University of Michigan Press, 2006.

Bailey, Robert. *Gay Politics, Urban Politics: Identity and Economics in an Urban Setting*. New York: Columbia University Press, 1999.

Beemyn, Genny. *A Queer Capital: A History of Gay Life in Washington, D.C.* New York: Routledge, 2015.

Bérubé, Allan. *Coming Out Under Fire: The History of Gay Men and Women in World War Two*. New York: Free Press, 1990.

Boag, Peter. *Same-Sex Affairs: Constructing and Controlling Homosexuality in the Pacific Northwest*. Berkeley: University of California Press, 2003.

Boyd, Nan Alamilla. *Wide Open Town: A History of Queer San Francisco to 1965*. Berkeley: University of California Press, 2003.

Brown, Kathleen Brown. "'Changed. . .into the Fashion of Man': The Politics of Sexual Difference in a Seventeenth-Century Anglo-American Settlement." *Journal of the History of Sexuality* 6 (1995): 171–193.

Brown, Tracy. "'Abominable Sin in Colonial New Mexico': Spanish and Pueblo Perceptions of Same-Sex Sexuality." In *Long Before Stonewall: Histories of Same-Sex Sexuality in Early America*, edited by Thomas Foster, 51–77. New York: New York University Press, 2007.

Butterfield, Herbert. *The Whig Interpretation of History*. 1931; New York: Norton, 1965.

Canaday, Margot. *The Straight State: Sexuality and Citizenship in Twentieth-Century America*. Princeton: Princeton University Press, 2009.

Chauncey, George. *Gay New York: Gender, Urban Culture, and the Making of the Gay Male World, 1890–1940*. New York: Basic, 1994.

Cleves, Rachel Hope. *Charity & Sylvia: A Same-Sex Marriage in Early America*. New York: Oxford University Press, 2014.

Collingwood, R. G. *The Idea of History*. 1946; New York: Oxford University Press, 1956.

D'Emilio, John. *Sexual Politics, Sexual Communities: The Making of a Homosexual Minority in the United States, 1940–1970*. Chicago: University of Chicago Press, 1983.

Eskridge, William. *Gaylaw: Challenging the Apartheid of the Closet*. Cambridge: Harvard University Press, 1999.

——. *Dishonorable Passions: Sodomy Laws in America*. New York: Viking, 2008.

Foucault, Michel. *The History of Sexuality: An Introduction*. New York: Random House, 1978.

Freedman, Estelle. "'Uncontrolled Desires': The Response to the Sexual Psychopath, 1920–1960." In *Passion and Power: Sexuality in History*, edited by Kathy Peiss and Christina Simmons, 199–225. Philadelphia: Temple University Press, 1989.

Godbeer, Richard. *Sexual Revolution in Early America*. Baltimore: Johns Hopkins University Press, 2002.

Gutiérrez, Ramón. *When Jesus Came, The Corn Mothers Went Away: Marriage, Sexuality, and Power in New Mexico, 1500–1846*. Palo Alto: Stanford University Press, 1991.

Hanhardt, Christina. *Safe Space: Gay Neighborhood History and the Politics of Violence*. Durham: Duke University Press, 2013.

Howard, John. *Men Like That: A Southern Queer History*. Chicago: University of Chicago Press, 1999.

Hurewitz, Daniel. *Bohemian Los Angeles and the Making of Modern Politics*. Berkeley: University of California Press, 2007.

Jacobs, Sue-Ellen, Wesley Thomas, and Sabine Lang, eds. *Two-Spirit People: Native American Gender Identity, Sexuality, and Spirituality*. Urbana: University of Illinois Press, 1997.

Johnson, David. *The Lavender Scare*. Chicago: University of Chicago Press, 2004.

Katz, Jonathan Ned. *Gay American History*. New York: Crowell, 1976.

——. *Gay/Lesbian Almanac*. New York: Harper, 1983.

Kennedy, Elizabeth Lapovsky and Madeline Davis. *Boots of Leather, Slippers of Gold: The History of a Lesbian Community*. New York: Routledge, 1993.

Krahulik, Karen Christel. *Provincetown: From Pilgrim Landing to Gay Resort*. New York: New York University Press, 2005.

Luibhéid, Eithne. *Entry Denied: Controlling Sexuality at the Border*. Minneapolis: University of Minnesota Press, 2002.

Meyer, Leisa. *Creating GI Jane: Sexuality and Power in the Women's Army Corps During World War II*. New York: Columbia University Press, 1996.

Meyerowitz, Joanne. *How Sex Changed: A History of Transsexuality in the United States*. Cambridge: Harvard University Press, 2002.

Mitchell, Pablo. *West of Sex: Making Mexican America, 1900–1930*. Chicago: University of Chicago Press, 2012.

Murdoch, Joyce and Deb Price. *Courting Justice: Gay Men and Lesbians v. the Supreme Court*. New York: Basic, 2001.

Murphy, Kevin P. *Political Manhood: Red Bloods, Mollycoddles, & the Politics of Progressive Era Reform*. New York: Columbia University Press, 2008.

Newton, Esther Newton. *Cherry Grove, Fire Island: Sixty Years in America's First Gay and Lesbian Town*. Boston: Beacon, 1993.

Rayside, David. "Electoral Politics." In *Encyclopedia of Lesbian, Gay, Bisexual, and Transgender History in America*. 3 vols, edited by Marc Stein. New York: Scribners, 2003. I:336–339.

Rayside, David. *Queer Inclusions, Continental Divisions: Public Recognition of Sexual Diversity in Canada and the United States*. Toronto: University of Toronto Press, 2008.

Rivers, Daniel Winunwe. *Radical Relations: Lesbian Mothers, Gay Fathers, and Their Children in the United States since World War II*. Chapel Hill: University of North Carolina Press, 2013.

Robertson, Stephen. "Shifting the Scene of the Crime: Sodomy and the American History of Sexual Violence." *Journal of the History of Sexuality* 19 no. 2 (2010): 223–42.

Romesburg, Don, Leila J. Rupp, and David Donahue, eds. *Making the Framework FAIR: California History-Social Science Framework Proposed LGBT Revisions Related to the FAIR Act*. San Francisco: Committee on Lesbian, Gay, Bisexual, and Transgender History, 2014.

Roscoe, Will. *Changed Ones: Third and Fourth Genders in Native North America*. New York: St. Martin's, 1998.

Rubin, Gayle. "Thinking Sex: Notes for a Radical Theory of the Politics of Sexuality." In *Pleasure and Danger: Exploring Female Sexuality*, edited by Carole S. Vance, 267–319. New York: Routledge, 1984.

Sears, Clare. *Arresting Dress: Cross-Dressing, Law, and Fascination in Nineteenth-Century San Francisco*. Durham: Duke University Press, 2015.

Serlin, David. "Bathhouses." In *Encyclopedia of Lesbian, Gay, Bisexual, and Transgender History in America*. 3 vols, edited by Marc Stein. New York: Scribners, 2003. I:122–125.

Shah, Nayan. *Stranger Intimacy: Contesting Race, Sexuality, and the Law in the North American West*. Berkeley: University of California Press, 2011.

Stein, Marc. "Policing and Police." In *Encyclopedia of Lesbian, Gay, Bisexual, and Transgender History in America*. 3 vols, edited by Marc Stein. New York: Scribners, 2003. II: 389–394.

——. *Rethinking the Gay and Lesbian Movement*. New York: Routledge, 2012.

——. *City of Sisterly and Brotherly Loves: Lesbian and Gay Philadelphia*. Chicago: University of Chicago Press, 2000.

——. *Sexual Injustice: Supreme Court Decisions from Griswold to Roe*. Chapel Hill: University of North Carolina Press, 2010.

Stewart-Winter, Timothy. *Queer Clout: Chicago and the Rise of Gay Politics*. Philadelphia: University of Pennsylvania Press, 2016.

Strub, Whitney. *Perversion for Profit: The Politics of Pornography and the Rise of the New Right*. New York: Columbia University Press, 2011.

Stryker, Susan. *Transgender History*. Berkeley: Seal Press, 2008.

Ullman, Sharon. "'The Twentieth Century Way': Female Impersonation and Sexual Practice in Turn-of-the-Century America." *Journal of the History of Sexuality* 5, no. 4 (1995): 573–600.

Wade, Holly Anne. "Discrimination, Sexuality and People with Significant Disabilities: Issues of Access and the Right to Sexual Expression in the United States." *Disability Studies Quarterly* 22, no. 4 (Fall 2002): 9–27.

25

LABOR

Sara R. Smith-Silverman

What do we imagine when we think of queer labor history? Our minds might immediately wander to, for example, the gay hairdresser, the lesbian construction worker, and the transgender sex worker. Clearly, each captures both stereotypes and structural realities, but also push us further. What comprises queer labor history might involve not only the study of kinds of work that can be defined as queer when performed by the "wrong" gender, but also how such work—and workers—became defined as queer in the first place. Queer labor history certainly also includes labor activism at work and in unions. More broadly, and with greater effort, historians are also documenting less visible and more furtive queer labor, including that which provides the context for same-sex intimacies as well as the experience of being queer in straight-dominated workplaces.

What makes up queer labor history is up for debate. This chapter makes two main arguments. First, historical developments in the economic systems governing people's labor have fundamentally shaped queer history. More specifically, the kinds of labor people have had access to have both helped and hindered people's ability to pursue sex with members of the same sex, identify as gay, bisexual or lesbian, and to be openly transgender and gender non-conforming. Second, the social movements of the 1960s and 1970s and the growth of employment in the public and service sectors of the economy particularly contributed to the emergence of a queer labor movement in the 1970s that is still gaining traction today, notwithstanding the challenges presented by AIDS and the rightward turn in American politics in the 1970s and 1980s.

As a field, queer labor history is relatively undeveloped. With important exceptions, few queer historians center the issue of labor. Though some scholars have examined the distinct shape that working-class queer communities have taken in US history, their analyses have largely not extended into the lives and struggles of queer people at work. Similarly, though labor historians have charted the history of labor unions, examined the effects of economic changes such as deindustrialization and globalization on workers and working-class life, and considered organizing by workers of color and women workers to challenge discrimination, very little in the labor history literature addresses queer labor.

That said, in the past few years in particular, there have been a handful of historians who have paved new ground. Allan Bérube's research on the queer, radical, and anti-racist Marine Cooks and Stewards Union, some of which was published in a posthumous collection of his work edited by Estelle Freedman and John D'Emilio, is pioneering, as is his analytical work in defining what actually makes certain kinds of work queer. "Queer work," according to Bérubé, is any kind of work for which gay men and lesbians "were supposed to be especially well suited."[1] Bérubé notes that the feminized work performed by gay white men, such as the work of stewards on luxury liners in the mid-twentieth century, had to first undergo a process by which it became feminized and racialized. Serving others was viewed as suitable for people of color, women, and eventually gay men. Historian Miriam Frank must also be credited as a pioneer in the field. She remains one of the only scholars whose extensive research has examined the history of queer workers' involvement in trade unions from the 1960s to the present. Phil Tiemeyer's book on the history of gay male flight attendants is also unique, being the only in-depth examination of the history of how one profession in particular became queer when performed by the "wrong" gender. Margot Canaday is currently working on a history of the queer workplace from 1945 to 2000, which promises to provide the first in-depth analysis of queer people's work lives, both in largely straight and queer workplaces.[2] The work of these scholars in particular is promising, signaling the emergent bubbling up of queer labor history after a long, slow simmer.

Queer Labor and the Expansion of Capitalism

In the foundational article "Capitalism and Gay Identity," John D'Emilio argues that the expansion of industrial capitalism in the nineteenth and twentieth centuries helped to make possible the emergence of public gay and lesbian identities and communities. Prior to the emergence of the market economy in the mid-1800s, a household economy organized around the nuclear family arranged labor and production in New England and elsewhere. In this system, the home was a workplace, and the members of the family—wife, husband, children (often many of them), extended family members, and any servants, indentured or free—depended on one another for economic survival. By the nineteenth century, capitalism drew men and women out of the household and into wage labor. With this transition the nuclear family underwent a transformation as well, becoming "an institution that produced not goods but emotional satisfaction and happiness." At the same time, sex became increasingly independent of procreation. Whereas in colonial New England couples had children to help with household labor, the rise of capitalism made procreation less economically imperative. D'Emilio maintains, "In divesting the household of its economic independence and fostering the separation of sexuality from procreation, capitalism has created conditions that allow some men and women to organize a personal life around their erotic/emotional attachments to their own sex."[3]

D'Emilio makes clear that workers experienced the sexually freeing effects of the expansion of capitalism unevenly. Race and gender influenced the kinds of wage labor to which people had access. Under capitalism white men have historically had access not only to a wider range of jobs than women and people of color, but also to jobs that paid better, allowing white men in particular to build a particular kind of personal life outside of the family earlier and with more ease. Under wage labor, women and people of color found it difficult to become financially independent and were thus less likely to pursue same-sex attachments and establish affiliated communities.

A handful of nineteenth-century professions allowed for women to pursue queer intimacies; in particular, the feminization of teaching gave unmarried young and especially middle-class white women the opportunity to live independently of men and pursue romantic friendships with each other.[4] In the mid-1800s teaching experienced a gender transformation when school districts determined they could pay women less than men to do the same work. Additionally, most school districts passed policies that only single women could be hired, based on the assumption that teaching prepared women for marriage and motherhood and that the proper place for women once they married was in the home. By 1920 women made up 86 percent of all teachers, and of these 91 percent were single, widowed, or divorced.[5] These "single" women's romantic friendships generally did not alarm the broader community because until the turn of the twentieth century, the public did not generally link same-sex romance to sexual desire or activity.

While romantic friendships were not supposed to replace heterosexual marriage, they sometimes did. Historian Rachel Hope Cleves discusses how two white women, Charity Bryant and Sylvia Drake, established a life-long bond in the early 1800s, made possible by their work as seamstresses. Charity and Sylvia established a tailoring business in their home and also shared a bed. Their mutually dependent labor provided a way to build a life-long intimate commitment to each other. Due to the low wages paid to women, however, they were able to support themselves "only through non-stop labor." They awoke before dawn and continued working by candlelight into the evening. As a result, both Charity and Sylvia suffered work-related injuries, including painful wrists and headaches from stitching. Their relationship appears to have been accepted by their families and the community of Weybridge, Vermont, where they had settled, but, as Cleves maintains, "communal acceptance of their union rested on its silencing."[6]

Unlike Charity and Sylvia, most women in romantic friendships eventually married men, due not only to family and community pressure but also to financial strain. Karen Hansen describes the challenge of Addie Brown and Rebecca Primus, two African American women in the mid-nineteenth century who shared a passionate friendship for nine years, but eventually married men. Paid less than white women and facing fewer job options, free black women found it financially difficult to pursue lives centered around same-sex love. Though Primus became a highly respected teacher, establishing a school for former slaves in the South in 1865, Brown primarily made a living as a domestic worker, one of the only jobs open to African American women in the South.

While the emergence of waged labor for women enabled limited openings for female same-sex relationships, capitalist expansion into the American West relied on male migrant labor, creating the conditions for relationships among men. According to Peter Boag, migrant men shared erotic intimacies in work camps, boarding houses, and saloons. These workers, who came from other parts of the country or as far as Asia and Latin America, labored in timber camps and saw mills, on farms and orchards, and constructed irrigation systems and railroads. As Nayan Shah has shown, South Asian immigrants working in various industries in the West, most prominently California's burgeoning agricultural industry, pursued sex with other migrant workers across racial and ethnic lines, including Chinese, Native American, white, and European immigrants. Thus, the development of the West created male homosocial worlds of work and leisure, and provided the conditions for same-sex erotic intimacies that crossed racial lines.

Immigrant workers laboring in the West experienced legal and often violent discrimination linked to race, sexuality, and gender. The anti-Asian movement that first formed in the mid-nineteenth century targeting Chinese workers extended into the twentieth century. During times of economic recession, in particular, white workers violently lashed out against their Chinese, Japanese, Korean, and South Asian fellow workers, blaming Asian workers for undermining their working conditions and charging them with taking jobs "belonging" to white workers. White workers also viewed Asian immigrants as a threat to normative sexuality. Laws, mobs, and myriad informal sanctions supposedly "protecting white womanhood" actively prevented male Asian immigrants from entering into interracial heterosexual relationships. As Shah details, white men, too, had to be "protected" against male Asian immigrants' perceived sexual predation and moral perversity.[7] This anti-Asian movement proved immensely successful, extending Chinese exclusion to all Asians with the passage of the Immigration Act of 1917.

Some people in the nineteenth century engaged in cross-dressing practices or identification as a gender other than the one assigned to them at birth in ways that were linked to their work lives. Some people, particularly women, might have dressed as men circumstantially, in order to pursue work opportunities otherwise not available to women. For instance, some women dressed and tried to pass as men in the mid-nineteenth century to work as miners during the Gold Rush in California. Some female prostitutes wore men's clothing as a way to advertise their sexual services. And some entertainers worked for wages by dressing in drag on stage. Other people identified in their lives more generally through a gender not assigned to them at birth (those we might today call transgender) or as masculine women or feminine men. Many undoubtedly experienced widespread discrimination for doing so. Municipalities across the United States, including San Francisco in 1863, passed laws criminalizing "cross-dressing." As Clare Sears has shown about San Francisco, these anti-cross-dressing laws did "not simply *police* normative gender by enforcing preexisting standards and beliefs but actively *produced* it by creating new definitions of normality and abnormality and new restrictions on participating in public life."[8]

Gender transgressive labor and same-sex work nonetheless enabled the formation of queer communities by the late nineteenth and early twentieth centuries. For instance, as Don Romesburg shows, while many teenage girls became prostitutes in order to contribute financially to their family's subsistence, teenage boys "for the most part seem to have sold themselves for themselves." Some newsboys took the opportunity to earn some additional cash by sidelining in same-sex sex work, while effeminate men and boys, or "fairies," became sex workers because it was one of very few occupations in the early twentieth-century that allowed them to express their gender—to be themselves—in public without hiding. Romesburg emphasizes that through sex work fairies "discovered and reaffirmed their connection to one another," facilitating community building.[9] However, male sex workers who sold sex to men did not necessarily do so because they identified as gay, or centered their lives more broadly around same-sex attraction; some teenage boys were motivated to sell sex to other men as way to earn enough cash to court women and girls. Though scholars have addressed, to some extent, the link between work, sexuality, and gender transgression, additional research is needed to fully comprehend this part of queer labor history.

By the turn of the twentieth century, in the context of industrial capitalism and the rise of the service economy, women increasingly found employment that permitted some measure of limited economic independence. Between 1880 and 1930, the number of female workers grew from 2.6 million to 10.8 million.[10] This allowed more women the economic self-sufficiency necessary to live outside of the traditional domestic sphere. They pursued same-sex intimacy and relationships, and established new lesbian subcultures in larger cities.[11] But because employers still assumed that their female workers had some support from their husbands or fathers, employers paid them low wages and many women, especially working-class women, had trouble making an independent living. As Joanne Meyerowitz has demonstrated, in order to survive, many women depended on each other; they pooled their money, shared households, and established cooperative housekeeping. It was in this context that, by the 1920s, visible lesbian communities formed in the furnished room districts of Chicago's Near North Side. To subsist financially, some lesbians had to resort to prostituting themselves to both men and women, while some lesbians depended on the help of more affluent female lovers.[12]

As anarchism grew in popularity in response to the rise of industrial capitalism, some anarchists extended their critiques of oppressive gender and sexual norms to a defense of people's right to pursue same-sex relations. The exploitation of labor under industrial capitalism—long work days, poor compensation, and unsafe working conditions—led to the emergence of a large labor movement and the growth of radicalism in the United States in the late nineteenth and early twentieth centuries. The nation's rise as a center of industrial growth drew immigrants from around the world, many of whom brought radical ideas with them. It was in this context that American anarchism experienced its heyday. Anarchists not only challenged capitalism as the cause of workers' exploitation, but also oppressive gender and sexual relations. Anarchist Emma Goldman, for instance, did not mince words in her denunciations of marriage as a fundamentally sexist institution. As Terence Kissack has illustrated, some anarchists, including Goldman, also advocated for sexual freedom, including the right to pursue same-sex intimacy without government intrusion. Kissack asserts, in fact, that key figures in the anarchist movement were the first in the United States to offer a political and very public defense of homosexuality, that these anarchists were "guided by their belief that women and men had the right to pattern their intimate lives free of interference from outside authority." This anarchist critique of anti-homosexual social mores and laws, moreover, was "part of a vision of complete and far-reaching social change." [13]

Heterosexuality in Crisis, and the Birth of the Modern Labor Movement, 1930s–1940s

The Great Depression of the 1930s created working conditions that sowed fears of the heterosexual family in crisis and also heralded queer participation in the left-led modern labor movement. By 1933, with about a quarter of Americans unemployed, great numbers of men could no longer play their expected role as the breadwinner earning a wage capable of supporting his wife and children. Marriages were postponed and divorces more common. Unemployment prompted widespread transiency, as men (and a small number of women) got in their cars and hopped on trains in search of work. Transiency was linked with non-marital sex including homosexuality; the nature of transient labor delinked men from the nuclear family and placed them in homosocial worlds where they were surrounded by other men in work camps, on farms, and in trains. In these situations, men had ample opportunity pursue sex with other men.

During the Great Depression, the federal government established welfare programs to shore up the straight nuclear family, indirectly using the state to exclude queer lives that did not also incorporate normative marriage and family from access to government support. The Works Project Administration, which employed people on public works projects and also provided work to artists, was mostly reserved for married men, effectively discriminating against women and unmarried queer workers. The government also established the Federal Transient Program (FTP) and the Civilian Conservation Corps (CCC) to assist men in need of work and financial assistance, providing residential camps and employment performing unskilled labor largely related to conservation and preserving natural resources. Both programs provided homosocial environments conducive to sex between men. The crucial difference was that the FTP provided financial assistance to individual male transients, and therefore offered a model of non-familial forms of state welfare. The CCC, on the other hand, was created in 1933 to offer assistance specifically to men *not yet* driven to transiency, who were required to send most of their income to dependants.[14]

Though the federal government viewed the living arrangements and work provided to unemployed men in the FTP and CCC camps as a way to solve what it viewed as moral degeneracy, because of the differences between programs the FTP could not shake the stigma of perversion and was ultimately shut down after a couple of years, whereas the CCC was one of the government's longest running and most popular welfare programs. Margot Canaday argues that the different fates of the FTP and CCC were part of a larger process of building a "straight state" that supported heterosexuality and discriminated against queer workers.

The modern labor movement emerged in the 1930s with the birth of the Congress of Industrial Organizations and the mass unionization of industry. Many left-led unions prioritized the unionization of workers of color and the broader struggle for racial equality. Little has been written about the involvement of queer workers in left-led unions in the 1930s, but a significant exception is Allan Bérubé's research about the radical, anti-racist, and queer Marine Cooks and Stewards Unions. In the 1930s and 1940s, the union's heyday, the Matson Liner hired white gay men to work on passenger ships to do work that was considered queer; they worked as waiters, florists, hairdressers, bedroom stewards, and pastry chefs, the kinds of denigrated labor reserved for men of color on other luxury liners, and women in similar positions on land. Because the Matson liners insisted on all-white crews, the company hired white gay men. The men on the Matson ships created a unique queer work culture, one that involved drag performances, calling each other "queens," and the campy renaming of ships—the *Lurline* became the "Queenline," and the *Matsonia* was renamed the "Fruit-sonia."[15] The gay stewards also promoted a queer labor politics within the Marine Cooks and Stewards Union. Queer workers became union leaders and challenged what they called "queen-baiting." This was in part made possible because the MCSU was led by leftists, including Communist Party members, who ensured that the union challenged racism within the union and on the ships.

The Cold War and the Lavender Scare, 1940s–1960s

In the late 1940s, the Marine Cooks and Stewards Union was destroyed by anti-communism, but homophobia was the final nail in the union's coffin. Because the MCSU was partially led by members of the Communist Party, in 1950 it was purged from its parent union, the Congress of Industrial Organizations (CIO). With the passage of the Port Security Act, extensive screening of maritime workers weeded out people deemed risks to national security. MCSU activists were purged for being gay, illustrating one manifestation of the much wider postwar "Lavender Scare" targeting LGBT people and those sympathetic to them from government and related employment. By January of 1951, nearly every leftwing MCSU steward was removed from the ships.[16]

Unfortunately, even the US Communist Party, by the late 1940s, had a homophobic party line, which derived from its tendency to conflate homosexuality with bourgeois decadence and condemn capitalism for corrupting working-class family life. Harry Hay, founder of the homophile group the Mattachine Society in 1950, was a former member of the Communist Party asked to leave because he was gay. Historian Bettina Aptheker has also written about the history of Party homophobia, including her personal experiences of being a lesbian. In the late 1940s the CP decided to expel its queer members because they were presumed likely to be blackmailed into betraying the Party. Aptheker, who grew up as a "red diaper baby" with parents belonging to the Communist Party, recalls that in the late 1940s and 1950s sexuality was simply not discussed. As an adult member of the Party, Aptheker was asked to write a position paper on women's rights in the 1970s. When she attempted to link the significance of lesbians to working women's struggles, the Party told her in no uncertain terms to abandon the effort. Because the Communist Party is so important to labor history, additional research is needed to determine the evolution of the Party's homophobia and its effect on members and left-led unions.

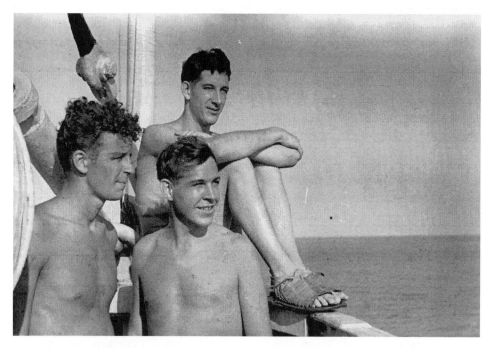

Figure 25.1 Ted Rolfs (center), onboard a Matson liner with fellow travelers in the Marine Cooks and
Stewards Union, which, in the 1930s and 1940s, supported queer workers and union
leadership before a late 1940s backlash.
Allan Bérubé collection, courtesy of GLBT Historical Society.

The destruction of the Marine Cooks and Stewards Union evidences the effects of the
Lavender Scare, which was intertwined with the Red Scare during the late 1940s through the
early 1960s. As gayness solidified as an identity after World War II, straight people became
increasingly aware and thus anxious about the existence of gay men, lesbians, and bisexuals.[17]
David K. Johnson has shown that pressure mounted to rid the federal government of its queer
workers because they were increasingly viewed as "security risks," easily blackmailed for fear
of their sexuality being exposed. Ultimately, thousands of gay and bisexual people were either
fired or denied employment.

This Lavender Scare filtered down to the state level, perhaps most prominently in the teaching
profession. Because teachers were expected to model and uphold social norms regarding
"appropriate" gender and sexuality for their students, gay, lesbian, and bisexual teachers came
under special scrutiny. Though additional research is needed about the pervasiveness of the
Lavender Scare in public schools, the purging of gay teachers in Florida serves as a compelling
case study. The Florida state legislature established an investigation committee in 1956 in an
attempt to impede desegregation efforts. When the committee's future was cast into doubt
by effective National Association for the Advancement of Colored People organizing, the
committee turned its sights on gay and lesbian teachers. The fear that teachers would "recruit"
students to homosexuality "reinforced demands that teachers act in accordance with a narrow
standard of normative behavior," argues Karen Graves.[18] In the absence of both gay rights
organizations capable of fending off persecution and legal anti-discrimination protections,
between 1957 and 1963 the state of Florida successfully fired and revoked the teaching

credentials of numerous teachers. Though once teaching had been a kind of labor lesbians could pursue to maintain their economic independence, between the end of World War II and the 1960s the repressive atmosphere of the Cold War generated increased policing of teachers' sexuality.

Gay Liberation and Queer Labor Activism, 1960s–1970s

Across the late 1960s and 1970s, the gay liberation movement emerged.[19] During the same time, in the context of the widespread unionization of the public and service sectors and the weakening of industrial unions, lesbian, gay, and bisexual service sector and public workers started to merge the labor and LGBT rights movements. Teachers in particular were at the forefront of such efforts. An early example of unions going on the record for lesbian and gay rights occurred at the California Federation of Teachers conventions in 1969 and 1970, when activists successfully convinced attendees to pass resolutions that opposed discriminatory laws against gays and lesbians, called for sex education programs at all levels of education that explained "various American lifestyles," and mandated the distribution of a pamphlet on how to mentor gay students.[20]

In the mid–1970s, the LGBT labor movement had its "coming out" moment when activists in San Francisco joined with unions to promote the boycott of Coors beer for its anti-union and anti-gay policies. Although queer labor activism had certainly existed before, the Coors boycott was more public and thus broader in its political reach than previous efforts. The alliance began in 1973 when Allan Baird, a representative of the International Brotherhood of Teamsters Local 888, approached Harvey Milk to ask him to organize support in the gay community for a boycott of Coors Beer, which was then refusing to agree to a union contract. Milk, soon to become the first out gay member of the San Francisco Board of Supervisors, agreed to build the boycott, but only if the Teamsters would also advocate for the right of gay people to work in the industry. Coors was not only anti-union and racially discriminatory, but it also administrated a lie detector test for potential employees that asked the question, "Are you a homosexual?" A positive answer would be ground for not being hired or being fired. An agreement in place, Milk, Howard Wallace and other gay activists publicized the boycott in the gay press and successfully convinced gay bars to boycott Coors beer. The boycott spread to the rest of California and eventually became a national movement.[21]

Though the rise of the anti-gay Christian Right in the late 1970s resulted in setbacks for LGBT rights in general, LGBT workers helped to push some sectors of the labor movement to speak out in defense of gay rights. In 1977 Anita Bryant became the most prominent anti-gay Christian Right spokesperson after she led a successful campaign to overturn an ordinance in Dade County, Florida prohibiting discrimination based on sexual preference in housing, employment, and public accommodations. Inspired by Bryant, California state Senator John Briggs put an initiative on the 1978 California state ballot proposing to forbid lesbians, gays, and their straight supporters from teaching or working in California's public schools. When a statewide campaign to defeat the "Briggs Initiative" emerged in cities and towns across California, gay, lesbian, and bisexual workers successfully pressured many labor unions to speak out and organize against the initiative, culminating in a large "Workers' Conference to Defeat the Briggs Initiative" in September 1978.

As my own research has shown, lesbian, gay, and bisexual rank-and-file teachers played a key role in the statewide campaign to defeat the "Briggs Initiative." These teachers formed groups independent of the teachers' unions to speak out in support of lesbian, gay, and bisexual students, school workers, and teachers. The independent groups also successfully influenced the California Federation of Teachers and the California Teachers' Association to lend a hand. Though it was the organizing of many gay-led groups that ultimately led to the defeat of the Briggs Initiative, the significant involvement of the labor movement marked a turning point in the history of LGBT labor activism.

In the 1970s and 1980s, due to the advancements of feminist and gay liberation movements, employment traditionally reserved for one gender opened up to workers who crossed gender lines. For instance, when conventionally masculine work in the steel mills and in construction started to open up to women, lesbians with a masculine gender expression were among the first to defy gender norms by pursuing "men's work." Whether straight, bisexual, or gay, women in workplaces traditionally reserved for men experienced intense sexism and "dyke-baiting," which Miriam Frank defines as "a clear and frequent expression of male hostility when men's power and privileges are threatened by women's transgressions of traditional gender roles."[22] As unions in the building trades rarely sought to defend straight women and lesbians subjected to sexism and homophobia, women formed independent groups in the late 1970s and early 1980s to support each other. In a recent study of queer workers in the steel mills of Gary, Indiana, Anne Balay writes that lesbians—particularly masculine lesbians—were sometimes able to fit into the "old-school macho" world of blue-collar work in the mills because they shared an interest in women with straight men, although this left the sexist machismo of the work culture relatively unchanged.

Gay liberation and feminism also helped to open up traditionally feminine work to queer men, including the flight attendant corps. Phil Tiemeyer shows that the post-World War II growth of homophobia, alongside a financial imperative to hire women who were paid less, resulted in the near-total exclusion of men from the flight attendant corps from the 1940s through the 1960s. By the late 1960s, only 4 percent of flight attendants were men, a figure that included Puerto Rican men hired at TransCaribbean Airways and Hawaiian men serving United flights to Honolulu. The Equal Employment Opportunities Commission's *Diaz v. Pan Am* decision (1971) determined that the female-only hiring policies of airlines violated the Civil Rights Act of 1964. The decision ushered in a new era in which men now could work side by side with women as flight attendants, an opportunity of which many gay men in particular took advantage.

The Rise of AIDS and Queer Union Activism, 1980s to the Present

Right as queer labor activism was getting off the ground, the rightward turn in American politics prompted a homophobic reaction to the AIDS epidemic in the 1980s, marking a retreat in the rights of queer workers.[23] But at the same time, queer workers fought back, forming queer labor caucuses to defend their rights and push labor unions to challenge homophobia and transphobia. Almost immediately upon his inauguration in 1980, President Ronald Reagan oversaw the crushing of the Professional Air Traffic Controllers' strike, launching a period of sharp decline in unions' political power and membership. At the same time, the rapid and devastating spread of AIDS generated widespread panic, and workers with HIV/AIDS faced harsh discrimination at work. Though there is still little written on the subject, historian Phil Tiemeyer considers the impact of AIDS on the male flight attendant corps. Many men working as flight attendants who survived the epidemic recall suffering tremendous loss, as friends, lovers, and colleagues died, one after another. Flight attendant Gaëtan Dugas, in particular, became infamous with the fabrication and spreading of the "Patient Zero" myth, which claimed that Dugas, a gay man diagnosed with AIDS in 1980, brought AIDS to North America through his sexual promiscuity. Tiemeyer also cites another lesser-known example: in 1983, United

Airlines grounded Gär Traynor due to his AIDS diagnosis, citing customers' fears about the spread of AIDS through casual contact. Traynor and a handful of other flight attendants with HIV/AIDS fought back, and through union arbitration proceedings were able to return to work in 1984. Then, in 1990 Congress adopted the Americans with Disabilities Act, a major victory, which stated that people with HIV/AIDS must be allowed to continue to work as permitted by their health.

Workers used unions to pursue contractual benefits particularly important for people with HIV/AIDS and educated fellow union members about the epidemic. Miriam Frank describes, for example, how the AIDS committee of Service Employees International Union (SEIU), Local 250, representing 30,000 hospital workers in the Bay Area, produced an educational leaflet in the mid-1980s in an effort to prevent homophobic and otherwise biased treatment of fellow workers and patients with HIV/AIDS. Further, as LGBT people founded AIDS clinics to provide medical, legal, and financial services, workers also began to unionize them. As is often the case in non-profits, employers often expected employees to view their work as a calling, requiring long hours and low wages. Frank recounts the successful unionization drives affiliated with the SEIU in the 1980s and 1990s at five HIV/AIDS service centers across the country.

In the late 1980s and into the 1990s, LGBT union caucuses blossomed, particularly in public sector unions, providing community and a further push for unions to address homophobia. These caucuses built on earlier organizing, such as independent groups in the 1970s, for example the Lesbian and Gay Labor Alliance, the Gay and Lesbian Labor Activists of Boston in the early 1980s, and the Lesbian and Gay Labor Network, formed in New York in 1986. Caucuses organized to push their unions to address the needs of LGBT workers, including incorporating related issues into contract negotiations—clauses ensuring non-discrimination based on sexual orientation, gender identity or expression, and HIV/AIDS status; domestic partner health benefits; transgender-inclusive health coverage; and so on. Caucuses also fought unjust firings and the daily discrimination LGBT workers often faced in straight-dominated workplaces. One significant example is the Lesbian and Gay Issues Committee within District Council 37 of the American Federation of State, County, and Municipal Employees (AFSCME), representing 135,000 New York City public sector workers, which gained official union recognition in 1990. The queer labor movement gained a major victory in 1997 with the entry of Pride at Work, which advocates for the rights of LGBT workers, into the AFL-CIO as a formal constituency groups. This was a historic moment, resulting as it did from decades of organizing by queer workers within the labor movement.

Very little has been written about the particular experiences and struggles of transgender workers in US history. In her broader queer labor history, Miriam Frank provides some anecdotes about transgender workers who have led efforts to challenge transphobic discrimination at work. This history includes organizing to incorporate trans issues in collective bargaining, including most prominently trans-inclusive health coverage—the service and procedures transgender people need to transition. The 2015 US Transgender Survey reveals how widespread discrimination in employment is, with 30 percent of respondents reporting being fired or denied a promotion, or experiencing other workplace mistreatment due to gender identity or expression discrimination.[24] Transgender women of color sex workers, in particular, experience tremendous violence. The study of transgender labor history is wide open. How have workers organized for the rights of transgender workers? What is the experience of coming out as transgender at work? How have trans men and trans women experienced work differently? How has the weakening of the welfare state affected trans people, who are more likely to experience unemployment and poverty because of their identity? These will be pressing issues for the next wave of queer labor history.

Conclusion

This chapter has traced the ways in which the economic systems governing people's labor have fundamentally shaped queer history. From the eighteenth through the mid-twentieth centuries, the kinds of labor people have been able to pursue have both assisted and obstructed people's ability to pursue sex with people of the same sex, center their lives around same-sex sexual attraction, and identify as transgender and gender non-conforming. With the rise of movements for queer liberation and the expansion of unions in the public and service sectors, we see the growth of queer labor activism, in which LGBT workers led efforts to challenge discrimination at work, in their unions, and in society more generally. Since the 1990s, queer labor activism has been on the upsurge, with more advancements made around queer labor rights than in the previous several centuries.

Where is queer labor history headed from here? Despite the weakening of academic programs in labor history, the recent increase of scholarship on queer labor gestures toward the possibilities of this fertile field. First and foremost, the existing scholarship is weighted toward the history of white men, and additional research is needed about the particular histories of queer workers of color and queer immigrant labor, as well as transgender and lesbian workers. In-depth studies of the history of specific kinds of queer work would be a boon to the field, as would a closer examination of unions that perpetuated homophobia and transphobia in addition to further research on unions that have promoted queer rights. A queer history of slavery in the United States would uncover the ways enslavement fostered or hindered same-sex intimacy and gender transgressions, as well as the use of same-sex sexual violence as a tool to protect slavery.[25] Queer labor history prior to World War II is wide open, including the history of workplace discrimination and the development of queer work cultures. An examination of the law in queer labor history would reveal how the state has discriminated against queer workers, as well as efforts to change the law to prohibit employment-based discrimination.

How might queer history and the history of labor and radicalism in the late nineteenth and early-twentieth centuries have overlapped? How has globalization affected queer migrant labor, and how have transnational labor circuits intersected with queer life?[26] How has the experience of hiding one's identity in straight workplaces affected queer workers? This is just a small sampling of the various research possibilities. The field of queer labor history is still relatively young, and the answers to these questions, and many other crucial arenas of scholarship, remain unwritten.

Notes

1 Allan Bérubé, "'Queer Work' and Labor History," in *My Desire for History: Essays in Gay, Community, and Labor History*, John D'Emilio and Estelle Freedman, eds. (Chapel Hill: University of North Carolina Press, 2011), 261.

2 According to her faculty profile at the Princeton University website, Canaday's book is tentatively titled *Pink Precariat: LGBT Workers in the Shadow of Civil Rights, 1945–2000*, www.princeton.edu/history/people/display_person.xml?netid=mcanaday. Accessed July 18, 2015.

3 John D'Emilio, "Capitalism and Gay Identity," *Powers of Desire: The Politics of Sexuality*, edited by Ann Snitow, Christine Stansell & Sharon Thompson (New York: Monthly Review Press, 1983), 103, 104.

4 For more on the nineteenth-century content of queer US history, see, in this volume, Rachel Hope Cleves, "Revolutionary Sexualities and Early National Genders (1770s–1840s)," and Clare Sears, "Centering Slavery in Nineteenth-Century History."

5 Jackie Blount, *Fit to Teach: Same-Sex Desire, Gender, and School Work in the Twentieth Century* (Albany: State University of New York Press, 2005), 59.

6 Rachel Hope Cleves, *Charity and Sylvia: A Same-Sex Marriage in Early America* (New York: Oxford University Press, 2014), 167, 192.

7 Nayan Shah, *Stranger Intimacy: Contesting Race, Sexuality, and the Law in the North American West* (Berkeley: University of California Press, 2011), 35.

8 Clare Sears, *Arresting Dress: Cross-Dressing, Law, and Fascination in Nineteenth-Century San Francisco* (Durham: Duke University Press, 2014), 13.

9 Don Romesburg, "'Wouldn't a Boy Do?': Placing Early-Twentieth-Century Male Youth Sex Work into Histories of Sexuality," *Journal of the History of Sexuality* 18, no. 13 (2009), 378, 379.

10 Joanne J. Meyerowitz, *Women Adrift: Independent Wage Earners in Chicago, 1880–1930* (Chicago: University of Chicago Press, 1988), xvii.

11 In this volume, for more on the queer historical context of the late nineteenth and early twentieth centuries, see Elizabeth Clement and Beans Velocci, "Modern Sexuality in Modern Times (1880s–1930s)"; for queer urban history, see Kwame Holmes, "The End of Queer Urban History?"

12 Meyerowitz, *Women Adrift*, 113–114.

13 Terence Kissack, *Free Comrades: Anarchism and Homosexuality in the United States, 1895–1917* (Oakland: AK Press, 2008), 3, 5.

14 Joan M. Crouse, "The Remembered Men: Transient Camps in New York State, 1933–1935," *New York History* 71, No. 1 (January 1990), 80, 118.

15 Allan Bérubé, *My Desire for History: Essays in Gay, Community, and Labor History*, ed. Estelle Freedman and John D'Emilio (Chapel Hill: University of North Carolina Press, 2011), 261.

16 Ibid., 315–317.

17 For the queer history of the postwar era, see, in this volume, Amanda Littauer, "Sexual Minorities at the Apex of Heteronormativity (1940s–1965)."

18 Karen L. Graves, *And They Were Wonderful Teachers: Florida's Purge of Gay and Lesbian Teachers* (Urbana: University of Illinois Press, 2009), xvii.

19 For the queer history of the gay liberation era, see, in this volume, Whitney Strub, "Gay Liberation (1963–1980)."

20 Sara Smith, "Organizing for Social Justice: Rank-and-File Teachers' Activism and Social Unionism in California, 1947–1978," (PhD Dissertation, University of California, Santa Cruz, 2014), 443–444.

21 Miriam Frank, *Out in the Union: A Labor History of Queer America* (Philadelphia: Temple University Press, 2014), 77–82.

22 Frank, *Out in the Union*, 24.

23 See also, in this volume, Jennifer Brier, "AIDS and Action (1980s–1990s)."

24 S. E. James et al., *The Report of the 2015 US Transgender Survey* (Washington, DC: National Center for Transgender Equality, 2016), 2.

25 For more on the exploration of the queer history of US slavery, see, in this volume, Sears, "Centering Slavery in Nineteenth Century Queer History" and Nayan Shah, "Queer of Color Estrangement and Belonging."

26 For discussions of queer history in relationship to the nation and transnationalism, see, in this volume, Eithne Luibhéid, "Queer and Nation," and Emily Hobson, "Thinking Transationally, Thinking Queer."

Further Reading

Anderson, Kelly, and Tami Gold. *Out at Work*. Documentary. New York: AndersonGold Films, 1997.

Aptheker, Bettina F. *Intimate Politics: How I Grew Up Red, Fought for Free Speech, and Became a Feminist Rebel*. Emeryville: Seal Press, 2006.

Balay, Anne. *Steel Closets: Voices of Gay, Lesbian, and Transgender Steelworkers*. Chapel Hill: University of North Carolina Press, 2014.

Bielski Boris, Monica and Gerald Hunt. "The Lesbian, Gay, Bisexual, and Transgender Challenge to American Labor." In *Sex of Class: Women Transforming American Labor*, ed. Dorothy Sue Cobble. Cornell, NY: ILR Press, 2007.

Bielski Boris, Monica. "Fighting for Equal Treatment: How the UAW Won Domestic Partner Benefits and Discrimination Protection for Lesbian, Gay, and Bisexual Members," *Labor Studies Journal* 35, no. 2 (2010): 157–180.

Blount, Jackie M. *Fit to Teach: Same-Sex Desire, Gender, and School Work in the Twentieth Century*. Albany: State University of New York Press, 2005.

Boag, Peter. *Same-Sex Affairs: Constructing and Controlling Homosexuality in the Pacific Northwest*. Berkeley: University of California Press, 2003.

Braukman, Lorraine. *Communists and Perverts Under the Palms: The Johns Committee in Florida, 1956–1965*. Gainesville: University Press of Florida, 2012.

Canaday, Margot. *The Straight State: Sexuality and Citizenship in Twentieth-Century America*. Princeton: Princeton University Press, 2009.

Fajardo, Kale Bantinque. *Filipino Crosscurrents: Oceanographies of Seafaring, Masculinities, and Globalization*. Minneapolis: University of Minnesota Press, 2011.

Foster, Thomas A. "The Sexual Abuse of Black Men Under Slavery." *Journal of the History of Sexuality* 20, no. 3: 445–464.

Frank, Miriam. *Out in the Union: A Labor History of Queer America*. Philadelphia: Temple University Press, 2014.

Gluckman, Amy, and Betsy Reed. *Homo Economics: Capitalism, Community, and Lesbian and Gay Life*. New York: Routledge, 1997.

Hansen, Karen V. "'No *Kisses* Is Like Youres': An Erotic Friendship between Two African-American Women During the Mid-Nineteenth Century." *Gender & History* 7, no. 2 (1995): 153–182.

Holcomb, Desma and Nancy Wohlforth. "The Fruits of Our Labor: Pride at Work." *New Labor Forum* 8 (Spring/Summer 2001): 9–20.

Hollibaugh, Amber. *My Dangerous Desires: A Queer Girl Dreaming Her Way Home*. Durham: Duke University Press, 2000.

Hunt, Gerald, ed. *Laboring for Rights: Unions and Sexual Diversity Across Nations*. Philadelphia: Temple University Press, 1999.

Johnson, David K. *The Lavender Scare: The Cold War Persecution of Gays and Lesbians in the Federal Government*. Chicago: University of Chicago Press, 2004.

Krupat, Kitty, and Patrick McCreery. *Out at Work: Building a Gay-Labor Alliance*. Minneapolis: University of Minnesota Press, 2001.

LaTour, Jane. *Sisters in the Brotherhoods: Working Women Organizing for Equality in New York City*. New York: Palgrave Macmillan, 2008.

Manalansan, Martin F. *Global Divas: Filipino Gay Men in the Diaspora*. Durham: Duke University Press, 2003.

Orleck, Annelise. *Common Sense and a Little Fire: Women and Working-Class Politics in the United States, 1900–1965*. Chapel Hill: The University of North Carolina Press, 1995.

Shah, Nayan. *Stranger Intimacy: Contesting Race, Sexuality and the Law in the North American West*. Berkeley: University of California Press, 2012.

Syrett, Nicholas L. "A Busman's Holiday in the Not-So-Lonely Crowd: Business Culture, Epistolary Networks, and Itinerant Homosexuality in Mid-Twentieth Century America." *Journal of the History of Sexuality* 21, no. 1 (2012): 121–140.

Tiemeyer, Phil. *Plane Queer: Labor, Sexuality, and AIDS in the History of Male Flight Attendants*. Berkeley: University of California Press, 2013.

Ward, Jane. "Gender Labor: Transmen, Femmes, and the Collective Work of Transgression." *Sexualities* 13, no. 2 (2010): 236–254.

26

CONSUMERISM

Stephen Vider

As legal recognition of same-sex marriage in the United States has expanded, wedding cakes have emerged as an unexpected site of controversy. In 2012, for example, a gay couple lodged a complaint with the Colorado Civil Rights Division against a baker who refused to create a cake for their wedding because he opposed same-sex marriage on the basis of Christian religious beliefs. The Civil Rights Division ruled in favor of the couple, as did a state appeals court, finding, in effect, that the rights of LGBT people as consumers are a fundamental component of their broader civil rights.[1] In the short term, the wedding cake cases might be understood as emblems of respectability politics for a neoliberal age, where LGBT consumer-citizens fight for recognition and equality within the constrained fields of marriage and the market. In a longer view, the cases are only the most recent scene in an ongoing and complicated romance between queers and commerce. The history of LGBT identity, community, and politics is bound up with the history of consumer goods, from paperback novels to poppers, as well as consumer spaces, from the Stonewall Inn in Greenwich Village to the Pulse nightclub in Orlando, Florida.

This chapter explores how consumerism has shaped LGBT life and politics from the early twentieth century to the present. It traces how acts, objects, and spaces of queer consumption played a central role in consolidating LGBT identities and communities, and provoked many of the earliest legal battles for gay, lesbian, and transgender rights. At the same time, it argues, consumerism has frequently functioned to reify gender, racial, and class divides among LGBT people, posing particular challenges for political activism and collective struggle for free expression and acceptance. The chapter is organized around five central themes in the historiography on LGBT consumerism: (1) identification; (2) performance; (3) space-making; (4) contestation; and (5) mainstreaming. These thematic sections draw together a wide range of historical research, as well as diverse actors, objects, and spaces, to point to common social and political meanings of consumerism over time, as well as changes in practices and opportunities for consumption among LGBT people and communities.

Identification

Much of the historical literature on consumption in the United States has focused on the ways consumerism has functioned to construct particular gender, race, and class identifications and sexual subjectivities.[2] Scholars of LGBT consumer culture have looked especially at print media, arguing that books and magazines played a critical role in enabling readers to see themselves as gay, lesbian, bisexual, and/or transgender.

Fiction proved particularly important for gay men, bisexuals, and lesbians from the 1920s into the 1960s. David Johnson, for example, in his study of 1930s Chicago, found that many young men's first introduction to the "gay world" was through the novels they borrowed from lending libraries throughout the city. Monica Bachmann's analysis of letters to author Jo Sinclair in the late 1940s shows particularly well how readers engaged with lesbian characters on the page. After the publication of her first novel, *Wasteland* (1946), Sinclair received many letters from women remarking on the character of Debby, a butch Jewish lesbian whose self-acceptance was practically unprecedented. One writer explained:

> Never before have I encountered a frank, tolerant public discussion of homosexuality, so this is the first time I have learned of anyone's views on the subject other than my own. At the point where Debby says, "I'm a person in this world. There's got to be room for me, too," I felt great relief and encouragement, as I have ever since reading *Wasteland*.[3]

Readers appeared to identify with Debby, even when they did not explicitly use the words "lesbian" or "homosexual."

Physique magazines and mail-order photographs targeted to gay consumers under the guise of "fitness" also encouraged the emergence of a self-conscious gay male subculture. Thomas Waugh notes that the circulation of physique magazines such as *Grecian Guild Pictorial* far exceeded that of homophile magazines *ONE*—and helped individuals, however isolated, to imagine themselves as part of a broader community: "the consumption of erotica was without question political: however furtive, however unconscious, however masturbatory, using pictures was an act of belonging to a community composed of producers, models, and most important, other consumers."[4] The act of purchasing and viewing physique magazines was an act of resistance and connection—validating same-sex desire. David Johnson has shown that physique entrepreneurs steadily expanded their offerings: 1960s mail-order catalogs such as *Vagabond* offered consumers greeting cards, drinking sets, erotic films, novels, as well as campy records and coloring books. By marketing to gay consumers, physique companies worked to refine a gay sensibility that did not depend exclusively on sexual acts. Instead they conceived homosexuality as a personality trait and gay men as a distinct subculture.

Early gay rights, or homophile, groups had a more ambivalent relationship to consumerism.[5] Early homophile periodicals including *The Mattachine Review*, *ONE*, and *The Ladder* were conceived more as educational than commercial projects. As Martin Meeker has shown, for example, *Mattachine Review* editor Hal Call strategically emphasized the magazine's "serious nature." Its open discussion of sex and obscenity laws, employment discrimination, and sexual psychology necessarily pressed on obscenity laws, but Call and others remained cautious about including information about gay bars and bathhouses, promoting physique magazines, or even sponsoring a pen pal club. Call's later efforts were less bound to maintaining a "mask" of respectability. By the early 1960s, Call and fellow Mattachine leader Don Lucas founded their own publishing company, Pan-Graphic Press, and with it, the mail-order catalog Dorian Book Service.[6] Initially, the book service, too, insisted on the literary and intellectual value of the books they sold. But as Whitney Strub has shown, by 1963, the catalog had begun including various pulp novels with titles such as *Male Bride* and *Homo Hill*, and in 1967, Call co-founded the Adonis Bookstore in San Francisco, selling both political and erotic work.

Looking to the East Coast, Marc Stein has documented how Clark Polak, a businessman in Philadelphia, aimed to bridge physique culture and homophile activism, mixing political and cultural commentary with erotic photography in his popular magazine *Drum*. While *Drum* became the most widely circulated gay periodical of its time, homophile groups criticized it as a threat to their veneer of respectability. In fact, *Drum* was far more representative of where the gay consumer market was headed: with the rise of the gay liberation movement in the late 1960s, gay periodicals such as *Gay*, *Fag Rag*, and *The Advocate* grew more forthright in celebrating gay sexuality and culture, at the same covering LGBT politics.

Scholars have begun to explore how an expanded lesbian consumer market in the 1970s shaped an emerging lesbian feminist community. Heather Murray, for example, shows that some lesbian feminists "refashioned business practices by taking on the role of artisans within a distinctive lesbian economy" and "reenvisioned feminity and domesticity through aesthetic and daily objects" including handmade jewelry and women's clothing sold from the pages of lesbian periodicals.[7] The feminist folk music recording company Olivia Records prominently, if not exclusively, featured lesbian artists, whose music promoted a sense of a distinct lesbian culture and sensibility.

Far less has been written about the impact of consumerism on the emergence of transgender identities in the United States after World War II. Robert Hill points to one important area for future research, in his study of the magazine *Transvestia*, published by Virginia Prince from 1960 to 1980. Hill argues that the magazine provided space for its audience to read about, and in their letters, articulate a spectrum of gender experiences and identities, often at odds with the respectability politics of the magazine's editors. The Digital Transgender Archive also contains scans of the groundbreaking magazine *Drag*, published by New York City drag queen Lee Brewster. Billed as a "magazine about the transvestite," it contained news, photographs of drag performances and competitions, personal ads, as well as advertisements for books and clothing that could be ordered from Lee Brewster's Mardi Gras Enterprises, an extension of the popular clothing store Brewster operated in Manhattan.

Similarly, few studies have considered the ways LGBT consumer goods, media, and catalogs tended to construct gay and lesbian identities as white. Tracy D. Morgan argues that the overwhelming whiteness of physique magazines, for example, produced a largely white imaginary for healthy gay masculinity in the 1950s and 1960s. In my study of Lou Rand Hogan's widely publicized 1965 book, *The Gay Cookbook*, I show that Hogan largely echoed American culinary trends in imagining an all-white readership while presenting foreign foods (Hawaiaan and Japanese, for example) as exotic additions. Lucas Hilderbrand suggests that the gay travel magazine *Ciao!*, published in the mid-1970s, might be read as both radically inclusive, in depicting men of a wide range of ethnic and racial backgrounds, and at the same time fetishizing those differences for an again presumed white reader. It would not be until the 1980s and 1990s when magazines targeted to queer people of color, including *BLK*, *Black/Out*, *Blacklines*, and *En La Vida*, would appear—and these remain largely unexamined by scholars.

Performance

Consumer practices can also be understood in terms of performance.[8] Consumption does not only shape subjective experiences of social identity, but also enables their public display. Within LGBT cultures, consumer performance has often taken the form of clothing and decoration—material goods whose display signifies a feeling of belonging, but also a sense of taste. Clothing has been a critical means of performing queer affiliation since the early twentieth century. As George Chauncey documents in *Gay New York*, from the 1910s through the 1930s, many "fairies"

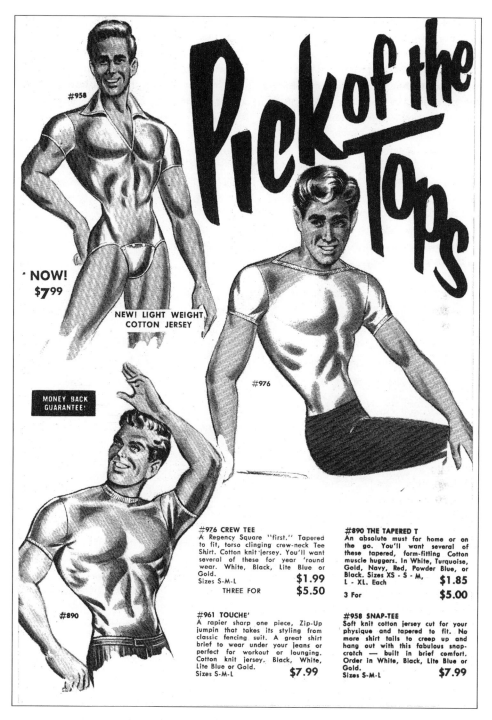

Figure 26.1 Page in the Los Angeles-based Regency Square menswear catalog (c.late 1960s), which used physique magazine and campy aesthetics to sell both its wares and the gay Southern California lifestyle they represented.

Courtesy of GLBT Historical Society.

adopted brightly colored or otherwise unconventional clothing, for example red ties and green suits, as a way of marking their difference, and making themselves identifiable to potential friends and sexual partners. In their classic study of a lesbian community in Buffalo, New York, Elizabeth Lapovsky Kennedy and Madeline D. Davis emphasize the importance of clothing in performing and differentiating butch and fem roles. Their oral history subjects discussed how the butch lesbians in their study wore conventionally masculine clothing—starched shirts, jackets, pants, and Oxford shoes—throughout the 1940s and 50s, with small but notable differences based on age, race, and class. Many women reported going to men's clothing shops or a particular tailor to purchase their clothes. Fems, on the other hand, took their clothing cues largely from mainstream women's fashion. For both Chauncey's and Kennedy and Davis's subjects, mannerism, hairstyling, and other bodily and vocal performances were key to performing queer affiliation, but clothing, shaped by both subcultural norms and larger cultural conventions, was essential.

Scholars have also documented the importance of clothing choices in the 1970s, when gay and lesbian fashion norms were reshaped by the counterculture, gay liberation, the women's movement, and lesbian feminism. Betty Hillman examines debates among feminists around clothing and self-presentation in the 1970s. Many lesbian feminists adopted and advocated for an androgynous look (or simply more practical clothes), rejecting makeup and high heels and dresses in favor of t-shirts, jeans, and boots. Other women expressed discomfort with a "masculine" aesthetic, and instead, emphasized their liberation to dress as they wished. In both cases, consumer choices were understood to be an expression of selfhood and solidarity with a larger political and social community.

Sociologist Martin Levine traced the rise of the "clone" look, a style of meticulous, muscled masculinity, among gay urban white men in the 1970s. The clone appropriated clothing associated with conventional working class male icons—the cowboy (denim jacket and cowboy shirt); the biker (leather jacket and cap); and the lumberjack (jeans and hiking boots)—and urbanized, eroticized, and stylized them, as a way of undermining conventional conceptions of gay men as effeminate. The resulting conformity, as the term "clone" suggests, was easily parodied: Hal Fischer's 1977 book *Gay Semiotics* warmly mocks the uniformity of San Francisco's gay clone culture, with annotated photographs documenting various looks ("Jock," "Hippie," "Basic Gay") as well as the handkerchief code (blue, right pocket for passive; blue, left active; or, Fischer noted, sometimes "used in the treatment of nasal congestion"). This uniformity was undoubtedly exclusionary, but it could also create a feeling of belonging and communal recognition.

Camp humor and performance have also been an important means of engaging with American consumer culture. While many scholars have written about camp's reappropriation of mainstream entertainment—for example, David Halperin's extended exploration of the film *Mildred Pierce* in *How to Be Gay*—fewer have written about gay male appropriation of material culture through decoration and design. Susan Sontag's classic essay, "Notes on 'Camp,'" is perhaps best where it explains the connections between taste and material culture. Camp, Sontag wrote, "is the love of the exaggerated, the 'off,' of things-being-what-they-are-not. The best example is in Art Nouveau, the most typical and fully developed Camp style. Art Nouveau objects, typically, convert one thing into something else: the lighting fixtures in the form of flowering plants, the living room which is really a grotto."[9] Sontag's most famous example of camp décor is the Tiffany lamp, with its stained-glass shade. In reclaiming "vulgar" objects, some gay men effectively short-circuited postwar modernist patterns of American consumerism, questioning dominant taste by reclaiming and revaluing the outdated.[10]

Space-making

Consumer spaces have also been essential for the creation of LGBT communities across the United States. This includes both the queer spaces created for and by LGBT people, and "straight" commercial venues that LGBT people have made their own. John D'Emilio's early essay, "Capitalism and Gay Identity," tied the emergence of gay and lesbian communities closely to the major shift of nineteenth-century capitalism—the decline of the household economy and the rise of free labor—which enabled men and women to leave their home communities and venture into the city. This shift also coincided with the expansion of urban leisure economies and a growing consumer market.

Scholars have long pointed to bars and nightclubs as primary incubators for LGBT community. In his groundbreaking 1983 book, *Sexual Politics, Sexual Communities*, John D'Emilio argued that the single most important change in LGBT life after World War II was the spread of bars that catered to gay men and lesbians across the United States. As D'Emilio wrote, "Alone among the expressions of gay life, the bar fostered an identity that was both public and collective."[11] Kennedy and Davis's study of lesbian culture in Buffalo bears this out, as bars served as the central meeting place for working-class lesbians in the 1940s and 1950s.

Perhaps the best-known commercial venue in LGBT history is the Stonewall Inn in Greenwich Village, where riots broke out among its diverse patrons and neighborhood regulars, including gay men, lesbians, trans people, and homeless youth, in response to a police raid. Within a year, the riots were widely commemorated as the beginning of a gay liberation movement. But the circumstances of the bar's operation also point to the complex intersections of commercial enterprise and queer life. As David Carter explains, the bar was unusually popular, in part because it had two dance floors. It was also operated by members of the mafia, who watered down the drinks and kept the prices high. Early gay liberation writer Carl Wittman specifically called out such exploitation as endemic to "gay ghettos," which he believed bred "self-hatred."[12]

Queer people have also historically depended on spaces of consumption that were not meant for them to create community. George Chauncey documents how some cafeterias and restaurants in Prohibition-era New York—both in Greenwich Village and the theater district—became known as queer gathering spots. Flamboyant, effeminate fairies took note of restaurants that would tolerate their behavior, and in some cases, became tourist spectacles in their own right. Nan Alamilla Boyd has traced how bohemian entertainment spots in 1930s and 1940s San Francisco also became known for gay, lesbian, and transgender performers and clientele. Allan Bérubé traced how bathhouses slowly emerged as gay sites, first as it became known which owners tolerated same-sex sexual behavior, and later as owners began to cater more openly to queer men. These spaces might be conceived, in French philosopher Michel Foucault's terms, as "heterotopias," spaces that exist in opposition to cultural norms. Spaces of entertainment and leisure do not merely produce new social conventions, but provide room to refract and invert everyday norms, including those of gender and sexuality, if only temporarily. They were, in Don Romesburg's phrase, sites of "contested leisure," where social and sexual convention as well as legal regulation challenged, and were challenged by, queer leisure.[13]

By the late 1960s and early 1970s, gay-owned or targeted businesses proliferated rapidly in major US cities. They produced new debates about acceptable and unacceptable social, sexual, and consumer practices. In 1967, for example, New York Mattachine veteran Craig Rodwell opened the country's first gay bookstore. As Jim Downs notes, Rodwell stocked classic gay literature as well as newer gay liberation and lesbian feminist non-fiction, but he would not stock explicit sexual material; not out of prudishness, he explained, but because such publications were sexually and economically exploitative. Martin Levine also documented an expansive number of sites in the late 1970s clone "circuit" of New York, including bars, restaurants, gyms, discos, bathhouses, and sex clubs. For Patrick Moore, such spaces gave gay men opportunities to explore sexuality as a creative art form, to initiate "an astonishing experiment in radically restructuring existing relationships, concepts of beauty, and the use of sex as a revolutionary tool."[14] It is precisely this sense of experimentation that Moore fears has been lost in the wake of HIV/AIDS.

Lesbians in the 1970s often had a more conflicted relationship to consumer space—in part because women generally had less economic and social capital to create spaces of their own. Despite the challenges (and feminist critiques of capitalism), many straight and lesbian feminists did seek to create consumer spaces of their own, including bookstores and restaurants, in hopes of building community and advancing women's culture and politics. Finn Enke chronicles the founding of feminist bookstores and coffeehouses in the Midwest in the early 1970s. While few of these spaces were exclusively targeted to lesbians, they were nevertheless important sites for building lesbian community and politics. At the same time, these businesses often struggled to make a profit, or were riven by internal debates over which women these spaces should ultimately serve. Far less has been written about lesbian bars in the 1970s and 1980s, perhaps in part because they did not as obviously serve feminist political aims.

A critical area for future research in studying LGBT consumer spaces are dynamics around racial inclusion and exclusion. Enke, for example, notes that lesbian bars in the Midwest in the 1970s were unlikely to be interracial, because of longer histories of segregation. Kent Peacock also notes, in a recent article on the homophile movement in Washington, D.C., that many gay bars practiced "double-carding"—asking people of color for multiple forms of identification. Such practices were common at gay and lesbian bars across the United States both before and after Stonewall. They were sometimes met with resistance. In the early 1980s *WomaNews* documented a protest at the popular lesbian bar The Duchess, for their discrimination against women of color.[15] In the early 1980s, as Kevin Mumford documents, the Philadelphia chapter of Black and White Men Together both investigated and protested racial profiling in the city's gay bars. Don Romesburg shows how San Francisco groups, including Black and White Men Together and the Asian Lesbian and Gay Alliance, worked over decades to draw attention to racist practices in the city's bars. Patrons responded less formally, too: In one of the poems in African-American artist Marlon Riggs's film *Tongues Untied*, the speaker recalls going to a new bar with a group of friends and the doorman demanding three forms of ID. He laments "I thought this shit was through," before snapping three times in the doorman's face, "She didn't know what hit her."

Queer people of color have often depended more on clubs or club nights specifically created for and/or by those within their communities. Khevon Lee LaGrone, for example, recalls two popular clubs in downtown Oakland, California: beginning in the mid-1980s, Cabel's Reef and Bella Napoli, only a block apart, drew black gay men from across the city and region. Many patrons felt the bars in San Francisco's predominantly white gay neighborhood, the Castro, simply weren't for them, as carding and other forms of discrimination frequently ensured. In his oral history study of Los Angeles in the 1970s and 80s, Eric Wat notes the creation of gay Asian bars was revelatory for many patrons: Although the bars were known to attract white men who fetishized men of Asian descent—so-called "rice queens"—they were also one of few places in the city where gay Asian men knew they wouldn't be turned away and they could meet others who shared both their sexual and racial identities. Darius Bost describes how Washington, D.C.'s race-stratified gay club scene in the 1970s and 1980s shaped HIV/AIDS cultural perceptions and activism in ways that powerfully shaped black responses to the epidemic. Historians need to continue extending analysis of racist practices and resistance within queer commercial venues.[16]

Contestation

Early LGBT historiography tended to distinguish between formal political activism and the "pre-political" communities centered in cultures of consumption, most notably bars. More recent scholarship on consumerism has questioned this strict divide. In *A Consumers' Republic*, for example, Lizabeth Cohen argues that American consumption in the twentieth century has often been mobilized and experienced as a mode of political citizenship. Scholars in LGBT history have similarly examined how LGBT consumer practices and spaces emerged as key sites of legal and political contestation. If consumerism has been a potent means of LGBT identity and community formation, efforts to restrict access have frequently been experienced as a major mode of oppression. It could lead to legal and political action.

Policing of bars was one of the most obvious and immediate legal challenges to LGBT life. Nan Alamilla Boyd, for example, notes a major shift in San Francisco's treatment of gay men and lesbians with the creation of the Alcoholic Beverage Control Board (the ABC) in 1955. The ABC expanded their interpretations of "public indecency" to include gender-non-conforming behavior and dress, as well as same-sex touching and dancing, effectively criminalizing homosexual assembly of any kind and making it far easier to revoke a bar's liquor license. Legal cases over the next six years would alternately affirm and challenge the ABC's authority, but the larger impact, Christopher Agee has argued, was to open space for more liberal, tolerant, and "cosmopolitan" views of homosexuality in the mainstream media. Local policing also led gay and lesbian bar owners to organize the Tavern Guild, which worked collectively to protect queer patrons, support each other's businesses, and support the city's broader homophile movement.

In his history of LGBT Philadelphia, Marc Stein also points to a series of sit-ins at Dewey's lunch counter, after the restaurant started refusing to serve gender non-conforming young people. One of the people who supported and joined the protest was Clark Polak, publisher of *Drum* magazine and head of the local gay rights group Janus. In a newsletter, Polak specifically challenged both the restaurant's practices and conventional homophile activism:

> All too often, there is a tendency to be concerned with the rights of homosexuals as long as they somehow appear to be heterosexual, whatever that is. The masculine woman and the feminine man often are looked down upon by the official policy of homophile organizations, but the Janus Society is concerned with the worth of an individual and the manner in which she or he comports himself.[17]

Through the 1950s and 1960s, gay and lesbian publishers also challenged censorship laws that restricted circulation of homosexual materials. The earliest gay censorship case to reach the US Supreme Court, *One Inc. v. Oleson*, overturned a decision by the post office that declared a 1954 issue of *ONE Magazine* too obscene to be mailed. The magazine ultimately won, with the court deciding that homosexual content was not in and of itself obscene. Still, as David Johnson explores, it was physique magazine publishers who faced the greater legal threat (nearly every major publisher was at some point arrested), and fought hardest for LGBT people's rights to consume erotic material—progressively winning the right to reproduce more and more explicit photography, and enabling more open discussions and depictions of homosexuality in other publications as well. The circle of transgender writers and readers around *Transvestia* also took considerable risk in sharing their stories and subscribing. As Robert Hill notes, several writers recounted being arrested or harassed by the police on charges of crossdressing. The magazine's founder, Virginia Prince, was also arrested in the 1960s for distributing material deemed obscene. She accepted a plea bargain with five years probation, but turned the situation to her advantage: her attorney arranged the stipulation that her probation would include giving educational lectures about gender variance, effectively allowing her to circumvent laws that forbid "masquerading" as a woman in public.[18]

Contestation of LGBT consumer restrictions could also take more spontaneous forms. The Stonewall riots are, again, the best-known example, but Susan Stryker has also documented earlier uprisings and protests in response to police harassment and arrests at consumer spaces. During the 1960s, Compton's Cafeteria in the Tenderloin district of San Francisco was a popular night spot for young transgender women, gay men, and sex workers. One night in 1966, the restaurant called in the police to remove one table of rowdy customers, but the patrons fought back en masse. That riot would not have the widescale impact of the Stonewall uprising a few years later, but still it indicates the ways LGBT people—even those who did not necessarily see themselves as activists—understood themselves as an oppressed group, who had the right to fight back. Consumer restrictions, of course, were not the only ways LGBT people were oppressed, but they were among the most widely experienced and persistent—and in public space, among the most obviously shared.

The new wave of lesbian and gay rights organizations, publications, and leaders that emerged after Stonewall increasingly recognized the political potential of queer consumption. In 1977, many activists called for a national boycott of Florida orange juice, after Anita Bryant, former spokesperson for the Florida Citrus Commission, led a successful campaign to repeal an anti-gay discrimination ordinance in Dade County. Discussion of the boycott made national headlines, and helped to consolidate a sense of a nationwide gay and lesbian political constituency. By the mid-1970s, gay activists including Harvey Milk joined with union leaders in advocating for a boycott of the conservative-owned Coors beer company, in protest against discriminatory labor practices. Calls for a boycott continued into the 2000s, even as the company began to reach out and market to gay and lesbian consumers.[19]

Mainstreaming

As Coors' outreach to gay consumers may suggest, among the most surprising shifts in American culture since the 1990s has been the identification of LGBT people as a marketing demographic by mainstream companies and advertisers. Marketing towards gay and lesbian consumers was not without precedent. As early as 1975, the *Wall Street Journal* had published an article on attempts by media producers to target gay audiences. Efforts to target a gay and lesbian market dramatically shifted in the early 1990s, as major companies placed custom ads in gay and lesbian periodicals, and as mainstream ads gradually included more and more gay and lesbian content. One major factor, Katherine Sender suggests in her book *Business, Not Politics*, is that while the stigma of HIV/AIDS kept many companies away from the gay market in the 1980s, by the early 1990s, responses to HIV/AIDS had also made gay men and lesbians more visible as a demographic than ever before. This change was coupled with increased media visibility more generally, and growing research on the supposed size and affluence of the gay market—white gay men in particular. At the same time, advertisers often hedged their bets: in 1997, business journalist Michael Wilke coined the term "gay vague," to refer to ads queer enough to resonate with LGBT consumers, but ambiguous enough to go over the heads of straight ones. The term also became a ranking on Wilke's website, The Commercial Closet (now Ad Respect), which has documented the rise of LGBT advertising in TV and print media for over two decades.

Gay and lesbian consumers, in turn, have often greeted targeted advertising by mainstream companies as a sign of cultural acceptance and civil rights. Yet many scholars have also critiqued the conflation of capitalist inclusion with political progress. In her book *Selling Out*, Alexandra Chasin argues that while the market has sometimes been a vehicle for lesbian and gay men to expand their political rights, an easy celebration of integration through consumer access masks greater social and economic injustice. As Chasin writes, "[T]he capitalist market makes possible, but also constrains, social movements."[20]

Lisa Duggan similarly implicates consumerism in her analysis of assimilationist LGBT identity politics, what she has influentially called, "homonormativity": "a politics that does not contest dominant heteronormative assumptions and institutions, but upholds and sustains them, while promising the possibility of a demobilized gay constituency and a privatized, depoliti-cized gay culture anchored in domesticity and consumption."[21] For Duggan, the potential of LGBT politics has been diminished by its acceptance of neoliberal policies and a conservative vision of civil rights that conflates freedom with the free market and equality with individual economic gains—nowhere more obviously than in the movement for same-sex marriage.[22] Nan Alamilla Boyd expands on this point in her analysis of the same-sex marriage movement's connections with the gay travel market. "The commodification of gay marriage via marketplace activity produces a new kind of queer citizen," she argues, "one that participates in civic life via the social rituals of marriage and the commercial rituals of conspicuous consumption."[23] The slow expansion of legal same-sex marriage in some states in the 2000s, alongside marriage bans in others, allowed for cities such as Boston to market themselves as wedding destinations, and uniquely gay-friendly tourist spots.

The flipside of the rise of the "respectable" gay and lesbian consumer might be the under-valuing, disappearance, and restigmatization of consumer spaces and practices that more openly challenge middle-class sexual and romantic norms. In their 1998 essay, "Sex in Public," Lauren Berlant and Michael Warner pointed to a new zoning law passed in New York City in 1995 under Mayor Rudolph Giuliani that placed restrictions on the size and number of adult book and video stores in a given area. Such laws, Warner and Berlant argue, have repercussions far beyond the businesses explicitly targeted:

> The gay bars on Christopher Street draw customers from people who come there because of its sex trade. The street is cruisier because of the sex shops. . . . Not all of the thousands who migrate or make pilgrimages to Christopher Street use the porn shops, but all benefit from the fact that some do.[24]

In the years since Berlant and Warner's essay, sexual commerce has increasingly moved online, along with the broader social and sexual culture it supported—though not entirely. Lynn Comella's research on feminist sex shops, including the lesbian-founded (and now multi-city and online) store Babeland, suggests how the market might still support queer communities and radical sexual and gender politics. This should not suggest that consumerism is the only or primary path forward for queer politics, but, to follow on Berlant and Warner's argument, it could still provide one avenue for building sexual and gender counterpublics, and imagining alternatives to homonormative social and sexual forms.

Conclusion: The Future of the Queer Consumer Citizen

The scope and meaning of LGBT consumerism has shifted radically since the publication of Sender's *Business, Not Politics* and Chasin's *Selling Out*. Not least among these shifts has been the expansion of online commerce and social media, allowing marketing to grow more targeted and personalized. Advertisers have also kept pace with the growing mainstream acceptance of white-centered, middle-class gay and lesbian couples and families. In 2015, Steven Petrow writing for the *Washington Post*, for example, offered a roundup of gay-inclusive TV commercials. This included a Campbell's soup ad, tied to the release of a new *Star Wars* film, featuring two dads feeding their son while quoting Darth Vader, "I am your father." Recent ads such as this one have regularly provoked outrage from One Million Moms, a project of the conservative Christian organization the American Family Association, but advertisers appear largely undeterred. Some mainstream advertisers have even begun to look, cautiously, towards transgender consumers.[25]

At the same time, many observers have noted the closing of older gay and lesbian businesses, especially bookstores and bars. Studying the history of LGBT consumerism can provide important context for understanding the implications of these shifts for queer communities and politics in the future. There are also significant gaps in the historiography on how consumerism has consolidated race, class, and gender divides within LGBT communities. Indeed, as consumer access has become a site and signifier of citizenship, those without financial resources and social capital have been increasingly left out of an imagined LGBT community.

As the LGBT consumer market becomes more assimilated into the mainstream, the history of queer appropriations of consumer culture may be particularly relevant. In *Out in the Country*, Mary L. Gray follows a group of queer young people in Kentucky who regularly head to a local Walmart to do drag in the aisles. As one participant explained:

> Why wouldn't we go there?! It's the best place to find stuff to do drag. They've got all the wigs and makeup and tight clothes and stuff. . . . Besides no matter how much we bug people doing what we're doing, we're still customers too.[26]

They can get away with drag at Walmart, Gray argues, because they are still legible as consumer citizens. Their queer use of Walmart's space resonates with Chauncey's study of fairies socializing in New York cafeterias a century earlier, and suggests the continuing potential for queer subjects to repurpose consumer spaces and goods for their own ends. Lisa Duggan's reading of consumption as an anchor of homonormativity in the twenty-first century is undeniable, and a critical frame for understanding how neoliberal capitalism undercuts queer political and community connection.[27] But history also reveals that consumerism has often been mobilized for more radical social and political ends as well. In the ages of Walmart, Amazon, and beyond, queer consumers will still question, subvert, and reclaim the market from within.

Notes

1 *Charlie Craig and David Mullins v. Masterpiece Cakeshop, Inc.* For an overview of the case, currently being reviewed by the US Supreme Court, see American Civil Liberties Union of Colorado website, http://aclu-co.org/court-cases/masterpiece-cakeshop. Accessed October 25, 2017.

2 See, for example, Jennifer Scanlon, *Inarticulate Longings: The Ladies' Home Journal, Gender, and the Promises of Consumer Culture* (New York: Routledge, 1995); Jennifer Scanlon, ed., *The Gender and Consumer Culture Reader* (New York: New York University Press, 2000); Kristin L. Hoganson, *Consumers' Imperium: The Global Production of American Domesticity, 1865–1920* (Chapel Hill: University of North

Carolina Press, 2007); Andrew R. Heinze, *Adapting to Abundance: Jewish Immigrants, Mass Consumption, and the Search for American Identity* (New York: Columbia University Press, 1990); Kenon Breazale, "In Spite of Women: *Esquire* Magazine and the Construction of the Male Consumer," *Signs: Journal of Women in Culture and Society* 20, no. 1 (1994): 1–22.

3   Monica Bachmann, "'Someone like Debby':(De)Constructing a Lesbian Community of Readers," *GLQ: A Journal of Lesbian and Gay Studies* 6, no. 3 (2000): 382.

4   Thomas Waugh, *Hard to Imagine: Gay Male Eroticism in Photography and Film from Their Beginnings to Stonewall* (New York: Columbia University Press, 1996), 217.

5   For the history of queer organizations, see, in this volume, Marcia Gallo, "Organizations."

6   Call's use of the term "serious nature" quoted in Martin Meeker, *Contacts Desired: Gay and Lesbian Communications and Community, 1940s-1970s* (Chicago: University of Chicago Press, 2006), 55. On Mattachine's "mask of respectability" as a political strategy, see also Martin Meeker, "Behind the Mask of Respectability: Reconsidering the Mattachine Society and Male Homophile Practice, 1950s and 1960s," *Journal of the History of Sexuality* 10, no. 1 (2001): 78–116.

7   Heather Murray, "Free for All Lesbians: Lesbian Cultural Production and Consumption in the United States during the 1970s," *Journal of the History of Sexuality* 16, no. 2 (2007): 258.

8   On performance as a mode of analysis, see Henry Bial and Sara Brady, eds., *The Performance Studies Reader* (New York: Routledge, 2016).

9   Susan Sontag, "Notes on 'Camp,'" *Against Interpretation: And Other Essays* (New York: Farrar, Straus and Giroux, 1966), 279.

10   In this volume, "The Apex of Heteronormativity," Amanda Littauer's chapter on 1940s-1960s US queer history, also contextualizes camp as a postwar-era sensibility, as does Sharon Ullman, "Performance and Popular Culture."

11   John D'Emilio, *Sexual Politics, Sexual Communities* (Chicago: University of Chicago Press, 1998 [1983]), 32.

12   Carl Wittman, "A Gay Manifesto," in *Out of the Closets: Voices of Gay Liberation*, ed. Karla Jay and Allen Young (New York: New York University Press, 1992 [1972]), 339.

13   Don Romesburg, "Gay Men's Leisure Lifestyles," in *Encyclopedia of Recreation and Leisure in America*, ed. Gary S. Cross, Vol. 1 (Detroit: Charles Scribner's Sons, 2004), 390.

14   Patrick Moore, *Beyond Shame: Reclaiming the History of Radical Gay Sexuality* (Boston: Beacon Press, 2004), 4.

15   Peg Byron and Audrey Roth, "When Women Protest, Duchess Listens," *WomaNews*, February 1981, 2.

16   See also, in this volume, Nayan Shah, "Queer of Color Estrangement and Belonging."

17   Quoted in Marc Stein, *City of Sisterly and Brotherly Loves: Lesbian and Gay Philadelphia, 1945–1972* (Philadelphia: Temple University Press, 2004), 246.

18   On Virginia Prince's arrest and probation, see Richard Ekins and Dave King, "Virginia Prince: Transgender Pioneer," *International Journal of Transgenderism* 8, no. 4 (2005): 5–15.

19   On Coors boycott, see especially Miriam Frank, *Out in the Union: A Labor History of Queer America* (Philadelphia: Temple University Press, 2014), 75–101.

20   Alexandra Chasin, *Selling Out: The Gay and Lesbian Movement Goes to Market* (New York: St. Martin's Press, 2000), xvii.

21   Lisa Duggan, "The New Homonormativity," in *Materializing Democracy: Toward a Revitalized Cultural Politics*, ed. Russ Castronovo and Dana D. Nelson (Durham: Duke University Press, 2002), 179.

22   For a more extensive discussion of queer history in the context of neoliberalism, see, in this volume, Margo Weiss, "Queer Politics in Neoliberal Times (1970s-2010s)."

23   Nan Alamilla Boyd, "Sex and Tourism: The Economic Implications of the Gay Marriage Movement," *Radical History Review* 100 (2008): 228.

24   Lauren Berlant and Michael Warner, "Sex in Public," *Critical Inquiry* 24, no. 2 (1998): 562.

25   Steven Petrow, "Advertisers Embrace Gay People in an Amazing Year of Firsts for Commercials," *Washington Post*, December 14, 2015; Chris Daniels, "Marketing to the T: Brands Get Inclusive of Transgender Consumers in LGBT Marketing," *PR Week*, February 24, 2016.

26   Mary L. Gray, *Out in the Country: Youth, Media, and Queer Visibility in Rural America* (New York: New York University Press, 2009), 97–98.

27   In this volume, see Margot Weiss's queer history of US neoliberalism, "Queer Neoliberal Times (1970–2010s)."

Further Reading

Abraham, Mark Joseph. "'You Are Your Own Alternative': Performance, Pleasure, and the American Counterculture, 1965–1975." Ph.D. dissertation, York University, 2014.

Agee, Christopher Lowen. *The Streets of San Francisco: Policing and the Creation of a Cosmopolitan Liberal Politics, 1950–1972.* Chicago: University of Chicago Press, 2014.

Baker, Dan. "A History in Ads: The Growth of the Gay and Lesbian market." In *Homo Economics: Capitalism, Community, and Lesbian and Gay Life*, edited by Amy Gluckman and Betsy Reed, 11–20. New York: Routledge, 1997.

Beins, Agatha, and Julie R. Enszer. "'We Couldn't Get Them Printed, so We Learned to Print': *Ain't I a Woman?* and the Iowa City Women's Press." *Frontiers: A Journal of Women Studies* 34, no. 2 (2013): 186–221.

Bérubé, Allan. "The History of Gay Bathhouses." *Journal of Homosexuality* 44, no. 3–4 (2003): 33–53.

Bost, Darius. "At the Club: Locating Early Black Gay AIDS Activism in Washington, DC." Special Issue on Race, Place and Scale, *Occasion* 8 (2015): http://arcade.stanford.edu/occasion/club-locating-early-black-gay-aids-activism-washington-dc. Accessed October 24, 2017.

Boyd, Nan Alamilla. *Wide-Open Town: A History of Queer San Francisco to 1965.* Berkeley: University of California Press, 2003.

Carter, David. *Stonewall: The Riots That Sparked the Gay Revolution.* New York: Macmillan, 2005.

Chauncey, George. *Gay New York: Gender, Urban Culture, and the Making of the Gay Male World, 1890–1940.* New York: Basic Books, 1994.

Clark, Danae. "Commodity Lesbianism." In *The Lesbian and Gay Studies Reader*, edited by Henry Abelove, Michèle Aina Barale, and David M. Halperin, 186–201. New York: Columbia University Press, 1993.

Clark, Philip. "'Accept Your Essential Self': The Guild Press, Identity Formation, and Gay Male Community." In *1960s Gay Pulp Fiction: The Misplaced Heritage*, edited by Drewey Wayne Gunn and Jaime Harker, 78–119. Amherst: University of Massachusetts Press, 2013.

Cleto, Fabio, ed. *Camp: Queer Aesthetics and the Performing Subject: A Reader.* Ann Arbor: University of Michigan Press, 1999.

Cohen, Lizabeth. *A Consumers' Republic. The Politics of Mass Communication in Postwar America.* New York: Alfred A. Knopf, 2003.

Colter, Ephen Glenn, ed. *Policing Public Sex: Queer Politics and the Future of AIDS Activism.* Boston: South End Press, 1996.

Comella, Lynn. *Vibrator Nation: How Feminist Sex-Toy Stores Changed the Business of Pleasure.* Durham: Duke University Press, 2017.

D'Emilio, John. *Making Trouble: Essays on Gay History, Politics, and the University.* New York: Routledge, 1992.

Downs, Jim. *Stand by Me: The Forgotten History of Gay Liberation.* New York: Basic Books, 2016.

Enke, Finn. *Finding the Movement: Sexuality, Contested Space, and Feminist Activism.* Durham: Duke University Press, 2007.

Escoffier, Jeffrey. *Bigger Than Life: The History of Gay Porn Cinema from Beefcake to Hardcore.* Philadelphia: Running Press, 2009.

Genter, Alix. "Appearances Can Be Deceiving: Butch-Femme Fashion and Queer Legibility in New York City, 1945–1969." *Feminist Studies* 42, no. 3 (2016): 604–631.

Halperin, David M. *How to Be Gay.* Cambridge, MA: Belknap Press of Harvard University Press, 2012.

Herring, Scott. "Out of the Closets, Into the Woods: *RFD*, *Country Women*, and the Post-Stonewall Emergence of Queer Anti-Urbanism." *American Quarterly* 59, no. 2 (2007): 341–372.

Hilderbrand, Lucas. "A Suitcase Full of Vaseline, or Travels in the 1970s Gay World." *Journal of the History of Sexuality* 22, no. 3 (2013): 373–402.

——. "The Uncut Version: The Mattachine Society's Pornographic Epilogue." *Sexualities* 19, no. 4 (2016): 449–464.

Hill, Robert. "'As a man I exist; as a woman I live': Heterosexual Transvestism and the Contours of Gender and Sexuality in Postwar America." Ph.D. dissertation, University of Michigan, 2007.

——. "Before Transgender: *Transvestia*'s Spectrum of Gender Variance, 1960–1980." In *The Transgender Studies Reader 2*, edited by Susan Stryker and Aren Z. Aizura, 364–379. New York: Routledge, 2013.

Hillman, Betty Luther. "'The clothes I wear help me to know my own power': The Politics of Gender Presentation in the Era of Women's Liberation." *Frontiers: A Journal of Women Studies* 34, no. 2 (2013): 155–185.

———. *Dressing for the Culture Wars: Style and the Politics of Self-Presentation in the 1960s and 1970s*. Lincoln: University of Nebraska Press, 2015.

Hogan, Kristen. *The Feminist Bookstore Movement: Lesbian Antiracism and Feminist Accountability*. Durham: Duke University Press, 2016.

Jacobs, Meg. *Pocketbook Politics: Economic Citizenship in Twentieth-Century America*. Princeton: Princeton University Press, 2005.

Johnson, David K. "The Kids of Fairytown: Gay Male Culture on Chicago's Near North Side in the 1930s." In *Creating a Place for Ourselves: Lesbian, Gay, and Bisexual Community Histories*, edited by Genny Beemyn, 97–118. New York: Routledge, 1997.

———. "Physique Pioneers: The Politics of 1960s Gay Consumer Culture." *Journal of Social History* 43, no. 4 (2010): 867–92.

Keller, Yvonne. "'Was It Right to Love Her Brother's Wife So Passionately?': Lesbian Pulp Novels and US Lesbian Identity, 1950–1965." *American Quarterly* 57, no. 2 (2005): 385–410.

Kennedy, Elizabeth Lapovsky, and Madeline D. Davis. *Boots of Leather, Slippers of Gold: The History of a Lesbian Community*. New York: Routledge, 1993.

LaGrone, Khevon Lee. "The Day the Unspeakable Screamed Its Name: My Memories of a Black Gay Men's Movement in 1990s Oakland," *Journal of Civil and Human Rights*, 2, no. 2 (2016), 186–206.

Levine, Martin P. "Gay Ghetto." *Journal of Homosexuality* 4, no. 4 (1979): 363–377.

Levine, Martin P., and Michael S. Kimmel. *Gay Macho: The Life and Death of the Homosexual Clone*. New York: New York University Press, 1998.

Loftin, Craig M. *Masked Voices: Gay Men and Lesbians in Cold War America*. Albany: State University of New York Press, 2012.

McGeehan Muchmore, Devin. "Like A Normal Business: Morality, Economy, and the Making of an Adult Entertainment Industry in the 1970s U.S." Ph.D. dissertation, Yale University, 2018.

Morgan, Tracy D. "Pages of Whiteness: Race, Physique Magazines, and the Emergence of Public Gay Culture." In *Queer Studies: A Lesbian, Gay, Bisexual, and Transgender Anthology*, edited by Genny Beemyn and Mickey Eliason, 280–297. New York: New York University Press, 1996.

Morris, Bonnie J. *The Disappearing L: Erasure of Lesbian Spaces and Culture*. Albany: State University of New York Press, 2016.

Mumford, Kevin J. *Not Straight, Not White: Black Gay Men from the March on Washington to the AIDS Crisis*. Chapel Hill: University of North Carolina Press, 2016.

Palmer, David. "Imagining a Gay New World: Communities, Identities, and the Ethics of Difference in Late Twentieth-Century America." PhD dissertation, University of North Carolina at Chapel Hill, 2011.

Roque Ramírez, Horacio N. "'That's my place!': Negotiating Racial, Sexual, and Gender Politics in San Francisco's Gay Latino Alliance, 1975–1983." *Journal of the History of Sexuality* 12, no. 2 (2003): 224–258.

Romesburg, Don. "Racism and Reaction in the Castro—A Brief, Incomplete History," IsBadlandsBad. com, 2004. www.academia.edu/9677965/Racism_and_Reaction_in_the_Castro_A_Brief_Incomplete _History. Accessed October 27, 2017.

Sender, Katherine. *Business, Not Politics: The Making of the Gay Market*. New York: Columbia University Press, 2012.

Stein, Marc. "Canonizing Homophile Sexual Respectability: Archives, History, and Memory." *Radical History Review* 2014, 120 (2014): 53–73.

Strub, Whitney. "Gay Male Pulp and the Narrativization of Queer Cultural History." In *1960s Gay Pulp Fiction: The Misplaced Heritage*, edited by Drewey Wayne Gunn and Jaime Harker, 43–77. Amherst: University of Massachusetts Press, 2013.

———. "Mondo Rocco: Mapping Gay Los Angeles Sexual Geography in the Late-1960s Films of Pat Rocco." *Radical History Review* 2012, 113: 13–34.

———. *Perversion for Profit: The Politics of Pornography and the Rise of the New Right*. New York: Columbia University Press, 2011.

Stryker, Susan. *Transgender History*. Berkeley: Seal Press, 2008.

Taylor, Verta, and Leila J. Rupp. "Women's Culture and Lesbian Feminist Activism: A Reconsideration of Cultural Feminism." *Signs* 19, no. 1 (1993): 32–61.

Vider, Stephen. "'Oh Hell, May, Why Don't You People Have a Cookbook?': Camp Humor and Gay Domesticity." *American Quarterly* 65, no. 4 (2013): 877–904.

Warner, Michael. *The Trouble with Normal: Sex, Politics, and the Ethics of Queer Life.* Cambridge: Harvard University Press, 2000.

Wat, Eric C. "Gay Asian Men in Los Angeles Before the 1980s." In *Contemporary Asian American Communities: Intersections and Divergences*, edited by Linda Trinh Võ and Rick Bonus, 75–88. Philadelphia: Temple University Press, 2002.

Weiss, Margot. *Techniques of Pleasure: BDSM and the Circuits of Sexuality.* Durham: Duke University Press, 2011.

27

QUEER PERFORMANCE AND POPULAR CULTURE

Sharon Ullman

An essay addressing the queer history of popular culture and performance in the United States raises an interesting challenge. Performance and queerness are so entangled historically and culturally that they feel twinned in the imagination. Performance on stage requires dressing up and pretending to be someone else, a labor reenacted in the everyday lives of millions hiding scorned gender variant presentations or sexual practices. Additionally, for centuries in the theater, men played women. This association of cross dressing would, by the early twentieth century in the US, ultimately cast theater in general as suspect and eventually mark everyone who participated as potentially queer. That history also provides a direct lineage for drag performance, which has for many decades now been distinctly queer. The histories of popular culture and queer representation unfold in profound symbiosis.

Practically speaking, what does the concept of "popular culture" really mean to someone looking at queer American history? What was popular culture during colonial settlement or the development of the new nation? Did it even exist, as Walter Benjamin noted long ago, before the "age of mechanical reproduction?"[1] American cultural historian Jim Cullen argues that popular culture can be seen as the art of democracy, in that it reflects widely shared values—for good and ill—that appeal to a broad audience. He notes that elites often viewed popular culture with dismay because it helped shepherd outsiders into the mainstream and provided a location for presenting resistant values. It evolves over time and is impacted by race, region, and gender. In the mid-to-late nineteenth century, for example, Shakespeare's plays were a form of popular culture in the United States, read eagerly by miners and laborers who also attended traveling performances with both knowledge and gusto. Popular culture can move from low to high and sometimes in reverse. Using Cullen's definition, and recognizing the significance of pop culture's ephemeral and evolving nature, the possibility for a richer understanding of American queer popular culture, from early settlement until today, comes more easily into view.

Despite the short-term memory of many, the 1990s sitcom *Ellen* is not the beginning of the story. We might begin instead in mid-eighteenth-century Philadelphia, with ribald novels highlighting sodomite characters such as *Roderick Random*, which historian Clare Lyons has shown was one of the most popular books purchased or borrowed from the city's lending libraries. Recognizing that those living in the colonial and early Republic periods had a wider knowledge of variant gender presentation and sexual practice than historians had previously assumed contextualizes the ways that queerness manifested in the popular cultures of those eras. Shared print culture that satirically explored sexual relations between men or unmercifully mocked the effeminate figure of the "fop" provide a clear sense of popular culture humor that directly engaged queer themes.[2]

As historian Lawrence Senelick revealed in his encyclopedic history of drag performance on stage, *The Changing Room: Sex, Drag, and Theater*, performance playing with gender assumptions was a mainstay of the theater long before it made an appearance in America, but it has a deep history in the United States, too. Senelick argues that such performances were inherently queer, even in an era when men played many women's roles, because drag forced the audience, either through willing suspension of disbelief, puzzled interrogation, or raucous laughter to ask what gender really meant.

After the Revolution and prior to the Civil War, as the population grew and expanded across the new country, popular culture grew dramatically. It could be seen in print culture, stage performances that included plays and novelty acts, travelling orators, as well as palaces exhibiting human and animal oddities, such as P.T. Barnum's American Museum in New York. The American Museum opened in 1841 and housed everything from elephants to the "Feejee Mermaid" until it famously burned to the ground in 1865. After the Civil War, dime museums were replaced by fairs, midways, and amusement parks that showcased those with "gender trouble" such as bearded women, fat ladies, and tiny men as a way to comment on and help police appropriate gender presentation. In the widely used original meaning of the word, some "queer" nineteenth-century popular culture highlighted the fascinating draw of "oddities" tantalizing precisely because they seemed so out of bounds.

However, the most significant form of nineteenth-century popular was the minstrel show. First seen in the 1830s, this travelling entertainment form reached a prominence by the late 1840s that it did not relinquish until the early twentieth century. Even after professional minstrel companies finally petered out under the competitive pressure of early film, the minstrel show's cultural influence remained (and can be seen even today). In these shows, white men (and some African Americans) used make up, usually burnt cork, to blacken their faces (the term "blackface" comes from this). The actors presented a series of "humorous" grotesque racial stereotypes to white audiences, few of whom outside the American slave-holding South had ever seen a black person. These nasty images became ingrained into white culture through constant and widespread repetition.[3]

Many of the white male performers who went on to fame and fortune in vaudeville in a variety of roles, including that as female impersonators, got their start on stage playing black women in minstrel performances. At a time when women had otherwise begun to appear on stage regularly, the minstrel show's exaggerated and vicious mimicry necessitated that only men played black female characters. In her essential study, *Queering the Color Line: Race and the Invention of Homosexuality in American Culture*, historian Siobhan Somerville reveals how important the ideologies governing race, many drawn from popular culture, were to the sexologists who "invented" the category of homosexuality in the late nineteenth century. The minstrel show not only created some of these ideologies, it became the dominant carrier of them throughout the country. How male performers understood and created female characters on stage during the mid-to-late nineteenth century—at the exact moment when notions of sexual identity were coming into being—emerged, in large measure, from the minstrel show. Historian Eric Lott unlocked the minstrel show's profound impact on white male social class in his classic *Love and Theft: Minstrelsy and the American Working Class*. White masculinity defined itself in attraction to and rejection of the black male bodies it desired, fantasized about, and, in response, treated with contempt. The minstrel show and its virulent racism dramatically influenced the development of US gender and sexuality norms.

Drag performers of the nineteenth century may well have helped develop what came to be known in the twentieth century as "camp." A self-presentational style that exaggerates and mocks dominant values and aesthetics, "camp" is deeply associated with gay men both in terms of community code as well as that of stage performance. While the origination of the style and even the appearance of the word itself to describe the behavior lie in some dispute, a camp sensibility was well established by the late nineteenth and early twentieth centuries. It can be seen in references to popular performances and audience reactions to queer performers in vaudeville and other traveling entertainments of the day.[4]

Until the popularity of film swamped it into oblivion, vaudeville offered a central location for queer performance and audiences. Vaudeville acts—singers, dancers, comedians, trained animals, and a host of other entertainers—traversed the country filling theaters everywhere from the 1880s until the 1920s. "Pansy" comedians propelling particular stereotypes of effeminate masculinity clearly understood by audiences as homosexual were a staple. Even more significantly, gender impersonators found a ready home both there and in burlesque.[5]

Female impersonation enthralled audiences with the spectacle of men who dressed as women to seeming perfection. Julian Eltinge, the leading female impersonator of his era, drew adoring mass audiences, had a theater named after him, and published a popular magazine for a period. Many others tried to replicate his success. Most female impersonators were judged by their accuracy in presenting female characters, although some, such as Bothwell Browne, focused more on comedy, with more overt queer overtones. Male impersonators, such as Kitty Donner, Kathleen Clifford, and Vesta Tilley, while never as popular, also had their heyday in the early twentieth century. Women dressing as men on stage were judged as "boys" and treated with a lighter touch by critics. Yet all gender impersonators came to be associated with fears of homosexuality and gender impropriety, despite—or perhaps because of—their popularity with audiences.[6]

Once the twentieth century arrived, the queer history of popular culture exploded in multiple directions. Historical changes that mark the twentieth century turn any discussion of queer popular culture into a very messy business. Large swaths of the population moved en masse from rural to urban areas and many localized communities, including queer communities, developed as a result. Popular culture expanded dramatically to meet a new leisure economy along with workers and urban dwellers with disposable income. Technology carved out new roads to create and carry popular culture. Innovations in mass print technology, movies, records, radio, television, the web, digital media, and whatever presentational platform is yet to come are the drivers of popular culture in the modern age.

One often overlooked site of twentieth-century queer popular culture were the widely circulated new exemplars of post–World War II cheap paper entertainments—male physique magazines, lesbian pulp novels, and even comic books. Magazines with such titles as *Body Beautiful*, *Physique Pictorial*, *Adonis*, and *Grecian Guild Pictorial* presented rousing photos celebrating well-toned nude male bodies in "artistic" poses revealing the beauty of the male form. Well understood to be a form of softcore gay pornography, hundreds of thousands of copies were sold between 1945 and 1970 and became treasured objects of pleasure for many men in the period.[7] According to scholars such as David Johnson, the circulation of these magazines provided not only an important site of affirmation for gay men, but also helped create the commercial undergirding for the nascent gay community that would later emerge in political form.

Figure 27.1 Female impersonator Karyl Norman (George Francis Peduzzi), "the Creole Fashion Plate," sold sheet music of original songs, such as "Nobody Lied (When They Said That I Cried Over You)" (1922), in addition to performing onstage in vaudeville and nightclubs across the country and beyond from the 1920s through the 1940s.

Don Romesburg personal collection.

Similarly, as Susan Stryker reminds us, lesbian pulp novels took advantage of the new mass market paperback book industry with their lurid covers and titillating stories of sexual "perversion." Sold in drugstores and bus stations across the country and animated by a growing public awareness of lesbian sexuality in the aftermath of World War II and the Kinsey reports, pulp novels such as *Women's Barracks*, (1950), *Spring Fire* (1952), *Odd Girl Out* (1957), and *Her Raging Needs* (1964) gave many women their first opportunity to read about lesbian desire. Famed author Patricia Highsmith (writing under the nom de plume Claire Morgan) wrote the classic of the era, *The Price of Salt,* in 1952, and actually afforded her central lesbian characters a happy ending, an unusual, albeit prescient, plot resolution.

Another prescient recognition from the annals of postwar paranoia was one propelled by crusading psychologist Frederick Wertham as he insisted that comic books were dangerous to children and could provoke homosexuality and social rebellion with their depictions of male bonded superheroes such as Batman and Robin and improperly gendered females such as Wonder Woman. In his best-selling 1954 book, *Seduction of the Innocent,*[8] Wertham demanded that comic books be censored and their evil influences condemned. As scholars such as Ramzi Fawaz make clear, Wertham had a point. These "New Mutants" carried the seeds of a radical potential revisioning of society as children who "didn't fit" suddenly could see themselves empowered by their own sense of difference. All these examples of "low brow" print matter in Cold War America carried with them a queer popular culture that ultimately helped build a queer political movement.

For many, movies and television are the primary vehicles for popular culture in the twentieth century. Scholars faced with such an overwhelming amount of such material have focused their energies in a series of overlapping directions. Initially some wanted simply to document the presence of iconic queer figures or sensibilities in popular culture. In this flag planting "we were here" style of popular history, a queer past could be documented in its most visible location, stage and screen. The act of revelation functioned to cement queer history, both in public and private, particularly prior to the modern LGBTQ civil rights movement. Vito Russo's classic *The Celluloid Closet* (1981), which explored how queer characters had been present from the beginning of cinema and persisted in different forms across the decades, kicked off a veritable cascade of scholarship on queer popular culture. Early film images were often direct transfers from the vaudeville presentations that preceded them. So, for example, the comedic "sissy" figure in vaudeville became a staple of early film as well, one that would remain from the days of silent movies until today. Russo documented a long and complex history, much of it painful and filled with seemingly negative stereotypes that helped shape the cultural image of homosexuality at large.

Studies looking at representations of homosexuality on film and television, sometimes direct, sometimes hidden, form a strong core to this discussion in the 35 years post-Russo. Scholars such as Boze Hadliegh, William J. Mann, Jim Elledge, Harry M. Benshoff, and Sean Griffin have continued Russo's work and traced this history in further depth. In doing so, they have propelled the argument that visibility brings with it not only positive effects, but inevitable costs and consequences. Others, in studying the Hollywood classical era (roughly the 1930s—early 1960s), have zeroed in on what they see as a queer gender disruption. Patricia White notes, for example, a subtle lesbian presence hanging over movies with strong female characters. Some, such as Gaylyn Studlar, Robert Corber, Steve Cohan, and Ina Rae Hark have focused on the ways that Hollywood both creates and disrupts notions of masculinity through a "queered" male figure. Hollywood masculinity, they argue, is always fundamentally fraught by virtue of its exaggerated stereotypes of masculinity. Inevitably, those images of an unattainable male ideal challenged masculine definition for the audience. Equally provocative were models of alternate masculinity through the presentation of such troubled and gender fluid "stars" as 1950's screen icons James Dean or Montgomery Clift.

Increased queer visibility in the streets led inevitably to an increased presence in popular media, documented early on by media scholars. The rise of the LGBT rights movement in the 1970s and 1980s was accompanied by a marked increase in gay psychopathic characters in mainstream film. Visibility has its discontents. These arguments became more elaborate with the rise of what B. Ruby Rich dubbed the "New Queer Cinema." Emerging in the 1990s, queer filmmakers such as Todd Haynes, Christine Vachon, Cheryl Dunye, and Tom Kalin, began to take the reins to create their own complex multifaceted queer images in movies such as *Poison* (1991), *Go Fish* (1994), *Safe* (1995), and *Watermelon Woman* (1996). Some objected to Tom Kalin's *Swoon*, which focused on the notorious 1920s's era murderers, Leopold and Loeb, who had fascinated Hollywood for years, but never with the overt recognition of the two men as lovers. Similarly, Gregg Araki's *The Living End* (1992) raised eyebrows with its on-the-road movie about two HIV-positive men on a nihilistic journey. *Swoon*, *The Living End*, and other New Queer Cinema films became embroiled in emerging debates over the question of "positive" and "negative" imagery in pop culture. In the age of civil rights activism and the struggle for dignity for people with AIDS, this became a thorny problem. Some assessed popular culture for either its liberatory power or persistent homophobia while, as Michele Aaron argues, voices of the New Queer Cinema dismissed the idea that they should be held responsible for so-called positive imagery, instead highlighting queer subjects on their own terms as a defiant act of political recuperation and liberation.

Traditional Hollywood slowly "discovered" affirming LGBT subjects when faced with a growing civil rights movement and increasing visibility. While some independent films such as *Longtime Companion* (1990) approached gay men struggling with the AIDS crisis with considerable nuance, Hollywood to a large degree avoided discussing AIDS for many years of the most acute crisis. Tom Hanks won a best actor Academy Award for playing a gay lawyer with AIDS in Jonathan Demme's *Philadelphia* (1992) in part because of the film's groundbreaking stature as the first big Hollywood movie about the subject—over a decade into the epidemic. Playing the part of a homosexual man often seemed to be Oscar bait for self-proclaimed heterosexual actors, such as William Hurt (*Kiss of the Spider Woman*, 1985), Philip Seymour Hoffman (*Capote*, 2005), and Sean Penn (*Milk*, 2008), while Charlize Theron garnered one for playing a lesbian serial killer (*Monster*, 2003). Cisgender actors have also found Oscar success playing trans characters, including Hilary Swank (*Boys Don't Cry*, 1999) and Jared Leto (*Dallas Buyer's Club*, 2013). The supposedly aggressively gender non-conforming roles seem to have given performers their Oscar boost. It remains unclear precisely what cultural work these "honors" do in imagining them as part of a queer pop culture scene.

That problematic double-edged sword was brought home most strikingly with the film *Brokeback Mountain*. This 2005 adaptation of a 1997 Annie Proulx short story depicted the thwarted love between two young men in the 1960s and 70s American west. The film was a box-office success and a critical darling. While director Ang Lee won an Oscar, its surprising loss of Best Movie was read as a sign of Hollywood's ongoing homophobia. Yet the movie was not without its own critique inside the queer community. Many raised concerns that film "degayed" the main characters; producers both resisted showing much actual sex between them and focused on the film's "universal" themes in trying to sell the movie. Despite the controversy, *Brokeback Mountain* shifted the conditions of possibility for queer-themed mainstream Hollywood. It is hard to imagine, for example, that *Milk* (the 2008 story of martyred gay politician Harvey Milk) or *The Kids Are All Right* (the 2010 family comedic drama about two wealthy, white lesbians and their sperm donor) could have been as successful without it. And Todd Haynes' brilliant films exploring queer pasts, *Far from Heaven* (2002) and *Carol* (2015), make clear that come of the best work exploring humanity and history come from the queer cinematic eye.

Scholars such as Richard Dyer, Alexander Doty, and Jose Muñoz drove studies of queerness and popular culture in new directions when cultural studies took off as a scholarly field from the 1980s on. For these authors, the potential within popular culture to denaturalize supposedly fixed norms could be seen as inherently queer. Dyer, using notions of camp and queer "excess," looked at the power of the Hollywood musical to structure visions of utopia and clarify the importance of "stars" to the audience's emotional universe. Doty, in his 1993 book *Making Things Perfectly Queer: Interpreting Mass Culture*, paved the way for a generation of scholars to queer all of popular culture and recognize that the line between queer and straight dissolved when one read popular culture with a queer eye. Muñoz's 1999 *Disidentifications: Queers of Color and the Performance of Politics* inspired a generation of scholars to reconceptualize performance theory with regards to racialized and queered bodies, focusing on the disruptive power of disidentification to both occupy and subvert exclusionary cultural and subcultural representations.

This scholarship deconstructed both audience and popular culture from queer points of view. When applied to popular culture, queer theory broadly recast the kinds of questions and answers popular culture might provide. To queer pop culture is to crack open the stories we tell ourselves about gender, sexuality, and what it means to be "normal" in varied forms of popular entertainment. In doing so, we have the opportunity to see the intense social power of popular culture and, potentially, to upend and change the meaning of the stories we tell.

The history of television—an entertainment form itself under dramatic refashioning in the twenty-first century—offers an excellent template for this analytical approach. Invented shortly before World War II, television became an essential entertainment form in post-war years. Building on networks constructed through radio, television presented a wide array of programming, much of it derived from earlier entertainment forms. Daily soap operas transferred from radio, as did evening dramatic programs and comedies. Vaudeville rituals found a home in television variety shows. These familiar entertainments, newly available through simultaneous national consumption that spanned regions and time zones, helped forge a distinct Cold War era mass culture. As Lynn Spigel argues, the intimacy of the TV set inside the home, designed initially as a location for family togetherness away from the crowd, inevitably reinforced notions of domesticity and gender norms. As a consequence, its potential for disruption has been equally great ever since. The growing queer presence on TV over the past generation helped shatter traditional definitions of the supposedly "normal" family that TV itself helped invent.

There is a direct line from vaudeville to the film "pansy" to, for example, comedian Paul Lynde's beloved "Uncle Arthur" character in the popular 1960s TV show *Bewitched*. After gay liberation groups began taking to the streets, the first openly gay characters with which the audience were expected to sympathize began to appear. Billy Crystal played a sympathetic gay character on the ABC comedy *Soap*, (1977–1981). Tony Randall appeared on *Love, Sydney* (1981–1983). Gay and lesbian characters showed up in isolated episodes on a wide array of popular network shows including *The Mary Tyler Moore Show* (1970–1977), *All in the Family* (1971–1979), *Hill Street Blues* (1981–1987), and a favorite nighttime soap opera, *Dynasty* (1981–1989). *Dynasty's* popularity was as much related to its camp quality as to the presence of a central gay character. Indeed, the camp quality of much of American television, from *Gilligan's Island* through *RuPaul's Drag Race*, reveals how queer much of popular culture truly has been, precisely because of it sense of excess and theatricality.

Dynasty also became a site of queer attention because one of its actors, famed post-war movie star and icon of hetero masculinity, Rock Hudson, announced he had AIDS in 1985. This outing of Rock Hudson—long an open secret—reframed not only the national conversation over AIDS but also the ways in which popular culture could be seen as a central location for a very large closet. With Hudson transformed from, as Richard Meyer described it in 1991, a "star body" to an "antibody," everyone in the country could be in on the game of "are they really?" Suddenly, it did seem as if queers were potentially "everywhere."

TV propelled the discussion of AIDS during the 1980s to a much greater degree than did cinema, with a significant number of episodic TV shows including an AIDS story line at some point. Usually the presentation was sympathetic (if often pathetic). In the case of a 1988 episode of a little-remembered crime drama *Midnight Caller*, however, an episode about a psychopathic AIDS patient deliberately infecting people resulted in national protests from the LGBT community. The backlash revealed a growing resistance to overly homophobic imagery on TV and an increasingly supportive national mood for the struggles faced by gay citizens.

Vice President Joe Biden once credited the TV show *Will and Grace* (1998–2006) for the success of the modern gay rights movement.[9] By that he meant that seeing LGBT people in TV had made them part of a national family and, in doing so, made the extension of basic rights and respect to gay people acceptable to many Americans. *Will and Grace*, a comedy centering on the deep friendship between a well-off white gay man and a heterosexual white woman, was a particularly welcomed vision of gay male life after the pathology and hardship that haunted gay male television representations during 15 years of the AIDS epidemic. This mainstreaming process had begun in earnest, however, with a lesbian. For the sitcom *Ellen* (1994–1998) starring Ellen DeGeneres, the comedian came out as a lesbian in 1997, first in real life in *Time Magazine* and shortly thereafter, as her character on the show. Ellen's "coming out" turned into a national event as the Gay and Lesbian Alliance Against Defamation (GLAAD), a national media watchdog organization, organized watch parties around the country. The episode is considered one of the most significant in television history. While widely praised at the time, the show was nevertheless cancelled the next year, largely from conservative backlash and criticism that the show had become too centered on gay plotlines to maintain a widespread mainstream audience share. DeGeneres herself went on to a long and successful career as a daytime talk show host, and her sitcom undoubtedly paved the way for *Will and Grace* and the many LGBT-inclusive programs that have followed.

If Vice President Biden understated the power of massive grassroots organizing and years of legal battles in the struggle to attain full citizenship rights for LGBT Americans, he had a point about the power of mainstream culture to help ease the way. More TV programs focusing on queer, primarily white, and usually male, protagonists followed *Will and Grace* such as *Queer as Folk* (2000–2005) and the reality television program *Queer Eye for the Straight Guy* (2003–2007). In addition, the 2000s brought visibility through the lesbian-centered serial, *The L Word* (2004–2009) and numerous shows added queer characters to their mix. More recently, principal transgender characters have seen their way onto television through online streaming networks, including *Transparent* (Amazon, 2014–present) and *Sense8* (Netflix, 2015–2017).[10] Scholars such as Amy Villarejo have tracked the changing social attitude toward LGBT rights by viewing the altered environment on TV programs, whether it is queer stories or supportive commentary from straight allies on programs such as Comedy Central's longstanding news commentary series, *The Daily Show* (1996–present).

Popular movies and TV, guided by the imperatives of broad based commercial capitalism, have been sites of particular influence but also specific struggles over censorship and an unwillingness to challenge what might be termed assimilationist images or values. Queer characters are often presented as "just like" straight characters in order to assuage the sensibilities of what is presumed to be a largely straight audience.[11] Similarly, queer characters are presented as largely white and middle-class. Queer characters of color are few and far between. Queer characters that challenge gender norms in any significant way rarely appear. As scholars such as Quinn Miller have documented, trans characters have only recently made any appearance in movies or television and the negotiation over such representation remains fierce as cis gendered actors vie for the "challenge" of portraying trans characters while actors who are themselves trans languish on the unemployment lines.

Theater, often more iconoclastic, perennially under-capitalized, and based commonly in urban areas, has had a richer and more complex queer history. Theater is widely seen as a home for the queer community because so many creators of theater have been queer. Moreover, their works have drawn queer audiences and the concepts of performance and performativity has come to mark queer theory more broadly. Recently, scholars have enriched the detailed historical processes by which theater and queerness came to be intertwined. Unruly bodies on stage, men dressed as women, and the inability to contain the parodic potential of theatrical performance has provoked fear and attempts to regulate theater from colonial times to the present. From outright bans in colonial Massachusetts to restrictions on government funding of queer artists in the 1990s, theater has historically been seen as a threat by many guardians of the gender and sexuality status quo.

"Theater is the queerest art," as Alisa Solomon and Framji Minalla noted in their 2002 volume, *The Queerest Art: Essays on Lesbian and Gay Theater* exploring this deep relationship.[12] Bernstein elaborates on this historically specific approach in her 2006 book, *Cast Out: Queer Lives in the Theater* and encourages us to resist "an essential, ahistorical affinity between performance and queerness itself."[13] These links have been forged by struggle, tragedy, and bold action. In the recent past, AIDS wreaked havoc on the theatrical community, driving many to shove through the oppressive homophobia that limited expression of overtly queer themes, and also dramatizing the urgency of open performance of queer hardship, controversy, and insistence on dignity.

In 1990, the director of the National Endowment for the Arts (NEA) vetoed recommended grants to several artists specifically because of queer content in their performances (Tim Miller, Karen Finley, and Holly Hughes). While the artists won a court battle, Congress soon decided to stop funding all individual artists in the future. Despite, or perhaps because of, this unpromising moment, queer theatre began to flourish. Tony Kushner's remarkable two-part play, *Angels in America: A Gay Fantasia on National Themes*, mounted on Broadway in 1993 and 1994. It focused on the AIDS crisis to illuminate the moral crisis at the heart of Reagan-era 1980s America. Considered one of the great twentieth-century plays, *Angels in America* won the Pulitzer Prize and the Tony Award for Best Drama, among many other honors. Mart Crowley's *Boys in the Band* (1968), Harvey Fierstein's *Torch Song Trilogy* (1982) and Larry Kramer's *The Normal Heart* (1985) had broken queer ground before *Angels in America*. But during the 1990s, numerous successful queer-themed plays and musicals began to appear on and off Broadway. Popular offerings included Terrence McNally's *Love, Valour, Compassion* (1995), the AIDS-themed musical *Rent* (1996), John Cameron Mitchell's rock opera *Hedwig and the Angry Inch* (1998), and the Matthew Shepard-based *Laramie Project* (2000). Into the 2000s, plays such as *Take Me Out* (2002), *Avenue Q* (2003), and *I Am My Own Wife* (2003), among others, made queer themed offerings a common sight on stages around the country. The trend has continued. In 2014, the musical adaptation of lesbian cartoonist Alison Bechdel's touching graphic memoir, *Fun Home*, won five Tony Awards, including Best Musical.

We find ourselves deeply drawn to know and understand histories of popular culture because they reach us on a deep emotional level. Popular culture, as American Studies scholar George Lipsitz noted all the way back in 1990, "ain't no sideshow." He argued that "time, history, and memory become qualitatively different concepts in a world where electronically communicated mass communication is possible." The circulation of images and ideology, initially in the late nineteenth and early twentieth century through traveling theater troupes, but soon, in dramatic and world changing fashion, through movies, radio, television, and most recently, the internet, fundamentally altered everyone's relationship to the past. Lipsitz reminds us that "consumers of electronic mass media can experience a common heritage with people they have never seen."[14]

Alison Landsberg carries Lipsitz's point further in her discussion of what she calls "Prosthetic Memory." Modern consumers of popular culture in all its forms take on the experiences they see and graft them onto their own sense of their own lives and 'shared' histories. These cultural forms "offer strategies for making histories into personal memories. They provide people with the collective opportunity of having an experiential relationship to a collective or cultural past they did not experience." But most importantly for those looking to excavate and reclaim a queer usable past, Landsberg calls us to recognize that:

> if these new encounters with the experiential can be imagined as an act of prosthesis, of prosthetically appropriating memories of a cultural or collective past, then they may make particular histories available for consumption across existing stratifications of race, class and gender.[15]

Both of these features—that popular culture and performance are in some manner always already queer and that a shared popular culture engenders an extraordinary progressive potential in a politics of empathy—has led to a deep investment in the history and theory of popular culture among scholars documenting and elaborating on what queer theorist Jack Halberstam calls "a queer time and place."[16] Thousands of books, essays, websites, and exhibits are devoted to this history, from the most all-encompassing scholarly treatises to blog entries engaged in the narrowest close reading of a particular television show or character. A short summary essay cannot do this topic justice, but it can, as I hope I have, lay out some of its key periods and claims. Most important is the point that, long before mass queer communities, movements, or even identities flourished, popular culture carried queerness from one generation to the next, offering many paths forward for those looking to see themselves. As queer communities and movements articulated more public and widely circulated possibilities, popular culture continued to generate spaces of self-recognition and mutual knowing, as well as pushing the rest of the country to open its hearts and minds to queer viability and accommodation. The soul of US queer history resides, in some ways, within in a popular culture that, curiously, provided a residence for queer individuals, knowledges, and possibilities long before they existed in the "real" world at large, even as it constrained the terms upon which they might be represented or consumed.

Notes

1 Walter Benjamin, "The Work of Art in the Age of Mechanical Reproduction," *Illuminations*, ed. Hannah Arendt, trans. H. Zohn (London: NLB, 1973, [1936]), 217–242.
2 For queer histories of early America, see, in this volume, Richard Godbeer, "Colonial North America (1600s–1700s)" and Rachel Hope Cleves, "Revolutionary Sexualities and Early National Genders (1770s–1840s)."
3 For more on this era, see, in this volume, Clare Sears, "Centering Slavery in Nineteenth-Century History."
4 Camp, as a mid-twentieth-century queer sensibility, is also explored in this volume in Amanda Littauer, "Sexual Minorities at the Apex of Heteronormativity (1940s–1965)" and Stephen Vider, "Consumerism."
5 For a wider context on the queer history of the early twentieth century, see, in this volume, Elizabeth Clement and Beans Velocci, "Modern Sexuality in Modern Times (1880s–1930s)."

6 Anthony Slide, *Great Pretenders: A History of Female and Male Impersonation in the Performing Arts* (University of Michigan: Wallace Homestead Book Co. 1986); Sharon R. Ullman, " 'The Twentieth Century Way': Female Impersonation and Sexual Practice in Turn-of-the-Century America," *Journal of the History of Sexuality* 5, no. 4 (1995): 573–600; Elizabeth Reitz Mullenix, *Wearing the Breeches: Gender on the Antebellum Stage* (New York: St. Martin's Press, 2000); Lesley Ferris, ed. *Crossing the Stage: Controversies on Cross-dressing* (New York: Routledge, 2005).

7 See also, in this volume, Vider, "Consumerism."

8 Frederic Wertham, *Seduction of the Innocent: The Influence of Comic Books on Today's Youth* (New York: Rinehart, 1954).

9 Quoted in EW.com, May 6, 2012. http://insidetv.ew.com/2012/05/06/joe-biden-will-and-grace-gay-marriage/ Biden made his remarks on *Meet the Press* on May 6, 2012. Accessed October 26, 2017.

10 Estimates from GLAAD in 2015 claim that approximately 4 percent of all characters on network TV were LGBT. This matches roughly what census figures claim is the percentage of the population that self identifies as LGBT (2.5–4 percent) but does not line up with their influence. GLAAD "Where We Are on TV: Report 2015" www.glaad.org/whereweareontv15. Accessed May 9, 2016. For census data see: Gary Gates, "LGB/T Demographics: Comparisons Among Population-Based Surveys," Williams Institute, UCLA School of Law, 2014.

11 For more on the context of mainstreaming some LGBT subjects in the historical era of our present, see, in this volume, Margot Weiss, "Queer Neoliberal Times (1970s–2010s)."

12 Alisa Solomon, and Framji Minwalla, eds. *The Queerest Art: Essays on Lesbian and Gay Theater* (New York: New York University Press, 2002). This volume grew out of a 1995 conference that brought together a wide range of scholars discussing this concept.

13 Robin Bernstein, *Cast Out: Queer Lives in the Theater* (Ann Arbor: University of Michigan Press, 2006), 9.

14 George Lipsitz, *Time Passages: Collective Memory and American Popular Culture* (Minneapolis: University of Minnesota Press, 1990), 3, 5.

15 Alison Landsberg, *Prosthetic Memory: The Transformation of American Remembrance in the Age of Mass Culture.* (New York: Columbia University Press, 2004), 33, 34.

16 Judith (Jack) Halberstam, *In a Queer Time and Place: Transgender Bodies, Subcultural Lives* (New York: New York University Press, 2005).

Further Reading

Aaron, Michele. *New Queer Cinema: A Critical Reader.* New Brunswick: Rutgers University Press, 2004.

Benshoff, Harry M., and Sean Griffin. *Queer Images: A History of Gay and Lesbian Film in America.* London: Rowman & Littlefield, 2006.

Cohan, Steve, and Ina Rae Hark, eds. *Screening the Male: Exploring Masculinities in the Hollywood Cinema.* New York: Routledge, 2012.

Corber, Robert J. *Homosexuality in Cold War America: Resistance and the Crisis of Masculinity.* Durham: Duke University Press, 1997.

Cullen, Jim. *The Art of Democracy: A Concise History of Popular Culture in the United States.* New York: Monthly Review Press, 2002.

Doty, Alexander. *Making Things Perfectly Queer: Interpreting Mass Culture.* Minneapolis: University of Minnesota Press, 1993.

——. *Out in Culture: Gay, Lesbian, and Queer Essays on Popular Culture.* Durham. Duke University Press, 1995.

Dyer, Richard. "Entertainment and Utopia. 1977." *The Cultural Studies Reader*, ed. Simon During. 271–283. New York: Routledge, 1993.

——. *Only Entertainment.* Hove, UK: Psychology Press, 2002.

——. *Heavenly Bodies: Film Stars and Society.* Hove, UK: Psychology Press, 2004.

Elledge, Jim. *Queers in American Popular Culture.* Santa Barbara, CA: Praeger, 2010.

Fawaz, Ramzi. *The New Mutants: Superheroes and the Radical Imagination of American Comics.* New York: New York University Press, 2016.

Hadleigh, Boze. *The Lavender Screen: The Gay and Lesbian Films: Their Stars, Makers, Characters, and Critics.* New York: Citadel Press, 2001.

Johnson, David K. "Physique Pioneers: The Politics of 1960s Gay Consumer Culture." *Journal of Social History* 43, no. 4 (2010): 867–892.

Keller, Yvonne. " 'Was It Right to Love Her Brother's Wife So Passionately?': Lesbian Pulp Novels and US Lesbian Identity, 1950–1965." *American Quarterly* 57, no. 2 (2005): 385–410.

Lott, Eric. *Love and Theft: Blackface Minstrelsy and Working Class Culture*. New York: Oxford University Press, 1993.

Lyons, Clare A. *Sex Among the Rabble: An Intimate History of Gender and Power in the Age of Revolution, Philadelphia, 1730–1830*. Greensboro: University of North Carolina Press, 2006.

Mann, William J. *Behind the Screen: How Gays and Lesbians Shaped Hollywood, 1910–1969*. New York: Viking Press, 2001.

Meyer, Richard. "Rock Hudson's Body." In *Inside/Out: Lesbian Theories, Gay Theories*. 259–288. New York: Routledge, 1991.

Miller, Quinn. "Television." *TSQ: Transgender Studies Quarterly* 1, nos. 1–2 (2014): 216–219.

Muñoz, José Esteban. *Disidentifications: Queers of Color and the Performance of Politics*. Minneapolis: University of Minnesota Press, 1999.

Rich, B. Ruby. *New Queer Cinema: The Director's Cut*. Durham: Duke University Press, 2013.

Russo, Vito. *The Celluloid Closet: Homosexuality in the Movies*. New York: Harper and Row, 1981.

Sears, Clare. *Arresting Dress: Cross-Dressing, Law, and Fascination in Nineteenth-Century San Francisco*. Durham: Duke University Press, 2014.

Senelick, Laurence. *The Changing Room: Sex, Drag and Theatre*. New York: Routledge, 2000.

Somerville, Siobhan B. *Queering the Color Line: Race and the Invention of Homosexuality in American Culture*. Durham: Duke University Press, 2000.

Spigel, Lynn. *Make Room for TV: Television and the Family Ideal in Postwar America*. Chicago: University of Chicago Press, 1992.

Stryker, Susan. *Queer Pulp: Perverted Passions from the Golden Age of the Paperback*. San Francisco: Chronicle Books, 2001.

Studlar, Gaylyn. *This Mad Masquerade: Stardom and Masculinity in the Jazz Age*. New York: Columbia University Press, 1996.

Villareal, Amy. *Ethereal Queer: Television, Historicity, Desire*. Durham: Duke University Press, 2014.

White, Patricia. *Uninvited: Classical Hollywood Cinema and Lesbian Representability*. Indiana University Press, 1999.

28

PUBLIC HISTORY AND QUEER MEMORY

Lara Kelland

Public historians create projects that interpret the past outside of textbooks and scholarly debates. Museum exhibits, walking tours, preserved historic buildings, podcasts, websites, archival collections, and other curatorial efforts nurture collective memory and provide various publics with an opportunity to engage with the past. Queer public history has experienced a significant growth in the past few decades, but it first emerged as a part of the cultural front of the Gay Liberation Movement. During the past half-century, queer public history has transformed from a grassroots cultural form of movement activism to a widely accepted cultural and intellectual practice that blends queer collective memory with the professional practices of the larger field of public history.

The rise of queer public history is deeply interwoven with the emergence of LGBTQ historical scholarship. Although most other twentieth-century social movements used historical narratives and public history projects to build identity and justify political demands, such cultural work usually enhanced or corrected existing scholarship. By contrast, the LGBT liberation movement of the 1960s, 1970s, and 1980s nurtured scholarly and popular history projects simultaneously, many of which became the institutional homes for late twentieth- and twenty-first-century queer public history. Such projects took varied forms, including travelling slide shows, community archives, and other visual and aural projects. This work also often intertwined with new scholarship, a fact that reflects the simultaneous development of queer public and academic history. As language and identity labels have changed significantly during the past half-century, I use "queer" and "LGBT" somewhat interchangeably here, although when possible I reflect the language that activists used to describe their own work. In most cases, I use "queer" as an umbrella term to indicate same-sex loving and gender-diverse history.

Beyond simple recognition of the longstanding existence of same-sex loving practices, a public articulation of a collective past was especially integral to developing a shared identity that was based on visibility and resiliency. As many LGBT people had been disowned by biological family and thus estranged from more traditional forms of heritage, the need to craft a new lineage was fundamental to the movement's success. By asserting the endurance of same-sex loving and gender diverse practices and individuals, activists (most of whom had recently came out of the closet and connected with other queer people for the first time) developed historical narratives of success and happiness as well as celebrations of the legacy of resistance. This quest for origin stories, as historian Jonathan Ned Katz declared in 1979, d as "an important contribution to our current struggle to dispossess the professionals d repossess ourselves" while simultaneously "finding spiritual nourishment in knowledge of our historical foremothers and fathers."[1] Thus, queer public history needs to be understood as a cultural front of a movement for social justice as well as an intervention into various public history professions.

Like other popular history efforts, queer public history practices varied across place and changed over time. The homophile movement of the 1950s and 1960s invoked earlier same-sex loving figures as a rudimentary step towards creating a public identity. The Daughters of Bilitis, a lesbian homophile organization active during the 1950s and 1960s, drew its name from a literary figure associated with the Greek poetess Sappho, an act that laid claim to the classic era of human accomplishment while also underscoring the literary focus of their monthly publication *The Ladder*. Though not explicitly offering historical essays, *Ladder* articles often mentioned other classic female literary figures, including references to their passionate relationships with other women. In one example, reprints of Sappho's poems lamented "with grief that so much has been lost."[2] This call to the past reflected a push by gay men and lesbians to begin to claim well-known historic figures as their ancestors. Such early approaches to gay and lesbian history stood in contrast to the cohesive cultural and social history that LGBT scholars would begin writing during the late 1970s. The Gay Liberation and lesbian feminist movements shifted public history efforts away from reclamation of famous figures and towards the exploration of a populist and broad-based gay and lesbian (if rarely bisexual and transgender-affirming) history.[3]

Moving beyond articles in community newspapers and magazines, activists identified an explicit need for popular education of movement members. In the mid-1970s, activists and scholars, some working independently and others in community organizations, developed a variety of queer memorial practices, including slide show lectures, conferences, films, and other programming to bring the new scholarship to the community. Many community historians developed their projects into books, videos, and exhibits, while others organized community archives and developed more institutionalized history projects. As a broader history began to emerge out of gay liberation and lesbian feminist movements, LGBT public historians struggled over whether community-based organizations or mainstream liberal institutions were the best place to preserve the community's historical assets. The outcome was development in tandem, sometimes in tension and often in close relationship, of LGBT history in both community and academic settings. The result was transformative: In less than two decades, a few loosely affiliated movement intellectuals produced a significant body of knowledge and a constellation of institutional homes in major cities across the country, such as the Lesbian Herstory Archives, the ONE archives (originally the Jim Kepner collection), the GLBT Historical Society in San Francisco, The History Project in Boston, the Gerber Hart Library in Chicago, Canada Gay and Lesbian Archives in Toronto, and more.

Like many other social movements of the 1960s and 1970s, Gay Liberation activists sought to use revised historical narratives as the basis for new political identities. Unlike other movements that had some scholarship (which was usually pathologizing or absurdly negative) to react to or refute, LGBT activists had to craft a new history out of fragmented memories and closeted documents that had mostly been kept from the scholarship records. To this end, a handful of academics and community intellectuals gathered in a New York City apartment in March 1973 and found both personal and intellectual kinship with one another, as well as a desire to change scholarly and popular representations of LGBT experience. This informal meeting led to the formation of the Gay Academic Union (GAU), a critical network during the early years of LGBT collective-memory building. The first GAU activists met to address the fear, hostility, and rejection they often experienced in the academy, as well as to begin networking around LGBT scholarship, although their efforts and interests were not confined by the walls of academe. Even though this first incarnation of GAU was relatively short-lived, it generated critically important social networks that came to be fundamental for cultivating queer collective memory. Out of the GAU, several lesbian and gay community-based history projects emerged, notably the Lesbian Herstory Archives in 1974 and The History Project in Boston in 1980.[4]

One of the oldest and most significant lesbian feminist history organizations in the United States, the Lesbian Herstory Archives, formed out of GAU meetings in late 1973 or early 1974. Women members of the GAU who felt a need for a women-only space formed a consciousness-raising group to address both a political desire for self-determination and a cultural need for lesbian history and representation. As the group focused its efforts more on the collective queer women's past, its members began to pool their personal collections and actively collect additional materials pertaining to women-loving-women.

For LHA collective members, the personal commitment to archival work did not end with the donation and collection of materials. Many of these women committed labor and leisure time to the project. Perhaps most notably, founding member Joan Nestle cared for the entire archives in her Upper West Side apartment from 1974 to 1991. Born and raised in New York City by a single mother, Nestle came out as a "Fem" in the late 1950s. Her experiences in the pre-Stonewall lesbian community grounded her own sense of self, even as post-Stonewall lesbians began rejecting butch-fem labels and expressions. In the early 1970s Nestle, unsettled that lesbian feminism dismissed the significance of butch-fem community and experience, determined to incorporate the earlier generation's experiences into the contemporary movement. During the years that Nestle maintained the collection in her apartment, the holdings grew from a few boxes to an archive filling several rooms of the apartment. Women from all over the world began to travel to the archives, and Nestle and other volunteers welcomed them, offering research support, camaraderie, and warm mugs of tea. This intimate space of the archives echoed the ethos of lesbian feminism, as LHA members were committed to creating a safe and personal space to preserve the community's collective past.[5]

At the same time, local gay and lesbian history projects continued to emerge across the country. In most instances, such endeavors came out of community researchers' own work, such as that of Greg Sprague and Allan Bérubé. Sprague, a Chicago-based graduate student in Education, got involved with the Gay Academic Union and began to organize community history endeavors in Chicago during the mid-1970s. Sprague's informal educational project, the Lavender University, led to the founding of the Chicago Gay History Project, which would eventually become the basis for the Gerber-Hart Library, the LGBT library and archives in Chicago. Bérubé, a college dropout turned antiwar activist, similarly pursued research interests in gay history and co-founded the Gay and Lesbian History Project in San Francisco. Both Bérubé and Sprague exemplified the intellectually diverse backgrounds that underpinned the new community history in the LGBT movement. Neither were formally trained in history, yet both were deeply committed to community education and the development of historical organizations. Similar efforts in Toronto led to the establishment of the Canadian Gay Archives just a few months before the founding of the GAU. Canadian activists formed alliances with their American counterparts in the GAU and other smaller community projects, and from these cross-national partnerships emerged the Lesbian and Gay Researchers Network, a professional organization that fostered dialogue around the challenges to, and methods for, preserving lesbian and gay history.

From the beginning, many LGBT public historians were deeply concerned about what sorts of control to impose over materials and collections. They expressed both a desire to make materials accessible to their community members and a need to reclaim intellectual control over their pasts from organizations that had closeted or pathologized their histories. As LHA grew, members of the collective fiercely held to their commitment of being a grassroots organization in the service of lesbians across the world. To this end, in a conversation with other lesbian and gay historians, Nestle underscored the importance of keeping the archives entirely separate from a patriarchal institution, insisting that lesbians "should be in control of our own materials, our own history."[6] Similarly, LHA prohibited men from using the space and collections, a policy that lasted well into the 1980s. LHA also maintained a strict commitment to a non-elite atmosphere. While LGBT researchers often found themselves barred from established institutional or academic archives due to a lack of institutional credentials, LHA upheld a policy of accessibility for all lesbians, a commitment which led to exclusion of non-queer women in addition to men.

Policies such as these produced archival spaces that functioned as much as community centers as repositories for historical materials. Book and slide show researchers comingled with recent mastectomy survivors who came to look at erotic images as a means of reclaiming sexuality. Throughout its organizational history, collective members remained committed to the LHA as "a cultural institution which, though it plays a dynamic role in the Lesbian community, is, at its core, a safe, nurturing environment, a mixture of library and family album."[7] This commitment led to the organization not simply serving as a historical resource for lesbians, but as a social and political organizing space informed by the project of lesbian public history.

Although all agreed on the importance of making materials more broadly available, LGBT public historians passionately debated one another over whether or not their materials should be kept within the community or mainstreamed into liberal institutions. Chicago GAU member Jim Monahan urged gay historians "to integrate the past into [mainstream] historical thinking."[8] Although Monahan recognized the importance of early community-based public history work, he argued vehemently against keeping such materials in separatist organizations, explaining that the "only separation and faction this archival movement can tolerate is one that allocates tasks, and divides the labor required to bring the gay archives into, and thereby creating, the major research centers that hold them."[9] While Monahan advocated for sensitivity and security for LGBT historical materials, his main concern was the consolidation of gay materials into one or a few centrally located repositories located within academic libraries.

In response, Joan Nestle came out against the removal of local and community control of historical materials. The occasion gave Nestle the opportunity to put forth a practice she termed *radical archiving*. Applied to the Lesbian Herstory Archives, *radical archiving* called for not only community ownership, but also for community responsibility for the archives. It included unfettered access of the archives for all lesbians in a lesbian-housed non-institutional space, and foregrounded LHA engagement in lesbian political struggles, egalitarian collection policies, community-based lesbian collection, curation, and funding.[10] For Nestle, the practices connected with maintenance of the archives were woven into the daily fabric of the community, and as such were intertwined with the political struggles and other needs of the community.

Part of the reason for mistrusting mainstream institutions was due to the closeting practices of librarians and archival staff. Early efforts at finding archival sources for same-sex loving experiences in the past proved to be daunting. Yet one of the first researchers to undertake a sizeable gay community history research project, Jonathan Ned Katz, remembered not a dearth of sources, but mainstream institutional barriers that silenced love letters and buried other traces of queer history, a result of what historian Michel Trouillot has called *archival power*. Tracking rumors proved to be a fruitful method for Katz, who received leads from other movement activists at parties or during informal chats about his work. Queer librarians and archivists, although often closeted themselves, also proved quietly useful in the early days of Katz' research, as they would surreptitiously point him towards relevant boxes. Early scholars and public historians working on LGBT topics shared information with one another on both methods and resources. Gregory Sprague corresponded with a variety of researchers regarding his projects to "hit pay dirt" as he mined what he could from traditional repositories. Judith Schwartz also corresponded with Jonathan Katz, alerting him to archival items in the FBI files at the National Archives that documented numerous lesbians who had not yet been written about. As Katz's papers at the New York Public Library show, scholars doing research for books, slide shows, films and community history courses wrote letters to one another, passing hints back and forth regarding how to locate sources. These letters illuminate the creative strategies necessary for LGBT historians working within an archive organized by forms of knowledge that did not recognize nor document gay and lesbian historical experiences.

To counteract these struggles and to lay the groundwork for future queer scholarly and public history, LGBT activists and organizations engaged in the task of making same-sex loving histories intelligible and accessible to all. For example, in April 1980, the Boston Area Lesbian and Gay History project published *A Beginning Handbook for Researching Lesbian and Gay History in the Boston Area*. This guide advised researchers to employ a long, oftentimes offensive, list of terms in card catalogs and indices, including *amazon, berdache, convent, flash in the pan, houseboy, interior decorating, lesbos, pederasty, social reform movement, spinster, suffragist, tribadism, uranian*, and the ever-useful *vice*. The handbook also republished a portion of the index from Jonathan Ned Katz's groundbreaking 1976 primary source book *Gay American History*, as well as etymological entries on *lesbian* and *gay*.

Similarly, the Circle of Lesbian Indexers produced a voluminous index of lesbian periodicals and subject thesaurus "to foster in our community a sense of continuity with the lesbian past."[11] The index, a project of LHA collective members as well as author J. R. Roberts and historian Claire Potter, served as a guide for researchers working on lesbian topics. The index was divided into sections, including a file of authors and subject entries; book reviews; lesbian writings; poems; and reproduced visual art. The 39-page subject file offered an extensive annotated topical list, traversing topics as broad as the *Back to the Land Movement, Feminist Wiccans, Conformity in the Lesbian Community, Plumbing Repair, Psychosurgery, Taxation* and the *Orange Juice Boycott*. While each of these initiatives had an impact on professional archival practices, their efforts also underscored a commitment to creating a community historical culture in the movement, where anyone might be inspired to undertake a new research project.

Throughout the development of queer public history, oral history interviews have served as a vital source for historic information, as a tool for community building, and as a memory practice that validated experiences and identities. Early oral history projects such as the Buffalo Women's Oral History Project, which led to the book *Boots of Leather, Slippers of Gold*, as well as projects such as Allan Bérubé's *Coming Out Under Fire* and the 1984 documentary *Before Stonewall* laid the groundwork for the centrality of oral history methods in queer public and scholarly history. For the past half-century, oral history has provided source material that fills in the significant gaps in the more traditional archival record. As queer public history has enjoyed unprecedented growth in the past two decades, the methods of queer oral history have been honed by a new generation of practitioners and researchers, as an edited volume by Nan Alamilla Boyd and Horacio Roque Ramirez attests.

While activist-archivists worked to improve the collection of, and access to, raw materials, movement historians also sought to return their research to the community in the form of curated projects that supported the development of new political identities. Out of this desire, they developed slide shows that were joyfully delivered and eagerly received. As improvised community centers filled to capacity with cheering crowds, young LGBT people coming of age during the 1970s and 1980s received an informal education in their own histories. The community slide show format was a central early medium through which to share findings. These events gave scholars an opportunity to show visual materials such as photographs, art, and book covers as they narrated LBGT historical narratives to enthusiastic audiences. John D'Emilio recalled a giddy euphoria sweeping over the audience as they watched images and listened to narration of a history they had long craved. Scholars would often travel with their shows, booking a full tour of LGBT gatherings and relying upon local organizers to turn out a full house, a task that seemed to be anything but difficult in communities filled with those eager to learn more of a past they could claim as their own.

Organizations such as the Lesbian Herstory Archives also embraced the slide show format, in one instance sending "Archivette" Alexis Danzig out on a cross-country motorcycle tour to promote the collections and share the stories of lesbian history. The slide show format emerged rather organically for LHA. As archive volunteers sought out opportunities to connect with the community, they also found travelling with archival objects a challenging task. Slides gave the presentation an exciting visual focus and were easily transported from one location to another. LHA representatives including Alexis Danzig, Deborah Edel, and Joan Nestle traveled significant distances to present in Toronto, Winston-Salem, NC, Louisville, KY, Santa Cruz, CA, Washington D.C., and around New York City and Upstate New York. Some slideshow screenings, such as the one at the Women's Studies Forum at SUNY Plattsburgh, complemented scholarly discussions, while women's bookstores organized others, sometimes as benefits for local women's groups.

Many community historians and LGBT history project activists utilized the communicative power of the slide show. On a given Friday or Saturday night during the mid-1970s to the mid-1980s, queer people in towns across the country could take in a traveling slide show on an impressive array of same-sex loving and gender diverse topics. Some focused on historical inquiries bounded by space and time, such as *Lesbians and Gay Men in Early San Francisco, 1849–1880*; *From the Gay and Lesbian Rights Movement to the Holocaust, 1860–1935*; and *100 Years of the Lesbian in Biography*. In other cases, slideshows reflected the growing transnationalism of the movement, covering non-US topics as broad as *Mayan and Mexican Goddesses* and *Gay Germany*. Topics that echoed gynocentric themes flourished within the lesbian community, including *The Goddess and the Witch*; *The Mother Goddess* and *Lesbian Erotica by Women Artists*. Cultural history themes also proved popular, including *What the Well-dressed Dyke Will Wear— Dyke Fashion, 1900-present*; *Gay Science Fiction*; and *Lavender Letters: Lesbians in Literature*.

Documentary films that attended to the historical experiences of same-sex loving folks such as *Word is Out* and *Before Stonewall* also blossomed during this period, further generating interest in LGBT history. As the production of both fiction and nonfiction queer film increased, communities began to organize film festivals across the country in the 1970s and 1980s. Film historian Vito Russo began to show his research in public as a filmography that featured same-sex attraction or gender-variant scenes from Hollywood films. This work would ultimately be published as *The Celluloid Closet: Homosexuality in the Movies* (1981), but its origins as a public performance reflect the significance of Vito's work to queer public history. Other filmmakers such as Barbara Hammer followed suit, using archival clips as a kind of queer public history via cinema.[12]

Although public history projects such as slide shows, films, and exhibits continued to be the focus of most community-based LGBT archivists and historians throughout the 1980s and into the 1990s, an imperative to mark the lost lives taken by the AIDS epidemic emerged and took hold. In 1986, San Francisco-based activist Cleve Jones founded the NAMES Project AIDS Memorial Quilt as a physical manifestation of grief and community rupture. Grieving friends and family from around the country began to send in panels commemorating the deceased, and in 1987 the quilt was displayed for the first time on the National Mall. As one scholar has noted, the quilt served as "an alternative site of memory for many who have been excluded from traditional means of mourning."[13] As other acts of LGBT memory had, the quilt was also deployed for movement-building purposes when activists toured it around the country in 1988. In addition to providing a space for grief, the tour served an educational purpose, raising money for AIDS service organizations and awareness about the epidemic.[14] Thus, in the 1980s and 1990s, many young LGBT folks who had heeded Harvey Milk's rejoinder to come out to their families of origin and found themselves isolated from traditional networks of support, used new means of commemoration such as the quilt to mark loss, process grief, and rearticulate their own meanings of family.

Over time, the quilt, which became the largest queer public history installation in ever and finally became too big to display in any one place, sought to remember the deaths of many individuals as a collective loss, a gesture that functioned as both an expression of grief and a demand for policy change. The quilt became a potent marker of queer memory, but it also expanded its function, as it by nature of the disease extended beyond LGBT identities. Although the disease was culturally marked as belonging to gay men, the fact that the memorial reflected the indiscriminate nature of infection rendered it a queer memorial that transcended simple identity categories. Beyond that shift, activists involved with the quilt envisioned the project as explicitly and broadly public, particularly using the quilt as a tool of education about the epidemic. Although certain other projects such as documentary films prior to this had sought to realize broad educational potential, the quilt marks a definitive shift in queer public history towards a commitment to reaching the widest possible audience.

Figure 28.1 The NAMES Project AIDS Quilt, first fully displayed on October 11, 1987, at the National Mall in Washington, D.C., during the National March on Washington for Lesbian and Gay Rights. It covered a space larger than a football field and included nearly 2,000 panels. After its final full display in 1996, it became too large to be displayed in any single place at once. Portions of the Quilt—there are now over 48,000 panels—continue to tour the world.

Photograph courtesy of Marc Geller.

LGBT academic and public history, borne out of private collections, rumors, living-room conversations, letters exchanged between friends, and informal networks, changed remarkably during the 1970s and 1980s. Although LGBT history still has a strong connection to community organizations such as archives and libraries, by the mid-1990s historical authorship had transitioned from primarily being located in grassroots community projects and individual labors of love towards a highly professionalized academic endeavor. As LGBT and queer studies became legitimate areas of research in the academy, the lines between community and scholarly history became more clearly drawn. However, even as the field became more polarized between popular and academic projects, collaborations between community groups and more traditional scholars echoed the grassroots origins of the field. Initiatives such as the Twin Cities Queer Oral History Project and the expansion of outhistory.org promoted dialogue between scholars and communities of memory, exemplifying both the collaborative ethos of early queer history projects and the professional standards of public history that foreground "shared authority" in the production of historical knowledge.

Similarly, as LGBT scholarly history enjoyed acceptance within the academy, mainstream public history organizations began to express interest in representing same-sex and gender-diverse historical experiences. Over time, the policy-oriented portions of the LGBT movement enjoyed much success in redefining same-sex relationships as normal loving human experiences, in significant part through the development of a political identity premised on the historical achievements and survival of same-sex loving individuals and communities. Some historians used their institutional affiliation and professional clout to argue for policy-based interventions, such as those who participated in producing the Amicus Brief for the landmark *Lawrence vs. Texas*. Acting as public intellectuals, beyond the scope of public history practice, they deployed historical arguments in support of federal policy revision. As the movement shifted away from community educational efforts towards a larger social intervention, the terrain of LGBT history shifted also from community-based organizations towards larger liberal institutions, from public history initiatives to K-12 curricular projects.

Because LGBT politics had experienced significant gains in mainstream US culture, by the 2000s queer historical representations had become part of the broader national narrative, making significant inroads into universities, museums, and other educational and cultural institutions. Although there have been museum representations of LGBT historical experience since the development of queer historical societies and archives, the 2000s brought about a new level of museumification of LGBT history, both within mainstream and community-based cultural organizations. Short-term, interaction-oriented exhibit practices emerged as an innovative method for reaching diverse audiences. In 2011, the Pop Up Museum of Queer History was founded in NYC, beginning as a one-night event and then developing into a museum-without-walls model of curation and interpretation. This model had precedence, as the GLBT Historical Society had developed a collaborative curatorial project called "Making a Case for Community History." This initiative brought diverse communities contained within the LGBT identity into the space of the museum and produced a series of touring exhibits. The popularity of these small informal exhibits sparked a desire for a permanent gallery space, and in 2003 the society moved to a new space, rooting the grassroots community history initiative in one of San Francisco's significant cultural institutions.[15] The 1990s and 2000s witnessed many LGBTQ historical organizations building new spaces, enhancing programming, and increasing professional engagement with other cultural institutions, including Lesbian Herstory Archive's new home in Brooklyn in 1993, Chicago's Leather Archives and Museum in 1999, and the ONE Archive's move to the University of Southern California Campus in 2000.

At the same time, some mainstream museums began to engage with LGBT historical topics to both build connections with queer communities and to tell stories to a more mainstream audience. In commemoration of the 25th anniversary of the Stonewall Uprising in 1994, The New York Public Library mounted the "Becoming Visible: The Legacy of Stonewall" exhibit. Similarly, major museums such as the Chicago History Museum and the Minnesota Historical Society began to undertake major interpretive projects and programming related to LGBT historical experience. Historic house museums such as Chicago's Hull House Museum also began to experiment with interpreting same-sex-loving experiences through methods such as exhibit labeling that promoted dialogue about identity and history. Likewise, the 2011 opening of CHM's *Out in Chicago* was the first major exhibit on LGBT experience in a large history museum.

Other forms of queer public history have experienced significant development in the past few decades. Digital history has provided new opportunities for the sharing and cultivation of LGBT collective memory. Founded by Jonathan Ned Katz, the OutHistory project is a model crowdsourcing archival project, gathering digitized documents and images from around the world. Many mainstream archives have prioritized the digitization of LGBT collections, including the New York Public Library, and other mutli-repository collaborations such as *LGBTQ History and Culture since 1940* have greatly enriched the number of resources available to online researchers. Public historians have also been working to increase the designation of significant built environments and public space. In 2014, the National Park Service announced a new initiative to identify historic sites relevant to the LGBT past. This project is intended to provide historical context for future nominations to the National Register of Historic Places and the National Historic Landmarks program, as well as provide a survey of significant heritage sites across the country. Beginning with a scholarly roundtable in 2014, the National Parks Service initiative sparked a two-year project of gathering information on site-based queer public history, culminating in the 2016 publication of *LGBTQ America: A Theme Study of Lesbian, Gay, Bisexual, Transgender, and Queer History*. The initiative signaled a federal commitment to the preservation and interpretation of the queer past, and institutionalized many grassroots projects attending to local queer historical experiences.

Activists seeking to change hearts and minds have long worked within cultural forms to alter perspectives and attitudes, and those working within the LGBTQ movement certainly took inspiration from other social movements regarding the power of the past in building new political identities. By the 2010s, with the embracing of LGBT history work within the larger public history profession via the National Park Service and mainstream museums, the grassroots memory work cultivated by earlier activists had comingled with the larger public history profession to integrate sexuality and LGBT identity into the national narrative. Queer public history has provided the larger movement with an important expression of precedence and perseverance, but it also provides the larger public history profession with a model for engaged and accountable politically effective cultural work that seeks social justice and democratic cultural representations.

Notes

1 Jonathan Ned Katz, "Why Gay History?" *Body Politic* 55 (August 1979): 19–20.
2 "Sappho of Lesbos," *The Ladder*, December 1, 1958, 12. For more on lesbian historical production, see, in this volume, Julie Enszer, "Lesbian History: Spirals of Imagination, Marginalization, Creation, and Erasure."

3 For more on the gay liberation and lesbian feminist context of early queer public history, see also, in this volume, Don Romesburg, "Introduction: Just a Moment or Momentous?", Whitney Strub, "Gay Liberation (1963–1980)," and Jen Manion, "Language, Acts, and Identity in LGBT History."

4 For more on the history of LGBT organizations generally, see, in this volume, Marcia M. Gallo, "Organizations."

5 For more on the Lesbian Herstory Archives and the history and subject of queer archives, see, in this volume, Kate Eichhorn, "Queer Archives: From Collections to Conceptual Framework."

6 "Gay History Meeting at Jonathan Ned Katz's apt. in Greenwich Village, January 28, 1978." Jonathan Ned Katz Papers, 41, Manuscripts and Archives Division, Humanities and Social Sciences Library, New York Public Library (New York, NY).

7 Deb Edel, "Building Cultural Memories: The Work of the Lesbian Herstory Archives," Ginny Vida, ed., *Our Right to Love: A Lesbian Resource Book* (New York: Prentice Hall, 1978), 270.

8 "Considerations in the Organizations of Gay Archives," Jim Monahan, *Gay Insurgent* 5, (1978).

9 Ibid.

10 Maxine Wolfe, "The Lesbian Herstory Archives: A Passionate and Political Act," Maxine Wolfe Papers, 1: "1995" Lesbian Herstory Archives (Brooklyn, NY).

11 "Mission Statement from the Circle of Lesbian Indexers," San Francisco Lesbian and Gay History Project Records, 1:10, GLBT Historical Society (San Francisco, CA).

12 In this volume, for the longer queer histories of consumerism, representation, and popular culture, see Stephen Vider, "Consumerism" and Sharon Ullman, "Performance and Popular Culture."

13 Christopher Capozzola, "A Very American Epidemic: Memory Politics and Identity Politics in the AIDS Memorial Quilt, 1985–1993," *Radical History Review* 82 (2002) 95.

14 For the queer US history of the AIDS epidemic, see, in this volume, Jennifer Brier, "AIDS and Action (1980s–1990s.)"

15 In 2011, the organization launched the GLBT History Museum, the nation's first freestanding museum of its kind, to international notice.

Further Reading

Adair, Peter, Nancy Adair, Andrew Brown, Robert P. Epstein, Lucy Massie Phenix, Veronica Selver, Mariposa Film Group. *Word Is Out*. American independents. New York, NY: New Yorker Video, 1992 [1997].

Bérubé, Allan. *Coming Out Under Fire: The History of Gay Men and Women in World War Two*. New York: Free Press, 1992.

——. *Lesbian Masquerade*, slide show, GLBT Historical Society, San Francisco.

Boston Lesbian and Gay Archives. *Our Boston Heritage*. Slide show, Boston Lesbian and Gay Archives, Boston.

Boyd, Nan Alamilla and Horacio Roque Ramirez, eds. *Bodies of Evidence: The Practice of Queer Oral History*. New York: Oxford, 2012.

Circle of Lesbian Indexers. "The Lesbian Periodicals Index and Thesaurus of Subjects," 3rd edition, September, 1981, Circle of Lesbian Indexers Collection, 1, Lesbian Herstory Archives. Brooklyn, NY.

Cowan, Liza, *What the Well-dressed Dyke Will Wear—Dyke Fashion*. Slide show, Lesbian Herstory Archives, Brooklyn, New York.

Ferentinos, Susan, *Interpreting LGBT History at Museums and Historic Sites*. Lanham, MD: Rowman and Littlefield, 2015.

Freedman, Estelle and Liz Stevens. *She Even Chewed Tobacco: Passing Women in Nineteenth Century America*. Slide show, GLBT Historical Society, San Francisco.

Katz, Jonathan Ned. *Coming Out! A Documentary Play*. 1972. http://outhistory.org/exhibits/show/coming-out. Accessed January 26, 2017.

——. *Gay American History: Lesbians and Gay Men in the U.S.A.* New York: Crowell, 1976.

Kennedy, Elizabeth Lapovsky and Madeline Davis. *Boots of Leather, Slippers of Gold: A History of a Lesbian Community*. New York: Routledge, 1993.

Koskovich, Gerard. "Displaying the Queer Past: Purposes, Publics, and Possibilities at the GLBT History Museum." *QED: A Journal in Queer Worldmaking* 1, no. 2 (2014): 61–78.

Morris, Charles E. III. "My Old Kentucky Homo: Lincoln and the Politics of Queer Public Memory," in Kendall R Phillips, ed. *Framing Public Memory*. Tuscaloosa: University of Alabama, 2004.

"Preserving our Words and Pictures," transcript of interview of Joan Nestle and Deborah Edel by Beth Hodge, circa 1980. Topical Files, "Publicity" Lesbian Herstory Archives. Brooklyn, NY.

Romesburg, Don. "Presenting the Queer Past: A Case for the GLBT History Museum." Special Issue: Queering Archives. *Radical History Review* 120 (Fall 2014): 131–144.

Schiller, Greta, Robert Rosenberg, John Scagliotti, Rita Mae Brown, and Media Network (U.S.). *Before Stonewall: The Making of a Gay and Lesbian Community*. MPI Home Video, 1989.

Trouillot, Michel-Rolph. *Silencing the Past: Power and the Production of History*. Boston, MA: Beacon, 1995.

Vider, Stephen. " 'Oh Hell, May, Why Don't You People Have a Cookbook?': Camp Humor and Gay Domesticity." *American Quarterly* 65, no. 4 (2013): 877–904.

INDEX